Teaching Children to Read

Teaching Children to Read

From Basals to Books

Second Edition

D. Ray Reutzel
Brigham Young University

Robert B. Cooter, Jr.
Austin Peay State University

Merrill,
an imprint of Prentice Hall
Englewood Cliffs, New Jersey   Columbus, Ohio

Library of Congress Cataloging-in-Publication Data

Reutzel, D. Ray (Douglas Ray)
  Teaching children to read : from basals to books / D. Ray Reutzel, Robert B. Cooter, Jr.—2nd ed.
          p.   cm.
  Includes bibliographical references (p.   ) and index.
  ISBN 0-02-399573-4
    1. Reading (Elementary). 2. Reading (Elementary)—Language experience approach.
  3. Language arts (Elementary).   I. Cooter, Robert B. II. Title.
  LB1573.R48   1996
  372.4'1—dc20   95-16834
                                                                            CIP

Cover art: Susan Sturgill
Editor: Bradley J. Potthoff
Developmental Editors: Linda James Scharp, Linda Montgomery
Production Editor: Mary Harlan
Copy Editor: Luanne Dreyer Elliott
Photo Editor: Anne Vega
Design Coordinator: Julia Zonneveld Van Hook
Text Design: Proof Positive/Farrowlyne Associates, Inc.
Cover Design: Julia Zonneveld Van Hook
Production Manager: Pamela D. Bennett
Electronic Text Management: Marilyn Wilson Phelps, Matthew Williams, Karen L. Bretz, Tracey Ward
Illustrations: Steve Botts

This book was set in Souvenir by Merrill/Prentice Hall and was printed and bound by R. R. Donnelley & Sons Company. The cover was printed by Phoenix Color Corp.

Earlier edition © 1992 by Macmillan Publishing Company.

Photo credits: All photos copyrighted Scott Cunningham/Merrill/Prentice Hall, except the following: Robert B. Cooter, pp. 449, 451, 511; KS Studios/Merrill/Prentice Hall, p. 52; Barbara Schwartz/Merrill/Prentice Hall, p. 170; Anne Vega/Merrill/Prentice Hall, p. 417; Tom Watson/Merrill/Prentice Hall, p. 349.

Printed in the United States of America

10 9 8 7 6 5 4 3 2

ISBN: 0-02-399573-4

Prentice-Hall International (UK) Limited, *London*
Prentice-Hall of Australia Pty. Limited, *Sydney*
Prentice-Hall of Canada, Inc., *Toronto*
Prentice-Hall Hispanoamericana, S. A., *Mexico*
Prentice-Hall of India Private Limited, *New Delhi*
Prentice-Hall of Japan, Inc., *Tokyo*
Simon & Schuster Asia Pte. Ltd., *Singapore*
Editora Prentice-Hall do Brasil, Ltda., *Rio de Janeiro*

For my wife, family, parents, and grandparents, who have always been there for me.
   —*DRR*

For my wonderful wife, Deb, and my parents, Toni and Bruce Cooter, who taught me that *everything* is possible.
   —*RBC*

ABOUT THE AUTHORS

D. Ray Reutzel

D. Ray Reutzel is Karl G. Maeser Research Professor and Chair of the Department of Elementary Education at Brigham Young University. He earned his doctorate in Curriculum and Instruction with an emphasis in reading and language arts from the University of Wyoming, Laramie, in 1982. He teaches courses in research design, reading, and language arts for preservice and in-service teachers at BYU. He has taught in kindergarten and grades 1, 3, 5, and 6 as an elementary school teacher.

Dr. Reutzel took a leave from his university faculty position to return to full-time, first-grade classroom teaching in Sage Creek Elementary School in 1987–1988. While in the elementary classroom, he established a model first-grade whole language classroom that has been visited by observers from throughout the country. In 1987, Dr. Reutzel received BYU's College of Education Excellence in Research Award. In the same year, his work was recognized by the American Educational Research Association (AERA) as one of the Distinguished Research Papers at the 1988 Annual Meeting.

Dr. Reutzel is the author of more than 80 articles, books, book chapters, and monographs. He has published in *Reading Research Quarterly, Journal of Reading Behavior, Journal of Educational Research, Reading Psychology, Reading Research and Instruction,* and *The Reading Teacher,* among others. He has served as an editorial review board member or guest reviewer for *The Elementary School Journal, The Reading Teacher, Reading Research Quarterly, The Journal of Reading Behavior, The Reading Teacher, The NRC Yearbook, American Reading Forum Yearbook, Reading Psychology,* and *Reading Research and Instruction.* Dr. Reutzel is an author of the *Literacy Place* program published by Scholastic, Inc. of New York.

Dr. Reutzel lives in Springville, Utah, with his wife, daughter, four sons, a dog, and a cat. His hobbies include reading, skiing, fishing, singing, playing the piano, and trying to keep up with his wife and children.

Robert B. Cooter, Jr.

Robert B. Cooter, Jr., is professor and dean of the College of Education at Austin Peay State University, where he teaches courses in reading and literacy education for preservice and practicing teachers. He has worked with teachers and administrators in school districts around the nation who are interested in developing balanced literacy programs, authentic assessment procedures, and process writing programs. He has taught grades 1, 3, 4, and 7 in the public schools and also served as a Title I reading teacher. Dr. Cooter previously served as chair of the Department of Curriculum and Instruction at Texas Christian University and, prior to that time, directed the Reading Center at Bowling Green State University in Ohio. Dr. Cooter earned his degrees at George Peabody College for Teachers of Vanderbilt University and the University of Tennessee.

In addition to this textbook, Bob Cooter has edited *The Teacher's Guide to Reading Tests* and co-authored *The Flynt-Cooter Reading Inventory for the Classroom.* He has recently completed a new textbook, *Teaching Reading in the Content Areas: Developing Content Literacy for All Students* (Merrill/Prentice-Hall). Dr. Cooter currently serves as editor of *Reading Research and Instruction,* an international professional journal, and has published articles in *The Reading Teacher, Journal of Reading, Reading Psychology, Reading Research and Instruction, The Journal of Educational Research,* and *Language Arts.* In addition, Bob is working on his first novel.

A native of Nashville, Tennessee, Bob Cooter enjoys sharing Southern folktales, cruising on Harley-Davidsons, sailing, listening to good blues, and dining on catfish and cheese grits. He lives with his wife, Deb, in Clarksville, Tennessee, is proud to have five children and two grandchildren (Joshua and Kaelee), and is owned by a hound dog of unknown breed or utility.

Preface

One of the greatest professional experiences we have had occurred several years ago when we decided to leave our university positions and return to teaching children. Our purpose was to try out many of the ideas coming from the whole language movement and discover how they might be integrated into traditional elementary and middle school classrooms. After our classroom experiences, we shared our knowledge and experiences with others through the first edition of *Teaching Children to Read: From Basals to Books*. In the second edition, we continue sharing concepts about making transitions toward what we call balanced reading and language instruction in elementary schools. The second edition represents the culmination of many years of work in the classroom, field, and office. It brings together our collective knowledge and experiences; the knowledge and experiences of many other recognized authorities in the field of reading education; and the experience, wisdom, and common sense of literally thousands of our teacher and student colleagues who continue to validate our ideas about initiating changes in reading instructional beliefs and practices.

The field of reading education has been, and hopefully will continue to be, in a state of constant flux and change. Although some view this process as simply a swinging of the educational pendulum back and forth between old and new, we believe that current calls for change in reading beliefs and instruction occur for two reasons. First, the language of change represents a fundamental shift in knowledge and understanding of the reading process. It reflects a new point of view, a profound change in how we view the world of language learning in elementary schools. Second, we believe that to revalue some traditions in the field fosters greater understanding of why we do what we do. As Frank Smith (1983) says, examining teaching traditions allows teachers at all levels to move beyond the confines of educational ignorance. We recognize that teachers who initiate changes in reading beliefs and instruction do so at great personal and professional risk.

Teaching Children to Read: From Basals to Books is a comprehensive, readable (some say even enjoyable) guide that assists preservice and in-service elementary school classroom teachers in examining their own beliefs about reading instruction. It is also an open invitation to teachers to embark on a stimulating professional journey. This journey involves teachers in a sustained professional change, moving unidirectionally from traditional reading instructional practices and beliefs toward balanced literacy instructional practices and beliefs. One reviewer of *Teaching Children to Read: From Basals to Books* stated, "It tells the true story of how teachers at all levels of training and experience can cross the bridge of transitions." Hence, this book is intended to serve as a text for a semester-long course on elementary school reading instruction. Moreover, it is intended to be a guide, support, and a continuing resource for teachers making transitions toward balanced literacy instructional beliefs and practices.

Major changes in this second edition of *Teaching Children to Read: From Basals to Books* are many. Aside from a general updating of previous content, this edition integrates two crucial sections throughout the text: helping students with special needs and assisting students who are culturally different and for whom English may be a second language. Reading theories are explicitly tied to specific reading instructional practices. Balanced literacy programs are discussed in detail. Thematic instruction in the content areas using trade books as a springboard into content area textbooks emphasizes a fresh approach to content reading. Color highlighting indicates whether a marginal note serves to define the word or concept (green bar) or has another purpose, such as adding a comment or asking a question (purple). New color photographs and illustrations, along with other new features, make the second edition of *Teaching Children to Read: From Basals to Books* more accessible and understandable.

The organization of the second edition reflects the usage of literally thousands of professors and students. We open with a brief discussion of the current state of affairs in reading/language education and why the transitions approach continues to be a necessary and useful model for the development of reading professionals. In Chapter 2, we explore basic belief systems and theoretical perspectives, both past and present, concerning the teaching of reading. The goal is twofold: to help teachers understand differing perspectives for the teaching of reading and to assist teachers in identifying their own current beliefs.

The remainder of the first half of the text is somewhat traditional in focus, yet it reflects current theory and practice. Chapter 3 focuses specifically on helping teachers understand the controversies and research related to children's development of reading and writing ability. In Chapter 4, we review the history, content, issues, and possibilities of basal reader instruction. In Chapter 5, we show teachers how to make transitions toward balanced literacy programs. In Chapters 6 through 8, we focus on helping children comprehend and compose text, develop reading and writing vocabulary, and develop word-identification strategies. The chapters are arranged to emphasize that comprehension is the first and primary focus of reading strategy development. Vocabulary and decoding instruction follow comprehension (Chapter 6) to indicate the supportive roles these processes play in connection with the construction of meaning.

Chapter 9 deals with practical organizational issues such as scheduling and structuring the classroom environment for literacy learning. Chapters 10 through 12 help teachers develop students' reading and writing abilities as these are applied to different age/grade levels from a balanced literacy perspective. Such key elements as balanced literacy program components, language routines, literature-based reading instruction, readers' and writers' workshops, and the writing process are described in some detail.

The final chapter deals with authentic assessment. The uses of portfolio assessment to document students' continuing growth and development in literacy is a main feature of Chapter 13. In addition, we have gone a step beyond most other authors in attempting to show how authentic assessment strategies can be used to satisfy such political realities as grading, an accountability issue and practice still required by most school systems. These proposals, or extrapolations, may cause some to speculate as to the appropriateness of using portfolio assessment components in this way. Others, in some cases practicing teachers, may feel the time has come for some of these real-world issues to be addressed. We simply hope the suggestions will prove to be helpful in stimulating further experimentation and debate in developing balanced programs.

Finally, we hope that readers will feel that the hallmark of this book is its practical nature. We have attempted to fill the second edition of *Teaching Children to Read: From Basals to Books* with numerous teaching activities, student work samples, literature response activities, descriptions of successful classrooms, lists of helpful materials, sample classroom schedules, and many other helpful illustrations. Contributions such as these come from our own classroom experiences and those of literally hundreds of teachers with whom we have worked. They are intended to breathe life into these pages and provide teachers with a handbook worth keeping and using in daily teaching. Any suggestions or successes the reader may wish to share are greatly appreciated and may help us all teach students to read and write more effectively and creatively.

Acknowledgments

After several years of planning, writing, and production, it seems an impossible task to thank all those involved in the revised edition of this book. For those we may inadvertently omit, we beg their pardon and patient understanding.

We owe a great deal of credit to the parents and children of the first-grade classes we taught as classroom teachers in 1987 to 1988. The insights of these child learners profoundly influenced our growing understanding of how children solve the language learning puzzle. We also wish to thank our teacher and administrative colleagues in Sage Creek Elementary School and Kenwood Elementary School, who have, through their dedication and risk taking, shared and clarified for us the way of transitions toward balanced literacy teaching. We are grateful also to those many teachers with whom we have worked in in-service projects throughout the country who have helped us clarify our transitions position and philosophy.

We owe a debt of gratitude to our students and colleagues at Texas Christian University and Brigham Young University who have been readers of and reactors to our evolving manuscripts of this revision and offered many hints for improvement. We must acknowledge the insights of the many professors, teachers, and students who used the first edition and shared their feelings and ideas. A particular debt of gratitude is extended to Kari Gali and Teresa Moss for their dedication to this project and many hours of careful work, and to Kathy Williams, Starpoint School. We should also express gratitude for the generosity and support of Brigham Young University and Texas Christian University for providing the use of computer equipment and office space during the writing of this text.

To Jeff Johnston, we express gratitude for sharing our vision and supporting this project. To Linda Scharp and Brad Potthoff, we express deepest gratitude for their unfailing excitement and creative vision for this project. To Linda Montgomery, Mary Harlan, and Luanne Dreyer Elliott, we express thanks for their meticulous attention to detail in the preparation and production of this text. To our many reviewers, we express deep gratitude for their words of encouragement, their timely insights, and their help in shaping the organization and content of the second edition of *Teaching Children to Read: From Basals to Books:*

Kathy Barclay, Western Illinois University
Carole L. Bond, Memphis State University
Martha Combs, University of Nevada, Reno

Susan J. Daniels, University of Akron
M. Jean Greenlaw, University of North Texas
Judith Mitchell, Weber State University
William J. Oehlkers, Rhode Island College
Timothy Rasinski, Kent State University
James E. Walker, Clarion University of Pennsylvania
Brad Wilcox, Brigham Young University

We hope all who venture into these pages may find useful knowledge, practical applications, and joyful insights into how children may be supported as language learners. Perhaps most important, we hope that readers of this text will come to understand that teachers, like children, are learners first. And teachers as learners need support and understanding as they make transitions toward balanced literacy instruction beliefs and practices.

Contents

Chapter 3

Chapter 4

Chapter 5

Chapter 6

Comprehending Text   196

Chapter 7

Acquiring a Reading Vocabulary   250

Chapter 8

Identifying Words in Print   276

Chapter 9

Designing Literacy Learning Environments   320

Chapter 10

Chapter 11

Chapter 12

Chapter 13

Teaching Children to Read

Chapter 1

Introducing a Transitions Approach to Reading

Focus Questions

When you are finished studying this chapter, you should be able to answer these questions:

1. What is the nature of the debate between whole language practitioners and traditionalists in reading education?
2. What is meant by "balanced literacy programs"?
3. What does Frank Smith (1983) mean by "soft-core ignorance" in education?
4. How does a transitions approach differ from an eclectic approach?
5. What are the key elements of the transitions model?
6. Why is it said that making transitions toward balanced literacy instruction is "evolutionary, not revolutionary"?
7. At what point in the transition is it appropriate to develop a system of beliefs? Explain.
8. The notion of "risk taking" is pervasive throughout the transitions philosophy. Who are the chief risk takers, and what are their risks?
9. Both preservice and in-service teachers face many obstacles in making transitions. What are some of the different challenges facing reading educators in transition?

Key Concepts

Transitions
Traditional Approaches
Whole Language
Balanced Literacy Program
Eclectic Approach

12 Principles for Supporting Literacy Development
Preservice Teachers
In-service Teachers

Transitions: A New Model for Teaching Reading

Teachers in transition are bridging the gap between traditional and whole language perspectives.

Traditional approaches rely heavily on teacher-directed instruction and basal readers.

What is whole language?

Balanced literary programs combine the richness of whole language with some of the structure of traditional approaches.

Transitions is a philosophical position that encourages teachers to initiate changes in reading beliefs and practices by building bridges, not walls, between traditional and holistic approaches. In recent years there has been a storm of controversy between reading educators favoring traditional basal reader programs and those advocating whole language perspectives. For our purposes, we define **traditional approaches** to reading instruction as those relying heavily on teacher-directed instruction, usually in conjunction with basal reader textbooks. These teachers tend to teach reading from a parts to whole perspective, or "skills-first, authentic reading later." **Whole language**, on the other hand, is not considered an approach or practice but a perspective or philosophical stance (Altwerger, Edelsky, & Flores, 1987). Whole language teachers attempt to integrate the four language modes of listening, speaking, reading, and writing across all curriculum areas. Reading in authentic literature and real writing and authoring experiences are two of the hallmarks of whole language teaching.

We take a stance of moderation when it comes to whole language perspectives, especially concerning (a) how quickly the transition is to occur and (b) whether or not teachers can use some ideas from traditional perspectives. We use the term **balanced literacy program** (also referred to as *balanced literacy instruction*) to differentiate our interpretation from a purist view of whole language. We concur with Routman (1988), who said, "I am also concerned about the possible misuse of the term 'whole language' as a new catch phrase that opportunists will exploit to their advantage" (p. 26).

Teachers drawn toward traditional basal programs argue that the basal is successful, especially as measured by standardized tests, competency tests, and other measures of reading achievement commonly used in most school systems. In addition, many teachers like the structured aspects of basal reader manuals, which save a great deal of time. Thus, many teachers feel that basal readers are efficient classroom tools, help children learn to read, and provide documentation of reading success.

In spite of the popular support of numerous administrators and teachers for these traditional modes of reading education, there is unrest among many teachers who feel required to use them. Even though the basals were substantially revised in 1994 and brought more in line with aspects of balanced literacy programming perspectives, many of the old problems remain. Routman (1988) states that for many years teachers have been dissatisfied with boring, isolated, and unrelated reading skills, drills, and worksheets; efficient but unfounded teaching methods; and "dumbed-down" stories and textbooks. But because of highly resistant forces and well-established traditions, teachers have sometimes come to disregard their own feelings, intuitions, and expertise as professionals. In some cases they have been subtly lulled into a state of educational ignorance. Frank Smith (1983) decried this problem in his essay entitled *The Politics of Ignorance:*

> Soft-core ignorance, which tends to be found in schools, is the ignorance of those who feel they need to be told what to do. Many teachers are trained to be ignorant, to rely on the opinions of experts or "superiors" rather than on their own judgment. . . . They express surprise or disbelief when it is suggested that their own experience and intuition might be as good a guide for action as the dogma of some expert. (p. 3)

Shannon (1989), in his book *Broken Promises,* asserted that during the past seven decades teachers have been gradually "deskilled" by an overreliance on basal readers—meaning that teachers are losing their ability to plan and make professional decisions about reading instruction largely because of an overdependence on commercially published basal readers. Shannon's assertion was corroborated by Duffy, Roehler, and Putnam (1987) when they reported "Neither the content nor the instructional design [of basals] offered much structure for decision making" (p. 360).

K. Goodman, Shannon, Freeman, and Murphy (1988), in their book *Report Card on Basal Readers,* declared "A promise is made to administrators that the basal eliminates teacher competence as a factor in successful reading development, provided that teachers follow the manual exactly" (p. 1).

List two problems associated with overreliance on basal reader programs.

Over time, teachers have become increasingly dependent on published materials to dictate the content, philosophy, and pedagogy of reading. To make matters worse, administrators have become equally dependent. They often mandate the strict and unquestioning use of basal materials and practices. Many times teacher evaluations are tied to the use of these materials and practices.

Whole language advocates, on the other hand, feel that their perspective does a better job of empowering students and teachers. This is accomplished in part through the integration of such activities as reading in real books, the writing process, and speaking and listening experiences. These activities are often based on students' own experiences and are assumed to be inherently more stimulating. Preliminary research suggests that students in whole language and balanced literacy programs tend to perform as well as students taught with basal readers (Reutzel & Cooter, 1990). Furthermore, balanced literacy instruction programs tend to foster positive attitudes toward reading as an elective activity (Reutzel & Cooter, 1990).

Balanced literacy programs help students develop skills as effectively as basals and also foster positive attitudes toward reading.

The struggle between traditional views of reading, whole language, and balanced literacy program innovations makes it difficult for teachers to reconcile changes against the two juxtaposed purposes held for schools. While educational researchers and theoreticians call for increased attention to respecting and meeting individual needs, parents, administrators, and school boards demand increased productivity and accountability to achieve societal goals. In conclusion, Mosenthal (1989) proclaims

Teachers trying to reconcile traditional and whole language perspectives often feel caught between a "rock and a hard place" (Mosenthal, 1989).

> by failing to provide teachers with the means to effectively deal with both approaches, whole language [and traditional] proponents are contributing to the problem of placing teachers between a rock and a hard place. (p. 629)

To better understand both the problems facing today's teachers, we recently returned to full-time classroom teaching. We explored the usefulness of many of the whole language and balanced literacy program strategies suggested by leaders in the field. So as not to fall into the "throwing out the baby with the bathwater syndrome," we also considered traditional strategies for teaching reading that might have value in a balanced literacy program. A major point of interest in our classroom experiences dealt with the challenges facing teachers moving from traditional forms of teaching to more balanced literacy programs. As a result of these experiences, we feel that we have come to a better understanding of the debate between whole language, balanced literacy, and traditionalist positions.

We believe the answer to the reading education dilemma is the creation of a third approach, one that bridges the gap between basal and whole language, balanced literacy instruction (Mosenthal, 1989). Instead of trying to draw teachers into either the whole language or basal reader "camps," teachers should be helped to build bridges between traditional views of reading instruction using basal readers and those views and practices they would like to develop.

A Transitions Approach to Reading Instruction

Transitions teachers are moving from traditional beliefs toward newer innovative practices gradually.

As stated earlier, *transitions* is defined as a philosophical position that encourages teachers to initiate changes in reading beliefs and practices by building bridges, not walls, between traditional and whole language approaches so as to arrive at a more balanced literacy perspective. This philosophical position asserts that teachers make changes by beginning from where they are and progressing to where they want to be—moving from the *known* in beliefs and instructional practices to the *new* (see Figure 1.1).

A transitions approach allows teachers to springboard from basal reader programs as their sole curriculum to such balanced literacy program practices as teaching the writing process and the use of popular children's literature for reading instruction. As teachers experience success with balanced literacy program approaches, a new spirit of adventure in teaching and learning enters the reading classroom. Several key elements of transitions are described in the following paragraphs.

Transitions Means Philosophical Movement

One aspect of transitions is the notion of movement. Over time, most teachers will gradually move toward more whole language-like strategies and further away from dependence on the basal approach. As Kenneth Goodman once remarked about whole language teaching, "It's contagious. It's a grass-roots movement, passed on from teacher to teacher. Once you see it in action, you can't go back" (Esch, 1991, p. D1).

One reason this notion of movement is important is because it distinguishes the transitions approach from those commonly referred to as "eclectic" approaches. In

Figure 1.1

Making transitions toward balanced literacy programs

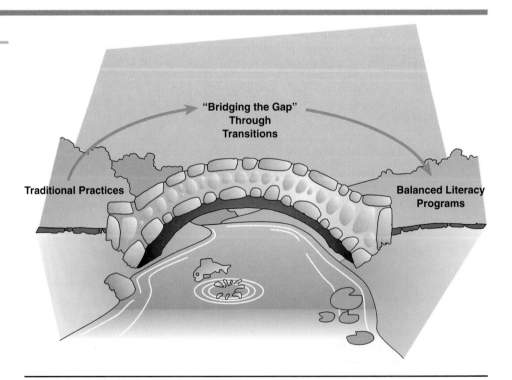

an **eclectic approach**, teachers simply borrow elements from two or more approaches to create their own approach. Eclectic approaches frequently grow out of what is considered new or trendy, rather than being organized according to one's articulated belief system. Once designed, an eclectic approach seldom changes; it is relatively fixed. Transition approaches, on the other hand, change continuously and move in a one-way direction toward more balanced teaching.

*Notice how **eclectic approaches** differ from traditional approaches to teaching.*

Transitions Takes Time

Transitions is also about time—time to learn, explore, and grow professionally as a teacher of reading. A transitions position emphasizes and acknowledges the fact that teachers will make changes toward balanced literacy program beliefs and practices in their own way and at their own rate. Rhonda Jenkins (1990), an Australian educational consultant, commented that teachers in the largest Australian school district were given a 10-year transitional period to learn how to change from traditional to more holistic or "balanced" reading and writing instruction. With this in mind, one must reasonably expect that teachers will make transitions toward balanced reading beliefs and instructional practices quietly, little by little, step by step, over a substantial period of time (Y. M. Goodman, 1986; Heald-Taylor, 1989; Routman, 1988).

Transitions means philosophical movement, changing over time at one's own pace, and involves curriculum integration.

Transitions Involves Curriculum Integration

One well-known teacher-in-transition, Regie Routman (1988), wrote about her gradual move toward whole language teaching and her struggle to change both her beliefs and practices to eventually reflect a more balanced literacy program perspective.

> At this point in time I am comfortable integrating the four language modes—listening, speaking, reading, and writing. . . . While many would say I am a whole language teacher, I am personally uncomfortable with the pureness that the term "whole language" implies for me. I cannot say at this time that I always have a whole language classroom. I don't always use thematic units; I occasionally teach from part to whole; I am still struggling hard to integrate more areas of curriculum with the language arts—an ideal that is very difficult to attain. I anticipate that this struggle will go on for years. (Routman, 1988, p. 26)

Transitions Involves Risk Taking

Closely related to the notion of allowing teachers time to make changes at their own pace and in their own way is the recognition that *risks* are associated with making these changes. Silvia Ashton-Warner (1963) acknowledged the risks associated with making changes in reading instruction when she wrote

> If only I had the confidence of being a good teacher. But I'm not even an appalling teacher. I don't claim to be a teacher at all. I'm just a nitwit somehow let loose among children. If only I kept workbooks and made schemes and taught like other teachers I should have the confidence of numbers. It's the payment, the price of walking alone. . . . It's this price one continually pays for stepping out of line. . . . But I must do what I believe in or nothing at all. (1963, p. 198)

Transitions teachers are supportive of each other and themselves. They build "safety nets" for themselves and others by understanding that transitions toward balanced literacy instruction take time and will not happen all at once. These safety nets

Moving toward balanced literacy instruction is evolutionary, not revolutionary.

are to be not only tolerated but appreciated as a normal evolutionary step. The movement toward balanced literacy instruction is evolutionary—not revolutionary (Pearson, 1989c), meaning it won't happen overnight. One teacher gradually transitioning into her own balanced literacy program remarked,

> The basal program acts like a safety net for me. I've used it successfully for years and I know that the curriculum objectives required by the school system will be met and documented when I use basal materials. But I do want more for my students. My transitions program allows me to keep my basal safety net while learning more about whole language. This year I reduced my classroom time in the basal to only three days per week. That allows me to begin to do more with the writing workshop and children's literature. Next year, I plan to use the basal even less to allow for more whole language activities. (Darlene DeCrane, Bowling Green, OH)

The Transitions Model: A Modest Proposal for Change

Making transitions toward balanced literacy instruction is a complex and multifaceted process. As discussed earlier, teachers make transitions in a variety of ways and at differing rates. For example, some teachers initially come into contact with balanced literacy programs through big books or trade books. Finding these reading materials both interesting and useful, these teachers begin to make their own transitions. Regardless of how, when, where, what, or why teachers begin, we have identified at least seven interrelated dimensions of making transitions represented in the model shown in Figure 1.2.

Notice that many dimensions are involved in making transitions.

An examination of the model in Figure 1.2 reveals that transitions toward balanced literacy instruction in reading involve gradual change along seven interrelated dimensions: (a) instructional beliefs, (b) reading materials, (c) curriculum design, (d) cultural diversity, (e) assessment, (f) classroom environments, and (g) community involvement. Transitions in instructional beliefs may range from an initial "combative" stance toward balanced literacy program beliefs to the opposite end of the continuum—an "advocate's" stance. Changes in the use of traditional instructional materials, while acquiring other instructional materials better fitted to the balanced teaching of reading, make up another dimension of transitions. Teachers' design of the reading curriculum may change during transitions from emphasizing isolated skills in reading toward integrating reading with the remainder of the school curriculum. Transitions in community involvement may range from classroom isolation to involving colleagues, parents, and administrators as integral parts of reading instruction. Transitions in classroom learning environments range from institutional environments to more home-like environments for learning. Another aspect of transitions is the shift from what may be termed monocultural views of society to a multicultural outlook created in the literacy learning classroom. Finally, transitions in assessment range from product—formal assessment best represented by criterion-referenced and standardized achievement tests—to process—informal (authentic) assessment, analyses of children's actual reading and writing processes.

The movement into transitions begins with the establishment of a system of beliefs. As Lucy Calkins (1986) stated,

> We must remember that it is not the number of good ideas that turns our work [teaching] into an art, but the selection, balance, and design of those ideas. Instead

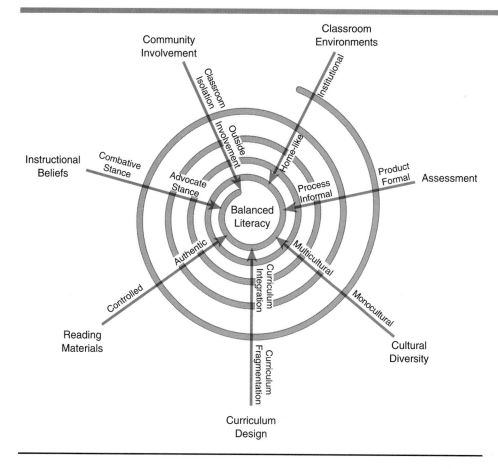

Figure 1.2

Dimensions of transitions: A model of change in reading instruction

of piling good teaching ideas into the classroom, we need to draw from all we know, feel, and believe in order to create something beautiful. (p. 9)

The next section is designed to help teachers begin to develop an understanding of principles consistent with a balanced literacy program philosophy for reading instruction.

Twelve Principles for Supporting Literacy Development

To begin making transitions toward balanced literacy instruction in reading, it is necessary to identify criteria by which teacher-held ideas about reading instruction or existing program elements may be judged. For practicing teachers, new program elements cannot be added until some of the more expendable program practices already in place are eliminated from the busy school day. A belief system helps teachers screen new ideas for philosophical and instructional congruence. We assembled a list of **12 principles for supporting literacy development** for this purpose, along with a description of each. Although this list may not be exhaustive, it should serve as a starting place for teachers to develop their own system of beliefs.

*The **12 principles** help teachers choose practices for their balanced literacy programs.*

- Principle 1: Sharing literacy
- Principle 2: Engaging prior knowledge and language
- Principle 3: Choice and independence
- Principle 4: Reading and writing are reciprocal processes
- Principle 5: "Read it again" using predictable literature
- Principle 6: Approximating, risk taking, and collaboration
- Principle 7: Teaching from whole to parts to whole
- Principle 8: Assessment for supporting learning
- Principle 9: Involving parents and community resources
- Principle 10: A curriculum rich in culturally relevant content
- Principle 11: A program that values multilinguistic and multicultural traditions
- Principle 12: Inclusion of students with literacy learning difficulties

Principle 1: Sharing Literacy

Immersing students in stimulating literacy-learning opportunities is a key to success.

Teachers need to immerse children in enticing literacy situations. The daily classroom lives of children should allow them to discover new and stimulating uses for reading and writing, should expose them to dynamic language use both verbally and in print, and should allow them to see real-life demonstrations of literacy events. These immersion tactics are often teacher designed and include such experiences as reading aloud exciting poems (e.g., Ahlberg & Ahlberg, *The Jolly Postman,* 1986; Prelutsky, *The New Kid on the Block,* 1984); entertaining songs (e.g., Bonne, *I Know an Old Lady,* 1985); and stories that create vivid pictures in the child's mind (e.g., Chase, *Grandfather Tales,* 1948; Davis, *Listening for the Crack of Dawn,* 1990; McKissack, *Flossie & the Fox,* 1986).

Principle 2: Engaging Prior Knowledge and Language

What is the role of prior knowledge in learning?

Each new concept or event encountered in life is stored in the human mind and used to help make sense of the world. Therefore, for children to make the best use of print, teachers should call to the mind of the reader past language and life experiences related to the text or story. Drawing these past experiences into reading experiences promotes deeper comprehension of text, facilitates word recognition, and creates opportunities for children to enjoy the reading experience. This is a critical role for teachers and may be accomplished through rereading favorite books, storytelling, audiovisual presentations, guest speakers, group discussion, and other appropriate means of stimulating the retrieval of memory structures.

Principle 3: Choice and Independence

Think about times when learning was easier for you because of high motivation.

One of the great motivators in life is choice. Teachers should structure learning situations in such a way that children are free to choose activities and materials within given limits. Practices such as individualized reading, self-selected reading (SSR), and self-selected writing (SSW) allow students to choose topics they find interesting and pleasurable. Choice promotes independence in learning, one of the ultimate goals of education.

Principle 4: Reading and Writing Are Reciprocal Processes

One of the most powerful tools for teaching reading is the teaching of writing, or authorship. When children become authors, they become "insiders" in reading (Calkins, 1986). In fact, it is not possible to teach the writing process without helping children become better readers. Children as writers become fascinated by new layers of meaning that can be created through written language. They notice words and phrases used by favorite authors and the way mental pictures can be created through language. Teachers who routinely involve children in the writing process discover that reading ability grows by leaps and bounds. Thus, writers become better readers, and readers become better writers.

As children develop as writers, they automatically grow as readers.

Principle 5: "Read It Again" Using Predictable Literature

All children seem to have books that they love to hear again and again. This "read-it-again" phenomenon produces for every child a body of favorite books. The massive practice that arises from this read-it-again process carries with it a sense of security, familiarity, and affection for different texts.

Instruction in reading should employ predictable language materials and activities at all levels of instruction. In the early years, this may be accomplished through the use of predictable language books (e.g., Martin, *Brown Bear, Brown Bear,* 1983; Skaar, *What Do the Animals Say?* 1972; A. Wood, *The Napping House,* 1984) and language experience charts. Strategies of prediction such as controlled cloze and the directed reading–thinking activity (Stauffer, 1975) should be used at both the micro- and macrolevels to emphasize the importance of thinking ahead.

In a study of beginning literacy (Reutzel & Cooter, 1990), teacher-made predictable language books, language experience, and developmental writing instruction were used with beginning readers in first grade. Not only did these children outperform their basal-only counterparts in other first-grade classes, one teacher remarked at midyear, "these kids think they can read and write anything!" In addition, their comprehension performance on measures regarding prediction and inferential thinking was significantly higher than the basal-only comparison group.

Principle 6: Approximating, Risk Taking, and Collaboration

Early learning in any developmental task is by nature clumsy and unskilled. Not only should this behavior be tolerated in reading instruction, it should be appreciated (Holdaway, 1984). Many times reading teachers expect word-perfect oral reading and penalize children when they fail to say each word just right! Instead, children should be praised in reading class for trying and for approximating the strategies of skilled readers. We know that learners take significant risks with their self-esteem whenever attempting new tasks. This spirit of risk taking should be encouraged so that children can begin to approximate adult standards of literacy. Teachers should do all they can to protect students ("safety netting") from peer criticism and competition in the classroom. The cost of learning must never become so high as to overshadow the benefits and joy of learning.

How is risk taking related to learning?

When children understand that school is a safe place where approximating is appreciated, a sense of community and belonging develops. Teacher-led activities such as shared book experiences, lively unison readings, and storytelling help to draw children further into the classroom community and involve them as active participants. Equally valuable are "collaborative" experiences in which children help each other succeed. Such activities as paired or assisted reading, teacherless writing groups, and other "buddy systems" reduce unnecessary competition and promote learning as a social process.

Principle 7: Teaching From Whole to Parts to Whole

Beginning skill instruction with whole text helps students better understand the value of what they learn.

Children learning to become better readers sometimes need to pay particular attention to aspects of print (Sulzby, 1985, 1991). However, that does not mean that instruction in such areas as phonics or comprehension should focus on these elements isolated from meaningful text (e.g., skill and drill workbook pages). To teach in this way confuses children as to what reading is all about and fails to connect new skills with the reading act (Durkin, 1981b). Reading instruction should begin with the reading or sharing of whole and meaningful text. Any reading skill or strategy to be learned should be taught within the context of a story or text. In the final stages of a

Students must know that the classroom is a safe place for risk taking.

reading lesson, the reading skill or strategy should be taken back into reading, that is, placed back into the original context, and applied later in other contexts (Department of Education, 1985). This whole-to-parts-to-whole way of teaching skills helps students understand the relevance and usefulness of what they have learned.

Direct instruction is often very useful in helping students understand thinking processes in balanced literacy program classrooms (Slaughter, 1988). Teacher modeling of strategic reading behaviors such as predicting, responding, self-correcting, and selecting cues can help children discover different ways of approaching literacy challenges. It is much like a carpenter who demonstrates his ability for an apprentice. By watching the master woodworker, the apprentice learns how carpentry skills are applied to create something beautiful out of raw lumber. Similarly, children in elementary classrooms need to have opportunities to observe their teacher and others as they apply literacy strategies to make sense out of the marks on a page. Whole-to-parts-to-whole instruction, sometimes using direct-teaching methods, is a powerful classroom combination.

Balanced literacy programs frequently make use of direct instruction.

Principle 8: Assessment for Supporting Learning

Classroom assessment should examine students' literacy processes as well as products. The goals of assessment should be to inform instruction and encourage the learner, not simply to document scores for an educational bureaucracy. Best assessments are conducted over time and compare students' past achievements to present abilities. This is partly accomplished through the accumulation of numerous learning artifacts collected using multiple methods of collection (Diffily, 1994). Thus, it is necessary to use authentic assessment techniques (e.g., portfolio assessment strategies, which may include student work samples, observation checklists, writing journals, etc.) as well as traditional assessment strategies to document the child's growth (e.g., standardized reading achievement tests). This view of assessment provides a comprehensive view of the learner's progress (Farr & Tone, 1994; B. Hill & Ruptic, 1994).

What are the goals of assessment?

Principle 9: Involving Parents and Community Resources

Schools cannot encourage literacy development alone, nor should they be expected to do so. Parents must become active participants and supporters in creating and maintaining homes that stimulate literacy growth (Rasinski & Fredericks, 1988). Learning is a three-way partnership between parents, children, and teachers. Without full participation from each, literacy learning is seriously compromised.

Principle 10: A Curriculum Rich in Culturally Relevant Content

Children should have opportunities to read and respond to the great literature, thoughts, and issues of our time (Hirsch, 1987). Within the bounds of good taste, we should not avoid content in an attempt to avoid controversy. Reading is language. Reading is the transmission of ideas. To remove diversity of thought is to reduce reading to a rote act of minor significance. Students should have the opportunity to graduate from our schools culturally literate. Learning materials and activities should be sought that help make this principle a reality.

Reading curricula should reflect the rich diversity of our world community.

Principle 11: A Program That Values Multilinguistic and Multicultural Traditions

Balanced literacy programs are inclusive by nature. They celebrate the rich cultural and linguistic diversity that makes up the mosaic of our nation. Reading and writing opportunities should open the door to learning about and respecting language and traditions from the peoples of the world. This is yet another way of encouraging risk taking in one's class; namely, letting children know that their heritage is not only okay, but invited. Some excellent books are available for read-aloud activities and literature-based reading instruction that serve as a catalyst for multilinguistic and multicultural literacy experiences (reading, language development, written composition, etc.). Some of our favorites for elementary audiences include *Crow Boy* (T. Yashima, 1983), *Hawk, I'm Your Brother* (B. Baylor, 1976), *Cuadros de Familia* (or *Family Pictures*) (C. L. Garza, 1990), and *Mufaro's Beautiful Daughters: An African Tale* (J. Steptoe, 1987).

Principle 12: Inclusion of Students With Literacy Learning Difficulties

What is meant by inclusion?

One of the great trends of the 1990s in American education is inclusion. Educators have come to realize that students with literacy learning difficulties can best be served, in many instances, in the regular classroom. Classroom teachers receive support from special education teachers in various ways so children can escape the stigma of "pull-out" programs and enjoy cooperative learning opportunities with peers. A successful balanced literacy program includes all children, recognizing that all students benefit from classroom diversity in ways that carry into adulthood.

Teachers making transitions toward balanced literacy instruction will likely find that the journey sometimes has a few pitfalls. According to Clarke (1989, p. 371), teaching is a lot like wind surfing: We have the basic instability of the board, shifting winds, the waves, and the sharks. If we are to embark on the adventure of teaching reading using a transitions approach, it may be helpful if we understand some of the "sharks" or obstacles that may cause difficulty. In the next section, some of the obstacles facing preservice and in-service teachers making transitions are explored.

Challenges Facing Teachers in Transition

Challenges Facing Preservice Teachers in Making Transitions

Preservice teachers, or students studying to become elementary school teachers, face special challenges in moving into balanced literacy instruction. Challenges facing preservice teachers are quite different from those of **in-service teachers** (those currently serving as classroom teachers). Preservice hurdles that can be addressed through the transitions approach include the following:

1. Past belief systems
2. Conflicting views among educators
3. Overcoming tradition in the schools

Past Belief Systems

Everyone who has ever attended elementary school as a child has some preconceived notions about what reading instruction is supposed to be. To maintain an open mind and overcome erroneous biases based on their past experiences, preservice teachers can do two things. First, preservice teachers should find out what beliefs they currently hold, then carefully review alternative philosophies and methods for teaching reading. This book is organized to facilitate this process. Once preservice teachers know what they know (and don't know), it becomes easier to begin making mental transitions toward new philosophies and strategies for teaching reading. It is important to remember that (a) everyone holds biases about education, either consciously or unconsciously, and (b) we should keep an open mind about teaching children until all possibilities have been explored.

Conflicting Views Among Educators

Another challenge for preservice teachers is the reality that not all educators agree as to which of the ways of teaching reading is best. For example, it is quite possible for students to take college courses from professors whose classroom experiences were very traditional and feel movement toward balanced literacy programs is not desirable. An important thing to remember is that colleges are organized, ideally, to present many different viewpoints. The purpose of collegiate work is education, not indoctrination. Maintaining an open mind is important if preservice teachers are to become as well informed and effective as they need to be.

Name some challenges for preservice teachers.

Overcoming Tradition in the Schools

Another obstacle is the feeling of inertia or tradition in schools. Many preservice teachers who are practice teaching in schools are intimidated and feel that they are know-nothings. Although it is true that preservice teachers by definition lack experience, it is not true that they are uneducated. Preservice teachers are part of the change process occurring in schools today. Many classroom teachers and administrators are still learning about balanced literacy programs. Preservice teachers play an important role in helping other teachers stay current and begin their own transitions. Preservice teachers should be viewed as change agents who contribute to the improvement of schools while gaining much needed experience from seasoned educators. When viewed in this way, preservice and in-service teachers become true professional partners who assist each other in making transitions toward balanced literacy instruction.

Preservice teachers contribute much to the cause of improving reading instruction.

Challenges Facing In-Service Teachers

Unlike preservice teachers, in-service teachers have had time to get used to the responsibilities associated with daily classroom teaching. The initial feelings of uncertainty have been replaced with a strong desire to find more effective ways of helping children become literate. As in-service teachers begin the process of moving into transitions, they almost immediately become aware of obstacles that can zap one's creative energies unless they are recognized and addressed. Most common hurdles for practicing teachers are related to (a) time commitment, (b) comfort zones, and (c) administrative risk taking.

Time Commitment

Developing balanced literary programs involves a significant time commitment for teachers.

Many reading teachers complain that transition programs require a great deal of time commitment in the early stages. For example, in addition to reading current professional books pertaining to balanced literacy programs (a short list is recommended at the end of this chapter), many teachers also need to become better acquainted with popular children's literature, pull together instructional resources, assemble teacher-made books and bulletin boards, order trade books and big books (for primary levels), review computer software and other technology, and perhaps design thematic units. (Note: These and many other teaching ideas are discussed fully in later chapters.) Teachers also need to find ways of reconciling performance objectives required by the school district with their own newly discovered notions of what the curriculum should include. Without doubt, transitions programs require significant planning time, especially the first few years. But once teachers are off and running, balanced literacy programs become relatively easy to maintain and modify. More importantly, the enjoyment both teachers and children experience in balanced literacy programs makes the effort worthwhile.

Comfort Zones

Another problem is that of comfort zones. That is, it is often difficult to get teachers who have been practicing their profession for even just a few years to begin something as different as transitions. In Chapter 9, we review various attitudinal stances teachers seem to evolve through as they approach change in the classroom environment. Ultimately, teachers who continue to experiment and update their teaching strategies throughout their careers tend to have greater successes with student development and performance, usually experience fewer discipline problems in these energized classrooms, and enjoy the teaching profession rather than burn out.

Administrative Risk Taking

Administrators join teachers in risk taking when making transitions in the curriculum.

Finally, a certain amount of administrative risk taking is involved whenever new program changes are considered. Many wonderful, innovative elementary principals are very supportive of classroom change. Some principals (like teachers), however, are somewhat resistant to change. Successful transitions teachers see as part of the process the necessity of educating administrators about what they are doing in their classroom, and why. They find ways to make the administrator part of the classroom family. They invite her into the classroom frequently and let her become meaningfully involved with children. It is important to remember that most people become teachers because they like to be around children. Principals are simply teachers who have administrative assignments (the term *principal* comes from the original title *principal teacher*). Giving your administrator "hands-on" opportunities with transitions will help inform her about your new literacy goals and build positive relationships.

A Walking Tour of *Teaching Children to Read: From Basals to Books*

Teaching Children to Read: From Basals to Books is intended to serve as a compendium of the best teaching ideas presently available to reading professionals. Because of the number and richness of ideas presented, it will probably not be possible

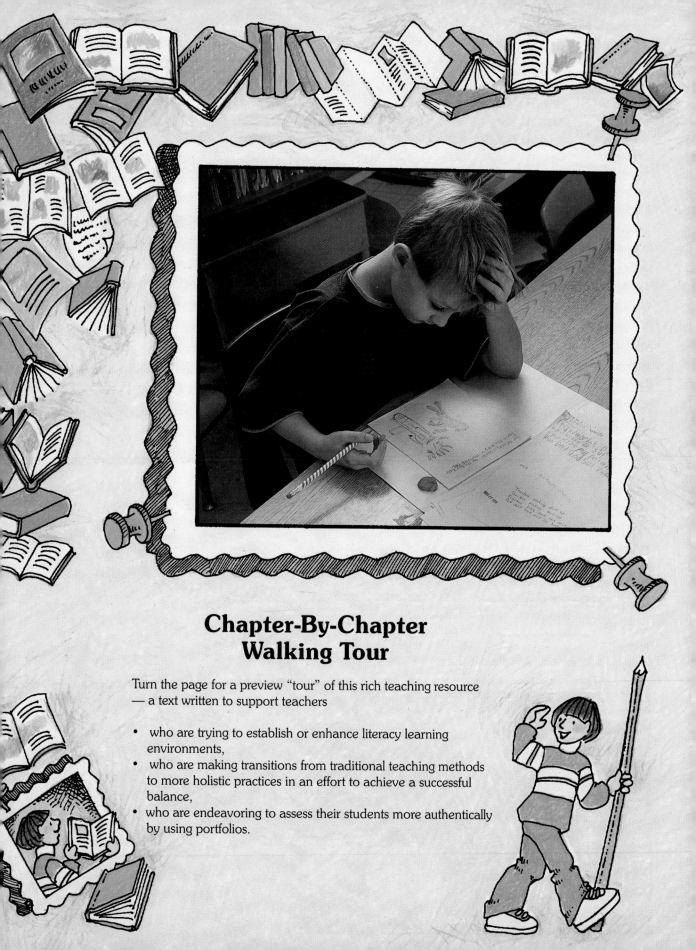

Chapter-By-Chapter
Walking Tour

Turn the page for a preview "tour" of this rich teaching resource
— a text written to support teachers

- who are trying to establish or enhance literacy learning
  environments,
- who are making transitions from traditional teaching methods
  to more holistic practices in an effort to achieve a successful
  balance,
- who are endeavoring to assess their students more authentically
  by using portfolios.

Introducing a Transitions Approach to Reading

Each child brings a unique set of experiences to your classroom. Part of the art of teaching is drawing on these experiences and connecting new learning to what children already know.

Understanding Reading: Defining and Refining Beliefs

As you examine the various beliefs and theories about reading, ask two crucial questions of yourself: "How do I believe children learn to read? How will I teach reading?" Some children have been read to extensively, some have limited experience with print, some will already know how to read. In what way will these differences among children influence your answers?

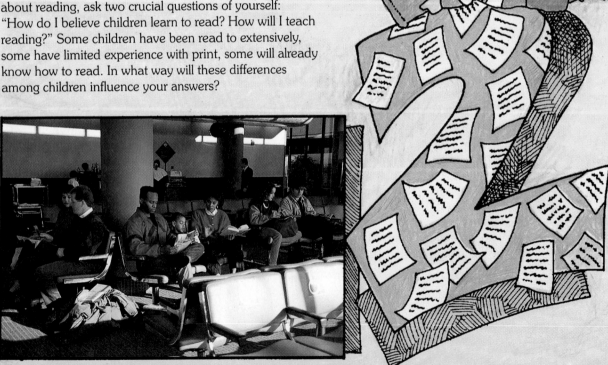

Understanding the Literacy Development of Young Children   Early literacy experiences are not limited to reading. Drawing or writing thank-you notes for gifts is one way even very young children are exposed to print.

Using Basal Readers Effectively   Most of today's basal reading programs contain unabridged versions of "real" children's literature. However, effective teachers need to manage published reading programs as part of a total literacy program. Understanding the strengths and weaknesses of published reading programs will help you redesign basal instruction to balance your teaching methods between skills-based instruction and more holistic practices.

**Making the Transition From Basals to Books:
Bridging the Gap** Murals, story maps, journals
— students can respond to literature in a variety of
ways. Once you have discovered and practiced
more traditional components of reading instruction,
you may want to use children's literature more
frequently and creatively in your classroom. This
chapter will guide you.

Comprehending Text Although you are in charge of
instructional decisions, you don't have to be the only teacher
in your classroom. Parent volunteers, teacher aides, computers,
and the children themselves can take a teaching role in certain
circumstances. Helping readers utilize text clues and connect
their background knowledge to their reading will enable them
to "make meaning" or comprehend what they read.

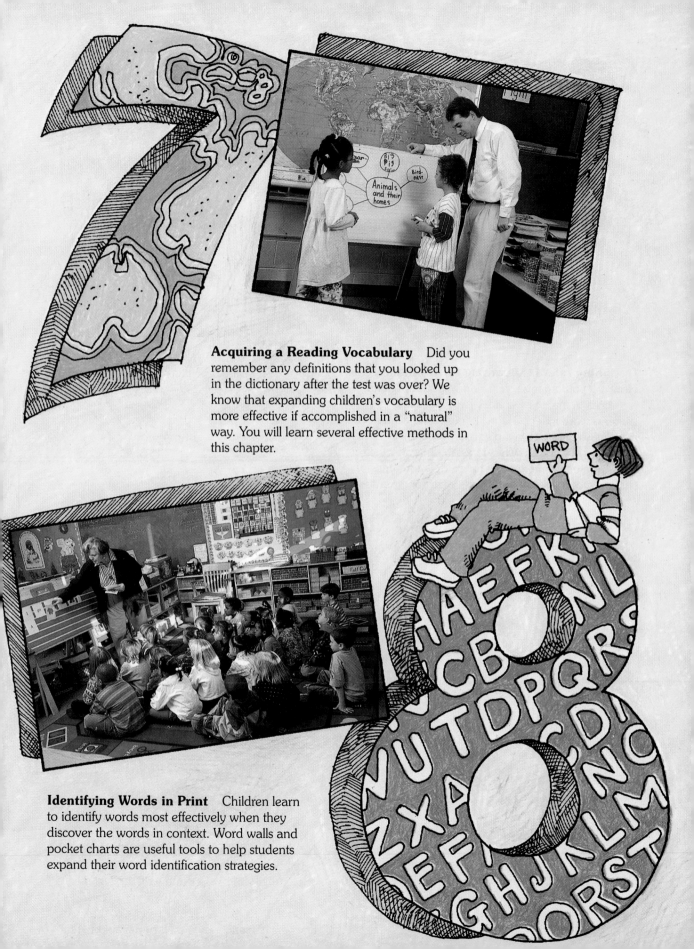

Acquiring a Reading Vocabulary Did you remember any definitions that you looked up in the dictionary after the test was over? We know that expanding children's vocabulary is more effective if accomplished in a "natural" way. You will learn several effective methods in this chapter.

Identifying Words in Print Children learn to identify words most effectively when they discover the words in context. Word walls and pocket charts are useful tools to help students expand their word identification strategies.

Designing Literacy Learning Environments
How will you organize classroom space, time, and
resources to maximize literacy learning? Having
students work independently at neat rows of desks is
not always the best way to encourage literacy. In this
chapter you will learn ways to establish a print-rich
classroom environment and to use different types of
student groups depending on your teaching purpose.

Reading and Writing in the Early Years Even
very young children can participate in classroom
communities of readers and writers. Recreating
stories in dramatic play or sharing personal responses
through talking or art are just some of the ways
teachers can encourage literacy development.

Reading and Writing in Grades 2 to 8

In this chapter, you will discover how to use reading and writing workshops as opportunities for students to respond to literature and to discuss their writing. Reading stories created and published by other student authors is one way to motivate reluctant readers.

Content Area Literacy Instruction

While literacy is important, it is not an end in itself. It is easy to think about computers and calculators as tools but reading and writing are also tools for learning science, mathematics, social studies, and health concepts. In this chapter you will learn strategies to help students read and learn in all content areas, as well as how to develop thematic units.

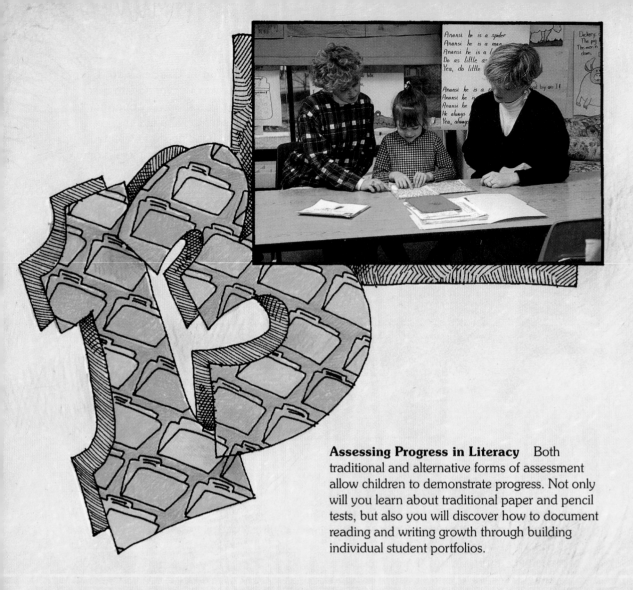

Assessing Progress in Literacy Both traditional and alternative forms of assessment allow children to demonstrate progress. Not only will you learn about traditional paper and pencil tests, but also you will discover how to document reading and writing growth through building individual student portfolios.

for the reader to absorb everything at once, and this is our intent. Rather, we hope that this book will serve as a useful companion to teachers as they make the transitions journey. Following is a brief "walking tour" or overview of the remainder of the text.

This book is intended to address two audiences: undergraduate and graduate students majoring in elementary education at teachers colleges, and in-service teachers wanting to know more about effective ways of teaching reading. The professional literature has been searched for philosophies and effective teaching strategies from traditional and balanced literacy program perspectives. Coupled with the literature review is our extensive classroom experimentation allowing for advocacy of ideas based on experience. From this combination of study and classroom experimentation has emerged a sense of organization that can aid teachers as they make their own transitions toward holistic teaching.

Chapter 1 presents and explains the transitions model of reading instruction. It provides teachers with a philosophy for moving from traditional to balanced literacy program perspectives. The remainder of the book offers an extensive review of traditional and balanced literacy practices that have proven to be effective. Chapter 2 helps teachers begin the transition process with theories of the reading process and instructional models that spring from these theories, and it provides readers with an opportunity to determine their current orientation toward the teaching of reading.

In Chapter 3 we describe the literacy development of young children. This includes such aspects as oral, reading, and written language development. A great deal of attention has been paid to emerging language in children over the past several decades, and this chapter helps readers better understand what is now known.

Many teachers in the early transition stages begin with the reading instructional materials they have on hand—the basal reader. We developed Chapter 4 to help teachers understand the pros and cons of basals and how they can be used effectively. We present many innovative uses of the newly revised basal series that have received much attention in the professional literature. We also demonstrate how basals may be used to teach minilessons in tandem with authentic literature.

Chapter 5 shows teachers how to cross the transitions bridge by springboarding from the basal toward innovative practices more closely associated with balanced reading and writing instruction. Three vignettes describe teachers who are at a traditional or early transitions stage as well as teachers who have progressed to an intermediate or advanced transitions stage.

The essence of reading is comprehension, or understanding the author's message. Over the years, many theories and teaching strategies have been advanced regarding text comprehension. Chapter 6 provides a thorough review of theory and practice in this field of study. Teachers reading this chapter will come to understand strategies children use to comprehend text and how teachers can facilitate the reading comprehension process through creative and stimulating teaching.

An important issue for reading teachers is skill instruction. Should phonics be taught in the early grades? Is it important to teach vocabulary words? What does reading research have to say about these concerns? Chapters 7 and 8 answer questions related to skill instruction and provide extensive information as to how reading vocabulary, decoding skills, and related strategies can be taught.

The latter part of the book presents ways to organize reading classrooms and help teachers move well into developing balanced literacy programs. A logical consideration in building balanced literacy programs relates to classroom reorganization—how to schedule the reading–language arts time period. Also of importance is how to set up the classroom so as to facilitate learning activities. Chapter 9 discusses in detail organizational alternatives including cooperative learning groups, classroom design principles, classroom area diagrams, ways of accommodating diversity, and a wide range of classroom instructional resources. Chapter 10 explains how literacy programs can be implemented to meet the needs of emergent learners in the early grades. Included in this chapter is a discussion of such program possibilities as themed literature units and thematic units. Chapter 11 discusses in detail how reading and writing can be developed for grades 2 through middle school. An exciting chapter for both preservice and in-service teachers, it offers the reader numerous ideas for teaching reading and writing. The chapter includes a recent, comprehensive literature-based model called the Reading Workshop. Similarly, a comprehensive review of the writing process and how it can benefit literacy development are discussed. As with literature-based reading, a classroom-tested model for writing instruction called the Writing Workshop is described. Chapter 12 is especially concerned with the integration and application of reading and writing in the content areas (e.g., science, social studies). Descriptions of how reference tools may be used and the development of interdisciplinary themed studies are important parts of Chapter 12.

The final chapter describes what is often considered the starting point for reading instruction, assessment. This chapter explores both traditional and authentic methods of assessing student progress in reading. A key feature of the assessment chapter is a detailed description of how authentic assessment practices can be successfully used to inform classroom instruction and satisfy typical school district requirements, such as student grades.

CONCEPT APPLICATIONS

IN THE CLASSROOM

1. Outline your reading and language arts block schedule or that of a teacher whom you have interviewed. Would you characterize this schedule as favoring a more traditional, basal-oriented approach, or does it include a number of balanced literacy program elements? Hint: Use the 12 principles to validate your judgment if you feel the schedule favors balanced teaching practices.
2. Consider your teaching environment (resources, principal's attitude, school board and central office policies, etc.) or that of an in-service colleague. What are some of the potential comfort zones? Will some administrative risk taking be required to facilitate transitions toward balanced literacy program teaching? Explain.
3. Draw up a comprehensive list of activities you are currently using in your classroom or those that you plan to use. Next, construct an evaluation checklist using the 12 principles as a guide. Evaluate each of your classroom activities using the 12 principles as the standard. Which of your activities qualify under two or more categories? Do any activities fail to meet any of the standards? If so, what should you do? (Possibly you will need to create some new principles.)

RECOMMENDED READINGS

Atwell, N. (1987). *In the middle: Writing, reading, and learning with adolescents.* Portsmouth, NH: Heinemann Educational Books.

Au, K. H. (1993). *Literacy instruction in multicultural settings.* Fort Worth, TX: Harcourt Brace Jovanovich College Publishers.

Calkins, L. M. (1994). *The art of teaching writing. New edition.* Portsmouth, NH: Heinemann Educational Books.

Heald-Taylor, G. (1989). *The administrator's guide to whole language.* Katonah, NY: Richard C. Owen.

Morrow, L. M. (1993). *Literacy development in the early years* (2nd ed.). Boston: Allyn & Bacon.

Routman, R. (1991). *Invitations.* Portsmouth, NH: Heinemann Educational Books.

Chapter 2

Understanding Reading: Defining and Refining Beliefs

Focus Questions

When you are finished studying this chapter, you should be able to answer these questions:

1. What can be said about reading habits in our society today and the need for reading ability in the future?
2. Why should teachers study and understand the reading process?
3. What are the cognitive, affective, social, and linguistic aspects of the reading process?
4. Which of the three major theories of reading drive three major approaches to reading instruction?
5. Where do your current beliefs place you on the continuum of reading instruction?
6. What is meant by the transitional model of reading instruction?

Key Concepts

Aliteracy
Zone of Proximal Development
Affective Aspects
Conative Aspects
Pragmatics
Linguistics
Psycholinguistics
Sociolinguistics
Language Acquisition
Prosodic Features

Bottom-Up Theory
Automaticity
Subskills Instruction
Interactive Skills Theory
Top-Down Theory
Skills Reading Instruction
Whole Language Theory
Balanced Literacy Instruction
Transitional Instructional Model

Reading in Today's Society

Television, newspapers, and magazines boldly proclaim society's failure to promote and sustain literacy as an enticing and rewarding enterprise for both youth and adults. Although many statistics declare that 23 to 25 million Americans cannot read at a functional level, the greater tragedy lies in the fact that many Americans can read but make a conscious choice not to do so (Chisom, 1989; Kozol, 1985). This problem, called **aliteracy**, is one of increasing concern to business and educators alike. A large number of adults in the United States were found to be illiterate in a 1993 report issued by Richard E. Riley, the U.S. Secretary of Education. In addition to these numbers, one must add the increasing numbers of immigrants who are admitted to the United States on a daily basis (Greaney, 1994). In the report *Who Reads Best* (Educational Testing Service, 1988), 55 percent of low achievers in reading claimed they had access to few reading materials in their homes, evidencing a decided lack of support for reading in the home. Thirty-three percent of low third-grade achievers in reading claimed to read for fun on a monthly basis or even less frequently. Nineteen percent of this same population claimed they had never read a book just for fun in school or out. Of adults questioned, only 23% claimed they had read a book in the previous year (Meade, 1973).

E. D. Hirsch (1987), in his book *Cultural Literacy,* claimed that not only do people fail to choose to read, their reading experiences in schools have focused so heavily on the development of skills that the transmission of culturally relevant content has been largely ignored. Ravitch and Finn (1987) explain why schools have opted for the teaching of skills rather than content:

> Unlike skill training, teaching the humanities requires people to make choices. Deciding what content to teach risks offending some group or individual, those who prefer a different version of history or different works of literature. How much easier, then, to teach social studies as skills rather than as history, offending practically no one; how much easier to teach the skills of language arts, to fill in blanks and circle words, rather than to bear the burden of selecting particular poems, plays, short stories, and novels and to have to figure out how to make them meaningful. (p. 8)

In *Becoming a Nation of Readers* (R. C. Anderson, Hiebert, Scott, & Wilkinson, 1985), the Commission on Reading reported that the average amount of time devoted to sustained reading of connected text in the typical first-grade reading instructional period was only 7 to 8 minutes. Forty-nine minutes, or about 50 to 70% of the reading instructional time, was spent in independent seat work completing worksheets (Rupley & Blair, 1987).

Although the preceding information paints a somewhat discouraging picture of literacy in schools and out, all is not lost. Between 45% and 48% of children in grades 3 and 4 report they read on their own for fun on a daily basis. These percentages, however, shrivel to half that number, 24%, in 12th grade (Educational Testing Service, 1988; National Assessment of Educational Progress, 1990). These data come to light just at a time when knowledge is increasing at astronomical rates and as societal trends move us rapidly away from smokestack industries toward information-service industries. Our society is quickly becoming one of the largest providers of information services; thus, today's children are growing up in an information age when reading and writing play a central and critical role economically and socially. Literacy cannot be oversold in today's economic marketplace. Now as never before, teachers need to understand how children develop into successful readers and writers. More importantly, teachers need to know how they can help children to develop this in their youth and sustain it into adulthood.

The Need for Understanding Reading

On one occasion, Frank Smith (1985), a well-known literacy authority, was asked by an exasperated group of teachers just what he would do if he had to teach 30 youngsters to read. He asserted that children have a right to learn to read with the aid of people rather than programs. Beyond this, his response included two valuable insights. First, teachers must clearly comprehend the *general process of how children learn and develop as human beings*. And second, teachers must understand the *specific processes of how children learn to read*.

How do young children become readers? This question is likely to provoke a flood of very different and sometimes emotionally charged responses. We asked our students to respond to this question in their course reflection journals; here is a sampling of their responses:

Reflect on how you learned to read and how you were taught to read in school.

"Little children start learning to read by being read aloud to."

"Kids learn to read from their parents and brothers and sisters."

"I remember learning the sounds of the alphabet letters and discovering how they made words."

"I remember memorizing a favorite book and reading it again and again until the letters and words made sense to me."

"Writing, that's how I learned to read. I asked my Mom how to write my name. That led to more questions about how to write other words and the names of other people."

Next, we asked our students to define reading. Here is a sampling of their ideas.

"I think reading is when you make the sounds of the letters and put them together to make words."

"Reading is understanding what is on the page."

"I learned to read from a little book with stories that used the same words over and over."

"Phonics is the first part of reading and comprehension is the last."

"Reading is the ability to put together what you know and what is on the page to understand."

"Reading is tracking the author's footprints in the sand along the beaches of the mind."

Of course, these responses led us to pose several additional questions to our students. What are the aspects involved in the reading process? Are there different beliefs on how children *learn* to read? Are there different beliefs on how children should be *taught* to read? How do these differ? These are critical issues to reflect on. Frankly, your definition and beliefs about how reading ability develops will influence the way you assist children in learning to read. Consequently, the remainder of this chapter is intended to help you understand and define reading. We also believe that in the process of defining reading you will begin to refine and articulate your own reading beliefs.

Aspects That Influence Reading Development

The process of learning to read is extremely complex; it is a web woven of intricate designs involving cognitive, affective, social, linguistic, physical, and experiential elements. All of these aspects combine in one unified whole to dynamically influence both the process and product we call *reading.* Although each of these aspects can be isolated for discussion here, we do not wish to imply that these should be separated for instruction. We agree with D. D. Johnson and Pearson, "language is indivisible" (1975, p. 758). We wish to emphasize how each of these aspects contributes to the holistic act of becoming a reader; how such knowledge is necessary for making informed decisions about reading instruction; and how this knowledge will help you to refine your beliefs about how children learn to read.

Cognitive Aspects

Piaget viewed language development as a product of cognitive growth.

To understand human development, a study of the relationship between language development and cognitive growth is essential. Piaget (1955) viewed changes in a child's expressive language ability as indicating intellectual growth or cognitive development. Thus, cognitive development was considered the primary impetus behind language acquisition. Piaget also asserted that language acquisition and cognitive development occurred as a result of maturational rather than environmental forces. These maturational forces directly influenced cognitive growth, which is thought to occur in a predetermined sequence of four stages. Although children were thought to progress through these cognitive stages sequentially, the ages at which they entered or exited each stage varied dramatically. Piagetians call this difference in timing or lag among children in moving from one stage of cognitive development to another *dé callage.*

*Children in the **sensorimotor** stage use language egocentrically to meet their own needs.*

During the first stage, the *sensorimotor stage* (birth to 2 years of age), children's oral language is called *egocentric speech,* meaning speech that is directed mainly at the self or one's own needs. Children at this stage of cognitive development do not see others as separate from themselves. The ability to take into account the view of others—called *socialized speech*—does not occur until much later, somewhere between the ages of 7 and 8 years. Although egocentric speech is audible to others, it is nevertheless directed at the self or self-related concerns.

*During the **preoperational** stage, conservation, reversibility, and decentration are cognitive concepts that are beginning to be learned.*

In the second stage, the *preoperational stage* (2 to 7 years of age), children's language becomes social. This means that children now see themselves as individuals, separate and distinct from others. They now use language to interact with others beyond the desire to meet their own needs. This change results from the process of maturation. Maturation changes children's view of the world, and this change is reflected in their understanding and use of language. During the preoperational stage, children begin to recognize the symbolic nature of language. Language can be used to represent an actual object, concept, or event. For example, the spoken word *baby* represents a real baby, separate and distinct from a picture. Acquiring this understanding is a critical prerequisite for furthering reading development. Children must realize that a word represents the meaning or identity of an object separate from the object itself or a picture to understand that words are merely symbolic representations of the objects and concepts themselves. According to Piaget, this understanding is related to the problem of relating and distinguishing classes or categories of concepts and objects.

It is also during the preoperational stage that children learn the idea that mass or substance does not change when the shape or form of an object is transformed. For example when a ball of clay is flattened, the mass or substance is not altered by the change in shape. This concept relates to Piaget's experiments on conservation. Another concept developed during the preoperational stage of cognitive growth is *reversibility*. Children in this stage do not understand that relationships between events and objects can be reversed. For example, a young boy at this age may recognize that he has a sister but does not realize that he is a brother to his sister. Attaining the ability to conserve concepts and reverse relationships helps young readers generalize their contextually tied recognition of words read in a familiar book or setting, such as a cereal box, to another, less familiar setting, such as the same words found on word cards, wall charts, and so on. During the preoperational stage of cognitive development, children develop the ability to relate the parts of an object to the whole. This development relates to the Piagetian concept of *decentration*—the ability to keep from centering attention on only one quality or attribute of an object or concept. This development is of particular importance because many children are introduced to reading in a manner that requires them to identify the parts of words first. Many children can learn and even memorize word parts before this stage of development, but understanding how these parts fit together to make a word or to access meaning requires an understanding of how the parts make up a constituent whole.

In the third stage, the *concrete operations stage* (7 to 11 years of age), children develop the ability to solve problems and think deductively while continuing their development and understanding of conservation, reversibility, and decentration. Language can now be used as a tool for discovering relationships such as sequence or order, cause and effect, and categories. Piaget maintains that much of this is learned from interacting with others and manipulating objects in the environment. Actual experience with and manipulating objects in the environment directly impact language development. Consequently, experience with language as a whole should precede a study of language parts. Only when language is experienced whole will the parts make sense to the learner. Vasily Sukhomlinksy, an acclaimed Russian educator, in his book entitled *To Children I Give My Heart,* clearly believed that experience and language are the fount of cognitive development.

Only when language is experienced whole will the parts make sense to the learner.

> I begin to take the children on journeys to the source of words: I opened the children's eyes to the beauty of the world and at the same time tried to show their hearts the music of words. I tried to make it so that words were not just names of people, places, things, or phenomena, but carried with them emotional coloration—their own aroma, subtle nuances. Until the child feels the aroma of words, sees their subtle nuances, it [sic] is not prepared to begin to study reading and writing. And if the teacher begins this too early, he or she dooms the children to a difficult task. . . . The process of learning to read and write will be easy if it is a clear, exciting bit of life for the children, a filling out of living images, sounds, and melodies. (Sukhomlinsky, 1981, pp. 125–126)

In the final stage, the *formal operations stage* of Piaget's (1955) cognitive development description (11 years of age to adult), children become able to think abstractly and logically. Now they use language to discuss distant concepts, events, and experiences. Language has become an important vehicle for transcending the

Formal operations *allow language to be used to transcend the boundaries of space and time.*

boundaries of time and space. Before this stage children needed to be in the presence of the object or event to manipulate or experience it; now thought can proceed without the immediate presence of objects or events. This use of language is crucial for reading development. Learning from text requires that the reader be able to abstract concepts, events, and experiences from text rather than from direct experience or manipulation of objects. In fact, it is hard to imagine a child learning from reading who cannot think abstractly.

Language learning, according to Piaget, is determined by increasingly sophisticated thought or cognitive growth. Cognitive growth is not determined by language use. Piaget's views lend support to current theories regarding the development of reading and writing among young children. Encouraging children to read and write whole texts and stories early in the schooling process allows children the opportunity of exploring, manipulating, and experiencing meaning in language. Piaget's views also support both actual and vicarious experiences to build children's background experiences in preparation for success in reading as well as using children's language and experience in the creation of reading materials.

Vygotsky (1896 to 1934), a famous Russian psychologist and educator, believed that an individual's cognitive capacity and the range of cognitive abilities among the general population were in large part predetermined by heredity. Contrary to Piaget's beliefs, Vygotsky (1962, 1978) believed that cognitive development was very much affected by language acquisition and its use in the course of interactions with other human beings in society. In short, Vygotsky believed that language meaning is negotiated in a society. This process of negotiating meaning between children and others in a society expands their ability and tools for thought. Hence, unlike Piaget (1955), Vygotsky (1962) maintained that meaning is not created in the mind of the child first and then conveyed to others; but through interaction with other language users in the environment, meaning arises and is established in the mind of the child. In short, when children find themselves in social situations, they use language as the tool for exploring their world. According to Vygotsky, when children use language to explore, they develop cognitively. When Piaget observed children in his research, he assessed their cognitive development in terms of how they could solve a problem without intervention or teacher assistance. From this work, Piaget maintained that there was no point in trying to teach a child to perform a particular task until she reached a certain stage of cognitive development when the solution to the task or problem was readily understood. Conversely, Vygotsky assessed cognitive development in terms of how well a child could perform a specific task in cooperation and collaboration with others. The difference between what a child can do alone and in collaboration with others is what Vygotsky called the **zone of proximal development**. Frank Smith described the zone of proximal development this way: "Everyone can do things with assistance that they cannot do alone, and what they can do with collaboration on one occasion they will be able to do independently on another" (1988, pp. 196–197).

Instead of withholding certain tasks from a child until a particular stage of cognitive development is reached, as suggested by Piaget (1955), Vygotsky (1978) recommended that once the zone of proximal development was identified, a teacher, parents, or peers could help a child perform a task she would not be capable of doing on her own. Vygotsky also differentiated between school and nonschool learning. Spontaneous concepts are learned outside of the schooling environment and are fairly concrete. Scientific concepts, for example, are usually fairly abstract and learned primarily in the school environment. Scientific concepts are most effectively learned when these are built on spontaneous concepts. Because Vygotsky valued the

Focus on two ways Piaget's views support current reading instructional practices.

Unlike Piaget, Vygotsky believed cognitive growth was the product of increasingly sophisticated language use.

The meaning of language is the result of a social negotiation and agreement.

*The **zone of proximal development** is working with a child to accomplish a task she cannot yet complete independently.*

role of language use and social interaction as a means for enhancing cognitive growth, tasks that are difficult or abstract would not be withheld from children in early schooling experiences. Instead, Vygotsky viewed language use and social interaction as the very vehicle that can support the child through the learning process.

The notion that social interaction plays a significant role in developing a child's cognitive growth and language ability is extremely relevant to current trends in reading instruction. When children are immersed in reading and writing early in the schooling experience while receiving support from peers and adults, their learning clearly reflects this belief. Further, Vygotsky's theory obviously supports a child-centered and activity-oriented reading curriculum, enabling children to negotiate the meaning of language while using language in a supportive learning environment.

Vygotsky views social interaction among learners as a primary force for developing cognitive abilities.

Affective and Conative Aspects

Attitudes, interest, beliefs, feelings, and values make up the **affective aspects** of the reading process, and desires, persistence, and motivation constitute the **conative aspects** of the reading process (Mathewson, 1994; Raven, 1992). Combined, affective and conative aspects influence whether children will choose to read and how much effort they will give to learning to read. Asher (1980), not surprisingly, has found that reading comprehension was positively affected when children were interested in the reading material. Interest was also shown to be a compensatory factor in reading. For example, some children may struggle with recognizing simple words like *the, at, and,* and *it*. On the other hand, these same children have little difficulty reading words like *dinosaur* and *tyrannosaurus rex* when they are interested in the material. Interest can also compensate for a child's lack of reading ability (Spangler, 1983). One way to ensure children's interest in a topic, book, or any other reading selection is to begin by enthusiastically sharing new reading materials through reading aloud or discussion. Another is to show children how to self-select their own books or stories for reading.

Affective aspects of reading include attitudes, motivation, interests, beliefs, feelings, and values.

Young children can often read books about dinosaurs but have trouble reading words like the, this, and that.

Children who have had positive experiences with learning to read will be more likely to continue to derive enjoyment from reading. Conversely, children who have had negative experiences with learning to read may have found the cost of learning to read too high in relation to the perceived benefit. Children who have had positive experiences with reading at home come to school expecting to learn to read. Parents who read to their children and discuss books with their youngsters create a positive attitude toward reading. Children are also highly motivated by the examples they see. If parents are seen reading and enjoying reading, this also can help mold positive reading attitudes.

When schools provide the same caring and supportive atmosphere for exploring language as the home, children form positive attitudes toward reading at school. Sensitive teachers can do much to positively affect children's attitudes toward reading. Reading aloud stories, books, poems, riddles, and jingles and singing songs together can immerse children in fun and supportive language activities. Providing time daily to explore, read, and talk about language and books children select themselves can also support the development of positive attitudes toward reading.

Parents and teachers should help students have positive initial reading experiences.

Children's reading attitudes can also be influenced by the format of the reading materials. Print size or style, the presence or absence of pictures, and the type of cover (soft or hard binding) in books all have been shown to influence children's reading attitudes and habits (Lowery & Grafft, 1967; Samuels, 1970). Attitudes

Think of a time when you selected a book to read. What physical characteristics influenced your choice?

toward reading have also been found to influence reading comprehension. Henk and Holmes (1988) and Reutzel and Hollingsworth (1991a) have found that negative and positive attitudes toward the content of reading selections among adults and children can influence reading comprehension. Teachers should actively monitor children's attitudes and interests in reading so that affectively appropriate selections may be chosen for classroom instruction (Cooter, 1994).

Grade level and gender have also been shown to influence reading attitudes. Girls tend to exhibit more positive attitudes for reading than boys in grades 1 to 6 (Parker & Paradis, 1986). Alexander (1983) reported positive attitudes toward reading at the end of grade 1 and continuing through the end of grade 3. Attitudes toward classroom reading showed sharp negative changes between grades 4 and 5 in the elementary school according to D. J. Brown, Engin, and Wallbrown (1979). Parker and Paradis (1986) found that positive changes in attitude between grades 4 and 5 were related to recreational, library, and general reading materials. It appeared that allowing for student self-selection of reading materials in the intermediate and upper elementary grade levels may play an even greater role than previously thought.

Allowing time for students to choose their own reading materials appears to be increasingly important in the intermediate and upper elementary grades.

Children who have feelings of inadequacy or inability may be afraid to take the risks associated with learning to read for fear they will fail. The student who reads aloud and is constantly corrected by the teacher or is the object of pointed humor by peers is likely to develop a poor reading self-image. These children often appear to have given up trying to learn to read for fear of failure. Children with positive self-images, on the other hand, attack new and uncertain situations in reading with poise and confidence. These students expect to learn. F. Smith (1988) maintains that children expect to be successful in learning. It is only when they have developed attitudes that they cannot be successful that learning fails.

Teachers can avert the development of poor reading attitudes in several ways. First, they should recognize and respect children's interests and preferences. Second, they can make reading easy by making reading easy (F. Smith, 1983). This means that children can begin reading with very simple and yet complete books like Mercer Mayer's (1976a, 1976b) *Hiccup* and *Ah-Choo* books. These books provide complete and enjoyable story lines while simultaneously limiting the difficulty of the text. Allowing children to choose their own books and having a supply of these limited vocabulary books available can do much to bolster young readers' confidence in their ability to successfully tackle the reading puzzle.

One final way teachers can help avoid the development of poor reading attitudes is to avoid labeling children. Exposing children to needless criticism, endless comparisons to other children, and membership in the low reading group can do much to damage a young child's self-image in the process of learning to read. Children should be supported in accomplishing what they are trying to do (F. Smith, 1988). Read-along tapes, older children, parents, grandparents, and choral reading can do much to support unsure readers while shielding them from criticism and comparison. The use of flexible grouping schemes can also help alleviate the problem and stigma attached to membership in the low reading group.

Social Aspects

As children interact with their environment and with significant others in their social circles, they discover that language is power. They learn that they can control the responses and behaviors of others through language. They learn that language can be used to get what they want and need. In short, they learn that language serves a wide variety of communicative purposes.

The study of how language is used in society to satisfy the needs of human communication is called **pragmatics.** Hymes (1964) describes pragmatics as knowledge about language functions and uses that is conditioned by the language environment into which one is born. In other words, children's and adults' language-related knowledge, habits, and behaviors are directly influenced by the culture or society in which they live and interact.

Pragmatics is knowledge of how, why, when, and where language is used in acceptable ways within a given society.

Halliday (1975), in a monumental exploration of cohesion in English, described three aspects of pragmatic language functions in our day-to-day lives: (a) ideational, (b) interpersonal, and (c) textual. F. Smith (1977) expanded and explained in greater detail Halliday's three pragmatic language aspects by describing 10 functions or purposes for which language can be used. The 10 pragmatic purposes or functions for using language are detailed in the following list[*]:

1. *Instrumental:* "I want." (Language is used as a means of getting things and satisfying material needs.)
2. *Regulatory:* "Do as I tell you." (Language is used to control the attitudes, behaviors, and feelings of others.)
3. *Interactional:* "Me and you." (Getting along with others, establishing relative status.) Also, "Me against you." (Establishing separateness.)
4. *Personal:* "Here I come." (Expressing individuality, awareness of self, pride.)
5. *Heuristic:* "Tell me why." (Seeking and testing world knowledge.)
6. *Imaginative:* "Let's pretend." (Creating new worlds, making up stories, poems.)
7. *Representational:* "I've got something to tell you." (Communicating information, descriptions, expressing propositions.)
8. *Divertive:* "Enjoy this." (Puns, jokes, riddles.)
9. *Authoritative/contractual:* "How it must be." (Statutes, laws, regulations, and rules).
10. *Perpetuating:* "How it was." (Records, histories, diaries, notes, scores.)

Once children understand the many uses for language in their own lives, they readily accept and recognize the purposes and meaning of language found in written language. In fact, success in reading depends very much on the degree to which the oral and written language children encounter in their early speaking and reading experiences mirror one another (Bridge, 1978; F. Smith, 1987).

In light of this fact, experiences with quality literature, extended discussions about literature, and opportunities to write and respond to literature become integral to success in early reading. It is in this setting children begin to make the critical connections between oral and written language uses. When texts support and relate to children's oral language uses and experiences, children can readily discover the fact that written and oral language are parallel forms of language and serve similar purposes for communication.

Linguistic Aspects

Language is a mutually agreed on symbol system that can represent the full range of human knowledge, experience, and emotions. Children and adults use language as a tool for getting needs met, for thinking, for solving problems, and for sharing ideas and emotions. Language can be both expressive and receptive. *Expressive language*

Linguistics is the study of language structure and how it is used by people to communicate.

---

[*]From "The Uses of Language" by F. Smith, 1977, *Language Arts, 54*(6), p. 640. Copyright 1977 by the National Council of Teachers of English. Reprinted with permission.

is used when the sender of a message encodes her thoughts into the symbol system of the language. *Receptive language* is used when the receiver of a message decodes the symbol system of the language into meaning.

Language study can be divided into at least four major fields: (a) linguistics, (b) psycholinguistics, (c) sociolinguistics, and (d) language acquisition.

Linguistics is the study of language structure and how it is used by people to communicate. In linguistics, language is grouped into four categories: phonemes, morphemes, syntax, and semantics. **Psycholinguistics** is the study of how language is used and organized in the mind. This branch of study is mainly concerned with how language relates to thinking and learning. **Sociolinguistics** is the study of how language relates to human and societal behaviors. It is concerned primarily with the social and cultural settings in which language is used such as regions of the country, churches, or schools, and also how levels of education and social class affect language use. **Language acquisition** is the study of how infants learn and use language to meet their needs and express their ideas. For the purposes of studying reading, the English language can be divided into three language cuing systems: semantics (the meaning of language), syntax (grammar, or the word order of language), and graphophonics (the letter symbol–speech sounds system).

Psycholinguistics is the study of how language is used and organized in the mind.

Language acquisition is the study of how infants learn and use language to meet their needs and express their ideas.

Semantics is the study of meaning.

Schemas are defined as packages of related concepts, events, or experiences. For example, on reading the word furniture, readers often activate their knowledge related to furniture.

The Semantic Cuing System in Language

Constructing meaning is the central reason for engaging in the act of reading. The semantic language-cuing system relates to the reader's background experience, knowledge, interests, attitudes, perspectives, and present context or situation in reading. R. C. Anderson and Pearson (1984) point out that constructing meaning from print depends in large measure on a reader's prior knowledge and experience within the content of the text. These prior experiences and knowledge are stored together in the mind in something researchers and theoreticians call *schemata,* or *schemas* (anglicized). *Schemas* are defined as packages of related concepts, events, or experiences. Rumelhart (1980) asserts that schemas are the basic building blocks of cognition—the foundation of the ability to think and comprehend. Readers use schemas to interpret their world, experiences, and print. Each new concept or event we encounter in life is stored and used to help us make sense of our world.

Schemas or the lack of schemas can affect the construction of meaning from a text in many ways. First, readers may have knowledge about the content of a text but may be unable to access their stored knowledge. Read the following passage from an experiment conducted by J. C. Bransford and Johnson:

> If the balloons popped the sound wouldn't be able to carry since everything would be too far away from the correct floor. A closed window would also prevent the sound from carrying, since most buildings tend to be well insulated. Since the whole operation depends upon a steady flow of electricity, a break in the middle of the wire would also cause problems. Of course, the fellow could shout, but the human voice is not loud enough to carry that far. An additional problem is that a string could break on the instrument. Then there could be no accompaniment to the message. It is clear that the best situation would involve less distance. Then there would be fewer potential problems. With face to face contact, the least number of things could go wrong. (1972, p. 719)

Did you experience difficulty in locating a schema to help you interpret the text? If you did, you are not alone. J. C. Bransford and Johnson's (1972) experimental subjects experienced great difficulty assigning the content of this passage to a particular topic. Pause for a moment and try to make a mental note of your best guess of what this passage was about. Now turn to page 40 and look at Figure 2.1. Reread the passage.

Were you able to recognize that the passage was a reenactment of the Romeo and Juliet serenade? Did you think the passage was about physics or electricity? Were you thinking about someone making a phone call? Although the word order or syntax was correct and you could pronounce all the words in the text, this was not enough information to allow you to interpret what you read. Once you were able to access a particular schema or set of topical knowledge, you were able to interpret the somewhat elusive meaning of the text. Even when the information in a text is relatively familiar, readers often access the most likely schema or knowledge base and later modify their choice as they gain more knowledge from the text. Read the following sentences (Sanford & Garrod, 1981, p. 114), and stop and picture what you see in your mind.

John was on his way to school.

He was terribly worried about the math lesson.

Now read the next sentence and notice what happens as you process the new information.

He thought he might not be able to control the class again today.

Did you notice a change in the schema accessed to interpret the text? Did your schema change from that of a young boy on his way to school worried about his math class and lesson to that of a concerned teacher? Now read the final sentence.

It was not a normal part of a janitor's duties.

Did you experience another change in selecting an appropriate schema? Not only do schemas help readers interpret what they read, but the text can influence the schema a reader selects. This back and forth influence of text on schema and schema on text is known as an *interaction*.

Researchers have found that the more you know about a topic or event in text, the more comprehensible the text becomes (Pearson, Hansen, & Gordon, 1979). They have also found that schemas that contain information that is contrary to the information found in a text can result in decreases in comprehension. Suppose a text was written to persuade you that the world was flat rather than round. You would tend to dismiss that information as incorrect. Thus, texts that are contrary to or refute a reader's prior knowledge can present comprehension difficulties (Alvermann, Smith, & Readence, 1985; Lipson, 1984). Finally, the perspective of the reader can influence what is recalled from reading a text. Goetz, Reynolds, Schallert, and Radin (1983) found that persons who read a test passage from the perspective of a burglar recalled distinctly different details than those who were instructed to read it from the perspective of the victim. It is clear, then, that your expectations, experiences, and perspectives help you anticipate and interpret meaning and relate this to your existing knowledge. The more we experience both directly and vicariously, the more our schemas are refined and elaborated, allowing us greater ability and flexibility in interpreting what we read.

Learning can be inhibited if text information is incompatible with information held in a specific schema.

The Syntactic Cuing System in Language

The syntactic cuing system concerns knowledge about the order of language. Proper use of the syntactic system results in grammatically acceptable phrases and sentences in speech and writing. In short, a knowledge of *syntax* is an understanding of how

Syntax *is an understanding of how language is ordered and how language works.*

Figure 2.1

The Romeo scene

language is ordered and how language works. Using accepted word order in language is important because it relates to how meaning is constructed. Suppose a reader picks up a book and reads the following:

> a is saying individual the is our aloud ability our in rarely purposes respond reader the silently only skill upon our is word of called conducted reading reading it Most by is private fluent that for element of to to use course one each to. (Chapman & Hoffman, 1977, p. 67)

Although each word can be read one by one, the meaning is obscured because word order is scrambled. When correct word order is restored, the meaning of the passage becomes easier to construct.

> The ability to respond to each individual word by saying it aloud is, of course, only one element in reading. It is a skill that the fluent reader is rarely called upon to use. Most of our reading is conducted silently for our own private purposes. (Chapman & Hoffman, 1977, p. 67).

Based on syntactic or grammatical knowledge, readers are helped to predict what comes next in a sentence or phrase. Syntax helps readers avoid overrelying on the print to construct meaning. For example, read the following sentence.

Hopalong Hank is the name of my green pet _____.

Even young children will fill in the blank with a noun. Although children may not be able to state a grammatical rule that accounts for the fact that a noun follows an adjective in a phrase or sentence, they are competent enough to know that only certain kinds of words are allowed in the blank. Moffett (1983) states that by the time children enter school they have mastered the contents of an introductory transformational grammar text. This commentary underscores the fact that young children have mastered to a large extent the grammar or syntax of their native tongue when they begin formal schooling; and they can, if allowed, use this knowledge in learning to read.

Graphophonic Cuing System in Language

The graphophonic cuing system concerns the relationship between letters and the sounds the letters are intended to represent. *Graphemes* or letters are mutually agreed on symbols for visually representing sounds and spoken language. Some graphemic systems use an alphabetic principle, whereas others represent unified concepts or events. For example, English uses a graphemic system that is alphabetic, whereas Chinese uses a logographic system that represents with pictures or logos entire concepts or events.

A *phoneme* is defined by linguists as the smallest unit in a spoken language. A *grapheme* is defined as a printed symbol representing a phoneme. The English graphophonic system is composed of 26 letters (graphemes) and approximately 44 sounds (phonemes). Opinions on the number of phonemes we use in English vary among scholars in the field. Ruddell (1974) states that English is composed of 21 consonant sounds, 3 semivowels, 8 unglided vowels, and four levels each for pitch, juncture, and stress—the commonly used and understood **prosodic features** of spoken language. In written language, punctuation (i.e., periods, commas, exclamation marks, quotation marks, etc.) is a means of graphically representing pitch, juncture, and stress found in speech. This brings the total to 44 phonemes. In addition to conventional forms of language study, other forms of sending messages involve using facial expressions, gestures, actions, and so on.

Chapter 8, "Identifying Words in Print," provides further information about the graphophonic cuing system.

*A **phoneme** is defined by linguists as the minimal or smallest unit in a spoken language. A **grapheme** is defined by linguists as a printed symbol representing a phoneme. The **graphophonic system** is composed of 26 letters (graphemes) and approximately 44 sounds (phonemes).*

Reading Theories and Their Relationship to Reading Instruction

Focus on several ways theory can be practical.

Theories explain the beliefs and assumptions teachers and researchers hold about how readers use aspects of the reading process to become proficient readers. Teachers, like researchers, hold theories about how children can be helped to become proficient readers. In fact, teacher instruction is theoretically based, although the theory or theories from which teachers make instructional decisions are often implicitly held; *this means that teachers' theories are seldom examined at a conscious level* (DeFord, 1985; Gove, 1983; Harste & Burke, 1977). In some instances, the mere mention of the word *theory* causes some teachers to dismiss information as impractical. However, Moffett and Wagner (1976) once said that nothing is so practical as a good theory. Nevertheless, teachers consistently use theories in their classrooms to make instructional decisions among various alternatives to help children become successful readers. Teachers' reading instructional practices are driven by beliefs, assumptions, and theories. Through examining theories of the reading process, teachers may come to identify, refine, value, and in some cases verify their own beliefs and how these assumptions impact their own instructional decisions at a practical level.

By definition, "a theory is a system of ideas, often stated as a principle, to explain or to lead to a new understanding" (T. L. Harris & Hodges, 1981, p. 329). Major theories of the reading process, at least for our discussion, are grouped into one of three categories. These include (a) bottom-up, (b) interactive, and (c) whole language theories. These three categories of reading theories represent three different and somewhat unique ideas used by teachers and researchers to explain or lead to an understanding of the reading process. It is important to realize that theories have been neither proven nor disproven; they are simply alternative ways of explaining the process of learning to read. Theories lead teachers to a variety of beliefs and are the motivation behind a number of instructional decisions and practices.

List two reasons why knowing reading theories helps teachers know how to help children more effectively.

In the next section of this chapter, we describe three theories of the reading process in some detail. Next we attempt to show how these theories of the reading process relate to or influence teachers' choices of classroom instructional practices that have been used to teach reading. We believe by making the link between theory and practice explicit, we can help teachers come to realize that all instructional choices are related to and derived from personally held theories about the reading process. Teachers who know how theory and practice relate are able to make logical connections between the reading process and instructional choices for teaching children to read.

Bottom-Up Theories and Their Relationship to Subskills Reading Instruction

Bottom-up *reading theories emphasize the importance of attending to the print and learning to decode the text symbols into spoken sounds.*

Bottom-up theories draw their theoretical roots from a branch of psychology called *behaviorism*. From the behaviorist's perspective, a stimulus causes a particular response in the subject, and this response is either strengthened or weakened through reinforcement. In bottom-up theories of the reading process, the stimulus for reading is the print on the page; thus, the reader begins with the letters on the page and constructs more complex levels of language: words, sentences, and paragraphs. In this process of stringing together letters into words, words into sentences, and sentences into paragraphs, readers glean the meaning from the print. In a very real sense, bottom-up reading theories view learning to read as progressing from the parts of language (letters) to the whole (meaning). Much like solving a jig-saw puzzle, bottom-up theories predict that the reading puzzle is solved by beginning with an examination of each piece of the puzzle one at a time and putting these together to make a picture.

One of the earliest models representing the bottom-up theoretical position about reading was the substrata model of Holmes (1953) and Singer (1960). Today, however, two other models of the reading process associated with bottom-up theories are most often discussed: (a) *One Second of Reading* by Gough (1972) and (b) *A Theory of Automatic Information Processing* by LaBerge and Samuels (1974).

Gough's (1972) *One Second of Reading* model described how print is processed by entering the mind through the eyes, being acted on by the mind in a serial, left-to-right sequence of language processing at several levels of language: first letters, then sounds, then word or concept identification, followed by sentence-construction rules or grammar, and finally meaning. Meaning is produced by Merlin, a magical entity in the model. The very presence of Merlin in this bottom-up explanation of the reading process punctuates the magical nature of deriving meaning from text. In short, the *One Second of Reading* model represents reading as a sequential process moving from the parts of words to the eventual and magical construction of meaning from the print on the page.

Notice some weaknesses associated with two of the earliest models representing the bottom-up theoretical position.

LaBerge and Samuels (1974), in their model of *automatic information processing,* separate reading into two distinct processes, decoding and comprehension. Readers' minds are conceptualized much like a computer. This theory hypothesizes that input is serially and sequentially entered in spite of the assertion that the mind or central processing unit is capable of doing more than one job at a time. This ability to perform more than one task at a time is known as *parallel processing.* Because each computer has a limited capacity available for these types of jobs, computer attention must be shifted from one to the other when doing parallel jobs. If one job requires computer attention, then attention is unavailable for another job. Like a computer, the mind of the reader has limited attentional capacity for doing parallel jobs. LaBerge and Samuels describe this concept as relating to **automaticity**. The term *automaticity* suggests that readers have limited attention capacity that can be shifted rapidly between the parallel processes of decoding and comprehension. If a reader is bogged down in decoding, she will not be able to shift attention to focus on comprehending.

*The term **automaticity** suggests that readers have limited attention capacity that can be shifted rapidly between the parallel processes of decoding and comprehension.*

For example, the novice reader who struggles with each word on the page has her attentional capacity focused on pronouncing the words. In this situation, attention cannot be shifted to comprehending the message. Like the novice reader, young children just learning to ride a bike focus intently on balancing, turning the handle bars, and pedaling. As a result, attention is unavailable for focusing on where they are going or on the warnings shouted from their parents to look out for the curb ahead. The novice bike rider is struggling so intently with the mechanics of bike riding that little attention remains for concerns about direction, potential dangers, and warnings. Similarly, if a reader is a poor decoder, this focuses attentional capacity on decoding and leaves little or no attention for comprehending.

In contrast, children who are accomplished bike riders can ride without hands, carry on a conversation with a friend, dodge a pothole in the road, and chew gum at the same time. Like the accomplished bike rider, the fluent reader can rapidly shift attention to processing the message when decoding no longer demands an excess of attention. In short, the LaBerge and Samuels (1974) model predicts that, if reading can occur automatically or without attentional demands focused on the decoding process, then improved comprehension will be the result. The bottom-up reading theory is represented visually in Figure 2.2. You may notice that this theory emphasizes

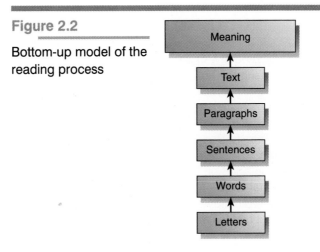

Figure 2.2

Bottom-up model of the reading process

the importance of the features of the text in the reading event (i.e., letters, words, etc.). Important features of this theory are summarized later in the left-hand column of Figure 2.4. Teachers who believe that bottom-up theories adequately explain how children become readers often select an approach to reading instruction called subskills.

Subskills Reading Instruction

Phonics is the foundation of reading in the subskills model with comprehension as the capstone.

According to Harste and Burke (1977) and Weaver (1988), phonics, decoding emphasis, or **subskills reading instruction** is depicted as a pyramid, with understanding sound–symbol relationships (the parts of language) at the base and comprehension (the meaning or whole of language) as the capstone. Chall (1979, 1983), a strong proponent of a phonics or subskills instructional model, characterizes the first stage of reading development as the initial reading or decoding stage. She describes what children must learn during the first stage of reading development.

> The essential aspect of *Stage One* is learning the arbitrary set of letters and associating these with the corresponding parts of spoken words [phonics]. . . . The qualitative change that occurs at the end of this stage is the insight gained about the nature of the spelling system of the particular alphabetic language used. (Chall, 1979, p. 39)

Instruction under a subskills model begins with the letters of the alphabet and the sounds these letters represent.

Phonics or subskill teachers typically focus on systematically teaching children letter–sound relationships during the early stages of reading instruction. Because the most important skill to be learned in early reading is the ability to *recode* the letters of print into the sounds of speech, letter-name and letter-sound instruction often precede allowing children to read words or books independently (as in programs such as CHAR-L or *Intensive Phonics*). Although comprehension is also important in a phonics-first or subskills model, the ability to comprehend is thought to depend largely on the ability to manipulate letter symbols and sounds and connect these with oral language. In effect, the subskills model (shown in Figure 2.3) represents the belief that efficient decoding results in comprehension ability.

Subskills models assume the primary cause of reading disability to be the inability to decode.

Subskills teachers believe that children must be taught phonics first with the letters of the alphabet and the sounds these letters represent *before* beginning to read books independently. Flesch (1955, 1979), among others, cautions that allowing children to attempt to read words or books without knowing the 26 letters and 44

Figure 2.3

Subskills instructional
model of reading

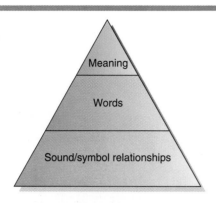

sounds of the letters could lead to potential reading failure and frustration. Thus, letter names and letter sounds become the basic building blocks of reading within a subskills instructional approach. The use of supplemental or external phonics programs along with phonically controlled readers often characterizes the components of this instructional approach. Early books or primers are often made up of words that follow the phonic generalizations the children have been learning, such as short vowel words like *can, man, fan.* This position is well illustrated in the *Becoming a Nation of Readers* report, "The important point is that a high proportion of the words in the earliest selections children read should conform to the phonics they have already been taught" (R. C. Anderson et al., 1985, p. 47).

Finally, teachers who believe in phonics-first or subskills instruction often consider a lack of decoding ability or phonics knowledge to be the fundamental cause of reading disability. Thus, teachers who believe in a bottom-up theory of the reading process tend to make decisions that result in subskills instructional practices. They believe that they can best help young nonreaders learn to read by directly and systematically teaching them to decode letters to sounds, and sounds to words, which are then matched with words in each child's oral speaking vocabulary. Once decoding is mastered, meaning can be derived from the print on the page. And finally, teachers who make instructional decisions based on a bottom-up theory of the reading process believe that reading skill is built from the smallest parts of language to the whole.

In Figure 2.4, the instructional process associated with subskills instruction as well as the connection between *bottom-up theories* and subskills instructional decisions are summarized. Note that *bottom-up theories* suggest that language is learned and processed from the part to the whole. Then observe the connection to practice as shown in the subskills instructional practices. Subskill teachers begin reading and writing instruction by teaching each of the parts of language as a prerequisite to reading words, sentences, and processing connected text. Notice how the theory of controlling text language results in instructional practices that limit students' exposure to words that are phonically regular and follow specific phonic generalizations. Finally, notice the fact that automatic decoding ability on the theory side is supposed to lead to automatic comprehension of text by virtue of word pronunciation and making the connection to one's oral language vocabulary on the practice side. Through this cursory examination, one can readily see how this theory relates to and influences classroom reading instructional practices.

Some authorities claim that automatic decoding ability leads automatically to comprehension ability.

Figure 2.4

Theory-driven reading instruction: Bottom-up and subskill reading instructional practices

Bottom-Up Theories of the Reading Process

• During reading and learning to read, language is processed from the parts to the whole, as in building a structure from blocks one at a time.
• Learning to read is based on Stimulus–Response chains posited by behaviorists.
• Learning to read is accomplished by reducing the skill of reading to its smallest parts to be mastered one at a time.
• Repetition in reading is focused on practicing the parts of the complex skill of reading to a level of overlearning or automaticity.
• Language stimuli for reading are carefully controlled to represent consistently identified language rules or patterns to be learned.
• Mastery of the smallest parts of reading is assumed to lead to competent understanding and performance of the whole act of reading.
• Automatic decoding of the smallest parts of language is a prerequisite to reading and comprehending connected texts or books.
• Correctness is expected; mistakes are to be corrected.
• Pronouncing words provides access to one's speaking vocabulary to enable comprehension.
• Comprehending words provides access to new vocabulary words and comprehension of text.

Subskill Reading Instructional Practices

• Reading instruction is begun by learning the 26 letters and the 44 sounds.
• Instruction proceeds to demonstrate the association(s) between the 26 letters and the 44 sounds.
• Blending the sounds represented by the letters in a word from left-to-right in temporal sequence or "sounding out" phonically regular words is taught.
• A limited number of high-frequency sight words are taught.
• Texts composed of carefully controlled words that are either known sight words or are phonically regular words are introduced to children for reading practice.
• More phonic patterns, rules, and generalizations are taught and learned.
• Texts are controlled to include new words as application for the patterns, rules, or generalizations learned.
• Control over text is gradually released, allowing phonically irregular words.
• Comprehending text is a direct outgrowth from the ability to pronounce words.

Interactive Theories and Their Relationship to Skills Instruction

Interactive skills theories of the reading process place an equal emphasis on the role of a reader's prior knowledge (what the child knows and has experienced) and on the print (what is on the page). In many respects, interactive theories of reading were developed as a reaction to the constant tension among theorists over purely bottom-up theories of reading and purely top-down theories of the reading process. Because we have already described the bottom-up theories of reading, we will briefly describe top-down reading theories, which when combined with bottom-up theories, form interactive theories of reading.

Interactive reading theories place equal emphasis on the role of a reader's prior knowledge and the print on the page.

The return of gestaltist psychological views to America in the early 1960s gave rise to the **top-down theory** of the reading process. To understand the gestaltist position, consider the classic example in Figure 2.5.

What did you see? Did you see the vase? Or did you see two persons facing each other? How did you decide to attend to one or the other interpretation of the picture? Did you notice that the stimulus did not change, but your perception of the stimulus changed?

According to Otto (1982), gestaltist views reconceptualized both the nature of the stimulus and the role of the subject in interpreting the stimulus. Stimuli are processed according to this theory from the whole to the parts. First, the sum or whole of a stimulus is seen. Then, how one perceives the parts of the stimulus are affected by the perception of the whole. People do not respond passively to physical stimuli by simply taking into their minds what is displayed. Rather, they actively organize and interpret stimuli. Because the whole of a stimulus influences the perception of the parts, gestaltists claim that the whole is greater than the sum of the parts.

Reading can be viewed similarly. Although reading is composed of several important aspects (e.g., cognitive, affective, linguistic, etc.), these aspects combine in such a way as to be both different from and greater than the sum of the individual aspects of reading. For example, when one reads, the words do not have meaning; rather, the reader brings personal meaning to the text from her background experiences. Word, sentence, and text meaning are conditioned, influenced, or shaped by the whole set of experiences and knowledge the reader brings to reading rather than the text jumping off the page into the reader's head and providing the mind with meaning.

Top-down reading theories imply that the information and experiences the reader brings to the print drive the reading process rather than the print on the page. In other words, reading begins with the reader, not the text. Reading is a meaning-construction process, not merely a process of carefully attending to visual clues or stimuli in the text. The top-down reading theory is represented visually in Figure 2.6.

Figure 2.5

The Rubin vase

Figure 2.6

Top-down theory of the reading process

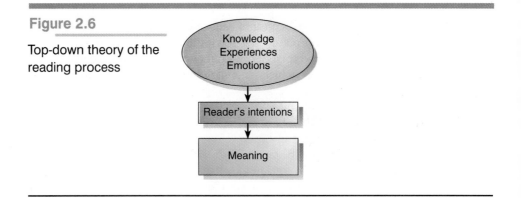

To better understand how reading can be driven by a reader's background knowledge rather than by the print, read a few lines from the well-known poem *Jabberwocky,* by Lewis Carroll (1872).

> 'Twas brillig, and the slithy toves
> Did gyre and gimble in the wabe;
> All mimsy were the borogoves,
> And the mome raths outgrabe.
>
> Beware the Jabberwock, my son!
> The jaws that bite, the claws that catch!
> Beware the Jubjub bird, and shun
> The frumious Bandersnatch!

Clearly, one cannot read or understand this poem by simply pronouncing the words on the page or attending more carefully to the visual stimuli on the page. As readers, we invoke all that we know about jaws, claws, and birds to deduce that the Jabberwock is some kind of creature. We also use all of our accumulated knowledge about grammar and language to determine that the Jabberwock is a thing, not an action or description.

Although these demonstrations are useful illustrations and argue strongly for top-down reading theories, several authors contend that there can be no pure top-down readers (P. C. Burns, Roe, & Ross, 1992; J. L. Vacca, Vacca, & Gove, 1991). Readers *must* attend to the print at some point in the reading process as well as using their entire set of background experiences and knowledge.

As theorists came to understand the reading process in greater depth, it was clear that neither the top-down nor the bottom-up theories could adequately explain the complexity of the reading process. As a consequence, interactive theories were developed in which the strengths of both top-down and bottom-up theories were combined while at the same time mitigating weaknesses associated with either single theory. In short, the interactive theory is a combination theory, as shown in Figure 2.7.

Interactive theories *of reading are drawn from cognitive psychology and represent a combination of bottom-up and top-down theories.*

Interactive theories propose that reading begins with a hypothesis about the text forged from their prior knowledge while simultaneously processing the print. Readers can begin with print and progress toward meaning or begin with meaning and support their selection of meaning by sampling the print. Processing print information in this manner seems to be most economical in terms of time and resources because elements from both bottom-up and top-down reading theories are combined in interactive theories of reading. Interactive theories draw their theoretical roots from a branch of psychology called *cognitive or constructive* psychology. From the cognitivist's per-

Figure 2.7

Interactive theory of the reading process

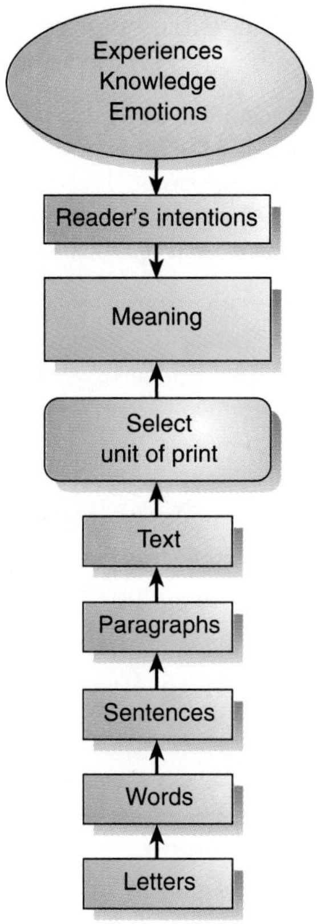

Experiences
Knowledge
Emotions

↓

Reader's intentions

↑

Meaning

↑

Select
unit of print

↑

Text

↑

Paragraphs

↑

Sentences

↑

Words

↑

Letters

---

spective, readers must integrate an array of information sources from the text and from their background experiences to construct a valid interpretation of the author's message recorded in the text. During this process of constructing interpretations of text, readers take on active and passive roles (J. L. Vacca et al., 1991). If a reader possesses a great deal of prior knowledge about a given text, then she will be more likely to form hypotheses about the text and, thus, use fewer text clues in reading. This is viewed as an active approach to reading. If a reader knows very little about a specific text, then the reader takes on a passive role, relying more heavily on the information on the printed page, because the absence of prior knowledge limits her ability to predict ahead of the print. For example, many of us have no trouble reading the following passage because we possess the prior knowledge of a birthday party.

Cody's Big Day

Today was Cody's birthday. He was 5 years old, big enough to go to kindergarten that fall. His mother had planned a sledding party up the canyon on the gently sloping foothills of the rugged mountains above. The sun shone brightly that day, and all the children had fun riding their sleds down the slopes. After the sledding party, Cody and his friends played games and opened presents. To top off the party, the boys and girls ate pizza, ice cream and cake. That night Cody went to bed as happy as any little boy could be.

Now, read the following passage. Although you may know a little about this topic, you must depend more heavily on the text to help you construct meaning because of a lack of adequate prior knowledge about both the topic and the structure of the text.

> But we must be careful not to exaggerate the extent to which a behavioral reinterpretation of intuition about form will clarify the situation. Thus suppose we found some behavioral test corresponding to the analysis of "John finished eating" suggested above. Or, to choose a more interesting case, suppose that we manage to develop some operational account of synonymy and significance. (Chomsky, 1975, p. 102)

Readers must integrate an array of information sources from the text and from their background to construct a valid interpretation of the author's message.

If you happened to have extensive prior experience with linguistics, this text presented little difficulty. You were able to rely on your prior knowledge and adopted an active reader role to construct meaning. Those who know very little about linguistics or transformational grammar have to rely heavily on the text to provide enough explicit information to allow comprehension of the passage. These readers adopt a more passive role. The interactive model of reading suggests that we use what is necessary, either text or background knowledge, to achieve the goal of making sense of text. Teachers who subscribe to interactive theories of the reading process will likely adopt a skills instructional approach for teaching children to read.

Skills Reading Instruction

Skills reading instruction arises from viewing reading ability as composed of a series of discrete skills, which are equally important and accessible to the reader. Each skill is taught directly, often in isolation, and is thought to be integrated by the reader when needed to construct meaning from text. The teaching of reading skills isolated from their use was well documented in studies by Mason (1983) and Reutzel and Daines (1987b). Skills reading instruction attends to meaning at the word level (Weaver, 1988). The belief here is that knowing how to pronounce each word and knowing the meaning of each word are all that is necessary for understanding sentences and larger units of text.

*The **skills model** is composed of three major skill areas: comprehension, vocabulary, and decoding.*

Teachers who use skills instruction see the act of teaching reading like making a tossed salad, in which the ingredients (tomatoes, lettuce, radishes, etc.) are mixed together rather than served in separate bowls. The major ingredients in a reading skills tossed salad are comprehension, vocabulary, and decoding. Even though major reading skill components are mixed together in the tossed salad act of reading, they can still be isolated if necessary for purposes of instruction and measurement. Thus, the act of reading becomes whole when readers integrate the isolated parts they are taught and practice. Pearson and Johnson described reading this way, "Reading (comprehension) is at once a unitary process and a set of discrete processes" (1978, p. 227).

After students read a story, three skill lessons are typically taught—one each on comprehension, vocabulary, and decoding.

Weaver (1988) illustrates skills instructional approaches in a circle, where reading is composed of three categories of skill instruction: (a) comprehension, (b) vocabulary, and (c) decoding (Figure 2.8). Decoding knowledge is not shown as the foundation in the model, but rather as an equal part of the reading instructional process. The three areas of reading skills become the focus from which individual reading skills may be sliced or isolated for instruction. In fact, the skills model is the most commonly accepted approach for providing reading instruction in schools today. This is most likely the case because skills approaches to reading instruction were the predominant form of instructional practice associated with basal reader series. In basal readers, reading skills are typically listed in a scope and sequence chart. The scope and sequence of skills is organized into the three major skills components of

Figure 2.8

Skills instructional
model of reading
(Weaver, 1988)

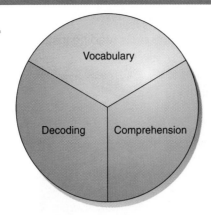

reading mentioned previously—decoding, comprehension, and vocabulary, as published in the teachers' edition.

Another characteristic of skills instruction involves the preteaching of new vocabulary words before reading a selection rather than allowing students to encounter these words in context (N. Gordon, 1984; Weaver, 1988). After students read a selection in a basal reader, teachers typically teach three skill lessons, one from each of the three skill components of reading. Thus, a comprehension skill lesson, a vocabulary skill lesson, and a decoding skill lesson are typically taught. Hence, skills reading instruction is predominantly occupied with teaching skill lessons, practicing these skills, assessing these skills, and reviewing these skills to maintain mastery. Although skills teachers also encourage the reading of stories in trade books and basal readers, reading of the text is usually only a diversion from teacher lessons dominated by skill instruction and practice.

The skills model treats comprehension as a set of discrete skills.

Another distinguishing factor of the skills model is the treatment of comprehension. Comprehension is seen as a set of discrete comprehension skills such as getting the main idea, noting the details, drawing conclusions, and using the context. Each of these comprehension skills is to be taught one at a time and reviewed in subsequent years. Skills reading instruction clearly focuses on the mastery and application of skills as a means to becoming a reader.

Several assumptions are associated with the skills reading instructional practices. First, reading ability is achieved by learning a skill + a skill + a skill, which is integrated by the learner to = reading. Second, instruction is designed to teach each of the language-cuing components—decoding, context, and meaning—separately. Third, when these skills are put together by a reader, they function in a unitary fashion. But, when these reading skills are learned in schools, they are often isolated from their use in text for instruction and practice. And finally, print contains the author's message, and the reader's job is to construct meaning from the text.

In Figure 2.9, the connection between interactive theories and skills instructional decisions is summarized. It is important to understand that interactive theories emphasize a blending of the elements of print and the reader's knowledge and experiences. This theoretical stance influences skills teachers instructional practices. They tend to provide a simultaneous emphasis on developing skills in decoding, vocabulary, and comprehension from the very outset of instruction. Language for reading materials is typically controlled to match students' hypothesized backgrounds and knowledge levels as well as to represent the most frequent or common words in

*Since **interactive theories** of reading emphasize a balanced emphasis on text and prior knowledge and skills instruction, notice how these influence the teaching of decoding, vocabulary, and comprehension skills.*

Figure 2.9

Theory-driven reading instruction: Interactive theories and skills reading instructional practices

Interactive Theories of the Reading Process

• During reading and learning to read, language is processed by balancing the features of the print with the reader's prior knowledge, culture, and background experiences.

• Learning to read is thought to be the *construction of meaning* through emphasizing information gained from the print and from the reader as posited by cognitive constructionists.

• Learning to read is accomplished by placing a balanced emphasis on mastering three skill areas: decoding, vocabulary, and comprehension.

• Language stimuli for reading practice are carefully controlled to represent words that are familiar to the child's background and used frequently in the language.

• Mastery of the skill areas of reading, decoding, vocabulary, and comprehension is assumed to lead to competent understanding and performance of the whole act of reading.

• A balanced emphasis on isolated lessons in each of the three skill areas of decoding, vocabulary, and comprehension is assumed to be integrated by each learner.

• Integration of the three skill areas is assumed to enable skilled, independent reading.

• Correctness is expected, although varying interpretations for meaning based on background knowledge are accepted.

Skills Reading Instructional Practices

• Reading instruction focuses on three skill areas in isolated lessons: decoding, vocabulary, and comprehension.

• Instruction begins in all three areas:
  - Decoding: Learning the 26 letters and 44 sounds.
  - Vocabulary: Learning high-frequency sight words in lists, e.g., *the*, *and*, *me*, *look*, etc.
  - Comprehension: Listening to stories read aloud for the main idea, sequence, or details.

• Instruction continues in the three skill areas in connection with the introduction of simple stories in books called "pre-primers."
  - Decoding: Letter–sound associations learned along with some blending and the sounds letters represent in selected sight words.
  - Vocabulary: New high-frequency sight word lists are learned along with attention to new conceptual knowledge focused around word meaning categories.
  - Comprehension: Simple comprehension skills related to short stories in the teacher's edition focus on main ideas and noting details.

• Instruction progresses to the use of a student's anthology of stories (some use controlled text, some use literature-based stories) and instruction in the three skill areas continues throughout the elementary years.
  - Decoding: Prefixes, suffixes, context clues, etc.
  - Vocabulary: Unfamiliar words, multiple meaning words, word categories, synonyms, antonyms, etc.
  - Comprehension: Sequencing, literary devices, following directions, etc.

printed English. Hence, skills teachers tend to rely on reading materials that limit language in texts to high-frequency words and sight words. Familiar and unfamiliar words are taught from a vocabulary list before reading each text. A purpose is set for reading, and comprehension is checked after reading each selection. The most notable practice in skills instruction is that after each story three skill lessons are to be taught in (a) decoding, (b) vocabulary, and (c) comprehension. From Figure 2.9, one can readily see that an emphasis on a reader's background knowledge and the aspects of the texts leads skills teachers to focus instruction on comprehension to validate and activate a reader's background knowledge as well as to teach lessons about decoding, vocabulary, and comprehension strategies to help children process the text. This connection between theory and practice clearly demonstrates how the tenets of interactive theories relate to and influence the practices of skill instruction.

Whole Language Theory and Its Relationship to Balanced Literacy Instruction

Whole language theories of reading have been eloquently articulated by a number of scholars in recent years (Cambourne, 1988; Edelsky, Altwerger, & Flores, 1991; Y. M. Goodman, 1986; Newman, 1985b). Whole language theories historically paralleled the development of interactive theories, which were viewed by whole language theorists as incomplete explanations of reading and writing development. Although many speak of whole language as though it were an approach, practice, or program, Altwerger, Edelsky, and Flores remind us:

> Whole Language is not a practice. It is a set of beliefs, a perspective. It must become practice, but it is not the practice itself. Journals, book publishing, literature study, thematic science units and so forth do not make a classroom *Whole Language*. Rather, these practices become Whole Language-like because the teacher has particular beliefs and intentions. (1987, p. 145)

*"**Whole language** is not a practice. It is a set of beliefs, a perspective." (Altwerger et al., 1987, p. 145)*

Whole language theories are rooted in the transactional theory of the literary work as explained by Rosenblatt (1978), whose work grew out of earlier writings of Dewey and Bentley (1949) entitled *Knowing and the Known* as well as the writings of early 20th-century literary critic theorists such as Bleich (1978). Unlike interactive theories of the reading process, whole language theories make a break with typically held views of behavioristic and cognitive psychology. According to Rosenblatt (1978), the term *interactive* suggests an artificial separation of reader, text, and the reading event or transaction into isolated categories. Whole language theory, on the other hand, views the reading process as holistic and indivisible. The text, the reader, and the social/situational context should be treated as an integral whole. When instruction does take place, it occurs within the context and constraints of the text, the readers' knowledge, and the classroom situation.

Whole language theories are rooted in transactional theories of literary criticism.

Likewise, whole language theories view language itself differently from interactive. Whole language theorists believe reading, writing, speaking, and listening are alternate forms of language used in society for the purposes of communication. Thus, whole language theories not only assume that reading, writing, speaking, and listening are integrated, but that these forms of language are simply different manifestations of the same underlying communication system called *language*. In other words, language may be expressed in different modes for a variety of purposes, but language as a communication system remains the same. Harste and Burke (1977) describe whole language philosophy as a three-dimensional meaning-centered lan-

Think about how whole language theory differs from bottom-up and interactive theories of reading.

guage sphere placed in a social context and composed of all levels of language. Because meaning construction is at the core of whole language theories, the unit of meaning and focus of instruction in whole language is the sentence rather than the word or letter as in previous theories. For specific word meanings to be correctly understood, a sentence context is necessitated, for example *minute* versus *minute*. When language is used to communicate, it is always embedded within a particular social setting, which conditions how it is used. The model of whole language theory in Figure 2.10 shows that when language is focused on for instructional purposes, it is not immediately reduced to words and letters. Rather, language is initially taught whole and undivided, which results in cutting across all the dimensions of the social setting as well as the three language-cuing systems (semantics, syntax, and graphophonic) available to readers and writers. In short, whole language theory results in teaching language from the whole to the parts to the whole again. And when language units smaller than a sentence are focused on for instructional attention, these subunits of language are always returned to their sentence- or story-level context.

Whole language theory suggests that there is an interdependency between individuals and their environment.

Consequently, another distinguishing feature of whole language theory is the attention paid to *ecological psychology,* a branch of psychological study that suggests that there is an interdependency between individuals and their environment (Barker, 1978; Brofenbrenner, 1977). Hence, whole language theories represent the language learner as embedded within specific surrounding environments called *social or situational contexts,* as shown previously in Figure 2.10. In short, this notion suggests that all language learners are influenced by their surrounding environment. The influence of the classroom environment, atmosphere, or situational context is of great importance in determining the way in which reading and writing are lived and experienced by learners. For example, when a teacher reads Wilson Rawls's (1961) story, *Where the Red Fern Grows,* a feeling of reverence and sensitivity interweaves with the reading of the story. The teacher's voice breaks a little bit toward the end, and this deepens the emotions for the children. The listeners wonder how love can sacrifice itself so tenderly, so completely, and yet so sadly that a red fern grew. When the teacher closes the book, there is silence in the room, and many eyes are filled with glistening tears. This is the silence of reverent reflection—a silence quite different in tone and mood from the silence in classrooms where every child is working individually on a reading skills workbook page or answering a line of comprehension questions. Also, classrooms rich with literacy tools and props, (e.g., books, notepads, message boards, appointment books, pencils, pens, stationery) prompt spontaneous literacy interactions among students (Neuman & Roskos, 1992). Thus, the social, situational context

Figure 2.10

Whole language theory

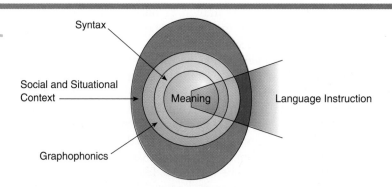

Syntax

Social and Situational Context

Meaning

Language Instruction

Graphophonics

for learning to read and write cannot be dismissed as incidental to the experiences children have as they develop and refine their understanding of reading and writing.

Whole language teachers believe that young children develop reading and writing ability in much the same way as they acquire oral language facility. They learn oral or spoken language in a supportive social environment where they see and hear language used by others for meaningful purposes. For example, when an infant cries, Mama asks if baby is dry, if baby is hungry, or if baby wants to play, while pointing to or holding the object being talked about (e.g., clean diapers, a bottle of milk, or a toy). The infant quickly learns to associate the spoken word with the object in a given situation. Parents also tend to be very accepting of baby's initial attempts to approximate adult speech. Baby mumbles, "ja ja." Daddy grabs her and wildly praises her for saying "da da," which, of course, she did not. Baby simply tried to speak, and for this she received lavish praise and affection. Rather than trying to teach baby to speak by following a predetermined curriculum, parents respond positively to what their infant is trying to do in learning to speak. Similarly, whole language teachers believe they must respond to the attempts of individual children who are learning to read. The careful act of observing children in classrooms to identify learning milestones has been called *kid watching* (K. S. Goodman, 1986).

Although whole language theory is not practice, Altwerger and colleagues (1987) indicated earlier that it must eventually become practice. For over two decades, the philosophy of whole language has become practice in many New Zealand and Australian classrooms. Educators such as Brian Cambourne, Jan Turbill, Andrea Butler, and Don Holdaway have described the practices that emanate from whole language theories of the reading process. We, along with others, refer to the translation of whole language theory into practice as *balanced literacy programs*.

Teachers whose beliefs can be ascribed to a whole language model feel that young children develop reading and writing ability in much the same way as they acquire oral language.

Think of something you have learned to do well. What processes did you employ?

Balanced Literacy Instruction

The elements of balanced reading and writing programs as described by New Zealand and Australian educators (Holdaway, 1979, Mooney, 1990; *Reading in Junior Classes* [handbook for New Zealand teachers, not referenced], 1985) are shown in Figure 2.11. These instructional elements include

- Reading aloud
- Shared reading and writing
- Guided reading and writing
- Language experience
- Supported reading and writing
- Independent reading and writing
- Assessment
- Designing literacy environments
- Instructional planning

In Figure 2.12, the whole language sphere has been penetrated by the instructional elements of a balanced literacy program to explain how teachers can provide reading and writing instruction to young learners.

An essential aspect of balanced literacy instruction is the belief that children learn to read by reading and learn to write by writing (Newman, 1985a). As a direct manifestation of this belief, children and teachers typically engage in daily sustained reading and writing activities using easy, sometimes graded or carefully leveled trade books, enlarged trade or big books, themed units, and self-selected writing projects.

Balanced literacy *instruction focuses on helping children learn to read and write by reading and writing TO, WITH, and BY children.*

Figure 2.11

Elements of a balanced
literacy program

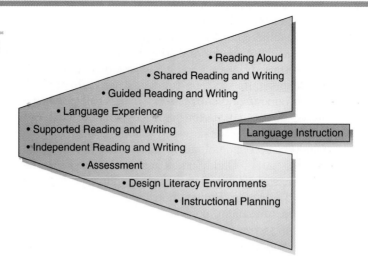

Based on Holdaway, D. (1979). *Foundations of Literacy.* Portsmouth, NH: Heinemann Educational
Publishers.

Teachers read aloud to children regularly, knowing that reading aloud to children
helps them see, understand, and develop appropriate concepts about and attitudes
toward reading and language. Books that children read contain real stories and natural language. Children are not asked to read books that contain artificial, controlled,
or instructionally contrived language. The environment of the classroom is made rich
with print from the everyday lives and learning of the children. The environment and
language of texts are designed to provide genuine opportunities for children to read
and write for authentic purposes. Favorite storybooks are read and reread in a shared
setting that supports children as they make sense of print. Early in the process, children's attempts to make sense of print are often assisted with sensitive demonstrations by other competent language users, such as older children, parents, grandparents, and teachers.

Figure 2.12

Balanced literacy
instruction

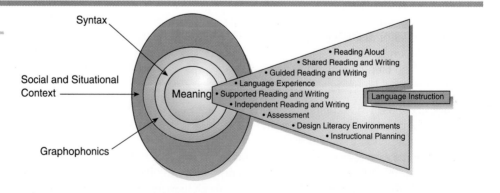

Based on Holdaway, D. (1979). *Foundations of Literacy.* Portsmouth, NH: Heinemann Educational
Publishers.

Teachers using balanced literacy instruction also believe that children's innate desire to use and learn language to express themselves and to meet their own social and personal needs ought to be respected by using children's oral language as the basis for creating reading and writing materials. This practice of using children's language and experiences is often known as the language experience approach. Such teachers believe that children do not begin reading by learning to read and then later on reading to learn. Balanced literacy practices include the use of carefully leveled emergent reading materials that children can read independently with the help and guidance of the teacher.

The object of guided reading is for the teacher to help children develop skills and strategies for successful reading as well as helping young readers discover and use the many language clues found in whole, connected texts. Finally, children must be given abundant reading materials and time to read personally selected reading materials independently each day. After all, balanced literacy teachers believe children learn to read by reading.

Similar practices in writing are incorporated into balanced literacy programs. When children write, they write for their own purposes and choose their own topics (Graves, 1983). They do not usually write about topics chosen by a teacher. Teachers demonstrate and reveal to children the many ways in which writing can be used: to tell the story of ourselves, to record ideas, to organize our efforts, to manage others' time and behavior, and so on. Not only are children exposed to these many ways of authoring ideas in writing, but they are helped to understand the form, features, and functions of these various writing approaches through demonstrations and guided writing activities. Children are given time to write each day. They are encouraged to keep notebooks, lists, and journals. Time for writing independently is provided daily because these teachers believe that children learn to write by writing. In summary, teachers practicing the elements of **balanced literacy instruction** put whole language theory into practice by teaching reading and writing strategies and skills in authentic ways that make sense to learners. They believe that children begin by making sense of print and expecting to learn; and in the process, they learn to read and write.

Several basic assumptions are associated with balanced literacy instructional practices.

1. Reading, writing, speaking, and listening are considered merely different mediums through which the concept of language may be manifested in communication.
2. Learning to read and write is and ought to be a natural process like learning to speak.
3. Meaning is at the heart of learning to read and write.
4. Reading and writing instruction focuses squarely on meaning by progressing from the whole to the parts and returning to the whole of language.
5. Learning to read and write are developmental processes.
6. Children learn to read in a supportive and rich literacy environment from the demonstrations of caring and informed people—not from published texts and instructional materials.

The connection between whole language theory and balanced literacy instructional practices is shown in Figure 2.13. Because whole language theory suggests that children learn to process language from encounters with connected texts, in supportive and authentic situations (e.g., bedtime reading), with real people providing demonstrations of reading and writing behaviors, it is clear that balanced literacy

Think of two ways in which whole language theory connects with balanced literacy instruction.

Figure 2.13

Theory-driven reading instruction: Whole language theories and balanced literacy instructional practices

Whole Language Theories of the Reading Process

• During reading and learning to read, readers process language by creating meaning dependent on their own purposes, the social and situational setting, and the semantic, syntactic, and graphophonic aspects of print.

• Learning to read is thought to be an event where a reader's response to a text is conditioned by the text, the people, the physical environment, and the cultural expectations of the situation as posited by literary criticism and transactional theory.

• Learning to read is accomplished by creating meaning through the use of semantic, syntactic, and graphophonic cues appropriate to the print, the context, the social or situational setting, and the reader's purposes.

• Language stimuli for reading practice are authentic, uncontrolled, and meaningful wholes including stories, songs, and poetry, etc.

• Approximating the demonstrations of competent language users—often with substantial guidance and support from these individuals—is assumed to lead to competent understanding and performance of the whole act of reading.

• Reading materials are practiced whole and undivided initially. After initial readings of the whole, instruction proceeds to look into the text for what one might learn about how language works and the parts of language. Instruction is tied directly to the text and context of the reading materials and learners.

• Mistakes are expected and seen as evidence of risk taking and progress among young learners.

• Demonstrations and modeling of conventional reading, writing, and spelling are integral for children and adults to learn how to make meaning that others will be able to understand and accept as appropriate.

Balanced Literary Instructional Practices

• Early reading instruction recreates the bedtime reading or lap reading situation through using enlarged print of stories, songs, or poems often found in "big books" read to and read with young children.

• Instruction demonstrates/emulates how competent readers read and write with fluency, expression, and use the language cues of pictures, semantics, syntax, and graphophonics to process and produce text.

• Instruction focuses on understanding the whole, then moves to understanding the parts, then returns to an understanding or integration of the parts with the whole.

• Because instruction focuses on meaning, language activities are often grouped around a topic, theme, author, or genre.

• Individual interpretations or diverse responses to a text are encouraged. Taking different perspectives on the same text is part of the instructional process.

• Integration of the language and learning approaches across traditional curriculum boundaries influences the use of themed units or thematic studies.

• Children read and write for personal or authentic reasons. Real literature books are read. Topics for writing are chosen by the writer.

• Classrooms resemble busy language workshops filled with literacy tools, print-rich environments, and lively literacy-based interactions between teachers and children.

• Balanced reading program elements include reading aloud, reading together, guided reading, supported reading, and independent reading.

instruction would re-create these authentic situations in the classroom. Teachers provide real stories and poems to be read. They provide exemplary models or demonstrations of reading and writing behaviors. They provide sensitive and helpful guidance about how to use skills and strategies to read and write. And they create a learning environment and specific classroom situations that mirror other authentic literacy and life-related events. Taken together, one can easily see that the practices associated with balanced literacy instruction are integrally related to and derived from the tenets of whole language theories.

Defining and Refining Instructional Beliefs

One characteristic of a knowledgeable and masterful teacher is the ability to clearly and succinctly state what she believes about teaching and learning. Articulating one's definition of reading is a critical step toward understanding the reading process. Teachers who do not possess a personal definition and understanding of the reading process are likely to adopt unexamined consensus beliefs and practices implicit in a given reading program or school setting. This leads to the possibility of teachers teaching from superstition and tradition rather than from knowledge, experience, and critical evaluation (F. Smith, 1985). Harste, Woodward, and Burke emphasize the importance of defining and refining teacher beliefs over time in this way:

Teachers who do not possess a personal definition and understanding of the reading process are likely to adopt unexamined the beliefs and practices implicit in a given reading program or school setting.

> We have come to believe that looking at teacher behavior in terms of beliefs held
> and assumptions made is more cogent and powerful than looking at behavior in
> terms of the supposed approach being used. . . . What this means practically is that
> in order to change behavior we must change beliefs. (1984, p. 7)

The Theoretical Orientation to Reading Profile

The Theoretical Orientation to Reading Profile (TORP) was designed and validated by Diane DeFord (1985) and is easily administered and scored (Figure 2.14). The purpose of the TORP is to help teachers clarify their own beliefs about how children learn to read and, consequently, how teachers believe reading should be taught. It also reveals which of three idealized instructional models teachers' beliefs about reading and reading instruction are currently associated with most strongly.

*The **TORP** was designed to help teachers clarify their own beliefs about how children learn to read and, consequently, how teachers believe reading should be taught.*

If you are a preservice teacher, you may find answering some of the TORP questions difficult. You may feel you do not yet have a belief system about reading instruction. However, we encourage you to take the risk and try by using the best sense you now have of the reading process. Remember that the TORP only reflects what you currently believe. It is in no way a reflection on the potential you have for becoming an excellent teacher of reading. All teachers began somewhere, and so must you. What is important is the understanding you gain about yourself, the reading process, and the direction and determination you have for continuing to grow and explore professionally.

We suspect that at the conclusion of this book you may want to take the TORP once again. You may surprise yourself at that time with the growth and perspectives you will have gained. Now stop here and complete the TORP in Figure 2.14 according to the directions given. Be sure after completing the TORP to follow the directions for scoring carefully. Your score will be interpreted for you in the next section.

Figure 2.14

The DeFord Theoretical Orientation to Reading Profile (TORP)

Directions: Read the following statements, and circle one of the responses that will indicate the relationship of the statement to your feelings about reading and reading instruction. *SA 2 3 4 SD* (select *one* best answer that reflects the strength of agreement or disagreement)

1. A child needs to be able to verbalize the rules of phonics in order to assure proficiency in processing new words.

   1 2 3 4 5
   SA   SD

2. An increase in reading errors is usually related to a decrease in comprehension.

   1 2 3 4 5
   SA   SD

3. Dividing words into syllables according to rules is a helpful instructional practice for reading new words.

   1 2 3 4 5
   SA   SD

4. Fluency and expression are necessary components of reading that indicate good comprehension.

   1 2 3 4 5
   SA   SD

5. Materials for early reading should be written in natural language without concern for short, simple words and sentences.

   1 2 3 4 5
   SA   SD

6. When children do not know a word, they should be instructed to sound out its parts.

   1 2 3 4 5
   SA   SD

7. It is a good practice to allow children to edit what is written into their own dialect when learning to read.

   1 2 3 4 5
   SA   SD

8. The use of a glossary or dictionary is necessary in determining the meaning and pronunciation of new words.

   1 2 3 4 5
   SA   SD

9. Reversals (e.g., saying "saw" for "was") are significant problems in the teaching of reading.

   1 2 3 4 5
   SA   SD

10. It is a good practice to correct a child as soon as an oral reading mistake is made.

    1 2 3 4 5
    SA   SD

11. It is important for a word to be repeated a number of times after it has been introduced to insure that it will become a part of sight vocabulary.

    1 2 3 4 5
    SA   SD

12. Paying close attention to punctuation marks is necessary to understanding story content.

    1 2 3 4 5
    SA   SD

13. It is a sign of an ineffective reader when words and phrases are repeated.

    1 2 3 4 5
    SA   SD

14. Being able to label words according to grammatical function (nouns, etc.) is useful in proficient reading.

    1 2 3 4 5
    SA   SD

15. When coming to a word that's unknown, the reader should be encouraged to guess based upon meaning and go on.

    1 2 3 4 5
    SA   SD

16. Young readers need to be introduced to the root form of words (run, long) before they are asked to read inflected forms (running, longest).

    1 2 3 4 5
    SA   SD

17. It is not necessary for a child to know the letters of the alphabet in order to learn to read.

    1 2 3 4 5
    SA   SD

From "Validating the Construct of Theoretical Orientation in Reading Instruction" by D. E. DeFord, 1987, *Reading Research Quarterly,* 20(3), pp. 351–367. Copyright 1985 by International Reading Association. Reprinted with permission of Diane E. DeFord and the International Reading Association.

18. Flashcard drill with sight words is an unnecessary form of practice in reading instruction.

1 2 3 4 5
SA   SD

19. Ability to use accent patterns in multi-syllable words (pho to graph, pho tog ra phy, and pho to graph ic) should be developed as a part of reading instruction.

1 2 3 4 5
SA   SD

20. Controlling text through consistent spelling patterns (The fat cat ran back. The fat cat sat on a hat.) is a means by which children can best learn to read.

1 2 3 4 5
SA   SD

21. Formal instruction in reading is necessary to insure the adequate development of all skills used in reading.

1 2 3 4 5
SA   SD

22. Phonic analysis is the most important form of analysis used when meeting new words.

1 2 3 4 5
SA   SD

23. Children's initial encounters with print should focus on meaning, not upon exact graphic representation.

1 2 3 4 5
SA   SD

24. Word shapes (word configuration, b i g) should be taught in reading to aid in word recognition.

1 2 3 4 5
SA   SD

25. It is important to teach skills in relation to other skills.

1 2 3 4 5
SA   SD

26. If a child says "house" for the written word "home," the response should be left uncorrected.

1 2 3 4 5
SA   SD

27. It is not necessary to introduce new words before they appear in the reading text.

1 2 3 4 5
SA   SD

28. Some problems in reading are caused by readers dropping the inflectional endings from words (e.g., jumps, jumped).

1 2 3 4 5
SA   SD

Scoring Directions

1. Identify items 5, 7, 15, 17, 18, 23, 26 and 27.

2. Score all other items 1, 2, 3, 4, 6, 8, etc.; by giving the number of points corresponding to the number circled in each item, i.e., if a 4 is circled, give 4 points, etc. Do not score items 5, 7, 15, 17, 18, 23, 26 and 27 when doing this.

3. Now score items 5, 7, 15, 17, 18, 23, 26, and 27 by reversing the process. If a 1 is circled, give 5 points. If a 2 is circled, give 4 points, a 3 = 3 points, a 4 = 2 points and a 5 = 1 point.

4. Add the total of the two scores for one total score and compare with the following scale.

    0 - 65 points indicates a decoding perspective.

    65 - 110 points indicates a skills perspective.

    110 - 140 points indicates a whole language perspective.

Where Do You Stand on Reading?

Scores on the TORP reflect current tendencies and beliefs. TORP scores do not reflect a rigid or exclusive category of beliefs and practices that cannot change.

According to DeFord (1985), teachers' beliefs can be placed along various points on a reading instruction continuum. For example, Figure 2.15 shows three reading instructional approaches along a continuum from left to right. Your beliefs about how children learn to read lie on this continuum somewhere between the subskills, skills, or whole language instructional practices. Now look at your score on the TORP, and find your place on the continuum. This gives you a general idea of where you currently stand with respect to a definition of the reading process.

If your score on the TORP placed you somewhere between the subskills and skills instruction, you have a tendency at present to view reading as a series of skills to be mastered. If your score places you a little closer to the subskills instruction, then you may be inclined to begin reading instruction with the letter sounds and letter names and bring in sight-word and listening comprehension instruction simultaneously or soon after having taught a few letter name–sound associations. If your score placed you between the whole language and skills instruction, you may continue to teach skill lessons while integrating more time for reading literature and self-selected writing projects into your classroom curriculum. You may want to go back and reread your answers for specific items, especially items 5, 7, 15, 17, 18, 23, 26, and 27. If your answers reflected the idea that children learn to read from natural rather than controlled language in books, and that the alphabet can be learned by reading whole books and writing, your beliefs reflect a whole language/balanced literacy orientation to the reading instructional process. Conversely, if your answers reflected a need for children to learn to read with controlled introduction of new words in their books, individual lessons on the letters of the alphabet, and so on, your beliefs cause you to lean more toward a skills and subskills reading instruction. You may feel uncomfortable with your current score on the TORP. Do not despair! You will learn more about how to help children learn to read in the remainder of this book. And as you do, your beliefs may change. You may be making transitions in your beliefs. We remind you once again at this point about the idea of transitions, as discussed in Chapter 1.

Transitional Instructional Model

Mosenthal (1989a) characterized the tension between the three instructional practices described earlier—subskills, skills, and balanced literacy—as putting teachers between a rock and a hard place. Initially, many teachers find elements within each of the three models with which they can agree (Heymsfeld, 1989). In fact, some teachers would very much like to believe and be empowered to teach balanced literacy programs; however, these same teachers become frustrated by those who portray the process of change and

Figure 2.15

Continuum of reading instructional models

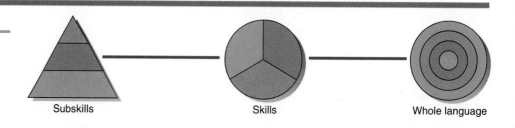

Subskills   Skills   Whole language

adaptation toward implementing balanced literacy practices as an all or nothing affair (Routman, 1988). This "wholier than thou" position is untenable for many teachers. Thus, as discussed in Chapter 1, the concept of **transitions** supports teachers who are attempting the difficult and time-consuming transition from skills or subskills instruction toward balanced literacy instructional practices and beliefs. Remember, however, that transitions is not another way of validating eclectic literacy instruction. Rather, transitions mean that teachers are changing the way they believe and engage in reading instruction in their classrooms consistent with holistic and balanced literacy practices, not just picking and choosing from all beliefs and practices to frame an eclectic stance.

*The **transitional instructional model** is discussed in detail in Chapters 1 and 5.*

Summary

The cursory survey of reading habits among the American population today presented in this chapter revealed significant problems for reading educators. While large numbers of individuals in the United States remain illiterate, the more insidious problem of aliteracy threatens to undermine the general reading habits and attitudes of American adults and children. Although not all indicators are negative, reading educators need to understand that now, more than ever, the ability to read is necessary to survive and prosper in a rapidly growing information society. The goal of producing able readers simply is not sufficient for today's schools. Teachers must become as concerned about developing positive reading habits and attitudes as they have been about ensuring reading achievement and ability. In short, children in today's schools must learn to *love* to read as well as to learn to read!

For teachers to achieve these objectives associated with reading instruction, they must study children and understand how these youngsters go about the business of learning about printed language. They must also clearly comprehend the various aspects of the reading process: cognitive, affective, social, and linguistic. What is more, they must have a working knowledge of three theories of reading: bottom-up, interactive, and whole language. Teachers must also understand that the assumptions and beliefs associated with specific reading theories lead to or drive instructional decisions and classroom instructional practices. Thus, the theories of reading supported three instructional approaches known as subskills, skills, and balanced literacy.

It is equally important to understand one's own beliefs about how children learn to read and how reading should be taught. Using the TORP (Figure 2.14), you were able to understand your current beliefs about how children learn to read and reading instruction. Finally, we briefly reexamined the transitional model of reading instruction as described in Chapter 1. This model explained that teachers need time to make the transition from current instructional beliefs and practices toward more holistic or whole language-like reading instructional beliefs and practices. Figure 2.16 summarizes the chapter.

CONCEPT APPLICATIONS

IN THE CLASSROOM

1. Conduct a poll in your college classes about the numbers of trade books (these exclude college textbooks) read in the last year.
2. Read more on Piaget and Vygotsky. Write a brief report contrasting the differences between these two theorists.

Figure 2.16

Chapter overview

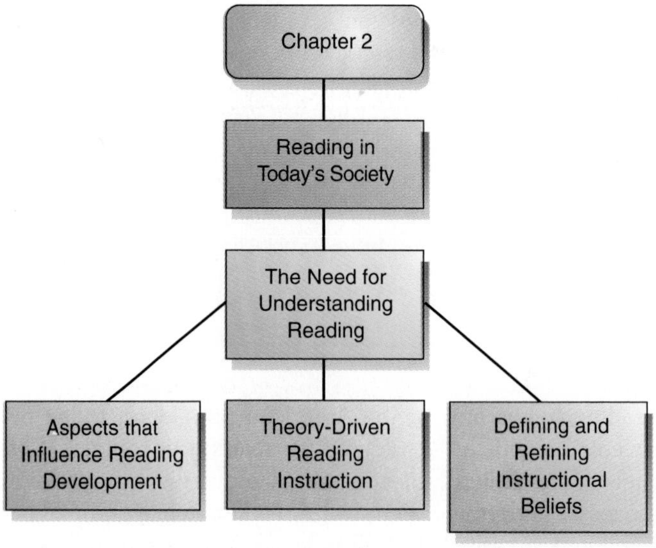

3. After taking the TORP and as you read the remainder of the book, keep a log of information you learn that may cause you to rethink your initial orientation to reading.
4. List the major assumptions and characteristics of each of three reading theories, and summarize each in writing.
5. List the major assumptions and characteristics of each of the three instructional models and summarize each in writing.

IN THE FIELD

1. Visit a kindergarten or first-grade classroom. Describe in detail how children are reading and writing. You may also be able to gather some writing samples to photocopy and return to the children. Make a list of the types of books you saw them reading. Which of the four reading theories best explains what you saw? Why?
2. Administer the TORP to a teacher. Visit her classroom, and determine if her beliefs on the TORP are reflected in her classroom instruction. Describe what you saw and how it related to one of the three instructional reading models.
3. Visit children in several different grade levels. Interview them using questions based on the Burke Reading Interview (Burke, 1987). Ask them:
    a. What is reading?
    b. Who do you think is a good reader in your class? Why?
    c. What would you do to teach someone how to read?
    d. How did you learn to read?
    e. What might you do to become a better reader?
   Record these for the different grade levels and compare. How do children's understanding of reading differ from grade to grade? Discuss these with a peer in your class. Did you both notice similar differences?

RECOMMENDED READINGS

Ashton-Warner, S. (1963). *Teacher.* New York: Touchstone Press.

Cazden, C. (1992). *Whole language plus: Essays on literacy in the United States and New Zealand.* New York: Teacher's College Press.

Chorny, M. (1985). *Teacher as learner.* Alberta, CA: Language in the Classroom Project.

Edelsky, C., Altwerger, B., & Flores, B. (1991). *Whole language: What's the difference.* Portsmouth, NH: Heinemann Educational Books.

Goodman, K. S. (1986). *What's whole in whole language.* Exeter, NH: Heinemann Educational Books.

Holdaway, D. (1979). *The foundations of literacy.* Exeter, NH: Heinemann Educational Books.

Newman, J. (1985). *Whole language theory in use.* Exeter, NH: Heinemann Educational Books.

Stahl, S. A. (1994). Separating the rhetoric from the effects: Whole language in kindergarten and first grade. In F. Lehr & J. Osborn (Eds.), *Reading, language, and literacy: Instruction for the twenty-first century.* Hillsdale, NJ: Erlbaum.

Stephens, D. (1991). *Research on whole language.* New York: Richard C. Owens.

Zarry, L. (1991). *Literacy through whole language.* Manitoba, Canada: Peguis.

Chapter 3

Understanding the Literacy Development of Young Children

Focus Questions

When you are finished studying this chapter, you should be able to answer these questions:

1. What is the difference between reading readiness and emergent literacy views about how children learn to read and write?
2. How do factors associated with reading readiness influence children's readiness for reading instruction?
3. What are three theories about children's oral language acquisition?
4. What are stages of children's oral language development?
5. What are stages of children's reading development?
6. How do children's storybook reading behaviors develop?
7. What are stages of children's writing and spelling development?
8. What is the role of environmental print in children's reading and writing development?
9. How do children develop a sense of story?
10. How do instructional language and terms influence the development of reading and writing abilities of young children?
11. What are children's perceptions of the purposes of reading and writing?

Key Concepts

Reading Readiness
Emergent Literacy
Auditory Discrimination
Phonemic Segmentation
Behavioristic Theory
Innatist Theory
Interactionist Theory
Telegraphic Speech
Analogical Substitution
Generative Language
Reading Development Continuum
Preindependent Reading
Independent Reading
Magical Stage

Self-Concepting Stage
Bridging Stage
Take-Off Stage
Independent Reading Stage
Skilled Reading Stage
Prephonemic Stage
Early Phonemic Stage
Letter-Naming Stage
Transitional Stage
Sense of Story
Story Grammar
Environmental Print
Print Concepts

On Becoming a Reader: Two Views of the World

A moment of magic is taking place right now. Children of all ages are discovering the world of printed language. Christopher, a 3-year-old boy, is going shopping with his mother. He runs down the cereal aisle at the local supermarket and stops abruptly, pointing to a box of cereal, "Look Mom, here's the Fruit Loops! You said they didn't have any!" Amber, age 2, sits on her porch with a well-worn copy of her favorite book held upside down in her hands and her doll on her lap. "Now listen while I read you this story," she whispers to her silent playmate. In a local day-care center, Jeremy, a 4-year-old preschooler, is busily scribbling with crayons on a neatly folded piece of paper. The teacher stops, looks at his work. She notices what looks like a picture of a cake with candles with some scribbles underneath the picture. At the bottom of the paper is the carefully scrawled signature of Jeremy. She pauses and asks, "Jeremy, what are you writing?" He replies with a smile, "I'm writing a birthday card to my Dad." "Really, tell me what you said to your Dad." Jeremy gladly points to each set of scribble marks and tells the teacher what he meant when he made the marks on the paper. These and many more illustrations indicate the wealth of knowledge children have already learned about the forms and functions of written language before formal reading and writing instruction in school.

Acting like a reader is part of becoming a reader.

Two views dominate the current literature on young children's early reading and writing behaviors: **reading readiness** and **emergent literacy**. One view, which categorizes the reading process into two distinct phases, reading readiness and beginning reading, is well illustrated by Chall (1983), who describes reading development in several stages. The prereading stage is labeled *stage zero,* implying that there is a point at which children cannot read. Stage one is labeled *initial reading* or the *decoding stage,* which implies that children begin reading when they have learned the arbitrary letter–sound and letter–name relations and can use these to decode print. The decoding stage also implies that children need to learn certain "basic skills" prerequisite to reading and writing. Although this perspective has long enjoyed popularity, recent research (Teale, 1987) challenges this view of how children learn to read and write.

Two views dominate the current literature on how children learn to read and write: reading readiness and emergent literacy.

The second view of how children learn to read and write is known by the label *emergent literacy.* Teale (1987) describes the forces that have shaped this perspective of the roots of literacy. The term *emergent* implies that becoming literate begins at birth and is a continuous, developmental process. Regardless of age, maturity, or intelligence, we may observe in the behavior of even very young children evidence of the process of becoming literate. Although the reading and writing behaviors of young children may not be conventional in the sense of those behaviors accepted by adults, young children are nonetheless making sense of the uses and conventions of printed language in a variety of situations and contexts from the cradle. The term *literacy* was chosen to represent the fact that reading and writing are closely related processes; and recent evidence suggests that reading and writing are reciprocal processes that dynamically influence each other.

From a historical perspective, the beginning reading and reading readiness perspective provides an interesting background against which the relatively new and developing perspective of emergent literacy can be understood and evaluated. For this reason, we believe that preservice and in-service reading teachers should understand both perspectives on how children learn to read and write.

Reading Readiness

According to Nila Banton Smith (1986), reading readiness became widely accepted during the late 1920s and into the 1930s. Because the concept of reading readiness has enjoyed such longevity, one might assume it is well understood and equally well defined. From a study of historical and current literature, that does not appear to be the case. The term *reading readiness* was coined to distinguish the readiness for reading from a general readiness to learn. Examples of how reading readiness has been defined include (a) the readiness to profit from reading instruction beyond the beginning level (Dechant, 1970) or (b) the adequacy of existing capacity in relation to the demands of a given learning task (Ausubel, 1959). Although these definitions provide some insight into the concept of reading readiness, another way that reading readiness can be understood is by identifying the assumptions that researchers and practitioners have held related to success in early reading.

One way to understand reading readiness is to identify the assumptions researchers and teachers hold about how children learn to read.

N. Hall (1987) describes several assumptions associated with the reading readiness perspective on how children become literate. First, reading is primarily a visual-perceptual process involving an understanding of phonic relationships. Second, children are not ready to learn to read until a certain stage of development or a given threshold is achieved. Third, children have to be formally, systematically, and

The search for related factors such as age and intelligence was undertaken to explain how children learn to read.

sequentially taught to learn to read. Fourth, children cannot learn to read until they learn a prerequisite set of basic skills. And fifth, the teaching of basic reading skills can be done in an isolated and value-free way. Because the concept of reading readiness has been based on these assumptions, much of the research related to reading readiness has resulted in a search for factors, such as age, maturation, and intelligence, that predict or relate to success in early reading achievement.

Several factors have been associated with early reading success in the reading readiness literature: age, gender, intelligence, visual and auditory discrimination, listening comprehension, learning modalities, perceptual-motor skills, and alphabetic knowledge. Because much of the research on reading readiness focused on the relationships between specific physical, cognitive, perceptual, and linguistic factors associated with early reading achievement, we discuss the most common of these in the following sections.

Age

One important assumption associated with the reading readiness concept is the idea that there is a portal or threshold through which children pass before possessing the ability to profit from reading instruction. For years, researchers, parents, and teachers have wondered at what point in time children reach this threshold. Logically, this concern resulted in inquiries into the relationship of a child's age to success in early reading. Research sought to determine the optimal age, if any, at which a child could be taught to read. Although some researchers maintained that the question of "when" children are ready for reading was the wrong question to ask (Gates, 1937; MacGinitie, 1969), still other researchers forged ahead, attempting to answer this question.

In 1931, Morphett and Washburne (1931) conducted a widely acclaimed and accepted study, which found that children were generally ready to receive reading instruction when they reached the mental age of 6 years and 6 months. An unfortunate misinterpretation of this finding in practice was that chronological age rather than mental age was a determiner of reading readiness. Although the Morphett and Washburne study was fraught with methodological problems and faulty assumptions, it supported the perpetual belief that reading instruction should be withheld from or delayed for most children. In a review of reading research, Singer dubbed the Morphett and Washburne study as "research that made a difference, but shouldn't have" (1987b, p. 59).

Some children learn to read without exposure to formal reading instructional methodologies.

Dolores Durkin conducted a series of studies aimed at identifying children who came to school already reading. In her classic report, *Children Who Read Early,* Durkin (1966) found that most children, nearly 99%, did not come to school reading. Those who did, however, had not been exposed to formal reading instructional methodologies. These early readers were found to maintain an advantage in reading achievement through the sixth grade over their peers who did not learn to read early. These findings seemed to suggest, that for some children, delaying reading instruction is unnecessary. In fact, research has demonstrated the fact that children learn to read successfully in countries where reading instruction is begun as early as 5 or as late as age 7 (A. J. Harris & Sipay, 1990).

Chronological age is a poor predictor of reading success.

Although some age advantages may be found for children who are older on admission to elementary school as late as in the third grade, by age 13 this advantage decreases substantially, and by age 17 disappears completely (P. Langer, Kalk, & Searls, 1984). A. J. Harris and Sipay (1990) indicate that age measured before reading instruction is one of the poorest predictors of reading success. From the research to date, children appear to have learned to read successfully regardless of chronological age on entering school, and chronological age appears to have little to do with success in early reading.

Gender

For many years, research supported the fact that boys learned to read more slowly than girls, as measured by reading achievement tests in the United States (Bond & Dykstra, 1967). In fact, older studies supported the idea that girls were developmentally ahead of boys, which afforded girls superior reading readiness skills, better initial reading achievement, and fewer reading failures (Durrell, 1940; Gates, 1961).

Gender as a predictor of reading achievement depends on the culture into which the child is born.

More recent research suggests that these earlier findings may have been culturally biased (Downing & Thomson, 1977; Gross, 1978; R. L. Thorndike, 1973). Dale D. Johnson (1973) conducted a large-scale investigation into the gender question in Canada, England, Nigeria, and the United States to determine the effect of gender on initial reading achievement. Of the 72 statistical comparisons between boys and girls, only 18 were significant. In England and Nigeria, boys tended to score higher than girls on tests of reading ability. However, in Canada and the United States, girls scored higher than boys. Johnson concluded that these results indicated that sex differences in reading ability among English-speaking students appeared to be the product of culture more than innate differences between the sexes. Studies to date indicate that gender differences are poor predictors of initial reading success.

Intelligence

In 1921, Arthur I. Gates conducted a study for his doctoral dissertation exploring the relationship between reading achievement and intelligence and found that the relationship between intelligence and reading achievement increased from grade to grade. From these data, he concluded that intelligence was only highly correlated with reading ability when the mechanics of reading were fairly well mastered. The research by Bond and Dykstra (1967) indicated only a moderate relationship between reading ability and intelligence. Spache and Spache (1977) found that intelligence tends to be a better predictor of reading ability for those students who have either a very high or very low intelligence quotient. Torrey (1979, p. 118) reviewed 11 studies of early readers and found that while most early readers were highly intelligent as measured by intelligence tests, some early readers' intelligence scores fell into average or below average ranges. Apparently, intelligence appears to be an unreliable predictor of potential reading achievement or ability.

Some children with low IQs learn to read well.

Visual Ability

It is generally accepted that the eyes play an important part in learning to read. Many teachers and parents have heard horror stories about the child who somehow advanced to the seventh grade making marginal progress and at that point was found to have vision problems. Consequently, every school should regularly screen young children's visual abilities to detect visual anomalies. Teachers should carefully watch children for headaches, squinting, and dizziness, which can signal visual problems, while working in classrooms. An excellent resource for schools to guide the design of a quality school vision-screening program is a book entitled *Screening Vision in Schools*

Focus on the indicator's potential visual problems.

by Jobe (1976). To help teachers, Bader (1984) described adjustments that can be made in instruction to accommodate visually impaired students. The checklist in Figure 3.1 can be used to help teachers make these needed adjustments.

Visual discrimination is the ability to distinguish similarities and dissimilarities among a set of two or more visual stimuli.

Another visual ability traditionally associated with reading readiness is visual discrimination. Visual discrimination is the ability to distinguish similarities and dissimilarities among a set of two or more visual stimuli. For readers, these visual stimuli are most often letters and words. However, some visual discrimination exercises have involved children in distinguishing between geometric shapes and pictures. Research has shown that training children to discriminate between letters and words produces greater transfer effects to the act of reading than does training with geometric forms

Figure 3.1

Instructional adjustments to vision problems

_____ was examined by

(student or client)

_____on _____

(vision specialist)   (date)

The results were:_____

_____

Glasses are to be worn   _____ at all times

_____ yes   _____ for far-point tasks

_____ no   _____ for near-point tasks

Recommended treatment is _____

He or she should be reevaluated by_____

(date)

Recommendations:

Procedures

1. _____ Restrict near-point vision tasks to _____ minutes.
2. _____ Restrict far-point vision tasks to _____ minutes.
3. _____ Permit a marker or use finger during reading.
4. _____ Give near-point copying tasks, only.
5. _____ Permit child to move closer to copy work.
6. _____ Encourage child to choose best seating to copy work.
7. _____ Restrict reading to charts or chalkboard.
8. _____ Restrict reading to near-point.

Materials

9. _____ Use manuscript print.
10. _____ oversize type (_____),
11. _____ a primer typewriter,

From "Instructional Adjustments to Vision Problems" by L. A. Bader, 1984, *The Reading Teacher*, *37*(7), pp. 568–569. Copyright 1984 by Lois A. Bader and International Reading Association. Reprinted by permission.

and pictures. Paradis (1974) found that most preschool and kindergarten children can already discriminate among shapes and pictures, rendering such activities useless even in the earliest years of schooling insofar as later reading ability is concerned.

Identifying geometric shapes has little to do with the ability to identify letters.

Auditory Ability

In reading programs where phonics play a large role in the introduction of reading, auditory ability becomes crucial. Here again, schools should provide regular auditory screenings to locate and help children who have problems hearing. Two auditory

12. _____ buff or pastel paper,

13. _____ line paper, wide spaces,

14. _____ soft large lead pencil,

15. _____ soft large chalk,

16. _____ a magnification device: _____,

17. _____ Avoid purple dittos.

Conditions

    Avoid high contrast. Use pale or muted colors for:

18. _____ reading, writing materials,

19. _____ work surfaces,

20. _____ walls,

21. _____ chalkboard.

    Reduce glare, use nonglare materials for:

22. _____ reading, writing,

23. _____ work surfaces,

24. _____ walls,

25. _____ Place light sources outside binocular field.

    Adjust working surface

26. _____ 20 degrees, off horizontal.

27. _____ Distance should not require tilting of head or body.

    Instruction

28. _____ Support visual instruction in reading and writing with VAKT (Visual-Auditory-Kinesthetic-Tactile) procedures.

29. _____ Remind student to practice visual training procedures.

30. _____ Work with teacher consultant for visually impaired.

31. _____ Other suggestions: _____

abilities are often helpful when learning to read: (a) auditory discrimination and (b) phonemic segmentation.

Auditory discrimination is defined as the ability to distinguish between the similarities and dissimilarities of two or more auditory stimuli. For many children, this means discriminating between, for example, the /f/ and /v/ sounds. Because many beginning reading programs demand auditory discrimination ability, the preponderance of reading readiness programs place great emphasis on developing this ability before formal reading instruction. Auditory discrimination is often considered a prerequisite for applying phonic skills through blending letter sounds into words. Paradis and Peterson (1975) found that the discrimination of initial consonant sounds was more difficult for young children than discriminating rhyming sounds. For auditory discrimination training to be useful, therefore, such training should focus on the discrimination of letter sounds and not on rhyming sounds or sounds in the environment. Although auditory discrimination is assumed by teachers and publishers to be a prerequisite for applying phonic skills in reading, research has failed to show this to be the case (Hammill & Larsen, 1974; Lyon, 1977; Neuman, 1981). Research has also failed to demonstrate a large discrepancy between good and poor readers directly related to auditory discrimination ability (Lyon, 1977).

Phonemic segmentation is defined as the ability to isolate in proper sequence the individual sounds found in a word. Research has shown that phonemic segmentation ability is often difficult for young children to acquire (Adams, 1990a; Allan, 1982; R. C. Anderson, Hiebert, Scott, & Wilkinson, 1985; Ehri & Wilce, 1985; Liberman et al., 1977; Wallach, Wallach, Dozier, & Kaplan, 1977, Yopp, 1988; Griffith & Olson, 1992).

Calkins (1986, p. 174) refers indirectly to phonemic segmentation ability when she mentions a technique called *word rubber-banding* used by young writers to invent spellings for words. Rubber-banding involves stretching a word to be able to isolate the individual sounds to approximate the spelling. For example, the word *run* would be stretched into *rrrrruuuuunnnnnn* to allow the writer to identify and segment the word into the phonemic values or sounds in the word. Roberts (1975) indicated that while blending seems to be needed for reading, phonemic segmentation seems to facilitate writing to a greater degree than reading. Thus, for young writers who use invented spellings, some training in phonemic segmentation may be helpful in showing children a useful strategy for approximating the spellings of words as they work to become independent spellers. On the other hand, young readers may need help with the blending process to facilitate the pronunciation of words unfamiliar to them in the printed form.

Learning Modalities and Learning Styles

A recurrent theme in reading education is the belief that children learn to read better when their dominant learning modality is identified and instruction is matched to the preferred modality. A *modality preference* is defined as a pronounced tendency toward selecting a particular modality for processing information, that is, visual, auditory, kinesthetic, or tactile. Although this belief may be intuitively appealing to some, no research has been reported in the field of reading to show that matching instruction to learning modalities positively influences reading achievement. In fact, H. M. Robinson (1972) concluded that with currently available instruments, only 11% of the students in her study could be reliably classified as "auditory" or "visual" learn-

---

Sidebar notes:

Auditory discrimination is defined as the ability to distinguish between the similarities and dissimilarities of two or more auditory stimuli.

Phonemic segmentation is defined as the ability to isolate in proper sequence the individual sounds found in a word.

No research has been reported in the field of reading to show that matching instruction to learning modalities positively influences reading achievement.

ers. Tarver and Dawson (1978) performed a meta-analysis of 15 studies dealing with modality preferences. Of the 15 studies analyzed, only two showed significant differences in reading achievement when reading instruction was matched to identified modality preferences. As such, Pikulski (1985, p. 128) concluded that the practice of matching modality preferences to reading instruction continues in spite of a scant if not "nonexistent" research base.

R. Dunn (1988) and Carbo (1988) have written extensively about learning styles. Learning styles tend to be thought of as the total combination of factors (e.g., environment, social aspects, physical conditions) that affect the way students learn. Carbo (1988) divides learners into global and analytic learners based on a series of evaluative criteria. Several problems continue to plague the learning styles literature. First, no definition of what constitutes a learning style has been generally agreed on in the literature. Second, the research in this area is in its infancy, and as of yet, no firm conclusions can be reached about the contributions of learning styles to reading achievement or reading readiness (A. J. Harris & Sipay, 1990; C. S. White, 1983).

As of yet, no firm conclusions can be reached about the contributions of learning styles to reading achievement or reading readiness.

Learning modalities and learning styles remain poorly defined, are difficult to reliably identify, and are not supported by a significant and well-regarded research base. As a result, using learning styles or learning modalities to determine if a child is ready to receive formal reading instruction seems inappropriate.

Listening Comprehension

Pearson and Fielding (1982) discussed the importance of developing young children's listening comprehension as a prelude to formal reading instruction. They noted a cross-modal transfer of learning with respect to listening comprehension. This means that comprehension abilities developed in the listening mode transfer to reading comprehension. The ability to discriminate and segment sounds is an important part of listening comprehension as well as listening for prosodic features of speech such as pitch, juncture, and stress. For example, "You are going to buy . . . that hat?" Or, "YOU are going to buy that hat!" Another auditory juncture example familiar to many is the "ice cream" versus "I scream." It is important to note that prosodic features operate in conjunction with the unfolding context of speech utterances to aid listeners in constructing meaning. Pearson and Fielding (1982) feel that young children should be given direct listening comprehension instruction. We feel that at the very least students should be given ample opportunities to listen to stories, plays, riddles, and the like under the guidance of a skillful teacher to develop an understanding of different text types before encountering these in reading.

Notice how students can be given ample opportunities to develop an understanding of different text types before encountering these in reading.

Alphabetic and Phonics Knowledge

Probably no topic in the field of reading is more likely to evoke an emotional response than phonics. After the dust settles, however, even the most adamant of whole-language advocates will admit that children need to learn phonics to become proficient readers and writers (Newman & Church, 1990). However, the necessity of phonics knowledge as a *prerequisite* to reading continues to be a point of heated debate. Groff (1984) argues that young readers do not need to know letter names to become readers but, rather, that letter-name knowledge is necessary for communication between teachers and children about language. Many researchers, however, point to the results of the famous first-grade studies reported in 1967 by Guy Bond

Phonics has never been shown to be a sufficient precondition to reading without concurrent exposures to connected and meaningful printed language.

and Robert Dykstra as conclusive evidence that early phonics instruction results in significantly better reading achievement at the end of first grade. Although these studies showed an advantage for basal and linguistic reading programs supplemented by an extrinsic phonics program as measured by end-of-first-grade reading achievement, phonics has never been shown to be a sufficient precondition for reading without concurrent exposures to connected and meaningful printed language.

In the report *Becoming a Nation of Readers* (R. C. Anderson et al., 1985), the authors state two important caveats for teachers with regard to phonics instruction. "The goal of phonics is not that children be able to state the 'rules' governing letter–sound relationships. Rather, the purpose is to get across the alphabetic principle" (p. 38). R. C. Anderson et al. also suggest three maxims for phonics instruction. "Do it early. Keep it simple. Except in cases of diagnosed individual need, phonics instruction should have been completed by the end of second grade" (p. 34).

Recent research into children's acquisition of the alphabetic principle indicates that once children establish the alphabetic insight (that letters and spoken sounds connect) for a few letters, this concept allows children to generalize other connections between letters and sounds from print (Byrne, Freebody, & Gates, 1992; Byrne & Fielding-Barnsley, 1990). Recent research related to phonic elements called *onsets* and *rimes* indicates that word parts called *rimes* (*at, ick,* etc.) are easier for young children to learn because of their rhyming nature (Goswami & Mead, 1992).

Hansen (1987) comments that some teachers may want to teach very brief, no more than 5-minute direct-instruction phonics lessons. She cautions, however, against using worksheets as practice for phonics instruction. Rather, she suggests that children practice phonics in reading connected text or writing.

At this point, the opportunity to learn the alphabetic principle and phonics patterns is an important part of any reading readiness program. Although the contribution of alphabet knowledge and phonics instruction to reading is at present poorly understood, most teachers feel that such knowledge and instruction are necessary prerequisites to success in early reading (Teale, 1987).

Word Recognition

In Chapter 8, look for the section on developing sight words.

In 1885, James Mckeen Cattell found that adult readers could recognize words as rapidly as single letters. This study lead to the proliferation of whole-word or sight-word instruction for reading. Although Cattell's work found that adult readers held a large supply of sight words in memory, the generalization of these findings to younger children and early reading instruction was clearly unwarranted (Singer, 1978b). However, studies of sight-word instruction since then have shown that sight-word instruction can benefit young readers' early reading achievement.

Some adults still remember the first words they learned to read.

Richek (1978) found that one of the major predictors of first-grade reading success was the ability to profit from sight-word instruction. Ehri and Wilce (1980) found differential effects for the way in which sight words were taught to children. If children were taught sight words in isolation or in lists, they were better at word-pronunciation and -discrimination tasks. When sight words were presented in a sentence context, students learned more about word meanings than they did about pronunciation or discrimination. Teaching sight words in conjunction with picture clues has also been researched. Research by Samuels (1967) and Braun (1969) indicated that words were not learned as well when they were taught with picture clues. Thus, the ability to learn sight words appears to be highly related to early reading achievement, and the way in which sight words are taught appears to influence how well children learn sight words, that is, pronunciation or meaning. Durkin (1989) recommends teaching sight words for one practical reason: Sight words allow children early access to the feeling of real reading. Such a reason may be justification enough for teaching children a stock of sight words as a part of reading readiness instruction.

Emergent Literacy

Reading research over the past two decades has gradually led to the conclusion that the reading readiness model has become theoretically and practically inadequate for studying how young children become literate. To make a clear distinction between the theoretical and practical assumptions undergirding the reading readiness model of literacy development and more recent perspectives on literacy, Teale and Sulzby (1986) have called for a shift in terminology to reflect this change. A. Bloom states that

Emergent literacy represents a profound change in how people believe early literacy is acquired.

> A new language always reflects a new point of view, and the gradual, unconscious popularization of new words, or of old words used in new ways, is a sure sign of a profound change in people's articulation of the world. (1987, p. 141)

Thus, the term *emergent literacy* has been selected to represent a profound change in the study and articulation of early literacy. As mentioned earlier, the term *emergent* symbolizes the view that literacy is a continuum that begins at birth and continues throughout life, and *literacy* embraces the abilities of both reading and writing.

N. Hall (1987) describes the assumptions surrounding the emergent literacy perspectives about how children learn to read and write. Some of these assumptions include the following:

1. Reading and writing are closely related processes and should not be artificially isolated for instruction.
2. Learning to read and write is essentially a social process and is influenced by a search for meaning.
3. Most preschool children already know a great deal about printed language without exposures to formal instruction.
4. Becoming literate is a continuous, developmental process.
5. Children need to act like readers and writers to become readers and writers.
6. Children need to read authentic and natural texts.
7. Children need to write for personal reasons.

From the earliest cognitive studies into language learning begun in about 1956, researchers in language acquisition carefully studied and observed young children to determine how they solved the puzzle of printed language. Durkin (1966) found that some young children could already read and write before exposure to formal schooling and instructional methodologies. This occurred in spite of the belief supported by the reading readiness research of the day indicating that children of this age were not yet ready for reading and writing instruction.

Clay's early work with 5-year-old children in New Zealand showed that "There is nothing in this research that suggests that contact with printed language forms should be withheld from any five-year-old child on the grounds that he is immature" (1967, p. 24). Thus, Clay rejected the notion of prereading and reading readiness stages as well as delaying exposure to books and other printed media based on a supposed lack of readiness.

Children may need extensive opportunities to experience books and stories before they can profit from school reading instructional practices.

Y. M. Goodman (1986) studied the knowledge of at-risk beginning readers and found that even these children possessed a great deal of knowledge about the functions and uses of printed language. Since the time of these early studies about how young children learn to read and write, many researchers have supported and extended these findings. For example, D. Taylor (1983) found homes rich with social and cultural examples of print and print use in the families she studied. In fact, she stated that, "Perhaps, it is only after children have shared stories and experienced reading and writing as complex cultural activities that they will be able to learn on an individual level through the traditional pedagogical practices of the first-grade classroom" (D. Taylor, 1983, p. 98). These studies are just a few examples of those that have led to the emergent literacy model of how young children become literate. In the next section, we discuss the research related to how children acquire spoken language, and in subsequent sections of this chapter, we discuss how the acquisition of oral language in many ways parallels the language learning processes associated with reading and writing.

Oral Language Acquisition

After the birth of a child, parents anxiously await baby's first intelligible speech. In the months that precede this much-awaited event, parents talk to baby, to each other, and to other individuals in their environment. The thought of withholding speech from their infant until he masters the mechanics of speech production never crosses the parents' minds. When baby finally utters his first intelligible speech sounds, these are often understood only by the parents or those most closely associated with the infant. Not until many weeks and months later will these utterances mean anything to the casual observer.

Several theories have been proposed in an attempt to explain how infants acquire an ability to speak their native tongue. The first theory to attempt an explanation of the origin and acquisition of oral language among infants emanates from the behavioristic tradition in the field of psychology.

Behavioristic Theory

***Behaviorists** believe that oral language is acquired through a process of conditioning and shaping that involves a stimulus, a response, and a reward.*

Behaviorists believe that oral language is acquired through a process of conditioning and shaping that involves a stimulus, a response, and a reward. The stimulus and reward are controlled by the adult role models in the infant's environment. Parents' or other care givers' speech acts as the stimulus in the speech environment. And when baby imitates the sounds or speech patterns of the adult models, praise and affection are given as a reward for attempts to learn language. Thus, the **behavioristic theory** of language acquisition states that infants learn oral language from adult role models through a process involving imitation, rewards, and rehearsal.

Behavioristic theories of language development fail to explain a number of important questions associated with children's language acquisition. For example, if a parent is hurried, inattentive, or not present when the child attempts speech utterances, the rewards for the desired speech response are not always systematically provided. Thus, if baby's language acquisition were simply motivated by rewards, speech attempts would cease without the regular and systematic application of rewards.

Another problem with the behavioristic theory of oral language acquisition centers on the fact that young children do not simply imitate adult speech. Imitation implies that when Mother says, "Baby, say Mama," baby would imitate Mother by saying, "Baby, say Mama." Anyone who has raised children knows this is not the case. In fact, baby may not say anything at all!

Behavioristic language acquisition theories do not account for speech terms invented by infants. For example, one girl used to call a sandwich a *weechie* even though no one in her home called a sandwich by any such name. While behavioristic theories may explain to some extent the role of the social environment and the importance of adult role models in shaping children's language acquisition, the explanation offered by this theory is at best incomplete and at worse erroneous.

Innatist Theory

A second theory pertaining to oral language acquisition among children is called the **innatist theory**. These theorists believe that language learning is natural for human beings. In short, babies enter the world with a biological propensity, an inborn device as it were, to learn language. Lenneberg (1964) refers to this built-in device for learning language as the language acquisition device (LAD). Thus, the innatist theory explains to some degree how children can generate or invent language they have never heard before.

Innatist theorists believe that language learning is natural for human beings.

N. Chomsky (1974, 1979) maintains that children use this LAD to construct an elaborate rule system for generating and inventing complex and interesting speech. Or put another way, just as wings allow birds to fly, LAD allows infant humans to speak. While the innatist theory provides what appears to be a plausible explanation for some aspects of oral language acquisition, researchers have failed to supply satisfactory supporting evidence. Menyuk asserts, "Despite the apparent logic of this position, there is still a great deal of mystery that surrounds it" (1988, p. 34).

Interactionist Theory

A third theory, known as the **interactionist theory,** appears to be a compromise between the behavioristic and innatist theories of language acquisition. Interactionists believe that many factors affect an infant's ability to acquire oral language (e.g., social, cultural, linguistic, biological, cognitive). Like Vygotsky (1962), interactionists believe that not only do cognitive and maturational factors influence language acquisition, but the process of language acquisition itself may in turn affect cognitive and social skill development. Thus, the relationship among the variables associated with language acquisition not only interact with one another, but the relationship among these variables appears to be reciprocal. While children may be born to learn language, as the innatists propose, the language that is learned is determined by the social and linguistic environment into which the child is born and the language role models available. Put another way, the innatist theory explains why babies learn language in the first place, and the behavioristic theory explains why babies born in the United States generally learn to speak English rather than German. Thus, the most reasonable of the three theories appears to be the interactionist theory, which blends both innatist and behavioristic theories.

*The **interactionist theory** appears to be a compromise between the behavioristic and innatist theories of language acquisition.*

Halliday (1975) (as discussed in Chapter 1) believes that language acquisition grows out of an active need to use language to function in society. Thus, infants learn language to survive, express themselves, and get their needs met. If you have forgotten this information, you may wish to reread Halliday's theories in Chapter 2 to

Parents interpret infants' early language rather than recognize it.

refresh your memory about a principle of literacy learning called *approximation*. Holdaway (1979, 1984) discusses this principle with regard to how children learn to speak. He says that *approximating* means that infants respond to speech stimuli in their environment by producing a rough, rather than an exact, reproduction of the speech stimulus. Over time, these crude attempts begin to resemble modeled speech more closely until an acceptable reproduction is achieved. This is what is meant by the term *approximation* with respect to the acquisition of oral language. Holdaway (1984) also makes special note of the fact that parents not only tolerate approximations in oral language learning but meet these unrefined attempts with appreciation and affection.

Stages of Oral Language Development

Teachers should become aware of the stages and average rates of oral language development. They should also bear in mind that oral language developmental rates may vary radically among individual children.

Parents' Baby Talk: One Way of Getting Attention

Across languages and cultures, adults use baby talk with their infants.

Parents use a special type of speech with their infants up to about 24 months of age called *baby talk* (Stern & Wasserman, 1979). Characteristics of baby talk include higher pitch and special intonation patterns. Studies have shown that infants respond best to high-pitch levels and to varied rhythms in speech (Kearsley, 1973; Kessen, Levine, & Wendrich, 1979). Other research has shown that the way in which infants react to adult speech affects the subsequent speech and behavior of their adult caretakers. In fact, adults usually use shorter speech patterns with significant periods of pausing to even encourage the infant to respond (Gleason, 1989). Thus, it appears that parents and adult care givers are intuitively intense kid watchers (Y. M. Goodman, 1986). They seem to scaffold their speech demonstrations carefully in response to the overt reactions and suspected needs of their infants (Harste, Woodward, & Burke, 1984). In conclusion, parents and adult care givers change their normal speech structures and prosodic features during interactions with their infants to encourage symbolic and verbal interaction.

The First 12 Months: A Time for Hope

Infant speech development begins with vegetative sounds.

During the first 2 months of life, babies cry to indicate their need to be fed, changed, or otherwise attended to in some manner. Because their tiny mouths are almost entirely filled with the tongue, and the vocal cords are still quite high in the throat, children at this age are unable to produce much variation in vocalization. The growth of the head and neck allows the infant to vary his vocalizations later to produce sounds already responded to and experienced in the environment. During this early stage of speech development, young infants also make what linguists call *vegetative sounds* such as burps, coughs, and sneezes.

Cooing, crying, and babbling are all means of the developing infant communication with others.

From about 2 to 5 months of age, babies begin to coo, much like the sound made by pigeons, although during this period, they may also begin to vary the consonant sounds attached to the pure "oo" vowel sound typical of cooing. These cooing sounds, along with sustained laughter, seem to typically occur during social and speech interactions with other care givers in the environment. Cooing and laughter, however, may also occur when baby is alone or even asleep. During this period of development, D'Odorico (1984) has discovered that babies develop three distinct types of crying: a need for comfort, call for attention, and rescue from distress. All of these speech developments seem to provide great pleasure and even a sense of relief and encouragement for parents and care givers.

From 6 months to 1 year of age, babies enter a period of oral language development called *vocal play and babbling*. This stage of development is marked by the ability to utter single syllables containing a consonant sound followed by a prolonged vowel sound such as "Maa Maa." While many other syllables (i.e., "Laa Laa") may be uttered during this period of development, only a few of these syllables will be retained into the next stage (i.e., "Ma Ma" and "Da Da"). These syllables are retained primarily because their use seems to bring a quick and delightful reaction from their parents or adult care givers. It is also during this period of speech development that children begin to use single words or *holophrases,* sounds, or invented words to represent complete ideas (Gleason, 1989). For example, while riding down the road, an infant of this age may point to a cow and squeal in delight "mooooo!" Or this same infant may point at the sink and say, "wa wa" indicating that he wants a drink of water.

From 1 to 2: By Leaps and Bounds

Language expands rapidly during the second year of development. Children continue to approximate the speech demonstrations of their parents and adult care givers to the point of reduplicating their gestures and intonation patterns. Children in this stage continue to make hypotheses about the rules that govern language use. In meaningful contexts, these children try out and refine these rules in the course of using language. During this year, toddlers achieve a significant linguistic milestone when they begin to put two words together. These words are typically selected from the large open classes of words known as nouns, verbs, and adjectives. Because these two word utterances sound much like the reading of a telegram, linguists have called this stage of speech development **telegraphic speech**. Typical utterances of the telegraphic type may include "Mommy Down!" or "Go Potty?" One recognizes readily the ability of these two-word, cryptic speech patterns to communicate an entire complex idea or need.

*Infants use two-word utterances called **telegraphic speech** to express their ideas and needs.*

From 2 to 3: What Does It Mean When I Say No?!

Oral language development continues to progress at rapid rates during the third year. The acquisition of words during this stage of speech development is remarkable. The broken and incomplete nature of telegraphic speech begins to give way to more complex and natural forms of speech. The use of descriptives such as adjectives and adverbs dramatically increases (Glazer, 1989).

One linguistic discovery made by the 2-year-old is the effect of negation. For many years, baby has heard the expression "No, No." Although over time he has learned what this expression implies for his own behavior, the child has not yet come to understand what the term *no* means when applied to the behavior of others. When asked, "Does baby want an ice cream cone?" baby responds, "No!" When he discovers that the ice cream cone to which he had said "No" is now denied, he begins to cry. Thus over time, the 2-year-old learns what "No" means for the behavior of others. In a sense, children at this age begin to establish their own identity—separate from others in their environment—and the "No!" response is evidence of this fact. The linguistic transformation of negation by using the words *no* and *not* are important changes in young children's language development.

From 3 to 4: The *Why* Years

*An **analogical substitution** is the overgeneralization by analogy of a language rule although small children rarely receive any formal instruction in these rules.*

By age 3, children begin to transform simple utterances by using complex sentences that include the use of prepositions, pronouns, negatives, plurals, possessives, and interrogatives. Children at this age have a speaking vocabulary of between 1,000 and 1,500 words (Morrow, 1989). Also at this age, children begin to use analogical substitutions in their speech. An **analogical substitution** is the overgeneralization by analogy of a language rule. These overgeneralizations often result in using an incorrect substitute term in speech. For example, a child may say, "Mom, will you put my boots on my *foots*?" In this case, the child has analogously overgeneralized the rule for pluralizing nouns by adding an *s* to the irregular noun *foot*. Another example of an analogical substitution is the overgeneralization of the language rule for changing verbs to their past-tense form. For example, Junior rushes into the house and yells, "Daddy, come quick. I *digged* up that mean bush with flowers and thorns on it!" Language "errors" such as these reveal the language rules children have been internalizing and how they go about refining their language hypotheses.

During this fourth year of oral language development, children begin to transform basic sentence structures into interrogative sentences. Before this time, these same children indicated the fact that a question was being asked by making a statement followed by a rising intonation pattern. Thus, questions were framed without the use of interrogatives or by transforming basic sentence structures. However by the time the child is 3, parents have become well acquainted with the interrogative "Why?"

For statements that appear to be perfectly obvious to adults, the 3-year-old will begin the typical line of questioning with "Why, why, why?" After several answers to this interrogative, parents realize they are trapped in a linguistic situation that is nearly impossible to escape with dignity. Bill Cosby once gave a solution to a problem similar to this one, which has been tried with 3-year-old children with reasonable success. The solution is simple. You ask why first! Regardless of the questioning nature of the 3-year-old, language development during the third to fourth year is an exciting experience for parents and care givers.

From 4 to 6: Years of Growth and Refinement

At 4 years of age, children seem to have acquired most of the elements of adult language.

At 4 years of age, children seem to have acquired most of the elements of adult language (Morrow, 1989). Vocabulary and syntactical structures continue to increase in variety and depth. Children at this age possess a vocabulary of about 2,500 words, which by age 6 will have grown to 6,000 words (D. A. Norton, 1993). Some children at age 4 or 5 continue to have trouble articulating the /r/ and /l/ sounds and the /sh/ at the end of words.

A son of one of the authors, Cody, has provided many examples of imaginative and **generative language**. One day Cody had purchased with his hard-earned money several plastic clips for his belt. With these he could hang his flashlight and plastic tools on his belt and make believe he was a working man. When his father first saw these clips on his belt, he inquired, "Cody, what are those things on your belt?" He responded, "Those are my *hookers,* Dad!"

On entering the world of school, kindergarten children often discover a genre of speech known as toilet talk and curse words. One day a young boy overheard his kindergarten teacher reprimanding some other boys for using inappropriate language. Sometime later during the day, his teacher overheard him remark regarding the subject of taboo words, "She means those words your Daddy uses when he gets real mad!" According to Seefeldt and Barbour (1986), adults find the way in which children of this age group use language imaginative and amusing. We certainly concur with these observations!

Understanding the development of oral language among children can be a source of increased enjoyment for parents and teachers. Knowing how children develop language helps adults recognize and appreciate the monumental achievement of learning to speak—especially when this occurs so naturally and in a space of just 6 short but very important years.

Development of Reading Behaviors

As explained earlier in this chapter, the emergent literacy model of the developing reader views reading acquisition as a continuum of development: Children pass through certain stages of reading development on the literacy continuum toward becoming independent and skilled readers, much as they do in acquiring their oral language. Although the reading readiness model also describes reading development in stages, the emergent literacy model does not view the beginning of reading as a point or threshold on the literacy continuum but rather as a continuous journey along the continuum. Hence, children are never thought of or talked about as nonreaders under the emergent literacy model.

Under the emergent literacy view of learning to read and write, children are never thought of or talked about as nonreaders or nonwriters.

Some years ago, two teachers had a discussion about what they meant by, "He is a beginning reader." These teachers began to gather data to support the construction of a **reading development continuum,** shown in Figure 3.2 (Cochrane, Cochrane, Scalena, & Buchanan, 1984). They divided the development of reading into two overarching categories: (a) preindependent reading and (b) independent reading. Within each of these two supercategories, Cochrane et al. describe three more subdivisions. Within the **preindependent reading** category are three subordinate divisions or stages: (a) the magical stage, (b) the self-concepting stage, and (c) the bridging stage. Within the **independent reading category** are three subordinate divisions or stages: (a) the take-off stage, (b) the independent reading stage, and (c) the skilled reading stage.

The Mystery of Reading: The Magical Stage

Long before children enter school, they begin noticing print in their environment and learn that printed language stands for words they have heard others use or that they have used themselves. Preschool children spontaneously learn to recognize billboards displaying their favorite TV channel logo. They can recognize a favorite soda brand logo or pick out their favorite cereal at the local supermarket. While they may not be able to read the print exactly on each of these objects, when asked to tell someone what the soda can says, they may respond with "soda" or "pop."

Figure 3.2

Reading development continuum

A. PRE-INDEPENDENT READING STAGES
  1. MAGICAL STAGE
     - Displays an interest in handling books.
     - Sees the construction of meaning as magical or exterior to the print and imposed by others.
     - Listens to print read to him for extended periods of time.
     - Will play with letters or words.
     - Begins to notice print in environmental context (signs, labels).
     - Letters may appear in his drawings.
     - May mishandle books—observe them upside down. Damage them due to misunderstanding the purpose of books.
     - Likes to "name" the pictures in a book, e.g., "lion," "rabbit."
  2. SELF-CONCEPTING STAGE
     - Self-concepts himself as a reader, i.e., engages in reading-like activities.
     - Tries to magically impose meaning on new print.
     - "Reads" or reconstructs content of familiar storybooks.
     - Recognizes his name and some other words in high environmental contexts (signs, labels).
     - His writing may display phonetic influence, i.e., *wtbo = Wally, hr = her.*
     - Can construct story meaning from pictorial clues.
     - Cannot pick words out of print consistently.
     - Orally fills in many correct responses in oral cloze reading.
     - Rhymes words.
     - Increasing control over nonvisual cuing systems.
     - Gives words orally that begin similarly.
     - Displays increasing degree of book handling knowledge.
     - Is able to recall key words.
     - Begins to internalize story grammar, i.e., knows how stories go together, e.g., "Once upon a time," "They lived happily ever after."
  3. BRIDGING STAGE
     - Can write and read back his own writing.
     - Can pick out individual words and letters.
     - Can read familiar books or poems which could not be totally repeated without the print.
     - Uses picture clues to supplement the print.
     - Words read in one context may not be read in another.
     - Increasing control over visual cuing system.

From *Reading, Writing, and Caring* (pp. 44–46) by O. Cochrane, D. Cochrane, D. Scalena, and E. Buchanan, 1988, New York: Richard C. Owen Publishers, Copyright 1988 by Richard C. Owen Publishers. Reprinted by permission.

- Enjoys chants and poems chorally read.
- Can match or pick out words of poems or chants that have been internalized.

B. INDEPENDENT READING STAGES

  1. TAKE-OFF STAGE
     - Excitement about reading.
     - Wants to read to you often.
     - Realizes that print is the base for constructing meaning.
     - Can process (read) words in new (alternate) print situations.
     - Aware of and reads aloud much environmental print (signs, labels, etc.).
     - Can conserve print from one contextual environment to another.
     - May exhibit temporary tunnel vision (concentrates on words and letters).
     - Oral reading may be word-centered rather than meaning-centered.
     - Increasing control over the reading process.

  2. INDEPENDENT READING
     - Characterized by comprehension of the author's message by reader.
     - Readers' construction of meaning relies heavily on author's print or implied cues (schema).
     - Desires to read books to himself for pleasure.
     - Brings his own experiences (schemata) to the print.
     - Reads orally with meaning and expression.
     - May see print as literal truth. What the print says is right (legalized).
     - Uses visual and nonvisual cuing systems simultaneously (cyclically).
     - Has internalized several different print grammars, i.e., fairy tales, general problem-centered stories, simple exposition.

  3. SKILLED READER
     - Processes material further and further removed from his own experience.
     - Reading content and vocabulary become a part of his experience.
     - Can use a variety of print forms for pleasure.
     - Can discuss several aspects of a story.
     - Can read at varying and appropriate rates.
     - Can make inferences from print.
     - Challenges the validity of print content.
     - Can focus on or use the appropriate grammar or structuring of varying forms of print, e.g., stories, science experiments, menus, diagrams, histories.

Reading is part of nearly every young child's life.

Magical stage readers readily recognize print in their environment.

Children at this stage of reading development love to have books read to them. In quiet moments, these children may crawl up into a large comfortable chair to hold, look at, and tell a story from the pictures of their favorite books. Jeremy, when he was 2 years old, enjoyed the naming of each animal in his favorite picture book. After naming each picture, he enthusiastically made the sounds of each, the roar of a lion or the crowing of a rooster. Parents and teachers of readers who find themselves journeying through the **magical stage** of reading development may see children who hold books upside down, turn the pages from the back to the front, and even tear out a page unintentionally. Although this may be concerning for parents on one level, children who behave in these ways evidence a need for exposure to and understanding of the purpose of books. Withholding books from these children because they do not know how to handle them or read them at this stage would most certainly prove to be detrimental.

Favorite books are requested to be read aloud again and again, indicating how young children want to practice learning to read.

Children in the magical reading developmental stage develop a marked preference for a single or favorite book. Willing adults are often solicited into reading this book again and again. Although parents and others may tire rapidly of this book, the affection and familiarity increases with each reading for the child. Favorite books are often repeatedly read to the point where the child memorizes them. Some parents even try to skip pages or sentences in these books, thinking their child will not notice, but they soon learn their child has internalized these books, and the unsuspecting adult will be caught every time.

The reading of entire contexts such as those found on product logos and in books constitutes evidence to support the fact that young children prefer to process printed language from the whole to the parts. Reading the entire context of a sign or label and memorizing an entire book are preferred by young children long before they want or need to focus on the details and parts of printed language.

"Look, Mom, I'm Reading": The Self-Concepting Reading Stage

The **self-concepting reading developmental stage** describes the child who has come to view himself as a reader. Although these children may not yet be able to read exactly what the print says, they are certainly aware of printed language and their own progress toward breaking the literacy barrier. Children in this stage will try to read unfamiliar books by telling the story from the pictures and from their own imaginations. Selected words are readily recognized, such as their own name, favorite food labels, and signs on bathroom doors. These readers will try to reconstruct the text of a favorite story from memory and picture clues. These children evidence an increasing awareness of words and sounds. They often ask questions about how words begin and rhyming words. If given a chance, these children can also fill in the rest of a sentence when asked to do so. For example, while reading the "Three Little Pigs," a teacher may say, "And the Big Bad Wolf knocked at the door and said, 'Little Pig, Little Pig'. . . . " Children at this stage will immediately fill in the hanging sentence with "Let me come in."

*Children in the **self-concepting stage** view themselves as readers.*

Spanning the Gap: The Bridging Stage

Children at the **bridging stage** of reading development can pick out familiar words and letters in familiar contexts and books. They often cannot, however, pick these same words out of an unfamiliar book or context when asked. Children in the bridging stage can reconstruct stories from books with greater precision than can children in the previous stage. In fact, children in the bridging stage can no longer reconstruct the story completely without using the print, although they will continue to use picture clues to augment their growing control over the print system.

Children in the bridging stage can also read back what they have written. It has long been a disappointment for us when teachers and parents fail to count these early behaviors as real reading by brushing them aside as cute. Parents or teachers will often remark, "She's not reading. She's got that book memorized." Only by understanding that reading is a developmental process and that memorizing favorite print and books is universal among children will parents and teachers be able to enjoy, recognize, and support the progress their children make toward conventional reading behaviors and skills.

Some parents and teachers discount memorizing books as an unimportant step in learning to read.

Blast Off!: The Take-Off Stage

If you are an unoccupied adult, look out for kids in the **take-off stage**. They are excited about reading and will perform for any reluctantly willing audience. In fact, they want to demonstrate their emerging ability as frequently as others will allow. Children at this stage of reading development have a clear understanding that print forms the basis for reading the story and constructing meaning. Words read in one book or context are now recognized in new or unfamiliar contexts. Signs and environmental print are subjects of intense interest among take-off readers. It seems as if print has a magnetic appeal for these children.

One autumn evening in a parent–teacher conference while one of the authors was teaching first grade, a parent said that her son, Curt, had requested new breakfast cereals. When his mother asked why, Curt responded, "There's not enough to read on these boxes." Mother bought him a box of cereal that seemed to contain enough print to satisfy his appetite.

Take-off stage readers may sound like worse readers than children in earlier stages because they are focusing so intently on the print.

Oral reading during the take-off stage may become word or letter centered. Although oral reading before this time may have failed to perfectly represent the print on the page, it was smooth, fluent, and filled with inflection. The fact that words and letters have been discovered at this stage of development may lead to a situation when children appear to temporarily regress in their reading development. Children in this stage need to focus on print details, which leads to less fluent and inflected oral reading for a time. With sustained opportunities to read and gain control over the reading process and print system, fluency and inflection will soon return.

I Can Do It by Myself!: The Independent Stage

*The **independent reader** has developed control over the entire reading process and cuing systems.*

Independent readers lack critical analysis skills.

The take-off reader wants an audience, but the **independent reader** takes great pride in reading books to himself for pleasure. The independent reader has developed control over the entire reading process and cuing systems. Reading is now carried on with simultaneous use of the author's printed clues and the reader's own store of background experiences and knowledge called *schemata*. Fluency and inflection have returned to oral reading. In fact, chunks or phrases are now read fluently instead of laboring over single words. The independent reader is predicting ahead of the print and using context to construct meaning not just as an aid to decoding (Stanovich, 1980). The ability to critically analyze print, however, has not yet been achieved. Thus, these readers may believe everything they read or may exhibit a tendency toward seeing anything in print as literal, truthful, and absolute.

Reaching the Summit: The Skilled Reader

Think of a time when you used print to support or extend your own thinking. What were you aware of at that time?

The skilled reader not only understands print but uses print to support and extend thinking. Although this stage is the final stage of reading development, it is not a destiny. The process of becoming skilled in reading is a lifelong journey. The journey to **skilled reading** involves processing print that is further and further removed from one's own experiences and knowledge. In other words, print is now used increasingly as a means to acquire new and unfamiliar information. The variety of printed media that skilled readers process increases from narratives and textbooks, to magazines, newspapers, TV guides, tax forms, and so on. The skilled reader can talk about different types of text organizations, make inferences from print, use print to substantiate opinions, challenge the surface validity of printed materials, and vary his reading rate according to the personal purposes for reading, such as skimming and scanning. Although more research is needed to corroborate the descriptions offered by Cochrane et al. (1984) in the reading development continuum, this model provides a useful framework for parents, teachers, and scholars through which they can view the becoming of a reader with increased understanding and a good deal less anxiety.

Development of Storybook Reading Behaviors

A more scholarly description of reading development is described in the work of Sulzby (1985). In this line of scholarly investigation, Sulzby (1985) researched and tested a classification scheme for describing children's emergent reading of story-books (Figure 3.3). In the earliest stages of storybook reading, children's behaviors seem to be largely governed by pictures. Children's earliest picture-governed but not well-formed storybook reading behaviors often included labeling, commenting, pointing, or even slapping at the pictures. Some children in this earliest stage of not well-formed storybook reading also became so caught up in the action of the pictures that they became part of the story as if the story were happening at the moment. For example, such a child might have said, "See, there he goes. He's getting away, and they don't even see him!" At a later stage in picture-governed storybook reading, children's storybook readings become more well suited or formed to the story in the book. Children engage in dialogic and monologic storybook reading. In *dialogic sto-*

Notice two main categories of Sulzby's storybook reading behaviors.

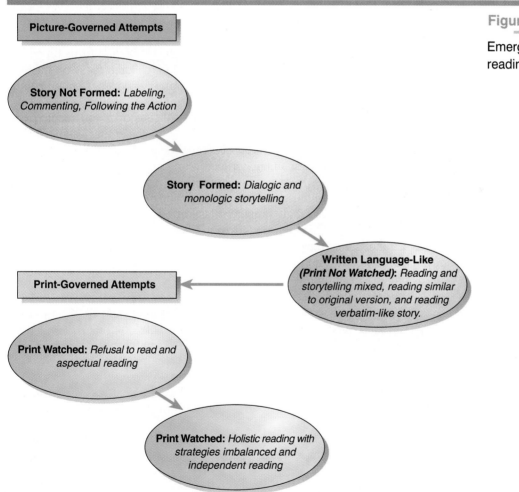

Figure 3.3

Emergent storybook reading behaviors

Picture-Governed Attempts

Story Not Formed: *Labeling, Commenting, Following the Action*

Story Formed: *Dialogic and monologic storytelling*

Written Language-Like (Print Not Watched): *Reading and storytelling mixed, reading similar to original version, and reading verbatim-like story.*

Print-Governed Attempts

Print Watched: *Refusal to read and aspectual reading*

Print Watched: *Holistic reading with strategies imbalanced and independent reading*

Based on E. Sulzby (1985).

rybook reading, children either create a "voice" for the characters in the story, or they tell the story by making comments directed to a listener of the story. Hence, characters are lived as if the child is in the story, or the child tells the story for the benefit of the listener. In any case, these story readings are often disjointed and difficult to follow. When children shift to *monologic* storytellings, a complete story is told and understood. The story is also told with a storytelling intonation rather than a reading intonation (Sulzby, 1985, p. 468).

After children reach the monologic storybook reading stage, they begin to tell well-formed stories that approximate written language. Children's written language-like reading attempts fall into three subcategories: (a) reading and storytelling mixed; (b) reading similar-to-original story; and (c) reading verbatim-like. Once children enter into these storybook reading behaviors, they tend to focus their attention partially on the print as a means for governing their reading. Consequently, they move into Sulzby's (1985) second supercategory of storybook reading behaviors, print-governed attempts.

Within this second supercategory of storybook reading behaviors, print-governed attempts, children often engage in three initial responses to storybook print: (a) refusal, (b) aspectual reading, and (c) holistic. In the first response, refusal, children refuse to try to read as they learn that print carries the story rather than the picture. For example, a child might remark, "I don't know the words. I can't read yet. I can't really read—I was just pretending." In the aspectual stage, children focus on one or two aspects of the print to the exclusion of others. Some children focus on memory for certain words, while others focus more intently upon specific letter–sound combinations for sounding out.

The final category, holistic, is divided into two subcategories: (a) reading with strategies imbalanced, and (b) reading independently. In the strategies-imbalanced stage, children might read a storybook by overdepending on certain strategies such as substituting known words for unknown words or sounding out every unknown word. In this stage, children have not yet learned to become strategic about their reading strategy selections and use during reading. In the independent stage, children have learned to self-regulate their strategy selection and balance the use of these strategies during reading. These youngsters sound like "word perfect" readers sometimes and at other times make deviations from the printed page but continue to demonstrate an awareness and control of the process of reading.

Sulzby remarks in summary,

> Finally, and most important, the development that was observed in these studies appears to make sense in light of theoretical ideas about general and language development and the findings of other current research. . . . These discoveries about literacy development appear to challenge traditional [readiness] assumptions about the nature of young children—assumptions built upon a conventional model. (1985, p. 479)

Emergent views of reading development do in fact challenge the more conventional views of reading readiness.

Development of Writing Behaviors

Laura, a 3-year-old neighbor girl, sat quietly on the couch next to her parents with four unlined, white 3- by 5-inch index cards and an old, teeth-marked pencil in her hands as her parents visited in the living room with a neighbor. After about 10 minutes, Laura slipped down from the couch and walked over to the visitor. Timidly, she approached, clutching one index card behind her back. Then impulsively, she thrust the card from behind her back into the waiting hand of the visitor. He studied the marks Laura had made on the card. "Wow! Laura," he exclaimed, "You are writing!" Laura's face broadened into a smile that stretched from ear to ear, "I really writed, didn't I!"

Laura had demonstrated her developing understanding that writing is a system for recording thoughts and feelings on paper to share with others. She had come to this understanding without formal spelling and writing instruction. By carefully watching others in her environment, Laura had taken the risk to act like a skilled writer and try out her tentative hypotheses about how printed language functions.

Writing can also be a system for developing thoughts and feelings.

Many of us have seen children attempting to solve the printed language puzzle through drawing and scribbling. Just as with reading, however, one may be tempted to dismiss these early attempts at writing as cute but certainly not *real* writing, as shown in Figure 3.4. This may be just as dangerous as rooting out a flower in the early stages of growth because the roots do not look much like the flower.

Figure 3.4

Laura's scribbles

Through careful study over a period of decades, researchers have discovered that young children pass through developmental stages similar to those discussed with respect to oral language and reading in their own writing and spelling development. An understanding of these stages of writing development will help teachers recognize the "roots" of writing and spelling development and, as such, be able to help nurture the roots of scribbling and drawing into the flower of writing.

Scribbling and Drawing Stage

Scribble writing is as important to writing development as babbling is to oral language development.

When young children first take a pencil or crayon in hand, they use this instrument to explore the vast empty space on a blank sheet of paper. In the earliest stages, children's writing is often referred to as scribbling by adult observers (Clay, 1987). These random marks are the wellsprings of writing discovery. As shown in Figure 3.4, Laura's scribbles appeared to be the result of acting on the paper just to see what happens without any particular intent. Her scribbles do not evidence much of what adults normally consider to be conventional or even purposeful writing. In Figure 3.5, Laura began to evidence an exploration of alternative forms to her previous scribbles. Circles, curved lines, and letter-like forms begin to appear as a part of Laura's writing exploration.

Sometime later, Laura's scribbles begin to look more and more like adult cursive writing. Note in Figure 3.6 that Laura's scribbles have become linear, moving from left to right. When questioned, Laura could tell what she meant with each of her scribbles. Unlike Figure 3.4, Laura's scribbling represented her meaning in a more conventional way. Because this writing sample was produced near Christmas time, Laura revealed that these scribbles represented a "Christmas Wish List." Often, letter-like writing or shapes as shown in Laura's Christmas list are used repeatedly in early

Figure 3.5

Laura's scribbles as exploration

Figure 3.6

Laura's scribble cursive
writing: Christmas list

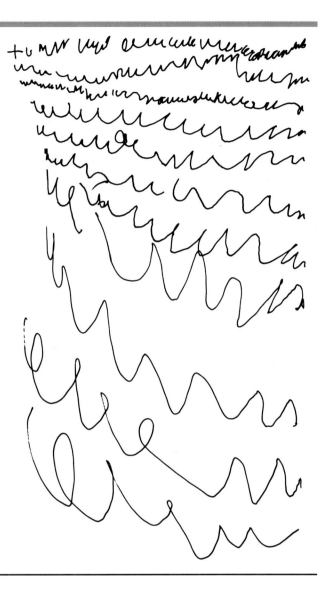

writing attempts. Clay (1987) calls the tendency to reuse and repeat certain scrib-
blings and drawings again and again *recursive writing*. The purpose behind recursive
writing seems to be a need for comfort and familiarity as children prepare to move
into the next levels of writing development.

   Weeks later, Laura produced the writing found in Figure 3.7. Note in this example
that drawings have begun to be used to carry part of the intended message. In addition, directly above the head of what appears to be a drawing of a young girl, one can
clearly see the emergence of letter-like forms etched in broken detail. When queried
about the intent of these letter-like forms, Laura responded, "That says Laura!" Evidently, Laura had discovered at this point in her development as a writer that drawings can be used to supplement the message but that writing is different from drawing.

   In another example, Toby, a 4-year-old child, produced the writing found in Figure 3.8. Toby used human-like forms to represent members of his family in his thank-

*Children soon discover that
drawing and scribbling are
alternate forms of written
expression.*

Figure 3.7

Laura's self-portrait

you letter. Randomly scattered about the page, one sees the use of letter-like symbols. Near the center, Toby signed his name. By looking carefully, one can see the upside-down letter *b* and what looks like a letter *y,* which Toby chose to represent his name. Thus, one can see that during this initial stage of writing development, Laura and Toby used scribbling, drawing, and disconnected letter-like forms to explore and record their meaning on paper. These children had likewise discovered that writing can be used to communicate meaning and that while drawing and writing are complementary processes, they are not the same.

Prephonemic Stage

The next stage of writing and spelling development among young children is often called the **prephonemic stage** (Temple, Nathan, Burris, & Temple, 1988). At this

Figure 3.8

Toby's thank-you letter

stage of writing development, children begin to use real letters, usually capital letters, to represent their meaning; letters do not represent their phonemic or sound values. Rather, they use letters as place holders for meaning, representing anything from a syllable to an entire thought. For example, Chaundra, a kindergartner, produced the writing in Figure 3.9. Note Chaundra's use of letters to represent her meaning. But only by asking the child to explain the meaning can one readily discern the fact that this child used letters as meaning placeholders and not to represent their phonemic values.

Clay (1975) points out that children in the prephonemic stage of writing development will usually produce a string of letters and proudly display them to a parent while asking, "What does this say?" or "What did I write?" We can remember our children doing this with the magnetic letters we have on our refrigerator doors. They would meticulously arrange a string of letters and then ask what they had written.

*In the **prephonemic stage,** children begin to use real letters, usually capital letters, to represent their meaning; letters do not represent their phonemic or sound values.*

Early Phonemic Stage

During the next stage of writing development, the **early phonemic stage** (Temple et al., 1988), children begin to use letters, usually capital consonant letters, to represent words. Children at this stage of writing development have discovered the fact that letters represent sound values. Words are represented by one or two consonant letters, usually the beginning or ending sounds of the word. In Figure 3.10, Samantha uses only the first consonant letters to represent the word *house* in her message.

Temple et al. suspect that the tendency for children in the early phonemic stage to represent a word with only one or two letters is due to an inability to "hold words

*In the **early phonemic stage,** children begin to use letters, usually capital consonant letters, to represent words.*

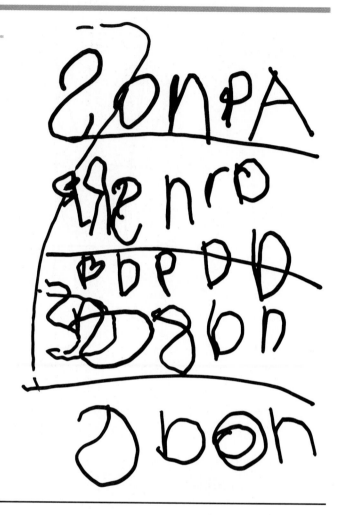

Figure 3.9

Chaundra's prephone-
mic writing

still in their minds" while they examine them for phonemes and match these to known letters (1988, p. 101). Although this may be true, it may also be possible that children at this stage may be continuing to learn certain letters of the alphabet. It may also be true that writers in this stage of development may not have developed the ability to segment more than the initial or final sounds in a word. Certainly, these possibilities would lead to the incomplete representation of words as found in the early phonemic stage of writing development. This is an area needing much more investigation (Teale, 1987).

Letter-Naming Stage

The **letter-naming stage** of writing development is a small but important jump from the early phonemic stage. This stage is recognized by the addition of more than one or two consonant letters used by young writers to represent the spelling of words (Temple et al., 1988). Chris, a kindergartner, produced an example of the letter-nam-

Figure 3.10

Samantha's early
phonemic writing: A
house

ing stage writing in response to his teacher's urgings to write about the rainbow he had seen the day before (see Figure 3.11).

While Chris continues to use capital letters exclusively, vowel letters have begun to appear in his writing. Chris had clearly discovered that words are made up of phonemes, both vowels and consonants; that these phonemes occur in an auditory sequence; and that these phonemes are properly represented in printed form from left to right. Although Chris was not yet reading independently, he had made important discoveries about print that nurtured his acquisition of reading; and his acquisition of reading will inform his acquisition of conventional spellings. With continued experiences in reading, Chris's writing will rapidly become more closely aligned with standard spelling and lead to the final stage of writing development—the transitional stage.

*The **letter-naming stage** is recognized by the addition of more than one or two consonant letters used by young writers to represent the spelling of words.*

Transitional Stage

Figures 3.12 and 3.13 illustrate the **transitional stage** of writing and spelling. Writing produced by youngsters in this stage looks like English, but the words are a mix of phonetic and conventional spellings. Typically, these writers neglect or overgeneralize certain spelling generalizations. For example, the final silent *e* is often omitted by these writers; familiar phonic elements are substituted for less familiar phonic elements; and double consonants are typically neglected.

***Transitional stage** writings look like English, but the words are a mix of phonetic and conventional spellings.*

Figure 3.11

Chris's letter-naming
stage writing: Rainbow

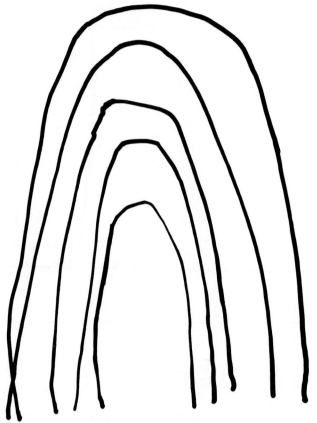

Devin, a first grader, wrote the story shown in Figure 3.12 during October. This example not only demonstrates some of the substitutions and omissions mentioned previously, but this young author chose to write his story in a top-to-bottom arrangement.

Figure 3.13 shows a note that Candice wrote to her parents during the fall of her second-grade year. Notice the spellings of *parents, hurting, guys,* and *special.* Some of the spellings are unconventional, but the writing of this child looks very much like English and communicates the message well. Candice's writing is also a good example of the characteristics of transitional writing mentioned previously—the mix of standard and nonstandard spellings. Note also the fact that transitional writers have discovered the use of other features of standard writing such as possessives, punctuation, and the standard letter- or note-writing format.

These examples demonstrate the progression of children's writing along a developmental continuum originating with their early attempts to make meaning on paper

Figure 3.12

Devin's Halloween story

through scribbling and drawing to later refinements including the use of conventional spelling, grammar, and mechanics.

One note of caution should be sounded at this point. Although we may discuss oral language, writing, and reading development in terms of stages through which children pass, we want to emphasize to teachers that they should not use this information to try to hasten development or to expect that children will or even should pass through each stage of development in the order described. Rather, teachers should use this information as a basis for understanding and supporting children's language learning by providing an environment rich in print and print use, gentle guidance, and enthusiastic encouragement as children struggle to solve the language and literacy puzzle. Just as children learned to speak within a nurturing home environment filled with supportive oral language users, children will develop naturally into readers and writers within print-rich school and home environments filled with the support, guidance, and encouragement of other competent and caring readers and writers. Figure 3.14 integrates information about oral language, reading, and

Notice at least two ways young children can be helped to develop into readers and writers.

Figure 3.13

Candice's note to her parents

writing development to show that these modes of language learning are developmentally similar.

Experience with books and stories has no reasonable substitute for helping children acquire a sense of story.

Developing a Sense of Story

In 1966, Durkin found that one characteristic common to the homes of early readers was parents who read books aloud to their children. Although we knew from Durkin's research that reading aloud to children seemed to be related to becoming a reader, we did not fully understand how reading aloud facilitated learning to read. During the 1970s, cognitive psychologists began to study the dimensions of how stories and narratives were constructed as well as how children developed a **sense of story** (Applebee, 1979). Out of this research grew the realization that authors seemed to be writing stories by following a set of implicitly held rules or schemas for

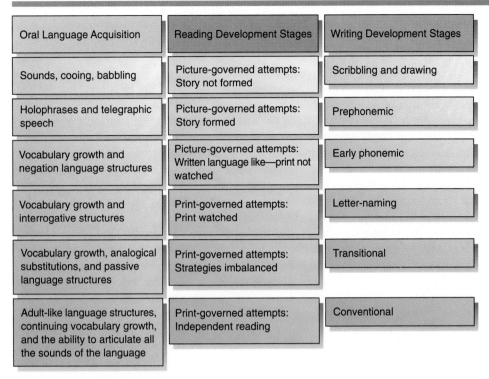

Figure 3.14

Development across the language modes of oral language, reading, and writing

Oral Language Acquisition	Reading Development Stages	Writing Development Stages
Sounds, cooing, babbling	Picture-governed attempts: Story not formed	Scribbling and drawing
Holophrases and telegraphic speech	Picture-governed attempts: Story formed	Prephonemic
Vocabulary growth and negation language structures	Picture-governed attempts: Written language like—print not watched	Early phonemic
Vocabulary growth and interrogative structures	Print-governed attempts: Print watched	Letter-naming
Vocabulary growth, analogical substitutions, and passive language structures	Print-governed attempts: Strategies imbalanced	Transitional
Adult-like language structures, continuing vocabulary growth, and the ability to articulate all the sounds of the language	Print-governed attempts: Independent reading	Conventional

how stories should be constructed. Thus, researchers developed a generalized set of rules to describe how narratives were composed. These rules were compiled and resulted in the development of several **story grammars** (Mandler & Johnson, 1977; Stein & Glenn, 1979; P. N. Thorndyke, 1977).

The elements found in a story grammar roughly parallel the description of the parts or plot of a story. A story typically begins with a description of the setting or location, the introduction of the main characters, and the general time frame of the events in the story. Stories may be composed of a single episode; however, complex stories may contain several episodes. Within each story episode, a series of events has been labeled by story grammarians. The labels may differ from one story grammar to another, but the elements generally include (a) a setting, (b) an initiating event, (c) an internal response, (d) goals, (e) attempts, (f) outcomes, and (g) a resolution.

The setting is described as a location, time, and the introduction of the characters. The initiating event or problem essentially starts the story action. This is followed by the reaction of the main character(s) to the initiating event, usually called an *internal response to the initiating event*. Next, the main character may devise some plan(s) to solve the problem set up in the initiating event. This is a process of setting goals to be achieved by the main character. This is followed by one or more attempts to achieve the goals or solve the problem. Finally, the outcome of the attempts are made known, and the story is concluded by describing the results of the character's success or failure in achieving the desired outcomes.

One question raised subsequent to the development of story grammars centered on how adults had come to know and use a story grammar for writing stories. It was

*Specific strategies for help-
ing young children develop
or elaborate story structure
knowledge will be presented
in Chapters 6 and 10.*

originally hypothesized that adult writers had learned the structure or grammar for stories by reading or hearing narratives throughout their lives. As a consequence, several researchers began to investigate whether or not young children had begun to develop a sense of story. A study of particular interest was conducted by Nurss, Hough, and Goodson in 1981 with a group of preschool children attending a local day-care center. These researchers concluded that preschool children had not yet developed a complete sense of story structure. Other studies (Olson & Gee, 1988; Stein & Glenn, 1979) demonstrated the fact that older children recalled stories more completely and could reorder scrambled pictures and story parts with greater precision than younger children. Thus, a concept of story structure appeared to be developmental in the sense that older children possessed more complete story structure knowledge than did younger children. One reason for this may be that older children had more experience with stories and as a result had more elaborated schemas for stories than did their younger counterparts.

Some researchers have attempted to directly teach a story grammar in the hopes that a sense of story may be imparted more efficiently and effectively to young children; these attempts have met with mixed and often disappointing results (Golden, 1992; Muth, 1989). Consequently, few if any reading experts now endorse such an approach (J. L. Vacca, Vacca, & Gove, 1987). Instead, most researchers recognize that experience with books and stories has no reasonable substitute for helping children acquire a sense of story. D. Taylor and Strickland (1986) recommend that parents read aloud regularly to their children to help them develop a sense of story. Nurss et al. (1981) suggest that story reading and discussion become an integral part of any preschool, nursery, or kindergarten program to help these children develop a concept of story structure. Morrow (1984) found that having children retell stories to other children or adults can significantly aid their development of a sense of story. Thus, the results to date indicate that children acquire a sense of story structure developmentally, over time, through reading or from hearing stories read aloud frequently.

Understanding Print Concepts and the Language of Instruction

Making sense of the purposes and symbols of reading and writing is a monumental task for young children. Research has demonstrated that children begin to attend to print at very young ages and come to school already having learned a great deal about the forms and functions of printed language (Y. M. Goodman & Altwerger, 1981; Harste et al., 1984). In our view, children must encounter the meaningfulness of printed language before they can make sense of school-based instructional practices (Lomax & McGee, 1987; Roberts, 1992). Thus, it is important for teachers to study how children develop an understanding of printed language to be able to effectively assist children through their learning experiences with printed language.

Understanding the Functions of Printed Language

*People read for different
purposes in everyday living.*

Teale suggests that a study of the functions of printed language may be viewed as a part of the "ongoing struggles of people to understand and deal with their lives" (1987, p. 48). Ken Goodman (1985) describes several purposes for which people learn to read and continue reading as a vital part of living:

- *Environmental reading* involves reading necessary to survive and function in a literate society such as ours. This type of reading includes reading street and regulatory signs, directions, labels, and store and product logos.
- *Occupational reading* is the type of reading demanded by one's vocation and may vary greatly. However, the average employee in the United States reads an average of 141 minutes per day on the job. This type of reading generally occupies the greatest share of readers' total time spent reading.
- *Informational reading* is another type of reading. Readers often need access to information they do not and would not store in memory. Hence, reference materials are printed such as TV guides, telephone books, and almanacs to be used for information.
- *Recreational reading* is used primarily to occupy leisure time as a pleasurable diversion from other pressures and stresses associated with daily living.
- *Ritualistic reading* is used in the culture of religions, clubs, and other service societies to fulfill the requirements of certain rites and rituals.

Of all these types of reading, perhaps the most important for understanding how young children learn to read and write is environmental reading.

Environmental Print Studies

Reading **environmental print** is described as reading printed language on signs, displays, billboards, and labels found in the environmental context of everyday living. In 1967, Ylisto conducted a print-awareness study involving 200 four-, five-, and six-year-old children. The subjects were presented with 25 printed word symbols taken from traffic signs and cereal boxes. The 25 items progressed in difficulty through six steps, from a highly contextualized setting (in a natural setting—photograph) to a more abstract setting (a page of book or word card). The youngest of these children were able to identify some of the symbols through each of the six steps.

Environmental print is described as printed language on signs, displays, billboards, and labels found in the environmental context of everyday living.

Romero (1983) and Y. M. Goodman and Altwerger (1981) conducted studies to investigate the print awareness of Anglo, African-American, Mexican-American, and Papago children ages 3, 4, and 5. These researchers found that 60% of 3-year-old children, and 80% of all 4- and 5-year-old children could read some environmental print. Harste et al. (1984) found that 3-year-old children could correctly identify environmental print or make a semantically acceptable "best guess." Hiebert (1978) found that children made significantly more errors recognizing words when they were presented without the environmental context. In other words, children seemed to be reading the entire context—not just the print. For example, if the word on a stop sign were transcribed onto a box of cereal, younger children would read the word *stop* as the cereal name about 38% to 50% of the time (Dewitz, Stammer, & Jensen, 1980). Thus, according to J. M. Mason (1980), children's early reading of environmental print is highly context dependent.

In another study that supported Mason's (1980) belief, Masonheimer, Drum, and Ehri (1984) found that young readers' errors increased when the unique print associated with a logo was removed from a full context. Even greater increases in errors were found when the unique print associated with a logo was replaced with conventional print. From these results, many researchers believed that children failed to devote attention to graphic detail; rather, children were reading the entire context. In a recent study, however, McGee, Lomax, and Head (1988) found that nonreaders did devote attention, although very limited, to graphic detail in recognizing environmental

Reading environmental print has been shown to be highly dependent on the context of the print.

print. In fact, attention to environmental print is now seen as an important means for introducing children to the world of written language (McGee & Richgels, 1990).

Student Perceptions of Reading

Children's perceptions about reading are closely tied to their teachers' beliefs and attendant instructional practices.

When a young girl attending an elementary school was asked about what she could do to become a better reader, she responded, "I would study my vowel rules and my phonics a lot because that's mostly reading" (DeFord & Harste, 1982, p. 592). Jerry Johns (1986) related that when a second-grade boy was asked, "What do you think reading is?" He responded, "stand up, sit down!" By this he meant that when he read his teacher requested that he stand and sit when he was finished. These are just a few of the perceptions students have about the purposes of reading.

In a pioneering study, Reid (1966) investigated the understanding of the purposes of reading held among 5-year-old children in a classroom in Edinburgh, Scotland. The children in this class were asked, "What is reading?" Their answers to this question indicated that they had a very vague notion about what reading was and how it was to be done. Some children, Reid reported, were unsure about whether one read the pictures or the marks on the page.

In a similar study, Weintraub and Denny (1965) found that children came to school with widely disparate perceptions about reading and that 27% of them could not verbalize anything intelligible about the reading process. Johns and Johns (1971) supported this finding with their own research. They found that 70% of kindergarten through grade 6 students gave vague, irrelevant answers or no response at all to the question of "What is reading?"

In a later and much larger study involving 1,655 students in grades 1 through 8, Johns and Ellis (1976) found that 69% of these students gave essentially meaningless responses to the question of "What is reading?" Nearly 57% of the responses to the question, "What do you do when you read?" were judged to be meaningless. In answer to the question "If someone didn't know how to read, what would you tell him that he would need to learn?" 56% of the respondents indicated something that had to do with pronouncing or decoding words and letters. This decoding perspective held among young readers on how reading could be improved was also replicated in a study by Canney and Winograd (1979).

An interesting insight into young readers' perspectives about reading is found in the work on Reutzel and Sabey (in press). These researchers examined how first-grade student perspectives about reading were influenced by teachers' theoretical beliefs about how children learn to read. Children were given the *Burke Reading Interview* (Burke, 1987), and teachers completed the *Theoretical Orientations to Reading Profile* (DeFord, 1985). Responses of students and teachers were examined and were found to be highly related to one another. Hence, students' perceptions of the act of reading seemed to be subject to the influence of their teachers' beliefs about reading instruction.

Very young students rarely perceive reading to be an act associated with constructing meaning for personal purposes.

From these studies, one may conclude that young readers have only vague notions about the purposes and mechanics of the reading process. Additionally, children's perceptions of the purposes and functions of the reading act are influenced by the beliefs their teachers hold about reading instruction. Finally, as children gain more experience with print, they are able to refine and better articulate their concepts about reading and are more likely to view reading as a meaning-seeking or constructive process.

Understanding the Forms of Printed Language

As children have opportunities to interact with print through reading signs, learning the alphabet, or reading books, they begin to pay closer attention to the details of printed language. **Print concepts** typically embrace an understanding of some of the following:

1. Directionality (left to right, top to bottom)
2. The difference between a word and a letter
3. The meaning and use of punctuation marks
4. The match between speech and print on the page
5. Many other technical understandings about how print and books work

Day and Day (1979) found that 80% of 51 first graders they studied had mastered book orientation and directionality by the end of first grade. However, only a small percentage could recognize incorrect words or letter sequences in a line of print or could explain the use of quotation marks. Downing and Oliver (1973) found that young children could not differentiate reliably between a word and a letter. Johns (1980) found that above-average readers evidenced greater print awareness than did below-average readers. Yaden (1982) concluded that even after a full year of reading instruction, some beginning reader's concepts about printed language remained incomplete and uncertain. Roberts (1992) and Lomax and McGee (1987) found that an understanding of print concepts is an important precursor of reading development among young children.

Young children learn as much about print concepts and word reading in a print-rich environment as they do with the addition of direct instruction on specific print concepts.

In view of these findings, Johns (1980) and N. E. Taylor (1986) cautiously recommended that print concepts and the language of reading instruction be explicitly taught to young readers. Other researchers believed children would learn printed language concepts as well in a print-rich environment where they interacted on a consistent basis with meaningful printed materials (Ferreiro & Teberosky, 1982; Hiebert, 1981; Holdaway, 1979; McCormick & Mason, 1986).

Recent research reported by Reutzel, Oda, and Moore (1989) showed that kindergartners learned as much about print concepts and word reading in a print-rich environment as they did with the addition of direct instruction on specific print concepts. Thus, it appeared that children learned print concepts as well in a print-rich environment with plenty of opportunities for interaction in meaningful ways with printed materials as with the addition of isolated, systematic print concept instruction.

Summary

In many respects, the acquisition of reading and writing parallels the acquisition of oral language among infants and young children. Children process print and speech from whole to part in supportive language environments. They begin by crudely approximating demonstrations of speech, reading, and writing behaviors and refine these attempts over time to become more like those they attempt to emulate. Adult language users play a critical role in youngsters' speech, reading, and writing acquisition. An informed teacher can do much to support youngsters in their attempts to become independent, skilled readers and writers.

See Figure 3.15 for an overview of this chapter.

Figure 3.15

Chapter overview

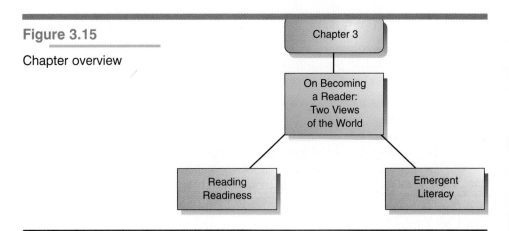

CONCEPT APPLICATIONS

IN THE FIELD

1. Interview two kindergarten teachers. Ask them what they believe contributes to a child's readiness for reading instruction. In a separate paragraph, contrast the differences and similarities.

2. Visit 15 minutes with two children about the same age. Record your visit on audiotape. Write a short essay about the features of spoken language you noted these children had learned well and those speech features for which they may need further demonstrations to support their learning.

3. For 1 week (1 hour/day), visit a kindergarten classroom. Make a listing of invented language used by children at this age. Publish your findings for the other members of the class.

4. Interview two parents about their young children's reading development. Ask them what their children are doing with books and print. Describe in writing the results of the interviews. Which stage(s) of reading development would best describe these two children's reading behaviors? Why?

5. Collect five samples of kindergarten or first-grade children's writing. Label each according to a stage of writing and spelling development described in this chapter. Explain your reasons for categorizing each.

6. Show a child several food product labels (at least 10) and ask him to read them. Record each answer. Ask the child to explain how he arrived at his answer. Discuss in writing each answer with respect to how the child answered and why.

7. Ask a child to tell you a story. Record the telling on audiotape. Analyze the telling using a story grammar. Describe in writing the parts of the story included and excluded in the telling. What can you conclude about this child's sense of story development from this sample?

8. Give two kindergarten or first-grade children a book that is handed to him by the spine and upside down. Ask him to:
   a. Show you where to begin reading.
   b. Show you which way your eyes should progress along the print.
   c. Show you a letter.

d. Show you a word.

e. Show you the end of the book.

Discuss in writing your findings for each child. Describe what this child knows and does not yet know about printed language concepts.

9. Ask three young children what they think reading and writing are. Record their responses on audiotape or in writing. Explain the perceptions these children have of reading and writing in a separate essay or in an entry in your learning log.

10. Ask a young child to read a book to you. After recording the event, reread the description of emergent storybook reading behaviors in Figure 3.3 (based on Sulzby, 1985). Where does this child fit within the developmental stages of storybook reading development?

RECOMMENDED READINGS

Butler, D., & Clay, M. (1979). *Reading begins at home.* Portsmouth, NH: Heinemann.

Clay, M. M. (1975). *What did I write?* Portsmouth, NH: Heinemann.

Clay, M. M. (1987). *Writing begins at home.* Portsmouth, NH: Heinemann.

Clay, M. M. (1989). Concepts about print in English and other languages. *The Reading Teacher, 42,* 268–277.

Cochrane, O., Cochrane, D., Scalena, S., & Buchanan, E. (1984). *Reading, writing and caring.* New York: Richard C. Owen Publishers.

Gentry, J. R. (1987). *Spel is a four letter word.* Portsmouth, NH: Heinemann.

Harste, C., & DeFord, D. (1982). Child language research and curriculum. *Language Arts, 59,* 590–600.

Temple, C., Nathan, R., Burris, N., & Temple, F. (1988). *The beginnings of writing.* New York: Allyn & Bacon.

Whaley, J. F. (1981). Story grammar and reading instruction. *The Reading Teacher, 34,* 762–771.

Yaden, D. B., & Templeton, S. (1986). *Metalinguistic awareness and beginning reading: Conceptualizing what it means to read and write.* Portsmouth, NH: Heinemann.

Chapter 4

Using Basal Readers
Effectively

Focus Questions

When you are finished studying this chapter, you should be able to answer these questions:

1. How have basal readers changed historically?
2. What are the major components associated with basal readers?
3. What are five strengths and five weaknesses of basal readers?
4. How are basal readers produced and organized?
5. How can the basal reader adoption process be improved?
6. What are at least three ways in which teachers can take control of their basal teacher's editions, that is, reconciled reading lesson, balanced reading programs, LEA, DRTA, and so on?
7. What are the sequence and parts of a directed reading activity?
8. How can teachers provide effective, explicit skill instruction?
9. How can teachers help students with special learning needs succeed with basal readers?
10. How can teachers help students with special language or cultural needs succeed with basal readers?

Key Concepts

Basal Readers ✓

Skill Instruction

Scope and Sequence Chart

Basal Reader Adoption

Themed Units ✓

Directed Reading Activity (DRA)

Literature Based

Teacher's Manual ✓

Balanced Reading Program

Reconciled Reading Lesson ✓

Basal readers are used daily in 9 of 10 primary classrooms in the United States.

The hornbook clearly illustrated the strong religious underpinnings of early American reading instruction.

Understanding the Basal Reader

Basal readers in one form or another have played an integral role in American reading instruction for centuries and are likely to continue to do so well into the future (McCallum, 1988; Reutzel, 1991). According to *A Dictionary of Reading*, a basal reading program is "a comprehensive, integrated set of books, workbooks, teacher's editions, and other materials for developmental reading instruction" (T. L. Harris & Hodges, 1981, pp. 30–31). In short, a basal reading program is a set of commercially prepared and sequenced materials for providing reading instruction in elementary and middle schools. Recent research indicates that basal readers are used daily in 92% to 98% of primary classrooms in the United States (Flood & Lapp, 1986). This evidence clearly demonstrates the integral role that basal reader instruction has played and continues to play in contemporary American reading instruction.

Today's basal readers have descended from a long ancestry of basal readers. The first in this line of predecessors was the hornbook, the earliest reading instructional material widely used and recorded in American history (N. B. Smith, 1965). Another ancestor of the modern basal published during this era of reading instruction was the New England Primer. Rooted deeply in the religious freedom movement of the American colonists, early reading instruction was aimed at helping children learn the theology necessary to work out their own salvation. This could only be accomplished by reading the Bible. A cursory examination of the hornbook clearly illustrates the strong religious underpinnings of early American reading instruction (Figure 4.1).

McCallum (1988) pointed out that, as the American citizenry moved away from government by the church to civil government, moral character, national interests,

Figure 4.1

A hornbook, with the alphabet, a syllabary, and the Lord's Prayer

Photo courtesy of The Horn Book, Inc.

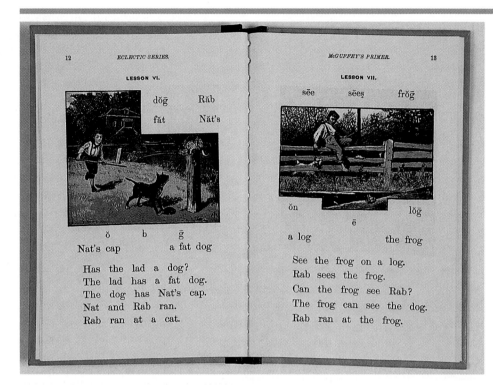

Figure 4.2

Sample pages from *McGuffey's Eclectic Primer,* Revised Edition, New York: Henry H. Vail, 1909.

and patriotism for a new nation influenced both the aims and content of basal readers. Consequently, the McGuffey Eclectic Readers (Figure 4.2) were introduced to the educational community in the 1830s by William H. McGuffey (Bohning, 1986).

In 1912, the Beacon Street Readers were published by Ginn & Co., located on Beacon Street in Boston. These readers reflected a strong emphasis on phonics, complete with elaborate articulation drills and diacritical markings (Aukerman, 1981).

Some may recall the *Dick and Jane New Basic Readers* (Figure 4.3), principally authored by William S. Gray and Marion Monroe and originally published by Scott, Foresman and Company in 1941. The *Dick and Jane* readers conveyed the stereotypic American dream pervasive in the United States during and following World War II and the Korean Conflict. The family depicted in the *Dick and Jane* basals owned a spacious, white, two-story home in a well-cared-for suburban neighborhood. Mother stayed home while Father worked at a successful career, providing for the family's needs. A car or two and a pet dog and cat also adorned the dream of the American family portrayed in this series. For those who remember the *Dick and Jane* readers fondly and wish to update their acquaintance, we suggest a modern humorous satire written by Marc Gallant (1986), entitled, *More Fun With Dick and Jane.*

Observe the language in Figure 4.3.

The basal readers produced during the mid-1960s and through the early 1970s reflected a serious-minded response to a perceived threat to national security by the successful launching of Russia's Sputnik into space. This perception prompted a quick return to basic and rigorous academics in American schooling. Additionally, the publication of Flesch's 1955 book, *Why Johnny Can't Read*, added fuel to the fire for the hasty return to phonics and basic **skill instruction** in reading. *The Reading Mastery Program* (Engelmann & Bruner, 1995) (Figure 4.4) was part of this movement.

Figure 4.3

Sample pages from the
Dick and Jane Readers

Look, Jane.
Look, Dick.
See funny Sally.
Funny, funny Sally.

18

Puff

19

From *The New We Look and See* by W. S. Gray, M. Monroe, A. S. Artley, and M. H. Arbuthnot, Chicago: ScottForesman. Copyright 1956 by ScottForesman. Reprinted by permission.

The basals of the late 1970s and early 1980s reflected an emphasis on back to basics and accountability.

Basals have been sharply criticized by whole-language advocates.

The basals of the late 1970s and the early to mid-1980s reflected a continued emphasis on a basic skills approach to reading instruction. This was accompanied by a major shift in the composition and content of basal readers. The stereotypic portrayal of men and women in basals was attacked and, as a consequence, revised. The failure of basal readers to fairly represent ethnic minorities was assailed by basal critics. Thus, compilers of the basals of this era reacted by attempting to equally represent the increasing complexity of modern American society while maintaining a continuing emphasis on back to basics and accountability (Aukerman, 1981).

Then as now, reading instruction was viewed as a principal means for affecting desirable change in American society. As the whole language philosophy became a force for change among reading professionals in the mid- to late 1980s, basal bashing came into style (McCallum, 1988). Basals were sharply criticized by whole language advocates for devaluing good literature, ignoring the needs of the learner by emphasizing skill instruction, controlling the vocabulary of stories, and prescribing, even usurping, teachers' practices and decisions. On the other hand, E. D. Hirsch (1987), among others, has called for the standardization of the school curriculum to produce a literate citizenry and work force for the future of the nation.

Thus, the interests of the aesthetic and the individual have run head on into the interests of society, business, and science. Mosenthal characterized this as "Teachers between a rock and a hard place" (1989b, p. 628). In fact, publishers of basal readers seemed to be caught in the same hard spot as teachers. In reaction, basal publishers scrambled to meet the divergent demands of this new split in the marketplace. On the one hand, whole language advocates declared the need for good literature, themed instructional units, natural language in basal stories, and guidance rather than prescription in teacher's editions. On the other hand, school boards, state offices of education, government, and businesses demanded standardized curricula, the use of scientific research findings and standardized test scores, basic skill mastery, accountability, and more, not less, prescription in teacher's editions. So dramatic was the polarization that some publishers actually published two teacher's editions to meet the needs of these two groups—for example, McGraw-Hill's integrated language arts edition and basic skills edition (Sulzby, Hoffman, Niles, Shanahan, & Teale, 1989).

During this time, the role of the basal reader became the focus of pointed debates. A book entitled *The Basal Report Card* called for major reforms in both the content and use of basal readers (K. Goodman, Shannon, Freeman, & Murphy, 1988). In a point–counterpoint series in *Reading Today* ("Point/Counterpoint," 1989), the bimonthly newspaper of the International Reading Association, the role of the basal reader was hotly debated. More recently, the debate over basal readers has involved concerns related to teachers' professional skills and decision making. Shannon (1989, 1992, 1993) has asserted that basal readers have contributed to a "deskilling" of teachers' expertise and decision making related to reflective and thoughtful reading instruction. Baumann (1992, 1993) has asserted on the other hand that teachers who are otherwise capable and intelligent decision makers are not

Figure 4.4

Sample page from the SRA *Reading Mastery* program

From *Reading Mastery I, Presentation Book A* (Rainbow Edition, p. 73) by S. Engelmann and E. C. Bruner, 1995, Columbus, OH: SRA Macmillan/McGraw-Hill. Copyright 1995 by SRA Division of Macmillan/McGraw-Hill School Publishing Company. Reprinted by permission.

falling prey to a mindless adherence to basal teacher's editions as Shannon indicates. In fact, Baumann maintains that such an argument is insulting. He asserts that teachers who otherwise think and make decisions do not stop making decisions when they approach reading instruction (Durkin, 1984).

Teachers and administrators need to understand the basal reader to make informed instructional decisions.

Because of the widespread, pervasive, and continued use of basal readers in American schools as the core for providing basic reading instruction (Flood & Lapp, 1986; Shannon, 1983), it is imperative that preservice and in-service teachers learn to use the basal reader with judgment and skill. The purpose of this chapter is to provide teachers with the information necessary for taking control of their basal reader teacher's editions. Teachers who are in control of reading instruction are empowered to make informed instructional decisions about how, when, and why to use basal readers for providing reading instruction.

Focus on the core materials that compose basal readers.

Anatomy of the Basal Reading Approach

Basal readers are typically composed of a set of core materials including the student's text (current series usually include some big books as part of the core in the early grades); the teacher's edition; student's and teacher's workbooks; supplemental practice exercises and enrichment activities (usually both of these are in the form of ditto masters); and end-of-unit or end-of-book tests. Other supplemental materials can be acquired at additional cost such as filmstrips, picture cards, picture with letter cards, letter cards, word cards, large charts, additional ditto sheet masters, classroom tradebook libraries, big books, and technology including videotapes and CD-ROM computer software. In addition, many basal reading series provide a system for record keeping, management of the reading skills taught and mastered, and assessment. Figure 4.5 shows an example of a 1995 teacher's edition basal reader. Because many teachers will employ a basal as the core component in a school reading program, we will describe each of the basal components along with examples.

The Teacher's Edition

*A **scope and sequence chart** describes in detail the range of concepts and skills to be taught in the basal program as well as the order in which these concepts and skills are to be presented.*

The long venerated Directed Reading Lesson has been dropped in many current basal readers and replaced with the Shared Reading Experience.

Perhaps the most important part of the basal reading program is the teacher's edition because the teacher's edition is the instructional guidance and in-service support that most teachers receive when they purchase and use a basal series. Within the pages of the teacher's edition, one usually finds three important features: (a) the scope and sequence chart of the particular basal reading program, (b) a reduced version of the student's text, and (c) a suggested lesson plan for the teacher. A **scope and sequence chart** like the one in Figure 4.6 describes in great detail the range of skills to be taught in a basal program as well as the order in which these are to be presented. A reduced version of the student's text, or facsimile, is included in the teacher's edition for the teacher's convenience. The lesson plan for each unit in the basal reader is already done for the teacher to save time. More recent editions of the basal reader (1993 and beyond) make subtle changes in the structure of reading lessons. Some basal readers are slowly moving away from the long venerated directed reading activity of E. Betts (1946) toward the lesson structure of the shared reading approach (Holdaway, 1979). This shift in pedagogy is most evident in the suggestions found in teacher's editions for reading aloud to students, reading with students, and reading by students (Mooney, 1990).

Figure 4.5

A current basal reader—a school textbook that contains a collection of literature

From *Treasury of Literature: A Place to Dream* (Teacher's ed., Level 3-1) cover illustration by J. Ransome, Orlando, FL: Harcourt Brace & Company, 1995. Copyright 1995 by Harcourt Brace & Company. Reprinted by permission.

It is important for teachers and administrators to understand that the teacher's edition is a resource to be used discriminatingly and not as a script to be rigidly followed. Teachers and administrators should not allow the teacher's edition to dictate the reading program. Rather, teachers should be encouraged to decide what is and what is not appropriate in the teacher's edition for use with a particular group of children.

The Student's Basal Text

The student's basal is an anthology of original and classic stories, poems, news clips, and expository text selections. Some selected original stories have been created expressly by authors for the student's basal reader, whereas other classic selections have been adapted from children's literature or trade books. High-quality artwork generally accompanies the selections in the contemporary basal reader; however, recently, rather than adapting the language of classic literature, basal reader publishers have engaged in cutting artwork from original picture stories (Larsen, 1994). Interspersed throughout the student's text, one may find poetry selections, jokes, riddles, puzzles, informational essays, and special skill and/or concept lessons. Some basal texts contain questions children should be able to answer after reading the stories. Upper level basal readers often contain a glossary of words that students can refer to when decoding new words or so that students can look up the meaning of new words found in the text.

Notice what is included in the student's basal text.

Although many basal readers include well-regarded children's literature, publishers continue to modify or adapt children's books in various ways for inclusion in basal readers.

Figure 4.6

Figure 4.6

A scope and sequence chart showing the range of skills to be taught in a basal program

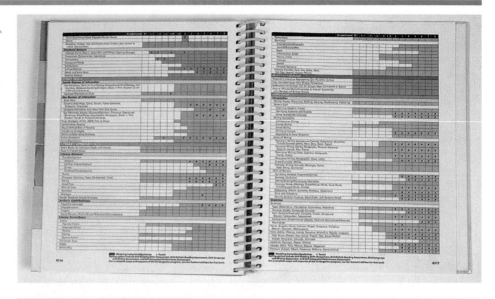

From *Treasury of Literature: A Place to Dream* (Teacher's ed., Level 3-1, pp. R116–R117), Orlando, FL: Harcourt Brace & Company, 1995. Copyright 1995 by Harcourt Brace & Company. Reprinted by permission.

*In some basals for beginning readers, called **primers,** the language is controlled to represent selected phonics generalizations.*

A hallmark of past and some current basal reader stories is carefully controlled vocabulary and text difficulty, particularly in the early grades, which allows for the introduction of a predetermined number of unfamiliar words in each new story. In years past, readability formulas often have been applied to the selections in basal readers to control for reading difficulty. Readability formulas, generally speaking, were used to measure the difficulty level of a text by counting the letters or number of syllables in a word and the number of words in each sentence. Reducing word size by using simpler words in place of longer words and shortening sentences supposedly renders a text less difficult to read. Research by Pearson (1974), however, challenges this concept that shorter sentences are easier to read. According to Pearson's research, short, choppy sentences tend to be more difficult to comprehend because explicit connecting or sequencing words such as *because, and, so, then, before,* and *after* are deleted from the text and consequently need to be inferred by the reader. In some basal readers, the earliest books or primers often contain language designed to reinforce a particular phonic generalization, as shown in the following excerpt (Beck, Armbruster, Raphael, McKeown, Ringler, & Ogle, 1989, p. 2):

> **The Map**
> Todd and Pam sat and sat.
> "What can we do?" said Todd.
> "Todd, look at Sampson," said Pam.
> "Look at him dig."

Although texts such as these may be useful in teaching phonics, children seldom encounter such contrived texts outside the boundaries of school textbooks. As a consequence, the twin practices of controlling vocabulary through the application of readability formulas or controlling vocabulary through contriving texts that adhere to a selected phonics generalization have been criticized sharply; these practices tend to distort the meaning of the stories, resulting in senseless, inconsiderate texts, and tend to suggest that reading is primarily a decoding task (Armbruster, 1984; Harste, Woodward, & Burke, 1984; K. S. Goodman, 1987). An examination of 1993 basal reader revisions reveals little if any tampering with the original language of children's authors. On the other hand, many companies, because of production and layout limitations, have engaged in cutting or moving the beautiful artwork that supports and sustains the language in many children's books (Larsen, 1994). This practice is perhaps as damaging, if not more so, than altering the text for young, emergent readers who may rely more heavily on the pictures for support through the text.

Think about some important criticisms of controlling vocabulary in early basal readers.

The Workbook

In past years, the most used part of any basal reading series was the workbook (Osborn, 1985). In fact, if any part of the basal reading lesson was neglected, it was seldom the workbook pages (Durkin, 1984; J. Mason, 1983). Although somewhat less the case today, workbook exercises remain firmly entrenched in many classrooms, as evidenced by their continued inclusion as a part and parcel of basal reading series.

Workbooks were designed to provide a means for students to independently practice skill instruction provided by the teacher.

Workbooks were designed to provide a means for students to independently practice skill instruction provided by the teacher. Also, workbooks often are used for assessing reading skills previously taught as well as those currently taught. In this way, workbooks play a dual role in classrooms, namely, practice and assessment. In some cases, teachers also have found that workbooks can serve a classroom management function. When children are engaged in completing worksheets, this frees the teacher to work with individual children or groups of children who most need help.

Recent research reveals that students spend up to 70% of the time allocated for reading instruction, or 49 minutes per day, in independent practice or completing worksheets, like those found in workbooks, while less than 10% of the total reading instructional time, or about 7 to 8 minutes per day, is devoted to silent reading in the primary grades. In fact, publishers indicate that there is an insatiable demand for worksheets (R. C. Anderson, Hiebert, Scott, & Wilkinson, 1985). Jachym, Allington, and Broikou (1989) reported that the cost of seat work that is due to the escalating demand for worksheets is the displacement of many more important aspects of reading instruction, such as the acquisition of good books and time for reading. Based on these findings, it seems obvious that workbooks have been misused and overused. However, when teachers judiciously select workbook exercises to support instruction, workbooks can provide students with valuable practice and feedback on progress in relation to specific reading skills. Osborn (1984) provides 20 guidelines for assessing the worth of workbook and worksheet-type reading tasks:

School reading instruction is often defined by children as "doing worksheets."

The cost of seat work has displaced many more important aspects of reading instruction such as the acquisition of good books and time for reading.

SOME GUIDELINES FOR WORKBOOK TASKS

1. A sufficient proportion of workbook tasks should be relevant to the instruction that is going on in the rest of the unit or lesson.
2. Another portion of workbook tasks should provide for a systematic and cumulative review of what has already been taught.
3. Workbooks should reflect the most important (and workbook-appropriate) aspects of what is being taught in the reading program. Less important aspects should remain in the teacher's guide as voluntary activities.

4. Workbooks should contain, in a form that is readily accessible to students and teachers, extra tasks for students who need extra practice.
5. The vocabulary and concept level of workbook tasks should relate to that of the rest of the program and to the students using the program.
6. The language used in workbook tasks must be consistent with that used in the rest of the lesson and in the rest of the workbook.
7. Instructions to students should be clear, unambiguous, and easy to follow; brevity is a virtue.
8. The layout of pages should combine attractiveness with utility.
9. Workbooks should contain enough content so that there is a chance a student will learn something and not simply be exposed to something.
10. Tasks that require students to make discriminations must be preceded by a sufficient number of tasks that provide practice on components of the discriminations.
11. The content of workbook tasks must be accurate and precise; workbook tasks must not present wrong information nor perpetuate misrules.
12. At least some workbook tasks should be fun and have an obvious payoff to them.
13. Most student response modes should be consistent from task to task.
14. Student response modes should be the closest possible to reading and writing.
15. The instructional design of individual tasks and of task sequences should be carefully planned.
16. Workbooks should contain only a finite number of task types and forms.
17. The art that appears on workbook pages must be consistent with the prose of the task.
18. Cute, nonfunctional, space- and time-consuming tasks should be avoided.
19. When appropriate, tasks should be accompanied by brief explanations of purpose for both teachers and students.
20. English major humor should be avoided.[*]

Workbooks, like TV, can be a tool that can assist or inhibit children's reading progress.

Additionally, completed workbook exercises can provide teachers critical evaluative information on the effectiveness of instruction as well as diagnostic information on the quality of students' learning. In short, workbooks can be a valuable resource when used correctly or can be a debilitating deterrent to students' reading progress when overrelied on or misused.

Assessment

The subject of testing and evaluation will be discussed in depth in Chapter 13.

Although workbook exercises can be used for formative assessment of reading skill development, most basal reading series provide end-of-unit or end-of-book tests for summative evaluation of student learning. These tests are generally criterion-referenced tests, which means that the items measured on these tests are directly related to the specific skills taught in that unit or book.

Just as workbook exercises can be abused, so it is with tests. Tests should provide teachers information about the quantity and quality of children's learning to direct future instruction. Tests should not be used to label children or teachers. No single test score should ever form the basis for making important decisions about children or teachers. Administrators and teachers must be extremely cautious in the use and interpretation of test scores.

---

[*]From "The Purposes, Uses, and Contents of Workbooks and Some Guidelines for Publishers" by J. Osborn, in *Learning to Read in American Schools* (pp. 110–111), edited by R. C. Anderson, J. Osborn, & R. J. Tierney, 1984, Hillsdale, NJ: Erlbaum. Copyright 1984 by Lawrence Erlbaum Associates, Inc. Reprinted by permission.

Record Keeping

Maintaining records to document teaching and learning is an important part of accountability. Most basal reading series provide a means for keeping records on children's progress through the skills outlined in the scope and sequence chart of the basal. Most often, the methods of assessment specified are paper-and-pencil testing or worksheet administration. The scores obtained on these exercises are entered into a master list or record, which follows the child throughout her elementary years. Such a skills-management system allows teachers to keep accurate records from year to year regarding each child's progress through the adopted basal reading program's scope and sequence of skills. Unfortunately, some teachers spend inordinate amounts of time keeping records of this kind, which leads to a most undesirable condition. Pearson captured this situation well when he stated:

> The model implicit in the practices of [this teacher] was that of a manager—[a] person who arranged materials, texts, and the classroom environment so learning could occur. But the critical test of whether learning did occur was left up to the child as s/he interacted with the materials.
>
> Children practiced applying skills; if they learned them, fine; we always had more skills for them to practice; if they did not, fine; we always had more worksheets and duplicating sheets for the same skill. And the most important rule in such a mastery role was that practice makes perfect, leading to the ironic condition that children spent most of their time on precisely that subset of skills they performed least well. (Pearson, 1985, p. 736)

To this we would like to add the comment that, disturbingly, teachers under this model spent the bulk of their time running off dittos, assigning, correcting, and recording rather than guiding, demonstrating, or interacting with children or books. Although elegant, record keeping should go well beyond keeping track of the worksheet type of evaluation. Fortunately, some basal readers now recognize this fact and include process as well as product measures of children's reading and reading habits. In fact, some basal readers now provide suggestions for designing individual assessment portfolios for each student. Figure 4.7 shows suggestions for a basal reader student portfolio. Unfortunately, many basal publishers still overrely on paper-and-pencil demonstrations for inclusion in student portfolios. They have yet to become serious about providing means for capturing students reading processes for inclusion in portfolios. For teachers who want to present students' reading demonstrations as evidence for a reading portfolio, they will need to obtain audiotapes of students' reading and analyze these (as shown in Chapter 13) on their own for the foreseeable future.

In summary, basal reading series are typically composed of a core of three elements; teacher's edition, student text, and workbooks, as well as a host of available kits, charts, cards, tests, additional practice exercises, and assessment/record-keeping systems to supplement the core elements of the basal series. In an effort to compete with trade-book publishers, basal publishers are also producing big books to complement the already expansive list of purchasable options listed previously. Teachers should be careful not to accept these new "basal" big books without careful examination. In some cases, big books published by basal companies are not big books at all—they are big basals!

Although the basal reader approach offers a resource for helping teachers provide systematic and sequenced reading instruction throughout the elementary and middle grades, even so, teachers must be careful to supplement this core program with trade books, silent reading time, group sharing, extensions of reading into writ-

Most basal reading series provide a means for keeping records on children's progress.

*A **skills-management system** allows teachers to keep accurate records from year to year regarding each child's progress through the adopted basal reading program's scope and sequence of skills.*

Although many basal readers provide assessment tools, the lack of a construction of a high-quality assessment rubric for constructing a portfolio remains a serious flaw.

Notice how teachers can supplement the basal reader core program.

Figure 4.7

One of the newer basals that recommend portfolio assessment

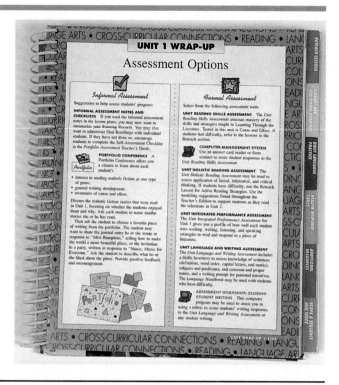

From *Treasury of Literature: A Place to Dream* (Teacher's ed., Level 3-1, p. T193), Orlando, FL: Harcourt Brace & Company, 1995. Copyright 1995 by Harcourt Brace & Company. Reprinted by permission.

ing, speaking, drama, music, and so on, as well as individual assessment of children's reading progress, behaviors, and attitudes. When this is understood and achieved, basal readers can provide a valuable service to schools, administrators, teachers, and children. In addition, basals provide a safety-net for many teachers, novice and experienced, as they make the transition toward balanced reading instruction.

Production and Organization of Basal Readers

Basal reading programs are typically known by the name of the publishing house that produces the basal.

Basal reading series are owned by large, diversified business corporations such as Xerox, Paramount, Inc., Raycon Inc., and Gulf-Western and are produced by a variety of publishing houses from coast to coast. The production of a basal reader is overseen by a managing editor with the assistance of a senior author team, a group of figures in the field of reading who are known and respected as experts. Basal reading programs are often known by the name of the publishing house that produces the basal (Figure 4.8).

Harcourt Brace	Macmillan/McGraw-Hill/SRA
D. C. Heath	Open Court
Holt, Rinehart & Winston	Scholastic
Houghton Mifflin	Silver Burdett & Ginn

Minor revisions of basal readers occur every few years. Major revision cycles occur every 5 or 6 years. Major revisions are usually slated for completion during the same year Texas and California consider basal readers for statewide adoption. Consequently, the "Texas and California" effect is known to exert considerable influence on the content and quality of new basal readers (Farr, Tulley, & Powell, 1987; Keith, 1981). In reading circles, one often hears the axiom, "as Texas and California go, so goes the nation."

Strengths and Weaknesses of Basal Readers

Although basal readers continue to be the mainstay of reading instruction in American schools, the basal reader approach to reading instruction has not gone unscrutinized. Criticisms of basal readers have ranged from the cultural to literary, from the linguistic to instructional. Because basal readers are used in over 90% of American classrooms, most teachers will inevitably have occasion to make use of the basal reader approach to reading instruction (Flood & Lapp, 1986; Zintz & Maggart, 1989). To make instructional decisions about how, when, and why to use the basal, teachers and administrators must know the strengths and weaknesses of the basal reader approach to reading.

In defense of basal reading series, basals possess certain positive qualities that contribute to their enduring popularity in American classrooms. Basal readers contain an organized and systematic plan for teachers to consult. More recently published basal readers often provide teaching suggestions from which transitional reading teachers make decisions about when and how to teach skills that are important and authentic reading related behaviors.

Basal readers contain an organized and systematic plan for teachers to consult in planning reading instruction.

Basal readers are sequenced from grade to grade, thus providing for continuous reading instruction throughout the elementary school years and continuity both within grades and across grade levels. The readily available tests and practice exer-

The subskills and skills reading instructional models are discussed in Chapter 2.

Figure 4.8

The level 6, grade 2 basal reader from Macmillan/McGraw-Hill

From *Window to the Sky,* 1993, New York: Macmillan/McGraw-Hill School Division. Copyright 1993 by Macmillan/McGraw-Hill School Publishing Company. Reprinted by permission.

Readily available tests and practice exercises found in the basal workbooks save teachers enormous amounts of time in materials preparation.

cises found in the workbooks save teachers enormous amounts of time in materials preparation. Reading skills are gradually introduced, practiced, and reviewed through the plan provided in the scope and sequence of the basal. The lesson plans found ready made in the teacher's editions also save teachers much preparation time. A variety of literary genres is available to teachers and students in current basal readers. The structure provided in basal readers is often very reassuring for novice or beginning teachers. Administrators can manage and provide accountability evidence more easily by adopting and using basal reading series. In short, basal readers do possess several characteristics that teachers and administrators find helpful and worthwhile.

ADVANTAGES OF THE BASAL READER APPROACH[*]

- A sequenced curriculum of skill instruction is provided. Skills instruction is arranged to provide for both initial instruction and a systematic review of skills taught.
- A continuous arrangement of instruction from grade to grade is supplied.
- To save teachers' time, a completely prepared set of stories, instructional directions and activities, instructional practice materials, and assessment and management devices is available.
- Stories are arranged in a sequence of ascending difficulty.
- Reading skills are gradually introduced.
- Teachers are provided structured lesson plans.
- Students are exposed to a variety of literary genre in basals.
- Organization and structure of basals are helpful to beginning teachers just learning about the reading curriculum.
- Organization and structure are reassuring to administrators and school patrons that important reading skills are being taught.

LIMITATIONS OF THE BASAL READER APPROACH

- Vocabulary control renders story content dull and repetitious.
- Cropping pictures removes supportive scaffolding for younger readers.
- Skill instruction is rarely applied in or related to comprehending the story content.
- The basal lesson design in teacher's editions very often fails to relate one part of the lesson, e.g., vocabulary introduction, to subsequent parts of the reading lesson, e.g., story comprehension discussion.
- Stories often do not relate to students' interests.
- The format of basals is often less appealing than the format of trade books.
- Special interest group censorship leads to the selection of stories that contain little real subject matter content, that deal with few real-life applications, or that present societal or ethical content for right-living.
- The application of readability formulas to text selections results in stories and text features that are void of content and inconsiderate of the reader's need to understand.
- Teacher's editions seldom contain useful directions on how to teach reading comprehension.
- A rigid adherence to the basal leaves little room for teacher creativity and decision making.
- The grading or leveling of basal readers promotes the use of traditional ability or achievement groups in classrooms.

[*]From "Understanding and Using Basal Readers Effectively" by D. R. Reutzel in *Effective Strategies for Teaching Reading* (p. 259) edited by B. Hayes, 1991, New York: Allyn & Bacon. Copyright 1991 by D. R. Reutzel. Reprinted by permission.

- Management demands of the basal program can become so time consuming that little time remains for students to self-select their own reading materials.
- Use of the basal reader approach has traditionally been associated with the use of "Round Robin" reading. Such a practice is encouraged by insisting that all children simultaneously attend to the same selection while another child reads orally.

Basal readers are not without significant deficiencies. Narrative selections in students' basal readers have been criticized repeatedly in the past two decades. They have tended in the early grades to be repetitive and boring—employing language patterns that are well below the speaking abilities of the children and dissimilar to the spoken or written language with which they have become familiar. Basal stories and selections have been condemned for their lack of literary worth. They have been indicted for failing to deal with real-life concerns and values; in short, basals represent contrived rather than authentic reading (Winograd, 1989). Although the variety of selections found in basals may be considerable, some educators are concerned with what appears to be genre and topic flitting in basal readers. Because of this criticism, most recently published basal readers now organize their selections into similar genres or center their selections on a theme or topic.

Although popular, basal readers are not without significant deficiencies.

Expository selections have been "dumbed down" to the point they contain little or no real content. These observations prompted an article in *The Reading Teacher* (1984) to ask, "Basal Reading Texts: What's in Them to Comprehend?" (p. 194). Many of the objections voiced about the stories found in the basals can be traced to publishers' efforts to fit story content into the straitjacket of readability formulas. Publishers ought not take the blame alone for the use of readability formulas on basal stories. Well-meaning but uninformed professors, textbook-adoption committees, teachers, and administrators pressured publishers into using readability formulas to measure reading difficulty. It should be noted, however, that recent basal readers have controlled vocabulary far less than in previous editions.

Many of the objections voiced about the stories found in the basals can be traced to publishers' efforts to fit story content into the straitjacket of readability formulas.

Basal readers have also been blamed for poorly representing societal groups and concerns. This is often attributable to the censorship of various special interest groups that enter into the **basal reader adoption** process, particularly in states that adopt statewide (Marzano, 1993/1994). Today, basals continue to be assailed for poor instructional design and content. Durkin (1981a) found that many teachers' editions contained an abundance of questions and evaluative activities mislabeled as instructional activities. What was labeled as instruction was often found to be nothing more than an assessment exercise. Reutzel and Daines (1987a) found that basal reading skills lessons seldom supported or even related to the selections to be read in the basals. These conclusions supported J. Mason's (1983) findings that teachers' reading instruction was more often than not unrelated to the text that children would be asked to read. In another study the same year, Reutzel and Daines (1987b) reported that even the parts of the reading units had little relation to one another. Eldredge, Reutzel, and Hollingsworth (1994) have demonstrated that reading instruction based on the shared reading approach (Holdaway, 1979) produces significantly greater growth in reading achievement than does the directed reading lesson (Betts, 1946). Despite these limitations, the basal "baby" simply cannot be thrown out with the bath water (Baumann, 1993; McCallum, 1988; Winograd, 1989). Basals have filled an important niche for many teachers and will likely continue to do so in the future. While awaiting improvements in the basal, teachers armed with an understanding of the strengths and weaknesses of basal readers, as described here, can enjoy the benefits associated with basals while moving gradually to overcome the weaknesses.

Organization of the Basal Reader

Basal readers are designed to take children through a series of books, experiences, and activities toward increasingly sophisticated reading behaviors. Each basal series typically provides several readers or books of reading selections at each level. For example, the *Macmillan/McGraw-Hill Reading/Language Arts: A New View* (1993) basal provides the following books for each grade level:

Grade 1: Level 1—*Books! Books! Books!*
Grade 1: Level 2—*Here We Grow!*
Grade 1: Level 3—*Goodness Gracious Me!*
Grade 1: Level 4—*Sing a Sweet Song*
Grade 1: Level 5—*The Very Thing*
Grade 2: Level 6—*Window to the Sky*
Grade 2: Level 7—*Make a Splash*
Grade 3: Level 8—*Catch a Sunflake*
Grade 3: Level 9—*Sing It to the Sea*
Grade 4: Level 10—*Beat the Story Drum*
Grade 5: Level 11—*Don't Forget to Fly*
Grade 6: Level 12—*Just Past the Possible*
Grade 7: Level 13—*Become the Music*
Grade 8: Level 14—*Dream a World*

An important feature to be found in teacher's editions is the scope and sequence chart. A scope and sequence chart is a curricular plan, usually in chart form, which includes the instructional objectives and skills associated with a specific basal reading program. These objectives and skills are arranged by the grade levels in which they are to be taught. It is in the scope and sequence chart that teachers can learn about the objectives of the basal program and the lessons designed to accomplish the objectives.

Some contemporary basal readers are organized into themed units.

Most contemporary basal readers are organized into **themed units**, with several basal selections organized around a selected theme or topic; still others are organized into arbitrarily divided units of instruction. Most basal readers continue to follow the **directed reading activity (DRA)** format originally developed by Betts in 1946. This format can be divided into six discrete parts or steps in the lesson:

1. Building background and vocabulary
2. Introducing and setting the purpose for reading
3. Guided reading
4. Comprehension discussion
5. Skill instruction and practice
6. Enrichment and/or language extensions

Building Background and Vocabulary

Notice what teachers should focus on when building story background.

Activities to build background and vocabulary involve the teacher and students in a discussion of the topic and unfamiliar concepts to be encountered in the story. Beck (1986) directs teachers to focus discussion on the central problem, critical concept, or central message needed to understand the story. This segment of the DRA is to provide students with the necessary knowledge to facilitate comprehension of the story content. Because comprehension of a story depends on owning the meaning of specific unfamiliar words, teachers should usually focus on activities designed to help students understand how new vocabulary words will be used in the context of the story.

Introducing and Setting the Purpose for Reading

The part of the DRA devoted to introducing and setting the purpose for reading is intended to provide motivation and purpose for reading the story. Introducing and setting the purpose for reading centers on reading the story title and subtitle(s) and looking at the pictures to predict the plot and outcome of the story. Students are often encouraged to make predictions from the titles and pictures. Finally, the teacher typically sets the purpose for reading by directing students to read to find the answer to a specific question. These activities guide students into purposeful reading.

Guided Reading

During guided reading, students read to answer questions or to confirm predictions. Many teacher's editions suggest that guided reading should be silent reading. Some teachers, however, especially primary grade teachers, insist that children read the stories orally to assess word-decoding abilities. This approach to guided reading is quite different from those in balanced reading programs (see the discussion of balanced reading programs later in this chapter and in Chapter 10).

Comprehension Discussion

After reading, a discussion of the story ensues through answering questions about the story content. Questions for conducting comprehension discussion are found interspersed throughout and following the story in the teacher's edition.

Skill Instruction and Practice

Skill instruction and practice focus on developing readers' skills in three areas of the reading curriculum: (a) decoding, (b) vocabulary, and (c) comprehension. Individual skill lessons from each of these areas usually follow the story in the teacher's edition. After instruction, students practice the skills in workbooks and on ditto sheets.

Enrichment or Language-Extension Activities

Activities concerning enrichment or language-extension activities focus on and extend the story content. Language-extension activities very often encourage students to go well beyond the content of the story or skill lessons to pursue related personal interests, related topics, or relevant skills.

Instructional Beliefs and Basal Readers

Although basal readers may be alike in many surface respects, they often differ with respect to authors' beliefs about how children learn to read and, consequently, how children should be taught to read.

Although basal readers may be alike in many surface respects, they often differ with respect to the authors' beliefs about how children learn to read and, consequently, how children should be taught to read. Some basal readers, for example, emphasize helping children acquire word-identification skills early and rapidly. Other basal reading series emphasize meaning at the outset of reading instruction. Children are initially taught a stock of sight words and then gradually introduced to decoding skills somewhat later using the sight words already learned for decoding instruction. Basals that take this approach to reading instruction reflect a skills belief on the reading instruction continuum, as discussed in Chapter 2. Thus, the differences in beliefs held by the authors of basal readers are typically reflected in both the structure and content of basal readers.

Subskills Basals

Basal readers founded on a strong subskills belief place an early and strong emphasis on decoding skills.

Basal readers founded on a strong subskills belief place an early and strong emphasis on decoding skills. In fact, these basal readers are often classified as "phonics first," explicit or synthetic phonics basal readers (R. C. Anderson et al., 1985; Flesch, 1955, 1981). Learning the letter sounds and names—usually one at a time until a child has mastered the 26 letter names and the 40-plus sounds those letters represent—is considered a prerequisite to reading words and connected text. Once children have learned these prerequisite letter names and sounds, this knowledge will allow them to crack the written code. Next, they are shown how to blend these sounds together to "sound out" words. For example, a child learns the letters *a, t,* and *c.* Blending sounds from left to right produces *c - a - t, cat.* Although all basal readers provide some type of decoding instruction, basals that represent a subskills belief can be distinguished by the following features: (a) teaching graphophonic relationships as a prerequisite to reading words and text, (b) teaching the blending of phonics elements to get words, and (c) reading phonically controlled texts written to conform to specific phonics generalizations. Subskill basals begin with the very smallest units of language first (Weaver, 1988). Examples of subskills basals include Science Research Associates (SRA) *Reading Mastery* (Engelmann & Hanner, 1983) and Economy Company's *Keys to Reading* (T. Harris et al., 1975). An example of a subskills basal is shown in Figure 4.9.

Literature-Based (Skills) Basals

Notice how skills basals have adapted to calls for changes in basal reader content and structure.

Skills basal readers present comprehension, vocabulary, and phonics skill lessons simultaneously from the very start of reading instruction.

In response to recent demands of teachers and textbook adoption committees to correct the weaknesses associated with basal readers in the past, many basal publishers have responded by making fundamental changes in both content and structure of their basal programs. These changes reflect a dramatic shift in beliefs, moving toward the balanced literacy end of the reading instructional continuum. Some of these changes include using greater amounts of existing, recognized children's literature. **Literature-based** (skills) basal readers, although interested in word identification, go well beyond the preoccupation evidenced in subskill readers to focus primarily on word meaning. These basals attend to issues of vocabulary development and comprehension as well as the requisite skills for identifying words (Weaver, 1988). For example, discussions build experiential background, and demonstrations help chil-

Figure 4.9

The Open Court basal:
A subskills basal that
includes literature

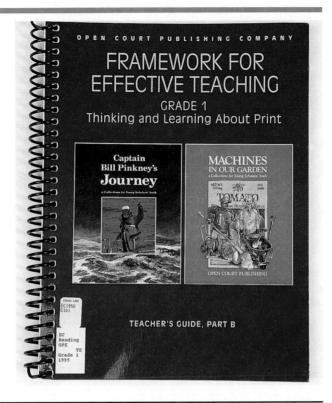

From *Collections for Young Scholars: Framework for Effective Teaching. Grade 1: Thinking and Learning About Print. Teacher's Guide, Part B* by M. J. Adams, C. Bereiter, J. Hirshberg, V. Anderson, and S. A. Bernier, 1995, Chicago: Open Court. Copyright 1995 by Open Court Publishing Company. Reprinted by permission.

dren draw on prior knowledge rather than simply teaching a list of new vocabulary words to enhance reading preparation. One example appears in Figure 4.10. In short, literature-based (skills) basal readers present comprehension, vocabulary, and phonics skill lessons simultaneously from the very start of reading instruction, whereas subskill basals delay emphasis on these components until word-identification skills have been mastered. Many basal readers, like the one in Figure 4.10, represent a skills belief about reading instruction. Reading selections in transitional or literature-based (skills) basals are often organized into themes (Figure 4.11). Some examples of skills basal readers include the Scott, Foresman; D. C. Heath; Houghton-Mifflin; and Silver Burdett & Ginn basal series.

As we mentioned, some transitional, or literature-based (skills), basal readers reflect a more holistic belief system applied to the use of basal readers. Some transitional, or literature-based, basal readers are imported from Canada, New Zealand, and Australia. Examples of these imported basals used in U.S. schools include *Networks,* from Nelson of Canada (McInnes, 1983), and *Impressions,* from Holt, Rinehart & Winston (Booth et al., 1985). More recently, U.S. publishers have provided examples of transitional, literature-based, basal readers with the child as the focus of the program rather than the skills developed throughout the program. Most prominent among these is the Scholastic *Literacy Place* program (1995) shown in Figure 4.12.

Reading selections in transitional, or literature-based, basals are often organized into themes.

Figure 4.10

An example of a theme in a literature-based teacher planner: Family days, family ways

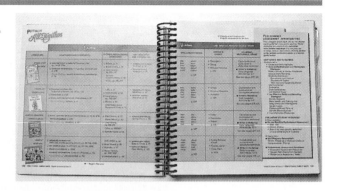

From *Window to the Sky* (pp. 10G–10H), 1993, New York: Macmillan/McGraw-Hill School Division. Copyright 1993 by Macmillan/McGraw-Hill School Publishing Company. Reprinted by permission.

Adopting and Evaluating Basal Readers From a Transitional Perspective

Few professional decisions deserve more careful attention than that of evaluating and selecting a basal reading series. Because many teachers will evaluate one or more basal reading series during their professional careers, they need to understand how to evaluate and select basal readers effectively. Learning about this process will also enable them to help reform, restructure, and strengthen future basal reading adoption processes.

Because many teachers will evaluate one or more basal reading series during their professional careers, they need to understand how to evaluate and select basal readers effectively.

Figure 4.11

A sample page from one of the new basals that show teachers ways to plan instruction around a theme

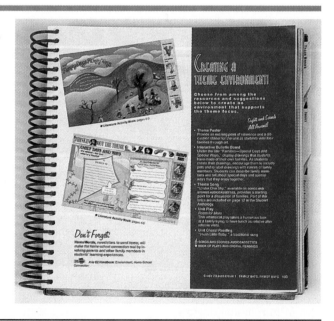

From *Window to the Sky,* New York: Macmillan/McGraw-Hill School Division. Copyright 1993 by Macmillan/McGraw-Hill School Publishing Company. Reprinted by permission.

From *Literacy Place. Literacy Source Book: Nature Guides,* 1995, New York: Scholastic. Copyright 1995 by Scholastic. Reprinted by permission.

Figure 4.12

The Scholastic *Literacy Place* program, embeds instruction in places where literacy is used, such as in nature

The Process of Basal Reader Adoption

Twenty-two states have adopted some form of highly centralized, state-level control over the evaluation and selection of reading basals. The remaining 28 states and the District of Columbia allow individual districts and schools to select basal reading series at the local level (Table 4.1). Regardless of whether evaluations and selections occur at state or local levels, the task of decision making is most often placed in the hands of a

Notice who is often charged with the responsibility for adopting a new basal reader.

Table 4.1

Textbook adoption policies by state

STATE ADOPTION	LOCAL ADOPTION
Alabama	Alaska
Arkansas	Arizona
California	Colorado
Florida	Connecticut
Georgia	Delaware
Hawaii	District of Columbia
Idaho	Illinois
Indiana	Iowa
Kentucky	Kansas
Louisiana	Maine
Mississippi	Maryland
Nevada	Massachusetts
New Mexico	Michigan
North Carolina	Minnesota
Oklahoma	Missouri
Oregon	Montana
South Carolina	Nebraska
Tennessee	New Hampshire
Texas	New Jersey
Utah	New York
Virginia	North Dakota
West Virginia	Ohio
	Pennsylvania
	Rhode Island
	South Dakota
	Vermont
	Washington
	Wisconsin
	Wyoming

Most basal evaluations amount to little more than a "flip test."

textbook adoption committee. Farr et al. (1987) indicate that these committees often use a locally produced checklist to evaluate basal readers. Unfortunately, most adoption checklists require the evaluators to determine only the presence of certain features in basals rather than to assess the quality of these features. Follett (1985) estimated that the average amount of time textbook adoption committee members spend evaluating basals is approximately 1 second per page, resulting in what Powell (1986) calls a "Flip Test" approach to evaluation and selection. Farr et al. (1987) proposed several guidelines for improving the basal reader adoption process found in Figure 4.13.

Although many of these recommendations will require major changes, improving the basal reader adoption process can itself contribute much to teachers' understanding of the reading curriculum and, as a result, can enhance the overall quality of reading instruction.

Evaluating Basal Readers From a Transitional Balanced Reading Perspective

Only after teachers are sufficiently well informed can they act to correct or adjust the use of the basal to benefit their students.

Although discussions about basal reader evaluations can sometimes be unpleasant, they are necessary to help teachers become aware of both strengths and limitations of the basal reader approach. Only after teachers are sufficiently well informed can they act to correct or adjust the use of the basal to benefit their students.

Dole, Rogers, and, Osborn (1987) recommend that to improve the evaluation of basal readers, those involved should focus on the following:

1. Identify the facets of effective reading instruction.
2. Delineate criteria to be analyzed in the basal readers related to effective reading.
3. Provide a means for carefully recording how well basal readers measure up to the established criteria.

Basic Assumptions

1. The selection of a reading textbook series should not be considered the same as the adoption of the total reading curriculum.
2. Basal reading adoptions should be conducted by school districts rather than by states.
3. The final decision regarding textbook selection should reside with the committee that spends the time and energy reviewing the books.

Selection of Reviewers

1. Reviewers should have the respect of other teachers in the school system.
2. We do not recommend in-service training in the teaching of reading, but we do strongly recommend training for reviewers in the review and evaluation of reading textbooks.

Establishing Criteria

1. The adoption committee's most important task is the determination of the basal reading series factors to be used in evaluating the programs.
2. As the selection criteria are established, the committee must agree on the meaning of each factor.

Procedures in Reviewing and Evaluating Basal Readers

1. Committees must be provided an adequate amount of time to conduct thorough evaluations of reading textbooks.
2. Committees should be organized in ways other than by grade level.
3. Procedures used to evaluate basal programs should be tested before the actual evaluation takes place.
4. Whatever evaluation procedures are used, committee members must do more than make a check mark.
5. Any person who wishes to address the entire adoption committee or any individual committee members should be allowed to do so.
6. Reading adoption committees need to consider carefully how much and what contact to have with publishers' representatives.
7. Pilot studies are useful if they are carefully controlled.
8. When the committee has completed its work, a report of the committee's evaluation procedures and findings should be made public.

Figure 4.13

Guidelines for basal reader adoption process

From "The Evaluation and Selection of Basal Readers" by R. Farr, M. A. Tulley, & D. Powell, 1987, *The Elementary School Journal, 87*(3), pp. 267–281. Copyright 1987 by The University of Chicago. Reprinted by permission.

In view of the fact that transitional reading teachers are concerned with curriculum changes that reflect a decided move toward more balanced literacy beliefs and practices in basal readers, Heald-Taylor (1989) authored a transitional basal evaluation checklist shown in Figure 4.14.

Transitional reading teachers can use this checklist to evaluate not only the presence but also the quality of basal features that reflect a whole language instructional approach. In this respect, Heald-Taylor's (1989) checklist satisfies many of the researchers' recommendations regarding evaluation and selection of basal reading series in addition to considering the relative strengths and weaknesses of basal reading series from a transitional and balanced literacy perspective.

Transitional Teachers Take Control of the Basal Teacher's Manual

Teachers should see their role as an instructional decision maker rather than the implementer of basal programs.

Basal readers were never intended to displace the teacher's instructional decision making in the classroom or to supplant opportunities for students to read a wide range of literary genres (Winograd, 1989). Rather, basals were intended as an instructional resource to help teachers provide basic, sequenced reading instruction for a wide range of student abilities (Squire, 1989). Although some teachers are content to sample or follow the teacher's edition, transitional reading teachers take control of the basal teacher's edition so that it truly becomes only one resource among many for the informed and discriminating teacher. Furthermore, moving away from total dependence on the basal teacher's edition is often the first step in beginning the transition (Altwerger & Flores, 1989). Because this is often a difficult step for some teachers, we offer detailed examples of how transitional teachers can begin to take control of their teacher's editions by using the edition as the basis for planning along with a variety of reading lesson structures within the familiar confines of the basal reader.

Balanced Reading Program

List the major components of balanced reading instruction.

A **balanced reading program** is described by Holdaway in 1979, in *Reading in Junior Classes* (a handbook for teachers in New Zealand, not referenced) in 1985, and is clearly and succinctly articulated by M. Mooney in her 1990 book entitled, *Reading TO, WITH, and BY Children*. Balanced reading instruction centers on using several key reading instructional practices:

> ### *Elements of a Balanced Literary Program*
> * Reading TO Children
>   Teacher read aloud
>   One-to-one reading
>   Lap reading
> * Reading WITH Children
>   Shared reading
>   Language experience
>   Guided reading
> * Reading BY Children
>   Buddy or assisted reading

Independent reading
Dramatic/performance reading

Transitional reading teachers recognize these elements of a balanced reading program and attempt to integrate these into their use of published basal reader series. For example, consider how the selection, *Tales of a Fourth Grade Nothing* (Blume, 1972), found in a current basal reader, could be taught by planning a lesson around the three areas of a balanced reading program.

Example Balanced Reading Lesson

Selection title: *Tales of a Fourth Grade Nothing* (Blume, 1972).

Reading TO Children: *Teacher Read Aloud.*   To set the context for the selection, read aloud the poem "Sister for Sale" by Shel Silverstein. Have a discussion about younger siblings and their habits that make you want to get rid of them. Make a list at the board of things younger siblings do to drive you crazy. Make a list of ways you have thought about getting rid of them or at least getting even. Next, tell children that you are going to be reading about a boy whose younger brother is named Fudge in the book *Tales of a Fourth Grade Nothing.*

Reading WITH Children: *Shared Reading.*   Begin by reading the first chapter of *Tales of a Fourth Grade Nothing* together. Several versions of choral reading: (a) unison, (b) echoic, (c) one line per child, (d) antiphonal, and so on could be used to vary the involvement of the group. Next, ask children to respond to the first chapter by sharing with a neighbor their favorite parts. After the discussion, ask children to remember words they had difficulty with during the reading of the story. List the difficult words on chart paper or a bulletin board. Invite children to add to this list as they read the remainder of the book. Next, determine questions, predictions, and goals for reading the selection, for example, how many chapters or sections will need to be read before the next stopping and responding point.

Reading BY Children: *Independent Reading.*   Allow children uninterrupted time to read the next chapter or section(s) of *Tales of a Fourth Grade Nothing.* Once children reach the agreed on stopping point, have several projects they can complete to respond to their reading such as a Character Report Card or Literary Passport (see Chapter 11). Once everyone has completed a response to the chapter or section(s), bring children together for a literature response group meeting to discuss their projects, perspectives, and feelings. Set a new goal for reading, and repeat the responding process. Be sure to note particular language and comprehension skills this book exemplifies for children. Focus on these at the conclusion of each response group meeting.

When the typical lesson format provided in most basal reader teacher's editions is altered to include elements of a balanced reading program, children experience the modeling of a teacher, join with the teacher and other peers in reading together, read independently, and join together to respond to their reading. In so doing, children and teachers pursue a common reading experience in a supportive social setting.

Reconciled Reading Lesson

Teachers recognize the importance of building adequate and accurate background information to prepare readers to successfully process text. The **reconciled reading**

Figure 4.14

Transitional basal evaluation checklist

	Ineffective	Somewhat Effective	Very Effective	Effective	
Literature How effective is this program in providing for: • quality literature selections? • unabridged literature selections? • variety of literary genre (patterns, poetry, informational, fictional)? • a variety of authors? • biographies of authors? • listings of high-quality literature, supplemental selections?					
Integration How effective is this program in providing for: • the integration of listening, speaking, reading, writing, drama, movement, and visual arts? • thematic organization of stories and student activities? • organizational strategies for the use of activity centers, such as book corners, listening post, drama center, construction area, art station, writing table? • the integration of other content areas, such as mathematics, science, social studies, music, and physical education?					
Instructional Strategies How effective is this program in providing for: • shared reading? • book talks? • choral speaking? • story reading? • storytelling? • listening activities? • co-operative learning? • dramatization, such as role play, puppet plays, mime, improvisation? • debates? • personal dictation? • problem-solving activities? • individualized reading? • encouraging students to use a variety of reading strategies, such as pictures, pattern of the text, meaning, memory, context, and phonetics?					

	Ineffective	Somewhat Effective	Very Effective	Effective
Instructional Strategies (continued) • student use of writing folders? • student use of writing process (prewriting, writing confer-encing, drafting, revising, editing, publishing)? • conferencing strategies? • peer conferencing? • experimentation with spelling, grammar, and usage? • revising strategies? • publishing strategies?				
Interpretive Activities for Students How effective is this program in providing for: • interpretive activities, such as drama, role play, improvisation, movement? • interpretive activities, such as discussions or debates? • interpretive activities, such as painting, drawing, cut-and-paste, modeling, and construction? • higher level thinking activities? • comprehension activities? • vocabulary study relative to the literature being read? • a variety of reading strategies, such as cloze exercises, pattern awareness, meaning, memory, picture clues, and phonetics? • phonetic activities that relate to reading and writing, oral as well as written? • skill activities based on the needs of students?				
Evaluation How effective is this program in providing for: • strategies for supporting teachers in observing students as they use language? • varieties of formats for collecting information such as language samples, checklists, running records, etc.? • opportunities for students to evaluate their language growth? • samples of typical language behavior inventories? • balance between standardized and informal evaluation procedures?				

*The **reconciled reading lesson (RRL)** reverses the traditional basal lesson instructional sequence.*

lesson (RRL) (Reutzel, 1985a, 1991) is useful for this purpose. The RRL recommends reversing the traditional basal lesson sequence, the directed reading lesson, by beginning with the basal suggestions for language enrichment and curriculum extenders and the like and working backward to vocabulary assessment as the last element in the lesson (Reutzel, 1985a). To begin an RRL, turn to the language enrichment and extension section of the reading lesson in the basal teacher's edition. The activities suggested in this part of the lesson are often excellent for building background knowledge and discussing unfamiliar concepts. In one major basal reader, for example, a lesson on the story "Stone Soup" (M. Brown, 1947) suggested that teachers make stone soup and have children write a recipe from their experience. Although these ideas could be used as excellent extensions of the story, the activities may be just as appropriate for background building before reading rather than as enrichment after reading.

The RRL recommends teaching reading skills before reading and relating them to the selection to be read.

The second modification that the RRL proposes to the basal lesson sequence centers on the place of reading skill instruction. The RRL recommends teaching reading skills before reading and relating reading skill instruction to the selection to be read. If this is not possible, teachers should select an appropriate reading skill that relates to the selection. By relating skills to the stories, teachers help children understand that reading skills are to be applied during reading. For example, the vocabulary skill of categorizing words was to be taught with the story in one reading lesson in a major basal reader. The words selected for the vocabulary-categorizing activity were unrelated to the words in the story. Putting this concern aside, one must ask the question, why teach this vocabulary skill in relation to a contrived list of words or using an instructional text snippet (Pearson, 1989a) when the skill could more aptly be applied to words taken from the story itself?

The decoding skill lesson associated with another basal story dealt with teaching children the vowel digraph /oa/. A quick glance over the text revealed the fact that only one word in the entire text contained that vowel digraph. Even worse, the stories preceding and following the story in the lesson contained no words with the /oa/ vowel digraph. This is just one demonstration of the findings that basal lessons seldom relate skill instruction to the selections children are expected to read (Reutzel & Daines, 1987b). Because of this failure on the part of some publishers, the teacher may often need to make explicit the relation between the skills taught and how (or if) these skills can be applied during the reading.

If the story does not lend itself to the reading skills to be taught, then adapt skill instruction to the story.

If the story does not lend itself to the reading skills to be taught, then adapt skill instruction to the story. For example, if the story is "Good Work, Amelia Bedelia," by Peggy Parish (1963), an appropriate comprehension skill to select for instruction would be understanding figurative or idiomatic expression. If the teacher's edition did not direct teachers to focus on this skill, the professional decision could be made to teach the prescribed skill lesson—such as getting the main idea—later during the year and to teach figurative or idiomatic expressions with this story. Instructional decisions such as these are characteristic of transitional teachers' taking control of their teacher's editions. In summary, the RRL recommends that skill instruction be taught before reading and be explicitly related to and applied in reading.

The third step in the RRL involves a discussion of the story intended to foster comprehension. The typical organization of the DRA provides for comprehension discussion through a list of comprehension questions following the selection in the teacher's edition. The RRL recommends that guided questioning, discussion, and prediction be included as an integral part of the prereading part of the reading lesson. Questions usually discussed after reading may be discussed before reading. Children are encouraged to predict answers to the questions before reading and to read to confirm their predictions. Such a practice can help students selectively focus their attention during reading.

The remainder of the RRL should be very brief. Students read the selection in the basal. Postreading activities focus primarily on assessment of comprehension and skill application. Questions can be asked such as, Did the students comprehend? How well did students predict answers to the prequestions? Did students revise their predictions as a result of the reading? Do the students understand the meanings of the new vocabulary words as they were used in the context of the story? In short, assessment is the primary purpose for postreading activities in the RRL.

Prince and Mancus (1987) and Thomas and Readence (1988) reported that using the RRL significantly increased students' comprehension and recall of text over the traditional DRA as well as other alternative lesson frameworks.

Research has shown that the RRL significantly increased students' comprehension and recall of text over the traditional DRA as well as other alternative lesson frameworks.

Using the Language Experience Approach With Basal Reader Lessons

The language experience approach (LEA) is often used with basal reading lessons by transitional reading teachers for two reasons. First, teachers can maintain their basal safety net by continuing to use the basal reader as the core component of reading instruction while gently making the transition toward more balanced literacy practices such as those found in the LEA. Second, transitional teachers can learn how to make basal lessons focus on integrating children's language and experience into the lesson and thereby make basal reading lessons more child, language, and experience centered.

Jones and Nessel (1985, p. 18) describe how LEA can be integrated with the basal approach. To begin, use the basic steps in obtaining dictated language experience stories:

Using LEA helps teachers integrate children's language and personal experiences into the basal reading lesson.

1. Through experiments, objects, activities, the teacher provides students with a stimulus that invites student participation.
2. Through discussion with the teacher and other students, the students develop concepts through observations and talking.
3. Children dictate to the teacher an account of the experience or activity. This dictation is usually recorded on large chart paper or poster board.
4. The teacher reads the dictated account back to the children. Next with teacher help, the students read the account with the teacher. The dictated story becomes the basis for phonics, structural analysis, and context usage lessons over the next few days.
5. Students read other books on related topics. They often reread the dictated story alone or in small groups during the day.
6. Learning from reading is reinforced with activities employing the other language skills. Writing and listening activities are used in this way to promote general communication growth.

To integrate this approach with the basal lessons, Jones and Nessel (1985) recommend that the teacher construct an experience to complement the basal story. For example, if the basal story is "The Lion and the Mouse," the teacher could tell a story about how one of her students once helped her teach another child. The teacher could describe how even a small child could help her when she needed it and that size does not tell us about whether a person can become a good friend. Children could then be invited to discuss how little friends can help big friends or little brothers or sisters can help older ones. These accounts could be recorded on the chart or on small paper for the children to reread during the next few days (Reimer, 1983). Words from the LEA-dictated story could be placed on word cards for practice. Usually, many of the words in the children's dictated stories are the same words that appear in the basal story. Thus, new or old vocabulary terms have been introduced or reviewed before reading the basal story. After reading the basal story, another story could be created by using words from both the original dictated story and the basal story. This story provides more opportunities to practice skills and sight words. Finally, reading skills can be taught using these stories to show children how reading skills can be applied to help them read a story. Using LEA-dictated stories and experiences is another way for transitional reading teachers to take control of their basal reader teacher's editions.

Reciprocal Questioning

ReQuest, or reciprocal questioning, is a structure for presenting reading lessons in which teachers and children silently read parts of a text and exchange the role of asking and answering questions about that text.

In 1969 Anthony Manzo outlined ReQuest, or reciprocal questioning, a structure for conducting reading lessons in which teachers and children silently read parts of a text and exchange the roles of asking and answering questions about that text. The ReQuest procedure can be used with individuals or with groups. The process begins with the teacher and students reading a preassigned portion of a text silently. Both the teacher and the students close the book after reading. Next, the students ask the teacher questions about the text, and the teacher answers these questions clearly and accurately. By answering the students' questions first, the teacher can demonstrate for students effective question–answering behaviors. Next, the roles between teachers and students reverse. This begins with the teacher and students reading the next part of the text and closing their books. At this point, students try to answer the questions the teacher asks. At some point in the lesson, usually predetermined by the teacher, students are asked to predict the potential events and outcome of the remainder of the text to be read. A list of predictions is constructed through discussion and shown at the board. Students read the remaining text to confirm or correct their predictions. After reading, the teacher leads a discussion to reconsider the original predictions.

Because children are encouraged to construct their own questions for reading, they become active readers to the extent that they (a) select their own purposes for reading and (b) engage in a proven reading strategy involving sampling, prediction, and reading to confirm or correct predictions.

ReQuest involves teachers and students equally in sharing the roles of participant and observer in the lesson as compared with the DRA, in which teachers frequently serve as the active participant in the lesson while the children spend their time looking on as passive observers. As a result, ReQuest helps children learn how to compose and answer questions about text through active observation and participation in the reading lesson.

Example ReQuest Lesson

Book title: *Franklin in the Dark* (Bourgeois & Clark, 1986).

> **Text:** "Franklin could slide down a riverbank all by himself. He could count forwards and backwards. He could even zip zippers and button buttons. But Franklin was afraid of small, dark places and that was a problem because . . . " (p. 1).

> **Student 1 question:** What's the turtle's name?

Teacher answer: His name is Franklin.

Student 2 question: What are things that Franklin can do?

Teacher answer: Franklin can slide down a riverbank, and button buttons, and zip zippers. Oh, he can also count forward and backward.

Student 3 question: What was Franklin afraid of?

Teacher answer: Franklin was afraid of small dark places.

Teacher question: What kind of animal was Franklin?

Student answer: A turtle.

Teacher question: Why do you think that being afraid of small, dark places can be a problem for a turtle?

Student 1 answer: Because then he wouldn't want to go deep under the water.

Student 2 answer: Because turtles hide in their shells, and if he was afraid of the dark, maybe he wouldn't want to hide in his shell.

Teacher comment: Those are both good answers. Let's read the next page and see why his being afraid is a problem.

Text: "Franklin was a turtle. He was afraid of crawling into his small, dark shell. And so, Franklin the turtle dragged his shell behind him" (p. 2).

After reading the second page of text:

Student 1 question: What was Franklin afraid of?

Teacher answer: He was afraid of getting into his shell because it was dark and small.

Student 2 question: What did Franklin do instead of getting into his shell?

Teacher answer: He had to drag it behind him.

Teacher question: What do you think Franklin could do so that he wouldn't be afraid of hiding in his shell?

Student 1 answer: He could take some medicine that wouldn't make him afraid anymore.

Student 2 answer: He could get a bigger shell so that it wouldn't be so small.

Student 3 answer: He could use a flashlight to light up his shell.

Student 4 answer: He could make a window in his shell so that it wouldn't be so dark.

Teacher comment: You're all really thinking hard about Franklin and his problem. Now let's read on to find out what Franklin does about his fear and see if what we thought was right.

Directed Reading Thinking Activity

In 1969 Russell G. Stauffer first developed the directed reading thinking activity (DRTA) to encourage readers to engage actively in a three-step comprehension cycle:

1. Sample the text.
2. Make predictions.
3. Sample the text to confirm or correct previous predictions.

*Notice the three steps used in the **directed reading thinking activity (DRTA)**.*

To use the DRTA, teachers give students a text selection and ask them to read the title, a few sampled lines of text, and examine the pictures to develop hypotheses about the text. Children generate hypotheses as they read from the text and from their own experiential backgrounds.

Teachers may adapt the DRTA in such a way as to sample the most important elements of a narrative or exposition based on the text structure employed. If the children are assigned a narrative or story to read, the DRTA could be based on the important elements of a story grammar or map, as suggested by Beck and McKeown (1981). These elements include setting, characters, initiating events, problems, attempts to solve the problems, outcomes or resolutions. For example, consider the sample DRTA lesson constructed using the story *Cloudy With a Chance of Meatballs* by Judi Barrett (1978).

Example DRTA Lesson

The teacher begins the lesson by showing the book and saying:

> **Teacher:** The title of the book we're going to read today is *Cloudy With a Chance of Meatballs.* What do this title and the picture make you think the story is about?
>
> **John:** It might be about an old man that makes a magic spell on the sky so that meatballs come down when he wants to eat them.
>
> **Lisa:** I think it might be about a place where any kind of food you want rains down from the sky.
>
> **Teacher:** Let's read and see how close your predictions are.

The teacher then reads until the town of Chewandswallow is described.

> **Teacher:** Now, do you still agree with your predictions?
>
> **Children:** It sounds like it's going to be about a place like Lisa described.
>
> **Teacher:** What makes you think so?
>
> **Jessica:** Because they haven't talked at all about an old man, the author only described the town and how food rained down for breakfast, lunch, and dinner.
>
> **Teacher:** Would you like to live in a town like Chewandswallow?
>
> **Susan:** I think it would be fun because then you wouldn't have to wait for your mom to cook dinner. You could just catch some extra food and eat when you were hungry.
>
> **Tyler:** I wouldn't like it cuz what would happen if it rained something heavy like barbecued ribs and you got hit on the head and got knocked out or died.
>
> **Teacher:** Tyler brought up a good point. Could there be some problems with living in this town?
>
> **Jeff:** It could rain heavy things and hurt you.
>
> **Maria:** If there were a storm of ice cream or something mushy, it would get really messy.
>
> **Teacher:** Good, now that you're thinking about what a place like Chewandswallow would be like, let's read on to see what happens in the town.

She reads until the weather takes a turn for the worse.

> ***Teacher:*** Now what do you think is going to happen in the story?
>
> ***James:*** It's about a town that rains food for breakfast, lunch, and dinner, and then one day the food starts coming down funny.
>
> ***Teacher:*** What do you mean by funny?
>
> ***James:*** I think that maybe too much food started coming down.
>
> ***Teacher:*** What makes you think that maybe too much food started coming down?
>
> ***James:*** Well, in the picture there is too much spaghetti in the road and the cars can't move.
>
> ***Teacher:*** Good, now let's continue reading to see if you are right.

The teacher now reads until the story describes a tomato tornado and then stops and asks questions again.

> ***Teacher:*** So, what happens in the town of Chewandswallow?
>
> ***Kayla:*** All kinds of food starts coming down. Some of it is yucky like peanut butter, mayonnaise, and brussels sprouts. And sometimes just too much of it comes down, like when they had a tomato tornado. Everything was a mess because the food was going crazy.
>
> ***Teacher:*** What do you think the town will do about it? Why do you think so?
>
> ***Frank:*** I think that they will hire a magician to put a spell on the clouds so that the weather will get straightened out because sometimes in the stories they can do that.
>
> ***Harold:*** I think that they have to leave if they can, before they all die. That's what I would do.
>
> ***Nancy:*** I think they need to find out who is in charge of making it rain so that they can ask them to stop it and make things go back to normal.
>
> ***Teacher:*** Those are good answers. Now I want you all to decide which of those you think is the most likely to happen and let's continue reading.

The teacher reads the rest of the book.

> ***Teacher:*** Did the people do what you thought they would do? Did you like how they solved their problem?
>
> ***Harold:*** Yes, that's what I thought they should do.
>
> ***Frank:*** No, I still think they should've called on somebody to help them so that they wouldn't have to leave Chewandswallow and have to buy groceries in the store.

A DRTA could also be extended for use with expository texts such as those found in the classroom science, health, and social studies textbooks.

Teaching Effective Reading Skill Lessons

Research has shown that reading skill instruction is a frequent practice in most class-rooms (Blanton & Moorman, 1985). Although basal reader lessons generally follow the structure of the DRA, an analogous structure for teaching reading skill lessons has not been widely articulated or accepted. In fact, research (Durkin, 1978, 1981a) has shown that skill instruction often involves relatively little or no instruction at all. Teachers themselves rate skill lesson directives in teachers' editions as only moderately helpful (Bacharach & Alexander, 1986). Because basal teacher's editions and curriculum developers have failed to provide a structure for teaching reading skill lessons, teachers often regard the assigning and monitoring of completed reading skill worksheets and dittos as instruction; thus, the assignment of reading skill worksheets often substitutes for meaningful reading skill instruction (R. C. Anderson, Osborn, & Tierney, 1984; Durkin, 1981a).

A direct or explicit model of instruction can be used to improve the quality of reading skill instruction.

Blanton, Moorman, and Wood (1986); Cooter and Reutzel (1987); and Reutzel and Cooter (1988) recommend the application of a direct or explicit instruction model to basal skills lessons to improve reading skill instruction. Educational researchers have demonstrated strong correlations between student achievement and the use of direct instruction procedures (L. Anderson, Evertson, & Brophy, 1979; Good, 1979; Rupley & Blair, 1978; Stevens & Rosenshine, 1981). Although direct instruction suggests that the teacher is central to and actively involved in the teaching act, direct instruction does not imply unengaged passivity on the part of students.

In addition to the use of a direct instruction model to improve reading skill instruction, Reutzel and Cooter (1988) suggest two research-based improvements for reading skill instruction. First, skill instruction should occur before reading rather than after the fact. Most basal teacher's editions encourage the teaching of reading skills following the reading. Reading skill instruction should precede reading of the text so that the reading skills taught can be applied during the act of reading. Second, basal reading skill instruction should be explicitly related to the story or text to be read. Because many basal teacher's editions fail to connect skill instruction with the reading selections to be read, teachers must examine and adjust the skill instruction suggestions in their editions to make clear the relation between learning a particular reading skill and how it can be applied to reading a text.

To help teachers use the suggestions outlined here to plan and present effective basal skill instruction, we present an example lesson based on Hunter (1984) using the comprehension skill of "getting the sequence." This skill was chosen because many teachers find this skill to be particularly difficult to teach before reading and then to relate to the reading of a selected story in the basal reader.

Anticipatory Set

An anticipatory set should create the need to know and desire to learn.

Teachers can begin the skill lesson by discussing several real-world situations in which "getting the sequence" is of critical importance such as using recipes, working verbal math problems, and assembling a bike. Teachers can ask children to recall a time when they failed to follow the correct sequence and the consequences that resulted. This discussion helps make critical ties between the skill taught and the experiential backgrounds of the children.

Objective and Input

Students are informed about the objective for the lesson.

Next, the teacher tells students that the objective for the lesson is "getting the sequence" and defines this skill as the ability to reorder the events that occur in a story or in life.

On an overhead projector, the teacher shows the entire group of children a piece of text about how to perform a magic trick. The teacher may list the steps for performing the trick on the board after reading. Next, the trick can be performed. For example, the teacher can show the children a water-glass trick by filling a glass of water, putting a heavy piece of paper over the glass, turning it over, and observing that the water remains in the glass without touching the paper. After this demonstration, the teacher leads a discussion of the sequence of steps recorded on the board for the water-glass trick. Particular emphasis is placed on locating sequence signal words, that is, *before, after, next, first, second, then,* and so on. To conclude the demonstration, the teacher can invite several children to come forward and, by following the sequence of directions recorded on the board, to perform the trick. Such an activity helps students immediately monitor their adherence to the sequence of events to successfully perform the water-glass trick.

Modeling

The role of the teacher during this stage of the lesson is to demonstrate the skilled reading and thinking behaviors related to getting the sequence. This can be accomplished by using a "thinking aloud" process: The teacher talks as if thinking aloud and reveals her mental strategies for determining the sequence of events in a preselected piece of text.

The role of the teacher is to demonstrate the desired reading and thinking behaviors pertaining to the specific skill.

Following this demonstration, another text selection can be placed on the overhead projector dealing with changing a flat tire. The teacher reads the passage aloud to the class and lists the steps involved in changing a flat tire. As the teacher orders the steps, she "thinks aloud" for the class. This allows students to witness the logical processes and verification strategies the teacher uses to successfully complete the task.

Once the demonstration is completed, the steps for getting the sequence are recorded at the chalkboard. Students may ask questions afterward and will frequently offer alternatives in logic that result in the same conclusions. When the teacher is reasonably certain that the students have grasped the essential elements of getting the sequence, the lesson proceeds.

Guided Practice

The purpose of guided practice is to practice the skill and assess whether or not the children have understood. Another reading selection can be chosen that closely parallels those previously used, and the group can engage in a discussion of how to get the sequence for this selected text.

The purpose of guided practice is to supervise the application of the skill and verify whether or not the children have understood the skill or concept being taught.

Checking for Understanding

Checking for understanding is an important element in direct instruction. Teachers continually assess student understanding throughout the instructional sequence and are prepared for reteaching activities as necessary. Crucial checkpoints seem to be directly following the modeling, guided practice, and independent practice segments of the lesson.

Independent Practice

The purpose of independent practice is to assess whether or not the children have understood the skill and can apply it to their own reading without requiring additional teacher assistance. At this point in the lesson, teachers may want to assign worksheets to individual students for practice. Teachers do not intervene during independent practice until the students have completed the assignment.

Assessment

Assessment is to evaluate and inform instruction.

A test from other selected texts or passages can be designed to assess students' ability to successfully perform the reading skill of getting the sequence. Observations of the students' completing real-life application projects can also be used to assess student learning.

This skill lesson structure can be applied to any skill lesson in the basal reader. It is not a script to be followed without careful thought and decision making. Teachers must decide which parts of the direct-instruction lesson model are appropriate.

Notice three ways to support students with special needs by using the basal reader.

Helping Students With Special Needs Succeed With Basal Reader Instruction

Historically, the basal reader has not served very successfully as a tool for reading remediation. There are several reasons for this situation. First, some teachers find the stories in basal readers to be bland and uninviting, especially for problem readers. What is needed most is literature that "turns on" the "turned-off" learner—an order too tall for many basals to fill. Second, if a child is failing to achieve success using one approach to reading instruction, in this case the basal reader, then common sense tells us that what is needed is an alternative strategy—not just more of the same. Finally, basal reader systems frequently do not allow students enough time for real reading. The multifarious collection of skill sheets and workbook pages tends to be so time-consuming that little time is left for reading.

In Chapter 1, we discussed 10 principles for encouraging literacy, some of which are most pertinent when using basals to help students with special needs. Three direct applications of these principles follow.

Reading the Basal Straight Through

Teachers working with special needs students recognize that what these children need most is regular and sustained reading. We suggest that skill sheets and workbook pages be used judiciously, or even avoided, to allow for more time spent reading. Children should be allowed to read basals straight through as an anthology of children's stories. The teacher may wish to skip stories that offer little for the reader in this setting.

Repeated Readings

In repeated readings, the teacher typically introduces the story as a shared book or story experience, then students attempt to read the book alone or with a friend (Routman, 1988). If the story has rhyme or a regular pattern, it may be sung or chanted. Repeated readings of stories help children achieve a sense of accomplishment, improve comprehension, and build fluency.

Supported, or Buddy, Reading

Many times, at-risk readers are very reluctant to become risk takers. Teachers simply must find ways of breaking the ice for them and create classroom safety nets. Supported, or "buddy," reading allows students to read aloud basal stories together, either taking turns or in unison. By rereading these supported selections, students' fluency and comprehension improve. Another variation is for teacher–student combinations to read together. Similar to the procedure known as neurological impress (P. M. Hollingsworth, 1978), the student and teacher read aloud in unison at a comfortable rate. For first readings, the teacher usually assumes the lead in terms of volume and pace. In subsequent repeated readings, the student is encouraged to assume the lead.

Chapter 9 provides more insights into how teachers can enhance the reading and writing environment as they begin making the transition from basal-only teaching to more balanced literacy perspectives and practices. In the process we will discover numerous opportunities for assisting students with special needs within the elementary classroom.

Chapter 9 provides more insights into how teachers can enhance the reading–writing environment as they begin making the transition from basal-only teaching to balanced literacy approaches.

Helping Students With Special Cultural and Language Needs Succeed With Basal Readers

Students who do not possess reading and writing ability in a first language should be taught to read and write in their native or first language to support and validate them as worthwhile individuals. In addition, reading instruction in the first language helps students capitalize on what they already know about their primary languages and cultures to build concepts that can facilitate the acquisition of English (Freeman & Freeman, 1992; Krashen & Biber, 1988). In any case, teachers must be sensitive to these students' special needs, which include (a) a need for safety and security, (b) a need to belong and be accepted, and (c) a need to feel self-esteem (Peregoy & Boyle, 1993).

Think about why students should be taught to read in their primary language.

Teachers should help English as a second language (ESL) or limited English proficiency (LEP) students feel at ease when they arrive in the classroom by assigning them a "personal buddy" who, if possible, speaks the language of the newcomer. This "buddy" is assigned to help the new student through the school day, routines, and so on. Another approach is to avoid changes in the classroom schedule by following a regular and predictable routine each day, which creates a sense of security. To create a sense of belonging, assign the student to a "home group" for an extended period of time. A "home group" provides a small social unit of concern focused on helping the newcomer adapt to everyday life as well as providing a concerned and caring peer group. Finally, self-esteem is enhanced when an individual's worth is affirmed. Opportunities for the newcomer to share their language and culture during daily events in the classroom provide a useful way to integrate them into the ongoing classroom culture.

To help ESL or LEP students succeed in classrooms where basal readers are the core of instruction, Law and Eckes (1990, pp. 92) recommend the following:

Describe three things that can be done to support second language learners when using a basal reader.

- Supplement the basal as much as possible with language experience stories (as discussed previously in this chapter).
- Encourage extensive reading: Gather basal textbooks from as many different levels as possible. Also acquire easier textbooks in content areas as well as trade books to encourage a wide range of reading topics.

• Expose children to the many different types of reading available in the "real" world such as magazines, *TV Guide,* newspapers, product labels, signs.

Summary

Basal readers over the past two centuries have become a veritable institution in American reading instruction. As social and political aims have changed over the years, basal reader content and structure have been altered to reflect these changing conditions. Modern basals are typically composed of several major components including a teacher's edition, a student's reader, workbooks, and tests. For teachers, basal readers represent a structured approach to teaching reading, which can save enormous amounts of preparation time. On the other hand, basal readers can in some instances displace teacher judgment to the degree that the basal becomes the reading program rather than a tool to be used to support the reading program. Basal readers are produced by large, business-oriented publishing houses. Senior authors on basal series are usually individuals widely known and respected in the field of reading.

Adopting a basal reader for use in schools is a task most teachers will likely face in the course of their professional careers. Hence, it is important for teachers to understand how basal readers have been adopted in the past as well as to perceive how the adoption process may be improved. Although basal readers can be useful tools for providing reading instruction, some teachers need to make conscious efforts to take control of their basal teacher's editions by changing the way in which they provide instruction. Suggestions in this chapter included using the balanced reading program, RRL, the LEA, ReQuest, and the DRTA, in addition to the DRA. Providing effective basal skill instruction focuses on relating skills to the reading selections, teaching skills before reading the selections, and using a direct-instruction lesson structure. Finally, readers with special needs who may be struggling can be helped by reading the basal straight through, allowing repeated readings of self-selected basal stories, and providing buddy or other forms of supported reading. ESL and LEP students can be helped to feel at home as newcomers in a school environment; the teacher can also take steps to supplement and extend basic basal reader text for these students. Figure 4.16 shows an overview of this chapter.

CONCEPT APPLICATIONS

IN THE CLASSROOM

1. Go to your local school district or university curriculum materials library. Locate two basal readers. Locate the following items in the teacher's edition: (a) the scope and sequence chart, (b) the parts of a directed reading lesson, (c) the skill lessons, (d) the workbooks, and (e) the book tests or assessment materials. Compare the instructional approaches and contents of each using a compare/contrast T chart.
2. Compare the contents of a current basal reader to the contents of the Dick and Jane or McGuffey basal readers. Write a brief essay on the differences you note.

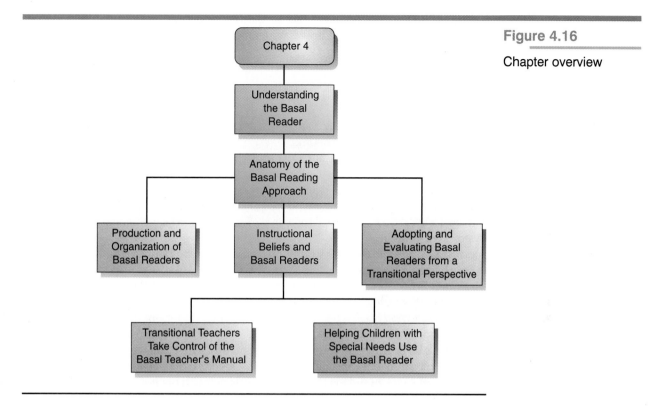

Figure 4.16

Chapter overview

3. Select a basal reader teacher's edition. Using the evaluation checklist in this chapter (Figure 4.14), evaluate the strengths and weaknesses of the basal you selected. Discuss this with a classmate or peer.
4. Select a basal reader lesson and story. Check the lesson for the major parts of the DRA. Describe in writing how the design of this lesson follows or fails to follow the description of the DRA.
5. Select a basal reader lesson and story. Redesign this lesson on your own by changing it to make use of (a) the RRL, (b) the LEA, (c) ReQuest, or (d) DRTA.
6. Choose one skill lesson. Redesign the skill lesson to incorporate the parts of an effective skill lesson as described in this chapter.

IN THE FIELD

1. Interview a teacher in the field about the strengths and weaknesses of the basal. Find out why this teacher uses or does not use the basal.
2. Visit a classroom in a local elementary school. Observe a teacher teaching reading with the basal. Which parts of the lesson did the teacher use? Which parts did the teacher omit? Write an essay about your observations.
3. Prepare a basal reading lesson to be taught in the schools. Secure permission to teach this lesson in a local grade-level appropriate classroom. Write a reflective essay on the experience detailing successes, failures, and necessary changes.
4. Select a basal reading lesson in a teacher's edition. Adapt the lesson in the teacher's edition by rewriting it using a balanced reading program, RRL, LEA, DRTA, and so on. Secure permission to teach this lesson in a local grade-level

appropriate classroom. Write a reflective essay on the experience detailing successes, failures, and necessary changes.

RECOMMENDED READINGS

Anderson, R. C., Osborn, J., & Tierney, R. J. (1984). *Learning to read in American schools.* Hillsdale, NJ: Erlbaum.

Aukerman, R. (1981). *The basal reader approach to reading.* New York: John Wiley & Sons.

Baumann, J. F. (1992). Basal reading programs and the deskilling of teachers: A critical examination of the argument. *Reading Research Quarterly, 27*(4), 390–398.

Cheney, L. V. (1990). *Tyrannical machines.* Washington, D.C.: National Endowment for the Humanities.

Goodman, K. S. (1987). Look what they've done to Judy Blume!: The 'basalization' of children's literature. *The New Advocate, 1*(1), 29–41.

Goodman, K. S., Shannon, P., Freeman, Y. S., & Murphy, S. (1988). *Report card on basal readers.* New York: Richard C. Owen.

A guide to selecting basal reading programs. Urbana, IL: Center for the Study of Reading, 1990.

Hoffman, J. V., & Roser, N. (Eds.). (1987, January). The basal reader in American reading instruction. [Special issue] *The Elementary School Journal, 87*(3).

McCallum, R. D. (1988). Don't throw the basals out with the bath water. *The Reading Teacher, 42,* 204–209.

Osborn, J., Wilson, P. T., & Anderson, R. C. (1985). *Reading education: Foundations for a literate America.* Lexington, MA: Lexington Books.

Perspectives on basal readers. [Special issue] *Theory Into Practice, 28(4),* 1989.

Shannon, P. (1992). *Becoming political: Readings and writings in the politics of literacy education.* Portsmouth, NH: Heinemann Educational Books.

Smith, N. B. (1986). *American reading instruction.* Newark, DE: International Reading Association.

Winograd, P. N., Wixson, K. K., & Lipson, M. Y. (Eds.). (1989). *Improving basal reader instruction.* New York: Columbia Teachers College Press.

Chapter 5

Making the Transition From Basals to Books: Bridging the Gap

Focus Questions

When you are finished studying this chapter, you should be able to answer these questions:

1. What are the six dimensions of change involved in the transitions model?
2. Which of the eight transitional stances in beliefs best describe(s) your current beliefs and why?
3. How can teachers begin to use their instructional materials differently?
4. How is a nonnegotiable skills list constructed and ratified by a faculty?
5. What are three levels of curricular integration associated with transitions?
6. How can teachers in transition involve colleagues and parents in reading instructional changes?
7. How does the classroom environment affect children's perceptions of learning to read?
8. What are some notable differences between traditional and balanced literacy assessment practices?
9. How can teachers come to cope with the changing demographics of the classroom, which are moving from monocultural to multicultural?
10. How are the three teachers described at the conclusion of this chapter alike and different?

Key Concepts

Transitions
Transitional Stances in Beliefs
Oral Recitation Lesson
Comprehension Interrogation
Outcome-Based Education (OBE)
Nonnegotiable Skills
Fragmentation

Curricular Integration
Language to Literacy
Institutional Environments
Home-like Environments
Portfolio Assessment
Reading Instructional Continuum

Transitions: Implementing Changes in Reading Instruction

Transitions involve a complex web of changes.

The **transitions** model of reading instruction is an invitation to risk change. At the same time, the transitions model of reading instruction provides an answer to the question of *how* teachers can safely but surely move out from between the rock and the hard place in reading instruction (Mosenthal, 1989b). As explained in Chapter 1, both preservice and in-service teachers need to work through a complex web of changes to make transitions in reading beliefs and practices.

Preservice and in-service teachers make transitions for different reasons.

Based on their own experiences as children in schools, preservice teachers frequently resist holistic reading beliefs and balanced literacy practices because these new beliefs and practices are very often incompatible with their own. In many cases, preservice teachers need to make transitions to survive student teaching or to gain initial employment in a school that remains committed to more traditional reading instructional approaches.

Similarly, in-service teachers risk a great deal when making changes toward holistic reading beliefs and balanced literacy instruction: employment security, professional reputation, and not the least, the potential progress and self-esteem of their students. Transitions allow for in-service teachers to initiate changes in reading instruction with minimal risks and maximal benefits.

> Anyone willing to take some risks can begin the exploration. Any teacher can handle the decision making. Every teacher can create the subtle structures that help shape the learning context. . . . With some support, every teacher can find his or her own way. (Newman & Church, 1990, p. 25)

The philosophy of transitions recognizes, in a very real way, each teacher's need to be safety-netted throughout the risky process of changing reading instructional beliefs and practices.

In addition to risk, making transitions toward balanced reading instruction is a complex process. Because of this complex web of interrelated changes, teachers make transitions in a variety of ways and at differing rates. We have identified seven interrelated dimensions of making transitions, shown in Figure 5.1.

The point where teachers begin transitions is a matter of choice.

We have observed that, regardless of the point of entry into the spiral of transitions shown in Figure 5.1, there is a domino effect that leads teachers from one dimension of change in the model to the next. Thus, teachers often begin with a single change that creates a domino effect leading from one change to the next in a spiral-like movement toward more holistic reading beliefs and balanced literacy instruction shown at the center of the model. Because the point of departure in the model and the speed of the domino effect are difficult to predict, the model can only represent the idea that transitions begin at a point or points in the model and move gradually toward the center of the model—balanced literacy instruction.

Once transitions are begun, teachers go through a series of changes.

The concept of transitions embodies the idea of lifelong professional changes and growth.

In the remainder of this chapter, we explain the dimensions and processes associated with making transitions. We begin this explanation by describing several stances or roles that teachers may adopt with respect to instructional beliefs throughout the process of making transitions. Next, we address necessary modifications of instructional materials and their uses. This is followed by a presentation on how teaching practices can be gradually changed toward balanced literacy and authentic instruction without ruffling too many feathers among colleagues, administrators, and school patrons. Then we discuss desired changes in classroom environments and assessment compatible with a balanced literacy philosophy. Finally, we share three

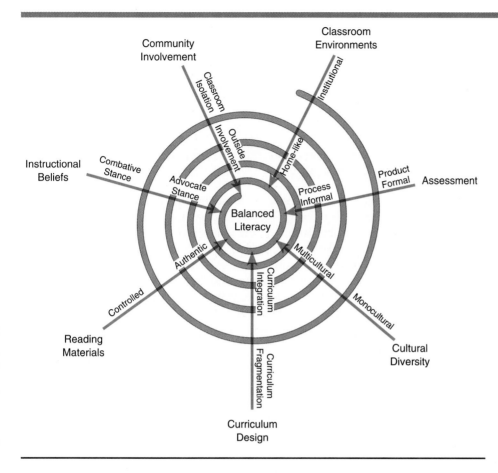

Figure 5.1

Dimensions of transitions: A model of change in reading instruction

case studies of teachers in transition. These case studies are offered in hopes of validating the fact that teachers make transitions at different rates and in very unique ways. What's more, we hope these case studies help teachers relax and enjoy the journey a bit more. Half the joy in embarking on the professional journey of making transitions is in the journey itself!

Transitions in Instructional Beliefs

Teachers approach transitions toward balanced reading instruction in many different ways. Some teachers just jump right in and try to make changes all at once. Others are more cautious, implementing just one or two carefully selected changes before attempting more. In fact, the authors of this book approached transitions differently and to varying degrees. For example, one jumped right into implementing balanced literacy instruction. The other continued using worksheets and basals as the core of reading instruction but supplemented these with generous amounts of literature, storytelling, writing, and teacher-made worksheets. Consequently, we hesitate to present transitions in a way that prescribes that *every* teacher must pass through specified stages in a predetermined order. On the other hand, we, along with others (e.g., Heald-Taylor, 1989), have noted with recurring frequency certain similarities in

Transitions in teacher beliefs often pass through several stages or stances. Think of a time you changed your beliefs. What were you aware of at this stage?

stances or roles adopted along the way by those who venture into transitions. For this reason, we discuss each of these **transitional stances in beliefs** as we have observed them. Because preservice teachers approach transitions from a different set of experiences, the first stance, *I Don't Know Enough Yet to Know Where I Stand,* is expressly directed at these individuals. The remaining stances are aimed most appropriately at in-service teachers who approach transitions in the wake of a wealth of teaching experience and tradition.

"I Don't Know Enough Yet to Know Where I Stand" Stance

Many preservice teachers do not know enough about their beliefs, others' beliefs, or their future circumstances to commit to a belief system.

Preservice teachers are often confused by the convoluted and conflicting world of reading education and research. From past experiences in school as youngsters, these teachers-to-be remember learning to read in small groups of children with special books. They recall vividly the completion of workbooks and other instructional materials designed to help them learn to read. These recollections often lead to a belief that these past practices must have been research based, effective, and worthy of continued emulation. Not until confronted with conflicting views of reading education in colleges of education and in elementary schools do preservice teachers entertain the possibility that their past experiences may not represent valid educational practice for today. In addition, preservice teachers often spend time as observers or apprentice teachers in elementary school classrooms that exemplify traditional reading instructional practices. Thus, innovative practices very often conflict with the realities of some classrooms they visit. In some cases, students encounter conflicting beliefs in their reading education courses. This conflict sets up further confusion and often a considerable degree of frustration. Hence, many preservice teachers surrender to traditional practices under the weight of confusion and conflict. At this point, preservice teachers often admit, "I don't know enough yet to know where I stand!" Melissa, a preservice teacher, wrote the following about her beliefs:

> The stance that best describes my beliefs, since I do not yet have my own class to teach, is the I Don't Know Enough Yet to Know stance. Just because I have this belief now (since I am not in the classroom) in no way means my beliefs will not change to a more holistic approach when I actually do get classroom experience. In fact, I would have to say that once I do have a classroom of my own I may very well become an advocate of holistic teaching. I really do love whole language philosophy, but I just don't know yet if I can make it work.

The need for classroom experience and an opportunity to test their own beliefs out in the classroom causes many preservice teachers to assume temporarily the "I don't know enough yet to know where I stand" stance. After acquiring classroom experience, however, many of these preservice teachers may be able to skip or move rapidly through the following belief stances as in-service teachers.

The Combative Stance

*A **combative stance** in reading beliefs is often provoked by external forces for change.*

Teachers who adopt a combative stance often feel threatened by change. They may resent a perceived authority figure, peer, or patron for making them feel they should change at all. They may feel cornered, even coerced by circumstances, into change.

Bonnie, a veteran second-grade teacher, had adopted a combative stance when we first met her. For many years, Bonnie had used the basal reader to teach reading and had experienced reasonable success. During summer vacation, however, the school principal and a few of Bonnie's colleagues became interested in balanced literacy philosophy and instruction after attending a local workshop. Because of the excitement generated by this workshop, the principal wrote a Chapter Two grant through the state office of education, which provided funds for in-service instruction to help the staff initiate transitions. But Bonnie was in no mood for this change. During the in-service sessions, she constantly pointed out that she did not feel a need to change. What she was doing to teach reading worked just as well as what we suggested. In fact, Bonnie just did not seem to want to entertain the very notion of change. When criticisms were raised regarding traditional instructional practices or basal readers, she rushed to their defense. When ideas were suggested to the other teachers who received them with enthusiasm, Bonnie stood by with the wet blanket of pessimism. She could catalog a much longer list of reasons why such changes were doomed to almost certain failure than we could conjure up in support.

To sum up, Bonnie was placed in the position of moving outside her instructional comfort zones before she was ready or willing. She was clearly committed to her program for teaching children to read and saw no reason to change. While the adage "people are generally down on what they are not up on" was obviously true in Bonnie's case, Bonnie was caught in the winds of change unwillingly. To her credit, Bonnie remained open-minded enough to examine new ideas in the privacy of her own thoughts. With time and reflection, many ideas Bonnie resisted at first led to a crack in the wall of her resistance. We have found that, like Bonnie, many in-service and preservice teachers take a combative stance when confronted with philosophical and practical suggestions that are incompatible with their own beliefs, schooling experiences, or long-standing practices.

> *Philosophical and practical suggestions that are incompatible with a teacher's own beliefs, schooling experiences, or long-standing practices can provoke a combative stance.*

Tentative Stance

While Bonnie remained combative on the exterior, she began to privately examine her own beliefs and practices. As the days and weeks rolled on, Bonnie listened intently as she overheard her colleagues talking about the events in their classrooms. Secretly, Bonnie confided at a later time, she hoped her colleagues would fail and her position would be exonerated. But this was not to be the case. Children in the other teachers' classrooms were enjoying reading and writing; the need to coax and cajole children into reading and writing had all but disappeared. Bonnie was troubled by the fact that she had to coax her students to read a book when they finished their work. These events combined to bring Bonnie to a tentative stance toward transitions. She noted that her colleagues seemed to be enjoying their work more, to say nothing of the fact that their students were reportedly enjoying reading and writing more. Cautiously, Bonnie began to ask questions of her colleagues about how these new changes in reading instruction were working out. The crack in Bonnie's wall of resistance began to widen. She was now ready to listen, tentatively, but willingly.

> *A **tentative stance** is signaled by an internal willingness to examine one's own beliefs and practices.*

Responsive Stance

In the faculty lounge, Bonnie continued to listen to the discussions of her colleagues with increased interest. She frequently asked others what they were doing in their classrooms while openly expressing surprise at their success. Secretly, Bonnie decided to try just one of the activities called silent sustained writing (SSW). This

> *Internal changes in beliefs become carefully externalized into selected practice in the **responsive stance**.*

seemed to be a reasonably unobtrusive change, even for her. She established 15 minutes of daily SSW in her classroom. Bonnie later confessed that she had made this change for nearly 3 months before telling her colleagues.

Explorative Stance

*Active searching for additional information characterizes a teacher in the **explorative stance.***

During the next school year, Bonnie requested from her colleague and best friend, Ann, materials she might read about balanced reading and writing instruction. She obtained from Ann a catalogue from which she ordered two books. Later that year, she attended with Ann a local balanced literacy instruction conference. On returning from the conference, Bonnie decided to make some additional changes—changes in the way and how much she used the basal reader. She invited Ann into her classroom to discuss how she might go about using the basal reader less and become more selective, including reducing her dependency on worksheets. Her primary concern centered on what to do to fill the void created by using the basal and worksheets less. Ann suggested several ideas for filling the void that she had tried the year before with good success. Bonnie decided on a few, selected strategies she would try and requested funds from the school principal for ordering specific materials to support her continued but carefully concealed exploration.

An Off-the-Record Stance

Practices found during exploration are used without revealing their use to others.

After several days of trying the selected strategies, Bonnie was surprised at the success she was experiencing. One day after school, Bonnie told Ann she was trying several of her suggestions and that things were working out fairly well. Then, Bonnie asked Ann several questions about what to do when certain problems arose in her classroom. Ann invited Bonnie to discuss these problems with several other faculty members who met once a month after school to share ideas and problems in a support group. Bonnie reluctantly agreed to come. But by accepting this invitation to attend a support group meeting, Bonnie's carefully concealed exploration eventually became apparent to her colleagues.

A Cautiously Out-in-the-Open Stance

A careful public exploration initiated with the knowledge and support of others exemplifies this stance.

After attending her first support group meeting, Bonnie's private indulgence in making a transition toward balanced literacy instruction was revealed. In many ways, Bonnie was relieved. Now she felt comfortable talking about her experiences—both her concerns and successes with peers. During subsequent meetings, she frequently asked questions about new practices.

In the months that followed, Bonnie continued to work on practicing and perfecting the strategies she had been using. In addition, she cautiously introduced several new strategies and practices into her classroom while continuing to use a few traditional strategies she was not willing to give up. Bonnie continued the slow but nonetheless directed process of making transitions during the year. At the end of the 2nd year, she was becoming convinced that balanced teaching of reading and language was worth the effort. Finally, Bonnie openly advocated the changes she had made while continuing her ongoing transitions.

An Advocate's Stance

Three years after we had met Bonnie, she had become one of the most respected reading teachers in her school. Other teachers visited her classroom, came to her with problems, and solicited information. She listened, supported, encouraged, and even offered her colleagues articles and books to read on balanced literacy instruction. Bonnie continued to study and change professionally. She attended reading and language conferences and workshops regularly to gain new insights and information. She shared information and ideas freely and openly with her colleagues. Today, Bonnie has not yet achieved the ideal of a totally integrated reading and language curriculum. She continues to occasionally use direct, isolated skill lessons, particularly those focusing on phonics and word-recognition skills. On the other hand, Bonnie has nearly abandoned basal readers and worksheets in favor of literature books, increased silent reading time, and reading response activities. She encourages her students to respond to their reading rather than interrogating them after reading with a list of questions. More and more, Bonnie integrates reading and writing in her classroom. She has even found that phonics can be practiced in writing and spelling, not just reading.

An advocate feels at ease with reading instructional change and supports others through the process.

While Bonnie has a ways to go toward total integration of the curriculum and teaching consistently from the whole of language to the parts, she has made significant strides toward that end. Those who talk to Bonnie today find her professionally vibrant and feeling very much in control of her classroom and curriculum. Figure 5.2 summarizes the major characteristics of each of the stances in reading beliefs.

Transitions in Using Instructional Materials

An important, even critical, dimension of making transitions is adapting or discontinuing the use of many traditional instructional materials. Using the basal reader like a textbook or script, assigning worksheets as practice for reading skills, and oral round-robin reading in ability groups are examples of classroom practices related to the use of specific reading instructional materials demanding change. Recent reports have pointed out that instructional materials have exerted significant effects on teachers and the teaching of reading for decades. K. Goodman et al. describe the effect of using basal readers:

Adapting or discontinuing the use of many traditional instructional materials is often a first step in making transitions.

> But just as [the basal] must control reading, language, and learning, the basal's central premise requires that it control the teacher. And the control of teachers, far from assuring their effectiveness, limits both their authority and their responsibility for the development of pupils. One of the great tragedies of the basals is the dependency they have built in teachers. (1988, p. 128)

In fairness, some scholars do not agree that basal readers are the *cause* of teachers' elected practices (Baumann, 1992). In fact, basal readers have been the cause of some recent changes in classroom practices (Baker, 1994). Because of the dependency on instructional materials, particularly basal readers, many teachers are timid about making decisions and sometimes resist taking responsibility for making instructional decisions that could affect change. Duffy, Roehler, and Putnam contend:

> As more is learned about the nature of reading and the effective teaching of reading, the need for elementary school teachers who will make substantive curricular decisions becomes more apparent. (1987, p. 357)

Figure 5.2

Transitions toward balanced reading beliefs: Typical teacher stances and behaviors

---

"I Don't Know Enough Yet to Know Where I Stand" Stance

Teachers may

___ Express confusion and frustration toward innovations in reading programs

___ Express commitment to their own experiences as school students and observers

___ Feel a need to conform to current norms or traditions in public and private schools

___ Express a concern regarding a lack of experience in real classroom settings as a teacher

___ Feel unsure of whether or not they can successfully implement a reading program based on holistic philosophy and associated instructional approaches

Combative Stance

Teachers may

___ Demonstrate hostility toward change

___ Defend traditional or existing reading programs

___ Enumerate obstacles to implementing whole language

Tentative Stance

Teachers may

___ Begin to privately examine their own reading beliefs and practices

___ Begin to listen in on teacher discussions of changes in reading beliefs and practices

___ Begin to ask questions about holistic reading strategies

Responsive Stance

Teachers may

___ Ask colleagues about their experiences in implementing holistic reading practices

___ Cautiously initiate unobtrusive holistic practices

___ Conceal from colleagues the initiation of holistic practices

---

For whatever reason, teachers who want to make transitions should pursue a cautious and well-thought-out plan for reducing dependency on basal readers as well as other basal-related reading instructional materials. Over time and with effort, teachers can move away from a reading curriculum dominated by basals, worksheets, and tests toward more authentic reading instruction. However, and somewhat paradoxically, to begin this journey, we suggest that the best point of departure for initiating transitions using instructional materials is the basal reader. With this in mind, we describe how teachers may use the basal as a springboard toward authentic reading instruction.

Basals as Springboards: Mitigating Weaknesses

Some reading experts recommend that teachers simply cut back on the use of the basal reader as a first step in transitions (K. S. Goodman, 1986). Although this may be a viable approach for some teachers, basal readers have come to fill an important

Explorative Stance

Teachers may

___ Request additional information about holistic reading instruction

___ Begin to attend conferences with colleagues

___ Try additional holistic reading strategies

Off-the-Record Stance

Teachers may

___ Share the positive and negative outcomes of the experience

___ Begin to ask "what do you do when?" types of questions

___ Accept invitations to attend in-school support group meetings

Cautiously Out-in-the-Open Stance

Teachers may

___ Begin to perfect the holistic reading strategies initiated

___ Begin to offer help to colleagues in transition

___ Replace more traditional strategies with holistic strategies

___ Show excitement by openly advocating positive results with students

___ Continue to use some traditional strategies

Advocate's Stance

Teachers will

___ Begin to share willingly with other teachers how holistic reading instruction is used

___ Use a predominance of holistic strategies while continuing selected traditional strategies

___ Share strategies with teachers who are just beginning

___ Read professional articles, journals, and books and share these with others

___ Visit other classrooms and receive visitors into their classrooms

niche in the instructional habits and practices of classroom teachers for well over 100 years (Pearson, 1989c). Cutting back may create much too large a void in classroom practices as a starting point. Simply cutting back also does nothing to help teachers think about instruction and make informed and reasoned instructional changes or adaptations in what often is the only instructional material they have on hand for teaching reading: the basal reader. We think a better approach is to rethink or adapt the use of the basal reader as an initial step in transitions. K. Goodman, Smith, Meredith, and Goodman propose:

> Teachers and schools wanting to adopt a whole-language approach to reading may find it most feasible to use the basal as a point of departure and adapt its use so that it ceases to be the focal point of the program. (1987, p. 264)

Using the basal as a springboard for departure from old practices requires that teachers understand several weaknesses inherent in basal readers and several common misuses of basals:

Learning to think about and use a basal reader differently is an important initial change in reading instruction.

- Reading the basal from front to back, *every story in order*, as a textbook rather than literature
- Skill lesson overkill: reading instruction as worksheets
- Teaching reading skills in isolation
- Oral round-robin reading: A practice high in risk, low in benefit
- Asking questions: the reading inquisition

Following are suggested ways to mitigate the weaknesses identified, which can help teachers begin the process of thinking about and adapting the use of basal readers in classrooms.

Treating the Basal as an Anthology of Literature—Not a Textbook!

The basal can be thought of as an anthology of reading selections. This concept was also discussed in Chapter 4.

Let students choose to read those selections in the basal anthology that interest them.

"What are basal readers, after all?" questioned a curious college student. "They are a school textbook containing stories, poems, and short informational selections. In a very real sense, basals are anthologies—collections of stories, expository articles, and poetry," we explain. "Are all works in an anthology of literature read in order from the front of the book to the back?" the student continues. "No, not typically! When reading an anthology, readers usually choose a story here or there, based on interest," we respond. The same should be true with a basal reader. Students should not be required to read the basal reader from front to back, every story in order. After all, publishers have never claimed that the selections in basal readers are perfectly sequenced by difficulty. The key issue here is capturing student interest. To capture students' interest, we must allow them to browse and choose interesting reading selections from the basal.

Basal reader visiting response groups or interest groups are discussed in Chapter 9.

If teachers could envision the basal reader as a small shelf of selected, individual storybooks that students can choose from, then browsing the basal shelf of stories seems to be a reasonable beginning point. We suggest that students be given 20 to 30 minutes at the beginning of each year to browse through the selections in the basal reader(s). They might be encouraged to make a list of their favorite selections. After browsing, teachers should conduct an interest inventory to determine the basal stories for which students seem to indicate high interest. This may be done by reading aloud the titles for each story in the table of contents and asking students to indicate by a show of hands which of the stories they are interested in reading. Another approach is to copy the table of contents, have students put their name on the copy, and mark which of the stories they would like to read. In this way, teachers learn which stories may be skipped in the basal because of little or no interest. After stories have been selected based on interest, teachers can form basal reader visiting groups or interest groups.

Working out of Worksheet Dependency: Toward Reader Response

Worksheets have filled a management role in reading classrooms—keeping children busy.

In recent years, several classroom observation studies have found that reading instruction is dominated by worksheets (R. C. Anderson et al., 1985; Durkin, 1978). Although this condition may be deplored by experts for important instructional reasons, classroom teachers have come to depend on worksheets for quite a different reason. Worksheets have served a role in the management of reading instruction

(Pearson, 1989c). Thus, calls for the complete, immediate, and total cessation of worksheets in classrooms send many teachers into worksheet withdrawal and eventual management shock.

One question teachers often ask is "If we don't teach and practice skills with worksheets, how will we know if students are learning?" or "How can we assign grades in reading without worksheet assignments?" "What will students do without worksheets when I am not working with their reading group?" These questions and many more emphasize teachers' real and legitimate concern over the use of worksheets for managing the reading classroom. How can teachers go about gradually working their way out of a worksheet economy in the classroom—an economy that breeds dependency for teachers? We suggest a two-part process that is aimed at reducing the number of worksheets while simultaneously improving the quality of those worksheets assigned to students.

First, reduce gradually the number of worksheets assigned during the reading instructional period. This can be accomplished by cutting out worksheets that emphasize content or skills for which students have already demonstrated sufficient understanding or ability. In place of worksheets, students can be given increased time for reading books, magazines, drama, and writing stories of their own choice. Increasing reading time is essential for year-to-year gains in reading achievement (R. C. Anderson, Wilson, & Fielding, 1988). Another means of reducing worksheets is for teachers to ask themselves questions such as "Where is this skill or strategy best demonstrated and practiced—in reading a text or on a worksheet?" Careful consideration of this question leads to the answer that reading skills or strategies ought to be embedded in an authentic context: the place where these skills are used in reading and society. Questions such as these will help teachers use worksheets more judiciously while replacing them with increased opportunities to read real books.

Notice two things the teacher can do to begin transitions with basal readers.

Second, the number of worksheets may be reduced by changing the very nature of worksheets to reflect more open-ended, divergent, or accepting formats. Worksheets such as these encourage students to write, draw, or otherwise interpret and respond to reading rather than requiring them to provide single answers, convergent or "correct" responses.

Although this recommendation defeats the time-saving advantages of many commercially produced worksheets, one advantage of custom designing worksheets is that other reading materials such as literature books, information books, or newspapers can be integrated into the reading program.

Change the nature of worksheet assignments. Use open-ended responses such as those suggested as literature-response activities described in Chapters 10 and 11.

Third, begin to substitute alternative ways to respond or record feelings about the reading of a book or story. Students can be asked to use drawing, art, dance, drama, music, or writing to record and share their responses to their reading. Wanted posters, murals, plays, radio readings, or learning logs can be used to engage students in activities that develop and refine skills as well as elaborate interpretations and comprehension (see Chapters 10 and 11).

Teaching With Text

Reducing dependency on worksheets leads to the realization that instruction can take place, perhaps more appropriately, within the context of printed language—the stories and books children read. For example, when teaching children about how graphophonic clues are helpful in decoding unfamiliar words in text, the best place to demonstrate this utility is in the texts that children have been reading or writing

Teach children reading skills and strategies using the print and books they are reading.

(Hansen, 1987). Specific literary devices or print-decoding skills are better demonstrated with excellent examples found in books rather than on worksheets. For example, helping children recognize figurative expressions is often taught using worksheets. Instead, it seems more reasonable to read stories containing rich examples of figurative language use such as *Amelia Bedelia* (Parish, 1963), *A Chocolate Moose for Dinner* (Gwynne, 1970) or *The King Who Rained* (Gwynne, 1976). Using children's reading and writing to teach specific language strategies makes good sense. We say this because there is no need to "transfer learning" from the unauthentic contexts of worksheets to real reading or writing events.

Oral Reading With Basals and Books: Breaking Away From Round-Robin Reading

*The **ORL** helps teachers move away from the practice of oral round-robin reading in their classrooms.*

Perhaps no practice, outside of using worksheets, figures as prominently in American reading instruction as does the practice of having children read aloud one at a time while other students listen and follow along. This practice is known as round-robin reading. Hoffman and Segel (1982) reviewed the historical literature on oral reading instruction in American classrooms in an attempt to locate the origin for round-robin reading. After an exhaustive search, these authors uncovered no work that could be used to determine a point in time at which round-robin reading assumed its prominent place in classroom reading instruction. Recent research on the effects of oral round-robin reading on students' reading achievement in regular classrooms has shown its negative effects as compared to other modes for providing group oral reading instruction and practice (Reutzel & Hollingsworth, 1993). Because recent research by Reutzel, Hollingsworth, and Eldredge (1994) indicated that the oral recitation lesson is a solid alternative for providing group oral reading instruction, we recommend Hoffman's (1987) oral recitation lesson as one approach for breaking away from an overdependence on oral round-robin reading practices.

Components of the Oral Recitation Lesson

The **oral recitation lesson (ORL)** consists of two basic components with a series of subroutines. The first of these two components is direct instruction.

    I.   Direct instruction
        A. Three subroutines
            1. Comprehension
            2. Practice
            3. Performance

    II. Indirect instruction
        A. Two subroutines
            1. Fluency practice
            2. Demonstrate expert reading

Notice two main components of the ORL.

Direct instruction consists of three subroutines: a comprehension phase, a practice phase, and a performance phase. When beginning an ORL, the teacher reads a story aloud and leads the students in an analysis of the story's content by constructing a story grammar map and discussing the major elements of the story such as setting, characters, goals, plans, events, and resolution. Students are asked to tell what they remember about these parts of the story, and the teacher records their responses at the board. In a sense, recording student responses is somewhat like a language experience dictation of their story recall. At the conclusion of this discussion, the story grammar map is used as an outline for students to write a story summary.

During the second subroutine, practice, the teacher works with students to improve their oral reading expression. The teacher models fluent reading aloud with segments of the text, and the students individually or chorally practice imitating the teacher's oral expressions.

Choral readings of texts can be accomplished in many ways. Wood (1983) suggests two that we have found useful for group choral readings: (a) unison reading and (b) echoic reading. To these we add a third, antiphonal reading. In unison readings, everyone reads together. In echoic reading, the teacher or a student reads, and the others in the group echo the reading. In antiphonal reading, the group is divided into two subgroups. One subgroup begins reading a segment of text, and the second subgroup echoes the first group's reading. A variation of this approach may involve the second group in reading the next line alternating with the first group. Text segments modeled by the teacher during the practice phase may begin with only one or two sentences and gradually move toward modeling and practicing whole pages of text.

Choral readings may also be used to break away from oral round-robin reading.

The third subroutine is the performance phase. Students select a text segment they want to perform for others in the group, and listeners are encouraged to comment positively on the performance.

The second major component of the ORL is an indirect instruction phase. During this part of the lesson, students practice a single story until they become expert readers. Hoffman (1987) defines an expert reader as one who reads with 98% accuracy and 75 words per minute fluency. For 10 minutes each day, students practice reading a story or text segment in a soft or mumble reading fashion. Teachers use this time to check students individually for story mastery before moving on to another story. The direct instruction component creates a pool of stories from which the students can select a story to use to become an expert reader in the indirect instruction phase. In summary, ORL provides teachers with a workable strategy to break away from the traditional practice of round-robin oral reading.

Asking Comprehension Questions: The Reading Inquisition

A common practice encouraged by basal reader teachers' manuals is to ask a line of questions following the reading of a basal story or selection. This practice is often mislabeled *discussion*. Durkin (1983) referred to the practice of asking a line of comprehension questions following reading as **comprehension interrogation.** Higgins (cited in Edelsky, 1988) referred to this practice as a "gentle (or not so gentle) inquisition" rather than as a grand conversation. Teachers should understand that basal reader comprehension questioning does nothing to improve comprehension; rather, its major utility is to assess comprehension. Hence, teachers should carefully review the practice of asking comprehension questions after reading.

Comprehension evaluation can be documented using retelling (described in Chapter 6) and completing reading response activities such as those found in Chapters 10 and 11.

In the real world, people do not discuss a book by one individual quizzing the other with a line of questions. For instance, when someone has just read a great book and is discussing it around the dinner table, those listening seldom ask questions to quiz comprehension (Atwell, 1987). Thus, asking a line of comprehension questions after reading ought to be discontinued on grounds of lack of authenticity.

Second, asking the line of questions in basal teachers' manuals fails to help children reconstruct the sequence of events in the story. Why? Because the questions in teachers' manuals are seldom, if ever, sequenced in the order of the story! Third, questions may probe only insignificant parts or details of the story. Consequently, Harp (1989b) warns that questioning may give a piecemeal view of a reader's comprehension of a story. Finally, children do not *want* to discuss answers to a list of questions in the teachers' manual. Instead, they would rather talk about how they felt about the book, a character in the story, the connections they made between their own experiences and those of the story characters, or ask their own questions.

Transitions in questioning first begin when teachers ask questions only about the major elements of the story's structure, setting, problem, goal, and so on, and in the sequence these events are found in the story. The second transitional step is for teachers to discontinue the use of question lists altogether and involve children in interpretive reading response activities, discussions, and retellings.

Transitions in Curriculum Design

"OBE is not the panacea. . . . Neither is it a pernicious movement to turn schools into factories, as its critics suggest" (Glatthorn, 1993, p. 363).

Curriculum fragmentation is a formidable obstacle to be overcome by teachers making transitions.

Curriculum reforms such as **outcome-based education (OBE)** are offered as a "success for all" panacea. The philosophy of OBE is based on the traditional philosophical grounding of competency-based education and mastery learning (Towers, 1992), which maintains traditional curriculum standards and perpetuates barriers to integration (Block, 1989). Although a more coherent approach to curriculum than in the past, Glatthorn suggests that "OBE is not the panacea. . . . Neither is it a pernicious movement to turn schools into factories, as its critics suggest" (1993, p. 363). Zlatos (1993) details the outrage of various religious and cultural groups toward the curriculum reforms proposed by the OBE movement. Hence, it is important to understand that curriculum reform is very much a political matter. Breaking down the artificial barriers constructed between the language arts, reading, writing, speaking, and listening, as well as other curriculum subjects in the elementary school presents teachers with a formidable task. To some, this task seems almost insurmountable. Teaching from the whole of language to the parts requires that teachers think about language, children, learning, and teaching quite differently from the well-established approach of teaching from the parts of language to the whole. Cutting across curricular boundaries to include science, math, social studies, art, music, and other curriculum subjects with reading, writing, speaking, and listening requires considerable thought, effort, time, and skill. And yet, a transitions philosophy advocates the gradual reintegration of the language arts and other curriculum subjects as a critical component of working toward balanced reading and language instruction. A reasonable point of departure for designing an integrated reading and language curriculum is to carefully examine the scope and sequence of reading skills.

Developing a Nonnegotiable Skills List

Recent studies indicate that many reading skills may be skipped or omitted without significant harm to reading test scores.

One problem associated with reading instruction in basal readers and in many school reading curriculum guides is the fragmentation of reading into minute skills and subskills. Because teachers and students spend up to 70% of reading instructional time on mastering a series of skills spelled out in district curriculum guides and in basal readers (R. C. Anderson et al., 1985), several researchers have conducted studies to examine the effect of skipping these so-called necessary skills on end-of-year or end-of-book tests. B. M. Taylor, Frye, and Gaetz (1990) found that without instruction and practice in these skills, many students' performance on skill tests remained high. This suggests that many students could be excused from these skill activities in basal programs and attention could be focused on other reading activities. Reutzel and Hollingsworth (1991b) found that students who were taught skills did no better on criterion-referenced skill tests than did students who had spent an equal amount of time reading self-selected trade books. In any case, it appears that teachers can reduce the endless lists of skills they have been made responsible to teach without serious detriment to students' reading progress or reading test scores.

Consequently, one important transitional step is to pare down the scope and sequence of skills to a list of a few important, **nonnegotiable skills**. These skills are judged by teachers to be those abilities essential to becoming a skilled reader. Santa (1990) tells of working with teachers in Kallispell, Montana, in an effort that resulted in creating a nonnegotiable list of reading skills teachers felt students needed to be taught in order to become skilled readers. The process for developing a list of nonnegotiable skills began when teachers met to discuss their grade level scope and sequence of skills with the goal in mind of cutting down to the essentials. Of course, such an effort should be supported by the building administrator if it is to be successful. In addition, reading research may be consulted to determine the most important reading skills to retain for instruction. From several literary and statistical analyses of reading comprehension skills, researchers have identified eight important reading comprehension skills (Rosenshine, 1980, p. 541):

*A **nonnegotiable skills list** is a carefully limited list of essential reading skills to be taught in school reading programs.*

- Recalling word meanings (vocabulary)
- Drawing inferences about the meaning of a word from context
- Finding answers to questions answered explicitly or in paraphrase
- Weaving together ideas in the content
- Drawing inferences from the content
- Recognizing a writer's purpose, attitude, tone, and mood
- Identifying a writer's literary techniques
- Following a structure of a passage

These seem to provide a reasonable guide for judging the relative value of reading comprehension skills in basal or district scope and sequence charts. In addition to these, the ability to use graphophonic cues along with other language cues should not be overlooked. In Chapter 8, we recommend seven phonic generalizations from among hundreds of phonic rules that deserve selective attention. By combining these seven phonic generalizations with the eight reading comprehension and vocabulary skills identified here, teachers can effectively cut skill lists containing hundreds of reading skills down to a list containing a manageable 15.

After grade-level groups meet and cut down to the minimum nonnegotiable list of skills, then the entire school faculty meets to cut down on unnecessary overlap and repetition of skills between grade levels. The final list of reading skills is ratified by a vote of the faculty. Faculty ownership of the process of cutting skills creates greater commitment to the end product. By reducing the almost infinite number of reading skills to a manageable few, teachers and students are released from the bondage of needless skill, drill, and practice. Teachers are freed to engage in activities related to reading real books with their students.

Studies of comprehension and vocabulary skills reveal only eight essential, distinct skills. Combined with the seven phonic generalizations, this yields a manageable list of only 15 nonnegotiable skills.

Levels of Integration:
Breaking Down Curriculum Barriers

An issue related to skill lists is the continued **fragmentation** of language in reading and writing instruction by isolating and compartmentalizing the reading and language curricu-

Fragmentation refers to the curricular practice of listing, teaching, and measuring reading skills in isolation from other language skills.

lum. Typically, the reading and language instructional curriculum has been divided into four separate curriculum blocks, periods, or times, such as 60 minutes for reading instruction, 30 minutes for language arts instruction, 20 minutes for spelling instruction, and 15 minutes for handwriting instruction. This practice was begun and maintained with the best of intentions. These included ensuring that each of the parts of the language arts received proper attention in the daily school curriculum as well as the ease of planning and managing instruction. Although these may be honorable motives, we have known for some time that the four modes of language (reading, writing, listening, and speaking) are interrelated and even inseparable in nature. D. D. Johnson and Pearson remind us:

> We know that language systems—the phonology, grammar, and lexicon—are interdependent. In essence, language is indivisible; yet skills management systems would seem to fractionate it and destroy its essential nature. Because of the interdependence of the language systems, there is really no possible sequencing of skills. (1975, p. 758)

Another important aspect of change to be undertaken in transitions is the reintegration of the school curriculum.

Harste, Woodward, and Burke warn against compartmentalizing the language curriculum when they state, "the reading and writing curriculum should not be isolated from other curriculum areas" (1984, p. 204). To this end, another important aspect of change to be undertaken in transitions is the reintegration of the school curriculum so that the ideal prescribed by Harste et al. can become a reality.

Integration involves putting skills of language and components of the language curriculum back together with the remainder to the school curriculum.

We have found that transitions toward **curricular integration**, or putting the curriculum back together, takes place in a three-phase process, as illustrated in Figure 5.3. The process of integration begins, somewhat paradoxically, with reducing fragmentation. By developing a nonnegotiable list of skills, as described earlier, teachers and administrators can discard some of the curricular artifacts that perpetuate fragmentation and compartmentalization.

Some practical applications of this level of language integration are illustrated by the language routine found in Chapter 10, the reading and writing workshops in Chapter 11, and the literacy units in the following section of this chapter.

The next step is to move to break down the curriculum barriers artificially dividing language-related areas: reading, writing, listening, speaking, handwriting, and spelling. Rather than scheduling four separate curriculum blocks for instruction, teachers may begin scheduling a single block of time devoted to *language learning* or *literacy education*. During this single time period, smaller blocks of time can be allocated to shared reading, silent reading, responding to books or stories through writing, discussions, sustained writing, and minilessons on reading strategies, writing mechanics, and authoring strategies. Teachers and students can read stories, discuss stories, write responses or summaries of stories, and practice a dramatization. In this way, the language-related curriculum components can become a unified whole again with subroutines during the period to support each part of language.

Figure 5.3

Levels of curricular integration

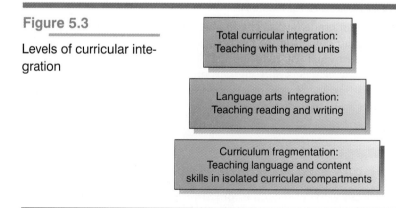

Total curricular integration:
Teaching with themed units

Language arts integration:
Teaching reading and writing

Curriculum fragmentation:
Teaching language and content
skills in isolated curricular compartments

The final step is to integrate the language skills with the remaining curriculum areas: math, science, social studies, art, music, physical education, and so on. When language skills are used to learn math concepts, record social studies learning, and document results of science experiments, they become the fundamental tools of learning in the elementary school. This level of curricular integration is very difficult to achieve and by recent estimates will probably require between 4 and 6 years of concentrated effort (Atwell, 1987; Newman & Church, 1990). Routman indicated the difficulty of reaching this final level of total curriculum integration when she wrote:

> At this point in time, I am comfortable with integrating the four language modes—listening, speaking, reading, and writing. . . . I am still struggling hard to integrate more areas of the curriculum with the language arts—an ideal that is very difficult to attain. I anticipate that this struggle will go on for years. (1988, p. 26)

When this final level of curricular integration is reached, teachers teach primarily with thematic units. In Figure 5.4, we show some examples of practices that demonstrate varying levels of curricular integration.

Teaching with thematic units is discussed in more detail in Chapters 11 and 12.

Language to Literacy Units With Basals and Books

Another program of promise for helping teachers reintegrate the four modes of language into a single unit of instruction is called the **language to literacy** program. Roser, Hoffman, and Farest (1990) describe four basic assumptions associated with this program:

*Another program of promise for helping teachers reintegrate the four modes of language into a single unit of instruction is called the **language to literacy program**.*

- Literacy acquisition is a developmental process.
- Oral language and literacy of printed language interact during development.
- Literacy is best developed in a positive environment that is opportunity filled, supportive, responsive, purposeful, and highly interactive.
- Literacy acquisition requires high teacher involvement.

Basic aspects of this program include several components that reflect a trend toward a balanced approach to reading instruction in which literature or basal stories are used as the basis for the program.

- Shared literature
- Writing with literature
- Fluency building
- Personalized reading
- Literature across the curriculum
- Parent as first teacher

Classroom teachers working with university faculty developed several types of language to literacy units (Roser et al., 1990). These included units that focused on authors, topics, literary genre, or themes. An author unit was developed that focused on the books of Eric Carle, *The Grouchy Ladybug, The Very Hungry Caterpillar,* and *The Very Busy Spider.* A topical unit was developed around the subject of dinosaurs. A themed unit was developed around the theme of "Being Different Makes Us Special." A genre unit was developed around the literary genre of biographies. Trade books were located for use in each of these literacy units. We suggest that with minimal effort basal language to literacy units can be developed using selected stories taken from basal readers similar to those already described. This is particularly true where access to literature is restricted.

For each literacy unit (Roser et al., 1990), teachers read aloud each of the trade books in the language to literacy units to the children. Conversation and response to

Figure 5.4

Selected practices reflecting levels of curricular integration

	Reading	Writing
Level 1 Integration Teachers remain mostly (more than 80% of the time) committed to basal programs. They supplement traditional practices with literature strategies and process writing opportunities. Traditional curriculum time blocks for separate reading, language, handwriting, and spelling periods remain intact.	Silent sustained reading (SSR) Open-ended worksheet activities Visiting basal response groups Reconciled reading lesson Direct reading thinking lesson The basal as an anthology Test wiseness units Core books study Directed reading thinking activity (DRTA) ReQuest Language experience approach (LEA) Story mapping	Journal writing Silent spontaneous writing Teacher-directed topic choice Mini lessons on writing skills Sentence-combining practice Word collection spelling lists Handwriting and calligraphy
Level 2 Integration Teachers spend less than 50% of time in basal programs and use literature-based process writing strategies the majority of the time. Curriculum blocks of reading, language arts, handwriting, and spelling have been collapsed into a single period of time.	Supported repeated readings Language to literacy units Author study Language routines: K–1 Reading workshop: 2–8 Sharing literacy Demonstrations and performances Literature response and transmediation Story frames Tradebooks Language experience Portfolio assessment Schema lesson Literature webbing	Writing process Writing workshop Student topic choice Sharing ways to become an author Conferencing and editing Strategic spelling instruction Handwriting models and review Sharing writing Publishing Tips for writing Portfolio assessment
Level 3 Integration Teachers spend less than 10% of their time in basal-oriented programs. They use literature-based reading and process writing curriculum almost exclusively. They have achieved total integration of the language arts and have begun to integrate the language arts with the remainder of the curriculum. Thematic curriculum units are the focus of instruction at this level.	Reading across the curriculum Themed studies Content area reading across the language modes Writing as reading assessment	Writing across the curriculum Logs Reports Projects Reading as writing assessment

books were fostered by the use of language charts. An example of a language chart for an author's language to literacy unit dealing with the books authored by Eric Carle is shown in Figure 5.5. In the language to literacy project (Roser et al., 1990), language charts were placed on the walls of the classroom. Children recorded their responses directly onto the language chart. Thus, language charts are a means of encouraging children to write about each of the books they have been reading as well as helping them make the connections between books. Children also recorded interesting vocabulary words onto vocabulary charts displayed on the walls of the classroom. After discussing the books of the language to literacy unit, children practiced reading one book chosen from the unit to an acceptable fluency level much like the procedures described in the previous section on the ORL. A tote bag filled with literature was sent home during each 2-week language to literacy unit. This bag was used to invite parents to read a book together with their child from the language to literacy unit. In this way, parents became informed and involved in their children's school reading experiences. Finally, science, drama, social studies, math, and other curriculum areas were planned into the language to literacy units as culminating activities. A summary of the process of using a language to literacy unit follows:

1. Teacher reads aloud the books to the class from the language to literacy unit.
2. Children discuss with the teacher individual responses to the books using a language chart.
3. Children record responses about the books on the language chart.
4. Children record selected vocabulary words on vocabulary charts for each book in the unit.
5. Children select a book for personalized reading and fluency building. Children practice the book or a segment of the book until they become expert readers.
6. Children and parents enjoy books read together from the language to literacy unit sent home in literature bags.
7. Culminating activities are planned that integrate the topic, theme, or author study of the language to literacy unit with other curricular areas.

__Language charts__ are used to discuss and record responses to books.

Sending books home involves parents in the school reading program.

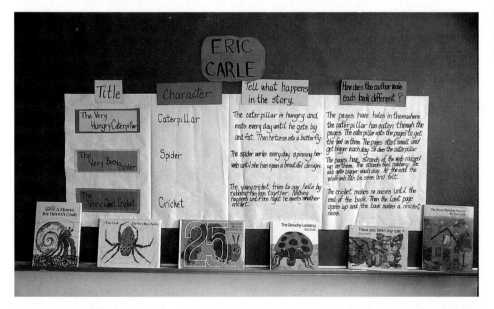

Figure 5.5

Example of a language chart for a literacy unit

At the final level of integration, teachers teach thematic units.

*Basal **language to literature units** can be developed using basal stories grouped around topics of themes.*

Because basal stories or a limited number of trade books can be used for developing and using language to literacy units, we see this program as one very useful transitional step toward balanced reading and language instruction. Teachers can use their basal stories to develop basal language to literacy units while they acquire an adequate number of trade books to develop language to literacy units. In fact, the development of language to literacy units around selected topics, themes, and author study can directly support the future selection and acquisition of trade books. We can easily envision teachers electing to limit the use of the basal reader to 2 or 3 days per week, and in its place, developing language to literacy units using basal stories or trade books to fill in the gap.

Transitions in Community Involvement: Seeking Support for Change

Think of a time when you "got into trouble" for failing to seek support from others. What were you thinking of at that time?

Making transitions is risky business. On one occasion, Jerry Harste (quoted in Newman, 1985b) warned that trying holistic reading and language instruction meant "getting into trouble" with teachers, principals, parents, and even children. Although this may be true, it certainly does not have to be the case. One way to prevent much of the trouble Harste foreshadows is to inform and involve parents, principals, and colleagues in efforts to change the school reading and language curriculum.

Parent Involvement: Information and Volunteerism

Rasinski and Fredericks (1989) asked parents in a survey what they thought of reading instruction in the schools. About 51% of parents surveyed thought that schools were teaching reading adequately. Another 36% responded the schools were doing a poor job of teaching reading. The parents who felt schools were doing a poor job of teaching reading were concerned about teaching the basics, especially the need to teach more phonics. A smaller percentage of parents (13%) expressed that the schools were doing a so-so job of teaching reading. Some comments from parents who were surveyed included, "Teachers should read to the class more; and children should get to read what they're interested in." Several parents mentioned their children characterized reading as "boring." From these responses, one thing is clear. Parents are aware of and concerned about the reading instruction their children receive. Hence, making dramatic changes in reading beliefs and instruction *without* informing and involving parents would most likely mean "getting into trouble."

Making transitions toward balanced reading instruction should include a strong commitment to parent involvement as one dimension of change. How can this be accomplished effectively? Fredericks and Rasinski (1990), in an article entitled, "Involving the Uninvolved: How To," list 14 different ways to involve parents and the community in reading curriculum changes. We have summarized, modified, and added to these suggestions as follows:

Making transitions toward balanced reading instruction should include a strong commitment to parent involvement as one dimension of change.

1. Provide parents with lots of written and visual informational materials over an extended period of time regarding your intended changes. One-shot information will not suffice.
2. Make parent involvement a schoolwide concern. Individual teachers cannot successfully implement and sustain a parent involvement program.
3. Provide a good deal of recognition for parents and students who become involved with the school and with school reading instructional changes.
4. Involve students wholeheartedly in recruiting parents to become involved through writing invitations, designing awards, and so on.
5. Encourage participatory projects that involve the entire family. Make reading a family concern. Suggest ways reading can be fostered in and by the entire family.
6. Don't focus school involvement programs on parents alone. Seek to involve other segments of the community, such as the elderly, business, and government.
7. Make the school a comfortable place. Encourage an open-door policy with a liberal and comfortable visitation and volunteerism plan. Let parents see and participate in school reading instructional changes. This will eliminate many fears, doubts, and suspicions.
8. Use the telephone as a means of communicating good news rather than bad news.
9. Find out why some parents distance themselves from involvement with the school and school reading changes. This will take time but can pay sizable dividends in the final analysis.
10. In scheduling involvement activities, provide for flexibility through various options and plans to accommodate those who are willing to participate.
11. Consider offering parents a "Parent Hot Line" through the PTA or PTO organizations to discuss concerns or provide needed information.
12. Solicit endorsements and advertisements of your school reading program from community business and government leaders, sports figures, and the like.
13. Document the special features of your school reading program through videotaping, photographs, and articles. Make these available to parents.

See Chapter 9 for more information on volunteers as an instructional resource.

14. When special events are held that require parent involvement, provide special services such as babysitting or escort service. Let parents know that you genuinely care about their attendance and involvement.
15. Survey parents periodically to gather their input. This practice helps parents feel ownership in the school reading program.
16. Hold periodic information or parent education seminars to help parents understand the desired changes in reading instruction.

In Chapter 9, we outline resources and provide a recruitment form for starting a school volunteer program.

Fredericks and Rasinski (1990) recommended five steps for establishing a quality volunteer program: (a) recruitment, (b) training, (c) variety, (d) recognition, and (e) evaluation. Because of the diversity associated with transitions, teachers will need to develop and implement their own volunteer training programs. We simply cannot anticipate the variety of training needs for every locale within the scope of this book. Recognition of volunteers is critical to the success of any such effort. All of us, parents and students, like to be recognized for our efforts. While we would like to believe that all persons serve others without recognition, this is often not the case. Small tokens of appreciation can go a long way toward sustaining a successful volunteer program. For example, in the school where one of the authors taught, the principal paid for volunteers to enjoy a free school lunch each day they volunteered. Finally, an annual assessment of the effectiveness of the school involvement program should be conducted. This effort may suggest options to be more effective or possibilities to sustain an already successful program.

Small tokens, such as certificates of appreciation or phone calls, have been used to foster a successful volunteer program.

Notice what can be done to better inform parents.

Parent education is an almost sure-fire means for avoiding unnecessary trouble when making transitions in reading instruction. Evening sessions, open houses, or seminars can be held, informing parents about how their children learned to speak

Parent volunteers are vitally important community resources.

and listen to language and about how these processes are similar to those the school reading program will be using to help them learn to read and write language. Another session may focus on tips for parents to use while reading aloud to their children. Still another session may focus on ideas that may be used at home to support transitions toward a balanced reading program. Fredericks and Rasinski (1990) suggested several ideas for supporting school reading programs at home. We have selected a few for the following list:

- Encourage parents to work with their children in keeping a family journal. Each member of the family would be expected to make a weekly contribution.
- Encourage parents to make audio or videotapes of their children's reading. These can be reviewed later and stored as family treasures.
- Encourage parents with young children to obtain wordless picture books. Children can write or dictate original stories to accompany the pictures in the books.
- Send home activities for parents and children to complete with certain books they may be reading at home.
- Send home holiday reading and writing packets to sustain the reading program through holiday vacations.
- Invite parents to share book talks with your class. These may be talks about books they have been reading with their youngsters at home.

To maximize the success of transitions, we need to elevate the sense of responsibility for reading and writing improvement to the level of community concern—not the sole responsibility of the schools and teachers (Asheim, Baker, & Mathews, 1983). When we accomplish this goal, our schools will truly become communities of readers and writers.

The sense of responsibility for reading and writing improvement needs to be elevated to the level of community concern—not the sole responsibility of the schools and teachers.

Seeking Administrative Support

The principal plays a critical role in ensuring the success of any curriculum innovations, especially in implementing balanced reading and language approaches (Heald-Taylor, 1989). Consequently, teachers in transition need to learn the art of carefully soliciting support and direction from their principals. Teachers can begin this process by simply mentioning an interest in improving classroom reading and language instruction to the principal. They may wish to hint at a particular interest in developing the ability to use the basal reader more effectively while incorporating more opportunities for students to read real literature books and to write for their own reasons. At the outset, we want to caution teachers against the use of labels such as *whole language* with administrators. It has been our experience that these labels often become fads or buzz words and tend to lead to greater misunderstanding or resistance by administrators than simply describing the desired instructional changes and reasons.

Teachers in transition need to learn the art of carefully soliciting support and direction from their principals.

Nonchalantly sharing books and articles with principals helps them develop a need to understand current changes in reading research and practice. Teachers should also be patient with their administrators. Principals will need time to make transitions just as teachers do. They learn to take risks, seek collegial support, and build a school consensus for change a little at a time, passing through similar transitional stages as teachers.

Teachers should be patient with their administrators as they learn to take risks, seek collegial support, and build a school consensus for change.

Once principals become interested in balanced reading instruction, encourage them to avoid mandating curriculum changes in reading instruction. They should seek to work with those teachers who are interested in change until other teachers decide to join in (Tovey & Kerber, 1986). As school administrators begin to ask questions and express interests in reading instructional change, teachers can suggest the need for outside consultant resources to support planning, implementation, and evaluation of potential curriculum innovations. At this point, it is appropriate to invite school administrators to attend conferences, workshops, professional meetings, and support groups to learn more about making transitions and balanced reading instruction. Finally, teachers should be sensitive to the financial constraints placed on administrators. However, as teachers purchase fewer worksheets and workbooks and depend less and less on basal readers, funds previously allocated for procuring these instructional materials can be redirected toward the acquisition of real literature books for classroom and school libraries.

For example, one elementary school faculty reviews current literature on reading instruction for a few minutes in each faculty meeting.

Faculty meetings can become a setting for reading and discussing books and articles on balanced reading instruction. Teachers can also investigate the difference in cost between implementing a locally designed literature-based reading approach as opposed to adopting a commercially published basal reader program. When teachers help their administrators, they become friends, not foes, of reading curriculum change. And when teachers have the support of their administrators, they can move forward in making transitions with confidence. By listening, providing resources, sharing ideas, encouraging open discussions, and working together, teachers and administrators can form a meaningful network of support for each other as they make transitions toward balanced reading instruction.

Colleague Collaboration: Establishing Support Groups

Some teachers in transition have begun to form small, informal study or support groups to discuss challenges, problems, and potential solutions.

Because making transitions tends to be a grassroots movement, some teachers feel alone or isolated even in their own schools. To sustain the energy necessary to continue transitions, some teachers have begun to form small, informal study or support groups. They meet to discuss challenges, problems, and potential solutions. They share success stories with each other and help each other work through problems. Sometimes they just encourage each other to stick with it or hang in there in the face of threatening and skeptical colleagues and administrators. We suggest that teachers affiliate with local professional groups such as the International Reading Association or the National Council of Teachers of English. Loose-knit support groups for sustaining transitions toward balanced teaching of reading are also forming known as *TAWL groups (Teachers Applying Whole Language)*. Once administrative support is secured, faculty meetings can begin to take on the characteristics of these support groups as whole faculties work together through the difficulties of making transitions.

Transitions in the Classroom Environment

Transitions toward balanced reading instruction involve an increased understanding of the role that classroom environments play in setting the stage for pleasurable reading, writing, and learning experiences.

In a quiet corner of one home, a mother sits at a desk carefully reconciling the family checkbook register with the most recent bank statement. Two children are in the kitchen, setting the dinner table. Father is sitting in a large overstuffed chair, reading to the youngest child in the family. Each nook and room in this home has its own atmosphere, climate, and function.

Every building has its own atmosphere, be it a church, court, hospital, or bar. Much like a home, a classroom that nurtures children in a literate environment provides a place that has its own atmosphere, climate, and function. Part of making the transition toward balanced reading instruction involves an increased understanding of the role that classroom environments play in setting the stage for pleasurable reading, writing, and learning experiences (Loughlin & Martin, 1987).

Institutional Versus Home-Like Classroom Environments

Teachers know that classrooms are special places for children and learning. This is evident in the way they adorn the walls, bulletin boards, and windows in their classrooms. But perhaps, the ornaments displayed in classrooms may "only create an atmosphere of inauthenticity, of mere busyness or shallow commitment" (Van Manen, 1986, p. 33). Some classrooms present an image and atmosphere of a department store display window. It is as if the classroom is on display to impress colleagues, administrators, and parents. Colorful but commercially produced bulletin boards seem to say, "This classroom is my classroom, not yours!" to children who enter. In some cases, classrooms mirror the **institutional environments** of our society such as prisons, warehouses, and factories rather than homes (Pino, 1978). Teachers in transition typically initiate changes in the classroom environment that invite children to learn and experience life. Consequently, planning and creating classroom environments to support and nurture children in becoming readers becomes an integral part of making transitions.

Institutional environments reflect the uniformity and warmth of such societal institutions as prisons, hospitals, and factories.

Classroom Design Considerations

When children enter classrooms they can feel the atmosphere—whether it invites and supports or threatens and controls.

> The lived in space of the classroom, its textural and spiritual qualities, first should remind us of what schools are for. School is a place where children explore aspects of the human world. (Van Manen, 1986, p. 34)

Beyond the walls and bulletin board arrangements, the physical arrangement of furniture and other objects in the classroom bespeaks a certain atmosphere. We carefully create an atmosphere in our homes. We consider colors on the walls and in the carpets. We concern ourselves with window coverings and lighting. We experiment with arranging the furnishings to create a sense of invitation and togetherness. Our homes are subdivided into work areas, recreation areas, messy areas, and quiet areas, which in themselves reflect different atmospheres. A transitional approach to balanced reading instruction emphasizes the need to make gradual changes in classroom environments that nurture and support children as they learn to read. For this reason, classrooms need to emulate **home-like environments** rather than institutional environments.

When entering balanced reading classrooms, one should immediately sense a climate that is responsive to children's needs for security, support, and collaboration. Display areas in the classroom should act as verification of the *known* and as an introduction to the *new* for learners. Morrow (1989) speaks of preparing print-rich environments for children to learn about how print works. Thus, display areas might provide commonly used words for concepts such as colors, numbers, directions, and labeled objects as well as information about schedules, procedures, and expectations in the classroom. Display areas could also provide opportunities for children to communicate with the teacher, with each other, and with parents. Sign-up boards, message boards, post offices,

Quality home-like environments are responsive to children's needs for security, support, and collaboration.

and the like recognize the need for using written communication in the classroom. Display areas ought to provide models or prototypes of acceptable written language use. Published compositions written by teachers and children, models of how to write personal letters, and models of standard handwriting help children understand the accepted standards of written language in the classroom. Finally, display areas should expand children's access to information beyond that of the home and neighborhood. Pictures of historical figures, time lines, current events, maps, forests, glaciers, and so on remind children of the larger world community to be experienced and enjoyed.

Classrooms should be physically arranged and adorned with literacy objects and tools that meet the needs of students as well as the preferences of teachers. For some teachers, classrooms will start out looking rather traditional, with the teacher's desk at the front of the room and rows of desks. Traditional classroom arrangements typically have few if any special purpose areas in the classroom. A transitions approach recognizes the need to subdivide spaces in the classroom for whole-class instruction, small-group interaction, or conferences with individual students. This may mean moving desks out of traditional rows into pods or clusters of desks. It may also mean removing desks altogether from the classroom and replacing them with tables. Decorating the classroom with plants, aquariums, soft pillows, rocking chairs, plush carpet, musical instruments, and bean bag chairs are just a few of the possible transitions in classroom arrangements. Like homes, transitions classrooms should gradually be changed to serve the various functions of learning to read and communicate using written language. Play areas such as post offices and kitchens, provided with literacy objects and tools, significantly impact the literacy learning of young children (Neuman & Roskos, 1992). In the final section of this chapter, we illustrate three transitional classroom floor plans to describe how these changes may occur. The important part of transitions in classroom learning environments is to remember that the classroom atmosphere is, as Van Manen (1986) puts it, a way of knowing and coming to know. Most importantly, the classroom environment and atmosphere determine for many of us the way we experience and remember schooling and learning to read.

Think of a classroom you have been in that evidenced a home-like environment. What are the qualities you remember?

Many ideas for subdividing the space in classroom environments are discussed in Chapter 9.

Transitions in Assessment

Changing assessment is perhaps the single most difficult transition to make in reading instruction. Tests are often misunderstood and misused by parents, administrators, and even lawmakers to make inferences about the teaching of reading and reading teachers' performance. Because of the political realities of testing, students and teachers are often obliged to allow their performance to be judged by using traditional and severely limited measures (Cambourne & Turbill, 1990; Clay, 1990). Moving away from traditional forms of assessment is a very scary proposition for teachers. While an integral part of making transitions means living with the political realities of current testing practices, this does not preclude augmenting traditional testing practices with more balanced and naturalistic documentation of reading growth and progress. Valencia and Pearson assert:

Changing assessment is perhaps the single most difficult transition to make in reading instruction.

Transitions means living with the political realities of current testing practices while augmenting traditional testing practices with more holistic and naturalistic documentation of reading growth and progress.

> What we need are not just new and better tests. We need a new framework for thinking about assessment, one in which educators begin by considering types of decisions needed and the level of impact of those decisions. (1987, p. 729)

Although this is the ideal, teachers in transition will of necessity continue to submit to traditional testing; but they will also recognize the purposes as well as the shortcomings of these obligatory practices. In addition, they will begin to design, create, and use balanced and naturalistic measures of reading progress to inform their teaching and to document student growth and progress in the context of authentic reading activities.

Freedom From the Bondage of Teaching to Tests

Research discussed earlier in this chapter has demonstrated the fact that children's standardized and criterion-referenced tests scores do not suffer appreciably when teachers skip skill lessons or devote increased time to authentic reading tasks. Although one may appreciate these facts at a cognitive level, they may not be fully accepted at a practical or political level. Some teachers say, "If I don't teach all of these skills, my students may not pass the tests." Fear, coupled with a shortage of jobs and the desire to help not hurt children, has forced many teachers to reduce the teaching of reading to an exercise in passing prescribed tests. As a consequence of this reality, students and teachers lose the joy of reading and responding to books.

Many individuals take practice tests and pay large fees to attend minicourses to prepare them to take the SAT, ACT, MCAT, LSAT, GMAT, or GRE examinations. One worthwhile suggestion for teachers who are reluctant to completely withdraw from teaching reading skills to pass the tests is to offer an annual minicourse in test-wiseness for their students before administering these tests.

Offer an annual minicourse in test-wiseness for students before administering standardized and criterion-referenced tests.

We suggest that teachers obtain similar, alternate forms of tests for practice or produce practice tests that cover the same objectives and concepts in a similar format to acquaint children with both the content, format, and language used in connection with these types of tests. We also wish to sound a note of caution. It is considered unethical (and sometimes illegal) to obtain the actual tests to be administered and practice taking these tests.

Teachers who have used an annual test-wiseness minicourse have found good success, have been able to help their students prepare and succeed on mandated tests, and have reduced test-related anxiety levels. Thus, offering minicourses in test-wiseness acted as a safety net for teachers as they made transitions in assessment practices.

Portfolios: Movies Not Snapshots

Imagine for a moment your ugliest photograph. Maybe you had braces at the time. Maybe you had just returned from a 3-day camping trip: Your hair was a mess, you hadn't bathed or changed clothes for several days, and to make matters worse, you hadn't slept very well. Now imagine that this photograph would be placed into an album that would be used by a principal to draw inferences about your appearance, personality, mental abilities, and future potential as a teacher. How well do you think such an album would represent you?

Portfolio assessment is a collection of evidence that demonstrates students' strengths.

Clearly, no one can honestly believe that one or even several standardized or criterion-referenced test scores—like single photos—can capture the sum total of one's life and learning. And yet, schools and governmental agencies insist on relying on one or even two test scores per year to represent the totality of a child's progress and growth in reading during a year of school. If this is an insufficient means of documenting reading progress and achievement, and it is, then what is the alternative? We, along with others, suggest **portfolio assessment** (Jongsma, 1989; Valencia, 1990; Valencia & Pearson, 1987).

In Chapter 13, we describe in greater detail the reasons for portfolio assessment and how portfolios can be developed.

Rather than relying solely on the snapshot variety of assessment associated with standardized and criterion-referenced tests, teachers ought to gather documentation of students' reading progress similar to a moving picture. This motion picture-like assessment of developing readers' abilities captures their ability to successfully complete a variety of reading tasks, to read and enjoy a wide assortment of texts, and to achieve in a broad array of situational contexts. When teachers build a portfolio, or collection of evidence, they demonstrate their students' strengths and best efforts rather than constructing files documenting students' weaknesses and failed efforts. For these reasons, portfolio assessment has great intuitive appeal. But perhaps the greatest appeal for portfolio assessment relates to the balance between instruction, practice, and assessment. Only a fixed amount of time is available for instruction, practice, and assessment of reading progress. Traditional programs of assessment have generally placed a greater emphasis on assessment, which meant detracting from time available for reading instruction and practice. Because portfolio assessment evidence for reading development is taken from authentic reading tasks, texts, and contexts, it does not detract from the time available for engaging in authentic reading activities. Alternatives in assessment are mentioned at this point because a major aspect of making transitions involves teachers in learning to cope with the continued political demands for traditional assessment while simultaneously developing the understanding and skill to document children's progress in reading through the use of balanced literacy assessment tools and portfolios. (See Chapter 13 for more detailed descriptions of Portfolio Assessment.)

Transitions in Diversity: Monoculture to Multiculture

By the year 2000, a near majority of the school-aged population will include persons of color, diverse cultural traditions, and a mixture of languages.

One increasingly obvious fact is that the racial, cultural, and linguistic purity of yesterday's classrooms is disappearing. By the year 2000, a near majority of the school-aged population will include persons of color, diverse cultural traditions, and a mixture of languages. Gone are the days of the American melting pot, welcome in the days of the "tossed salad," when each part of the culture makes a unique contribution to the American experience (Ramirez & Ramirez, 1994). Because of changing demographics in this nation, teachers who have experienced a monocultural background are recognizing a need to understand and honor the contribution of other cultures to history, literature, and art of the United States (Taxel, 1993). There is one danger in recommending that teachers adopt a multicultural view. Typically, one assumes that making the transition from monocultural experiences to an understanding of multiculturalism is only incumbent on those people who belong to the cultural, linguistic, and racial majority. This is not true. Because most individuals come from monocultural backgrounds, multiculturalism argues for all peoples to move outside their own cultures to experience, understand, and appreciate the traditions, perspectives, and contributions of others.

Minimizing differences between home cultures and the school culture is a major step in helping children succeed in school.

Minimizing differences between home cultures and the school culture is a major step in helping children succeed in school. Maxim (1989) suggests that one way to enhance children's self-esteem is to respect their culture. It is suggested that one way in which teachers and children can open the world of multiculture is to read multicultural children's literature (Rasinski & Padak, 1990). From these experiences, monocultural teachers come to better understand children, their cultures, and communities, as well as broaden their view of the world. Harris asserts, children of color—African, Asian, Hispanic, and Native American—need multicultural literature. The inclusion of multicultural literature in schooling can affirm and empower these children and their culture. . . . Children can derive pleasure and pride from hearing and reading . . . and seeing illustrations of characters who look as if they stepped out of their homes and communities. (quoted in Martinez & Nash, 1990, p. 599)

We list below several ideas that may be helpful to classroom teachers as they learn about and use multicultural children's literature to make the transition from mono- to multicultural classrooms.

Describe five criteria for selecting multicultural literature for transitional classrooms.

- Encourage children to respond to a story or illustration by sharing connections they make to their own cultures, languages, and traditions.
- Note and list the motifs that appear in different cultural tales.
- Discuss how the literature refers to other cultural groups' contributions to history, art, music, science, and so on.
- Discuss the social traditions of various cultures.
- Produce story-related cultural artifacts.
- Engage in culturally relevant games, traditions, and events through simulations.
- Invite parents of children from various cultures to share cultural traditions including art, music, and dance.
- Purchase multicultural literature for the classroom library.
- Post lists of available multicultural books in the school or community library.
- Note behaviors and beliefs that are universals among all people as well as those that are specific to a cultural, racial, or linguistic group.
- List ways in which certain cultures are stereotyped, and discuss how these stereotypic labels are inappropriate.

As teachers, we must take a proactive role in understanding and effectively dealing with the increasing diversity in classrooms. One way to accomplish this is to apprise ourselves of the available literature and share these books with each other and children. A short list of multicultural literature for teachers has been compiled by Livingston and Birrell (1994) and is shown in Figure 5.6.

From Caterpillar to Butterfly: The Metamorphoses of Three Transitional Reading Teachers

To help in-service and preservice teachers understand different ways teachers make transitions, we present three vignettes of reading teachers and reading classrooms at various stages in transition. The first vignette describes a novice second-grade teacher, Ms. Scott, who begins with a traditional classroom design, whole-group skill lessons, basal reader instruction, and ability grouping. In this early transitions classroom, we describe how Ms. Scott has begun to integrate practices and beliefs into her classroom, which are moving her cautiously but surely along the **reading instructional continuum** (shown in Chapter 2) toward more balanced reading instruction. In a second vignette, we describe a fifth-grade teacher, Mr. Helms, who has been making transitions for several years and who has been able to successfully integrate some balanced literacy practices and beliefs into his classroom while preserving his basal reader program safety net. We call this developmental stage *intermediate transitions*. In the final vignette, we describe a first-grade teacher, Ms.

Figure 5.6

Multicultural literature
by theme

Artistic Contributions
Rising Voices (Hirschfelder/Singer; poetry and essays of young Native Americans)
Neighborhood Odes (Soto: Hispanic urban poems)
A Coconut Kind of Day (Joseph; poetry reflecting celebration of tribal and family traditions)
Alvin Ailey Dancers (Pinkney; history of the famous modern dance company)
The Piñata Maker (Ancona; the life of a Mexican village piñata maker told in Spanish and English)
The Real McCoy (Towle; story of African-American inventor of the automatic oil cup for trains)

Civil Rights Movement
Road to Memphis (Taylor; family saga of racial discrimination in the 1940s)
Plutie and Little John (Edwards; inequality and discrimination in the lives of two young men from different racial backgrounds)
Year of Impossible Goodbyes (Choi; a family's ordeal during the Japanese occupation of Korea)
Devil's Arithmetic (Yolen; family chronicle of the holocaust)

History and Life-styles
Abenaki to Zuni (Wolfson; illustrated guide to 28 tribes, their customs, habitats, and other useful information)
A to Zen (Wells; alphabet picture book of Japanese events and ideas)
A Migrant Family (Brimner; a photographic essay on the lives of migrant workers)
Mennorahs, Mezuzahs, and Other Jewish Symbols (Chaikin; symbols, ideas, and traditions of Judaism)

Contemporary Children's Stories
Love, David (Case; challenges of mixed-race girl growing up in South Africa)
Hello, Amigos (Brown; photographic essay of Hispanic family life)
Pueblo Boy: Growing Up in Two Worlds (Keegan; adapting to tribal tradition and current American life)
Day of Ahmed's Secret (Heide/Gilliland; young boy in contemporary Cairo finds success in a hard life)

Self-Esteem
Amazing Grace (Hoffman, a young girl finds self-confidence and grows with courage)
312 Valentines (Cohen; gifted and talented black student seeks his own identity)
Year of the Boar and Jackie Robinson (Bao Lord; girl emigrating from China learns to love American life)
Local News (Soto; short stories about Hispanic life in an urban neighborhood)

Folktales, Fairytales, and Legends
Raven (McDermott; Pacific Northwest tale of how Raven found the sun)
The Rainbow People (Yep; Chinese folktales that sustained immigrant laborers)
Lon Po Po (Young; Chinese Little Red Riding Hood)
The Singing Snake (Czernecki/Rhodes; Australian folktale about the invention of the didgeridoo)
The Uninvited Guest and Other Jewish Holiday Tales (Jaffe; A collection of stories providing insight into Jewish life and culture)

Compiled by Livingston and Birrell (1994).

Valdez, who has been successful in approximating practices and beliefs most closely aligned with balanced reading and language instruction, or what we call *advanced transitions.* But as Regie Routman wrote in her book *Transitions,* "[This teacher doesn't] always use thematic units, [this teacher] occasionally [teaches] from part to whole; [this teacher is] still struggling hard to integrate more areas of the curriculum with the language arts—an ideal that is very difficult to attain. [This teacher anticipates] that this struggle will go on for years" (1988, p. 26). We begin with an example of early transitions by looking into a second-grade classroom with Ms. Scott.

Early Transitions: Ms. Scott, Second Grade

Ms. Scott had just graduated from college with her endorsement in elementary education. She interviewed with several school districts before deciding to accept the offer of Riverside School District to teach second grade. She walked into her empty classroom to look it over for size, furniture, arrangement, and instructional resources. Before arriving in her classroom, she stopped to talk with two teacher colleagues in second grade. They told her that they used a basal reader in the school and that she would be expected to use the basal also. They implied that the principal insisted on following the basal scope and sequence carefully so as to teach children the necessary skills associated with skilled reading. Ms. Scott's colleagues informed her that they used ability grouping by classroom to meet the needs of the children and that she would have the opportunity to work with the poor readers this year. This would allow her to use her recent training in reading.

After her brief visit with her new colleagues and to her new classroom, Ms. Scott began to think about how she could satisfy the expectations her school colleagues held for her professional behavior, classroom, and instruction; and how she could use what she had learned in her college training about a balanced approach to reading instruction. In fact, she was a bit perplexed by the conflict between her college-based beliefs and the school-based practices she was expected to use. But determined to be successful, Ms. Scott began planning her classroom to conform to the espoused expectations of her school, principal, parents, and colleagues while simultaneously planning a gradual introduction of the balanced literacy practices in which she had come to believe.

First, Ms. Scott sat down and designed how she would arrange her classroom. She realized that she would be teaching an entire class of low readers. Because of this assignment, she thought she might be able to support these children through selected whole-group reading activities. Thus, she designed a large area of the classroom with desks for whole-group instruction. She also knew that not all low readers have the same instructional needs or interests. So, she planned a small-group instructional area for guided or targeted reading lessons with children of differing needs and abilities within her low-ability classroom. She also felt children should have a time and place to choose their own books to read silently or with a partner, so she set up a reading nook in her classroom. The result of her thinking and planning is seen in her arrangement of the classroom (Figure 5.7).

Figure 5.7

Early transitions, second-grade classroom arrangement

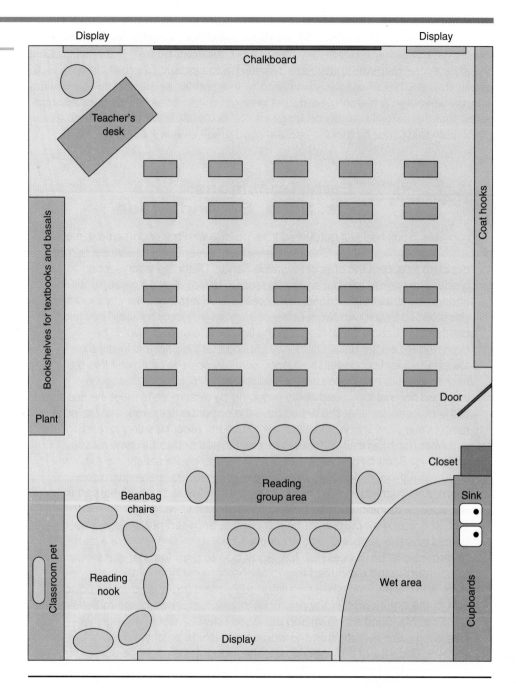

Next, Ms. Scott began creating her daily routine for reading instruction. In Figure 5.8, Ms. Scott portrays her daily routine within the framework of a weekly reading plan. While Ms. Scott's beliefs were aimed toward whole language-like instruction, her classroom and lesson plans reflected a more traditional approach. She began her reading instructional time with 20 minutes of sustained silent reading (SSR). She chose this activity because she believed children need to have time to read

books of their own choosing. During SSR time, she also read a book—
knowing that children learn to read from example. Next, Ms. Scott taught
a 20-minute whole-group skill lesson as outlined in her basal teacher's
manual. Although Ms. Scott did not quite know whether she believed skill
instruction was necessary, her district and colleagues expected documentation for having taught these skills. Because Ms. Scott was unsure
of the curriculum and the reading process as a novice teacher, she chose
to remain on the safe side of the issue, at least for a while. On Monday,
she taught a decoding lesson on several consonant blends. On Tuesday,
she had children practice these skills on the assigned workbook pages.
On Wednesday, she taught a skill lesson on using the glossary; on Thursday, children participated in a skill lesson on sequencing; and on Friday,
children practiced these skills by completing assigned worksheets.

Following the daily skill lesson or practice, Ms. Scott worked directly
with her whole class for 20 minutes on a basal reading story. The whole

	M	T	W	Th	F
8:40 A.M.	Silent sustained reading	→			
9:00 A.M.	Reading skill lesson sn, sm, sc, consonant blends	Practice reading skill lesson Workbook pp. 3–7	Practice reading skill lesson Looking up glossary words	Reading skill lesson Getting the sequence	Practice reading skill lesson Workbook pp. 8–9
9:20 A.M.	Basal Story Introduction: *Ugly Duckling*	Read-aloud together	Read again together in pairs	Skill instruction with story / Word recognition	Extensions into other curriculum areas: Play
9:40 A.M.	Daily language sharing time: LOGOS	Poem: *How Not to Have to Dry Dishes*	Song: *I've Been Working on the Railroad*	Book: *Jumanji*	Sniglets and pundles
10:00 A.M.	Language arts skill lesson: Using commas in a series	Skill practice: identifying nouns in sentences	Creative writing: Story starter: *Mouse on the Mayflower*	Free writing: Personal topic choice	Creative writing
10:30 A.M.	Handwriting	practice →			
10:40 A.M.	Spelling pretest: Unit 6	Spelling practice: Writing list words in sentences	Spelling practice: 6-step spelling strategy with partner	Spelling practice: Spelling bee	Spelling post-test:
10:50 A.M.	Daily journal writing	→			

Figure 5.8

Early transitions, second-grade weekly reading plan

class read the same basal story together because Ms. Scott believed whole-class work supported struggling and shy students. She conducted whole-class discussions and background-building experiences with the group on Monday in preparation for reading as well as preteaching the vocabulary words listed in the teacher's manual. During subsequent days, Ms. Scott provided various repeated and supported reading activities for the whole group or with small groups pertaining to the story *The Ugly Duckling,* which they had read on Monday. She also taught a skills lesson on Thursday in relation to some of the words found in the *Ugly Duckling* story. On Friday, she extended the story through drama, music, art, or other language arts activities.

On a daily basis from 9:40 to 10:00 A.M., Ms. Scott read aloud to children, had them share books they could read, sang songs with words projected on the overhead screen, and played word and language games. She did this to help children enjoy the playful nature of language and to broaden their literary horizons.

For 30 minutes, during the language arts instructional block, Ms. Scott followed her teacher's manual carefully. However, 1 day a week, on Thursday, she allowed children a topic choice in writing, remembering this as important from her college training. Daily handwriting and spelling practice were also a regular part of Ms. Scott's day. As a final daily activity, Ms. Scott encouraged her students to make an entry in their personal journals. She encouraged children to share what they had written in their journals with her and the class if they so chose.

Ms. Scott provides an excellent example of a teacher's practices lagging well behind her belief system temporarily until time and conditions change to allow further transitions. As Ms. Scott becomes more sure of herself, her students, the curriculum, and the reading process, she will begin to make additional transitions toward the next stage of instructional implementation, intermediate transitions. In summary, Ms. Scott has carefully and selectively initiated changes in her classroom as well as her lesson plans to arouse little attention from others at the present. This allows her the opportunity to make changes without undue resistance or pressure. This is typical of those in the early stages of transitions.

Intermediate Transitions: Mr. Helms, Fifth Grade

Mr. Helms has been teaching fifth grade for 3 years at Brookville Elementary school. During his 1st year of teaching, Mr. Helms attended a state reading conference, where he had first learned about balanced reading instruction. During the next year, Mr. Helms read about balanced reading instruction and learned late in the year about a group of teachers meeting in a support group to discuss balanced reading instruction. During his 3rd year of teaching, Mr. Helms began attending support group meetings regularly and felt that he was making substantial changes in his reading beliefs and as a consequence his classroom practices. Also during Mr. Helms's 3rd year of teaching, the school district adopted a new basal reading series. He noted that the new basal series contained much better literature than previous editions and that the reading skill lessons were more often related to the stories. Although Mr. Helms had been exploring, implementing, and changing over the 3 years, he still felt that the basal was a necessary part of his classroom reading program. In fact, he recognized that the basal provided a structure and safety net for his teaching he still needed. It was also clear that the district supported the use of the new basal and expected teachers to use it. Although Mr. Helms needed and felt somewhat obligated to make use of the basal in his classroom, his attendance at the local whole language support group was helping him realize he could teach reading without a total reliance on the basal. As he began planning his 4th year of teaching, he decided to move ahead with further changes.

First, Mr. Helms decided to implement a writing process approach during the language arts instructional block. This meant that he needed to provide time, demonstrations, and locations in the classroom for activities such as drafting, brainstorming, peer conferencing, editing, and publishing. Consequently, he placed peer conference and individual reading conference sign-up boards around the room. Tables were located around the room for conferencing and editing. He arranged desks into pods or groups to facilitate greater interaction among students during drafting. An area for publishing and binding was also added in one corner of the room.

As Mr. Helms contemplated changes in the reading instructional block, he wanted to continue an opportunity for children to read books of their own choosing each day. Thus, a reading nook and SSR remained from years previous. This year, however, he decided to use the basal differently. He had heard his friends talk about not "basalizing literature" in his support group. One teacher who still used the basal raised a question that captured Mr. Helms's attention. She asked, "Do you think I could try to 'literaturize the basal' instead?" Mr. Helms decided to try to treat the new basal as if it were a collection or anthology of literature books all boxed up together. He would also treat the basal stories with the respect due good literature rather than just as so much more text to practice reading. Also, this year he would use visiting basal reader response groups with the basal reader. So, he established an area in the room for visiting basal reader response group meetings. Because he still felt a need to explicitly teach many of the reading skills in the basal reader scope and sequence, he left the desks close to the front of the room for whole-group skill instruction. The results of Mr. Helms's planning can be found in Figure 5.9.

The next step for Mr. Helms was to plan his daily routine in such a way as to incorporate the changes he intended to make this year. His modified daily routine, shown in the format of a weekly reading lesson plan, can be found in Figure 5.10.

Like Ms. Scott, Mr. Helms began his daily routine with 20 minutes of SSR. At 8:30 A.M., he planned to hold an input sharing time. Mr. Helms realized that just as computer operators say, "garbage in, garbage out; nothing in, nothing out," so it goes with children and language. In Mr.

Figure 5.9

Intermediate transitions, fifth-grade classroom arrangement

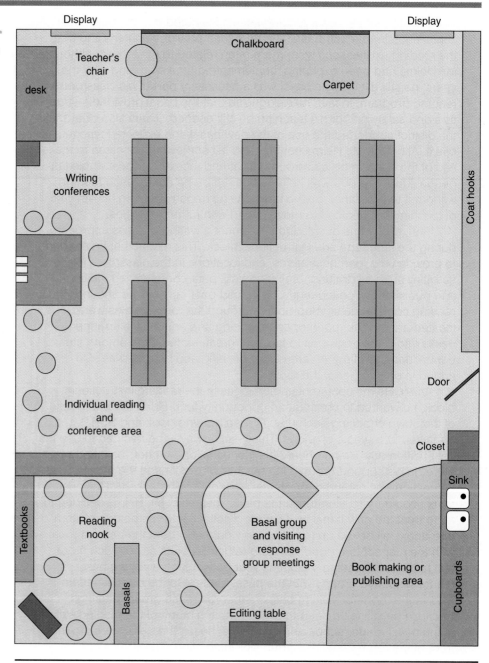

Helms's mind, sharing time was a time for input of reading and writing examples and the literature of the culture. During the week, Mr. Helms shared songs with the words projected onto an overhead screen; read riddles, poetry, and books aloud; and encouraged children to play with language through sharing spoonerisms, changing the initial sounds of two words (i.e., *silly boy* changed to *billy soy*). At 9:10 A.M., Mr. Helms

	M	T	W	Th	F
8:30 A.M.	Silent sustained reading →				
8:50 A.M.	Input sharing time → Singing favorite songs on overheads	Riddles day: Highlights	Spoonerisms fun	Read aloud book: *Ben and Me*	Poetry 1: *A Light in The Attic*
9:10 A.M.	Whole Group — Dividing words into syllables	Skill lessons → The prefix "un"	Understanding figurative language	Locating and noting details	Selecting the main idea
9:30 A.M.	Basal story	Basal visiting response group 1	Basal visiting response group 2	Basal visiting response group 3	Basal visiting response group 4
		Practice: Wkbk 17–19	Practice: Wkbk 20–21	Practice: Wkbk 22	Practice: Wkbk 23–24
	Visiting response groups or skills application and practice				
10:00 A.M.	Writing process (drafting, minilessons, conferencing, editing) Time →				
10:20 A.M.	Spelling minilesson pretest	Spelling practice: 6-step spelling strategy with partner	Handwriting: Upper case cursive "W"	Handwriting: Lower case cursive "z"	Spelling post-test:
10:35 A.M.	Journal writing →				
10:45 A.M.	Closing Sharing time	(Author's chair, read-alouds, performances, etc.) →			

Figure 5.10

Intermediate transitions (upper grades), fifth-grade weekly reading plan

presented a skill lesson from the basal teacher's manual. He tried to use examples in the skill lessons from the children's basal reader stories, library books, and their writing in order to make skill instruction relevant. He taught skill lessons on syllabication, prefixes, figurative language, noting details, and main ideas, to mention just a few.

At 9:30 A.M., children either practiced their skill lesson instruction on assigned worksheets or they attended a *visiting response group* meeting. Having selected a favorite story from the basal (see "Basal Reader Visiting Response Groups" in Chapter 9 for how these groups are formed and their function), children met with Mr. Helms to respond to their basal story. They talked about how they felt about the story. They discussed where they had experienced trouble understanding. They discussed what they liked best or least about the story. They also discussed how they could extend the story into other language arts such as writing, performing, art, music, and so on.

Next, for 20 minutes each day from 10:00 to 10:20 A.M., children in Mr. Helms's room engaged in the writing process, selecting their own topics to write about, drafting, soliciting peer responses, editing, and publishing selected works. For 15 minutes after writing time, Mr. Helms conducted spelling, handwriting, or punctuation lessons. He held a firm conviction that children needed to practice the mechanics of accepted spelling, handwriting, and punctuation regularly, although he knew that some of his peers who used balanced literacy instruction did not agree with the isolated teaching of spelling, handwriting, and writing mechanics. Next, for 10 minutes each day, the children and Mr. Helms wrote in their journals. At 10:45 A.M., they met together as a group for sharing time. They shared their books through reading aloud, book talks, and journal entries, and they performed plays for the whole class or read their own published writings to small groups of interested peers.

Mr. Helms is an excellent example of a teacher who has begun to make substantial changes in the way he believes and practices his beliefs in the classroom. Although his practices continue to lag somewhat behind his beliefs, he is becoming comfortable with taking charge of his beliefs and practices despite opposition by both the school system and some members of his support group. As Mr. Helms became more uncomfortable about differences between his beliefs and classroom practices and those espoused by members of his support group, he continued to make additional transitions. Over time, Mr. Helms will progress toward the most sophisticated stage of balanced reading instruction to attain, advanced transitions.

Advanced Transitions: Ms. Valdez, First Grade

Ms. Valdez was in her 5th year of teaching first grade. When she graduated from college, she was employed in a nearby school district. The university from which she graduated began a state writing project the year after she graduated. As the newest teacher in her building, she was approached by her school principal and asked if she would like to represent their school as a participant in the state writing project. She agreed to participate. The principal informed her she would need to share the information she learned with her colleagues in faculty meetings.

Ms. Valdez attended the meetings of the writing project and learned a great deal about the writing process. That year and in subsequent years, she was very much involved in implementing the writing process with her first graders from the very first day of school. As she worked more with the writing process, she sensed that her beliefs and instructional practices related to writing were in large measure inconsistent with her beliefs about reading and reading instruction. The daily reading routine just didn't feel right. Ms. Valdez began reading and attending classes at her local university to work on an advanced degree. She signed up for the required course work as well as a class in emergent literacy. In this course she was exposed to recent research on how children develop as readers and to a way of thinking about children, language, and learning called *whole language.* This whole language approach fit well with what she had been learning about the writing process. She realized that she needed to put the principles she had once learned in her writing work-shop experience to work in her reading instruction. She began reading voraciously anything she could find about whole language. She studied, talked, and began trying to implement her whole language beliefs in the classroom. In fact, incorporating whole language into her reading instruc-tion became her terminal project report for her advanced degree. As she planned for the coming year, after many years of study, learning, and try-ing, some of the results of her sustained efforts were reflected in her classroom design and daily reading routine.

Ms. Valdez designed her classroom to use various grouping schemes including whole group, small group, and individual work. She provided specific areas in her classroom for whole-group instruction at the front of the room. Tables with chairs, rather than desks, were arranged around a large carpeted area at the front of the room. Because Ms. Valdez felt that singing songs was a fun and functional way to learn to read, she had an electronic keyboard for accompanying songs chil-dren liked to sing. Easels with large sheets of chart paper were used to enlarge song lyrics, poetry, jokes, and riddles, and for taking children's dictation. These easels were located at the front of the room. Another easel was purchased for displaying and reading big books together dur-ing shared reading time.

Areas for signing in and writing messages were located next to the door of the room. A book-making and publishing area was located in the back of the room for publishing children's written products. An area for collaborative writing projects and literature response group meetings was established near the center of the room. On the back wall, sign-up boards for editing, peer conferences, and reading conferences were dis-played. One bulletin board on the back wall was used to post logo or environmental print that children brought from home to school. Two small tables at the back of the room were set aside for holding writing peer conferences and editing sessions.

A reading nook was provided in a back corner of the classroom. It was complete with a rocking chair, a small chair, a bathtub filled with pil-lows, and bean bag chairs. Each day an elderly "reading grandmother" volunteer visited Ms. Valdez's classroom and sat in the rocking chair. She listened to children read to her while they sat next to her in the small chair or on her lap in the rocking chair. Bookshelves surrounded the reading nook. Trade books, big books, child-authored books, personal storage bins, writing binders, and so on were stored in the bookshelves. Next to the reading nook was a librarian area. Here one student was chosen each week to function as a class librarian to check out and keep track of reading materials taken from the classroom reading nook library.

An area of the classroom that was particularly popular was the theme center. Here, children listened to music, made art projects, engaged in science reading and experiments, and played math games—all related to a selected topic or theme. A table with taped sto-ries was also provided for young readers in Ms. Valdez's classroom to allow them to practice old favorite books again and again with support. Next to this area were two chairs for holding individual reading conferences near Ms. Valdez's desk. For 5 years, Ms. Valdez had been gradually implementing her changing beliefs about reading and writing instruction into her classroom. These changes are shown in Figure 5.11.

Ms. Valdez also tried something different this year in relation to her lesson planning. For 2 years she had been using Holdaway's (1984)

Figure 5.11

Advanced transitions, first-grade classroom arrangement

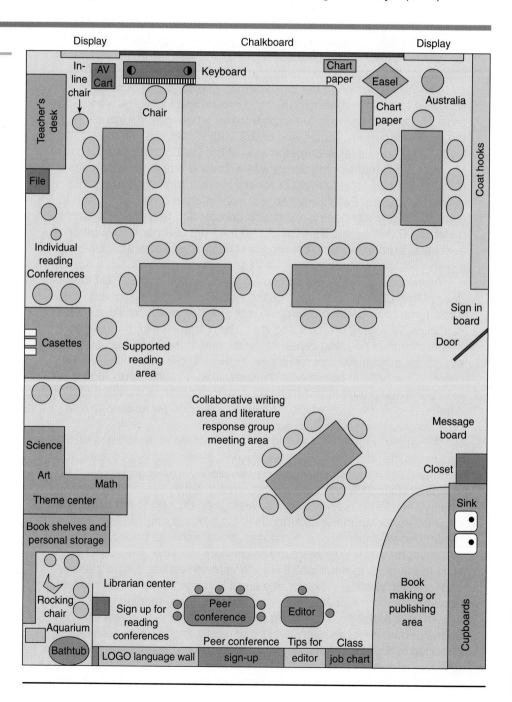

Theme: Bears

	M	T	W	Th	F
8:30 A.M.	**Tune in:** *Going on a Bear Hunt*	Song: *The Bear Went Over the Mountain*	*B–E–A–R*	*Ten Little Bears*	*T–E–D–D–Y* (Bingo Song)
8:45 A.M.	**Old favorites** *The Three Bears*	*The Three Bears*	*Brown Bear, Brown Bear*	*Brown Bear, Brown Bear*	*Hairy Bear*
9:00 A.M.	**Learning about language:** *Teddy Bear Picnic*	Literature webbing	Counting and graphing # of cinnamon bears	Read a book to your teddy bear	Drawing your favorite part of our bear stories
9:15 A.M.	**New story:** *Brown Bear, Brown Bear* (big book)	(small book) *Ira Sleeps Over*	*Hairy Bear* (big book)	*Bear in Mind: A Book of Bear Poems*	(small book) *Ten Bears in My Bed*
9:30 A.M. 10:30 A.M.	Independent activity: Centers rotation 1 = Writing/publishing center: Language experience dictation stories this week 2 = Writing workshop: Minilessons on handwriting, spelling, or authoring favorite bear posters 3 = Read-along (taped books) with small books 4 = Paired reading of songs on charts, word bank cards, big books 5 = Reading work: Read alone, with Grandma Volunteer or with third-grade helpers 6 = Themed centers work: Work on science, art, and music projects about the bear theme 7 = Response group meeting: Children and teacher meet to discuss a big book read during "New Story" time.				

Figure 5.12

Advanced transitions (lower grades K–1), first-grade weekly reading plan

reading routine including "Tune-In," "Old Favorites," "Learning About Language," "New Stories," and "Independent Output Activities." In spite of this routine, she had been struggling long and hard to integrate her reading–writing curriculum with other curricular areas. During the summer months, Ms. Valdez had designed several themed lesson units using Holdaway's (1984) reading routine, wherein she integrated reading and writing with other curricular areas. The first week's lesson plan involved a themed unit focusing on bears. The results of her planning are found in Figure 5.12.

Each day at 8:30 A.M., "Tune-In" time began. During this time, Ms. Valdez shared with children the enlarged text of a new song, poem, or chant on the easel at the front of the classroom. She pointed to the words of the text as she sang or read aloud the text. The children followed along as she pointed. During this week, four songs and a poem about the theme of bears were introduced to the children.

At 8:45 A.M., "Old Favorites," books that had been read on previous occasions, were read again. Assuming that many children had heard the story of the three bears before, Ms. Valdez chose this book as an old favorite to begin the year. Later during the week, after another book had been introduced in the new story part of the routine, *Brown Bear, Brown Bear* (B. Martin, 1983) became the old favorite to be read again.

At 9:00 A.M., Ms. Valdez had selected specific experiences she felt might enhance her students' understanding of the theme or the new story for the day. On Monday, the children took their teddy bears on a picnic. On Tuesday, the children predicted from a literature web the plot of the story *Hairy Bear.* Wednesday, they counted and graphed cinnamon bears. (After the lesson, they ate them!) Thursday, they brought a book from home or borrowed one from the class library to read to their teddy bear. Friday, they drew pictures of their favorite bear of the week.

At 9:15 A.M., Ms. Valdez read aloud, in standard size or in a big book format, a new bear story each day. At 9:30 A.M., independent activity time began. Seven centers or stations were located about the room. Children rotated through three of these centers each day. Each child was assigned to a flexible traveling group. A large multicolored wheel with each group on the face of it was rotated at 15-minute intervals to indicate to the children where to move in the rotation of the seven stations.

Ms. Valdez's classroom design and lesson planning exemplify extraordinary effort sustained over many years. Ms. Valdez has worked hard to attain the degree of integration and organization found in her classroom. In many respects, Ms. Valdez's classroom design and instructional practices closely represent whole language beliefs and practices. Although it has taken years to make the transition to this point, Ms. Valdez has just now reached the stage of instructional implementation we characterize as advanced transitions.

To a large extent, Ms. Valdez has studied children and the reading process for years to succeed in implementing reading instruction at the advanced transitions level. In Chapter 3, we presented vital information for understanding how children develop reading and writing ability. This information should help preservice and inservice teachers understand how they can support children more effectively as they learn to read and write.

Summary

In this chapter, seven dimensions of change involved in transitions were depicted. Eight transitional stances also were described, ranging from "I don't know enough to know where I stand" to advocacy stances. Springboarding from the basal reader is a good place to begin transitions with instructional materials. Thinking of the basal as an anthology of literature, making careful decisions about the use of worksheets, and doing away with asking a line of questions after reading to evaluate comprehension are some transitional steps in using instructional materials. Constructing and ratifying

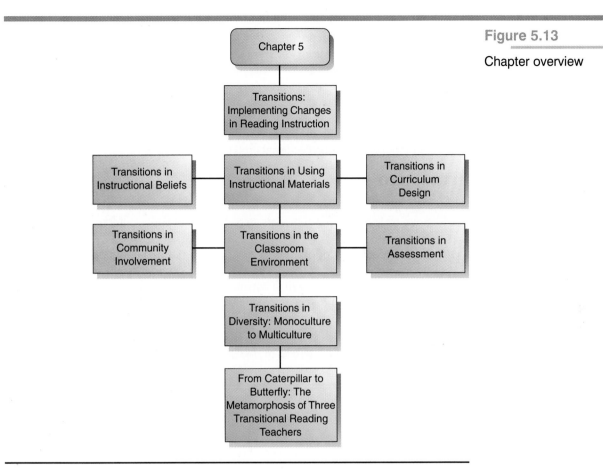

Figure 5.13

Chapter overview

a nonnegotiable list of reading skills in schools is a means to reduce the teaching of unnecessary reading skills in schools. Involving parents, seeking administrative support, and attending colleague support groups provide important assistance for teachers as they make the transition from traditional to balanced reading instruction.

The significance of modeling the classroom learning environment after home-like environments rather than other societal institutions was emphasized. Developing and teaching test-wiseness units and introducing the concept of portfolio assessment are ways for teachers to cope with problems associated with transitions in assessment. Finally, vignettes of three teachers, Ms. Scott, Mr. Helms, and Ms. Valdez, demonstrated various ways and degrees to which teachers make transitions. Figure 5.13 shows an overview of the chapter.

CONCEPT APPLICATIONS

IN THE CLASSROOM

1. Describe the transitions in beliefs stance that best describes you. Tell why.
2. Make a language to literature unit for a favorite set of books written by the same author.

3. Design your own parent involvement program for making changes in reading and language instruction.

4. Make a drawing of your classroom arrangement. Explain your reasons for the arrangements, furnishings, display areas, and so on.

5. Make a week-long lesson plan for your reading–language instruction. Put this lesson plan into a week-long schedule, as shown in this chapter.

6. Describe in an essay which of the three teachers—Ms. Scott, Mr. Helms, or Ms. Valdez—you most identified with and why. Describe a 5-year transitional plan for your own professional growth.

IN THE FIELD

1. After observing reading instruction in a school classroom, make a list of transitions in instructional materials and their uses you would recommend to the teacher.

2. Visit a teacher support group or attend a reading–language conference in your area. Write a brief response about your experience.

3. Make arrangements to visit an inner-city school to visit with the teachers about the types of diversity experienced in these urban settings. Discuss issues of language, culture, socioeconomic status, mobility, achievement, and so on of these schools. Explore with teachers at least three strategies they have found helpful in succeeding with children schooled in these settings.

RECOMMENDED READINGS

Asheim, L., Baker, D. P., & Mathews, V. H. (1983). *Reading and successful living: The family school partnership.* Hamden, CT: Library Professional.

Goodman, Y. M. (1987). *Supporting literacy.* New York: Teachers College Press.

Loughlin, C. E., & Martin, M. D. (1987). *Supporting literacy: Developing effective learning environments.* New York: Teachers College Press.

Newman, J. M. (1990). *Finding our own way.* Portsmouth, NH: Heinemann.

Taylor, D. (1983). *Family literacy.* Exeter, NH: Heinemann.

Taylor, D., & Strickland, D. S. (1986). *Family storybook reading.* Portsmouth, NH: Heinemann.

Tovey, D. R., & Kerber, J. E. (Eds.). (1986). *Roles in literacy learning.* Newark, DE: International Reading Association.

Van Manen, M. (1986). *The tone of teaching.* Ontario, Canada: Scholastic.

Chapter 6

Comprehending Text

Focus Questions

When you are finished studying this chapter, you should be able to answer these questions:

1. What is the difference between *teaching* and *testing* reading comprehension?
2. What are the major differences between strategies and skills?
3. What are the meaning and implications of schema theory and generative learning theory?
4. What are the components of the Gradual Release of Responsibility model of instruction?
5. What are the narrative and expository text-comprehension instructional strategies?
6. What are some types of metacognitive training lessons described in this chapter?
7. What are some strategies suggested for knowledge- and experience-based comprehension instruction?
8. What are the strategies for effective questioning discussed in this chapter?
9. What are the steps involved in reciprocal teaching?
10. What are some strategies for helping limited English proficiency (LEP) or English as second language (ESL) learners in your classrooms comprehend better?

Key Concepts

Teaching Versus Testing
Schema Theory
Slot Filling
Instantiation
Accretion
Tuning
Restructuring
Generative Learning Theory
Story Grammar
Discussion Webs

Cloze
Cohesive Ties
Typographic Features
Prereading Plan (PReP)
Metacognition
Repair Strategies
Think Aloud Lessons
Question–Answer Relationships
(QARs)
Contextual Diagrams

Teaching reading comprehension is the very heart and soul of teaching children to read. Parts of written language such as words and letters exist only to facilitate the crucial process of constructing meaning or comprehending. Although words and letters are easily taught and measured, teachers and children must never lose sight of the purpose for reading—comprehending. In fact, from their first encounters with text and reading instruction, children should expect that books and reading instruction will make sense.

During the late 1960s and throughout the 1970s, reading comprehension was taught in school classrooms by asking questions and by assigning skill sheets as practice for separate reading comprehension skills such as getting the main idea, determining the sequence, following directions, noting details, and cause and effect. During this same period, the process and instruction of reading comprehension enjoyed unparalleled research attention. This interest and attention, spanning nearly a decade of concentrated effort, resulted in identifying several key issues, theories, and instructional solutions that give form and substance to current understandings of how to teach reading comprehension.

During the 1970s and early 1980s, reading comprehension enjoyed unparalleled research attention.

This chapter begins with a discussion of issues that emanated from the comprehension research of the 1970s and 1980s. Next, the important theoretical understandings gained during this same era of research are discussed. This discussion is followed with a presentation of comprehension instructional strategies designed to enhance text-based and reader-based comprehension. The chapter concludes with a description of several strategies. First, a strategy called *reciprocal teaching* is described for those students with special comprehension needs. Second, two strategies, contextual diagrams and active listening, are described for helping those students with diverse cultural and linguistic needs.

Issues in Teaching Reading Comprehension

Teaching Versus Testing

Durkin (1978) observed that less than 1% of total reading or social studies instructional time was devoted to the teaching of reading comprehension.

Note the differences between teaching and testing comprehension.

In 1978, Dolores Durkin reported a study in which she investigated the state of reading comprehension instruction in public school classrooms. After observing a variety of teachers engaged in reading instruction in both reading and social studies classrooms, Durkin concluded that teachers spent very little time actually teaching children how to understand, work out the meaning of, or comprehend text units larger than a single word. In fact, less than 1% of total reading or social studies instructional time was devoted to the teaching of reading comprehension. This finding led to another question: What was happening in the name of reading comprehension instruction in America's classrooms? Durkin's answers to this question were both distressing and insightful. She characterized teachers as "mentioners," "assignment givers," and "questioners." She defined a *mentioner* as a teacher who said "just enough about a topic (e.g., unstated conclusions) to allow for a written assignment to be given related to it" (Durkin, 1981a, p. 516). Attention to new vocabulary words was often brief, even "skimpy" (p. 524). Teacher's manuals were usually consulted for only two purposes: (a) to study the list of new vocabulary words and (b) to ask the comprehension questions following the reading of a selection. Classroom reading comprehension instruction was dominated by ditto sheets that were in reality nothing more than informal tests. Thus, Durkin concluded that teachers apparently did not differentiate the concepts of **teaching** and **testing** reading comprehension.

Durkin's research pointed out the need for understanding the difference between asking children to read and perform comprehension tasks and assisting them in their efforts to comprehend a text. She described comprehension instruction as helping, assisting, defining, demonstrating, modeling, describing, explaining, or otherwise guiding students' efforts to construct meaning from text larger than a single word. From this description, we can see that effective reading comprehension instruction involves teachers and students in an active pursuit of constructing meaning from text. This view of comprehension instruction implies that teachers must become far more proactive in providing comprehension instruction. Teachers should feel an ethical obligation to share the secrets of their successful comprehension with students as well as how to monitor and repair comprehension when it fails to take place. Simply asking students to respond to a worksheet or to a list of comprehension questions does nothing to instruct those who fail to successfully complete these tasks. The conclusion to be drawn from Durkin's research on comprehension instruction is that teachers must vigorously engage in instructional processes that reveal for students the secrets of successful comprehension.

Basals Don't Teach Reading Comprehension

Later, in 1981, Dolores Durkin conducted a second study (1981b), in which she investigated the comprehension instruction found in five nationally published basal reading series. Her conclusions in this study essentially supported her earlier study. She concluded that publishers, like teachers, failed to understand the differences between teaching and testing reading comprehension. Basal teacher's manuals offered little or no help for teachers about *how to teach* children to comprehend text. Instead, reading basals often presented a preponderance of reading comprehension assessment activities mislabeled as instruction rather than testing.

*Basal teacher's manuals offered little or no help for teachers about **how to teach** children to comprehend text.*

Don't Be Afraid to Teach

While Durkin's comprehension studies made a strong case for active teacher involvement in comprehension instruction, other trends in reading and language arts education have had an opposite effect. Lucy Calkins (1986) and P. David Pearson (1989b) describe a trend associated with the process writing and whole-language movements that may undermine the role of the teacher in teaching reading comprehension. In an effort to respect the choice and interests of individual readers and writers in classrooms, some teachers have been led to believe that they should never take an active role in guiding or directing students' learning. Thus, some teachers may have become fearful of "taking ownership" of students' learning or "taking over" for students if they intervene in any way.

Calkins gives examples of teachers who have developed sly ways of avoiding teaching by asking questions or making comments such as, "I wonder if there is another sentence you could use as a lead?" (1986, p. 165). From such practices, students often conclude that teachers know how to help them but would rather conceal their knowledge. Calkins is very clear in her admonition to teachers, "We should not relinquish our identities as teachers in order to give students ownership of their craft" (p. 165).

C. J. Gordon said teachers should take "a proactive rather than an indirect approach" (1985, p. 445) when teaching reading comprehension. P. David Pearson recommends a new role for teachers in the 1990s:

> I would like to propose a new model . . . in which the teacher assumes a more central and active role in providing instruction. . . . They become sharers of secrets,

A trend associated with the process writing and whole-language movements is that some teachers have been led to believe that they should never take an active role in guiding or directing students' learning.

The key for teachers is to assist students toward better comprehension.

coconspirators, coaches, and cheerleaders. . . . They become willing to share the secrets of their own cognitive successes (and failures!) with students. (1985, p. 736)

*The **zone of proximal development** is discussed in Chapter 2.*

Classroom teachers must feel that they have the professional prerogative, even the ethical obligation, to share what they know and have learned with their students. Hence teachers often must walk a tightrope between taking over for students and relinquishing their role as teachers. We believe simply that teachers ought to be teachers; people who recognize that they can assist and help children toward better reading comprehension. Vygotsky's (1962) zone of proximal development certainly indicates the importance of the teacher's role in assisting children in those tasks they cannot yet complete for themselves. However, we believe the teacher should gradually release the responsibility for comprehending to the child. In keeping with this understanding of the proper role of the teacher and the learner, Pearson (1985) recommended a model of instruction called the Gradual Release of Responsibility model of instruction. This instruction model as related to reading comprehension instruction is discussed in more detail later in this chapter.

Teaching Skills Versus Strategies to Improve Reading Comprehension

Teachers need to teach students reading strategies rather than isolated reading skills.

Too often, reading instruction focuses on the bits and pieces of language rather than on the entire process of reading. D. D. Johnson and Pearson (1975) contend that reading has been effectively redefined as its components or skills, rather than as the sum of its components or skills. Those authors criticized the use of skills management systems as "psycholinguistic naivety." They concluded:

We know that language systems—the phonology, grammar and lexicon—are interdependent. In essence, language is indivisible; yet skills management systems would seem to fractionate it and destroy its essential nature. Because of the interdependence of the language systems, there is really no possible sequencing of skills. (D. D. Johnson & Pearson, 1975, p. 758)

Imagine a child who had read aloud the following:

Daddy bought a new saddle. He went out to the corral to catch our *house* named Patch. He put the saddle on Patch's back.

From a skills teacher's perspective, instructional feedback may focus exclusively on the miscue *house* by asking, "Look at that word carefully. Does it look like the word *house?*" This same teacher may focus on yet a smaller part of language by asking, "Does the word house have an *r* sound in it?" Thus, the skills teacher treats the miscue *house* for horse as if the word *horse* stands alone in the text. Instructional feedback was focused on skills for identifying words, not on strategies for gathering and evaluating information.

An alternative approach that can be used to develop comprehension strategies, rather than focusing on skills for word identification, might involve the following instructional feedback for the miscued word *house* for *horse*. "Think about what you just read. What was Daddy doing? If you had a saddle and went to a corral, would you be planning to put that saddle on a house? What would you put the saddle on?"

Understanding the difference between teaching skills and strategies is important. Strategies are generalized schemata or plans for gathering, evaluating, and using text information to construct meaning such as predicting, sampling, confirming, and correcting. Skills tend to focus on parts of language as if they stand alone or are isolated from other parts of language, from a text as a whole, and from meaning such as noting details, getting the main idea, and using context clues. In fact, when properly understood, skills are selected as tools during the use of strategies, as shown in Figure 6.1. Teachers can help children develop and use effective reading strategies in two ways: (a) through demonstrations and (b) by encouraging wide and varied reading opportunities. Teacher demonstrations of strategies should use connected texts and show how one goes about gathering, monitoring, evaluating, and processing text information effectively and efficiently. In addition, reading widely and talking about and responding to text are integral aspects of maintaining a focus on comprehension strategies rather than on isolated skills or bits and pieces of language.

Strategies are generalized schemata or plans for gathering, evaluating, and using text information to construct meaning such as predicting, sampling, conforming, or correcting.

Theories About Comprehending Text

Schema Theory

In the 1970s and 1980s, one theory of the comprehension process called **schema theory** led to substantial progress in unraveling the complex and puzzling processes a reader employs to construct meaning using the ink marks on a printed page. Schema theory explains how people store information in their minds and how previously acquired knowledge is used to inhibit or assist the learning of new knowledge. A *schema* (plural is *schemata*, or anglicized *schemas*) can be thought of as a package of knowledge composed of related concepts *(chairs, birds, ships)*, events *(weddings, birthdays, funerals)*, emotions *(anger, frustration, joy, pleasure)*, and roles *(parent, judge, teacher)* drawn from the reader's life experiences (Rumelhart, 1981).

*A **schema** is a package of knowledge containing related concepts, events, emotions, and roles experienced by the reader.*

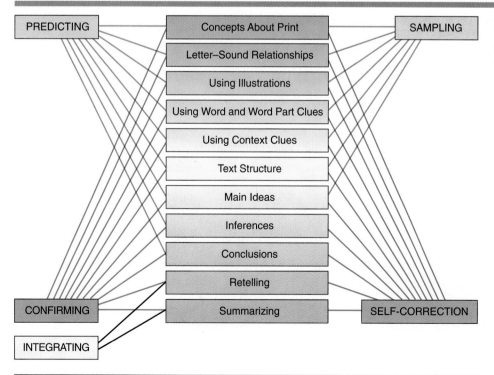

Figure 6.1

Strategies and skills: The relationships

*Each **schema** contains a set of defining attributes or semantic features, such as wings and feathers associated with a bird schema.*

Schemata are composed of defining attributes called *semantic features*. For example, the semantic features associated with a bird schema may include examples of birds such as eagles, robins, blue jays, and so on; characteristics of birds such as wings, feathers, beaks; and categories into which a particular bird belongs such as birds of prey. Hence, schemata are organized in memory by associations, categories, examples, and meaning rather than by temporal, or time, order, or some other means of organization. Because of this organization, schemata are accessed in memory much like looking up a topic in an encyclopedia. For example, when looking up the topic of *birds* in an encyclopedia, one usually encounters information about birds including attributes, categories, and examples of birds. Pearson, Hansen, and Gordon (1979) found that children who already knew a great deal about the topic of spiders remembered more from their reading than did children who knew little or nothing about spiders. One inescapable fact drawn from this research on schema theory is the simple yet profound conclusion: Previous knowledge helps readers acquire new knowledge.

Notice how researchers have represented schemas.

Researchers have visually re-represented schemata as networks of associated meanings (A. M. Collins & Quillian, 1969; Lindsay & Norman, 1977). Each schema is connected to another related schema, forming an individual's vast interconnected network of composite knowledge and experiences. The size and content of each schema are influenced by past opportunities to learn. Thus, younger children generally possess fewer, less well-developed schemata than mature adults. For example, consider Figure 6.2, which represents a first grader's schema about birds; then in Figure 6.3, examine the bird schema of a high school student just completing a biology class.

Younger readers generally possess less well-developed schemata than older readers.

*Adding new information to an incomplete schema is called **slot filling**.*

Because individuals store personal meanings in memory, teachers may not assume that all children in a classroom possess identical or similar associations for a given concept or event. Although readers' schemata often share common features as are shown in Figures 6.2 and 6.3, the first grader's schema is less well elaborated than the high school student's. Thus, schemata are never complete; they simply provide a framework for storing new information. It is clear that the first grader's bird schema has great potential for growth, as evidenced by the many potential slots of information not yet filled in by experience compared with the high school student's bird schema. A concept fundamental to schema theory is the idea of adding to a schema through a process called **slot filling**. In conclusion, a schema can be thought of as an abstract, flexible, and growing cognitive framework with slots that can be filled in by the personal and vicarious experiences of a reader.

Understanding the Process of Comprehending Text

The act of comprehending a text is extremely complex. Thus, some simplification of this process is necessary when explaining reading comprehension. Based on schema theory, we describe the comprehension of text in four stages:

Figure 6.2

First grader's bird schema network

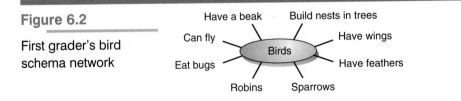

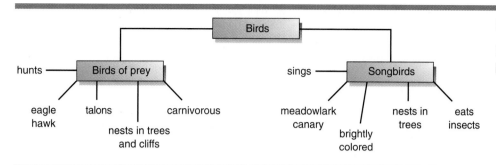

Figure 6.3

High school student's
bird schema network

1. Searching for an appropriate schema by attending to minimal meaning clues taken from the situational context and the print
2. Applying the selected schema to guide the interpretation of print
3. Selecting and evaluating information to be retained or discarded by using the selected schema
4. Composing a new text that is integrated into the existing schema or used to create a new schema. This process is illustrated in Figure 6.4.

***Comprehending** can be thought of as a four-step process: searching, applying, selecting and evaluating, and composing.*

Essentially, the process, as illustrated in Figure 6.4, shows that when readers begin reading, they bring with them their collective set of schemata to help them construct meaning from the print. Expectations concerning the nature and content of print are influenced by two factors: (a) the function of the reading materials, such as labels, road signs, bus schedules, books, or newspapers, and (b) the situational context in which the act of reading takes place, such as a supermarket, a car, a bus terminal, a book store, or an easy chair at home. These contextual factors—function and situation—help readers efficiently select an initial or tentative schema for interpreting the print.

For example, imagine going to a local laundromat to wash your own clothes for the first time. As a novice, you will probably look around the laundromat for information to help you accomplish the task. On a nearby wall, you read the following sign posted above the washing machines:

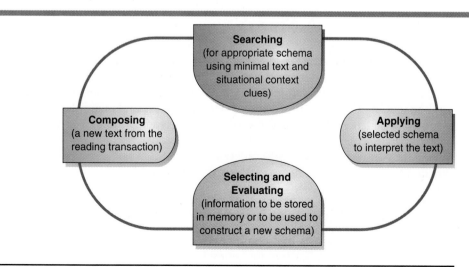

Figure 6.4

A schema-based explanation of processing text information

The procedure is actually quite simple. First you arrange the items into different groups. Of course one pile may be sufficient depending on how much there is to do. If you have to go somewhere else, due to lack of facilities that is the next step, otherwise you are pretty well set. It is important not to overdo things. That is it is better to do too few things at once than too many. In the short run this may not seem important but complications can easily arise. A mistake can be expensive as well. At first, the whole procedure will seem complicated. Soon, however, it will become just another facet of life. It is difficult to foresee any end to the necessity for this task in the immediate future, but then, one never can tell. After the procedure is complete one arranges the materials into different groups again. Then they can be put into their appropriate places. Eventually they will be used once more and the whole cycle will then have to be repeated. However, that is part of life. (J. D. Bransford & Franks, 1971, p. 719)

If you had not read these directions on a sign in the situational context of the laundromat, you may have had greater difficulty limiting your search for the correct schema to the act of washing clothes. Thus, the function of a sign and the situational context of reading (the laundromat) helped you limit your search to the most likely schema—washing clothes.

Once the most likely schema is selected, it is applied by the reader to interpret the text. In the laundromat scenario, the reader interprets the word *procedure* in the text to mean the act of, or steps involved in, washing clothes. If the reader had selected a postmaster schema by mistake, then the word *procedure* may have been interpreted as the act of, or steps in, sorting letters into post office boxes. Thus, the selected schema is used to guide the interpretation of each word in the text as well as the collective meaning of all the words in the text.

Schemata also provide a structure or framework for assimilating new information from text. The empty slots in a novice's laundry schema are filled in from the connections made between existing knowledge about laundry and the information conveyed in the sign. Thus, the empty slots in readers' schemata help them select and evaluate information. By referencing new information against existing schemata, readers can decide which information is important to add to the laundry schema for future use.

Schemata guide the construction of each word meaning as well as the meaning of the entire text.

During this ongoing process, readers compose a new text, which represents the unique information retained from reading the laundry sign. In this sense, comprehending a text is very much like composing a text (Tierney & Pearson, 1983). The resulting text version of the sign as represented in the head of readers is not the same as the version posted on the wall. Instead, the text on the wall has been transformed into a new and personal re-representation of the meaning by using existing knowledge and the relevant information from the text. Thus, one change resulting from the reading transaction is that readers are changed. They now possess greater knowledge about doing the laundry than before reading the sign on the wall. The sign on the wall has changed, in a sense, because it has been transformed in the mind of the reader to re-represent personal meaning construction. Hence, the act of comprehending a text can be thought of in terms of a dialogue between reader and author that takes place in a specific situational context. The product of the reading transaction is best represented by the fact that the function of the text, the reader, and the situational context have combined, resulting in a new and personal text that replicates the original and intended meaning of the author's laundry text posted on the wall.

Explaining Comprehension Difficulties

Rumelhart (1984) suggests that comprehension difficulties can be traced to four schema-related problems. Each of these problems is discussed with examples to help you gain an understanding by experiencing first-hand the difficulties students may encounter in comprehending.

- *Difficulty 1:*   Students may not have the necessary schema to understand a specific topic. Without a schema for a particular event or concept, they simply cannot construct meaning for the text.

For example, without the necessary schema, readers cannot appropriately interpret individual word meanings in the following passage, and they cannot construct a clear meaning for the overall text.

> a—Machine-baste interfacing to WRONG side of one collar section ½" from raw edges. Trim interfacing close to stitching. b—Clip dress neck edge to stay stitching. With RIGHT sides together, pin collar to dress, matching centers back and small dots. Baste. Stitch. Trim seam; clip curve. Press seam open. (Gibson & Levin, 1975, p. 7)

Although those individuals who possess a sewing schema can readily interpret this passage, those without a sewing schema experience great difficulty in making any sense out of selected words *(baste, interfacing)* in the text or the text as a whole.

- *Difficulty 2:*   Readers may have well-developed schemata for a topic, but authors may fail to provide enough information or clues for readers to locate or select a given schema.

In some cases, readers know a great deal about the topic to be read. Some authors, however, may fail to provide enough clues that connect with the slots found in a reader's schema for a specific topic. For example, read the following text to see if you can locate your schema on this well-known topic.

> Our hero bravely defied all scornful laughter that tried to prevent his scheme. "Your eyes deceive," he had said, "An egg not a table correctly typifies this planet." Now three sturdy sisters sought proof, forging along sometimes through calm vastness. (J. C. Bransford & Johnson, 1972)

The authors, by failing to include relevant clues in the text such as explorer, ships, and America, make selecting the *Christopher Columbus* schema extremely difficult. Why? Because these key clues call up specific slots *(associations)* found in the Columbus schema. For the Columbus schema to be located and selected for interpreting this text, enough of these key clues must be found or **instantiated** by the text.

- *Difficulty 3:*   Readers may prematurely select a schema for interpreting a text, only to discover later that the text information does not instantiate the slots in the selected schema.

When this happens, readers may shift from using one schema to using another to interpret a text. You may recall the following example from Chapter 2. Read each sentence, stop, and picture what you see in your mind.

> John was on his way to school.

> He was terribly worried about the math lesson.

Now read the next sentence, and notice what happens as you process the new information.

> He thought he might not be able to control the class again today.

Difficulty 1: Students may not have the necessary schema to understand a specific topic.

Difficulty 2: Readers may have well-developed schemata for a topic, but authors may fail to provide enough information or clues for readers to locate or select a given schema.

Difficulty 3: Readers may prematurely select a schema for interpreting a text only to discover later that the text information does not fit the slots in the selected schema.

Did you notice a change in the schema you accessed to interpret the text? Did your schema shift from that of a young boy on his way to school worried about his math class and lesson to that of a concerned teacher? Now read the final sentence.

It was not a normal part of a janitor's duties. (Sanford & Garrod, 1981, p. 114)

Did you experience another change in selecting an appropriate schema? Not only do schemata help readers interpret what they read, but text information influences the schemata selected.

Difficulty 4: The cultural experiences a reader possesses may affect her stance or perspective when selecting a schema to interpret a text. This leads to an "understanding" of the text but a misunderstanding of the author.

- *Difficulty 4:*   The cultural experiences a reader possesses may affect her stance or perspective when selecting a schema to interpret a text. This leads to an "understanding" of the text but a misunderstanding of the author.

To illustrate this point, Lipson (1983) conducted a study and found that Catholic and Jewish children comprehended texts better that were compatible with their own religious beliefs than those that conflicted with their religious schemata. Alvermann, Smith, and Readence (1985) found that schemata that conflicted with text information were strong enough to override text information. Reutzel and Hollingsworth (1991a) found that attitudes toward a particular schema were strong enough to influence comprehension of incompatible texts about a fictitious country called *Titubia*. S. J. Read and Rosson (1982) found that attitudes influenced recall of compatible and incompatible texts read about nuclear power. Thus, information represented in schemata can act to facilitate or inhibit assimilating new information from text. To illustrate this difficulty, R. C. Anderson, Reynolds, Schallert, and Goetz (1977) asked people to read the following paragraph:

> Tony slowly got up from the mat, planning his escape. He hesitated a moment and thought. Things were not going well. What bothered him most was being held, especially since the charge against him had been weak. He considered his present situation. The lock that held him was strong but he thought he could break it. He knew, however, that his timing would have to be perfect. Tony was aware that it was because of his early roughness that he had been penalized so severely—much too severely from his point of view. The situation was becoming frustrating; the pressure had been grinding on him for too long. He was being ridden unmercifully. Tony was getting angry now. He felt he was ready to make his move. He knew that his success or failure would depend on what he did in the next few seconds. (R. C. Anderson et al., 1977, p. 372)

Think of a time when your schemata inhibited or facilitated the process of assimilating new information from text. What were you aware of at that moment?

Most people in the study thought the passage described a convict planning his escape. There is, however, another possible interpretation. When physical education majors read the foregoing passage, they thought the passage was about wrestling. Thus, the cultural background of the readers influenced their perspectives by leading them to select entirely different schemata for interpreting the text.

Instructional Implications of Schema Theory

Although schema theory has provided researchers with powerful explanations about how readers comprehend text, these discoveries can only benefit children when teachers clearly understand the instructional implications that arise from schema theory. Rumelhart (1980) discusses three different types of learning that are possible in a schema-based learning system: accretion, tuning, and restructuring.

***Accretion** involves adding new information to an existing schema.*

Accretion refers to learning new information that is added to existing information in a schema. Thus, *accretion* means that several of the potential slots in any given schema become filled, or instantiated. For the bird schema, perhaps children learn that the bones in a bird's body are hollow. This information is then added to the bird schema.

Tuning involves major modification of an existing schema to fit new information. A schema may be tuned by making major changes that allow the schema to become useful in interpreting a larger class or concepts or events. This is called *concept generalization.* For example, the bird schema is changed to include the idea that birds are not the only creatures whose young are hatched from eggs. Another schema change in connection with the concept of tuning relates to altering the schema structure to fit conflicting information. For example, not all birds have the ability to fly; penguins are one example.

Restructuring relates to the idea of creating new schemata from old. For example, the bird schema may be used to create a schema for pterodactyl—a flying dinosaur. These three learning modes suggest several implications for the teacher of reading.

When preparing students to read a text, the teacher must understand the critical role that schemata play in the comprehension process. Students may need the teacher's assistance to help them learn effectively from text. Teachers may provide this assistance in one of five ways. First, teachers will want to assess the background knowledge of their students to provide relevant and meaningful learning experiences. Second, the teacher may help students activate or select the appropriate schema for interpreting a text. Activation and selection of schemata may be accomplished in a variety of ways, discussed later in this chapter. Third, if teachers find that some students need to create a new schema for an unfamiliar concept, they should build the necessary background before asking students to read. Fourth, if teachers find that some students need to tune or modify their schemata to include other unfamiliar or incompatible concepts, they may provide examples and discussion to help them make the necessary changes. Finally, if teachers discover that students possess a fairly complete understanding of a concept or event, then reading may be assigned with relatively brief background-building discussions or lessons. One caution should be sounded at this point. Such a determination must emanate from *assessment* of prior knowledge—not from a teacher's *assumption!*

Generative Learning Theory

Generative learning theory adds a noteworthy dimension to understanding schema theory and proposes significant implications for effective comprehension instruction, so we discuss it briefly here.

Generative learning theory (Doctorow, Wittrock, & Marks, 1978; Wittrock, 1974) grew out of the work of early cognitive researchers. This model of learning suggests that for reading comprehension to occur readers must actively construct relationships between the information in the text and their background knowledge. The generative model of learning advances the idea that teachers can enhance reading comprehension by providing learning experiences that cause readers to actively make connections between their background knowledge and text information. Comprehension strategies such as summarizing, illustrating, writing headings, giving the main ideas of text, and retellings are just a few of the many strategies developed to generatively teach reading comprehension.

In the remainder of this chapter, we discuss practical applications of schema and generative learning theories as well as a model for providing effective and proactive reading comprehension instruction. The strategies selected for presentation integrate schema and generative learning theories into successful classroom practices that attend to the importance of background knowledge and to the active, generative involvement of students in making personal connections between text and their background knowledge.

Tuning involves major modifications or changes to existing schemata to fit new understanding.

Restructuring is the process by which new schemata are constructed from existing schemata.

Students may need assistance to help them locate and use their schemata to comprehend text. For example, sometimes a picture can be very helpful.

Generative learning theory suggests that readers need to actively construct relationships between the information in the text and their background knowledge.

A Model for Effective Comprehension Instruction

Gradual Release of Responsibility Instruction Model

*The **gradual release of responsibility model** depicts the idea that responsibility for comprehension tasks should be shifted gradually over time from the teacher to the student.*

Growing out of Durkin's (1978) research findings showing that reading comprehension instruction was nearly nonexistent in the nation's schools, Pearson and Gallagher (1983) designed a model for providing effective comprehension instruction. These authors believe that the completion of any comprehension task requires some varying proportion of responsibility from teachers and students. In Figure 6.5, the diagonal line from the upper left-hand corner extending downward toward the lower right-hand corner represents the varying degrees of responsibility teachers and children share in accomplishing a comprehension task.

The upper left-hand corner in Figure 6.5 shows teachers carrying the major share of the responsibility for task completion, while the lower right-hand shows students carrying the major share of the responsibility. The model depicts the idea that responsibility for task completion should be shifted gradually over time from the teacher to the student. In this way, teachers transfer responsibility to the students, who then become capable and independent learners. In practice, the gradual release of responsibility is accomplished during the *guided practice* phase of comprehension lessons under the teacher's supervision. Guided practice continues until the transfer of responsibility from teacher to student is complete and success is ensured.

The concepts associated with this model of comprehension instruction may be applied as a general framework to any of the comprehension strategy lessons presented in the remainder of this chapter. It is important at this point to recall again

Figure 6.5

The gradual release of responsibility model of instruction

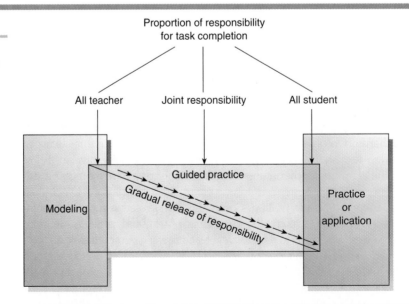

From "The Instruction of Reading Comprehension" by P. D. Pearson and M. C. Gallagher, 1983, *Contemporary Educational Psychology, 8*(3), pp. 317–344. Copyright 1983 by Academic Press. Reprinted by permission.

Vygotsky's (1962) zone of proximal development, which reminds us that children need to be helped to do those things they cannot yet do independently. By releasing the responsibility for task completion gradually to children, the Gradual Release of Responsibility model of instruction provides a useful framework for working into and out of the zone of proximal development.

Text-Based Comprehension Instruction: Focus on Narrative Structure

Narrative Structure: Story Grammars

Perhaps one of the most important aspects of teaching reading comprehension is developing a schema for narrative text or stories. A story schema, or a *sense of story structure*, can be described by using the elements of one of several published story grammars. By definition, a *grammar* describes principles or rules that govern the order of language. Thus, a **story grammar** describes the order of language found in a story. Regardless of several slight differences among story grammar descriptions, researchers generally agree on the following elements for describing a story grammar: setting, problem, goal, events, and resolution.

Developing a sense of how stories are formed helps readers predict with greater facility, store information more efficiently, and recall story elements with increased accuracy and completeness. In light of these findings, several researchers have described instructional procedures for developing readers' story structure awareness and knowledge. C. J. Gordon and Braun (1983) recommend several guidelines for teaching story schema. We have adapted these recommendations as follows:

*For more on the concept of **story grammars**, consult Chapter 3 on developing a sense of story.*

1. Instruction in story schema should use well-formed stories such as *Jack and the Beanstalk* (D. W. Johnson, 1976). A visual organizer can be used to guide the introduction of the concept of story schema (see Figure 6.29). For the first story used in story schema instruction, read the story aloud, stop at key points in the story, and discuss the information needed to fill in the diagram. For stories read after introducing the concept of story schema, use the visual organizer to introduce and elicit predictions about the story before reading. During and after reading, the visual organizer such as a story grammar map (shown later in this chapter) can be used to guide a discussion.
2. Set the purposes for reading by asking questions related to the structure of the story. Questioning structured to follow the story's structure will focus students' attention on major story elements.
3. After questioning and discussing story structure, specific questions about the story content can be asked.
4. For continued instruction, gradually introduce less well-formed stories so that students will learn that not all stories are "ideal" in organization.
5. Extend this instruction by encouraging children to ask their own questions using story structure and to apply this understanding in writing their own stories.

Although instruction of story parts and story structure, as described by C. J. Gordon and Braun (1983), have been researched and found to be reasonably effective, the most effective route for helping children understand story structure is finding ways to encourage them to read great numbers of stories. In the following sections, we suggest two alternative approaches that have been shown to improve comprehension of narrative text.

Story Mapping

Story schema can be enhanced by teaching students the major structural elements of stories.

Story maps re-represent stories in a visual diagram to highlight specific story elements such as title, setting, plot, and the relationships among those constituent elements in a story such as simple sequencing, comparisons, and cause-and-effect chains. According to Reutzel (1985b, 1986c), story maps help teachers accomplish two major comprehension goals. First, by creating story maps, teachers become involved in thinking about the structure of stories and how story elements are related to one another. This degree of teacher involvement presumably leads to increased planning and better organization of comprehension instruction because of the teacher effort involved in creating a story map. The second goal accomplished by using story mapping is that students are led to understand the important parts of stories as well as how these parts relate to one another.

To design a story map, Reutzel (1985b) lists the following steps:

1. Read the story. Then, construct in sequence a summary list of the main ideas, major events, characters, and so on that make up the plot of the story.
2. Place the title or topic of the story in the center of the story map.
3. Draw enough ties projecting out symmetrically from the center of the map to accommodate the major elements of the story's plot and attach the elements from the summary list to these ties.
4. Draw enough ties projecting out symmetrically from each major element of the plot to accommodate the important details associated with these major plot elements and attach this information to the map from the summary list.

Story maps help teachers and students think about the important elements of stories and visualize the story structure.

After creating the story map, children are introduced to the story by viewing a copy of the story map on an overhead projector or the chalkboard. Questions such as "What do you think the story we will read today is about?" are asked. Children focus their attention on the story map to guide their answers and predictions. Further discussion can be facilitated by asking about details represented in the story map such as "Who do you think the characters are in the story? Can we tell anything about this character from the information in the story map?"

In a lesson focusing on a story entitled *Haunted American History,* Reutzel (1985b) discussed the story map shown in Figure 6.6 with his students as described. Following the initial discussion, Reutzel asked the children if the story could be true and discussed their predictions and supporting reasons. He asked students to read the story to see if their predictions based on the story map were accurate. During reading, children referenced the unfolding story against the information contained in the story map. In this way, the story map acted as a metacognitive aid to help students determine whether or not they were comprehending the elements and sequence of the story events as well as the relationship among these events. After reading, students were asked to write a summary of the story with the story map withdrawn, or they were asked to make their own recall and summary story map.

Story maps can be adapted to focus on important elements of the story plot such as showing logical relationships like cause and effect and making comparisons among characters, as shown in Figures 6.7 and 6.8.

A variation of story mapping that is particularly useful as a prediction strategy for improving reading comprehension is the cloze story map (Reutzel, 1986a, 1986b). To design a cloze story map (like that in Figure 6.9), a story map is first developed. Next, a deletion pattern is chosen. Reutzel (1986a) suggests proceeding around a story map in clockwise motion and deleting every fifth concept or event found in the map and replacing it with an empty circle, which marks a place for prediction. Cloze

Figure 6.6

Story map: Main idea—sequential detail

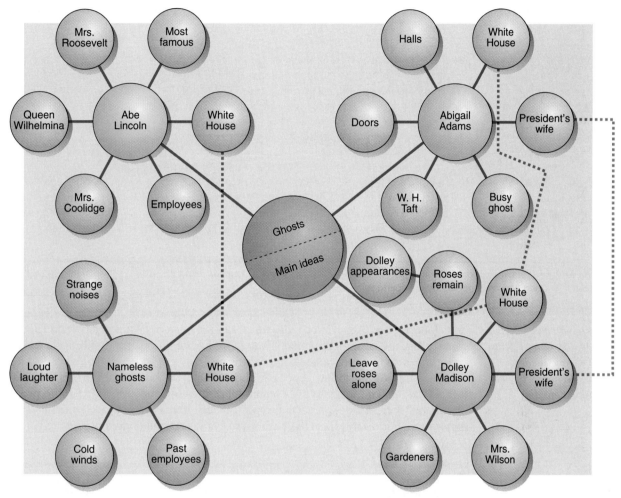

From "Story Maps Improve Comprehension" by D. R. Reutzel, 1985, *The Reading Teacher, 38*(4), pp. 400–411. Copyright 1985 by International Reading Association. Reprinted by permission.

story maps have been shown to result in increased comprehension of stories over discussions or adjunct questions inserted into the text (Reutzel, 1986b).

In summary, story maps can be used before, during, and after reading a story to visually represent the major elements of the story plot and the relationships among those elements. By using story maps, teachers plan and implement more purposeful, focused reading lessons, which lead to increased recall and comprehension.

Story maps can be used before, during, and after reading to improve comprehension by helping children visualize the organization of a story.

Story Frames

Fowler (1982) and Nichols (1980) recommend using story frames and paragraph frames to develop comprehension among elementary and secondary students. Cudd

Figure 6.7

Alternative story map: Compare–contrast

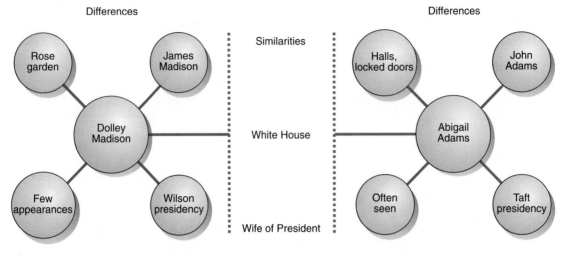

From "Story Maps Improve Comprehension" by D. R. Reutzel, 1985, *The Reading Teacher, 38*(4), pp. 400–411. Copyright 1985 by International Reading Association. Reprinted by permission.

Story frames can be used with a variety of ages, text structures, and reading strategies to improve reading comprehension.

and Roberts (1987) presented story frames as a means of helping first-grade children develop a sense of story structure. Thus, story frames can be used effectively with all ages of readers to improve text comprehension.

Because not all stories, especially those found in early basal primers, are well-formed stories (i.e., they do not contain all of the elements of a story in the proper order), teachers can design several types of story frames to improve students' comprehension. For most stories, the basic story frame is useful (Figure 6.10).

Figure 6.8

Alternative story map:
Cause–effect chain

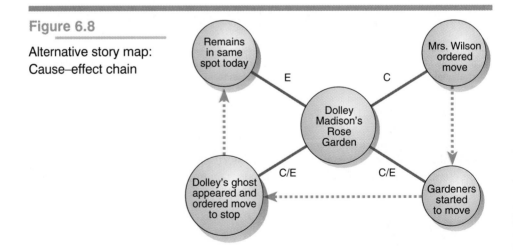

From "Story Maps Improve Comprehension" by D. R. Reutzel, 1985, *The Reading Teacher, 38*(4), pp. 400–411. Copyright 1985 by International Reading Association. Reprinted by permission.

Figure 6.9

Sample deletion pattern for a cloze story map

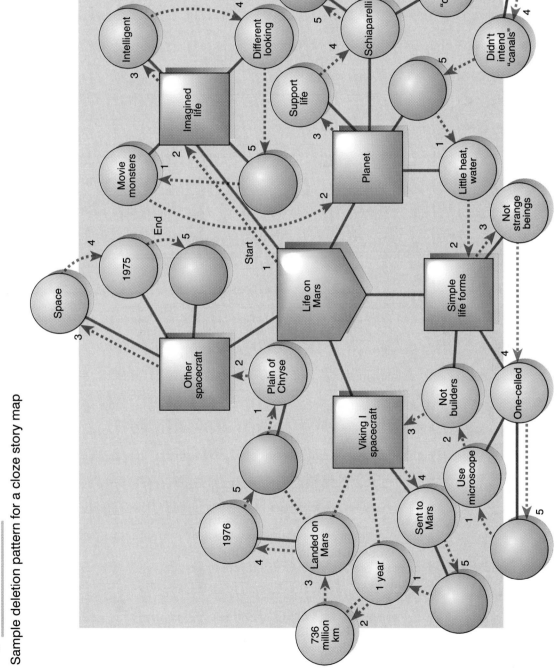

From "Clozing in on Comprehension: The Cloze Story Map" by D. R. Reutzel, 1986, *The Reading Teacher*, 39(6), pp. 524–529. Copyright 1986 by International Reading Association. Reprinted by permission.

Figure 6.10

Basic story frame

Title _The Best Birthday_

In this story the problem starts when _Maria gets sick and she can't have a birthday party_

After that, _her friends want to make her feel better._

Next, _they go get a clown and ask him to help._

Then, _the clown goes to Maria's house_

The problem is finally solved when _the clown makes Maria laugh_

The story ends _when Maria says this is the best Birthday ever._

Figure 1 from "Using story frames to develop reading comprehension in a 1st grade classroom" by Evelyn T. Cudd and Leslie L. Roberts, *The Reading Teacher,* October 1987, p. 75. Reprinted with permission of Evelyn T. Cudd and the International Reading Association.

Other types of story frames can be designed to facilitate comprehension of specific stories, short stories, or stories that contain no logical sequence of events such as those often found in early basal preprimers and primers. Other story frames may be designed to focus on the main idea or plot of the story or on the comparison and analysis of characters. Figures 6.11 through 6.14 illustrate different story frames that do not follow all of the elements of story structure in the proper order.

We have also found that story frames, especially the basic story frame, can be used to encourage children to make predictions about a story after having introduced a story by reading the title, looking at the illustrations, and a brief discussion. By displaying the story frame on large chart paper, predictions can be recorded for the group. Individual copies of the story frame can be distributed, and students can write their own predictions in the story frame before reading. We suggest that children write these predictions in pencil so that they can be changed during or after reading the story. Used in this way, story frames help children focus their thinking on important questions and information to be understood from reading a story.

After reading, we list the major story elements, such as setting, initiating events, and attempts, at the board. The predictions recorded on the group story frame displayed on the chart paper are discussed. Next, we cut parts of the story frame chart apart and scramble them up. Individual students or small groups are given one of the pieces of the story frame chart. They discuss which part of the story schema they have in their hands.

By pointing to the card at the board such as *setting,* we ask children to raise their hands if they think they have this part of the story. We progress through the entire story structure until all of the parts of the story frame have been classified under one of the story structure headings at the board. A side benefit we have noticed from using story frames as a prediction and review discussion guide is that predictions and review discussions are sequenced in the typical order of story elements. This process seems to focus attention on and facilitate recall of major story parts. In this indirect way, we have been able to successfully alert children's attention to the structure of stories and thereby improve their comprehension.

Cudd and Roberts (1987) have also found story frames helpful in focusing children's attention on specific text elements. In Figure 6.15, a story frame is used to focus attention on key sequencing word clues embedded in the text.

Story frames can be adapted to many levels and elements found in narrative text. Benefits associated with using story frames include students' asking themselves and their peers questions based on their story structure knowledge. Students are also able to use their knowledge of story structure to help them predict, sample, and process narrative text more productively, resulting in increased recall and enjoyment of stories. Students seem to develop a sense for stories as whole and meaningful units of text to be enjoyed.

Story frames also help students develop a sense of story structure and story order.

Perhaps the greatest benefit associated with using story frames is that students begin to read more like writers. They pay attention to structure, sequence, and sense in reading and expect text to be well formed and sensible. Further, their writing is improved because they begin to write stories that are more considerate of their readers. So, in this sense, students begin to write more like readers.

Schema Stories

Watson and Crowley (1988) suggest a strategy lesson for improving comprehension called *schema stories.* In this lesson, children use what they know about sentence and story structure to reconstruct a story. The key to this lesson is to select text that

Figure 6.11

Basic frame with no sequence of events

Title __The new pet__

The problem in this story is ___Chen wanted a___

puppy

This was a problem because __his apartment was too__

small for a dog

The problem was finally solved when __his mother got__

him a kitten

In the end, ___Chen played with the kitten___

Figure 2 from "Using story frames to develop reading comprehension in a 1st grade classroom" Evelyn T. Cudd and Leslie L. Roberts, *The Reading Teacher,* October 1987, p. 76. Reprinted with permission of Evelyn T. Cudd and the International Reading Association.

Figure 6.12

Story-specific basic frame

Title _The sad mule_

In this story a _mule_ had a problem. His problem was _he was too old to work_

This was a problem for him because _the farmer was going to sell him_

Then one day a _hen_ had a good idea. She _told the farmer's children to ride on the mule's back_

This solved the mule's problem because _the children had fun and they wanted to keep the mule._

In the end, _the farmer said yes and they were happy._

Figure 3 from "Using story frames to develop reading comprehension in a 1st grade classroom" Evelyn T. Cudd and Leslie L. Roberts, *The Reading Teacher,* October 1987, p. 77. Reprinted with permission of Evelyn T. Cudd and the International Reading Association.

contains highly predictable structures such as "once upon a time" and "they lived happily ever after." The schema story strategy lesson can also be used with expository text such as science and social studies textbooks.

Schema stories are used to teach children to predict and confirm story predictions.

After selecting the text, prepare the lesson by physically cutting the story or text into sections, each of which is long enough to contain at least one main idea. Usually, one or two paragraphs will be sufficient in length to accomplish this purpose. To begin

Figure 6.13

Short summary frame

Title _Two cats_

A country cat came to the _city_ to see _his brother_. But he didn't like _the cars_, and he didn't like _the noise_. Then the city cat went to _the country_. The city cat liked _the soft grass_, and he liked _the old barn_, but he didn't like _the big dogs_. He ran back to _the city_ and stayed there.

Figure 4 from "Using story frames to develop reading comprehension in a 1st grade classroom" Evelyn T. Cudd and Leslie L. Roberts, *The Reading Teacher,* October 1987, p. 77. Reprinted with permission of Evelyn T. Cudd and the International Reading Association.

Figure 6.14

Main episode frame

Title _Red Tail Learns a Lesson_

The problem in this story begins because _a greedy squirrel doesn't want to share his acorns_

The other animals warn Red Tail that _someday he might need their help_

After this, _a big storm comes and knocks Red Tail's house down_

Then, all of the acorns _are gone_ because _the tree fell in the river_

Finally, _the other animals share with Red Tail_

Red Tail's problem is solved when he learns _that it is better to share_

In the end _Red Tail and his friends sit down and eat_

Figure 6 from "Using story frames to develop reading comprehension in a 1st grade classroom" Evelyn T. Cudd and Leslie L. Roberts, *The Reading Teacher,* October 1987, p. 79. Reprinted with permission of Evelyn T. Cudd and the International Reading Association.

the lesson, each section of text is distributed to a small group of students (five to eight students). A student is selected in each group to read the text aloud in her group. The teacher invites the group that thinks it has the beginning of the story or text to come forward. The group must state why it believes it has the requested part of the story, and consensus must be reached by the class before proceeding on to the next segment of text. If agreement cannot be reached, a group decision is made by a majority vote, and the dissenting opinion(s) is noted by the teacher. This procedure continues as described until all of the segments of the text have been placed into order.

Schema story lessons make excellent small-group or individual comprehension lessons that can be placed into a center or station devoted to comprehension strategies. All of the segments of a text can be placed into an envelope and filed in the center. Small groups of children or individuals can come to the center and select an envelope and work individually or collectively on reconstructing the story. A key for self-checking can be included to reduce the amount of teacher supervision.

As children work through a schema story strategy lesson, they talk about how language works, the way in which authors construct texts, and how meaning is used to make sense of the scrambled elements of a text or story. In this way, children learn

Figure 6.15

Story frame with key
sequence words

Title _Mike's House_

A little boy made a _play house_ out of a box.

First, he _made windows_ on the sides.

Next, he _made a door_ on the front.

Then, he _put a rug_ on the floor.

Finally, he _put a sign_ on the door.

The sign said _Mike's House_.

Figure 5 from "Using story frames to develop reading comprehension in a 1st grade classroom" Evelyn T. Cudd and Leslie L. Roberts, *The Reading Teacher,* October 1987, p. 78. Reprinted with permission of Evelyn T. Cudd and the International Reading Association.

about the structure of language and text as well as the importance of attending to meaning as they read an unfamiliar text or story.

Discussion Webs

Notice five steps for using discussion webs.

Discussion plays an important part in guiding students' comprehension and interpretation of reading selections (Alvermann, Dillon, & O'Brien, 1987). Children are encouraged during discussions to examine more than one point of view as well as to refine their own comprehension of a text. **Discussion webs** are based on an adaptation of the cooperative teaming approach by McTighe and Lyman (1988) known as "Think–Pair–Share." The aim of using discussion webs is to encourage children to adopt a listening attitude, to think individually and critically about ideas, and to involve typically less verbal children in the ongoing discussion of a reading selection.

Alvermann (1991) describes a five-step process for using discussion webs:

1. Begin by preparing students to read a selection by activating their background for the selection, introducing unfamiliar vocabulary terms and concepts, and setting a purpose for reading. An example may be based on the story *Tales of a Fourth Grade Nothing* (Blume, 1972), as shown in Figure 6.16.
2. After reading the selection, students are introduced to the discussion web. Students are placed in pairs and asked to discuss the pros and cons of the question in the center of the web, "Was Fudge really a bad kid?" Children take turns jotting down reasons for the yes and no continuum of the web.
3. Once children have had sufficient time to discuss the question in pairs and jot their ideas down on the web, one pair of students is placed with another pair of students. This group of four students discusses and shares their thinking around the central question in the discussion web. Children are told to keep an open mind and to listen carefully during this part of the sharing. They are also reminded that it is appropriate to disagree with others in appropriate

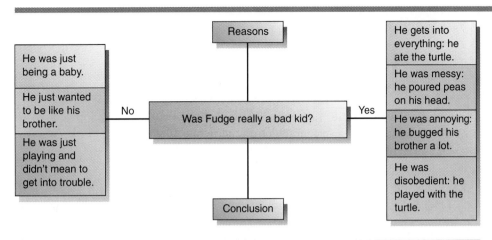

Figure 6.16

Discussion web based on *Tales of a Fourth Grade Nothing* (Blume, 1972)

ways. The children work as a group toward a concluding statement that can be placed in the web.

4. When each group of four has reached a conclusion, a spokesperson is selected to represent the conclusion during the general group discussion. Spokespersons are encouraged to represent dissenting points of view as well as the group's majority conclusion.

5. As a follow-up, children are asked to complete their own discussion webs by filling in their own ideas as well as those of the groups with whom they participated. These individual responses in the discussion webs should be prominently displayed in the classroom when completed.

Discussion webs help teachers lead students to deeper understandings of characters, story outcomes, how two sides of an issue may be considered, and using critical thinking strategies to make reasoned judgments.

Text-Based Comprehension Instruction: Focus on Expository Structure

Expository Structures

In expository text, authors use several predominant patterns for structuring the presentation of information. According to Armbruster and Anderson (1981) and Meyer (1979), the patterns most textbook authors use are time order (putting information into a temporal sequence); cause and effect (showing how something occurs because of another event); problem and solution (presenting a problem along with a solution to the problem); comparison (examining similarities and differences among concepts and events); and simple listing (registering in list form a group of facts, concepts, and events). Research has shown that readers who use an author's organizational pattern to structure their memory for reading recall more than those who do not (Bartlett, 1978; Meyer, Brandt, & Bluth, 1980). Poor readers are less likely to use an author's organization of text to facilitate recall than are good readers. For students to compre-

Expository text patterns include time order, cause and effect, problem and solution, comparison, and simple listing.

hend expository text with ease and facility, teachers must help them understand and use the organizational patterns found in expository text.

Pattern Guides

Olson and Longnion (1982) recommend several steps for using pattern guides to provide students practice in identifying the structure of expository texts. We have modified these recommendations as follows:

*Notice reasons why teachers would use **pattern guides**.*

1. Identify a few important concepts in the text to be taught.
2. Determine the expository pattern used by the author.
3. Make a chart or a diagram for the students to complete that represents the text organization and the important concepts to be learned.
4. Model for students how to use the guide with the first paragraph or two of the text on an overhead projector.
5. Make sure the printed directions provided on the pattern guides are clear and understandable.
6. After modeling, distribute the pattern guides for independent use.

Examples of pattern guides for science and social studies texts are shown in Figures 6.17 through 6.22. Note that each example also uses a different type of text organization. Students' comprehension of expository text can be enhanced by helping them recognize and use the text organizational patterns found in their content area textbooks. Practice in identifying text organization as well as important information related to text organization results in better recall of information among both good and poor readers.

Figure 6.17

Pattern guide for "Kinetic Theory"

Cause–Effect

The kinetic theory explains the effects of heat and pressure on matter. Several ramifications of the theory are discussed in this chapter. Be alert to causal relationships as you read.

1. Gas exerts pressure on its container because
   A. *p. 261, par. 1* _____
   B. *p. 261, par. 1* _____
2. What causes pressure to be exerted in each arm of the manometer?
   A. *pp. 261–262* _____
   B. _____
3. The effects of colliding molecules that have unequal kinetic energy are *p. 266*
   _____
4. What causes the particles of a liquid to assume the shape of the container?
   p. 269, par. 1 _____
   _____

Pattern guide created from *Chemistry, A Modern Course* (Smoot & Price, 1975).

Figure 6.18

Pattern guide for "Organizing the Forces of Labor"

> ***Cause–Effect***
>
> In this section, look for cause-effect relationships in the situations mentioned below. Add the cause or effect in the proper column.
>
> | | |
> |---|---|
> | 1. | 1. Saving money was difficult or impossible for unskilled labor (p. 400). |
> | 2. Owners felt it was necessary to keep labor costs as low as possible (p. 400). | 2. |
> | 3. | 3. Only the boldest workers dared to defy management and join labor organizations (p. 400). |
> | 4. By 1800s, wages of unskilled workers exceeded skilled artisans (p. 401). | 4. |
> | 5. | 5. The workingmen's parties supported Jackson after 1828 (pp. 402–403). |

Pattern guide created from *The Adventure of the American People* (Craft & Krout, 1970). From "Pattern Guides: A Workable Alternative for Content Teachers" by M. W. Olson and B. Longnion, 1982, *Journal of Reading, 25*(8), pp. 736–741. Copyright by the International Reading Association. Reprinted by permission.

Concept–Text–Application

Wong and Au (1985) developed concept–text–application (CTA) as a structure for lessons to improve comprehension of expository text. The CTA lesson organization is based on several assumptions of effective comprehension instruction. First, quality comprehension instruction should create or build on students' existing background knowledge. Second, expository text requires special instructional attention because it

Figure 6.19

Pattern guide for "The United States Divided"

> ***Contrast and Compare***
>
> Using pages 264–265, you will contrast and compare the repercussions in the South and the North to the Supreme Court's decision in the Dred Scott Case.
>
> | ***The South*** | ***The North*** |
> |---|---|
> | 1. (Hint: newspapers) | 1. |
> | 2. (Hint: Democratic Party) | 2. |
> | 3. | 3. |
> | 4. | 4. |

Pattern guide created from *The Adventure of the American People* (Craft & Krout, 1970). From "Pattern Guides: A Workable Alternative for Content Teachers" by M. W. Olson and B. Longnion, 1982, *Journal of Reading, 25*(8), pp. 736–741. Copyright by the International Reading Association. Reprinted by permission.

Figure 6.20

Pattern guide for "Sleep, Fatigue, and Rest"

> ***Listing***
>
> This section of your textbook lists many causes of fatigue (pp. 96–97). Some of the causes are physical and some are mental. Fill in the causes under the appropriate heading.
>
> I.   Physical causes of fatigue
>   A.   short burst of intense effort
>   B.   rapid growth
>   C.   lack of important food
>   D.   p. 96, par. 3
>   E.
>   F.
>   G.
> II.   Mental causes of fatigue
>   A.   p. 96, par. 1
>   B.

Pattern guide created from *Investigating Your Health* (Miller, Rosenberg, & Stackowski, 1971). From "Pattern Guides: A Workable Alternative for Content Teachers" by M. W. Olson and B. Longnion, 1982, *Journal of Reading, 25*(8), pp. 736–741. Copyright by the International Reading Association. Reprinted by permission.

CTA is appropriately used with readers in second grade on up and is conceptually similar to the processes discussed in Chapter 12 for analyzing content area reading materials and planning instruction for content area reading lessons.

contains heavy concept and vocabulary loads, placing unusual demands on the reader. Third, expository text structure is less familiar for young readers than narrative text, prompting comprehension difficulties (Alvermann & Boothby, 1982).

A CTA lesson is composed of four stages: (a) planning; (b) concept assessment and development; (c) guided reading of the text; and (d) application, during which the teacher helps students draw relationships between the text information and their own background experiences. To clarify the CTA lesson structure, following is a lesson based on a book entitled, *The Life of the Butterfly* (Drew, 1989).

Figure 6.21

Pattern guide for "Religious Change in Western Europe"

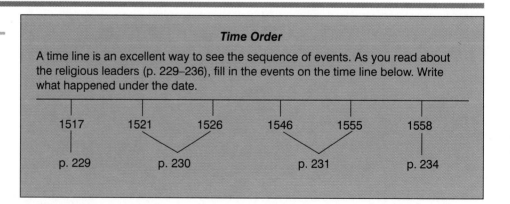

Pattern guide created from *People and Our World: A Study of World History* (Kownslar, 1977).

Figure 6.22

Pattern guide for "A Time of Conflict"

Time Order

Religious factions caused by the Reformation triggered a number of religious wars in the 1500s and 1600s. Rewrite the events below in the order they occurred. Place the date of each event beside it (pp. 237–248).

1.   The son of King Charles I was called back to England for the return of the monarchy.

2.   The Thirty Years War involved almost all major European countries.

3.   Most people in the northern half of the Spanish Netherlands became Protestant.

4.   In England, conflict between the king and Parliament led to Civil War.

5.   Sweden revolted against the Catholic king of Denmark and declared its independence.

6.   The Act of Succession was agreed to by William and Mary.

1.

2.

3.

4.

5.

6.

Pattern guide created from *People and Our World: A Study of World History* (Kownslar, 1977). From "Pattern Guides: A Workable Alternative for Content Teachers" by M. W. Olson and B. Longnion, 1982, *Journal of Reading, 25*(8), pp. 736–741. Copyright by the International Reading Association. Reprinted by permission.

Planning

To plan a CTA lesson, the teacher follows three steps. She reads the book to determine the major concepts and main ideas in the text for which concepts will be developed in the concept assessment and development part of the lesson. Second, she rereads the text to look for major points to bring up during the discussion, formulate attention-focusing questions, and note important vocabulary concepts that may need to be pretaught. When using CTA, many teachers find it useful to represent their planning by creating a visual organizer like that found in Figure 6.23. The final step in planning involves the teacher in thinking about ways the information learned from reading the text about the life of a butterfly can be shared, used, and extended into other related curriculum areas.

A CTA lesson is composed of four stages: (a) planning, (b) concept assessment and development, (c) guided reading of the text, and (d) application.

Concept Assessment and Development

Wong and Au (1985) tell teachers using CTA that capturing children's interest at the outset of the lesson is critical to success. This can be accomplished by asking questions that invite students to engage in dialogue about their own background experiences in interesting and imaginative ways. For example, while teaching the CTA using the book *The Life of the Butterfly* (Drew, 1989), the teacher began the lesson with the following introduction and question.

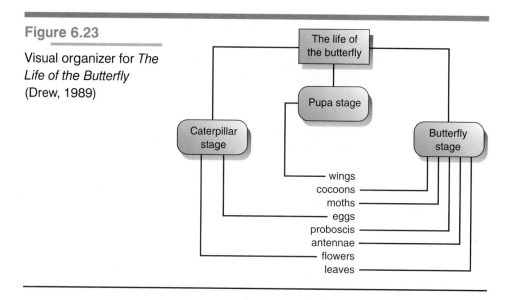

Figure 6.23

Visual organizer for *The Life of the Butterfly* (Drew, 1989)

Teacher: (while holding the book up for the children to see) In this book, we will learn about how a caterpillar becomes a butterfly. Can you tell me what you know about caterpillars and butterflies?

After this initial discussion, subsequent questions could focus attention on critical or possibly unfamiliar concepts and vocabulary related to butterflies. For example, children may need to learn the vocabulary terms *spiracles, pupa, antennae,* and *proboscis.*

Text

At this point in the lesson, the teacher moves into guided reading of predetermined parts of the text. Through questioning and discussion, teachers and children negotiate a purpose for reading each segment of the book. The lesson proceeds by alternating purpose setting, silent reading, and discussion for each segment of the text.

A visual organizer plays a central role in the alternating activities of purpose setting, reading, and discussion. By displaying an organizer, the teacher directs reading and discussion toward filling in the organizer. So, for each cycle of the lesson, the teacher fills in the organizer with additional information until it is complete. The lines are drawn in after the discussion to show which of the items previously discussed belonged with the phases of the life of a butterfly. In this way, the teacher represents the author's structure for conveying the information in the text. Thus, the text information is mapped onto the organizer, which visually depicts the organization and content of the information the author presented in the text.

Wong and Au (1985) alert teachers to look for opportunities to teach other useful concepts and vocabulary not presented in the text. They also recommend that teachers remain alert to opportunities to build or elaborate on children's existing butterfly schemata. For example, explaining that moths build cocoons and butterflies develop in a chrysalis is a topic with which the text deals only briefly.

Application

After the entire text has been read, the teacher helps students draw relationships between the text and their own background knowledge. By using the visual organizer, students are encouraged to synthesize and summarize the information discussed throughout the lesson.

Following the discussion or on another occasion, students may become involved in extension activities. These may range from something as simple as illustrating a selected butterfly to something as complex as building a three-dimensional diorama of collected and labeled butterflies. By following the steps in a CTA lesson, teachers offer students quality comprehension instruction in processing expository text at the whole-text level. Although we have offered many selected strategies for improving comprehension of narrative and expository text, these do not represent all of the possible strategies available. In the next section, we focus attention on microelements of the text that affect reading comprehension. These include sentence comprehension, cohesion elements, and typographical features in text.

Teaching Reading Comprehension: Focus on the Sentence

The Cloze Procedure

As described in the Bullock Report (D.E.S., 1975), the **cloze** procedure is "the use of a piece of writing in which certain words have been deleted and the pupil has to make maximum possible use of context clues available in predicting the missing words" (p. 93). According to Rye, the cloze procedure is a useful instructional strategy because "the human mind has a tendency to complete incomplete patterns or sequences" (1982, p. 2). When cloze was first introduced by W. L. Taylor in 1953, it was proposed as a means of measuring reading ability. Since that time, a variety of instructional uses have been developed using cloze to improve children's reading comprehension and word identification. In the following paragraphs, we describe several instructional uses to improve children's reading comprehension.

The most familiar version of cloze involves an every *n*th-word deletion pattern. Typically, every fifth or tenth word in a passage of 250 words is deleted and left for students to complete using the context, or surrounding familiar words, in the sentence. Look at the following example, which uses an every fifth-word deletion pattern.

Use of cloze as an assessment procedure is also discussed in Chapter 13.

The most familiar version of close involves an every nth-word deletion pattern.

> Many scientists believe that there are other forms of intelligent life some-
> where in space. These forms may not _____ the way we do. _____
> often show life forms _____ space with silly-looking _____. Movies
> often show them _____ frightening monsters. But have _____ ever
> wondered what those _____ life forms might think _____ us?

Primary-aged children experience greater success with the every tenth-word deletion pattern than with the every fifth-word deletion pattern because deleting every tenth word provides children with more context clues to use before encountering the next deletion.

With **selected deletions**, *teachers delete selected words depending on their instructional goals and the observed needs of their students.*

Watson and Crowley (1988) describe another approach using the cloze procedure for instruction called *selected deletions.* This approach encourages children to use all the linguistic and experiential clues available to them to fill in deleted information. The advantage to this approach is that teachers can delete selected words depending on their instructional goals and the observed needs of their students. To help students recognize comprehension clues embedded in text, teachers may delete structure words in sentences. Words that signal the sequence of text *(first, second, next, before, after)*, words that refer back to or ahead to other words in the text *(he, she, this, those, which)*, words that show location *(behind, on, under, next to)*, words that signal an explanation *(thus, because, so, therefore, as a result)*, words that signal comparisons *(but, yet, although, similarly)*, and words that signal an example *(such as, for example, that is, namely)* can be selected for deletion. Words or phrases can be selected for deletion that are easy for students to fill in using the meaning and sentence structure clues found in the text. By using selected deletions in this way, students develop a sense for using language clues to fill in missing information. Examples for some of these selected deletions follow:

Many scientists believe that there are other forms of intelligent _____ somewhere in space. These _____ may not look the way we do. Movies often show life _____ from space with silly-looking _____. _____ often show them as frightening monsters. But have you ever wondered what those other _____ forms might think of us?

Zip Cloze Procedure

Zip cloze *is used to help students use intrasentence and intersentence clues in text to construct meaning.*

Blachowicz (1977) suggests using zip cloze to help students use intrasentence and intersentence clues (clues within and between sentences, respectively) in text to construct meaning. A zip cloze lesson is begun by making an overhead transparency of a section of a story or chapter in a textbook. Next, the teacher selects the words for deletion. By cutting masking tape into small, narrow strips, the teacher can cover the words selected for deletion with masking tape, peeling the edge of the masking tape back so that the tape can be easily removed. The teacher then places the overhead transparency onto the projector and has the class read the story as a group either in unison or echo reading. At the covered words, the teacher has the children predict what the word might be and uncovers the word all at once or a letter at a time. When the children correctly predict the word using minimal text clues, the teacher zips the masking tape off and reveals the word. She continues this process until the text has been completely read. During this presentation, discussions may focus on how context was used to determine the appropriate word(s) for filling in the blanks.

Maze

When using **maze**, *only nouns and verbs are deleted.*

Maze is another cloze approach for improving readers' use of text clues to aid comprehension. Although many contexts will allow children to predict deleted content words successfully, some materials will not. This is particularly true for first-grade and second-grade reading instructional materials. The maze procedure proposed by Guthrie, Seifert, Burnham, and Caplan (1974) helps to compensate for this problem. When using maze, only nouns and verbs are deleted. However, instead of deleting these content words and leaving a blank to fill in, three choices are provided for each deletion. The three choices provided are carefully prescribed by the authors of this approach. First, one choice is the word deleted from the text. The second choice is a word that is the same part of speech as the word deleted. The third choice is a word that is a different part of speech than the word deleted. An example of a maze follows:

Chapter 8 discusses three more varieties of cloze that are particularly useful for helping children identify unfamiliar words: **successive, regressive,** and **progressive** cloze procedures.

box

The boy in the forest lived in a log _____. cabin

run

Many more varieties of cloze are available for teaching children to attend to details in text for improving both reading comprehension, inferencing, and word identification (E. M. Carr, Dewitz, & Patberg, 1989).

Cohesive Ties

Another important research finding related to reading comprehension focuses on the relationship between cohesion and comprehension. Moe and Irwin describe cohesion as "a type of [language] redundancy that links one sentence or phrase with another" (1986, p. 3). Research has found that the organization of text, or global coherence, is only one important means for rendering a text cohesive (Perfetti & Lesgold, 1977). Local coherence in text is established by using words that link sentences together, called **cohesive ties**. Some examples of cohesive ties follow:

Words that link sentences together are called **cohesive ties**.

Type of Cohesive Tie	Example
Reference Includes many pronoun types, location words, and time words.	Austin went to the park. *He* climbed the slide. "Mom, look at that car! Can we go over *there?*"
Substitution Replacing a word or phrase with another.	"My dress is old. I need a new *one.*" "Do you know him?" "No, *do* you?"
Ellipsis Omitting a word or phrase resulting in an implied repetition.	"Were you laughing?" "No, I wasn't." Ralph wears expensive sneakers. His look nicer.
Conjunction Connects phrases and sentences using additive, adversative, causal, and temporal ties.	Jeremy went to the store *after* dinner. He didn't eat fish *because* he dislikes them.
Lexical Using synonymous or category terms to establish ties in text.	The bear went fishing. This large *mammal* likes to eat fish.

Teachers should be selective about which cohesive ties they teach. We suggest beginning with reference ties—especially common pronouns. A good rule of thumb for selection, however, is to observe the comprehension difficulties of your students.

Teachers should be selective about which cohesive ties they teach.

If children are experiencing difficulties with lexical cohesive ties, then instruction should focus on these.

We remind the reader that Durkin (1978) found very little reading comprehension instruction in classrooms—particularly explicit instruction that helped children work out the meaning of text larger than the meaning of a single word. Cohesion is an area for comprehension instruction needing increased attention for many students. Reutzel and Morgan (1990) found that even prior knowledge did not compensate for the absence of (causal) cohesive ties in text.

Pulver (1986) and Baumann and Stevenson (1986) recommend several elements that should be included in lessons when teaching students about cohesive ties in text:

- Directly explain the cohesive link and how it works in text by providing examples.
- Orally model the cohesive link by describing your own thought processes as a reader.
- Ask questions of students to encourage discussion and description of their own thoughts about the cohesive tie.
- Spend time in group practice activities.
- Provide independent practice activities.

Typographic Features

Typographic features include punctuation marks, italics, bolded text, bullets, or boxes.

As with cohesive ties, other text features affect the comprehensibility of text. When authors write, they use **typographic features**. Many of these include punctuation marks such as the period, comma, question mark, exclamation mark, capitalization, semicolon, and colon. Aside from these punctuation features, authors will sometimes use *italics,* **bolded text**, bullets, or boxes to highlight text features and make text more reader friendly. We suggest that teachers draw attention to these features during group readings to heighten students' awareness of their presence and functions in text. For example, we assign a unique vocal sound to mark the presence of each punctuation mark during oral reading. Then, during a unison choral reading, we make each of the assigned sounds for the punctuation marks as we encounter them in the print. This approach is both fun and instructive for readers.

Knowledge- and Experience-Based Comprehension Instruction

Building Background for Reading: Targeting the Discussion

Teachers who understand schema theory realize the importance of activating and building their students' background knowledge in preparation for reading. In fact, many recent basal reader teacher's manuals now contain sections entitled "Building Background for the Story," or "Building Background Knowledge." The unfortunate consequence of this feature in the teacher's manual is that teachers may think they do not need to analyze the recommendations for building background offered in the teacher's manuals.

Analyses of several basal teacher's manuals show instances of problems in the pre-reading component. Some manuals suggest that teachers focus on tangential concepts that are irrelevant to the upcoming selection; sometimes the suggestions for presenting the concepts would encourage far-ranging discussions that could distract the children from what is important. Even under the best conditions, the teacher's manuals may suggest concepts inappropriate for a specific group of children. (Beck, 1986, p. 15)

We therefore caution against an overreliance on basal manuals and suggest some directions for teachers as they consider activities and plan lessons for activating or building their students' background knowledge in preparation for reading. An example may best illustrate the problem.

A recently published basal reading series contains suggestions in a second-grade-level teacher's manual for building background in preparation for reading the story *The Ugly Duckling* (H. C. Andersen, 1965). The teacher's manual suggested focusing the background-building discussion on the differences between a duck and a duckling, a chick and a chicken, and so on. The concept under development revolved around the fact that infant or young animals often are called by names different from those of adult or mature animals. Although such a concept may be appropriate for a text dealing with the topic of the life of a duck, it was totally misdirected for the story of *The Ugly Duckling*.

Teachers can be led to believe that focusing on the topic of a story is the important thing to do when building background for reading. Although this may be true of some types of expository text, authors of narrative text seldom write to communicate cold, bare-facts information. Authors of narrative text generally write a story to convey a message or teach a lesson through the medium of a story. On the other hand, authors generally write expository text to convey information and to clarify concepts, events, and processes. Thus, background-building activities for these two types of texts should differ based on the author's purposes. As we have discussed previously, readers may experience a comprehension difficulty when they "understand" a text but miss the author's intended message. In the case of *The Ugly Duckling*, focusing discussion on the differences between young and mature animal names seems to miss the message the author intended to convey and leads teachers and students into "far-ranging discussions that could distract children from what is important" (Beck, 1986, p. 15).

In the story *The Ugly Duckling*, Hans Christian Andersen wrote about himself as a youth—his lack of self-confidence resulting from previous peer criticism and his later realization that all along he was a lovable and capable individual. Building background for this story in particular is obviously more appropriately targeted toward understanding self-worth—the author's purpose for writing this story. To build background for this story, the teacher may put a sign with the letters IALAC, which represent the words "I am lovable and capable," around the neck of a volunteer in the class. The student volunteer then may be told that she is to assume a new name and that a story will be read aloud about her as this fictitious person. Each time the volunteer hears something in the story that makes her feel badly about herself or erodes her self-worth, she is to tear a piece of the IALAC sign off, which represents the gradual destruction of her feelings of self-worth. Children in the class may then be led to understand how the story of *The Ugly Duckling* is very much like this story and that the author was attempting to share a message similar to the IALAC story with his readers.

It is unfortunate, but true, that when suggesting background building activities for instruction most basal reader teacher's manuals tend to treat stories and exposi-

Notice how some teacher's manuals suggest that teachers focus on tangential concepts that are irrelevant to reading the upcoming selections.

When reading stories, teachers should focus background discussions on the author's message or purpose for writing the story rather than on the topic of the story.

tions as if they were written for the same purposes. Not all text lends itself equally well to a cognitive–conceptual approach to background building. Stories, unlike expositions, often require background-building activities that are centered on emotions and are more closely aligned with affective message approaches to background building rather than cognitive–conceptual approaches. Because of this condition, teachers need to exercise caution when using basal teacher's manual suggestions for building background. We suggest three questions teachers need to ask themselves to evaluate the background-building ideas provided in basal teacher's manuals:

- What is the purpose of this selection (story or expository)?
- If a story, what was the author trying to convey as a message to the reader?
- If expository, what was the concept, event, or process the author was attempting to explain or clarify?

Once teachers answer these questions, they can appropriately direct and focus background-building activities and discussions to prepare students for successfully comprehending a text. By understanding the subtle but real relationship between a reader's background and the author's intent, teachers can ensure that students do not miss important information in expositions or the author's intended message in narratives.

Prereading Plan

One way to activate prior knowledge of a topic for expository text or the message of narrative text is to use J. Langer's (1981) **prereading plan (PReP)**. Begin a PReP lesson by examining the text to be read. Look for key words, phrases, and illustrations that relate to the topic or message of the text depending on the type of text to be read (narrative or expository). You may be reading a passage about Mississippi river boats. Words such as *steamers, barges,* and *dredging* may be selected along with illustrations for this lesson. Langer suggests that students' prior knowledge of a selection be assessed before beginning instruction. The key words from the selection can be listed on a handout and numbered. Students are asked to write down what they know about each of the selected words. Scoring can be accomplished by assigning each prior knowledge response a qualitative ranking ranging from 0 to 3.

0 = *Neither prior knowledge of nor response to the item.*

1 = *Little prior knowledge.* This is evidenced by responses that include words that sound like the stimulus word in the list, a short personal experience that is for the most part irrelevant, and supplying word parts, such as suffixes and prefixes.

> dredge–ledge
> I think my grandpa lived by a dredge.
> Dredge, is that like dredging?

2 = *Some prior knowledge.* This level of prior knowledge is evidenced by responses containing examples, attributes, and definition of characteristics related to the stimulus term.

> Isn't dredging like digging?
> Don't you have to have a steam shovel or something like it to dredge?

3 = *Much prior knowledge.* This level of prior knowledge is evidenced by responses containing definitions, analogies, and category concept names (superordinate concept labels).

> A dredge is like a shovel.
> An apparatus for scooping up mud and debris.
> A tool for digging.

After assessing the general status of prior knowledge among students in the classroom, teachers are better prepared to focus on students' prior knowledge needs to facilitate presenting the PReP lesson.

PReP is composed of three distinct phases: (a) association, (b) reflections on associations, and (c) organizing knowledge. The lesson is begun by asking students to free associate with a selected term or idea such as *steamboats.* This can be done by saying, "Tell me anything you think of when you hear the idea of the *steamboats.*" These responses can be written at the board or recorded on chart paper for later reference. After jotting down the associations of the group, the teacher requests that students think about their associations. This may be done by saying, "What made you think of . . . ?" Following this phase of the lesson, students discuss any new ideas or knowledge they formulated during the previous phases of the lesson. These ideas should be recorded at the board or on chart paper as well. Before reading, tell students they should set some purposes for reading. This can be done by suggesting, "Write down several questions before beginning to read. These should be questions for which you want to find answers by reading the passage or story." After reading, students can summarize and organize their questions and answers. Both the questions and answers can be shared with the group.

PReP is a useful knowledge-based teaching strategy for helping students activate and elaborate what they know about a topic before reading to improve reading comprehension. PReP can also help students develop the ability to monitor the state of their own understanding. By engaging students in revealing their knowledge about a topic, concept, or event before reading, students become aware of how much or how little they know. Thus, PReP is helpful for assessment, activation, and elaboration or prior knowledge to improve readers' comprehension of text.

List two things PReP helps students do to succeed in reading expository text.

K-W-L

Another strategy that can be used to develop comprehension through activating prior knowledge is called K-W-L. Ogle (1986), the originator of K-W-L, asserts that this strategy is best suited for use with expository text, although we see no reason why it cannot be applied to stories with minor modifications.

Notice three steps for using K-W-L.

Step K: What I Know

K-W-L strategy lessons begin with step K, what I know. This step is composed of two levels of accessing prior knowledge: (a) brainstorming and (b) categorizing information. Begin by asking children to brainstorm about a particular topic (in the case of a narrative, brainstorm a particular theme or message). For instance, children may be asked what they know about bats. A list of associations is formed through brainstorming. When students make a contribution, Ogle (1986) suggests asking them where or how they got their information to challenge students into higher levels of thinking.

Next, teachers should help students look for ways in which the brainstorming list can be reorganized into categories of information. For example, teachers may notice that the brainstorming list shows three related pieces of information about how bats navigate. These can be reorganized into that category. Children are encouraged to look at the list and think about other categories represented in the brainstorming list.

Step W: What Do I Want to Learn?

During step W, students begin to recognize gaps, inaccuracies, and disagreements in their prior knowledge to decide what they want to learn. Teachers can play a central role in pointing out these problems and helping students frame questions for which they would like to have answers. Questions can be framed by having students use the question stem "I wonder." After the group generates a series of questions to be answered before reading, they are directed to write down personal questions for which they would like answers. These can be taken from those generated by the groups as well as others generated by individuals.

Step L: What I Learned

After reading, have students write down what they learned. This can take the form of answers to specific questions they asked or a concise written summary of their learning. These questions and answers may be discussed as a group or shared between pairs of students. In this way, other children benefit from the learning of their peers as well as from their own learning. In summary, K-W-L has been shown to be effective in improving reading comprehension by causing students to activate, think about, and organize their prior knowledge as an aid to reading comprehension (DeWitz & Carr, 1987).

Generating Reciprocal Inferences Procedure

Notice how teachers model the process of making an inference in the first stage of the GRIP strategy.

P. M. Hollingsworth and Reutzel (1988) emphasize the fact that one important part of reading comprehension involves the ability to make inferences. A two-stage approach is used to help students develop this ability in the generating reciprocal inferences procedure (GRIP). First, the teacher models explicitly how an inference is made by reading, and then the teacher highlights key or clue words in the text. For example, the teacher may read aloud the following passage, after which she highlights certain clue words in the text, as shown:

> The <u>elevator ride</u> was great fun. Now Kathy and Becky <u>looked down</u>
> through the wire fence as the wind whistled in their ears. The <u>people</u> and the
> <u>cars on the street looked</u> just like <u>tiny</u> toys. Although they were <u>very high up,</u>
> the girls were not frightened. It was exciting to <u>see the whole city</u> spread out
> before them.

Where were Kathy and Becky? This passage requires the reader to make a certain kind of slot-filling inference—a location inference. The teacher makes this inference after highlighting the clues in the text that led to that conclusion. After highlighting the relevant text clues and making the inference, the teacher justifies the inference by pointing out how each text clue, combined with prior knowledge, supported the inference that Kathy and Becky were on a high building overlooking a city—the location.

The GRIP lesson continues with four more paragraphs. These paragraphs are needed to gradually release the responsibility for inferencing from the teacher to the students. In the next paragraph, the teacher highlights the words, the children make the inference, and the teacher justifies the inference the students made. The third paragraph is read, the children highlight the key words, the teacher makes the inference, and the students justify the inference. In the fourth and final passage, the students highlight the key words, make the inference, and justify the inference.

After children are able to assume full responsibility for finding key words, inferencing, and justifying the inference, they move into *generating* reciprocal inferences. Children are paired to write their own inference paragraphs. This is done by generating a list of five or more key words and writing the text, incorporating the clues without giving away the inference to be made. After writing, the students in each pair exchange paragraphs, mark key words, make the inference, and justify their inferences to the author. This process can continue as long as needed and as long as interest remains high. Variations of this approach include placing the paragraphs written by children on overhead transparencies and inviting children to locate the key words, make an inference, and justify their own inferences in writing. Another variation to this approach involves a game board activity (Figure 6.24) with directions for playing the game (Figure 6.25).

In the second stage of the GRIP strategy, students compose inferential text for peers to make inferences.

GRIP has been shown to increase children's abilities to make inferences across a wide variety of measures and under several conditions (Reutzel & Hollingsworth, 1988a). GRIP is a useful implementation of the Pearson and Gallagher (1983) model of gradual release in comprehension instruction, which improves inferential and global reading comprehension.

Retellings

Gambrell, Pfeiffer, and Wilson (1985) found that using retellings following silent reading enhanced reading comprehension as measured by answers to literal and interpretive questions. Wilson and Gambrell (1988, pp. 53–54) speculate that retellings of text improve comprehension because students engage in rehearsing the structure and content of text. In the following list, we have modified Wilson and Gambrell's five tips for helping students retell text successfully:

Focus on five steps for helping students retell successfully.

1. Teachers can model retelling by taking a few minutes to retell a portion of a story, including the modeling of accurate sequencing.
2. Teachers can retell a portion of an event in a story and ask the students to finish retelling the story.
3. Students can be asked to tell about what they thought was the most important or interesting event or episode in a story.
4. Teachers can pair students off for retelling a story after reading. They can be instructed to tell their peer the story as if they had not read it.
5. During individual reading conferences, students can be asked by the teacher to retell what they have read as an assessment of reading comprehension. Retellings can be scored for major ideas or story grammar components, that is, setting, initiating event, attempts, resolution, and so on.

Retellings are an effective comprehension instructional strategy because they involve students in activating their prior knowledge for remembering stories and expositions. By requiring that readers select information from a text that is worth remembering, retellings help students focus selective attention on relevant information in text as well as increase sensitivity to a variety of text structures.

Figure 6.24

Generating Reciprocal Inferences Procedure (GRIP) game board

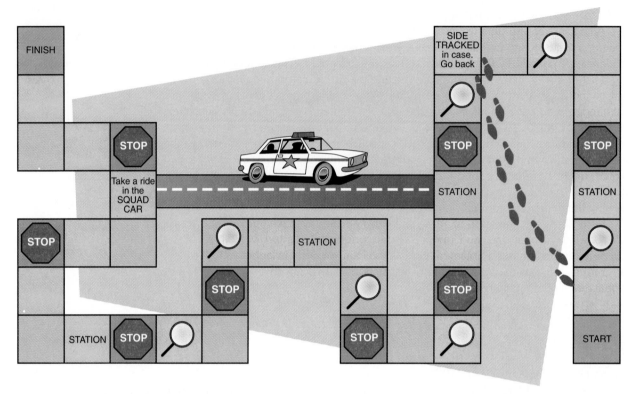

From "Get a GRIP on Comprehension" by P. M. Hollingsworth and D. R. Reutzel, 1988, *Reading Horizons, 29*(1), p. 78. Copyright 1988 by Reading Horizons. Reprinted by permission.

Metacognition and Fix-Up Strategies

Metacognition involves readers in checking the status of their own understanding and taking steps to repair failing comprehension when necessary.

In addition to activating, elaborating, or modifying prior knowledge to improve comprehension, readers must learn to monitor the status of their own ongoing comprehension and know when comprehension breaks down. The act of monitoring one's unfolding comprehension of text is called **metacognition**, or sometimes *metacomprehension*. The ability to plan, check, monitor, revise, and evaluate one's unfolding comprehension is of particular importance in reading. If a child fails to detect comprehension breakdowns, then she will take no action to correct misinterpretations of the text. However, if a child expects that text should make sense and has the ability to strategically self-correct comprehension problems, then reading can progress as it should.

To help students develop the ability to monitor their own comprehension processes, H. K. Carr (1986) suggested a strategy called "click or clunk." This strategy urges readers to reflect at the end of each paragraph or section of reading by stopping and asking themselves if the meaning or message "clicks" for them or goes "clunk." If it clunks, what is wrong? What can be done to make sense of it?

Although the ability to detect when comprehension breaks down is important, it is equally important to know which strategies to select in repairing broken comprehension

Figure 6.25

Directions for Generating Reciprocal Inferences Procedure (GRIP) game board

Children play the GRIP board game in pairs. Before the game begins, each child needs to understand the rules for playing the game and follow them carefully. We begin by discussing the game rules with the children:

1. Requires two players to play the game.
2. Write four sentences that go together to make a story. Underline the clue words in each sentence.
3. Select a marker.
4. Place marker on START.
5. Throw the die, letting the highest start the game.
6. Each player moves his/her marker the number of spaces shown on the die.
7. If you land on STATION, have the other player read a sentence.
8. If you land on MAGNIFYING GLASS, move to the nearest STATION, have the other player read a sentence.
9. A different sentence is read at each STATION.
10. You must be on STATION to guess, and you only get one guess.
11. If you land on STOP SIGN, go back to the space from which you started your turn.
12. You can be on the same space as the other player.
13. If you land on SIDETRACKED, follow the feet.
14. If you land on SQUAD CAR, follow the road.
15. Whoever guesses what the story is about is the winner, and the game is over.

When the GRIP Board Game is introduced, play the game with one child while the other children in the classroom watch. This makes the transition from discussing the rules to playing the game easier.

as well as when to use these strategies. Consequently, students may know that they need to take steps to repair comprehension but may not know which steps to take or when to take them. As a consequence, children should be introduced to the options available to them for repairing broken comprehension. A. Collins and Smith (1980) suggest the following **repair strategies** for use by readers who experience comprehension failure.

- Ignore the problem and continue reading.
- Suspend judgment for now and continue reading.
- Form a tentative hypothesis, using text information, and continue reading.
- Look back or reread the previous sentence.
- Stop and think about the previously read context, reread if necessary.
- Seek help from the environment, reference materials, or other knowledgeable individuals.

To help students develop a sense for when to select these strategies for repairing failing comprehension, teachers may consider using a think-aloud modeling procedure. The teacher begins by reading part of a text aloud, and as she proceeds, comments on her thinking. By revealing to students her thinking, the hypotheses she has formed for the text, and anything that strikes her as difficult or unclear, the teacher demonstrates for the students the processes successful readers use to comprehend a text. Next, the teacher reminds students of the click or clunk strategy. Gradually, she releases the responsibility for modeling metacognitive strategies to the children during follow-up lessons on metacognitive monitoring. She displays the repair strategies shown previously in a prominent place in the classroom and draws students' attention to these strategies throughout the year.

Notice six things a think-aloud lesson would emphasize.

For students needing additional help with metacognitive strategy development, we recommend Baumann, Jones, and Seifert-Kessell's (1993) **think-aloud lessons**. In think-aloud lessons, students are explicitly taught what the strategies of metacognition are through definition, description, and examples. Next, children are told why learning these strategies is important for helping them become better readers. Finally, students are taught how to use these strategies through a sequence of instruction using (a) verbal explanation, (b) teacher modeling, (c) guided practice, and (d) independent practice. The think-aloud lesson centered on the following topics:

- Self-questioning (see self-questioning later in this chapter)
- Sources of information (see question–answer relationships, QARs, later in this chapter)
- Think-aloud modeling introduction (see GRIP, previously in this chapter)
- Think-aloud review and extension (see GRIP)
- Predicting, reading, and verifying
- Understanding unstated information
- Retelling a story (see retellings Chapter 10)
- Rereading and reading on (see preceding discussion)
- Think-aloud/comprehension-monitoring application

We recommend this procedure because it brings together in an integrated fashion all of the elements of excellent, research-based metacognitive reading instruction, which has been shown to be very effective in helping students acquire a broad range of metacognitive strategies.

Strategies for Effective Questioning

Questions are an integral part of life both in and out of school. From birth, we learn about our world by asking questions and then by testing our answers against the confines of reality. In school, teachers ask questions to motivate children to become involved in learning. Because questions are so much a part of the schooling process and can affect the quality of children's comprehension, teachers must know how to effectively use questioning to deliver quality reading instruction.

For many years, the only means of teaching comprehension was through questioning students.

Questioning Taxonomies

For many years, teachers thought they were teaching children to comprehend text by asking questions. Although it is true that questions may be used to teach, Durkin (1978, 1981a) found that the preponderance of teacher questions were used as comprehension evaluation and assessment rather than as comprehension instruction. Herber (1978) asserted that the development of questioning taxonomies was an attempt to consolidate and simplify the task of teaching reading comprehension by reducing the long and elaborate lists of comprehension skills found in basal readers. During the past several decades, a variety of questioning taxonomies such as B. Bloom's (1956), T. Barrett's (1972), and Taba's (1975) taxonomies were published along with impassioned appeals for teachers to ask more higher level questions. Figure 6.26 illustrates Bloom's taxonomy.

Questioning taxonomies played an integral role in early efforts to improve teacher questioning.

In addition to simplifying the task of teaching reading comprehension to the act of asking questions at a few levels of thinking, taxonomies were thought to help teachers develop a sensitivity to the levels of questions they asked. Research of the day supported the proposition that teachers' questions and questions in basal teacher's manuals were mostly lower level questions. By observing and classifying teacher questions, Guszak (1967) found that 70% of questions teachers asked during reading instruction were at a literal, recognition, or recall level. Such questions, he contended, did not foster higher level thought processes such as evaluation, application, generalization, or synthesis questions. In 1985, Shake and Allington found that the ratio of higher level to lower level questions had not changed markedly since 1967.

Others have challenged the idea that asking higher level questions leads to higher level thinking abilities (Gall et al., 1975). More recently, Farrar (1984) has objected to the concept that higher level questions are necessarily better at disposing students toward higher level thinking. While much can be and will be argued about asking higher level questions for some time into the future, the fact is that students remain unaided in developing strategies for answering the host of questions they encounter on a daily basis in schools.

Asking higher level questions does not necessarily lead to higher level thinking abilities.

Pearson and Johnson (1978) devised a three-level questioning taxonomy (Figure 6.27) describing the sources of information available to students for answering questions rather than describing levels of thought processes. These authors contend that teachers should help students answer questions—not just ask questions. The Pearson and Johnson taxonomy helps students and teachers realize that they can draw on two basic information sources for answering questions: the text (text explicit), their own knowledge (script implicit), or a combination of both sources (text implicit).

Asking questions is not enough; teachers must help students learn how to answer questions.

Question–Answer Relationships

A direct application of Pearson and Johnson's (1978) questioning taxonomy for training students to successfully navigate the obstacle course of questions encoun-

Figure 6.26

B. Bloom's (1956) taxonomy of the cognitive domain

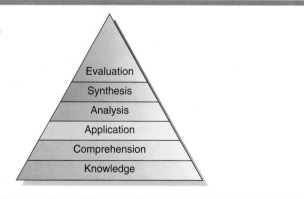

Figure 6.27

Pearson and Johnson (1978) questioning taxonomy

Text implicit: Answers are not as obvious, but are found on that page.

Text explicit: Answers are obvious right there on the page.

Script implicit: Answer is found in the reader's head.

tered in school classrooms can be found in Raphael's **question-answer relationships (QARs)** (1982, 1986). The purpose of QARs is to teach children how to identify the types of questions asked of them as well as to determine the appropriate sources of information necessary to answer those questions.

Raphael (1982, 1986) identified four QARs to help children identify the connection between the type of question asked and the information sources necessary and available for answering questions: (a) right there, (b) think and search, (c) author and you, and (d) on my own. Figure 6.28 shows examples of each of these four types of QARs.

Instruction using QARs begins by explaining to students that when they answer questions about reading there are basically two places they can look to get information: *in the book* and *in my head.* This concept should be practiced with the students by reading aloud a text, asking questions, and having the students explain or show where they found their answers. Once students understand the two-category approach, expand the *in the book* category to include *right there* and *putting it together.* The distinction between these two categories should be practiced by reading several texts along with discussion. For older students, Raphael (1986) suggests that students be shown specific strategies for locating the answers to *right there* questions. These include looking in a single sentence or looking in two sentences connected by a pronoun. For *putting it together* questions, students can be asked to focus their attention on the structure of the text, such as cause–effect, problem–solution, listing–example, compare–contrast, and explanation.

Next, instruction should be directed toward two subcategories within the *in my head* category: (a) *author and me,* and (b) *on my own.* Here again, these categories can be practiced as a group by reading a text aloud, answering the questions, and discussing the sources of information. To expand this training, students can be asked to identify the types of questions asked in their basal readers, workbooks, content area texts, and tests as well as to determine the sources of information needed to answer these questions. Students may be informed that certain types of questions are asked before and after reading a text. For example, questions asked before reading typically ask students to activate their own knowledge. Therefore, questions asked before reading will usually be *on my own* questions. However, questions asked after reading will make use of information found in the text. Therefore, questions asked after reading will typically focus on the *right there, putting it together,* and *author and me* types of questions.

Using the QARs question–answering training strategy is useful for at least two other purposes. First, it can help teachers examine their own questioning with respect to the types of questions and the information sources students need to use to answer their questions. Second, some teachers may find that by using QARs to monitor their own questioning behaviors they are asking only *right there* types of questions. This discovery should lead teachers to ask questions that require the use of other information sources. Students can use QARs to initiate self-questioning before and after reading. Children may be asked to write questions for each of the QARs categories and answer these questions. Finally, a poster displaying the information in Figure 6.28 can heighten children's and teachers' awareness to the types of questions asked and the information sources available for answering those questions.

Raphael and Pearson (1982) provided evidence that training students to recognize these question–answer relationships resulted in improved comprehension and question–answering behavior. In addition, evidence also shows that teachers find the QARs strategies productive for improving their own questioning behaviors.

In the Book QARs

Right There
The answer is in the text, usually easy to find. The words used to make up the question and words used to answer the question are **Right There** in the same sentence.

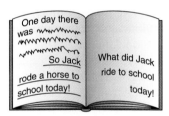

Think and Search (Putting It Together)
The answer is in the story, but you need to put together different story parts to find it. Words for the question and words for the answer are not found in the same sentence. They come from different parts of the text.

In My Head QARs

Author and You
The answer is *not* in the story. You need to think about what you already know, what the author tells you in the text, and how it fits together.

On My Own
The answer is *not* in the story. You can even answer the question without reading the story. You need to use your own experience.

Figure 6.28

Illustrations to explain question–answer relationships (QARs) to students

---

Figure from "Teaching Question Answer Relationships, Revisited" by Taffy E. Raphael, *The Reading Teacher,* February 1986. Reprinted with permission of Taffy E. Raphael and the International Reading Association.

Asking Prereading Versus Postreading Questions

Prequestions act to focus the reader's attention on relevant items, whereas postquestions have a "reviewing" effect on students' recall.

The amount of attention a reader can give to remembering what has been read is limited. Requiring students to read to remember everything is simply not possible and interferes with memory (F. Smith, 1985). Tierney and Cunningham (1984) indicate that questions asked before reading can both restrict and facilitate readers' recall. When specific information is to be recalled from reading a selection, detail questions should be asked before reading. Prequestions act to focus the reader's attention on relevant items while screening out other less pertinent information. If extracting specific information from the text is not the objective, prequestions can restrict the reader's search to specifics in the text, thus leading to a fragmented understanding of the entirety of the text. If students are to read to get the gist or plot of a story, questions are best asked after reading. Postquestions have a "reviewing" effect on students' recall. Obviously, not all questions fall neatly into these two dichotomous categories. Rather, for questions to be effectively used for learning from text, teachers must make sure that the questioning practices employed are consistent with their instructional goals.

Reciprocal Questioning

*Refer to Chapter 4 for an in-depth discussion of **ReQuest**.*

Students must at some point become responsible for their own learning (Manzo, 1969). A major goal of comprehension is to stimulate students to monitor their own comprehension (Baker & Brown, 1984). Teachers can serve as a much needed model of questioning; but perhaps even more importantly, they can stimulate children to think about their own thinking and comprehension. One way to get students to think about their own comprehension is to help them to ask their own questions about reading. Singer (1978a) and Shanklin and Rhodes (1989) have declared that the end goal of teacher questioning should be student-generated questions. Although this procedure was designed to be used one-on-one, reciprocal questioning (ReQuest) can be modified to involve whole groups by pairing students off for questioning. Carefully supervised by a caring teacher, ReQuest has been shown to improve reading comprehension (Dreher & Gambrell, 1985; Tierney, Readence, & Dishner, 1985).

Wait Time

Teachers can improve their questioning by waiting at least 3 seconds after asking a question before rephrasing, redirecting, or answering the question.

With the current emphasis on "pacing and content coverage" in the teacher-effectiveness literature, teachers may become tempted to embrace a "faster is better" teaching philosophy. Although these characteristics of "effective" teaching are important, we must not forget the fact that not all children operate in the fast lane. Kagan (1966) first coined the concept of a "cognitive tempo." This term implies that one student might be an impulsive thinker, quick to respond, perhaps disregarding accuracy, while another student might be a more reflective thinker, slow to respond, but more concerned about accuracy. A fast-paced classroom environment, especially related to the pacing of questioning, may in fact lend itself to one cognitive tempo and not another, thus unintentionally impairing the thinker with a slower cognitive tempo.

In 1974, Rowe investigated the pacing of teacher questioning during science lessons. Her primary unit of observation centered on the length of the interval between the time a teacher asked a question and then expected a response, redirected the question to another student, or rephrased the original question. This interval was called "wait time." Rowe (1974) found that the average teacher wait time was only 0.9 seconds. On the other hand, Rowe (1974) observed that, when teachers allowed at least a 3-second wait time, both teacher questioning characteristics and student answering behavior evidenced appreciable improvement. Improved teacher questioning characteristics included asking fewer but higher quality questions. Flexibility toward student responses considered acceptable increased, and the teachers' expectations for slower students changed. On the other hand, student responses were also affected positively by the increased wait time. Shy and slow students answered more questions. Students' answers to questions were more elaborated, and greater confidence in their answers to questions was reflected in their vocal inflection. Knowing that a wait time of only 3 seconds holds the potential to improve both teacher questioning and student question-answering behavior, teachers should make concerted efforts to observe a 3-second wait time.

Questions Can Help Students Reconstruct a Model of the Text for Remembering

Beck and McKeown (1981) and Sadow (1982) suggested that teachers follow a rational model of the text for questioning. The rational model of text proposed to guide questioning was based on story grammars and was called *story grammar mapping* (Mandler & Johnson, 1977). Subsequent to their proposal, Beck, Omanson, and McKeown (1982) provided evidence that mapping the questioning of a story using a story grammar produced improved reading comprehension.

Teachers should ask questions about the major elements of a story and the order of the story.

At first glance, story grammars like that in Figure 6.29 look very similar to the major characteristics traditionally used to summarize a story's plot. According to Rumelhart's (1975) story grammar, the major elements of a story grammar include setting, problem, goal, events, and resolution. Questions about the setting generally request information about the time, locale, or props used in the story. Questions about the beginning of the story center around an event that precipitated the initiation of an event in the story. Questions concerning the reaction examine the response of the protagonist in the story to the beginning event. A goal question asks the reader to provide information about the motives or objectives of the story characters. An attempt question asks that the reader provide information about what the story characters do to achieve the goal. To evaluate the success or failure of the characters' planned efforts to achieve a goal, readers can be asked questions regarding the outcome. A question about the ending can be asked to cause the reader to draw a conclusion or make a final judgment about the story episode(s).

Evidence from research on story grammars suggests that good readers have well-developed internal representations of story structure, whereas poor readers do not (Whaley, 1981). The motivation for using a story grammar in the design of questioning is to help increase readers' awareness of story structure and to provide a logical framework both for guiding teacher questioning and for students' remembering—all of which lead to improved comprehension.

Increasing Student Involvement

During the typical reading lesson, students respond one at a time to teacher questions. But what might happen to student question-answering behavior if *every* child could respond to *every* question? First, students could become more actively

Figure 6.29

Story grammar map of "Jack and the Beanstalk"

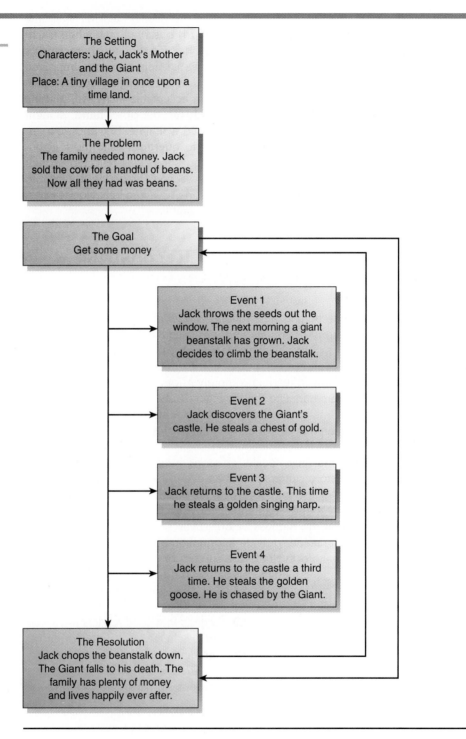

The Setting
Characters: Jack, Jack's Mother and the Giant
Place: A tiny village in once upon a time land.

The Problem
The family needed money. Jack sold the cow for a handful of beans. Now all they had was beans.

The Goal
Get some money

Event 1
Jack throws the seeds out the window. The next morning a giant beanstalk has grown. Jack decides to climb the beanstalk.

Event 2
Jack discovers the Giant's castle. He steals a chest of gold.

Event 3
Jack returns to the castle. This time he steals a golden singing harp.

Event 4
Jack returns to the castle a third time. He steals the golden goose. He is chased by the Giant.

The Resolution
Jack chops the beanstalk down. The Giant falls to his death. The family has plenty of money and lives happily ever after.

involved in answering questions. Second, teachers could observe the correctness of all student responses in lieu of sampling only a selected few. Third, shy students could answer questions without having to risk becoming the focus of attention. These few benefits alone should be enough to motivate teachers toward more frequent use of choral response methods in questioning.

Choral response to questions increases student involvement and allows for on-the-spot evaluation of all students' comprehension.

Hopkins (1979) recommended several ways teachers can make use of whole-group response methods. For word recognition, students could be given yes–no cards to respond to questions asked about words. True–false cards could be used to assess students' comprehension of the various aspects of stories. Stick figures could be used to answer questions about story characters.

Extensions of Hopkins's (1979) ideas for choral response to questions include the use of lap-sized chalkboards or magic slates that can be erased and reused to respond to questions. Another advantage to chalkboards and magic slates is that they need not be prepared before students use them, thus saving teacher time.

Teachers who use choral response methods soon recognize that students become more actively engaged in the reading lesson, and teachers receive more extensive feedback about the state of students' comprehension. In sum, both teacher and learner benefit from choral response techniques used during reading instruction.

Helping Students With Special Comprehension Needs

Reciprocal Teaching

Palincsar and Brown (1985) designed and evaluated an approach to improve the reading comprehension and comprehension monitoring of students who scored 2 years below grade level on standardized tests of reading ability and reading comprehension. Their results suggest a teaching strategy that is useful for helping students who have difficulties with comprehension and comprehension monitoring and is called *reciprocal teaching*. Essentially, this strategy involves teachers and students in exchanging roles, which increases student involvement in the lesson.

Reciprocal teaching is a useful strategy for helping students who have difficulties with comprehension and comprehension monitoring.

The reciprocal teaching lesson is composed of the following four phases or steps:

1. *Prediction:* Students are asked to predict from the title and pictures the possible content of the text. The predictions are recorded by the teacher.
2. *Question generation:* Students generate purpose questions after reading a predetermined segment of the text, such as a paragraph or page.
3. *Summarizing:* Students write a brief summary for the text by starting with "This paragraph was about . . . (p. 299)." Summarizing helps students capture the gist of the text.
4. *Clarifying:* Students and teacher discuss a variety of reasons a text may be difficult or confusing, such as difficult vocabulary, poor text organization, unfamiliar content, or lack of cohesion. Students are then instructed in a variety of comprehension fix-up or repair strategies (as described earlier in this chapter).

Once teachers have modeled this process with several segments of text, the teacher assigns one of the students (preferably a good student) to assume the role of teacher for the next segment of text. The teacher may also, while acting in the student role, provide appropriate prompts and feedback when necessary. When the next segment of text is completed, the student assigned as teacher asks another student to assume that role.

Teachers who use reciprocal teaching to help students with comprehension difficulties should follow four simple guidelines suggested by Palincsar and Brown (1985). First, assess student difficulties and provide reading materials appropriate to students' decoding abilities. Second, use reciprocal teaching for at least 30 minutes per day for 15 to 20 consecutive days. Third, teachers should model frequently and provide corrective feedback. Finally, student progress should be monitored regularly and individually to determine whether the instruction is having the intended effect. Palincsar and Brown (1985) have reported positive results for this intervention procedure by demonstrating dramatic changes in students' ineffective reading behaviors.

While reciprocal teaching was originally intended for use with expository text, this intervention strategy may be used with narrative texts by focusing discussion and reading on the major elements of stories. By using reciprocal teaching with narrative texts, teachers can intervene earlier with those who are experiencing difficulties with comprehension and comprehension monitoring rather than delaying intervention until expository text is typically encountered in the intermediate years.

With minor changes, reciprocal teaching can be used with narrative as well as expository texts.

Helping Students With Special Cultural and Language Needs

Contextual Diagrams

Contextual diagrams allow LEP students to learn needed vocabulary before entering an unfamiliar societal setting.

For many second language learners, pictures or diagrams of social or situational settings wherein objects and actions are labeled are of significant help for acquiring ability to speak, listen, read, and write in a largely unfamiliar language. The purpose of **contextual diagrams**, such as the one shown in Figure 6.30, is to allow students to learn language for settings outside the school classroom. Diagrams of the kitchen, bedroom, or bathroom at home can help students begin to learn and associate second language terms with familiar or even somewhat unfamiliar objects in another setting. Diagrams of stores, libraries, mechanic shops, or hospitals wherein objects and actions are labeled can move students' potential for language comprehension well beyond the physical and social confines of the school classroom. Hence, diagrams of whole, meaningful, and naturally occurring situations serve a purpose of expanding the language learning contexts of English as second language (ESL) and limited English proficiency (LEP) students in schools.

Active Listening to First- and Second-Language Literature

Active listening has been shown effective for both LEP and non-LEP students.

Walters and Gunderson (1985) studied the effects of listening to stories read aloud in students' first and second languages on reading achievement. Results from the 16-week study showed that children benefited from listening to stories read aloud in both the first and second languages. For students with limited first-language proficiency, listening to stories read in the first language helped them to understand that print represents spoken language (Gunderson, 1991). On the other hand, students with LEP who also had an ability to read in the first language learned how terms from the first and second languages map onto one another (Heald-Taylor, 1991).

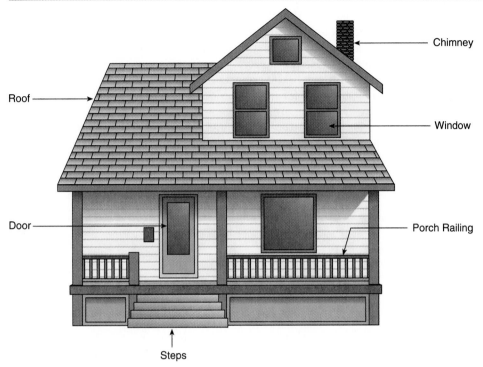

Figure 6.30

Situational context diagram

Chimney

Roof

Window

Door

Porch Railing

Steps

The most important part of active listening involves the selection of material that is interesting to the students. For some beginning students, *wordless picture books* are a good place to begin. Read the story or look at the book in small, preplanned sections. If possible, read so that the students can see the print as it is read. In the case of using wordless picture books, students could dictate the print that tells a story to match the pictures. The print can then be recorded so that students could return to the book later and read their own dictated language, telling the story of the pictures. This may mean that the text will need to be enlarged for some groups. However, the active listening strategy can be used with individual students as well.

When using high-interest books selected for reading aloud, stop at strategic points and ask students, "What will happen next?" As a follow-up question, ask students to explain why they think a particular event will take place next in the story. It may even be appropriate when a story employs a repeated pattern, such as, "Little Pig, Little Pig, Let me _____ _____," for the teacher to stop and invite the students to complete the pattern orally. In this way, students are drawn into careful and continuous active listening while hearing a text read aloud.

Summary

Teaching comprehension, unlike testing comprehension, involves teaching behaviors such as explaining, demonstrating, and defining. Teachers must not assume they are teaching children to comprehend text when they mention or assign comprehension skill practice sheets.

Schema theory, a theory about one's storehouse of prior knowledge and experience and how these influence the ability to comprehend text, was depicted in the context of a simplified model of text comprehension involving searching, applying, selecting and evaluating, and composing.

The Gradual Release of Responsibility model of instruction was discussed to provide a comprehensive framework for effective comprehension instruction. Other effective instructional strategies for improving comprehension of narrative text and expository text as well as focusing on comprehending text parts such as sentences, words, and typographic features were highlighted throughout the chapter.

Finally, readers were shown several effective lesson strategies dealing with building background for reading, effective questioning strategies, and helping readers with comprehension difficulties. (See Figure 6.31 for an overview of the chapter.)

Figure 6.31

Chapter overview

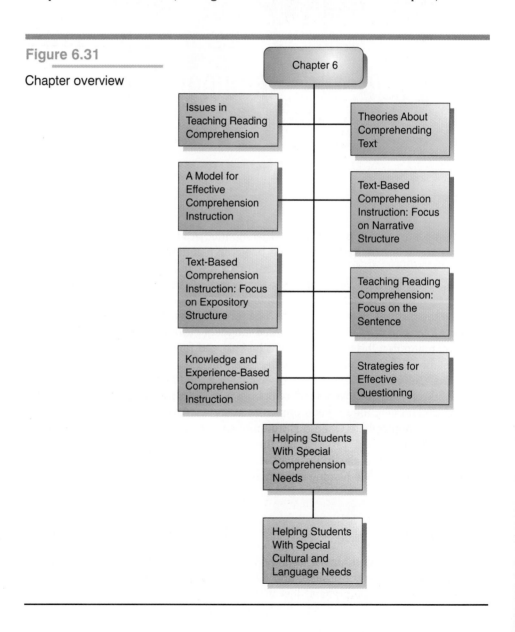

CONCEPT APPLICATIONS

IN THE CLASSROOM

1. Examine a basal reader scope and sequence listing of comprehension skills. Choose those that represent skills and those that represent strategies. Provide a written rationale for your choices.
2. Pick a favorite story. Describe the story grammar parts of your selection. Make a story map, a schema story lesson, or design a story grammar questioning map.
3. Select a chapter from an elementary science, health, math, or social studies text. Identify the organizational pattern used by the authors. Make a pattern guide.
4. Choose a literature or basal textbook selection. Design two metacognitive monitoring lessons of the 10 possible lessons described by Baumann et al. (1993) in this chapter. Be sure to include each of the lesson parts, that is, (a) verbal explanation, (b) teacher modeling, (c) guided practice, and (d) independent practice.
5. Take a 250-word passage from a story or expository text. Show how you could use two cloze techniques on this passage by preparing two cloze lessons.
6. Make some group response cards or boards for use in your classroom to respond to questions.
7. Evaluate the recommendations for background building in a basal reader. If necessary, describe how you would alter the recommendations.

IN THE FIELD

1. Make arrangements to visit a public school classroom. Carefully observe and record the time devoted to teaching versus testing reading comprehension.
2. Visit with a classroom teacher about the skills she thinks are important for helping students become skilled readers. Summarize these views in a brief essay.
3. Devise a lesson to train children to use QARs. Try it out in an elementary school classroom. Reflect on this experience by making an entry in your professional journal.
4. Prepare a reciprocal teaching lesson. Make arrangements to visit a local resource or Chapter 1 classroom to teach your lesson.
5. Prepare a situational context diagram. Make arrangements to work with LEP or ESL students in an elementary school classroom. Use your diagram to teach a language lesson and report on your findings.

RECOMMENDED READINGS

Alvermann, D. E., Dillon, D. R., & O'Brien, D. G. (1987). *Using discussion to promote reading comprehension.* Newark, DE: International Reading Association.

Carr, E., Dewitz, P., & Patberg, J. (1989). Using cloze for inference training with expository text. *The Reading Teacher, 40,* 380–385.

Irwin, J. W. (1986). *Teaching reading comprehension processes.* Englewood Cliffs, NJ: Prentice-Hall.

Johnston, P. H. (1983). *Reading comprehension assessment: A cognitive basis.* Newark, DE: International Reading Association.

McNiel, J. D. (1987). *Reading comprehension: New directions for classroom practice.* Glenview, IL: Scott, Foresman.

Pearson, P. D., & Johnson, D. D. (1978). *Teaching reading comprehension.* New York: Holt, Rinehart & Winston.

Robinson, H. A., Faroane, V., Hittleman, D. R., & Unruh, E. (1990). *Reading comprehension instruction 1783–1987: A review of trends and research.* Newark, DE: International Reading Association.

Wilson, R. M., & Gambrell, L. B. (1988). *Reading comprehension in the elementary school.* Reading, MA: Allyn & Bacon.

Chapter 7

Acquiring a Reading Vocabulary

Focus Questions

When you are finished studying this chapter, you should be able to answer these questions:

1. What are the four hypotheses as to how vocabulary is learned? Describe.
2. For many decades, two views have been expressed in the research as to how vocabulary is best taught: intensive phonics and concept development. What are these two dominant positions?
3. What are the four guidelines suggested here for effective vocabulary instruction?
4. Compare and contrast semantic-based and keyword strategies for vocabulary development. Which appears to be the strongest approach according to the research? Which strategy would be most practical for teachers to implement?
5. What are at least five strategies that teachers may use to assist students in building background knowledge?
6. Many words in our language have multiple meanings. What activities might a teacher use to help students extend their knowledge of new vocabulary meanings?
7. One of the ultimate goals of education is to help students become independent learners. What are three strategies students can use to acquire new vocabulary on their own?
8. How does the study of various word functions (e.g., synonyms, euphemisms, onomatopoeia) enable students to better communicate and understand the messages of others?

Key Concepts

Instrumental Hypothesis
Aptitude Hypothesis
Knowledge Hypothesis
Access Hypothesis
Semantic-Based Strategies
Keyword Method
Guidelines for Vocabulary Instruction
Cluing Technique
Predict-O-Gram
Frayer Model
Opin
Word Cards
Structured Overview

Semantic Maps
Semantic Feature Analysis
Exclusion Brainstorming
Concept Ladder
Free-Form Outlines
Capsule Vocabulary
Individual Interest Sheet (IIS)
Recasts
Vocabulary Overview
Word Map
Synonyms
Antonyms
Euphemisms
Village English Activity

The acquisition of a reading vocabulary is one of the most essential aspects of literacy development. Reading vocabulary knowledge involves a cross section of such literacy prerequisites as word identification, prior knowledge, semantics, phonics, context, and basic comprehension. Research has confirmed that vocabulary difficulty and the type of vocabulary instruction students receive can have a significant effect on reading comprehension (Stahl & Jacobson, 1986; Stahl, Hare, Sinatra, & Gregory, 1991). So it is not surprising that many reading programs have been developed to provide significant amounts of time building reading vocabulary. In their zeal to develop reading vocabulary, however, some program developers have gone a bit too far. Just as reading is more than phonics, reading is likewise much more than the simple learning of words. In one study, researchers concluded that approximately 88,500 distinct words are found in school English and that "even the most ruthlessly systematic direct vocabulary instruction could neither account for a significant portion of all the words children actually learn, nor cover more than a modest proportion of the words they will encounter in school reading materials" (Nagy & Anderson, 1984, p. 304).

Although it is our position that the development of a reading vocabulary is an essential element of elementary reading instruction, we temper this position with the realization that this perspective has practical limits. Nevertheless, preservice and inservice teachers should understand that vocabulary acquisition is simply one tool among several in the arsenal of skillful readers.

In this chapter, we discuss four prominent theories related to vocabulary acquisition, followed by some basic guidelines for effective vocabulary instruction in the classroom. The remainder of the chapter is devoted to various learning and teaching strategies that may be used in transition and balanced classrooms.

Four Hypotheses About Vocabulary Acquisition

For many years, linguists, psychologists, educational researchers, psycholinguists, and others have concerned themselves with the questions of how children learn new words. This puzzle is yet to be fully pieced together. Several tenable hypotheses, however, that may shed some light on this complex learning phenomenon have come forward in recent years. Three views have been articulated by R. C. Anderson and Freebody (1981) and a fourth by Mezynski (1983), which we summarize in the following sections.

The Instrumental Hypothesis

Instrumentalists believe performance on vocabulary tests is closely related to word knowledge.

Hypotheses concerning vocabulary acquisition are often linked to how well students do on standardized vocabulary tests. The **instrumental hypothesis** (R. C. Anderson & Freebody, 1981) is one such view. It suggests that children who do well on a vocabulary test are likely to know more words in school texts and other readings they encounter than children who do not do as well on these tests. The important assumption here is that knowing words directly empowers students for successful reading comprehension. But one may ask where this vocabulary knowledge comes from. This is a troubling and important question apparently not fully addressed by subscribers of this position.

The Aptitude Hypothesis

Another view drawn in part from vocabulary measures is the **aptitude hypothesis**. Aptitude is related to the propensity or ability of students to learn words quickly. The assumption is that persons with large vocabulary knowledge comprehend better and possess superior mental agility and/or quicker minds (R. C. Anderson & Freebody, 1981), possibly as a result of heredity. In the classroom, this means that superior vocabulary-aptitude students will learn more word meanings with the same amount of exposure to information as other students.

Aptitude is the ability to learn words quickly.

The Knowledge Hypothesis

The **knowledge hypothesis** states that experience or first-hand knowledge of a concept under study is directly related to comprehension (R. C. Anderson & Freebody, 1981). For instance, if a child grows up working with his parents in the sporting goods business, he is likely to understand that the word *spinner* has something to do with fishing. This same knowledge will likely help him understand a fishing story in a favorite magazine that contains words other than *spinner*, such as *dry fly, tackle,* or *leader.* The knowledge hypothesis differs significantly from the instrumental hypothesis, even though they appear to be virtually the same at first glance. The instrumental hypothesis emphasizes individual word meanings, but the knowledge hypothesis is directly related to the development of knowledge structures, or schemata (see Chapter 2 for a discussion of schema theory). The knowledge hypothesis also provides us with some idea(s) as to how vocabulary is acquired.

Consider ways experience can influence reading comprehension.

The Access Hypothesis

Mezynski (1983) describes an **access hypothesis,** which essentially states that aptitude is related to a blend of trainable subskills. These vocabulary-learning subskills have to do with locating, or accessing, word meanings and using those meanings efficiently while reading. Educators and researchers subscribing to this hypothesis have as their goal a kind of automatic behavior or *automaticity* (LaBerge & Samuels, 1985) in reading as accessing and comprehension take place. According to Mezynski, the classroom implication of the access hypothesis is that the amount of practice is an important factor in word learning. Words taught must become a permanent part of the child's knowledge to be useful in reading.

The ability to think of correct word meanings quickly and efficiently is crucial to reading comprehension.

Which Hypothesis Is Correct?

Because the research at this point has failed to arrive at absolute conclusions, it is difficult to say that one, or any, of the preceding views is correct. We tend to favor the knowledge hypothesis, based on recent comprehension research. Even though the theoretical picture may be a little unclear, we feel it is possible to draw some important inferences from the research that can help guide teachers as they attempt to promote vocabulary development. First, there is little doubt that first-hand experience helps children learn new concepts and vocabulary. Parents can do much to help their children succeed by taking them on vacations, answering their child's questions about new experiences, and helping them to read about and discuss new ideas in the home. Similarly, teachers can select learning activities that give students concrete

The search for a workable hypothesis has led researchers to some interesting conclusions.

opportunities to learn. In Chapter 12, we offer a pyramid of classroom experiences, which may help teachers to select concrete concept and vocabulary-building activities. Second, students need to become actively engaged in vocabulary learning tasks (Guthrie, 1982). Teachers need to provide learning opportunities that stimulate children and help them find exciting ways to use language. These learning experiences should help students acquire initial knowledge of new words and embellish or extend meanings of previously learned words or concepts.

Guidelines for Effective Vocabulary Instruction

Research on Concept and Vocabulary Development

Reading ability and successful comprehension involve many important factors. Knowledge of words and word meanings is one of the most critical of all factors to be developed by teachers. As D. D. Johnson and Pearson point out:

> It is not the words themselves that are so critical. Rather it is the rich reservoir of meaning—the conceptual base underlying words that matters. The words become a summary symbol for all those concepts, a set of abbreviations that allow us to communicate a lot of meaning in a brief amount of space and time. (1984, p. 1)

Words frequently summarize broader concepts.

Other researchers support the notion that teachers should not merely teach words but should teach concept knowledge (R. C. Anderson & Freebody, 1981). K. S. Goodman (1976) states that new vocabulary should be learned in the context of acquiring new knowledge. This means that memorizing long lists of isolated words is not likely to give students an increased understanding of what they read. We believe that teachers need to avoid these rote exercises and teach new words and concepts using meaningful language and books.

Reading research in recent decades has focused some attention on two aspects of word learning: phonic analysis approaches and the teaching of whole words and concepts. Although many researchers and teachers in past decades placed almost exclusive emphasis on the importance of phonics in early reading, research results indicate that there is more to reading success than phonics alone. The chief finding is that intensive phonics programs produce students who are better at pronouncing words, but who may not do as well in comprehension. Not only can intensive phonics programs negatively affect reading comprehension, they may also harm other important factors such as interest, attitude toward reading, and motivation (D. D. Johnson & Baumann, 1984). Although phonics knowledge may help children recognize and pronounce words that are new to them in print, concept and vocabulary knowledge help children finish the reading process by attaching meaning.

Semantic-based strategies spark meaning connections in the brain.

Research has shown two effective vocabulary teaching strategies: semantic-based and mnemonic strategies. **Semantic-based strategies** rely on students' knowledge of words, and of the world, to spark meaning connections in the brain. For example, the use of context clues and semantic mapping (discussed later in the chapter) to develop concept and vocabulary understandings are instructional practices consistent with the semantic-based view. Research suggests that helping children learn to use semantic information embedded in sentences, or context clues, along with helping them define words according to what they already know, facilitates the learning of new words.

Mnemonics uses word and picture associations to help students remember new words. A particularly effective mnemonic strategy has been tested extensively through research in upper elementary and middle school/junior high settings known as the **keyword method** (Levin et al., 1984; Levin, Levin, Glasman, & Nordwall, 1992). Levin et al. offer the following description:

> As an example of keyword method use, consider the vocabulary item *carlin,* meaning *old woman.* In the first stage of the process, one *recodes* the unfamiliar vocabulary word *carlin* into a more familiar concrete proxy that resembles (orthographically or acoustically) some part of *carlin.* A good recoded "keyword" for this example is *car.* Then, in the second stage of the process, one *relates* the keyword to the vocabulary word's definition . . . such as *an old woman driving a car.* With this method, when one is later asked to recall the definition of *carlin,* an efficient systematic retrieval path is now possible: from the vocabulary word *carlin* to the keyword *car* to the interactive representation of *an old woman driving the car* to the definition *old woman.* (1992, p. 157)

*Develop a **keyword method** example using a word or words from a favorite children's book.*

Another example offered by Levin et al. (1984) for the keyword *angler* uses the word *angel* as a "word clue" along with a mnemonic picture (Figure 7.1).

Research comparing semantic-based and mnemonic strategies indicates that mnemonics tend to work best for helping students recall definitions (Levin et al.,

ANGLER (ANGEL) a person who likes to go fishing

Figure 7.1

Keyword illustration for the word *angler*

1992). Although keyword and other mnemonic strategies may prove useful, it seems impractical for teachers to develop mnemonic pictures for every new word to be introduced. Teachers, however, should seek out additional strategies that help students relate what they already know, both in terms of words and experiences, in recalling word meanings and pronunciations.

Guidelines for Instruction

From results of the research cited previously, it is possible to develop a list of guidelines for teachers to consider concerning reading vocabulary instruction. They are based in part on the work of Stahl (1986), who conducted a rather extensive meta-analysis of 52 vocabulary instruction studies. Stahl found three principles that characterized effective vocabulary instruction. Each is presented below, along with a brief explanation.

Principle 1

Teachers should offer both definitions and context during vocabulary instruction. As children learn new words, they do so in two different ways. First, they learn basic definitions or information that helps determine the logical relationship of a word compared to others, as in a dictionary definition. This can be accomplished by simply providing the definition, or through other comparisons such as synonyms, antonyms, classification schemes, word roots, affixes, and so on.

Context helps readers choose the correct meaning for multiple-meaning words.

Context information has to do with knowing the basic core definition of a word and how it varies, or is changed, in different texts. For example, the word *run* is generally thought of as a verb meaning "to move swiftly." When looking for this simple word in the dictionary, one quickly realizes that the word *run* has approximately 50 separate definitions, which are determined by the context. There is the word *run*, as in "running a race"; "a run of bad luck"; or, the run women sometimes get in their hosiery. Without context, it is impossible to say with certainty which meaning of the word *run* is intended. Therefore, it is important for teachers to help students understand both the definitional and contextual relations of words. Vocabulary instruction should include both aspects if reading comprehension is to benefit.

Principle 2

Deep processing *connects new vocabulary with existing knowledge in students.*

Deep processing of reading vocabulary should be encouraged. Deep processing of vocabulary has two potential meanings: relating the word to information the student already knows and/or spending time on the task of learning new words. Stahl (1986) defines three different levels of processing for vocabulary instruction:

- *Association processing:* Students learn simple associations through such language permutations as synonyms and word associations.
- *Comprehension processing:* Moves the student beyond simple associations by having them do something with the association, such as fitting the word into a sentence blank, classifying the word with other words, or finding antonyms.
- *Generation processing:* Involves taking the comprehended association and generating a new or novel product (sometimes called *generative comprehension*). This could involve a restatement of the definition in the student's own words, creating a novel sentence using the word correctly in a clear context, or comparing the definition to the student's own personal experiences. One caution relates

to the generation of sentences by students. Sometimes students generate sentences without really processing the information deeply, as with students who begin each sentence with "This is a . . . " (Pearson, 1985; Stahl, 1986).

Principle 3

Students need to have multiple exposures to new reading vocabulary words. Providing students with multiple exposures to information about new words and multiple exposures to the new word in varied contexts appears to improve comprehension. Amount of time also seems to be a relevant factor for improving comprehension. The more time teachers are able to devote to comprehension, the greater the opportunity for learning to take place.

E. Carr and Wixson (1986) suggest some **guidelines for vocabulary instruction** that correspond well to the principles stated previously. Classroom strategies for implementing each of these guidelines are presented in the next section of this chapter.

Notice that multiple exposures to new vocabulary improve comprehension.

1. *Vocabulary instruction should help students link new vocabulary to their background knowledge.* A variety of techniques should be used to link new vocabulary to already known information in children's minds. This process helps the new words to become personalized and relevant in children's lives. Without this linkage, new vocabulary remains abstract and irrelevant.

2. *Vocabulary instruction should help students develop a depth and breadth of word knowledge that goes well beyond simple memorization.* As noted, many common words carry multiple meanings. For vocabulary knowledge to be maximally beneficial and functional, words need to be understood within a variety of contexts (E. Carr & Wixson, 1986; D. D. Johnson & Pearson, 1984).

3. *Vocabulary instruction should provide for active student involvement in learning new words.* Too often, students are placed in a passive role in which it is easy to tune out. For vocabulary instruction to "stick," students must become actively engaged so that generative thinking can occur. Teachers must constantly search for learning activities that make generative thinking about words a reality.

Students should be actively involved in vocabulary development, not just passive listeners.

4. *Vocabulary instruction should help students develop strategies for acquiring new vocabulary independently.* One of the goals of education is to help people become independent learners for life. This goal is made specific here in stating that the job of vocabulary instruction is not truly complete if teachers fail to help students develop strategies of their own for selecting new words for study. Paris, Lipson, and Wixson (1983) refer to this phase of instruction as helping students become "strategic" readers.

Which Words Should We Teach?

Finally, M. McKeown and Beck (1988) have addressed an important issue in their research, namely, which vocabulary should be taught in elementary classrooms? They point out that one problem with traditional vocabulary instruction in basal readers has been the egalitarian treatment of all categories of words. As an example, a mythology selection in a basal reader about Arachne, who loved to weave, gives the word *loom* as much attention as the word *agreement*. McKeown and Beck point out that while the word *loom* may be helpful in understanding more about spinning, it is a word of relatively low use compared to the word *agreement*, which is key to understanding the story and of much higher utility as students move into adult life.

Students enjoy word play activities as part of vocabulary learning.

Not all words are created equal, especially in elementary classrooms. As McKeown and Beck put it:

> The choice of which words to teach and what kind of attention to give them depends on a variety of factors, such as importance of the words for understanding the selection, relationship to specific domains of knowledge, general utility, and relationship to other lessons and classroom events. (1988, p. 45)

They add that students should be expected to seek new words outside of class and discover vocabulary to learn on their own. This helps children continue to develop as lifelong learners and users of the building blocks of language fluency.

Strategies for Building Students' Background Knowledge

In Chapter 2 we discussed the role of schema development in reading comprehension. It is important that children find ways to link new information to what they already know. These mental connections do not always happen through normal encounters with their environment, nor by accident. Therefore, an important task for teachers is the structuring of learning situations wherein new conceptual frameworks can be formed. This section describes several classroom-proven possibilities for teachers to consider. We suggest that this section be viewed as a small resource book of ideas for preservice and in-service teachers.

Gipe's Cluing Technique

Research by Joan Gipe (1980, 1987) indicates that new word meanings are best taught by providing appropriate and familiar context. Gipe's **cluing technique** introduces new vocabulary through a series of sentences that rely heavily on context clues, or cluing. A four-step procedure is recommended. First, students are given a passage in which the beginning sentence uses the new word appropriately, thus providing valuable semantic and syntactic (context clues) information. Second, the next sentence of the passage describes some of the characteristics or attributes of the new word. With all of the sentences in the cluing technique, the context should be filled with familiar words and situations. The third sentence in the paragraph defines the new word, again with care being taken to use familiar concepts (Gipe, 1987, p. 152). The final sentence provides a generative thinking opportunity by asking students to relate the new word to their own lives. This is achieved by having them write an answer to a question or complete an open-ended statement requiring application of the word meaning. Gipe provides the following example in her book *Corrective Reading Techniques for the Classroom Teacher:*

> The boys who wanted to sing together formed a quintet. There were five boys singing in the quintet. Quintet means a group of five, and this group usually sings or plays music. If you were in a quintet, what instrument would you want to play? (1987, p. 152)

After students complete this reading and writing exercise, responses can be shared in a group discussion. Answers to the final question or open-ended statement might be written on the chalkboard or chart paper in much the same fashion as a language-experience chart. If students are keeping individual and/or a classroom word bank, these new words can be added. This will make the words easily available for future writing projects and thus provide natural repetition.

Cluing uses teacher-made passages loaded with context clues related to the new word.

Predict-O-Gram

The **Predict-O-Gram** (Blachowicz, 1986) is a charting process that asks students to organize vocabulary in relation to the structure of the selection. In the case of narrative text, this structure is the story grammar (setting, characters, problem, actions taken, resolution, etc.). To begin, teachers might write the new vocabulary and/or concepts on the chalkboard or an overhead transparency. Note that this occurs before students have read the story. After a brief introductory discussion of the words, we recommend that teachers give students a copy of the story grammar elements and ask students to predict how the author might use the words and concepts in the story. As a final step before reading the selection, the class might discuss the predictions and why they were judged to be in their respective categories.

Notice that a key element of ***Predict-O-Grams*** *is prediction.*

To illustrate the Predict-O-Gram procedure, let's say that important vocabulary for the book *Why Mosquitoes Buzz in People's Ears* (Aardema, 1975) includes *mosquito, iguana, farmer, reeds, burrow, feared, gathered, alarmed, council, killed, plotting, sticks,* and *whining.* After a quick run-through for definition purposes, the students, either independently or as a class, predict how each word might be used in the story. The results of the prediction might look something like what is presented in Figure 7.2.

Figure 7.2

Predict-O-Gram for
*Why Mosquitoes Buzz in
People's Ears*

Directions: Predict how the author may use these words in our story.

The setting	The characters	The problem/goal
reeds	mosquito	feared
burrow	iguana	alarmed
	farmer	whining

Actions	Resolution	Other things
gathered	killed	sticks
	plotting	council

After reading the selection, the teacher and class should return to the Predict-O-Gram to verify and/or modify the predictions based on new information from the selection. In our example in Figure 7.2, the words *killed* and *whining* are in incorrect categories and would be moved to the correct columns.

Frayer Model

*Examples and nonexamples are used to analyze new concepts in the **Frayer model**.*

The **Frayer model** was developed to provide students with a systematic means for analyzing and learning new concepts. The steps of the Frayer model, along with examples described by McNeil (1987, p. 116), follow:

1. Describe the necessary characteristics that are common to the concept in all situations. For example, a necessary characteristic for the concept *globe* is *spherical*.
2. Differentiate relevant from irrelevant characteristics concerning the concept. For example, *size* is an irrelevant characteristic for the concept *globe*.
3. Provide an example for the concept, such as showing students a classroom globe.
4. Provide a nonexample for the concept, such as a chart (because it is not spherical).
5. Compare the concept to a lesser or subordinate concept, such as a ball.
6. Relate the concept to a superordinate term, for instance *global*.
7. Compare the concept to a coordinate or related term, such as *map*.

To use the Frayer model, teachers begin by reviewing the reading selection to locate new vocabulary and concepts that are important to the topic. After a quick reading or discussion of the selection, teacher and students together try to write meanings for the new concepts, based on information presented by the author. Then, students try to think of nonexamples and examples for the concepts. The final step is to compare examples and nonexamples to discover necessary characteristics for the concepts. Be sure to choose examples that are best examples of the concepts to avoid confusion. For instance, *tomato* would probably not be a best example for *fruit* because it is often used as a vegetable.

Opin

Opin is a procedure that has children, working in small group settings, come up with responses to cloze passages. Originally developed by Greene (1973), Opin is easy to implement and requires little preparation time. The following steps are suggested by Searfoss and Readence (1989):

1. Begin by forming groups of three children each. Distribute several Opin sentences to the groups. For primary grades, it may be desirable to distribute the sentences one at a time. This is also true for all age groups when initially explaining or modeling this activity.
2. Each child should choose a word that makes sense and spend a minute or so trying to convince the other group members their answer is correct. The group is to decide on one answer they think is best.
3. Then, the whole class/group assembles to hear the choice from each small group. The one rule is that the group must explain why their choice makes sense. This final step provides teachers with an excellent opportunity to point out how context can determine the choice of words.

Examples of Opin sentences and possible vocabulary words follows:

A fireman's _____ curves down in the back to allow water to drain off without getting his clothes wet. (helmet, hat, cap)

A person who is honest and truthful is said to have _____. (integrity, candid, fair, moral)

Many people feel _____ when moving to a new city or neighborhood. (anxious, sad, happy, scared)

Opin uses modified cloze passages to help students use context to understand new words.

Key Vocabulary and Word Banks

Two very effective activities that help facilitate both concept and vocabulary development are key vocabulary (Ashton-Warner, 1963) and the use of word banks. Because both of these activities are extremely helpful in promoting word identification, we have included full discussions of each in Chapter 8.

Word banks are student-made "dictionaries."

Word Cards

E. Carr (1985) suggests the use of **word cards** to help students record and recall new vocabulary. The idea is to have students write the new word on an index card or word bank card. Then each student should record a word, phrase, name, and the like that remind the child of the new word's meanings. Finally, short definitional words should be added to clarify the correct usage of the word.

The end result looks something like a diagram (Figure 7.3).

Structured Overview

A **structured overview** is a graphic organizer usually presented by the teacher before silent reading, then referred to by students during silent reading and reread as a guide to postreading discussions (Manzo & Manzo, 1990, p. 106). As a tool for building concept knowledge, the structured overview arranges both new and known

Chapter 12 describes in detail how to construct structured overviews.

Figure 7.3

Word card

> **vivacious**
>
> –Jennifer
>
> –lively, energetic, bouncy

concepts and vocabulary into a kind of diagram illustrating the relationships between the new word and known concepts and vocabulary. Structured overviews belong to a class of teacher-constructed instruments usually applied to content area subjects (e.g., science, social studies) known as *graphic organizers*. This refers to any pictorial representation of concepts, meanings, or vocabulary. The idea is to arrange synonyms, definitional words, examples, and other pertinent information into a kind of flowchart that moves from known information toward the new concept. While the flow usually moves from the top down (known to new), a structured overview can actually be constructed in any form that makes sense. The procedure for constructing structured overviews along with an example are included in Chapter 12.

Strategies for Extending Students' Vocabulary Knowledge

Semantic Mapping

Semantic maps depict relationships between concepts.

Semantic maps are diagrams or graphic depictions of concepts that help children see how words relate to each other. An excellent activity for extending students' vocabulary knowledge, semantic mapping enables children to see known words in new contexts. The process for constructing semantic maps involves the following steps:

Step 1:   Select a vocabulary word or concept important to the story, text, or book.

Step 2:   Write the word or concept in the center of the chalkboard or an overhead transparency.

Step 3:   Ask the class to help think of other words that have something to do with the word or concept at the center of the chalkboard or transparency.

Step 4:   Group related words into categories and agree on labels for these categories.

A discussion should follow in which the relationships of these words are examined. In essence, the teacher helps children to construct new schema structures for background knowledge enhancement. A completed semantic map is shown in Figure 7.4.

Semantic Feature Analysis

Class, example, and property are three relationships of vocabulary.

D. D. Johnson and Pearson (1984) explain in their book *Teaching Reading Vocabulary* that concepts have certain relationships known as *class, example,* and *property.* Class relations are those in which the stimulus concept, or concept under study, belongs to the class of things indicated by the related response. For example, *guppies* are related to the class

Figure 7.4

Semantic map

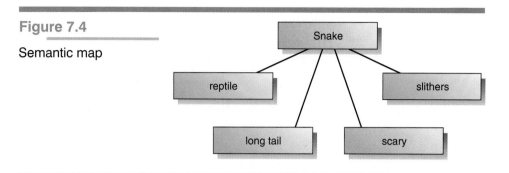

known as *fish*. Example relations represent examples of class relations. *Cocker spaniel* is an example for the class known as *dogs*. Finally, *property relations* specify the properties or attributes associated with concepts. Dogs bark, have hair, and often perform tricks. These are examples of properties associated with the class *dogs*. Through semantic mapping or feature analysis strategies, students can graphically illustrate these various relationships.

Semantic feature analysis builds on and expands the categories of concepts tucked away in students' memory banks (D. D. Johnson & Pearson, 1984). The object is to complete a grid or matrix that identifies common and unique traits of words classified into the same category. A classroom experience based on semantic feature analysis may proceed as follows:

1. Present to the class a list of words that have some common features. The category of *flying machines,* for example, might include words such as *jet, Hovercraft, balloon, blimp,* and *rocket.* List these words in the vertical column at the far left of the grid on the chalkboard, chart paper, or overhead transparency.
2. Begin to list some features, with the assistance of the students, commonly associated with one or more of the flying machines. List these features across the top of the grid.
3. Children should complete the grid by putting either a "+" (meaning the example has that feature) or "−" beside each word under each feature.
4. Group discussion of the grid or matrix should follow so as to lead the children to a better understanding of each word and to an understanding that no two words have exactly the same meaning.

An example of a semantic feature analysis matrix and grid is provided in Figure 7.5.

Figure 7.5

Semantic feature analysis for *flying machines*

	has wheels	passengers	has wings/fins	very fast
jet	+	+	+	+
Hovercraft	−	+	−	+
balloon	−	+	−	−
blimp	−	+	−	−
rocket	−	+/− (sometimes)	+	+

Figure 7.6

Exclusion brainstorming

	The Red Pony	
colt	tricycle	kids
currying	California	saddle

Exclusion Brainstorming

Blachowicz (1986) describes an activity called **exclusion brainstorming** in which students use their prior knowledge to anticipate new concepts. This activity is begun by creating an activity sheet or overhead transparency with the title or topic of the selection across the top. Beneath the title or topic, the teacher writes a few well-chosen words that either come from the story and fit the topic, some words that clearly are not consistent with the topic, and others that are ambiguous. One example for Steinbeck's (1937) *The Red Pony* is shown in Figure 7.6.

Students begin by deciding which words they think will not be found in the selection and underline those they think will appear. Students should be expected to explain, either orally or in print, why they think the way they do. From this point in the discussion, the teacher can highlight important words and concepts found in the passage. Exclusion brainstorming offers teachers a wonderful blend of schema activation and vocabulary analysis, and both are directly linked to the reading of a selection.

Concept Ladder

Teachers often need students to focus on single words that carry meaning for broader concepts. Gillet and Temple (1986) describe an activity known as the **concept ladder** that can serve this purpose quite well. It provides a graphic depiction of how multiple concepts are related to other words and concepts they already know. This procedure creates a kind of semantic network for each term. Figure 7.7 displays a concept ladder for *ships*.

Figure 7.7

Concept ladder for *ships*

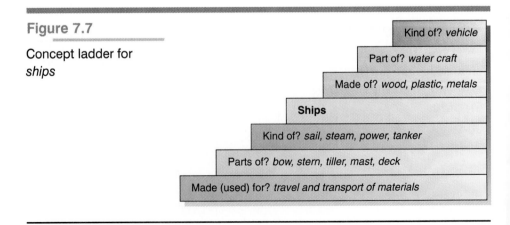

Kind of? *vehicle*

Part of? *water craft*

Made of? *wood, plastic, metals*

Ships

Kind of? *sail, steam, power, tanker*

Parts of? *bow, stern, tiller, mast, deck*

Made (used) for? *travel and transport of materials*

Free-Form Outline

Free-form outlines are postreading diagrams that include webs, maps, and radial outlines. Like the structured overview discussed earlier, they provide a visual framework for new vocabulary and concepts (E. Carr & Wixson, 1986). Free-form outlines, however, generally are not hierarchical and are generated by the students themselves at the conclusion of a selection or unit of study. Figure 7.8 shows a free-form outline based on the book *Charlotte's Web* (E. B. White, 1952).

In the free-form outline in Figure 7.8, the student has focused on characters and events related to the characters. In constructing free-form outlines, students select new vocabulary, link the new words (in this case, the words were *egg sac, terrific,* and *radiant*) to background knowledge gained from the text and make associations between the important concepts.

List three examples of free-form outlines.

Capsule Vocabulary

Capsule vocabulary (E. Carr & Wixson, 1986; Crist, 1975) encourages word learning by involving the four language modes: listening, speaking, reading, and writing. Students are presented a list of words related to a topic under study. If the class is studying computers, then the list of words might include *keyboard, CRT, disk, hard copy, laser printer,* and *word processing.* Students work in pairs, with one student discussing the topic for 5 minutes using the designated words, then the partners switch roles. After the talk sessions, each student writes a summary of the topic using the designated terms.

Cloze Passages

Cloze passages offer teachers another interesting way to improve both vocabulary knowledge and word-identification abilities. Various uses of the cloze passage are discussed in Chapters 6 and 8.

Charlotte
Spider
Friends with pig
Writes "messages" on her web
Produces an "egg sac" for her babies

Fern
The Arable's daughter
Saves Wilbur the pig from death
Is a true friend to Wilbur

Templeton
Rat
Befriends Charlotte and Wilbur
Saves Charlotte's "egg sac"
Wilbur promises a reward

Wilbur
Beloved pig
Charlotte's best friend
Feels "radiant" (p. 101) and "terrific"
Is allowed to live a long life

Figure 7.8

Free-form outline of *Charlotte's Web*

Strategies for Helping Students Acquire New Vocabulary Independently

The ultimate task for educators is to help students become independent learners. The selection and learning of new vocabulary throughout life is unquestionably a key to continuing self-education. In this section, we feature ways students may help themselves become independent learners of new words they encounter while reading.

Encouraging Wide Reading

Wide reading is a natural and powerful way to build vocabulary knowledge.

Reading is a cognitive skill that in some ways mirrors physical skill development. As with physical skills, the more one practices reading, the more one's ability level increases. Over the years in our work with at-risk students, we have come to realize that if we can simply get children to read every day for 15 to 20 minutes (or more), their reading ability will increase quickly and exponentially. In one study, Reutzel and Hollingsworth (1991c) discovered that allowing children to read self-selected books 30 minutes every day resulted in significantly improved scores on reading comprehension tests. These children performed as well as students who had received direct instruction on the same tested reading comprehension skills for the same amount of time each day. These results suggest that regular daily reading is probably at least as effective as formal reading instruction, and the child can do it on his own!

Surveying student interests helps teachers select free-reading materials.

So the question for teachers is, how can we encourage children to read independently on a regular basis? The answer probably lies in helping them recognize their interests and finding books they can read. The interest issue can be resolved in two steps. First, the teacher should administer an interest inventory to the class at the beginning of the year (see Chapter 13) to determine what types of books are indicated for classroom instruction. These results, however, could be taken a little further. We suggest that the teacher start an **individual interest sheet (IIS)** for each child

What are some motivational ways teachers can encourage wide reading?

based on these results and present it to children during individual reading confer-ences (see Chapter 11). The IIS sheet simply lists topics that appear to be of interest to the child and suggests books available in the school library. Over time, the child can list additional topics he discovers to be of interest and can look for books in that area. This is much the same principle as having children keep a list of topics they would like to write stories about, which is discussed in Chapter 11. Figure 7.9 shows an example of an IIS, along with new interests written in by the student.

A useful reference for teachers attempting to match children's interests with qual-ity literature is Donna Norton's (1995) book *Through the Eyes of a Child: An Intro-duction to Children's Literature.* Most high-interest topic areas are discussed in this text and are matched to several possible book titles. Book suggestions include brief descriptions of the main story line to help in the decision-making process.

Shared Reading and Vocabulary Learning

M. Senechal and Cornell (1993) have studied ways vocabulary knowledge can be increased through shared reading experiences (those where adults and children read stories together). The methods investigated included reading the story verbatim (read alouds), asking questions, repeating sentences containing new vocabulary words, and what has been referred to as recasting new vocabulary introduced in the selection. **Recasts** build directly on sentences just read containing a new word the teacher (or parent) may want to teach the child. Verbs, subjects, or objects are often changed to recast the word for further discussion and examination. Thus, if a child says or reads, "look at the *snake,*" the adult may recast the phrase by replying, "It is a large striped *snake.*" In this example, the same meaning of the phrase was maintained, but adjec-tives were added to enhance understanding of the word *snake.* Interestingly, Senechal and Cornell concluded that activities that involve requesting students' active participa-tion, such as questioning and recasts, did not boost children's vocabulary learning (p. 369). Reading a book verbatim to a child was just as effective. This does not mean that we should abandon these strategies; they are effective. Rather, we should under-stand that reading passages aloud to students can be just as potent as direct teaching

List two ways teachers can enhance vocabulary learn-ing, according to Senechal and Cornell (1993).

Individual Interest Sheet

Mrs. Harbor's Sixth Grade

Sunnydale School

Name: Holly Ambrose

Things I am interested in knowing more about, or topics that I like . . .

Topics	Books to consider from our library
horses	*The Red Pony* (J. Steinbeck)
getting along with friends	*Afternoon of the Elves* (J. Lisle)
romantic stories	*The Witch of Blackbird Pond* (E. Speare)
one-parent families	*The Moonlight Man* (P. Fox)

Figure 7.9

Individual interest sheet (IIS)

strategies. We need to do both: read aloud regularly *and* discuss passages containing new vocabulary with students in challenging ways.

Computer-Assisted Vocabulary Learning

Computer-assisted vocabulary instruction is a powerful option for teachers.

As computers become more accessible to students and teachers, the question arises: Can some of the new computer applications available help students learn new vocabulary? Reinking and Rickman (1990) studied the vocabulary growth of sixth-grade students who had computer-assisted programs available to them. They compared students who read passages on printed pages accompanied by either a standard dictionary or glossary (the traditional classroom situation) with students who read passages on a computer screen. These computer-assisted programs provided either *optional assistance* (on command) for specific vocabulary words or *mandatory* (automatic) assistance. They learned two very interesting things from their research. First, students reading passages with computer assistance performed significantly better on vocabulary tests focusing on the words emphasized than students in the traditional reading groups. Second, students receiving automatic computer assistance with the passages also outperformed the more traditional reading group on a passage comprehension test relating to information read in the experiment. This strongly suggests that computer programs that offer students passages to read with vocabulary assistance can be helpful. Further, this suggests to us another possible computer advantage: the value of teaching students to use what might be termed a *vocabulary enhancer,* such as a thesaurus program, with students' writing. This could help students discover on their own new synonyms and antonyms for commonly used words. Most word processing programs, such as Microsoft Word, have a thesaurus program already installed for *easy use.*

Vocabulary Overview

Vocabulary overviews *involve student self-selection of words to be learned.*

In classroom settings, teachers can usually anticipate vocabulary that may be troublesome during reading and teach these words through brief minilessons. But when children read independently, they will need to compensate and find ways to learn new words on their own. An activity that serves this purpose is developing a vocabulary overview. **Vocabulary overviews** help students select unknown words in print and use their background knowledge and context clues from the passage to determine word meaning.

One way of helping students develop their own vocabulary overviews is Haggard's (1986) vocabulary self-selection strategy (VSS). Our version of the VSS begins with a small-group minilesson to learn the process. Students are asked to find at least one word they feel the class should learn. They are asked to define the word to the best of their ability, based on the context of the word in the text and any other information from their own background knowledge. On the day the words are presented, each child takes turns explaining (a) where each word was found, (b) his context-determined definition for the word, and (c) why he thinks the class should learn the word.

As students practice the VSS, they become more cognizant of vocabulary that may require further investigation or extra thought. After practicing the VSS in small-group settings, the next step is to apply the strategy during self-selected reading (SSR) times. Words found in SSR books should be one of the topics of discussion during independent one-on-one reading conferences between the teacher and student. The heightened awareness that comes from student-generated vocabulary overviews eventually transfers and becomes an automatic reading strategy.

Word Maps

A **word map** (Schwartz & Raphael, 1985) is a visual rendering of a word's definition. It answers three important questions about the word's meaning: *What is it? What is it like? What are some examples?* Answers to these questions are extremely valuable because they help children link the new word or concept to their prior knowledge and world experiences, a process known to have an effect on reading comprehension (Stahl et al., 1991). An example of a word map is shown in Figure 7.10.

Word maps graphically portray word meanings.

Introducing this vocabulary-acquisition strategy to students is a relatively easy task. First, the teacher introduces the students to the idea of using picture strategies to understand new word meanings and explains that the word map is one example. Next, students should work with the teacher to organize familiar information in terms of the three questions used in the word map. In early practice exercises, simple concepts should be used. This will help students learn the map as a tool. For example, a practice map might be constructed using the word *car*. Answers for each of the story map questions that might be offered by elementary students follow:

Word: *car*

What is it? (transportation, movement)

What is it like? (four wheels, metal, glass, lights, moves, steering wheel)

What are some examples? (Corvette, station wagon, Firebird, convertible)

After working through several examples with the whole group or class, teachers should give students opportunities to practice using the word map. In the beginning, whole-class practice works best, followed by independent practice using narrative and expository texts of the students' or teacher's choosing.

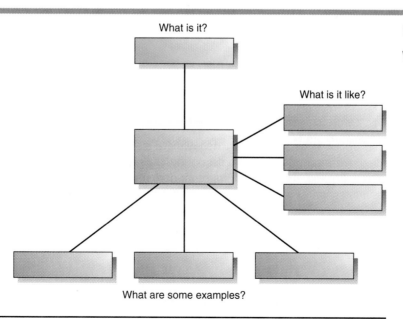

Figure 7.10

Word map

Studying Word Functions and Changes

Synonyms

Synonyms are words that have similar, but not exactly the same, meanings (D. D. Johnson & Pearson, 1984). No two words carry exactly the same meaning in all situations. Thus, when teaching children about new words and their synonyms, teachers should provide numerous opportunities for students to see differences as well as similarities. As with all reading strategies, this is best done within the natural context of real books and authentic writing experiences.

Think of interesting reading materials that might be used to teach students about synonyms.

One very productive way to get children interested in synonyms in the upper elementary grades is teaching the use of a thesaurus with their writing. Children can begin to see how the use of a thesaurus can "spice up" their writing projects. This tool is best used during revising and editing stages of the writing process (see Chapter 11). For instance, children sometimes have a problem coming up with descriptive language in their writing. A character in a story may be tortured by hostile savages, and the child may write that the victim felt "bad." If this word is targeted for thesaurus research, then the child may come up with synonyms for *bad* such as *rotten, unlucky, putrid, futile, rough, poorly,* or *nasty.* Following are several other common words that children overuse that could be researched using a thesaurus.

good	big	thing
pleasant	vast	object
glorious	grand	item
wonderful	enormous	entity
delightful	huge	organism

One way to involve children with books and synonyms is to take text from old favorite books and revise selected words. Teachers might want to develop a modified cloze passage, deleting only certain kinds of words, then let the children use synonyms to complete the blanks. Take, for example, the following excerpt from a book well suited for early to intermediate grade readers, *The Grouchy Ladybug*:

"Good morning," said the friendly ladybug.
"Go away!" shouted the grouchy ladybug. "I want those aphids."
"We can share them," suggested the friendly ladybug.
"No. They're mine, all mine," screamed the grouchy ladybug.
"Or do you want to fight me for them?"*

One option is to delete words following a statement (e.g., *said, shouted, suggested, screamed*) and put them in a list on the chalkboard with possible synonyms, such as *hinted, greeted, growled, yelled, reminded, mentioned, pointed out,* and *offered.* The resulting rewrites may look something like the following:

"Good morning," *greeted* the friendly ladybug.

"Go away!" *growled* the grouchy ladybug. "I want those aphids."

---

*From *The Grouchy Ladybug* by E. Carle, 1986, New York: HarperCollins. Copyright 1986 by HarperCollins. Reprinted by permission.

"We can share them," *hinted* the friendly ladybug.

"No. They're mine, all mine," *yelled* the grouchy ladybug.

"Or do you want to fight me for them?"

Class discussions might relate to how the use of different synonyms can alter meaning significantly, thus showing how synonyms have similar meanings, but not the exact same meanings. For example, if we took the sentence

"Go away!" *shouted* the grouchy ladybug.

and changed it to read

"Go away!" *hinted* the grouchy ladybug.

it would be easy for children to understand how the author's message had been softened considerably. This cross-training with reading and writing experiences helps synonyms to take on new relevance as a literacy tool in the hands of children.

Antonyms

Antonyms are word opposites or near opposites. *Hard–soft, dark–light, big–small* are examples of antonym pairs. Like synonyms, antonyms help students gain insights into word meanings. When searching for ideal antonym examples, teachers should try to identify word sets that are mutually exclusive or that completely contradict each other.

Several classes of antonyms have been identified (D. D. Johnson & Pearson, 1984) that may be useful in instruction. One class is called *relative pairs,* or *counterparts.* Examples include *mother–father, sister–brother, uncle–aunt* because one term implies the other. Other antonyms reflect a complete opposite or reversal of meaning such as *fast–slow, stop–go,* and *give–take.* Complimentary antonyms tend to lead from one to another such as *give–take, friend–foe,* and *hot–cold.*

Word opposites, or near opposites, are **antonyms**.

Antonym activities, as with all language-learning activities, should be drawn from the context of familiar books and student writing samples. By using familiar text with clear meanings, it is easy for children to see the full impact and flavor of differing word meanings. Remember, in classroom instruction involving minilessons, teaching from whole text to parts (antonyms in this case) is the key. Thus, if the teacher decided he wanted to develop a kind of antonym worksheet for students, then the worksheet should be drawn from a book that has already been shared (or will be shared) with the whole class or group. One example of a fun book for this exercise is *Weird Parents* by Audrey Wood (1990), which could yield sentences like the following (in the space provided, students write in antonyms for the underlined words):

1. There once was a boy who had <u>weird</u> (   ) parents.
2. In the <u>morning</u> (   ), the weird mother always walked the boy to his bus stop.
3. At 12 o'clock when the boy <u>opened</u> (   ) his lunch box, he'd always have a weird surprise.

Another possibility is to ask children to find words in their writing or reading for which they can think of antonyms. A student in sixth grade reading *A Wrinkle in Time* (L'Engle, 1962) might create the following list of book words and antonyms:

Wrinkle Words/Page No.	Antonyms
punishment/13	reward
hesitant/63	eager
frightening/111	pleasant

If a student in third grade had written a story about his new baby sister, he might select some of the following words and antonyms:

Baby Story Words	Opposites
asleep	awake
cry	laugh
wet	dry

One way to assess the ability to recognize antonyms is through multiple-choice and cloze exercises. The idea is to choose sentences from familiar text and let students select which word is the correct antonym from among three choices. The choices may include one synonym, the correct antonym, and a third choice that is a different part of speech. Following are two examples taken from the book *The Glorious Flight* (Provensen & Provensen, 1983):

1. Like a great swan, the *beautiful* (attractive, <u>homely</u>, shoots) glider rises into the air. . . .
2. Papa is getting *lots* (<u>limited</u>, from, loads) of practice.

Of many possible classroom activities, the most profitable will probably be those in which students are required to generate their own responses. Simple recognition items, as with multiple-choice measures, do not cause children to go within themselves nearly as deeply to find and apply new knowledge.

Euphemisms

According to Tompkins and Hoskisson (1991, p. 122), **euphemisms** are words or phrases that are used to soften language to avoid harsh or distasteful realities (e.g., *passed away*), usually out of concern for people's feelings. Euphemisms are certainly worth some attention, because they not only help students improve their writing versatility but also aid in reading comprehension.

Euphemisms soften language.

Two types of euphemisms include *inflated* and *deceptive* language. Inflated language euphemisms tend to make something sound greater or more sophisticated than it is. For example, *sanitation engineer* might be an inflated euphemism for *garbage collector*. Deceptive language euphemisms are intentional words and phrases meant to intentionally misrepresent. Children should learn that this language often is used in advertisements to persuade an unknowing public. Several examples of euphemisms based on the work of Lutz (cited in Tompkins & Hoskisson, 1991, p. 122) follow:

Euphemism	Real Meaning
dentures	false teeth
expecting	pregnant
funeral director	undertaker
passed away	died

previously owned	used
senior citizen	old person
terminal patient	dying

Onomatopoeia and Creative Words

Onomatopoeia is the creation of words that imitate sounds *(buzz, whir, vrrrrooom).* Some authors, such as Dr. Seuss, Shel Silverstein, and others, have made regular use of onomatopoeia and other creative words in their writing. One instance of onomatopoeia may be found in Dr. Seuss's book *Horton Hears a Who!* (1954) in the sentence "On clarinets, oom-pahs and boom-pahs and flutes." A wonderful example of creative language is found in Silverstein's (1974, p. 71) poem "Sarah Cynthia Sylvia Stout Would Not Take the Garbage Out" in the phrase "Rubbery blubbery macaroni. . . . "

Dr. Seuss and Shel Silverstein are two authors who create words for effect.

Children can be shown many interesting examples on onomatopoeia and creative words from the world of great children's literature. The natural extension to their own writing comes swiftly. Children may want to add a special section to their word banks for onomatopoeia and creative words to enhance their own written creations.

Assisting Students in Multicultural Settings With Vocabulary Development

Vocabulary development in spoken and written English is at the heart of literacy learning (Wheatley, Muller, & Miller, 1993). Because of the rich diversity found in American classrooms, teachers need to consider ways of adapting the curriculum so that all children can learn to recognize and use appropriate and descriptive vocabulary. In this section, we consider three possible avenues proven to be successful in multicultural settings.

Linking vocabulary studies to a broad topic or novel. We know that there is a limit to the number of words that can be taught directly and in isolation. K. Au (1993) tells us that students in multicultural settings learn vocabulary best if the new words are related to a broader topic. Working on vocabulary development in connection with students' exploration of content area topics is a natural and connected way to learn new words and explore their various meanings. In Chapter 12 we go into further detail about how vocabulary instruction can be conducted in content units, including the use of special computer-assisted programs.

Wide reading as a vehicle for vocabulary development. Reading for enjoyment on a daily basis helps students increase their vocabulary knowledge, not to mention myriad other reading abilities. Teachers can help students become regular readers by assessing their reading interests (see Chapter 13), then locate books that "fit the reader." Matching books and students is a simple way of encouraging the kinds of reading behaviors that pay dividends. Helping students learn how to choose books on their developmental level (see "Rule of Thumb" in Chapter 11) is an important way students can learn to independently select books.

List several ways to stimulate greater vocabulary learning in multicultural settings.

The Village English activity. L. Delpit (1988) writes about a method of teaching Native Alaskan students new vocabulary that works well in most multicultural settings. This **Village English activity** respects and encourages children's home languages while helping them see relationships between language use and power realities in the United States (Au, 1993, p. 133). The Village English activity begins with the teacher writing "Our Language Heritage" at the top of half a piece of poster board, and "Standard American English" at the top of the second half. The teacher explains to students that in America people speak in many different ways and that this makes our nation as colorful and interesting as a patchwork quilt. For elementary students, we think this would be a good time to share *Elmer* by David McKee (1990), a book about an elephant of many colors (called a "patchwork elephant") and how he enriched the elephant culture. The teacher can explain that there are times when adults want to speak in the same way so they can be understood by people of all cultures, and that these times are usually formal situations. In formal situations, we speak Standard American English. When at home or with friends in our community, we usually speak the language of our heritage. It is like the difference between a picnic compared to a "dressed up" formal dinner. On the chart, then, phrases used in the native dialect can be written under the heading "Our Language Heritage," and comparative translations are noted and discussed on the side labeled "Standard American English." These comparisons can be noted in an ongoing way throughout the year as dialect or other forms of language are naturally encountered in the context of speech or reading activities. The Village English activity can be an interesting way to increase vocabulary knowledge while also valuing language differences.

Summary

A student's knowledge of words directly affects his success as a reader. Hypotheses (e.g., instrumental, aptitude, knowledge, access) have been advanced to help explain how children learn new words. From these theories, we understand that parents can help their children succeed in expanding concept and vocabulary knowledge by exposing them to new experiences and helping them to read about and discuss new ideas in the home. Teachers can select learning activities that give students concrete opportunities to learn. These activities should help students internalize new words and concepts so that reading can become an automatic process. Learning experiences should help students acquire initial knowledge of new words and embellish or extend meanings of previously learned words or concepts. Ultimately, the task is to help students internalize strategies for the lifelong process of learning new words independently. The chapter overview in Figure 7.11 diagrams vocabulary acquisition from the classroom perspective.

CONCEPT APPLICATIONS

IN THE CLASSROOM

1. Design a minilesson introducing word maps to fifth-grade students. You should be certain that the lesson follows the "whole-to-parts" principle, as described in Chapter 1.
2. Create a "Deceptive Language" bulletin board, either formal design or collage, that shows various uses of euphemisms in advertising aimed at children as consumers. Create a second board showing how these same tactics are used on adults through advertising (and perhaps by political leaders!).

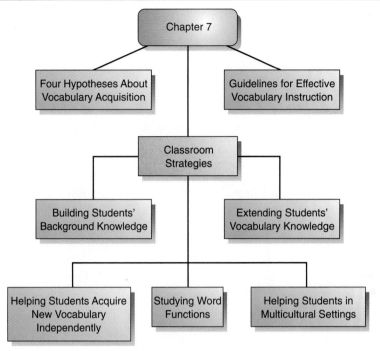

Figure 7.11

Chapter overview

IN THE FIELD

1. Do an interest inventory with five students in a local elementary school. Next, prepare an IIS that matches at least four of their interests to popular children's literature. Ideas for the books should be recommended by the school librarian or drawn from D. Norton's (1995) book *Through the Eyes of a Child: An Introduction to Children's Literature.* Finally, present the IIS forms to each child, and explain how they are to be used. Copies of both forms should be turned in to your college instructor, along with a journal entry explaining how each child reacted.

2. Prepare and teach a minilesson demonstrating the VSS. Develop a simple handout for the students with helpful hints about collecting new words for investigation.

3. Locate an elementary classroom in which the writing process (discussed in Chapter 11) is practiced. Working with two child-volunteers, prepare a minilesson on synonyms and antonyms using samples they permit you to borrow from their writing folders.

RECOMMENDED READINGS

Au, K. H. (1993). *Literacy instruction in multicultural settings.* Fort Worth, TX: Harcourt Brace Jovanovich College.

Johnson, D., & Pearson, P. D. (1984). *Teaching reading vocabulary.* New York: Holt, Rinehart & Winston.

McKee, D. (1990). *Elmer.* London: Red Fox.

Norton, D. E. (1995). *Through the eyes of a child: An introduction to children's literature* (4th ed.). Englewood Cliffs, NJ: Merrill/Prentice Hall.

Chapter 8

Identifying Words in Print

Focus Questions

When you are finished studying this chapter, you should be able to answer these questions:

1. What are the differences between explicit and implicit phonics perspectives?
2. How do context clues fit into an overall word-identification strategy for early readers?
3. What is the concept of "bridging," and how is it facilitated in the classroom?
4. In the book *Why Johnny Can't Read* by Rudolf Flesch (1955), an argument is made that phonics instruction has the potential to cure the reading ills in America. What are some of the pros and cons of such an intensive phonics position?
5. Compare and contrast the teaching of onsets and rimes to phonics instruction. How are they similar? How are they different?
6. What are the four types of sight words that can be developed in the elementary classroom? Describe at least one strategy for helping children learn each type of sight word.
7. What are the main structural analysis elements? Provide at least five different examples of words containing each element.
8. How are songs and chants useful in the teaching of word-identification strategies?
9. What are some of the advantages and disadvantages of commercial alphabet books versus teacher-made alphabet books?
10. How can children in multicultural settings be helped to develop phonemic awareness?

Key Concepts

Explicit Phonics
Implicit Phonics
Context Clues
Phonemic Awareness
Alphabetic Principle
Onsets and Rimes
Word-Identification Strategy
Cloze Techniques
Phonics Generalizations
Word Banks
Discovery Words

Drastic Strategy
Morphemes
Structural Analysis
Minilessons
Test-Wiseness
Alphabet Books
Invented or "Temporary" Spellings
Word Rubber-Banding
Sequential Decoding
Hierarchical Decoding

A key concern for reading educators is helping children solve the puzzle of what to do when they encounter unknown words in print. There are generally two types of unknown words for elementary students to identify: those words that are actually known in the child's listening and speaking vocabulary but have not been added to her reading and writing vocabulary, and words that are completely unknown to the child. Most of this chapter focuses on how children can be helped to identify the first of these types of unknown words.

Word identification involves the use of context clues and simple phonics generalizations.

Teachers are primarily concerned with helping children learn the role of context and phonics in the word-identification process. When children understand the ease and utility of using context clues to guess or predict the identity of an unknown word combined with simple phonics generalizations to confirm or refine the predictions, the puzzle of unfamiliar words in print can be quickly solved. Similarly, when children learn the proper function of a dictionary in the word-identification process, words that are completely unknown can likewise be dealt with independently and efficiently.

This chapter begins with a brief discussion of issues related to word identification. Many of these issues have been debated by education scholars for well over a century. Throughout the chapter, some of the most important word-identification factors, according to the research, are discussed. In the final section of this chapter, effective classroom strategies for teaching word-identification skills are discussed.

Issues Related to Word Identification

*Notice that **explicit phonics** methods are linked to bottom-up theories of learning.*

Implicit phonics *instruction relies on deductive reasoning abilities in students.*

Almost since the beginning of formal reading instruction in public schools, controversy has surrounded the subject of teaching word-identification skills. The trail of protests over changes in reading methodology seen through the decades reflects earnest concern on both sides (Adams, 1990b)—a desire to offer children the best possible reading instruction. Perhaps the most vigorous discussion has surrounded the teaching of phonics. Some have argued that phonics is the essence of reading and should be the chief, if not the only, concern of beginning reading instruction (Flesch, 1955). Beginning reading instruction that depends on the teaching of isolated letters, letter sounds, and phonics generalizations is known as the *alphabetic,* or *explicit phonics, method.* **Explicit phonics** methods are based on bottom-up theories of learning (see Chapter 2), indicating that readers process information letter by letter, word by word, sentence by sentence until meaning is constructed. Others, beginning with Cattell in 1885, have argued that early success in reading can be achieved by teaching whole words and that phonics can be learned by analogy or through implicit phonics instruction. **Implicit phonics** methods are more interactive theoretically (see Chapter 2). Implicit processing advocates call for the teaching of whole words at the outset of beginning reading instruction, thus allowing meaning cues to assist the reader as she builds comprehension as well as analogical deduction of letter sounds. In a review of over 100 years of research on beginning reading, Marilyn Jager Adams (1990b) concluded that two factors correlate highly with early reading success: knowledge of letter names and the ability to discriminate phonemes auditorially. Adams's review of the research is discussed in more detail in the next section.

A second major issue pertaining to word identification is method of instruction. For more than 30 years, much of what has been offered to children as word identification strategies has taken the form of workbook pages and skill sheets. According to

Durkin (1981b), however, skill sheets and workbook pages are little more than assessment tools and are not effective in helping children to internalize word-identification strategies. In other words, skill sheets and workbook pages do not teach, they test!

In recent years, a rather fierce debate has gone on between teachers who prefer traditional methods, as described above, and whole language advocates. Some have falsely denounced whole language teachers for not failing to include phonics instruction in their reading programs. To resolve this issue, many teachers developing balanced reading programs have proposed the reduction or elimination of skill sheets and workbook pages in favor of word-identification lessons drawn from real books and texts. These activities, proponents feel, are much more authentic and provide students with opportunities to practice word-identification strategies in real reading situations. In the section of this chapter entitled "Some Classroom Strategies That Really Work" is an example of a minilesson using real text.

Assessment of word identification is a related issue that concerns many educators. Traditionally, word identification has been assessed using skill sheets and other tests that isolate and measure skills in artificial settings devoid of real text. An example modeled after these isolated skill sheets is provided in Figure 8.1. Educators who believe in more balanced literacy assessment strategies are discovering ways to assess word identification in more authentic reading settings.

Authentic assessment is discussed in detail in Chapter 13.

Finally, there is some discussion as to which word-identification strategies are worth teaching. Is it really necessary, for example, for students to be drilled on dozens of phonics generalizations, structural analysis elements, and other related skills? Probably not. For example, virtually *every* basal reading series includes exercises on how to detect *diphthongs in words*. Dennis Joseph, a mathematics educator, once jokingly asked if diphthongs were "those funny little shoes people put on when they get out of a swimming pool!" (Actually, diphthongs are defined as the glided sound made by such vowel combinations as *oi* and *oy* as heard in the words *boy, toy,* and *oil.*) The important question in this instance is, do successful strategic readers stop and look for diphthongs when encountering unknown words in print? Common sense suggests they do not. Strategic readers, however, routinely do use *some*

Many word-identification skills included in basals do not need to be taught directly.

Name _____

Words ending in -*er* and -*or*

Some words end with the letters -*er* or -*or*, which means "a person or thing having to do with." For example, the word *actor* means "one who acts," and the word *builder* means "one who builds."

Choose from the following words those that mean "a person who does something," and write them in the spaces provided at the bottom of the page.

boxer   singer   wander   developer

inner   sailor   gather   water

_____   _____

_____   _____

_____   _____

Figure 8.1

Skill sheet for the -*er,* -*or* word endings

word-identification strategies, which probably should be taught to all children. The use of context clues is a good case in point.

Understanding and Using Context Clues in Word Identification

One of the early dilemmas for beginning readers is what to do when coming to an unknown word in a story. With most basal readers of the past and present, students have been taught isolated skills to help "attack" unknown words. Scores of these isolated skills are taught throughout the child's schooling. It is assumed that readers will be able to apply whichever skills might be needed when encountering unknown words in print.

There are two problems with this approach to word identification. First, it assumes that young children will somehow be able to quickly decide which of the dozens of skills they have been exposed to are appropriate as they encounter problems in reading. To expect such sophisticated and abstract reasoning behavior of children seems rather optimistic at best. Second, most skill instruction in basal readers is done apart from real reading situations. Skills are often taught in isolation and rarely applied in real text. Thus, the connection between the skill or strategy being taught as applied to real reading is often minimized or overlooked (Durkin, 1981b). This form of teaching is called "parts-to-whole" instruction, in that a part of language (e.g., beginning sounds in words, consonant blends, prefixes, etc.) is being taught out of the context of reading whole text. A more holistic or balanced approach we recommend later in this chapter is called "whole-to-parts-to-whole" teaching.

Context clues, as the first step in word-identification, remind students that comprehension is the main goal.

What children need is an easy-to-understand strategy for using word-identification skills in real reading situations. An important first step in helping children develop such a strategy is teaching them to use context clues. **Context clues** are semantic and syntactic cues contained in written text that suggest to the reader possible meanings of unknown words. For example, the word *run* has over 50 possible meanings listed in many dictionaries. It is only through context clues that readers can decide which meaning is correct. In the two examples below, the reader can easily see which meanings are being implied using context at the sentence level.

Jake will *run* in the Boston Marathon next year.

Deb felt she was experiencing a *run* of bad luck.

Teachers usually explain the use of context clues to children by saying something along these lines, "Girls and boys, sometimes when we're reading we come to a word we don't know. When that happens, think about which word might make sense, guess, then continue reading. As you continue reading, you will usually be able to decide if you guessed correctly." The use of context clues should be the first skill taught as part of the word-identification strategy because it emphasizes, first and foremost, that the main goal in reading is trying to discover meaning. It is also quick and will not cause students to forget what they have just read in the sentence.

Approaches expecting students to sound out words can result in loss of sentence comprehension and fail to remind students of the primary goal in reading—comprehension. However, we do not mean to suggest that phonics instruction is not necessary. On the contrary, it is an essential element of a balanced reading program. In the next section, we discuss the starting points in teaching letter–sound relationships.

The Alphabetic Principle and Phonemic Awareness

Research in recent years has focused a great deal of attention on two aspects of word identification: *phonemic awareness* and the *alphabetic principle.* **Phonemic awareness** is an understanding that speech is composed of a series of individual sounds (Yopp, 1992). When most children begin their schooling, they come equipped with a sizable vocabulary and a fairly well-developed knowledge of syntax. However, they usually lack phonemic awareness. For instance, the word *dog* is known to many 4- and 5-year-olds only as a domestic animal that walks on four legs. They usually lack the awareness that *dog* is comprised of three phonemes, /d/, /o/, and /g/. Numerous studies have been conducted to determine whether phonemic awareness is necessary for children to become successful beginning readers. The answer seems to be that phonemic awareness is an important factor, but that it will not ensure reading success alone. Rather, instruction in phonemic awareness should be viewed as an important element of a balanced reading program in the early elementary grades.

A great deal of research suggests that phonemic awareness is an important early literacy tool.

Yopp (1992) has identified and categorized several types of phonemic awareness instruction offered by teachers: sound matching activities, sound isolation activities, sound blending activities, sound addition or substitution activities, and segmentation activities. A number of recommendations have been suggested (National Association for the Education of Young Children, 1986; Yopp, 1992) for the selection of phonemic awareness activities.

- Learning activities should help foster positive feelings toward learning through an atmosphere of playfulness and fun. Drill activities in phonemic awareness should be avoided, as well as rote memorization.
- Interaction among children should be encouraged through group activities. Language play seems to be most effective in group settings.
- Curiosity about language and experimentation should be encouraged. Teachers should react positively when students engage in language manipulation.
- Teachers should be prepared for wide differences in the acquisition of phonemic awareness. Some will catch on quickly, while others will take much longer. Teachers should avoid making quick judgments about children based on how they perform in phonemic awareness activities.

Phonemic awareness combined with letter-sound knowledge is necessary for students to attain a new level of understanding called the *alphabetic principle* (Byrne & Fielding-Barnsley, 1989). The **alphabetic principle** is the knowledge that speech sounds can be represented by a certain letter(s) and that when a given sound occurs anywhere in a word it can be represented by the same letter(s). Discovery of the alphabetic principle is thought to be necessary for students to fully master reading, although this is not all there is to reading; for instance, the ability to use context clues is essential. Therefore, teachers need to seek out activities that help students learn (a) the alphabet letters and the sounds they make, (b) that speech is made up of individual sounds that can be represented by specific letters and letter combinations, and (c) that these letter representations remain generally constant in words and across the

List two prerequisites for children learning the alphabetic principle.

various books or texts they encounter. In Chapter 10 we suggest a number of ways teachers can introduce the alphabetic principle to elementary youngsters.

Onsets and Rimes

The next developmental step for students' learning to identify words independently is the ability to recognize beginning and ending sounds in words. This can be a tricky proposition because many of the beginning and ending sounds in written English are irregular. However, a promising alternative has been unearthed through educational research.

Adams (1990b) states that linguistic researchers have proposed an instructionally useful alternative form of word analysis known as *onsets* and *rimes*. An **onset** is the part of the syllable that comes before the vowel; the **rime** is the rest (Adams, 1990b, p. 55). Although all syllables must have a rime, not all will have an onset. In the following list are a few examples of onsets and rimes in words:

Word	Onset	Rime
A	—	A
in	—	in
aft	—	aft
sat	s-	-at
trim	tr-	-im
spring	spr-	-ing

Onset and rime are of greater use than many phonics generalizations.

One may wonder what the usefulness of onset and rime is in the classroom, at least as far as word-identification instruction is concerned. First, some evidence seems to indicate that children are better able to identify the spelling of whole rimes than of individual vowel sounds (Adams, 1990b; Barton, Miller, & Macken, 1980; Treiman, 1985). Second, children as young as 5 and 6 years of age can transfer what they know about the pronunciation of one word to another that has the same rime, such as *call* and *ball* (Adams, 1990b). Third, although many traditional phonics generalizations with vowels are very unstable, even irregular phonics patterns seem to remain stable within rimes. For example, the *ea* vowel digraph is quite consistent within rimes, with the exceptions of *-ear* in *hear* compared to *bear*, and *-ead* in *bead* compared to *head* (Adams, 1990b). Finally, there appears to be some utility in the learning of rimes for children. Nearly 500 primary-level words can be derived through the following set of only 37 rimes (Adams, 1990b; Blachman, 1984):

-ack	-at	-ide	-ock
-ain	-ate	-ight	-oke
-ake	-aw	-ill	-op
-ale	-ay	-in	-or
-all	-eat	-ine	-ore
-ame	-ell	-ing	-uck
-an	-est	-ink	-ug
-ank	-ice	-ip	-ump
-ap	-ick	-ir	-unk
-ash			

The application of onset and rime to reading and word identification seems obvious. Students should find it easier to identify new words in print by locating familiar rimes and using the sound clue along with context to make accurate guesses as to the words' pronunciation. Spelling efficiency may also increase as rimes are matched with onsets to construct "invented" (we call them "temporary") spellings.

One teacher recently remarked that the easiest way to teach rimes is through *rhymes!* She was exactly right. Children learn many otherwise laborious tasks through rhymes, songs, chants, and raps. Any of these that use rhyming words can be very useful to teachers. For example, a teacher may wish to use an excerpt like the one shown below from the book *Taxi Dog* by Debra and Sal Barracca to emphasize the *-ide* and *-ill* rimes. The rimes are noted in bold type for easy identification by the reader.

Rhymes, songs, and chants are fun ways to teach onsets and rimes.

> It's just like a dream,
> Me and Jim—we're a team!
> I'm always there at his s**ide**.
> We never stand st**ill**,
> Every day's a new thr**ill**—
> Come join us next time for a r**ide**! (1990, p. 30)

When we bring together all that we know about how children develop word-identification abilities, a reasonably clear and sure progression emerges. Students begin to comprehend stories using context clues provided by pictures and oral language clues. These context clues may be provided in the beginning by adults reading to the child or through the child's knowledge of some words known on sight. In any event, students begin to understand that reading is a process of constructing meaning. Phonemic awareness emerges next, followed by addition of the alphabetic principle. These abilities help students to sound out many words for themselves, thus providing more context clues for constructing meaning. The fourth word-identification ability to emerge is the child's knowledge of beginning and ending sounds in words including, hopefully, his awareness of onsets and rimes. Finally, blending and other phonetic nuances are added, which helps the reader to be even more independent in constructing meaning from text.

As students become more and more proficient in using word-identification abilities, they cross the threshold of new reading possibilities. What is then needed is a strategy or "assembly routine" (Byrne & Fielding-Barnsley, 1989) that helps children logically and easily attack unknown words in print using all available information. In the next section, we suggest a strategy we have found to be most effective in our own classrooms and those of many other successful teachers.

Children need an easy-to-use word-identification strategy.

A Word-Identification Strategy for Balanced Reading Programs

A **word-identification strategy** is a process for decoding words in print that is simple enough for children to use in everyday reading. It begins with the use of context or other meaning cues supplied in the text, followed by a logical application of key phonic elements. The word-identification strategy we recommend can be illustrated with the following example drawn from a children's book entitled *The Teacher From the Black Lagoon* (Thaler, 1989), with the word in parentheses representing an unknown word.

It's the first day of school. I wonder who my teacher is.
I hear Mr. Smith has dandruff and warts,
and Mrs. Jones has a whip and a wig.
But Mrs. Green is **(supposed)** to be a *real* monster.
Oh my, I have *her!*
Mrs. Green . . . room 109.
What a bummer! (Thaler, 1989, pp. 1–4)

Step 1: Context Clues

Think of strategies you use to identify unknown words. Aren't these a search for meaning?

A context clue is information from the immediate sentence, paragraph, or surrounding words that might help readers determine the meaning and/or pronunciation of an unknown word. When encountering an unknown word in print, students should first ask themselves what word would make sense and make a guess or prediction. This keeps the focus of reading where it belongs—comprehending the author's message. If this is not possible, as when the unknown word is the first word in the sentence, then the reader should simply skip the word and continue reading. After the student finishes the sentence or paragraph, the unknown word often becomes clear. In the example preceding, the word *supposed* is one of only a few words that could make sense in this context.

Context clues are derived from two sources: semantic and syntactic cues. *Semantic cues* are meaning cues within the passage. They are the answer to the "what makes sense" question. *Syntax* has to do with the grammar or structure of the sentence and what kind of word normally fills a given grammatical slot (noun, adverb, adjective, etc.). For instance, the word *super* begins with the same sounds as *supposed* but does not fit this passage because it fails to make sense (semantics) and is not the correct part of speech (syntax).

Step 2: Beginning Sounds

Use of beginning sounds is the single most effective phonics skill for identifying words when used with context clues.

When context alone is not enough for positive identification of the unknown word and perhaps when there is more than one possible word that makes sense, then the reader should apply her knowledge of beginning sounds. In the example, several words could fit the context (*supposed, said, presumed, understood, about, apparently, evidently, truly*), so further verification is needed. The single most powerful phonics strategy that can be applied in this situation is identifying the beginning sounds in words. In most situations, when a student encounters an unknown word in elementary texts, if she will apply context clues first, then verify the guess with beginning sounds in words, she can make positive identification. This process is both simple and quick. Remember, if word identification is not quick, then the student may very well sacrifice comprehension of the text.

Of all the possible words mentioned previously, for example, only two begin with the letter s—*supposed* and *said*. Of more than 250,000 words in the English language, children may quickly and efficiently narrow their search to two possibilities. If the unknown word had been *truly* or *understood,* the word-identification process could stop here, as is usually the case. But positive identification will require a little more effort with this particular example.

Step 3: Ending Sounds

When more than one possible word exists that fits the context and has the same beginning sound, then children may use a second phonics strategy, ending sounds in words. If the unknown word was either *about* or *apparently,* then the ending sound clue would be enough for positive identification, because *about* ends in *t* and *apparently* in *-ly.* But in this example, *supposed* and *said* both end with the same sound, therefore, a final step is needed.

Step 4: Medial Sounds

Medial, or middle, sounds in words are not usually a necessary step in early reading materials but nevertheless come into play in many reading situations. What most readers notice in this example is the double *p* sound in the middle of the word *supposed.* This final step will make it possible to positively identify the unknown word. All four steps can easily be taught in grades 1 and 2 and can be used by students quickly and accurately.

This procedure will allow readers to quickly identify unknown words in most instances. Sometimes, however, children encounter words completely unknown or unrelated to their background experiences or listening and speaking vocabulary. When this happens, the usual strategy is to use dictionary skills to determine the pronunciation and meaning of the new word. Skills related to dictionary usage are usually taught throughout the elementary school experience. In the primary grades, children learn alphabetical order. In intermediate grades, children are usually exposed to the concept of multiple meanings. At some point in the upper elementary grades, children become acquainted with pronunciation symbols. These skills can be combined into a word-identification strategy for unknown words that will serve the students throughout their lives.

The only reliable way to identify completely unknown words on your own is to use a dictionary.

What About the Role of Onsets and Rimes?

As noted earlier in the chapter, a problem that often arises in teaching decoding is the reliance on beginning sounds, which are often quite irregular and unreliable. Because research supports the teaching of onset and rime as a reliable alternative to beginning and ending sounds, it seems logical to include them in our word-identification strategy—but where?

In most cases involving primary reading materials, onsets will be most valuable as part of a word-identification strategy when noticed at the beginning of the word. Likewise, rimes will often be of most use when noticed at the end of a word. Therefore, onset should be considered as part of Step 2 of the word-identification strategy, or "Beginning Sounds *and* Onsets," and rimes should be included as part of Step 3, or "Ending Sounds *and* Rimes."

Onsets and rimes, combined with context, work well in most primary reading materials for word identification.

As an example, let's revisit our excerpt from *The Teacher From the Black Lagoon* (Thaler, 1989). Assume that the word *whip* in the following line is unknown to the reader in its print form. That is, the reader knows the word *whip* when spoken but has not yet learned to recognize it in print.

> I hear Mr. Smith has dandruff and warts,
> and Mrs. Jones has a **whip** and a wig.

The onset *wh-* is quite common and is familiar to the reader from such words as *which, where,* and *whistle.* He can easily transfer this beginning sound or onset from previous experiences with text. The rime *-ip* is a highly regular one appearing on the list of 37 common rimes mentioned earlier in the chapter and has been taught in class by the teacher using various songs and favorite rhymes. Using context clues plus his knowledge of this particular onset and rime, the student quickly identifies the word *whip* and continues reading.

To summarize, the proposed word-recognition strategy uses the following clues in combination (as needed):

1. Use of context clues
2. Beginning sounds and onsets in words
3. Ending sounds and rimes in words
4. Medial sounds and onsets and rimes in words

Although this word-recognition strategy includes the most frequently recommended means for identifying unknown words in print, good readers occasionally employ other strategies, such as onset and rimes, or structural analysis. Phonics strategies and structural analysis strategies are discussed later, following a discussion on the needs of and strategies for helping young children who have just begun to attend to print.

The bridging stage occurs when children learn to recognize known letters and words in familiar books.

Focusing Attention on Print: Bridging From Memory to Text

One of the early stages in reading development is known as the bridging stage of literacy development (see Chapter 3), when children can call out known words and letters in familiar books and contexts. At this stage, however, they cannot pick out the same words and letters in an unfamiliar book or context. In short, they have not generalized and transferred their budding word-identification abilities to other reading situations. For children to progress to the next stage of reading development, they need to begin to "bridge" word recognition from known books and contexts to new reading situations. In this section we describe several classroom strategies teachers may use to help children who have memorized text, story, or books to begin to focus their attention on the features of print rather than relying solely on meaningful and memorable features of familiar text. Many of these ideas are adapted for this purpose from the book *Literacy Through Literature* by T. D. Johnson and Louis (1987) and from Reutzel (1995). Once children move beyond this stage, they are ready for other aspects of the word-identification process.

Recognition

To begin, reread a text sample taken from a familiar and popular print source (a familiar book, big book, language experience chart, poem, chant or song). Once completed, this text sample may be used to support the following print recognition transfer activities.

Identification and Matching

Pocket charts are used to help students with identifying and matching skills.

Begin by asking your students to listen and follow along as you read aloud related sentences, lines, phrases, words, or letters displayed in a *pocket chart*. Then, using text from a different familiar selection, have children find the same part of language in the pocket chart (see Figure 8.2). The idea is to transfer students' ability to recog-

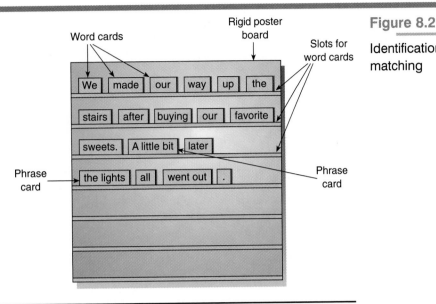

Figure 8.2

Identification and matching

nize specific words in a familiar book or text to new books and text. Several other ways children may be helped to bridge from known to new text using cloze procedures are presented in the next section.

Cloze Techniques

Three variations of the **cloze techniques** procedure may be used to help students bridge from memorized text: *progressive, regressive,* and *successive cloze.* With progressive cloze, teachers cut sentence strips into individual words and place them into a pocket chart. Next, have children read the words after removing one or two words from the sentence at a time (Figure 8.3). Structure words, such as *the, but, and, a,* should not be removed. As a verbal place holder, have children snap their fingers or say "blank" when they come to each missing word.

Regressive cloze is essentially the reverse of progressive cloze. Start with only the structure words from a sentence, line, or phrase. Replace one word at a time, and have children read what is in the pocket chart. Ask them to predict the full message of the sentence after each new word is added (Figure 8.4).

List and describe three cloze variations.

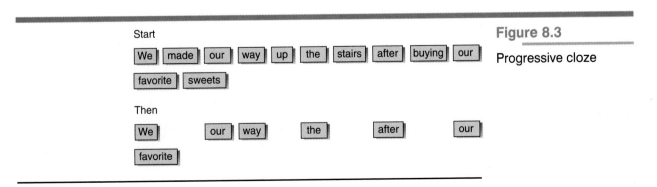

Figure 8.3

Progressive cloze

Figure 8.4

Regressive cloze

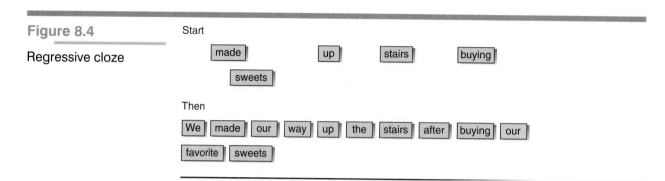

Successive cloze is done by masking the beginning or ending letter of a word. Enough spaces for each missing letter are provided to help children use context and letter clues for solving words (Figure 8.5).

Substitution

Take a word from one sentence strip and substitute it for a word in another strip without telling students which word has been substituted. Tell the students what the strip said before the substitution was made. Ask them to locate the word that has been switched (Figure 8.6).

Error Detection

Students search for words that don't make sense in error detection.

Error detection is very similar to substitution. Take a sentence or phrase strip and substitute a word that does not make sense. Ask students to find the word that does not make sense.

Spoonerisms

Spoonerisms take the first letter(s) of two words and transpose them to alter their pronunciation. This results in humorous nonsense words that children enjoy immensely. Spoonerisms can be used to help children focus on initial letter sounds in words using self-stick memo notes in big books, overheads, or sentence strips in a pocket chart (Figure 8.7).

Vowel Substitution

Substitute initial, final, or medial vowel sounds from two or more words in a sentence, line, or phrase strip. Ask children to read the strip with the changes in place. For example, "Humpty Dumpty sat on a wall" . . . becomes "Himpty Dimpty sit on a will."

Figure 8.5

Successive cloze

We made our way up th|s_____| after buying our favorite sweets.

A little bit | | the lights all went | |

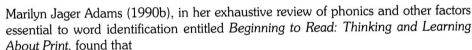

Figure 8.6

Substitution

What Is Phonics Instruction All About? Values and Myths

Marilyn Jager Adams (1990b), in her exhaustive review of phonics and other factors essential to word identification entitled *Beginning to Read: Thinking and Learning About Print,* found that

> prereaders' letter knowledge was the single best predictor of first-year reading achievement, with their ability to discriminate phonemes auditorily ranking a close second. (p. 36)
>
> Approaches in which systematic code instruction is included along with the reading of meaningful connected text result in superior reading achievement overall, for both low-readiness and better prepared students. (p. 125)

Adams also noted that these conclusions seem to hold true regardless of the instructional approach through which reading is taught. However, it should be noted that very few, if any, studies have been conducted comparing balanced literacy word-identification teaching strategies with more traditional skills instructional models or basal readers. Thus, Adams's review of the research appears to have a decided bent in favor of decoding and skills-based instructional methods. At any rate, one cannot deny that there is a compelling need to include phonics as at least one part of a comprehensive reading program.

Those who support the use of intensive phonics instruction in beginning reading cite several benefits of this practice (Chall, 1967; Flesch, 1955, 1981). One argument is that English spelling patterns are relatively consistent; therefore, phonics rules can aid the reader in approximating the pronunciation of unfamiliar words. As a result, phonics rules can assist the reader in triggering meaning for unfamiliar words if they are in the reader's listening and speaking vocabulary. It is felt that when phonics rules are applied in conjunction with semantic (meaning) and syntactic (grammar) cues in the passage, the reader can positively identify unknown words in most elementary reading level materials.

Letter knowledge is the single best predictor of early reading success in young children.

List some benefits to intensive phonics cited by its proponents.

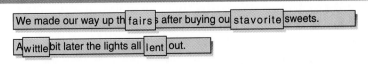

Figure 8.7

Spoonerisms

Those opposing intensive phonics programs cite a number of justifications for their position as well. The chief complaint is that the English language is *not* all that regular and that phonics generalizations often have many exceptions (A. J. Harris & Sipay, 1990). Focusing on ambiguous details in words, to the exclusion of such comprehension-based strategies as context clues, can actually cause children to miss appropriate meaning and word clues.

Readers taking too long to identify words risk losing comprehension.

Another problem with overreliance on phonics cues is the time factor for processing the author's message. When engaged in the act of reading, the reader stores the author's message—as represented by each word, sentence, and paragraph—in the reader's short-term memory. As thoughts are constructed from the text, they are then more fully processed and may become part of long-term memory. If a reader who encounters an unknown word spends too much time trying to figure out the identity of a single word, then she risks forgetting (or losing from short-term memory) that earlier part of the message already processed. That is why many teachers tell children to "skip" unknown words and let the context of the passage "do the work for them." When considering how many phonics rules and generalizations exist, it is not hard to see why some teachers feel that overreliance on phonic analysis, to the exclusion of context, is not helpful to emerging readers.

Balanced Reading Programs Include Phonics Instruction

Phonics instruction is an important part of balanced reading programs in the early grades.

As mentioned earlier in the chapter, some teachers have expressed the belief that holistic teaching means that "you don't teach phonics in whole language classrooms." Nothing could be further from the truth (Newman & Church, 1990). In an article entitled "Myths of Whole Language," Judith Newman and Susan Church stated

> A good deal of what people have had to say reflects a serious misunderstanding of what whole language is really about. . . . No one can read without taking into account the grapho-phonemic cues of written language. . . . Whole language teachers do teach phonics but not as something separate from actual reading and writing. . . . Readers use graphophonic cues; whole language teachers help students orchestrate their use for reading and writing. (1990, pp. 20–21)

Thus, the question in building a balanced reading program is not whether one should teach phonics strategies. Rather, the appropriate questions have to do with *how* to teach phonics strategies and *which ones to teach*. The following section answers the "which-ones" question. How to teach phonics and other strategies are discussed later in the classroom strategies section of this chapter.

Seven Phonics Generalizations

Seven phonics generalizations are fairly reliable and should be taught along with the word-identification strategy.

According to May and Elliot (1978), only a few **phonics generalizations** have a fairly high degree of utility for readers. When students use phonics generalizations in conjunction with the word-identification strategy discussed earlier in the chapter, they should be able to successfully identify most words found in elementary reading materials. Each of seven phonics generalizations are discussed in the following paragraphs. (Note: explanations in some cases are adapted from Hull, 1989.)

The C Rule

The letter *c* is an irregular consonant letter that has no phoneme of its own. Instead, it assumes two other phonemes found in different words, *k* and *s*. In general, when the letter *c* is followed by *a, o,* or *u,* it will represent the sound we associated with the letter *k,* also known as the *hard c* sound. Some examples are the words *cake, cosmic,* and *cute.*

On the other hand, the letter *c* can sometimes represent the sound associated with the letter *s.* This is referred to as the *soft c* sound. The *soft c* sound is usually produced when *c* is followed by *e, i,* or *y.* Examples of the *soft c* sound are found in the words *celebrate, circus,* and *cycle.*

The G Rule

G is the key symbol for the phoneme we hear in the word *get* (Hull, 1989, p. 35). It is also irregular, having a *soft* and a *hard g* sound. The rules remain the same as they are for the letter *c.* When *g* is followed by the letters *e, i,* or *y,* it represents a *soft g* or *j* sound, as with the words *gently, giraffe,* and *gym.* If *g* is followed by the letters *a, o,* or *u,* then it usually represents the *hard* or regular sound as with the words *garden, go,* and *sugar.*

The C and G rules are essentially the same.

The CVC Generalization

When a vowel comes between two consonants, it usually has the short vowel sound. Examples of words following the CVC pattern include *sat, ran, let, pen, win, fit, hot, mop, sun,* and *cut.*

Vowel Digraphs

When two vowels come together in a word, the first vowel is usually long and the second vowel silent. This occurs especially often with the *oa, ee,* and *ay* combinations. Some examples are *toad, fleet,* and *day.* A common slogan used by teachers, which helps children remember this generalization, is "when two vowels go walking, the first one does the talking."

The VCE (Final *E*) Generalization

When two vowels appear in a word and one is an *e* at the end of the word, the first vowel is generally long and the final *e* is silent. Examples include *cape, rope,* and *kite.*

The CV Generalization

When a consonant is followed by a vowel, the vowel usually produces a long sound. This is especially easy to see in two-letter words such as *be, go,* and *so.*

R-Controlled Vowels

Vowels that appear before the letter *r* are usually neither long nor short but tend to be overpowered or "swallowed up" by the sound. Examples include person, player, neighborhood, and herself.

Other Common Phonics Terms and Skills

Even though the seven phonics generalizations offered here are the most useful, most basal reading programs focus attention on many others. In the interest of thoroughness, following are several terms, definitions, and examples of other phonics skills related to consonants and vowels not already discussed in this chapter.

Consonants

- *Consonant digraphs*—Two consonants together in a word that produce only one speech sound *(th, sh, ng)*.
- *Consonant blends or clusters*—Two or more consonants coming together in which the speech sounds of all the consonants may be heard *(bl, fr, sk, spl)*.

Vowels

- *Vowel digraphs*—Two vowels together in a word that produce only one speech sound *(ou, oo, ie, ai)*
- *Schwa*—Vowel letters that produce the *uh* sound *(a in America)*. The schwa is represented by the upside-down *e* symbol: ə
- *Diphthongs*—Two vowels together in a word that produce a single, glided sound *(oi in oil, oy in boy)*.

Developing Sight Words

Word Banks

Sight words are high-frequency words that account for much of what is written.

Understanding text in part relies on the immediate recognition of often-used words, or sight words. Studies of print have found that just 109 words account for upward of 50% of all words in student textbooks, and a total of only 5,000 words accounts for about 90% of the words in student texts (Adams 1990b; J. B. Carroll, Davies, & Richman, 1971). Knowledge of these high-frequency words logically can help the fluency of readers. Many of these high-frequency words carry little meaning but do affect the flow and coherence of the text being read, such as words like *the, from, but, because, that,* and *this,* sometimes called *structural words.* The actual meaning of the text depends on the ready knowledge of less frequent, or *lexical words,* such as *automobile, aristocrat, pulley, streetcar, Martin Luther King,* and *phantom.* Adams et al. state that

> while the cohesion and connectivity of English text is owed most to its frequent words (e.g., *it, that, this, and, because, when, while*), its meaning depends disproportionately on its less frequent words (e.g., *doctor, fever, infection, medicine, penicillin, Alexander, Fleming, melon, mold, poison, bacteria, antibiotic, protect, germs, disease*). (1991, p. 394)

Word banks help students collect and use new words for reading and writing.

As with phonics instruction, the question for teachers is, how to go about helping students acquire a large knowledge of words they can recognize immediately on sight. **Word banks** are used to help students collect and review sight words. Word banks also can be used as personal dictionaries. A word bank is simply a student-constructed box, file, or notebook in which newly discovered words are stored and reviewed. In the early grades, teachers often collect small shoe boxes from local stores for this purpose. The children are asked at the beginning of the year to decorate the boxes to make them their own. In the upper grades, more formal-looking word banks are used to give an "adult" appearance. Notebooks or recipe boxes are generally selected. Alphabetic dividers can also be used at all levels to facilitate the quick location of word bank words. Alphabetic dividers in the early grades also help students rehearse and reinforce knowledge of alphabetical order. Figure 8.8 shows an example of a word bank.

Once students have word banks, the next problem for the teacher is helping students decide which words should be included and from what sources. At least four sources can be considered for sight-word selection and inclusion in word banks. Each is briefly discussed in the next section.

Key Vocabulary

Silvia Ashton-Warner, in her popular book *Teacher* (1963), describes key vocabulary words as "organic," or words that come from within the child and her own experiences. Ashton-Warner states that key vocabulary words act as captions for important events in life that the child has experienced. The child comes to the teacher at an appointed time or during a group experience and indicates which words she would

Key vocabulary words are organic. The come from the child's own experiences.

Figure 8.8

A word bank

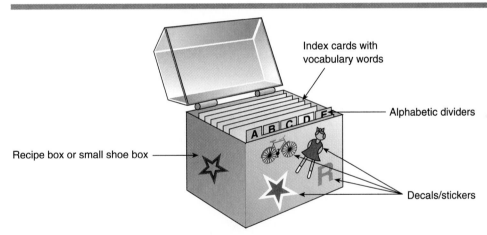

A word bank is a box in which children keep/file new words they are learning. The words are usually written in isolation on one side of the card, and in a sentence on the back of the card (usually with a picture clue).

Example:

Front	Back
bicycle	Jason rode his bicycle to school.

like to learn. For instance, the teacher may ask "what word would you like to learn today?" The child may respond with a word of her choice such as *police, ghost,* or *sing.* Ashton-Warner found that the most common categories of key vocabulary words for children were fear words *(dog, bull, kill, police),* sex (as she called them), or affection words *(love, kiss, sing, darling),* locomotion words *(bus, car, truck, jet),* and a *miscellaneous* category that generally reflects cultural and other considerations *(socks, frog, beer, Disneyland, Dallas Cowboys).*

Ashton-Warner (1963) calls key vocabulary "one-look words" because one look is usually all that is required for permanent learning to take place. The reason that these words seem so easy for children to learn is that they usually carry strong emotional significance for the child. Once the child has told the teacher a word she would like to learn, the teacher writes the word on an index card or a small piece of tag board using a dark marker. The student is then instructed to share the word with as many people as possible during the day. After the child has done so, the word is added to her word bank.

Basal Words

Basal words are vocabulary taught in basal readers.

Many teachers are concerned that students will not learn high-frequency words if they do not use basal readers. Basal readers often use stories written using high-frequency words and market their reading series with that factor as a major selling point. Overreliance on high-frequency words, however, causes basal stories to sometimes seem stilted and unnatural. One remedy is to add several words per week to students' word banks from the high-frequency word lists offered by the adopted basal readers. These words can be used by children when needed in writing and other experiences. Basal words can be taught in a whole-group setting and reviewed periodically. By so doing, the teacher is free to use (or not use) the basal, trade books, or language experience activities as she pleases.

Reviewing selected words in the word bank is a good activity for parent volunteers or teacher aides to conduct with small groups of students. Figure 8.9 presents the Fry (1980) word list of the 300 most common words in print for teachers not having access to a basal series word list.

Discovery Words

For example, a fourth grader brought to school a cocoon, leading to the discovery of words such as chrysalis, monarch butterfly, and antenna.

During the course of a typical school day, students are exposed to many new words. These words are often discovered as a result of studies in the content areas. Such words as *experiment, algebra, social, enterprise, conquest, Bengal tiger, spider,* and *cocoon* find their way into students' listening and speaking vocabulary. Every effort should be made to add these discovery words to the word bank as they are discussed in their natural context. Such words often find their way into new compositions in student writing.

Function ("Four-Letter") Words

Many words are very difficult for students to learn because they carry no definable meaning. Typical words in this category are *with, were, what,* and *want.* Referred to earlier in the chapter as structural words (also known as *functors, glue words,* and *four-letter words*), these words are most difficult to teach because they cannot be

Figure 8.9

Fry New Instant Word List

The first 10 words make up about 24% of all written material, the first 100 words about 50% of all written material, and the first 300 about 65%.

1. the	44. each	87. who	130. through	173. home	216. never	259. walked
2. of	45. which	88. oil	131. much	174. us	217. started	260. white
3. and	46. she	89. its	132. before	175. move	218. city	261. sea
4. a	47. do	90. now	133. line	176. try	219. earth	262. began
5. to	48. how	91. find	134. right	177. kind	220. eyes	263. grow
6. in	49. their	92. long	135. too	178. hand	221. light	264. took
7. is	50. if	93. down	136. means	179. picture	222. thought	265. river
8. you	51. will	94. day	137. old	180. again	223. head	266. four
9. that	52. up	95. did	138. any	181. change	224. under	267. carry
10. it	53. other	96. get	139. same	182. off	225. story	268. state
11. he	54. about	97. come	140. tell	183. play	226. saw	269. once
12. was	55. out	98. made	141. boy	184. spell	227. left	270. book
13. for	56. many	99. may	142. following	185. air	228. don't	271. hear
14. on	57. then	100. part	143. came	186. away	229. few	272. stop
15. are	58. them	101. over	144. want	187. animals	230. while	273. without
16. as	59. these	102. new	145. show	188. house	231. along	274. second
17. with	60. so	103. sound	146. also	189. point	232. might	275. later
18. his	61. some	104. take	147. around	190. page	233. close	276. miss
19. they	62. her	105. only	148. form	191. letters	234. something	277. idea
20. I	63. would	106. little	149. three	192. mother	235. seemed	278. enough
21. at	64. make	107. work	150. small	193. answer	236. next	279. eat
22. be	65. like	108. know	151. set	194. found	237. hard	280. face
23. this	66. him	109. place	152. put	195. study	238. open	281. watch
24. have	67. into	110. years	153. end	196. still	239. example	282. far
25. from	68. time	111. live	154. does	197. learn	240. beginning	283. Indians
26. or	69. has	112. me	155. another	198. should	241. life	284. really
27. one	70. look	113. back	156. well	199. American	242. always	285. almost
28. had	71. two	114. give	157. large	200. world	243. those	286. let
29. by	72. more	115. most	158. must	201. high	244. both	287. above
30. words	73. write	116. very	159. big	202. every	245. paper	288. girl
31. but	74. go	117. after	160. even	203. near	246. together	289. some-
32. not	75. see	118. things	161. such	204. add	247. got	times
33. what	76. number	119. our	162. because	205. food	248. group	290. mountains
34. all	77. no	120. just	163. turned	206. between	249. often	291. cut
35. were	78. way	121. name	164. here	207. own	250. run	292. young
36. we	79. could	122. good	165. why	208. below	251. important	293. talk
37. when	80. people	123. sentence	166. asked	209. country	252. until	294. soon
38. your	81. my	124. man	167. went	210. plants	253. children	295. list
39. can	82. than	125. think	168. men	211. last	254. side	296. song
40. said	83. first	126. say	169. read	212. school	255. feet	297. being
41. there	84. water	127. great	170. need	213. father	256. car	298. leave
42. use	85. been	128. where	171. land	214. keep	257. miles	299. family
43. an	86. called	129. help	172. different	215. trees	258. night	300. it's

From "The New Instant Word List," by Edward Fry, *The Reading Teacher,* December 1980, pp. 284–289. Reprinted with permission of Edward Fry and the International Reading Association.

made concrete for children. Just imagine trying to define or draw a picture of the word what!

Patricia Cunningham (1980) developed the **drastic strategy** to help teachers solve this difficult instructional problem. This six-step process follows:

*The **drastic strategy** is useful for teaching function words, those having no real meaning, for example, what, with, and that.*

Step 1: Select a function word, and write it on a vocabulary card for each child. Locate a story for storytelling, or spontaneously create a story, in which you use the word many times. Before you begin your story, instruct the children to hold up their card every time they hear the word printed on their card. As you tell the story, pause briefly each time you come to the word in the text.

Step 2: Ask children to volunteer to make up a story using the word on their card. Listeners should hold up their card each time they hear their classmate use the function word.

Step 3: Ask the children to study the word on their card. Next, go around to each child and cut the word into letters (or have them do it for themselves). Have the children try to arrange the letters to make the word. Check each child's attempt for accuracy. They should mix up the letters and try to make the word again several times. Each child should be able to do this before moving on to the next step. Put the letters into an envelope and write the word outside. Children should be encouraged to practice making the word during free times.

Step 4: Write the word on the chalkboard and ask children to pretend their eyes are like a camera and to take a picture of the word and put it in their mind. Have them close their eyes and try to see it in their mind. Next, they should open their eyes and check the board to see if they correctly imagined the word. They should do this three times. The last activity is for them to write the word from memory after the chalkboard has been erased, then check their spelling when it is rewritten on the chalkboard. This should be repeated three times.

Step 5: Write several sentences on the board containing a blank in the place of the word under study. As you come to the missing word in the sentences, invite a child to come to the board and write the word in the blank space provided.

Step 6: Give children real books or text in which the function word appears. Ask them to read through the story, and whenever they find the word being studied, they should lightly underline (in pencil) the new word. When they have done this, read the text to them, and pause each time you come to the word so the students may read it chorally.

We recommend one final step to the drastic strategy: Add the word under study to the child's word bank for future use in writing. There is one drawback to the drastic strategy—*time*. This process can take quite a bit of time, therefore it is not always necessary to teach each and every step in the drastic strategy for all words. Teacher judgment should determine which steps are most needed.

Structural Analysis and Morphemic Clues

Words are made up of basic meaning units known as **morphemes**. Morphemes may be divided into two classes—*bound* and *free*. Bound morphemes must be attached to a root word (sometimes called a *base word*) to have meaning. Prefixes and suffixes are *bound* morphemes (e.g. pre-, un-, dis-, en-, inter-, extra-, -ed, -ies, -er, -ing). *Free* morphemes *(base words,* or *root words)* are meaning units or words that can stand alone and have meaning. The word *retroactive* has both a bound and free morpheme: *retro-*, the bound morpheme (prefix) meaning "backward," and *active*, the free morpheme meaning "working." Sometimes two free morphemes combine to form a new word, such as **dog**house, **out**doors, **play**ground, and **to**night. Studying words to identify familiar word elements is known as **structural analysis**.

Morphemes are meaning-bearing units of written language.

Teachers can help children begin to practice structural analysis in the same ways as for onset and rime. The idea to get across to students is that whenever a good reader comes to a word she cannot identify through context alone she sometimes looks within the word for a recognizable base (root) word and its accompanying prefix, suffix, or endings (Durkin, 1989; Lass & Davis, 1985). In other words, look for something you know within the word.

To demonstrate the use of structural analysis, a whole-to-parts-to-whole minilesson is described in the next section. Begin by reading a whole story or text to the class, then focus on a single page that has several words with structural elements that you wish to focus on during the lesson. The final step is to select another page from the selection and have students identify words with structural elements and discuss their meanings. The following selected examples of root affixes are adapted from *The Reading Teacher's Book of Lists* (Fry, Polk, & Fountoukidis, 1984).

Prefixes

Prefix	Meaning	Prefix	Meaning
intro-	within	ad-	to, toward
pro-	forward	para-	beside, by
post-	after	pre-	before
sub-	under	per-	through
ultra-	beyond	ab-	from
dis-	off, away	trans-	across

Suffixes

Suffix	Example(s)	Suffix	Example(s)
-ant	servant	-ee	payee
-ist	pianist	-ary	library
-ence	violence	-ity	necessity
-ism	capitalism	-ette	dinette
-s	cars	-al	natural
-fy	terrify	-ing	singing

Some Classroom Strategies That Really Work

Minilessons

One of the most useful structures for teaching word-identification strategies is the **minilesson**. Minilessons are typically whole-class or group lessons that last approximately 5 to 10 minutes each and may be used to teach strategies and skills, promote literary response or to teach a necessary procedure (Hagerty, 1992). (Note: In Chapter

Minilessons are the cornerstone of direct language instruction.

9 we explore further these three types of minilessons in greater detail.) Minilessons allow teachers to quickly get to the point and end the lesson before student attention fades. Thus, if a teacher wishes to teach a word-identification strategy, such as context clues, then a minilesson can be offered once each day until students learn the strategy.

Another characteristic of minilessons is that they teach reading strategies from whole to parts to whole. Unlike basal readers that teach reading strategies from parts to whole (workbook activities in isolation to whole stories), minilessons begin by using whole stories or text and work down to the essential strategy or skill to be developed. This process allows students to see the relevance of the strategy being emphasized to real reading tasks. Following is a sample minilesson schedule for teaching context clues in the early elementary grades.

Minilesson Schedule (Whole to Parts to Whole)

Word-Identification Strategy: Context Clues
Materials Needed: Big book version of *More Spaghetti, I Say!* (Gelman, 1977), overhead transparencies adapted from page 9 of the book, and teacher-made practice sheets in a modified cloze format.

Day 1 Activity: Shared Book Experience.   Using a big book version of *More Spaghetti, I Say!* read the book aloud with the class and discuss the class's favorite parts.

Notice that minilessons begin with whole text that makes sense.

Day 2 Activity: Teacher Modeling.   The teacher begins the minilesson by rereading portions of *More Spaghetti, I Say!* to remind the children of the story line. Next, she explains that sometimes when reading we come to words that we do not know. Good readers usually guess what the word might be and continue reading. As they read, the meaning of the story helps them to know whether their guess was correct or not (context clues).

Why is it important for teachers to serve as models?

Figure 8.10

Page 9 of *More Spaghetti, I Say!* intact text

No. I can **not**.
I can **not** jump and play.
Can't you see?
I need more.
More spaghetti, I say!

From *More Spaghetti, I Say!* by Rita Golden Gelman, illustrated by Jack Kent. Text copyright © 1977 by Rita Golden Gelman, illustration copyright © 1977 by Jack Kent. Reprinted by permission of Scholastic Inc.

The essence of modeling is the teacher thinking aloud for students so they can understand thought processes used to solve literacy problems. To illustrate context clues, the teacher may begin by showing a transparency copy of page 9 from the book on the overhead projector (Figure 8.10). The teacher and class reread the page chorally. Next, the teacher puts another copy of page 9 on the overhead projector, this time with selected words deleted and replaced with blanks in a kind of modified cloze format (Figure 8.11). The teacher reads the passage aloud, and she "thinks" or "guesses" out loud what the missing word might be for each of the blanks. The emphasis should always be on "what makes sense" within the context of the passage. Notice that for the sentence "I _____ more" the words *need* and *want* would both make sense. This realization could easily lead into a later minilesson related to the word-identification strategy of beginning sounds in words. When beginning sounds are used in conjunction with context clues, a child could easily determine that the unknown word is *need* because "it begins with the right sound." After this demonstration, the children are asked if they have any questions. They are now ready for the next minilesson.

Modeling is the act of showing students how adults use the new skill.

Day 3 Activity: Guided and Independent Practice.   Children at this point have seen context clues demonstrated and have some understanding of the strategy. To make this strategy their own, they must practice it themselves. Another familiar page of text, for example, page 24, is selected from *More Spaghetti, I Say!* and a practice sheet is produced in the same format as was demonstrated by the teacher (Figure 8.12). Children complete the practice exercise, with assistance from the teacher or in collaboration with other students, if desired. The teacher or parent volunteer then reviews the sheet for accuracy. Remember, as long as the student response makes sense, it should be accepted.

The final step at this stage is a final practice sheet from the book, such as page 26, which the child completes without any assistance from others. If this exercise is

As minilessons proceed, responsibility shifts from the teacher to learners.

Figure 8.11

Page 9 of *More Spaghetti, I Say!* modified cloze for context clues lesson

No. I can **not**.
I can ___ jump and play.
Can't you ___?
I ____ more.
More _____, I say!

Adapted from *More Spaghetti, I Say!* by Rita Golden Gelman, illustrated by Jack Kent. Text copyright © 1977 by Rita Golden Gelman, illustration copyright © 1977 by Jack Kent. Reprinted by permission of Scholastic Inc.

completed without difficulty, the minilesson is concluded. If there are problems, however, then reteaching should be done.

Students should be taught test-taking skills so they can fully demonstrate their abilities on state-mandated tests.

Day 4 Activity: Test-Wiseness Lesson.   To satisfy testing requirements, most teachers are required to give some sort of mastery test to children on the various reading strategies. They may take the form of end-of-basal tests, standardized achievement tests in reading, or district-constructed tests. In the preceding example, one can be reasonably

Figure 8.12

Practice sheet developed from text on page 24 of *More Spaghetti, I Say!*

"Oh, Minnie,
that look on your ____!
You ____ bad.

____ look big.
You look green.
You look ____ .
You look sad."

Adapted from *More Spaghetti, I Say!* by Rita Golden Gelman, illustrated by Jack Kent. Text copyright © 1977 by Rita Golden Gelman, illustration copyright © 1977 by Jack Kent. Reprinted by permission of Scholastic Inc.

sure that all children have acquired the ability to use context clues, at least on a novice level, but one more step may be needed to help students apply the strategy on a mastery test. Recognizing that most districts rely on end-of-basal tests because of their easy access (they already own basal series), one or two of the basal reader "skill sheets," dealing with context clues in this case, may be duplicated for each student (Figure 8.13 is an example). By working through an example or two with the teacher and then completing the remainder of the practice sheet themselves, students will become acquainted with the format of the test but not the actual test itself. This final step in the teaching process to prepare children for mandated testing is known as a **test-wiseness** lesson.

Songs and Chants

Sometimes children are required to learn rather lengthy and abstract word-identification concepts, such as the alphabet, vowel generalizations, and various phonics rules. Teachers developing balanced reading programs have discovered that many of these concepts can be learned easily and quickly through songs and chants.

Songs and chants serve at least two purposes. First, they make rote learning tasks, such as the alphabet and vowel generalizations, easy to memorize and later transfer to real reading situations. Second, songs and chants provide a springboard into rich experiences with literature, song, drama, and other art activities.

Songs and chants can transform rote learning into delightful experiences.

Figure 8.13

Skill sheet on context clues for test-wiseness lesson

Skill Lesson 22: Decoding Practice
Context Clues

Name _____

Sometimes the words in a sentence can help you figure out a word you don't know how to read yet. In the example below, the words _____ and

_____ help you to know that the word _____ completes the sentence.

On a hot day, I like to go to the _____ pool.

ice	swimming	day	up

Directions: Complete the sentences below using a word from the box that makes sense.

theater	gym	flavor	vacation

1. Sean likes to play basketball in the _____ at school.

2. My favorite _____ of ice cream is chocolate.

3. Celeste and I went to the movie _____ to see the movie *Little Mermaid*.

4. Our family likes to go to Florida every summer on _____.

Many songbooks are available for teachers that help children learn useful language and word-identification elements. The most obvious is the "Alphabet Song." It is probably a very safe bet that most American children learned the alphabet in this way. Students can also learn many fun and funny songs filled with rhyme with the help of Marsha and Jon Pankake's (1988) songbook entitled *A Prairie Home Companion Folk Song Book*. As noted earlier, the instruction of onsets and rimes can easily be facilitated through these wonderful songs.

"The Vowel Song" teaches basic vowel generalizations.

In one of the first studies of the effectiveness of whole-language teaching as compared to basal readers (Reutzel & Cooter, 1990), Reutzel developed a song for teaching the long- and short-vowel generalizations. "The Vowel Song" was found to be easy enough for first graders to learn almost at once. The words are presented in Figure 8.14 ("The Vowel Song" can be sung to the tune of "Twinkle, Twinkle, Little Star"). Once children learned the vowel song, they began little by little to apply the words of the song to real reading and writing situations with occasional reminders from the teacher.

Two other vowel songs have been prepared by Reutzel, one for "Silent *E*" and the other for "Vowel Pairs" (Figures 8.15 and 8.16).

Silent *E* Song and Vowel Pairs Song

Chants and raps can be used to teach word-identification skills.

Chants or "raps" can be equally effective with students as songs. With the popularity of rap music, students are naturally drawn to rhyming rhythms. Cooter, in the study mentioned (Reutzel & Cooter, 1990), used "The Vowel Song" strictly as a rap in his first-grade classroom. The first time he introduced "The Vowel Song," the children were instructed to snap their fingers in a moderately slow, steady rhythm with the teacher and listen as he

Figure 8.14

The vowel song

The Vowel Song

The vowels we know
And you will see,
That we can say each perfectly,
a as in *apple*
a as in *ate*
And don't you think that we are great!
e as in *egg*
e as in *eat*
And don't you think that we are neat!
i as in *it*
i as in *ice*
And don't you think that we are nice!
o as in *pot*
o as in *no*
And don't you think it's time to go!
u as in *cut*
u as in *cute*
Now it's time to light the fuse!
     Boom!!!

Figure 8.15

Silent *e* song

> ### Silent e
>
> When you have an *e*
> at the end of a word,
> The *e* is silent so it's never heard.
> The first vowel almost always
> says its name,
> Follow this rule below
> you'll find it's the same . . .
> c-a-m-e is *came*
> P-e-t-e is *Pete*
> l-i-k-e is *like*
> h-o-m-e is *home*
> c-u-t-e is *cute*
>
> Remember this and be sure to use
> The first vowel's name
> in this reading game!

performed the rap. The rap was written in large letters on poster paper in a kind of big-book fashion so the children could read along as it was performed. After the teacher went through the rap a few times, the children were invited to join in. Soon the rhythmic chant could be heard on the playground as children jumped rope. Within a week or so, every child in his first-grade class could recite "The Vowel Song" rap easily. They even developed hand gestures and dance movements to use while "performing" the rap.

It should be noted that songs and raps do not immediately transfer to application. Students are attracted to the aesthetic qualities of these art forms first; application and transfer occur gradually over a period of time.

Miss Mary Mack (J. Cole & Calmenson, 1990) is one book that might prove helpful to teachers interested in trying chants for the first time. Joanna Cole and Stephanie Calmenson have put together various children's "street rhymes" categorized as *hand clapping, ball bouncing, counting out, just-for-fun,* and *teases and comebacks.* One example from *Miss Mary Mack* that works well as an introductory chant follows:

> Number one, touch your tongue.
> Number two, touch your shoe.
> Number three, touch your knee.
> Number four, touch the floor.
> Number five, learn to jive.
> Number six, pick up sticks.
> Number seven, go to heaven.
> Number eight, shut the gate.
> Number nine, touch your spine.
> Number ten, do it all again.

Many other books can provide fuel for chants and raps in the classroom. Shel Silverstein's (1974) book of poetry entitled *Where the Sidewalk Ends* has several poems especially well-suited to teaching rhyme. The following poem is instructive both in the areas of rhyme and words that are almost alike.

Figure 8.16

Vowel pairs song

Vowel Pairs

When you have two vowels
you have a pair.
The first vowel's name
is the name they share.
When you see two vowels
side by side,
The second vowel's name
will usually hide.

ee says *e* as in *meet*
ea says *e* as in *read*
ay says *a* as in *day*
oa says *o* as in *boat*
ai says *a* as in *paid*

If by chance you find
that this won't do,
Then try the second vowel's name
this might work, too!

THE LITTLE BLUE ENGINE[*]

The little blue engine looked up at the hill.
His light was weak, his whistle was shrill.
He was tired and small, and the hill was tall,
And his face blushed red as he softly said,
"I think I can, I think I can, I think I can."

So he started up with a chug and a strain,
And he puffed and pulled with might and main.
And slowly he climbed, a foot at a time,
And his engine coughed as he whispered soft,
"I think I can, I think I can, I think I can."

With a squeak and a creak and a toot and a sigh,
With an extra hop and an extra try,
He would not stop—now he neared the top—
And strong and proud he cried out loud,
"I think I can, I think I can, I think I can!"

He was almost there, when—CRASH! SMASH! BASH!
He slid down and mashed into engine hash
On the rocks below . . . which goes to show
If the track is tough and the hill is rough,
THINKING you can just ain't enough! (p. 158)

Alphabet Books

Aside from the traditional way of teaching the alphabet (using the famous song), teachers can construct highly predictable **alphabet books** (Cooter & Flynt, 1989) to teach letter names. Developed by Carol Berrey and Ruth Marie Carter in Chetopa, Kansas, alphabet books help students achieve two important goals in kindergarten or first-grade settings: Develop (a) a sense from the first day of school that they can read and (b) a working knowledge of the alphabet and the sounds they represent.

These teacher-developed predictable books tend to follow one of several patterns. Some follow a "sentence that grows" pattern. These books begin with a kernel sentence, which is repeated, and added to, on each successive page. When the sentence becomes about as long as a beginning reader can handle, a new kernel sentence is put into play.

Another alphabet book format uses a repeating word that simply changes the rest of the sentence each time. *The Egg Book* (Carol Berrey & Ruth Marie Carter) for the letter *e* is one example. This book is made in the shape of a fried egg (sunny side up). The center of the book, where the yellow part of the egg appears, has the word *egg* on every page. The script for *The Egg Book* is in Figure 8.17.

A third possible alphabet book format takes familiar songs, such as "One Little, Two Little, Three Little Indians," and rewrites lyrics to comply with a given theme, such as *cats* for letter *c*. This alphabet book is made in the shape of a cat and should be sung to the familiar song's tune.

Alphabet books teach letter names and sounds in highly predictable formats.

Commercial Alphabet Books

Teachers wanting to use alphabet books may not have the necessary time at first for making their own books. Many books already available in most school libraries could be used for the same purpose. For instance, one could use Bill Martin's (1983) *Brown Bear, Brown Bear, What Do You See?* book for the letter *B* theme. The book entitled

Many wonderful alphabet books are available from commercial sources.

Figure 8.17

The Egg Book for the letter *e*

page 1:	Ed is an *egg* lover.
	For breakfast, he ate a . . .
page 2:	happy *egg.*
page 3:	Ed ate a boiled *egg.*
page 4:	Ed ate a fried *egg.*
page 5:	Ed ate a scrambled *egg.*
page 6:	For lunch, Ed ate an egg McMuffin (Don't forget to draw in the "Golden Arches!")
page 7:	Ed ate *egg* salad.
page 8:	Ed ate a deviled *egg.*
page 9:	And, Ed ate an *egg* sandwich.
page 10:	Ed went on an Easter *egg* hunt.
page 11:	Ed found a bird's *egg.*
page 12:	Ed found a chicken's *egg.*
page 13:	Ed found a duck's *egg.*
page 14:	Ed found a dozen *eggs.*
page 15:	Ed likes *eggs.* Don't you?

Courtesy Carol Berrey and Ruth Marie Carter.

What a Mess! (Cowley, 1982), distributed by the Wright Group, could be used for the letter *M* theme. Sometimes teachers may wish to introduce alphabet letter themes using a book like *Animalia* (Base, 1986), which features all of the alphabet letters with multiple pictures of animals whose name begins with that letter. The main thing to remember in selecting commercially produced alphabet books is that the objects or characters pictured should be easy to identify and should not have more than one commonly used name (D. Norton, 1995). Several commercially available alphabet books follow:

Baldwin, R. M. (1972). *One hundred nineteenth-century rhyming alphabets in English.* Carbondale, IL: Southern Illinois University.

Bayer, J. (1984). *My name is Alice* (Steven Kellogg, illustrator). New York: Dial Books.

Hague, K. (1984). *Alphabears: An ABC book* (Michael Hague, illustrator). New York: Holt, Rinehart & Winston.

MacDonald, S. (1986). *Alphabatics.* New York: Bradbury.

Martin, B., & Archambault, J. (1989). *Chicka chicka boom boom.* New York: Simon & Schuster.

Musgrove, M. (1976). *Ashanti to Zulu: African traditions.* New York: Dial.

Using Alphabet Books

Once alphabet books have been written and produced for classroom use, several possibilities exist for their use. A format adapted from the first-grade study mentioned previously (Cooter & Flynt, 1989) is described in this section.

Children enjoy reading alphabet books chorally.

First, the teacher introduces a letter theme for the day using a collage bulletin board featuring many familiar objects in the environment of the children that begin with the letter sound. For example, the letter *c* might feature pictures cut from magazines such as a *car, cop, calendar, carpenter,* and *cat.* After identifying these objects, the teacher gathers the children into the shared reading experience area to listen to the alphabet book. The teacher holds the book up for the class to see as she reads the story aloud. The book is much easier to use if it has been made into a big book. After the teacher has read the alphabet book aloud once or twice and discussed its story, the children are invited to join in for choral rereading of the book several more times.

At this point in the lesson, the children return to their seats. In the Cooter and Flynt (1989) study, each child was then given a mimeographed copy of the alphabet book made from the pattern of the teacher's copy ($8\frac{1}{2} \times 11$-inch size). The story was read again chorally once or twice more, then the children were allowed a few minutes to color some of the pictures. The student copies were brought out again at the end of the day and reread chorally once or twice. Alphabet books went home in a large envelope with each child to read to as many people in the home as possible. A home reading response form (Figure 8.18) was attached to the envelope to be signed by each person who listened to the child read. This envelope was returned each day and checked by the teacher to confirm home support of the reading process.

Reproductions and Innovations
With Alphabet Books

Children can combine reading and writing modes with alphabet books to increase emergent literacy opportunities. Typically, teachers establish a writing center in their

Figure 8.18

Home reading
response form

> ### Home Reading Response Form
>
> Directions: Please indicate below that your child has read to you his/her book or that you have read it with him/her. Your child should then return the envelope and receive a new book tomorrow.
> Thank you!
>
> | **Name of the Book** | **Adult Partner** | **Date** |
> |---|---|---|
> | | | |
> | | | |
> | | | |
> | | | |
> | | | |
> | | | |
> | | | |

classrooms in which students can create both reproductions and innovations of alphabet books already shared. A reproduction is a student-made copy of the original alphabet book. Children copy the text on each page exactly and draw their own illustrations. Innovations borrow the basic pattern of the alphabet book but change key words. For instance, one group of first-grade students took the book *Brown Bear, Brown Bear, What Do You See?* (Martin, 1983) and performed an innovation based on Halloween characters. Part of the students' text read

Reproduction and innovation books are wonderful activities for writing centers.

> Brown spider, brown spider,
> What do you see?
> I see a black cat looking at me!

> Black cat, black cat,
> What do you see?
> I see a white skeleton looking at me.

These reproductions and innovations help students take ownership of the text and encourage good-spirited risk taking in the classroom.

Benefits of Alphabet Books

One of the great benefits of using alphabet books in either kindergarten or first grade is that no matter what the socioeconomic advantages or disadvantages of the chil-

Children are drawn to teacher-made alphabet books.

Alphabet books provide massive practice with high-frequency words.

dren, every child ends up owning at least 26 readable books at the conclusion of the units. Children love these books and read them time and again.

Another benefit of these books is the massive practice it gives children with high-frequency and high-interest words. In the study mentioned earlier (Cooter & Flynt, 1989), the teacher carefully went through each of the alphabet books and verified which words were also found in the basal series adopted by the school district. All of the basal words were found in both the alphabet books and the first three preprimers of the first-grade basal series, with the exception of 10 words (e.g., *Buffy, Mack,* and other proper nouns).

Alphabet books can also be used as a springboard to other activities such as handwriting practice of each letter, word identification and phonics instruction through minilessons, and other lessons related to the reading and writing process. Cooter and Flynt reported

> At the end of the [alphabet book units] each child has read 26 books . . . acquired basic handwriting skills including the formation of all letters (upper and lower case), developed a basic understanding of beginning, medial, and ending sounds in words, mastered most basic concepts about print, and something about authoring. (1989, p. 278)

Using the Writing Process to Teach Word Identification

Word-identification strategies have traditionally been taught in basal reading groups using bottom-up procedures, or parts to whole. One could argue that because most people have learned to read in such programs that they must be effective. Perhaps they are, to some degree, but many reading educators feel that such instructional processes do not produce individuals who enjoy reading or want to continue reading into adulthood as a recreational pastime. Therefore, the search has continued for more effective and interesting ways to help children acquire word-identification strategies.

In recent years, many teachers developing balanced literacy programs have decided to teach word-identification strategies as part of the writing workshop (discussed in detail in Chapter 11). These teachers argue that such literacy skills as phonics knowledge, grammar, word identification, and basic writing mechanics can be taught effectively in the context of writing (Calkins, 1980; Varble, 1990). Regarding the teaching of phonics through the writing process, Jane Hansen writes "Phonics is a servant. It serves the message. In our reading/writing program young children learn the purpose of phonics when they write" (1987, p. 101).

Children use phonics skills as they write.

In this section, several possibilities are reviewed for teaching word-identification strategies through the writing process. Because the superiority of these practices is only partially validated by research, readers may wish to set up their own classroom comparisons with traditional methods to judge their effectiveness.

Invented or "Temporary" Spellings

Children as young as preschoolers can use their knowledge of phonology to invent spellings of words (C. Read, 1971; Tompkins & Hoskisson, 1991). Years ago, teachers thought that allowing children to use these **invented spellings** (we prefer the term **temporary spellings** because that better conveys to children and parents what is meant) might be detrimental in that students would be learning an "incorrect" form of the word and have to later *un*learn it in favor of the correct spelling. More recently, educators have realized that some important benefits may be derived by learners when temporary spellings are encouraged.

First of all, temporary spellings allow children to put into practice what they know about phonemes. In early grades, this means that children may spell favorite words with a single letter, such as *d* for *dinosaur,* *g* for *goat,* *r* for *ring,* and so on. This early application of what is known helps students begin to transfer rote learning of such things as the "Alphabet Song" to actual literacy communications. Children also begin to feel that they are successful writers on a level they find rewarding.

Another benefit of temporary spellings is that students begin to apply simple phonics knowledge. As was pointed out earlier in the chapter, phonics strategies that seem to have the greatest utility when combined with context clues are beginning, ending, and medial sounds in words. As children progress in temporary spellings, they tend to mirror these very same strategies. Thus, for the word *dinosaur,* children will tend to progress in their early (semiphonetic) invented/temporary spellings from *d,* to *dr,* to *dinosr.* This kind of spelling and writing metamorphosis has direct benefits in reading. As the student becomes aware of the structure and functions of the written word and letters, word identification through sounding out or blending prominent letter sounds begins to make sense.

Temporary or invented spellings develop phonic awareness in children.

As alluded to, a third important benefit of temporary spellings is related to spelling development itself. After more than a century of formal spelling instruction, educators now know that attempting to teach words using spelling lists is not very effective. Children simply use short-term memory to temporarily conquer the spelling list and pass a test, then quickly forget the words through a lack of use. Richard Gentry (1987), in his book entitled *Spel . . . Is a Four-Letter Word,* mentions several

Writing activities provide a natural setting for applying temporary spellings.

important keys to encouraging spelling growth, which in turn affect invented spellings and transfer to word-identification strategies:

- Kids learn to spell by inventing spelling. Inventing spellings allows children to engage in thinking about words and to demonstrate their acquired skills.
- Purposeful writing is the key to learning to spell.
- Spelling is a constructive developmental process.
- Allowing children to take risks in their own writing is the best technique. (Gentry, 1987, p. 28)

Word Rubber-Banding

Word rubber-banding helps children with both spelling and reading development.

Word rubber-banding is a simple technique that can be used to help students pronounce unknown words in print and also as a strategy for invented spellings. In the classroom, the teacher may explain word rubber-banding by saying "Stretch (the word) like a rubber band . . . and listen to the sounds. . . . What sounds do you hear?" (Calkins, 1986, p. 174). Students should begin by using context as a word-identification strategy to think about which word might make sense in the text they are reading. By stretching the word out phoneme by phoneme, or perhaps by onset and rime, sound clues are provided to the student that help solve the word-identification puzzle.

As an invented spellings strategy, children are encouraged to stretch out the word they wish to spell vocally. Teacher modeling through minilessons is needed in the beginning to help children understand the process. For example, during the Christmas season, students may well want to write stories about Santa Claus. The teacher could offer the following model for her students for the word Scrooge after explaining the concept of word rubber-banding:

Teacher: Listen while I stretch out the name Scrooge as I say it out loud. Ssssccr-rooooogggge. I sounded kind of like Marley's ghost when I said it like that, didn't I? Now, watch as I write the name Scrooge while saying it like Marley's ghost.

Observations: As the teacher rubber-bands the name Scrooge again orally, she writes the following letters that are easily heard. S-c-r-o-o-g.

Teacher: Now that I have written the word Scrooge, I can begin to check it for accuracy, to see if I spelled it accurately. Where could I find the correct spelling of Scrooge, class?

Child Volunteer: Maybe a dictionary. Maybe in the book *A Christmas Carol?*

From that point, the class and teacher can discover the correct spelling through some light research. The point is that once an invented spelling has been created the word can be found using reference sources. Children have an opportunity to practice these skills in the context of real writing, and it all makes sense.

Editing Sessions

Editing sessions between writing "experts" and students can be most constructive for developing word-identification strategies. Usually conducted in a one-on-one or small group setting, the focus is always on making sense. That is, the composition should use semantic and syntactic constructions that help the reader understand the author's message. Therefore, the focus of these sessions can be such topics as invented spellings and grammar. When we remind ourselves that *reading and writing are reciprocal processes,* it is easy to see how to help students with word-identification through editing sessions. For example, let's say that a student named Shelley has been writing a story about motorcycle racing. The character in the story is leading in a big race, and the motorcycle on which she is riding begins to suffer some mechanical problems. When examining the story, the writing expert (teacher, parent volunteer, peer tutor from an upper grade) notices the following sentences:

Editing sessions focus on making sense of print.

> As Laura made it through the curve she felt something hot down her leg. A quick down told her that she had a bad oil leak, probably from the new injection system Rob had installed just that morning.

The editor first wants to commend Shelley for her idea and writing. They are certainly action packed and reveal some understanding of her topic. By beginning with positive comments, the editor is building a sense of acceptance and creating a safety net in the learning environment so that Shelley will be encouraged to continue to be a risk taker. Next on the agenda is to discuss possible ways the story could be improved, remembering that Shelley as author has the final say-so regarding changes. After discussing a few minor alterations, this portion of the story is revised. The new version appears below with changes noted in bold type.

> As Laura made it through the **tight hairpin** curve she felt something hot down her leg. A quick **glance** down told her that she had a bad oil leak,

probably from the new injection system Rob, the **mechanic**, had installed just that morning.

Several ideas come to mind that the editor might emphasize to help Shelley improve her word-identification skills in reading. Some possible minilesson topics follow:

Correction: *tight hairpin*

Word-identification strategy description: Context clues. Words immediately preceding a noun are typically descriptive words that help the reader create a clear mental picture of the setting. When coming to a word that is not known in this sort of context, descriptive word guesses will usually make sense.

Correction: *glance*

Word-identification strategy description: Grammar. In this instance, a necessary word was missing. Through the use of simple context, an appropriate word could be chosen that made sense.

The strategy then for word identification in reading is *when coming to an unknown word, use context and knowledge of sentence grammar to make an appropriate guess.*

Helping Students With Special Needs Develop Word-Identification Strategies

Students with special needs in reading often were derailed early in their learning of word-identification strategies. Learning to identify words in print is a complex process, enough so that many elementary students can lose sight of the main purpose of reading—understanding the author's message.

We have observed that many students having reading problems, in the early grades especially, essentially have not internalized the four aspects of the word-identification strategy described earlier in this chapter:

- Use of context clues
- Beginning sounds and onsets in words
- Ending sounds and rimes in words
- Medial sounds and onsets and rimes in words

Where teachers' well-intentioned efforts to help special needs students sometimes break down is at the point of intervention. They frequently focus on sophisticated decoding strategies well ahead of the student's zone of proximal development (see Chapter 2 for a review of this concept) instead of first making sure that the word-identification strategy has become automatic for the child. For example, it makes no sense to teach about the consonant-vowel-consonant (CVC) generalization when the student has not yet mastered beginning sounds and onsets as part of the word-identification strategy! S. McCormick explains that there are two levels of word identification or decoding development:

Sequential decoding is learned first, followed by hierarchical decoding (Ehri, 1991). In **sequential decoding**, students learn simple one-to-one correspondences between letters and the sounds that the letters typically stand for—for example, that the sound typically associated with *f* usually is the sound heard at the beginning of *fat.* . . . In **hierarchical decoding**, more complicated understandings are developed, such as the concept that sometimes letters cue the sounds of other letters, as in certain common spelling patterns. (1995, p. 303)

Thus, one must carefully assess where students are in their development of the word-identification strategy, which is essentially a sequential decoding act. In Chapter 13, we discuss a number of authentic assessment methods teachers may use to assess word-identification abilities. If the word-identification strategy is well-internalized, then the teacher may wish to develop hierarchical decoding abilities. However, our experiences suggest that students who have internalized the word-identification strategy rarely have problems with decoding, especially in elementary grades.

> *Word identification is essentially a sequential decoding act.*

Because many students with learning needs in reading have not yet internalized the word-identification strategy, it may be necessary to seek out alternative teaching strategies when the usual minilessons are not successful. Writing activities can be quite effective with special needs students because they involve both the encoding and decoding of written language. The more students write, the more they engage the elements of successful reading—use of context, sounds in words (invented/temporary spellings), and so on. In this section we present a few quick and easy activities that help students internalize aspects of the word-identification strategy.

> *Writing activities involve both encoding and decoding.*

Writing Pattern Stories to Develop Context Clues Awareness

Tompkins and Hoskisson (1995) describe pattern stories as those having a repetitive pattern or refrain. Numeroff's (1985) *If You Give a Mouse a Cookie* and Viorst's (1972) *Alexander and the Terrible Horrible No Good Very Bad Day* are cited as two very popular examples of this type of writing. In writing pattern stories, begin by sharing a pattern book, song, or poem so that students get a feel for the original text. (Note: Some teachers prefer to share the original text last so that students can compare what they developed with that of the author.) Next, present students with a copy of the book, song, or poem with key elements deleted and ask them to re-create the story in their own way. This will require the use of context to determine the kind of word or phrase needed and also allow students to use their own background knowledge to complete the story. Allow volunteers to share their compositions in small groups or author's chair (see Chapter 11).

One fun example uses the well-known song "I Know an Old Lady Who Swallowed a Fly," which is also available in book form. Figure 8.19 shows an excerpt of the original text (about midway through) with deletions/blanks that have been completed to create a pattern story/song:

Creating Crazy Stories to Practice Using Rimes

Crazy stories (S. McCormick, 1995) is a simple activity that has students change the first part of underlined words (onsets) in a story excerpt to another letter or letters so that the rime in the last part of the word takes on new meaning. If students wish, they can create an illustration to go with the altered story. Figure 8.20 shows an excerpt from the book *Earrings!* (Viorst, 1990, pp. 2–3) that has been converted into a crazy story.

Figure 8.19

Writing a pattern story to develop context clues awareness

I know an old _donkey_ who swallowed a _rat_ .

Imagine that, to swallow a _rat_ !

_He_ swallowed the _rat_ to catch the _goldfish_ ,

_He_ swallowed the _goldfish_ to catch the _worm_

That _squirmed_ and _turned_ and _churned_

inside _him_ ;

_He_ swallowed the _worm_ to catch the

apple ,

But I don't know why _he_ swallowed the _apple_ ,

I guess _he won't_ die!

Vowel and Consonant Sound Practice

S. McCormick (1995) suggests an interesting and sometimes challenging way for students to rehearse what they know about context clues, consonant sounds, consonant clues, and vowel sounds all at once. Provide students with one- and two-sentence passages that contain words with all vowels deleted. Their task is to translate the sentence by filling in the missing vowels. Following is an example from Babette Cole's (1983) book *The Trouble With Mom* (she's a witch!):

Th__ tr____ble w__th m__m __s th__ h__ts sh__ w____rs . . .

Figure 8.20

Creating crazy stories to practice using rimes

Weird Hair!   Weird Hair   Cool dudes!   Singers   Movie stars

~~Earrings!~~ Beautiful ~~earrings~~ for ~~Pierced ears.~~ ~~Teachers~~ and ~~lady dentists~~

it   Fabio   Johnny Depp   has   it!

have ~~them.~~ ~~Mothers~~ and even ~~grandmothers~~ ~~have them.~~

Weird Hair?

Why won't my mom and my dad let me have ~~pierced ears.~~

Assisting Students in Multicultural Settings Develop Phonemic Awareness

Yopp (1992) has stated that most children enter kindergarten with a rather sizable vocabulary and a serviceable knowledge of English syntax. This may not always be the case, however. Some students may be learning English as a second language (ESL) and have to learn a new listening and speaking vocabulary before they can experience much success. Others may have limited language ability because of linguistically deprived home environments.

In Chapter 7, we suggested ways that teachers can develop vocabulary so that these challenges do not become obstacles. As students from multicultural settings build vocabulary knowledge, teachers must then help them acquire word-identification strategies.

One of the most crucial word-identification abilities, which also has great use in the writing process, is phonemic awareness. Following are a few activities found to be quite effective and enjoyable for children (Yopp, 1992) and equally useful in multicultural settings.

Some ESL students must develop a listening and speaking vocabulary before they can be successful readers.

Sound Matching

In sound matching, students are asked to identify words that begin with a specified phoneme. This is a relatively easy task, which allows students to use words already in their listening and speaking vocabularies. The following simple lyric is used with the tune of "Jimmy Cracked Corn and I Don't Care." Note that the sound of the phoneme (in this case /m/), not the name of the letter, is used.

Who has an /m/ word to share with us?

Who has an /m/ word to share with us?

Who has an /m/ word to share with us?

It must start with the /m/ sound.

After a word is identified by a class volunteer, the whole group sings the following together:

Mask is a word that starts with /m/

Mask is a word that starts with /m/

Mask is a word that starts with /m/

Mask starts with the /m/ sound.

Sound Isolation

A similar activity to sound matching is sound isolation, which uses lyrics sung to the tune of "Old MacDonald Had a Farm" and helps children to hear sounds at the beginning, middle (or medial position), or end of words. Following are examples for sounds in the medial position:

What's the sound in the middle of these words?

Creep and *deep* and *seat*?

(wait for a response)

/ee/ is the sound in the middle of these words:

Creep and *deep* and *seat.*

With an /ee/, /ee/ here, and an /ee/, /ee/ there,

Here an /ee/, there an /ee/, everywhere an /ee/, /ee/,

/ee/ is the sound in the middle of these words:

Creep and *deep* and *seat.*

Blending

Blending helps students assemble segmented sounds to pronounce words.

Blending is a task that requires students to combine individual sounds to form a word. Yopp and Troyer (1992) developed an activity called "What am I thinking of?" wherein the teacher calls out the segmented sounds one at a time (e.g., /r/ - /a/ - /t/), then children try to blend them to guess the word (e.g., *rat*). As with the previous phonemic awareness tasks, blending can be sung using the following lyrics combined with the tune "If you're happy and you know it, clap your hands":

If you think you know this word, shout it out!

If you think you know this word, shout it out!

If you think you know this word,

Then tell me what you've heard,

If you think you know this word, shout it out!

(Then say a segmented word, then children respond)

Segmentation

In segmentation activities, students must isolate individual sounds in a spoken word. This is a very difficult activity for many students, but one that can be important to developing an effective word-identification strategy. One activity suggested by Hallie Yopp (1992) is for students to sing favorite songs and repeat initial phonemes in key verses. For instance, in the old favorite (for kids) "I'm Looking Over, My Dead Dog Rover," the first verse might be sung "I'm l-l-l-looking over, m-m-m-my d-d-d-dead dog R-R-R-Rover. . . . " Another idea that Yopp suggests is a song that helps students with complete segmentations and can be sung to the tune "Twinkle, Twinkle, Little Star":

Listen, listen

To my word

Then tell me all the sounds you heard: *place*

(say slowly)

/pl/ is one sound

/a/ is two

/s/ is the last in *place*

It's true.

(repeat verse with new words)

Thanks for listening

To my words

And telling all the sounds you heard!

Summary

How to identify new words in print has been the subject of research and debate for over a century. Some educators favoring an explicit phonics perspective feel it is best to teach letter sounds in the very beginning and lead students to an understanding of whole words, sentences, and complete text. Others believe an implicit way of teaching using whole words first is best. We have presented a word-identification strategy that uses context clues in conjunction with effective phonic-analysis skills for quick identification of new words. This strategy uses what we know about letter–sound relationships and the role of text comprehension in ways that make sense to children. Seven phonic generalizations that seem to be reasonably reliable were also discussed.

New research has emerged in recent years suggesting that onsets and rimes may be helpful in word-identification instruction. Hundreds of early elementary words can easily be learned on sight as children internalize familiar rimes. Songs, poetry, and chants are interesting vehicles for these learning experiences. Likewise, the teaching of the alphabetic principle seems to be an important key to effective word identification.

Word learning can be enhanced through the use of word banks. These individual or class "dictionaries" assist children in reading and writing experiences as they acquire what have been termed key vocabulary, discovery words, basal words, and "four-letter," or function words. The drastic strategy is especially helpful for the teaching and learning of function words.

Several ideas were presented for emergent readers and writers in the word-learning and identification process. Two of these were bridging strategies and word rubber-banding. Bridging strategies help children transfer knowledge of known words from familiar books to new reading situations in unfamiliar books. Word rubber-banding is a teaching activity during which children learn to say new words slowly to facilitate invented spellings. Invented spellings help students hear word parts and phonic elements, skills that directly benefit both reading and writing processes. Finally, ways of helping students in multicultural settings develop phonemic segmentation abilities were offered.

Figure 8.21 shows an overview of the chapter.

CONCEPT APPLICATIONS

IN THE CLASSROOM

1. Construct a minilesson teaching the use of beginning sounds in words as a decoding strategy for a second-grade class. The lesson should begin with whole text, preferably using a children's book, and proceed to parts (beginning sounds in words) and conclude by reapplying the strategy in whole text.

2. Develop a model word bank for third graders. It should be made using inexpensive materials found around the home or a typical classroom. An old children's shoe box is about the right size. Remember to decorate your word bank and include the four kinds of words discussed in this chapter.

3. Write a minilesson helping first-grade children to think of key vocabulary words. You may want to use themes such as scary words, funny words, or happy words.

4. Make an innovation book modeled after a favorite read-aloud book at a grade level of your choice. You may want to consider the following books:

Figure 8.21

Chapter overview

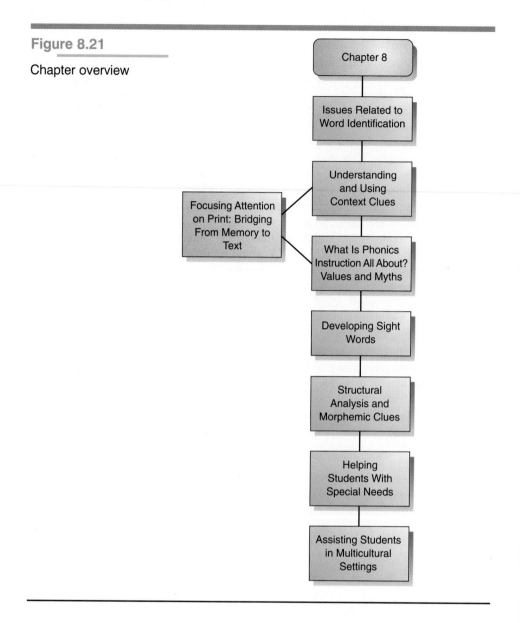

The True Story of the 3 Little Pigs! by A. Wolf (Scieszka, 1989), or *Gila Monsters Meet You at the Airport* (Sharmat, 1980).

5. Put together a collection of poems that can assist children in learning at least 10 of the rimes listed in this chapter that have high utility and frequency in words.

RECOMMENDED READINGS

Adams, M. J. (1990). *Beginning to read: Thinking and learning about print.* Urbana-Champaign, IL: Center for the Study of Reading.

Ashton-Warner, S. (1963). *Teacher.* New York: Touchstone.

Fry, E. B., Polk, J. K, & Fountoukidis, D. (1984). *The reading teacher's book of lists.* Englewood Cliffs, NJ: Prentice-Hall.

Gentry, R. (1987). *Spel . . . is a four-letter word.* Portsmouth, NH: Heinemann.

Johnson, T. D., & Louis, D. R. (1987). *Literacy through literature.* Portsmouth, NH: Heinemann.

McCormick, S. (1995). *Instructing students who have literacy problems.* Englewood Cliffs, NJ: Merrill/Prentice Hall.

Tompkins, G. E. (1994). *Teaching writing: Balancing process and product.* Englewood Cliffs, NJ: Merrill/Prentice Hall.

Yopp, H. K. (1992). Developing phonemic awareness in young children. *The Reading Teacher, 45(9),* 696–703.

Chapter 9

Designing Literacy
Learning Environments

Focus Questions

When you are finished studying this chapter, you should be able to answer these questions:

1. What are four ways literacy props affect the environment–behavior relationships found in classrooms?
2. What are several areas into which classroom space may be subdivided for specific classroom activities?
3. What are several instructional resources available to classroom teachers?
4. Name at least two software programs that may be used to improve reading comprehension abilities. What specific reading comprehension strategies do these programs help develop?
5. Compare and contrast the technologies known as *hypertext* and *hypermedia*.
6. How can teachers implement a classroom literacy volunteer project?
7. What are at least three alternative grouping plans to ability grouping?
8. What are at least three cooperative learning grouping plans?

Key Concepts

Aggregation
Whole-Class Learning and Sharing
   Area
Writing and Publishing Area
Collaborative Writing Area
Conference Area
Editing Area
Publishing Area
Silent Reading Area
Supported Reading Area
Reading Conference Area

Thematic Studies Area
Trade Books
Hypertext
Hypermedia
Ability Grouping
Basal Reader Visiting Response
   Groups
Literature-Response Groups
Cooperative Learning
Minilessons
Flexible Traveling Groups

Designing the Classroom Environment

A supportive and inviting reading classroom is integral to achieving a balanced and successful reading instructional program. Often, when planning effective literacy classrooms, teachers become so involved in managing children, materials, time, and space they lose sight of the fact that what goes on within the classroom environment is what really counts. The way teachers design the classroom environment will in large measure affect the value children attach to literacy and literacy instruction.

> Schools too have atmosphere. . . . For a young child the school can have the feel of an alien and threatening place, or it can create an atmosphere which shelters the child and inspires him or her with security and confidence. (Van Manen, 1986, p. 32)

Describe two ways classroom environments are an important part of the total learning experience for elementary school-aged readers.

Thus, the environment of the literacy learning classroom can contribute much to a child's sense of well-being in the school setting. The climate, atmosphere, and environment in a classroom begin with the teacher's beliefs, behaviors, and attitudes. Children are quick to pick up on a teacher's sensitivity to their needs and interests as well as their personal enthusiasm for reading and writing. When teachers evidence sensitivity for children and enthusiasm for reading and writing, the classroom climate results in a supportive and productive worklike atmosphere in which children are treated with respect and affection—the result of which is that the risks commonly associated with learning to read become minimized and the benefits maximized.

Balanced Literacy Classrooms: Understanding the Dynamics of Classroom Environment

Recent research demonstrates a clear relationship between classroom environments and literacy-related behaviors and learning.

The physical environment of the literacy classroom can be a powerful tool in support of literacy learning or an unrecognized and undirected influence on teaching and learning behaviors (Loughlin & Martin, 1987). Although generally accepted as an important part of literacy instruction for many years, too little attention has been focused on what the literacy environment of the classroom brings to children and their learning. Research by Neuman and Roskos (1990, 1992) demonstrates a clear relationship between classroom environments and literacy-related behaviors and learning. Teacher decisions related to classroom literacy environments generally include two types: (a) what they *decide* about the environment and (b) what they *do* in the environment. Based on recent literacy environmental research, we have developed a model entitled Balanced Literacy Classrooms: Understanding Environment Behavior Relationships (Figure 9.1) to help teachers understand the aspects of the environment–behavior relationships that condition and shape literacy learning in school classrooms.

To help teachers understand how classroom environments shape literacy learning, we discuss in some detail each of the four quarters of the model in Figure 9.1 separately.

Providing Literacy Props Affects Children's Literacy Learning Opportunities

Research by Neuman and Roskos (1990, 1992) has shown that enriching play centers for young children with a variety of literacy props leads to dramatic increases in child literacy learning. They showed that literacy behaviors during play became more

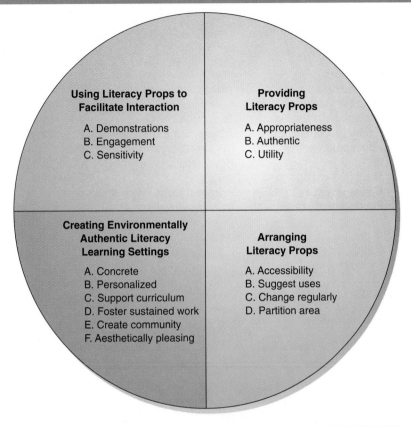

Figure 9.1

Balanced literacy classrooms: Understanding environment–behavior relationships

purposeful when centers included more artifacts, props, or provisions for literacy learning. Children's play behaviors became more literacy learning centered or connected; more literacy interaction occurred when children employed speaking, listening, reading, and writing behaviors spontaneously and purposefully; and children more readily adopted roles appropriate to specific play areas, such as kitchen, post office, business office, or libraries. In Figure 9.2, we provide a partial listing of possible props for literacy classrooms as examples of the types of literacy props.

When provisioning classrooms with literacy props, it is important that teachers consider the reasons for including specific literacy props. Neuman and Roskos (1990) provide some guidance for teachers in relation to these decisions. First, teachers should consider whether or not the props selected fit the criterion of *appropriateness.* To determine *appropriateness,* teachers might ask questions such as, Are the props age-/maturity-level appropriate? Can my children use this prop safely? Can my children use this prop in purposeful ways? Can my children use this prop in natural ways to communicate and interact? Second, teachers should decide if a selected literacy prop fits the criterion of *authenticity.* To determine whether or not a literacy prop fits this criterion, teachers may ask, Is this prop an item children would find in other environmental settings that people really use to perform the literate behaviors of speaking, listening, reading, and writing? Finally, teachers should consider if a literacy prop fits the criterion of utility. In relation to this criterion, teachers might ask, Does this prop serve a literacy function that is familiar or found in *everyday* life? We

Literacy behaviors increase with the number of literacy props provided in the classroom environment. For example, when children have a message board, they tend to write more often to their peers.

Figure 9.2

Possible literacy props to enrich literacy learning environments

Books, pamphlets, magazines	Posters of children's books	Appointment book
Ledger sheets	Small drawer trays	Signs (e.g., open/closed)
Cookbooks	Library book return cards	File folders
Labeled recipe boxes	A wide variety of children's books	In/out trays
Personal stationery		Business cards
Grocery store ads/fliers	Telephone books	Self-adhesive notes and address labels
Empty grocery containers	A sign-in/sign-out sheet	
Note cards	ABC index cards	Bookmarks
Pens, pencils, markers	Small plaques/decorative magnets	Post Office mailbox
Trays for holding items		Computer/address labels
Message pads	Assorted forms	Calendars of various types
Envelopes of various sizes	Blank recipe cards	
	Emergency number decals	Posters/signs about mailing
Racks for filing papers		Stamps for marking books
Index cards	Food coupons	
Clipboards	Play money	Typewriter or computer keyboard
Stationery	Small message board	
Stickers, stars, stamps, stamp pads	Notepads of assorted sizes	Telephone
A tote bag for mail	Large plastic clips	Paper of assorted sizes

have found that these criteria are very useful for deciding what might be included in a classroom literacy environment.

The Arrangement of Literacy Props Affects the Quality and Quantity of Literacy Learning in Classrooms

Notice three qualities associated with the arrangement of literacy props.

Research by Morrow and Rand (1991) has shown that the arrangement of literacy props in classroom play centers significantly increased children's literacy learning. Issues specifically related to arranging classroom literacy props for optimal effectiveness focused on three major points. First, literacy props should be kept in clearly marked or labeled containers that can be easily accessed and easily put away. Children will not use literacy props as readily if they must ask teachers to access them. Likewise, teachers will not want to allow children access to materials if they must take responsibility for their cleanup and storage. Second, teachers should suggest possible uses for literacy props. For example, a message board in the classroom might be used to post announcements, ask questions, or send personal communications. Used in a kitchen play center, a message board may be used to post a grocery list or take telephone messages. Used in an intermediate-grade science center, a message board may be used to list materials needed to conduct an experiment, record the steps of an experiment, or make a diagram for displaying the process. In any case, suggested uses for literacy props help children see the many potential uses for these objects as they learn and communicate. Third, teachers should change the availability of literacy props regularly. Just like adults, children grow weary of the same old things. To add excitement to learning, literacy props should be added to, deleted from, and rotated on a regular basis. The four points related to arranging literacy props in classrooms are summarized in Figure 9.1.

Literacy Props Help Focus Human Interaction Toward Acquiring Literacy Behaviors

F. Smith (1988) described three environmental conditions that must be present for literacy learning to successfully take place: (a) demonstrations, (b) engagement, and (c) sensitivity. When people have access to literacy props, they demonstrate what it means to be literate and how reading and writing are done. When children engage in the literacy demonstrations of others or engage on their own using available literacy props, they "learn by doing." It is important to understand that children do not choose to engage in literate behaviors spontaneously without a degree of personal sensitivity to the literate demonstrations of others. Consequently, children and teachers must understand and assess the sensitivity of self and others to the available demonstrations in literacy environment.

When teachers share their favorite books such as *Poems for Laughing Out Loud* (Prelutsky, 1991) and chuckle or laugh or read the *Bridge to Terabithia* (Paterson, 1977) and tears stream down their cheeks, children learn that books, one type of literacy prop, evoke an emotional response that teachers and children share, discuss, and ponder. When a child brings the teacher some cookies from home and finds a thank-you card on her desk the following morning, she learn that cards, a writing prop, facilitate the mutual sharing of gratitude between teacher and child. In each of these examples, demonstrations using various literacy props help children see the value, utility, and purposes of becoming literate—learning to read and write.

Having seen, experienced, and understood the value and power of reading and writing through demonstrations, children choose to engage in literacy themselves or with others. It is no longer enough to allow teachers the singular privilege of using literacy props. Drawing on the demonstrations provided in the classroom environment and the available literacy props, children engage in reading books, writing notes, telling stories, and listening to poems. In short, they come to explore, experiment with, and use literacy props in ways that approximate the demonstrations they have experienced. This decision does not occur without sensitivity to previous literacy demonstrations.

Children do not engage in literate acts without a belief or confidence that learning to read and write is possible. In fact, F. Smith (1985) maintains that the major precursor of reading and writing difficulties is a belief that learning to read and write is hard, painful, or impossible. Hence, student attitudes and interests frame the motivation for engagement. Literacy props, particularly a variety of these tools, provide for a broad spectrum of attitudes and interests that spark desire and *press* children into engaging in literacy learning. A typewriter in the corner of the room may be just what is needed for a child with illegible handwriting to move ahead with literacy. A telephone for talking and a notepad for taking down messages may be just the set of tools needed to influence a reluctant student to write. Literacy props influence the motivations or sensitivity of children to engage in literate behaviors in the first place. And conversely, children's engagement in literacy in the classroom affects the tone, the feel, and the available demonstrations of literate behavior for the other children

Describe the concept of press as related to establishing literacy environments.

in the classroom as well. Taken together, literacy props affect the dynamics of the classroom learning environment.

Literacy Props Can Be Used to Create Authentic Literacy Learning Settings

Designing the environment of classrooms has received considerable attention in recent years (Morrow, 1993; Neuman & Roskos, 1993; Rhodes & Shanklin, 1993). Recommendations regarding the way in which classrooms can be provisioned with literacy props fall into three broad categories, according to Neuman and Roskos (1993): (a) creating spatial boundaries, (b) displaying literacy props, and (c) using personal touches. At the core of each of these recommendations is the concept of organization—organizing the classroom to inform children in concrete and personal ways.

Classrooms, as research suggests, should be broken up into smaller specific activity settings such as those shown on the cover of this book. Doing so encourages quieter classrooms, sustained engagement in literacy learning, more cooperative behaviors, and a sense of privacy to pursue personal projects. The nuts and bolts of creating a variety of these spaces in the classroom is discussed later in this chapter. The arrangement of furnishings is one way of cordoning off specific activity areas in the classroom. Another way of designating activity areas is through the use of displays, labels, and signs. Each of these objects should attract attention, teach, and inform children as they roam the room.

Aggregation means that literacy props are collected into a related network of materials or objects for a particular purpose.

The key to displays and storing literacy props is the concept of **aggregation.** This means that props are collected into a related network of materials or objects for a particular purpose. For example, when designing a classroom library area, teachers aggregate or collect literacy props such as library books, cards, due date stamps, book marks, posters of favorite children's books, pictures of authors, and advertisements of new books for display and use in this area. There might be a card catalogue, a librarian's desk, a rotating wire book display rack, and a check out. Bookshelves are labeled with section headers such as biographies, fiction, fables, folk tales, and fairy tales.

Other displays and areas in the classroom focus on themes taken from curriculum subject areas such as science or social studies. An area focusing on the Civil War where children make and view "crankies" on the various issues, personalities, and events of the Civil War could also be constructed. Each of these areas should enjoy a personal touch from home. Here again, furnishings and objects provide the key to this concept. Plants, bean bag chairs, pillows, children's portraits, mailboxes, message boards, galleries for artwork, and mobiles for displaying the main characters in books, enhance the "personal" nature of the classroom. All combined, these elements of classroom design create a press for children to engage in literacy as an ongoing and enjoyable source of learning, creating, and growing.

In addition to these compelling reasons for using literacy props to create authentic settings for learning literacy, several other reasons are worthy of consideration. First, literacy props properly organized can be used to extend and enrich every other area of the curriculum. Second, because children enjoy using literacy props, children tend to remain on task for longer periods of time. They can sustain their attention and effort longer. As children work together in activity areas using literacy props to learn, they develop a sense of independence as well as a strong network of interdependence with other classroom peers. And finally, when properly organized, authentic literacy learning settings are aesthetically pleasing to children. A warm, comfortable, well-lit reading nook with the quiet bubbling sound of an aquarium has a calming and tranquilizing effect on children's behaviors. This is a place to go to think, experience quiet, and share a peaceful moment with print and others. Thus, organizing literacy props into environmentally authentic literacy learning settings provides not only an aesthetically pleasing learning environment but one indispensable to children's personal language progress.

Practical Considerations for Organizing the Classroom Environment

For both the novice and the experienced teacher, one of the immediate problems demanding attention is the physical arrangement of classroom space and instructional resources to facilitate a collaborative, effective, and supportive learning environment. Faced in late summer with an empty classroom soon to be filled with lively and anxious children, teachers must somehow plan to make effective use of classroom space.

Classroom furnishings need to be arranged to facilitate easy movement between classroom areas and to provide access to necessary materials, a clear view of chalk-

A quiet, comfortable reading nook should invite children to read silently.

Signs or labels set the standard for printed products in the classroom as well as provide children with an opportunity for environmental reading.

boards and demonstration areas, as well as specific areas in the classroom for children to express their ideas and feelings. Areas for storing and reading books should be comfortable and well lit. Each area in the classroom should be clearly labeled with neatly printed or handwritten signs. Neatness is important because these signs or labels set the standard for printed products in the classroom as well as provide children with an opportunity for environmental reading. A major objective of the physical design of any literacy classroom is to encourage children to learn from the environment, each other, and the teacher. As teachers plan layouts and schedules for their classrooms, they often begin simply. Later, they may wish to subdivide the classroom into functional work areas. Much like homes—which are divided into smaller areas for performing specific tasks such as kitchens, recreation rooms, quiet areas, and sleeping rooms—classrooms can be divided into functional areas for accomplishing desired literacy tasks. Several useful areas to have in a classroom include whole-class learning and sharing areas, writing and publishing areas, silent reading areas, supported reading areas, reading conference areas, display areas, and storage areas. In the following sections, these areas are discussed in greater detail for teachers to consider as they carefully plan their classroom literacy learning environments. It should be noted that these suggestions are to be viewed as potential classroom components that may be added to the typical classroom floor plan and schedule as teachers develop sufficient control and expertise to manage a more complex learning environment.

Whole-Class Learning and Sharing Area

*A **whole-class learning area** is useful for whole-class activities such as singing from a chart or performing a play.*

A **whole-class learning and sharing area** is logically located near chalkboards and well away from designated quiet areas in the classroom. A large piece of well-padded carpet may be used to comfortably seat the entire class of children in the area. Audiovisual equipment may include overhead projectors; tape players; easels for displaying enlarged print of stories, poems, riddles, songs, group experience charts, and discussion summaries; electronic keyboards for music accompaniment; and cardboard or wooden easels for reading commercial or child-produced big books. Audiovisual equipment needs to be located near the whole-class sharing area. The sharing area should also be clear of obstructions. The whole-class learning and sharing area may occupy up to 25% of the total space in the classroom (Figure 9.3).

Writing and Publishing Area

A **writing and publishing area** (Figure 9.4) can be subdivided into three smaller working areas:

- Work area for collaborative writing projects, conferences, and editing
- Quiet area for silent sustained writing
- Publishing area with necessary supplies

The writing process is discussed in much greater detail in Chapter 11.

The writing and publishing area is designed to be used with a process-writing approach in the classroom. A **collaborative writing area** is designated for children to interact with teachers and peers about their writing projects—projects that may have been authored by individuals or groups or may have been co-authored. Because of the nature of the activity in the collaborative writing area, it should be located away from the other quiet writing areas designated for silent sustained writing. A **conference area** with table and chairs can function as a location for conduct-

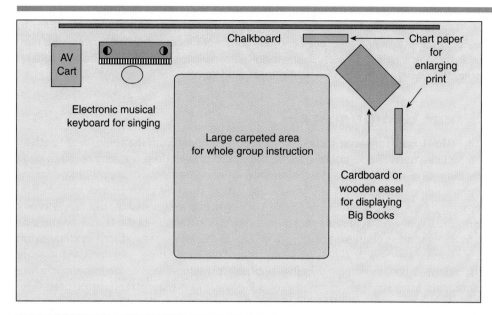

Figure 9.3

Whole-class learning and sharing area

ing peer–student or teacher–student conferences about emerging writing projects. An **editing area** can be located at a desk near the conference area. An older student, the teacher, or adult volunteer can function as an editor for student-authored works in the classroom. An editor's visor, printer's apron, various writing and marking media, and a poster displaying editorial marks can be located here for the editor's use. The **publishing area** should be stocked with pencils, pen, markers, stapler, and various papers (colors and sizes) for covers. Binding materials also should be available for students to bind or publish their final writing products in a variety of ways.

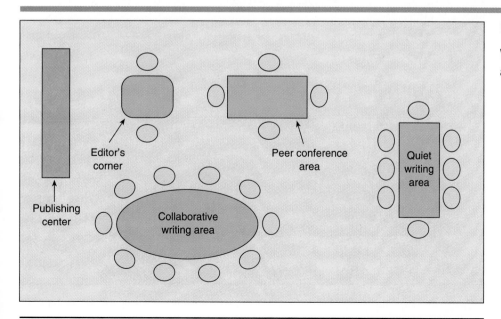

Figure 9.4

Writing and publishing area

The location for each of the many supplies in this area can be indicated by a printed label or an outline of the object. Doing so makes it easier for students to help in keeping the publishing area neat and tidy. Student works published in this area may take the form of big books, shape books, microbooks, accordion books, letters, notes, lists, posters, bulletin boards, murals, and so on.

Silent Reading Area

A *silent reading area* needs to provide a comfortable, inviting environment for enjoying books.

The **silent reading area** should be located well away from the mainstream activity of the classroom. Trade books may be organized into sections for easy reading, early reading, and advanced reading materials in the classroom library. Within each of these three categories of reading difficulty, books may be organized in alphabetical order by titles. When multiple copies of a single title are available, old cereal boxes cut in half, covered in contact paper, and displaying the title of the books on the side can be used to store these books as a group. Big books can be stored in shelves, on hooks, pant hangers or easels near this area. This location can also be used to store the adopted basal readers. Whether a basal or multiple copies of trade books are used, this area is ideal for small-group or one-to-one story reading or literature-response group meetings. It should be comfortable and well lit. Carpeting, bean bag chairs, a bathtub filled with pillows, pillow chairs, and the like can be used as a com-

Storing big books for reading is easily accomplished with clothes hangers.

Name of student _____

Monday—Date _____

Book Titles _____

_____Time in Minutes _____

Tuesday—Date _____

Book Titles _____

_____Time in Minutes _____

Wednesday—Date _____

Book Titles _____

_____Time in Minutes _____

Thursday—Date _____

Book Titles _____

_____Time in Minutes _____

Friday—Date _____

Book Titles _____

_____Time in Minutes _____

Figure 9.5

Book title and time log

fortable place for children to curl up with a favorite book. A large rocking chair can be located here for lap reading with younger children. Plants, aquariums, and so on can do much to create a peaceful atmosphere for this part of the classroom. Record keeping for silent reading can be easily managed by using a book title and time log for each child, as found in Figure 9.5. The children record the amount of time in minutes spent reading silently and the titles they had sampled or finished that day.

If books or basals are to be checked out from this center for out-of-school reading, a librarian's center can be located near the silent reading area for check outs (Figure 9.6). Children who serve as librarians keep records on books checked out and those overdue from the class library. All children are asked to be responsible for keeping the classroom library orderly.

Based on the book *Alexander and the Terrible Horrible No Good Very Bad Day* by Judith Viorst (1972), teachers might establish an Australia Escape Corner. When things in the classroom or a student's personal life are just too much to handle at the moment, they may retreat to Australia, just like Alexander, for 10 minutes, no ques-

Figure 9.6

Silent and supported
reading area

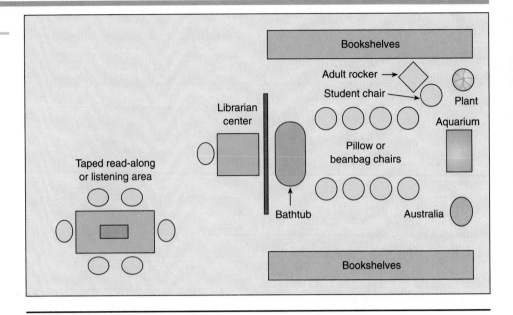

tions asked, once a day. If they need to remain longer than 10 minutes, they should explain their reasons. Teachers may also retreat on occasion to Australia. This action alone was found to be one of our best classroom discipline techniques!

Supported Reading Area

Younger readers need to be supported as they learn to read by the provision of read-along tapes, buddy readers, or "grandparent helpers" from the community.

The **supported reading area** is a spot in the classroom where children can be supported by other competent readers in learning to read. As such, the supported reading area is typically found in grades kindergarten through 2 but may continue in upper grades on a more limited basis for children who experience unusual difficulties in learning to read.

Opportunities for collaborative reading activities between children, teachers, parent volunteers, older children, and senior citizen volunteers are made available in the supported reading area. One means of supporting emergent readers is to station a tape player for children to follow along with a prerecorded tape of the books or basal stories in this area. Another idea is to display large charts containing poems, song lyrics, and riddles in this area for buddy reading or singing. A bank of word cards

Figure 9.7

Reading conference
area

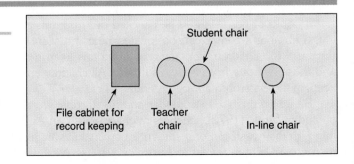

taken from children's language experience charts, big books, basals, and other shared reading materials can be located in this center. Children may also choose to work in pairs on word cards in the class word bank by reading them together, to each other, or by matching the word cards back into the books, stories, or charts from which they were taken. In terms of classroom space allocation, the whole-class sharing area can often double as the supported reading area because the two functions do not occur simultaneously in the classroom.

Reading Conference Area

The **reading conference area** is usually small and quiet (Figure 9.7). It is used for conducting individual reading conferences between teachers and individual students. Students are asked to make an appointment to meet with the teacher for an individual reading conference by signing up on the individual reading conference sign-up board, which is shown in Figure 9.8. The teacher and an individual student meet together briefly to read and discuss a selected trade book or a story taken from a

Individual reading conferences provide an ideal setting for assessing a student's progress in reading, as is discussed in Chapter 13.

Figure 9.8

Individual reading conference sign-up board

Monday—Date _____

8:00 A.M.

Name _____ Book Title _____

_____ Page Numbers _____

8:10 A.M.

Name _____ Book Title _____

_____ Page Numbers _____

8:20 A.M.

Name _____ Book Title _____

_____ Page Numbers _____

Tuesday—Date _____

8:00 A.M.

Name _____ Book Title _____

_____ Page Numbers _____

8:10 A.M.

Name _____ Book Title _____

_____ Page Numbers _____

8:20 A.M.

Name _____ Book Title _____

_____ Page Numbers _____

The guidelines for selecting and developing integrated theme units are discussed at length in Chapters 11 and 12.

*A **thematic studies area** is designated for in-depth study of a selected topic or theme.*

basal reader. While the student reads, the teacher listens, encourages, records performance, and supports the child.

Thematic Studies Area

The **thematic studies area** of the classroom is designated for in-depth study of a selected topic or theme. For example, children may express interest in the topic of *magic* as a result of having read the book *James and the Giant Peach* (Dahl, 1961).

Figure 9.9

Theme center activity log

Name of Student _____

Monday—Date _____

Activity _____

Response _____

_____

_____

Tuesday—Date _____

Activity _____ Response _____

_____

_____

Wednesday—Date _____

Activity _____ Response _____

_____

_____

Thursday—Date _____

Activity _____ Response _____

_____

_____

Friday—Date _____

Activity _____ Response _____

_____

_____

The teacher identifies resources available for investigating this topic. After brainstorming with the children, she designs several activities to focus the curriculum on the theme of magic. Children may listen to music about magic in this area, produce art that employs different media and that may seem magical such as crayon-resist drawings or turpentine swirl painting. Geometric puzzles or math problems from *I Hate Mathematics* (M. Burns, 1987) provide several magical math problems and solutions. Last, the teacher must design a way to schedule opportunities for children to use the center and provide a means of record keeping. An example of a theme center activity log can be found in Figure 9.9. Children record in this log the activities they complete each day and write a short essay response to the activity.

Display Areas

Display areas can be located almost anywhere in the classroom. Displays should be student- rather than teacher-produced where possible. The reason for having classroom displays is to immerse students in an environment of interesting and functional print. A message board for leaving messages is one means for teachers and students to communicate with each other. A sign-in board encourages even the very youngest children to write their names to begin the school day. Window writing using pens with water-soluble ink allows students to transcribe their stories, poems, jokes, riddles, and song lyrics onto the window glass. Windows are a fun and novel way to publish writing projects. Many children were very intrigued by window-published writing projects. A logo language or environmental print bulletin board can be devoted to print that children bring from home. Logo language is both fun and instructionally useful because it helps even the youngest child to know she can already read. Children bring labels from cans, cereal boxes, old packages, bumper stickers, newspaper ads, and so on to display on a logo language wall. This wall can be a resource for guided language lessons throughout the year. (Be sure to remind children that they must label the contents of a can if they remove the label before it is used!)

An informational display located in a prominent place in the classroom can be used for posting rules, calendars, lunch menus, TV guides, and posters. In addition, informational displays can be used to exhibit information about classroom routines, time schedules, hints on successful reading, the writing process, steps and media for publishing writing, lists of words the class knows, songs the class likes, favorite books, and so on. Scheduling displays can be used for making appointments with peers and teachers for reading and writing conferences as well as editing sessions. Figures 9.10 and 9.11 show examples of scheduling displays for these purposes.

Labeling objects in the classroom can be done by even the youngest children. Children may invent spellings for objects in the classroom and write these on cards. For example, we have seen the following object labels written by young children: *seling (ceiling), klok (clock), weindos (windows), dr (door), fs (fish),* and *srk (shark).* During subsequent language lessons, children can be alerted to look for these words in their reading and revise them. Within a matter of weeks, many teachers find that invented spellings used to label classroom objects will be revised to reflect conventional spellings (Calkins & Harwayne, 1987).

Other areas in the classroom can be used to display helpful reference information such as numbers, colors, alphabet letters, lunch time, and classroom helpers. Teachers should remember that displays should be neatly produced to set the standard for published works in the classroom.

Think of a classroom environment where children can use the walls, ceilings, windows, and floor to learn to read and to demonstrate their learning to read. What characteristics are you thinking of in such a classroom?

Figure 9.10

Writing peer conference
sign-up board

Monday—Date _____
8:00 A.M.
Name of Author _____ Names of Peers _____
_____
8:15 A.M.
Name of Author _____ Names of Peers _____
_____
8:30 A.M.
Name of Author _____ Names of Peers _____
_____
Tuesday—Date _____
8:00 A.M.
Name of Author _____ Names of Peers _____
_____
8:15 A.M.
Name of Author _____ Names of Peers _____
_____
8:30 A.M.
Name of Author _____ Names of Peers _____
_____

Storage Areas

Storage areas should be neat, well-organized, and easy to maintain.

Selected areas in the classroom need to be devoted to storage of classroom and student materials. A writing storage area for children's emerging writing products is a must. Author's folders, response logs, and learning logs can be neatly filed in corrugated cardboard file boxes. Children's writing drafts can be stored in a three-ring binder in an accessible location such as a bookshelf. A small tablet for recording spelling words can be inserted in the pocket of this writing draft binder. Writing draft binders should have each child's name on them. Personal storage areas using rubber tubs for each child in the classroom can serve dual purposes. First, these tubs can be used to store children's personal writing materials, pencil boxes, and belongings. Second, these tubs can double as post office boxes. Each tub can have a name and a P.O. box number written on the front. These tubs can be stored in specially constructed shelves or along coat racks and window sills. Properly cleaned and covered with contact paper, 2- to 5-gallon ice cream buckets can be stacked along coat racks, cupboards, and window sills for the same purposes without the expense of purchasing rubber tubs.

A publishing storage area houses materials such as staplers, paper punches, construction paper, and unlined paper. Publishing materials need to be arranged for easy accessibility. The proper location of each item in this area needs to be labeled to facilitate cleanup and maintenance. Sorting baskets or bins properly labeled can do much to ease the cleanup of this area and improve its appearance. The publishing storage area should also be located near other busy and potentially noisy areas in the classroom.

Book storage areas need to be properly located to facilitate retrieval, cleanup, and accessibility. A reading nook, loft, or corner should provide adequate shelf space for a classroom trade-book library. Books in this area can be organized and stored as discussed earlier. Word cards can be stored in old, labeled shoe boxes in this area on the bookshelves. Child-authored books should be afforded the same respect as commercially produced books. A library card pocket and a checkout card can be placed in each child-authored book. These books should be afforded a section in the classroom library where they can be read, reread, and checked out. Child-authored big books and charts can be given a prominent display area and/or stored along with

---

Figure 9.11

Editing session sign-up board

Monday—Date _____

8:00 A.M.

Name of Author _____ Name of Editor _____

_____

8:15 A.M.

Name of Author _____ Name of Editor _____

_____

8:30 A.M.

Name of Author _____ Name of Editor _____

_____

Tuesday—Date _____

8:00 A.M.

Name of Author _____ Name of Editor _____

_____

8:15 A.M.

Name of Author _____ Name of Editor _____

_____

8:30 A.M.

Name of Author _____ Name of Editor _____

_____

other commercially published big books. Plastic pants hangers can be used with clothespins to store or display big books and chart tablets effectively.

Reference material storage, such as dictionaries, atlases, *The Guinness Book of World Records,* encyclopedias, almanacs, and spellers, should be placed near the editing area in the classroom but accessible to students and the editors. Writing media should be placed near where they are needed in the classroom. Small rubber baskets, boxes, cut-down milk containers, and the like can be used for both storage and sorting of writing materials. Crayons, markers, pencils, pens, erasers, and chalk can be placed in individual containers for storage. In this way, children can easily sort and clean up writing materials scattered during busy writing output times. Other containers should be made available into which small quantities of writing media may be placed from large-capacity storage bins for transport to other classroom areas. These small transport containers can be taken to conference areas and collaborative project areas for use and returned and sorted for storage and cleanup.

Instructional Resources

The availability of classroom resources for instruction is another of the many concerns facing teachers of reading. Schools often provide a wide array of possible instructional resources and supports for teaching reading. A discussion of the most common instructional resources available to teachers follows.

Trade Books

A balanced literacy classroom typically requires a minimum classroom library of 250 to 300 trade books.

Picture books and storybooks not written for the express purpose of teaching reading and typically found in libraries or available for purchase in local bookstores are called **trade books**. The size and content of a trade-book library varies with the purpose this library will serve in a classroom. If the classroom library is to be used for self-selected, silent reading purposes or in an individualized reading program, Veatch (1968) suggests a minimum of at least three different books for each student in the classroom. For the average-sized traditional or individualized classroom, this translates into about 75 to 90 different books. On the other hand, if a balanced literacy program is contemplated, Stoodt (1989) recommends 10 books per student as a minimum. For the average-sized, balanced literacy classroom, this translates into a minimum of 250 to 300 books.

Trade books should vary in terms of the content as well as their length and difficulty. A variety of trade books might include wordless picture books, big books, books with limited print, and books with chapters. The PTA can help acquire books by sponsoring bake sales and school stores where children can buy books or other school supplies and by soliciting donations for books from local merchants. The school librarian can often be a source of trade books. Local thrift and second-hand stores are an inexpensive source for acquiring books. Garage and attic sales are also possible sources for acquiring trade books. Book auctions, where children bring their own trade books and auction them off to their peers for reading, are an exciting way to provide expanded trade-book access for children in schools.

Teachers working in conjunction with their principals may make a decision to use funds allocated for the purchase of consumable classroom supplies such as workbooks to purchase classroom trade-book libraries or multiple copies of paperback books.

Encouraging children to purchase their own paperback books through book clubs is a common practice among teachers for acquiring trade books to add to classroom collections. For every book purchased by an individual child in these book clubs, the teacher collects points toward free copies of books for the classroom library.

Some teachers solicit book donations from parents. Used children's books donated from parents whose children have outgrown these books are a valuable resource. Parents can be asked by the PTA to donate a book to the classroom or school library in the name of their child rather than sending treats to school on the child's birthday. The possibilities for acquiring a vast supply of trade books for use in schools is only limited by the imagination and innovation of teachers and administrators.

In summary, it is important that teachers and school administrators not relegate the acquisition of trade books to the level of bake sale fund raisers indefinitely. Rather, school administrators and teachers must elevate the acquisition of quality trade books to the status of a regular line item in school budgets.

Teachers and school administrators should make the acquisition of quality trade book literature a priority in school budget planning.

Basal Readers

Because basal readers are used in over 90% of schools today, teachers will not need to look very far to find a basal series for reading instruction in most schools. Recently published basals have made concerted efforts to include a greater variety and improved quality of children's literature selections. Newer basal teacher's manuals encourage the integration of the reading, writing, listening, and speaking modes of language. Some recently published basals are also thematically organized, allowing children to thoroughly explore a topic rather than flitting from one topic to the next with each subsequent story in the reader. T. D. Johnson and Louis (1987) suggest that basal stories can also be used in the younger grades for extensive modeling and choral readings. We suggested in Chapter 5 that basal readers can be used as a springboard into literature-based or balanced literacy programs. For many teachers, especially novice teachers, the basal becomes simultaneously the beginning point and the departure point in making the instructional transition toward a more balanced literacy instructional program.

Chapter 4 provides a more in-depth discussion of the basal.

Many recent basals have been organized around themed literature units.

Workbooks and Worksheets

Many teachers believe that workbook pages are an important component of the reading program. This is evidenced by the fact that children frequently spend as much time completing workbook pages as they do interacting with teachers and real books. Teachers often use workbook pages unnecessarily or for classroom management purposes (Osborn, 1984).

The report *Becoming a Nation of Readers* (R. C. Anderson, Hiebert, Scott, & Wilkinson, 1985) states that children spend up to 70% of the time allocated in classrooms for reading instruction engaged in independent seat work, completing workbooks and worksheets. Durkin (1981a) informed the profession that workbook pages are typically used for assessment rather than for teaching reading. Suffice it to say at this point that teachers should carefully weigh the relative value of workbook activities as they plan reading instruction in their classrooms. From the currently available data, workbook and worksheet activities appear to dominate reading instruction in classrooms at the expense of reading and instructing with real stories and books (Osborn, 1984; Rupley & Blair, 1987; Tunnell & Jacobs, 1989).

The topic of workbooks and worksheets is treated in greater depth in Chapter 4.

Workbook and worksheet activities appear to dominate reading instruction in classrooms at the expense of reading and instructing with real stories and books.

Computers

Although computers have become available in most schools, the educational application of computer technology is in the "horse and buggy days" (Blanchard, Mason, & Daniel, 1987, p. 1). Today, computers are used for a variety of purposes in classrooms ranging from drill and practice activities to assessment and record keeping. A number of promising new avenues involve computers in reading instruction. In this section we take a quick look at some of these useful technologies.

Word Processing Programs

Notice two ways word processing programs assist students in creating compositions of a narrative or expository nature.

Word processing programs are quickly gaining favor with teachers because they enable children to create compositions, use invented spellings, revise and edit at will, and print compositions that have a professional appearance. There are even public domain (free) programs available for classroom use. One very popular source for public domain software is the Minnesota Educational Computing Corporation (MECC), 3490 Lexington Avenue North, St. Paul, MN 55126.

Comprehension-Development Software

A number of newer software packages assist in reading comprehension development. Just a few follow:

The Puzzler helps children make, confirm, and revise story predictions.

***The Puzzler* (Sunburst, 1987)**   Caverly and Buswell (1988) describe a computer software program known as *The Puzzler*, which encourages students to make and confirm predictions based on meaning cues from text. This package includes 10 stories on two computer disks. Students begin by making a prediction of what the story is about using only the title. One story in the program, "Zingles," will not permit students to see the first page of the story until at least one prediction has been made. After reading, some of the story predictions can be revised. Once revisions are made, the reader can progress to the next part of the story. *The Puzzler* is just one of many new programs that have reading comprehension dimensions.

***The Semantic Mapper* (Kuchinskas & Radencich, 1986)**   This package provides character, setting, and action maps that allow students to immediately begin to formulate ideas about crucial story elements. Wepner (1990) explains how this program could be applied to the book *Jelly Belly* (R. K. Smith, 1981), a story about Ned, the heaviest kid in fifth grade. *The Semantic Mapper* might be used to create a character map of Jelly Belly's family and friends, setting maps of Jelly Belly's experiences at home, school, and at camp, and action maps that describe his tricks to get fattening food and attempts to diet. (See Chapter 6 for more information on semantic maps, called *story maps*.)

Super Story Tree creates branching, interactive stories with multimedia effects.

***Super Story Tree* (Brackett, 1989)**   This program offers multimedia capability (e.g., fonts, graphics, sound, and music) that can be used to create branching interactive stories (Wepner, 1990). Among choices available to young readers and writers are various title screens, clip art that may be pasted into stories, music, and sound effects, which help create a rather dramatic rendering of the student-authors' compositions.

The *Playwriter* Series   *Playwriter* is a series of interactive fiction programs that allow students to help complete either adventure episodes or autobiography texts. Appropriate mostly for intermediate grades or above, "Tales of Me" and "Adventures in Space" are two examples that use student responses to create personal narratives

(Dowd & Sinatra, 1990). In these narratives, questions appear on the computer screen that require either multiple-choice or fill in the blank responses. Single words, whole phrases, or sentences may be required to complete blanks about the main character, her interests, or reactions to story events. Although this program is more structured than some, it may be helpful to reluctant readers and/or writers as a first step.

Hypertext and Hypermedia

Blanchard and Rottenberg (1990) have described new technologies with applications in reading instruction known as *hypertext* and *hypermedia*. **Hypertext** (Blanchard & Rottenberg, 1990; Nelson, 1988; Whitaker, Schwartz, & Vockell, 1989) is a program that links information in a nonsequential or nonstandard manner. For example, a reader of science topics interested in "mammals" may select a computer program dealing with this topic. Once the mammals screen appears, she may then go to a second screen focusing on water mammals, such as the whale, or may need to go to a more detailed explanation of a term mentioned on the first screen. The advantage of organizing information in this way is twofold. First, arranging information by such nontraditional patterns as webs is multidimensional, much like schema webs in the brain. Myriad aspects of a topic may be considered at once. Second, these nontraditional patterns are preferred over linear or sequential patterns because traditional patterns invariably carve up or divide information to the point that it becomes not only ungovernable but unlocatable as well (Blanchard & Rottenberg, 1990, p. 656).

> *Hypertext* links information in a nonsequential or nonstandard manner.

    Hypermedia is a computer format in which several media, such as film, graphics, text, animation, newsreels, still images, and music, can be viewed in an order determined by the teacher or user. Hypermedia can be especially useful for teachers who are seeking more holistic ways to connect the content of their instruction with students' learning. For example, the computer user may decide to view a movie clip about the death of Mahatma Ghandi before reading a paragraph about his accomplishments as a national leader (Dillner, 1993–1994, p. 260). A chief advantage of hypermedia is its nonlinear multimedia ability; users can select any preprogrammed option in virtually any order instead of having to view the program from start to finish in a predetermined order.

> *Hypermedia* is a mixture of technologies managed by hypertext technology.

    Hypertext and hypermedia are still very much in their infancy and can be expensive. They require computers with large random access memories (RAM) and large hard disk drives. Other equipment, such as laserdisc, videodisc, compact disc (CD) and player, and high-resolution monitors may also be needed (Blanchard & Rottenberg, 1990).

Technology and Thematic Units

Wepner (1993) has described a number of computer software programs that can help teachers in planning thematic units. Thematic units, according to Wepner, offer teachers "endless opportunities to use literature for extending and enriching learning across disciplines," and "technology provides yet another vehicle for helping students to understand key concepts and engage in activities related to an overriding theme" (p. 442). Following are several computer/technology programs recommended by Wepner for a thematic unit on Japan listed according to discipline area.

Social Studies   *Science Explorers: Nutrition* (Apple and MS-DOS) is a program useful in helping students learn more about different food cultures and the nutritional content of foods that we eat. Tutorials titled "Food and Energy" and "The Foods You Eat" lead students into a simulation called "Nutrition Explorer," a bar graph activity showing the balance of fat, protein, and carbohydrates with foods they select. In spite of the somewhat misleading title of this package, it can enhance students' knowledge of other cultures encountered in the social studies.

Language Arts   *The Bank Street Writer* (Macintosh). To use this program, you will need a Macintosh PC or IIsi's built-in microphone to digitize messages, music, and sound effects. This newly revised program has a hypertext function offering three options: note buttons that can help students provide definitions related to what they are writing; file buttons that help students create data bases or other "chain files;" and sound buttons to place sounds in students' documents.

Art   *Bulletin Board Maker—Happy Habitats: The Pond* (Apple). This program produces huge posters, signs, newsletters in four sizes, announcements, and other possible creations. *The Pond* option includes graphics of fish and animals found around ponds.

Science   *WorldClassroom*. This is a great program for classrooms equipped with a modem, communications software, and access to a telephone. *WorldClassroom* is a "global on-line computer education network that enables students to use real-life data to make decisions about themselves and their environment" (Wepner, 1993, p. 444). Students are able to confer with peer-colleagues around the world as they work through investigations in science or other content areas.

Compact Disk Read-Only Memory Books

CD ROM books are easy to handle programs that allow children to access information by simply double-clicking the mouse at the beginning of each sentence.

A most exciting technology for teachers is the advent of books on CD read-only memory (ROM) disks. The same kind of technology that has revolutionized the music industry is now making its way into the reading classroom. One company in this field is Discis Knowledge Research, which publishes a complete library of 10 volumes. Discis Books, made for the Apple Macintosh Plus computer, allow children to simply double click the mouse button on a word, picture, page corner, or the speaker icon at the head of each sentence to make things happen (McKuen, 1990). Even beginning readers can learn this program easily. If students become lost and do not understand what to do, a talking question mark guides them through all the possibilities.

Several options available with Discis Books (McKuen, 1990) can be most helpful in reading instruction. Students can keep and recall lists of words, slow the reader's voice or speed it up, change font styles and sizes, and use an electronic bookmark that returns students to where they left off. Sound effects complement the dialogue without overly distracting the reader. Some of the book titles include Beatrix Potter's (1953) *The Tale of Peter Rabbit,* Sean O'Huigin's (1988) *Scary Poems for Rotten Kids,* and *The Paper Bag Princess* by Robert Munsch (1980).

Stories and More (requires IBM CD-ROM drive, speech adapter, and MCGA or VGA color display) is a literature-based, read-aloud program for primary students produced by IBM (Wepner, 1992). Some 36 stories are included, mostly from original books; 16 stories come with voice-supported options plus interactive computer activities, whereas the remaining stories have the read-aloud option only.

Computers and At-Risk Students

Elementary teachers are constantly seeking creative ways to help at-risk students break the cycle of failure and discouragement they perceive in reading–writing instruction. A program in Texas (Werner, 1990) has demonstrated success with at-risk elementary students using innovative software to (a) motivate them to read, (b) facilitate writing, and (c) integrate the reading–writing processes. Reading motivation has been accomplished largely through the use of software programs featuring on-screen texts and graphics. The most popular program of this type has been the *Choose Your Own Adventure* series (Bantam, 1985), which has students read high-interest adventure stories and make choices at strategic points. The plots of the stories then change according to the choices made by the reader (p. 14). Another successful program for younger readers has been the *Talking Text* (Scholastic, 1986) series featuring various folktales, fairy tales, and fables, with on-screen graphics and a speech synthesizer that can read the stories to children as they follow along.

Computer programs can be very motivating for at-risk students, can facilitate writing, and can provide activities for integrating reading–writing processes.

Some computer programs can be quite helpful in integrating the reading–writing processes. One such program is *The Writing Adventure* (Developmental Learning Materials, 1985), a comprehensive program for children ages 9 and older. It provides a number of story starters in the format of adventure scenes and prompting questions (Werner, 1990, p. 15). Children use *The Writing Adventure* to first watch scenes and make notes on computerized "note cards," then use their notes to begin drafting their own stories using the story writer part of the program. Stories are later revised, edited, and printed for group sharing.

The Writing Adventure helps at-risk students move into writing by combining adventure story starters and computerized note cards to begin first drafts.

Perhaps the greatest value of computer programs for at-risk students is the novel way they can offer a fresh start. When the cycle of failure has been in force for some time, computer media can help break through the psychological roadblocks that prevent children from enjoying the world of books and literacy.

Volunteers

Because children have a right to learn to read from people, volunteers can form the backbone of the reading program in schools. Helping children become readers ought to become a community concern. All sorts of people can be recruited as volunteers for helping with the classroom reading program. Ervin (1982) suggests using parents, retired teachers, college students, student teachers, high school students involved with Future Teachers of America Clubs, and community and government service organizations. Cassidy (1981) suggests using Grey Power or senior citizens in the classroom as volunteers for tutoring, instructional aides, and producers of instructional materials. Recruitment of volunteers can be accomplished in various ways. Announcements made in PTA meetings, notices sent home to parents, pamphlets to community service organizations, and advertisements in local radio, television, or newspapers are just a few ideas. Figures 9.12 and 9.13 show a listing of volunteer recruitment resources and sign-up forms for volunteers.

Schools can and should make reading a community concern by implementing strong literacy volunteer programs that involve businesses, parents, retired teachers, service clubs, and the like.

Instructional Organization: The Question of Grouping

Because teachers vary greatly in their experience and expertise in coping with the complexity of classrooms, the question of grouping in a classroom is of critical importance. The use of more groups and a greater variety of grouping plans add to the complexity of coping with a classroom. Although the choice to use a particular grouping plan may reduce the administrative complexity of managing a classroom,

Grouping decisions need to be based on benefits for both teachers and children.

Figure 9.12

Resources for reading
program volunteers

- In-school personnel, e.g., principal, secretary, custodians
- Parents
- Grandparents
- Senior citizens
- Local rest homes
- Service clubs, e.g., Kiwanis, Lions, Rotary, Elks
- Government agencies
- Sponsoring businesses
- High school students
- Future Teachers of America
- Eagle Scout projects
- Older children in the school
- Church organizations
- News media organizations
- College students
- Student teachers
- Chamber of Commerce
- Reading Is Fundamental groups
- Retired teachers

the potential consequence of such a choice may be that individual students' needs may not be met. Thus, a decision to use a particular grouping plan should be made with full knowledge of the potential consequences. The ideal for most reading teachers is to begin with a simple and manageable grouping plan and gradually expand their efforts toward effectively using a wide range of grouping plans to provide for individual differences, allow for free choice, foster collaboration, support individual readers as they develop, and encourage social interaction.

Grouping classrooms into smaller groups often fills a niche for teachers who wish to bridge the gap between whole-class grouping and complete individualization of instruction. Perhaps one of the most controversial grouping plans is grouping children by ability for reading instruction.

Ability Grouping

Ability grouping is an organizational practice where students are placed into a group to receive reading instruction based on a score(s) on reading achievement tests or other less formal measures.

Dividing children into reading groups on the basis of reading ability or achievement, called **ability grouping**, continues to be a popular practice in many classrooms. Although teachers most often rely on standardized reading test performance scores as a means for assigning children to an ability group, other factors such as personality attributes, general academic competence, work habits, and home background are also weighed in the decision to assign children to ability groups (Haller & Waterman, 1985). Ability grouping is often associated with the use of graded basal readers, workbooks, and skill lessons designed to follow a published scope and sequence of skill development. Many teachers use ability, achievement, or homogeneous grouping of children to accommodate individual student needs, and this practice is rooted in the idea of the capacity to profit from instruction. This latter reasoning is inconsistent with teachers' desire to meet individuals' instructional needs. Teachers group children by ability to conform to the demands of instruction rather than modifying the instruction to conform to the needs of the students.

Notice three ways teacher expectations for students are influenced by their ability group membership.

Numerous negative outcomes have been associated with the use of ability groups despite their administrative ease and intuitive appeal. For example, children in low-ability groups spend more time in oral round-robin reading and reading workbook assignments than do their peers in high-ability groups (Allington, 1983; Leinhardt, Zigmond, & Cooley, 1981). Teachers tolerate more outside interruptions in low-ability groups than in high-ability groups (Allington, 1980). In the spring of the school year, children assigned to low-ability groups for reading instruction exhibited

Volunteering for the School Reading Program

Figure 9.13

Volunteer sign-up form

Children learn to read from other people who can read. Please help children learn to read by volunteering your time.

Name:_____ Street Address: _____

City: _____ Home Phone: _____

Business Phone: _____ Occupation: _____

Grade Level Preference (if any): _____

Teacher Preference (if any): _____

Do you have a child in the school? Yes _____ No _____

Name of child if applicable _____

When can you help? (Please check one)

Daily_____ Weekly_____ Monthly _____

How much time can you give on this basis? _____

Please list available times (e.g., Tuesday/Thursday 8–10 A.M.)

Where would you like to help? (Please check one or more)

____Classrooms ____Local library ____In parents' home

____Special classrooms ____Day-care center ____In your own home

____Library ____Local businesses

How would you like to help?

(Please indicate your first three preferences with the numbers, 1, 2, & 3)

____Read to students in a group   ____Give presentations on selected topics

____Help children with reading   ____Solicit books for class library

____Help with record keeping and progress evaluation   ____Write with small group of children

____Produce instructional materials   ____Make puppets

____Conference with children about their writing projects   ____Give book talks

____Help children edit writing projects   ____Help children make books

____Tell stories   ____Help children rehearse a play or other dramatic production

____Teach children songs   ____Take children's dictation and make little books from dictation

____Share your own writing

____Read with individual students

____I have no particular preference, please place me where I am needed most

Please list any special talents, abilities, experiences, or knowledge you would be willing to share: _____

*Low-ability group readers
receive double the decoding
instruction of high-ability
group readers.*

three times the number of inattentive behaviors exhibited by their counterparts assigned to high-ability groups (Felmlee & Eder, 1983). Children in low-ability groups tend to have lowered academic expectations and self-concepts (Eder, 1983; Hiebert, 1983; Rosenbaum, 1980). Time devoted to decoding instruction and practice is fully double for low-ability group readers as compared to high-ability groups (Gambrell, Wilson, & Gnatt, 1981). Teachers tend to interrupt low readers more often when they miscue while reading than they do high readers (Allington, 1980).

Weinstein (1976) found that as much as 25% of the variation in reading achievement at the end of first grade could be attributed to group assignment. Kulik and Kulik (1982) analyzed the results of 52 studies and determined that (a) ability grouping generally has small effects on achievement, (b) high-ability readers profit from ability grouping in terms of achievement, and (c) the effects of ability grouping on average- and low-ability children's achievement is only trivial. On the other hand, children's friendships tend be increasingly influenced by continuing membership in an ability group (Hallinan & Sorensen, 1985). Eder (1983) showed that even 1 year in an ability group caused some children to begin to question the reasons underlying their group membership. Although reading achievement may be minimally affected by ability grouping, children's self-images and social circles appear to be profoundly affected (Oakes, 1992). Although ability or homogeneous grouping may be deemed necessary in some instances, it should only be considered on a temporary basis not to exceed 1 month in duration. Alternative grouping plans such as those suggested in the following discussion should be strongly considered.

Whole-Class Instruction

*Whole-class reading activities
provide a safety-net for struggling and shy readers by
shielding them from singular
attention during reading.*

Whole-class grouping is an effective means for safety-netting emerging readers as they develop more conventional and sophisticated reading strategies. Whole-class reading and sharing activities shield learners from the potentially harsh emotional and psychological consequences of individual risk taking by acting as a safety net to catch and support readers who are learning to read. Whole-class reading activities can also reduce some of the negative effects associated with ability grouping or other labeling that occurs in schools, such as *slow learners, resource rooms,* and *learning disabled.* Although some may contend that whole-class grouping might fail to meet the needs of individual learners, we assert that whole-class reading activities put children in touch with the social nature of reading and learning to read while safety-netting the risks associated with this learning.

Because learning to read is a social event, and because reading selections are meant to be shared, whole-class reading and sharing activities should be a regular and integral part of every reading classroom. Activities such as storytelling; dramatizations of stories; children reading books aloud and sharing their own authored stories, poems, songs; reading big books together; reading the enlarged text of songs, poems, raps, and jingles; sustained silent reading and writing; participating in an experiment or experience; and creating language experience charts are just a few examples of potentially appropriate activities for whole-class teaching.

Basal Reader Visiting Response Groups

*Using the basal as a literary
anthology is discussed in
Chapter 5.*

Teachers in transition can develop the ability to use literature response groups, described next, by using their basal reader stories and beginning with **basal reader visiting response groups**. Students are invited to spend about 20 minutes browsing through the basal reader table of contents, looking at the pictures, and scanning the stories as they might in a library of literature. This requires that teachers and students think about the basal reader as an anthology of literature to be a resource for reading material. Then each title in the table of contents can be read aloud by the teacher. Students can indicate their interest in each story by raising their hand, and the teacher records interest levels by recording this information in their teacher's manual table of contents. This process provides a quick means of gauging interest for each story in the basal reader. Next, the teacher should look at story titles in the table of contents for possible common themes or topics. Then, basal stories can be grouped by themes, genre, or authors to provide several related basal story units for organizing basal reader visiting response groups. At a later time, the teacher describes each basal story unit to the students. Then, students can elect their first and second choices for group membership. The remaining steps for forming basal reader visiting response groups are the same as described later for literature response groups. Basal reader visiting response groups have been recommended by the Commission on Reading in the report *Becoming a Nation of Readers* (R. C. Anderson et al., 1985) and represent an effective transitional step toward teaching a balanced reading program. One final note: Basal reader visiting-response groups can be used with the reading workshop as described in Chapter 11 (Reutzel & Cooter, 1991).

For some recently published basal readers with theme story selections, see Chapter 4.

Literature-Response Groups (Literature Circles)

Literature-response groups or **literature circles** use trade books or literature books as the core for reading instruction. To form literature-response groups, begin by having children look through several selected titles of literature books available for small-group instruction. (This means that multiple copies of each title will be needed! We recommend that teachers purchase about 10 copies of each title rather than purchasing classroom sets for use with literature-response groups.) At the conclusion of this period, the teacher reads available book titles aloud and asks how many students would like to read these books. In this way, teachers can get a quick idea of which available books seem to interest the students most and which engender no interest. The teacher selects from these high-interest trade books three to four titles, depending on how many groups he can reasonably manage. Next, the teacher works up a "book talk" on each of the selected books to present to the students the next day. A book talk is a short, interesting introduction to the topic, setting, and problem of a book. After presenting a book talk on each of the books selected, the teacher asks older children to write down the titles of their first two choices. For younger children, the teachers asks them to come to the chalkboard and sign their name under the titles of their two favorite book titles. Only one literature-response group meets each day with the teacher to discuss and respond to a chapter, or to read a predetermined number of pages in a trade book. It is best if the teacher meets with each literature-response group after children have indicated their choices to determine how many weeks will be spent reading the book and how many pages per day need to be read to reach that goal. The remaining steps for organizing literature-response groups are summarized in the following list:

Teachers give "book talks" on selected trade books before organizing literature-response groups.

The teacher meets with only one literature-response group per day to discuss and respond to parts of the books.

1. Select three or four titles you believe children will be interested in reading from the brief interest inventory of literature titles available in the school or classroom, as described.
2. Introduce each of the three book titles by giving a "book talk" on each.
3. Invite children to write down the titles of their two top choices.
4. Depending on the number of multiple copies of trade books available, fill each group with those children who indicated the book as their first choice. Once a

Teachers and students set group goals for daily reading, to arrange meeting dates, and to decide how the group will respond to the literature.

See Chapter 11 for possible literature-response activities.

group is filled, then move remaining children to their second choice until all children have been invited to attend the group of their first or second choice.

5. Decide how many days or weeks will be spent reading this series of book choices.
6. Meet with each of the literature-response groups and determine
   a. How many pages per day will need to be read to complete the book in the time allowed.
   b. When the first group meeting will be. (The teacher meets with only one group per day.)
   c. How children will respond to their reading. This may involve writing in a reading response log, character report cards, or other possible responses. (See Chapters 10 and 11 for response activities.)
7. Help children understand when the first or next meeting of their literature-response group will be, how many pages in the book will need to be read, and which type of response to the reading will need to be completed before the meeting of the literature-response group.
8. Near the completion of the book, the group may discuss possible extensions of the book to drama, music, art, and so on.

Peterson and Eeds (1990), in their book *Grand Conversations*, suggest a checklist form that teachers may use to track student preparation and participation in literature-response groups (Figure 9.14). Based on this concept, we have modified this

Figure 9.14

Checklist for teachers to track student preparation and participation

Record of Goal Completion for and Participation in Literature Response Groups

Name _____ Date _____
Author _____ Title _____

Preparation for Literature Study

Brought book to literature response group.	Yes____	No____
Contributed to developing group reading goals.	Yes____	No____
Completed work according to group goals.	Yes____	No____
Read the assigned pages, chapters, etc.	Yes____	No____
Noted places to share (ones of interest, ones that were puzzling, etc.)	Yes____	No____
Completed group response assignments as they came to the day's discussion.	Yes____	No____

Participation in the Literature Response Group

Participation in the discussion	Weak ____	Good ____	Excellent ____
Quality of verbal responses.	Weak ____	Good ____	Excellent ____
Used text to support ideas	Weak ____	Good ____	Excellent ____
Listened to others.	Weak ____	Good ____	Excellent ____

From *Grand Conversations* by R. Peterson and M. Eeds, 1990, New York: Scholastic. Copyright 1990 by Scholastic. Adapted by permission.

form to be used with the literature-response groups as we have described their use in the Reading Workshop (Reutzel & Cooter, 1991), discussed in detail in Chapter 11.

On completion of the trade book, literature-response groups are disbanded and new groups are formed for a new series of trade books. Thus, students' interests are engaged by encouraging choice, and the problem of static ability-grouping plans can be avoided. Further, children only visit the group for the length of time taken up in completing the trade book, and then new groups are formed.

Both basal reader visiting response groups and literature-response groups change regularly to prevent the stagnant nature of fixed ability groups.

Cooperative Learning Groups

One form of organizing for effective reading and writing instruction recently made popular is called **cooperative learning**. Cooperative learning groups are heterogeneous groups ranging in size from two to five children working together to accomplish a *team task*. Bill Harp (1989a) indicates four characteristics that identify cooperative learning groups.

***Cooperative learning groups** are heterogeneous groups ranging in size from two to five children working together to accomplish a team task.*

- First, each lesson begins with teacher instruction and modeling.
- Second, the children in the group work together to accomplish a task assigned by the teacher to the group.
- Third, children work on individual assignments related to a group-assigned task. Each student must be willing to complete his part of the group shared assignment.
- Finally, the team is recognized by averaging individual grades and assigning the group grade to each member of the group.

Much research indicates that children in cooperative learning groups have consistently shown greater achievement than children who participate in traditional grouping schemes (D. W. Johnson, Maruyama, Johnson, Nelson, & Skon, 1981; Jongsma, 1990; Slavin, 1988; Stevens, Madden, Slavin, & Farnish, 1987a, 1987b; Topping, 1989; Webb & Schwartz, 1988; K. D. Wood, 1987). In a synthesis of research on cooperative learning, Slavin (1991) found that cooperative learning not only increased student achievement but also increased student self-concept and social skills.

Cooperative learning groups have consistently shown greater achievement than children who participate in traditional grouping schemes.

Manarino-Leggett and Saloman (1989) and K. D. Wood (1987) describe several different grouping alternatives associated with the concept of cooperative learning. A few of these selected cooperative learning grouping alternatives are briefly described in Table 9.1.

How do children learn to read and write from each other in cooperative learning groups?

Table 9.1

Alternative grouping plans for encouraging cooperative learning

---

Collaboration is an important part of cooperative learning groups allowing children time to talk, plan, and work with other children to complete a task.

Dyads can be very beneficial for young at-risk readers.

Jigsaw groups involve students in reading and retelling assigned parts of an assigned text.

Book-Response Pairs

Students interview a peer or partner about a book they have read. After the interview, they write a report on their partner's book.

Cooperative Integrated Reading and Composition (CIRC)

CIRC is a programmatic approach to teaching reading and writing in the intermediate elementary grades (Stevens, Madden, Slavin, & Farnish, 1987a, 1987b). This program consists of three elements: (a) basal-related activities, (b) direct instruction in reading comprehension, and (c) integrated language arts writing.

Composition or Coauthoring Pairs

One of two students explains what she plans to write while the other student takes notes or outlines the discussion. Working together, the two students plan the lead-in, thesis, or opening statement. One student writes while the other student explains the outline or notes. They exchange roles as they write a single composition, or they can exchange roles to help each other write their own composition.

Computer Groups

Students work together on a computer to accomplish a given task. Students adopt specific roles such as keyboard operator, monitor, and checker throughout the process. Roles should be regularly rotated to allow each student to experience all three roles.

Drill Partners

Students pair off for drill activities such as working with words from personal or classroom word banks or rereading books to improve fluency.

Dyads

K. D. Wood (1987) assigns roles to each student in a dyad, or pair, of readers. Each student reads silently, or in some cases orally in unison, two pages of text. After reading these two pages, one student acts as recaller. This student verbally recounts what the two had read. The other student acts as listener and clarifier for the recaller. Dyad reading is an effective means for supporting young children's reading development, especially for at-risk readers (Eldredge & Quinn, 1988).

Focus Trios

Children may be randomly assigned or may form social groups of three students for the purposes of summarizing what they already know about a reading selection and developing questions to be answered during reading. After reading, the trio discuss answers to the questions, clarify, and summarize answers.

Group Reports

Students research a topic together as a group. Each person is responsible for contributing at least one resource to the report. Written or oral reports must involve all students in the final report.

Group Retellings

Students read different books or selections on the same topic. After reading, each student retells what she has read to the other group members. Group members may comment on or add to the retelling of any individual.

Groups of Four

Groups of four are randomly assigned task-completion groups. Each individual is given a responsibility to complete some phase of a larger task. For example, when writing a letter, one student could be the addresser, another the body writer, another the checker, and so on. In this way, all students contribute to the successful completion of the task. Roles should be exchanged regularly to allow students to experience all aspects of task completion.

Jigsaw

Students in a group are assigned to read a different part of the same selection. After reading, each student retells what she has read to the others in the group. A discussion usually ensues, during which students may interview or question the reteller to clarify any incomplete ideas or correct misunderstandings. After this discussion concludes, students can be invited to read the rest of the selection to confirm or correct the retellings of other group members.

Adapted from Manarino-Leggett and Saloman (1986) and K.D. Wood (1987).

Metacomprehension Pairs

Have students alternate reading and orally summarizing paragraphs or pages of a selection. One listens, follows along, and checks the accuracy of the other's comprehension of the selection.

Playwrights

Students select a piece of reading they wish to dramatize as a play. Students work together to develop a script, the set, costumes, and practice the play with individuals serving in various roles as director, characters, and other necessary functions. The culmination of the group is the performance of the play for a selected audience.

Problem-Solving and Project Groups

Having children work together cooperatively in pairs or small groups to solve reading or writing problems is another effective classroom practice involving the use of other children as a primary resource for enhancing classroom instruction. Problem-solving groups are small groups initiated by children who wish to work collaboratively on a self-selected reading or writing problem. In project groups, children are encouraged to explore a wide variety of possible reading and writing projects, such as plays, puppetry, reader's theater, research, authoring books, poetry, lyrics to songs, notes, invitations, and cards. The products resulting from project groups are to be of publishable quality. Thus, the culmination of a project group is sharing the project or product with an authentic audience.

Reading Buddies

In the lower grades, upper grade children can be selected as reading buddies to assist emergent readers. These buddies can be selected for a short period of time, say a week, then other children can be selected. This allows ample opportunities for upper grade readers to assist lower grade readers. In upper and lower grades, reading buddies can pair off and share a favorite book with a friend by reading exciting parts of the book or just discussing the book.

In the lower grades, upper grade children can be selected as reading buddies to assist young readers.

Strategy Teachers and Concept Clarifiers

Students work together in pairs on reading strategies, such as prediction, sequencing, making inferences, until both can do or explain these concepts or strategies easily.

Test Coaches

As students prepare for a test, a group of students can be given a prototype test. The group can divide the test items into even groups for each individual in the group. Each individual completes her part of the test. The group meets together to review the answers of each of the students, and check, confirm, or correct each answer.

Think-Pair-Share

Lyman (1988) recommends that students sit in pairs as the teacher presents a reading minilesson to the class. After the lesson, the teacher presents a problem to the group. The children individually think of an answer, then with their partners discuss and reach a consensus on the answer. A pair of students can be asked to share their agreed-on answer with the class.

Turn-to-Your-Neighbor

After listening to a student read a book aloud, share a book response, or share a piece of published writing, students can be asked to turn to a neighbor and tell one concept or idea they enjoyed about the presentation. They should also share one question they would like to ask the reader or author.

Worksheet and Homework Checkers

When teachers deem it necessary to use worksheets to provide practice for a concept or strategy taught during a reading minilesson, students can be organized into groups to check one another's work and provide feedback to each other.

Writing Response Groups

When a writer completes a publishable work or needs help with developing a draft, groups can be organized to listen to the author share her work. Afterward, group members can share ideas on how to improve the draft. If the piece is complete, group members should compliment the work and ask the author questions about her presentation.

Reading Minilessons and Needs Groups

Notice three possible opportunities for teachers to intervene using minilessons.

Minilessons are an integral part of planned daily routines, but they may also arise as teachers and children work together collaboratively or individually on a selected story or text (Atwell, 1987; Calkins, 1986). Minilessons can be presented to an entire class or small groups. They are not always meant to be lessons where outcomes are required. Sometimes minilessons are simply invitations to engage in some literate behavior as part of immersing students in language.

Selected strategies for teaching minilessons in comprehension, vocabulary, and word identification are covered in Chapters 6 to 8.

Hagerty (1992) describes three types of minilessons: procedural, literary, and strategy/skill. A listing of possible minilesson topics is found in Table 9.2.

A procedural reading minilesson, for example, might involve the teacher and students in learning how to handle new books received for the classroom library as well as how to repair worn books in the classroom library. The teacher may demonstrate how to break a new book's binding in by standing the book on its spine and opening a few pages on either side of the center of the book and carefully pressing them down. Cellophane tape and staplers may be used to demonstrate how to repair tears in a book's pages or covers. A heavy-duty stapler is used to reattach paperback book covers in another demonstration on caring for books. Minilessons are a major vehicle in balanced literacy programs for providing children access to guided, and when needed, explicit demonstrations of skilled reading and writing behaviors, necessary procedural knowledge, and a greater understanding of literary and stylistic devices.

Procedural, literary, and skill/strategy are three different types of potential minilessons.

One example of a literary minilesson for early readers might involve a child presenting the teacher with a small booklet written at home in the shape of a puppy that retells favorite parts from the book *Taxi Dog* (Barracca & Barracca, 1990). This may constitute an opportunity for the teacher to share the book with his students as one demonstration of how another student shared his ideas using the writing process in the form of a shape book. After such sharing, a rash of shape books is likely to result. An upper elementary-level student may assemble a poster resembling the front page of a newspaper to show major events from a novel just read, such as Betsy Byars's (1970) *The Summer of the Swans.*

An example of a strategy/skill minilesson for early readers might occur during the reading of a big book entitled, *Cats and Mice* (Gelman, 1985), where the teacher notes the fact that many of the words in the book end with the participle form of *-ing.* Noticing this regularity in the text, the teacher draws children's attention to the function of *-ing.* For example, while rereading the big book the next day, the teacher may cover the ending of each word ending in an *-ing* with a small self-adhesive note. During the group rereading of the book, the teacher reveals the *-ing* ending at the end of the words covered. On subsequent readings, the teacher invites students to join in the reading while emphasizing the *-ing* sound at the end of words. Other words that children know are written at the board, and an *-ing* ending is added. Children take turns pronouncing these words with the *-ing* added. A minilesson for more advanced readers might pertain to patterns used by nonfiction writers to make abstract information better understood (i.e., cause–effect, description, problem–solution, comparisons, etc.). This could involve (a) describing the patterns used; (b) searching for examples in science, mathematics, and social studies materials; then (c) students' writing/creating their examples of these patterns pertaining to a topic of choice.

Flexible Traveling Groups

With the use of multiple centers or stations in a classroom, some transitional and balanced literacy teachers may find it necessary to group children into temporary

Table 9.2

Possible minilesson topics

Procedural Minilessons	Literary Minilessons	Strategy/Skills Minilessons
Where to sit during reading time	Differences between fiction and	How to choose a book
Giving a book talk	nonfiction books	Selecting literature log topics
How to be a good listener in a	Learning from dedications	Connecting reading material to
share session	Books that show emotion	your own life
What is an appropriate noise level	Books written in the first, second,	Tips for reading aloud
during reading time	or third person	Figuring out unknown words
What to do when you finish a	Author studies	Using context
book	How authors use quotations	Substituting
What kinds of questions to ask	How the story setting fits the story	Using picture clues
during a share session	Characteristics of different genres	Using the sounds of blends,
Running a small group discussion	Development of characters, plot,	vowels, contractions, etc.
Self-evaluation	theme, mood	Using Post-its to mark interesting
Getting ready for a conference	How leads hook us	parts
How to have a peer conference	How authors use the problem/	Monitoring comprehension (Does
Where to sit during minilessons	event/solution pattern	this make sense and sound
Taking care of books	Differences between a picture	right?)
Keeping track of books read	book and a novel	Asking questions while reading
Rules of the workshop	Titles and their meanings	Making predictions
	Characters' points of view	Emergent strategies
	Examples of similes and	Concept of story
	metaphors	Concept that print carries
	Examples of foreshadowing	meaning
	How authors use dialogue	Making sense
	Predictable and surprise endings	Mapping a story
	Use of descriptive words and	How to retell a story orally
	phrases	Looking for relationships
	How illustrations enhance the	Looking for important ideas
	story	Making inferences
	Secrets in books	Drawing conclusions
		Summarizing a story
		Distinguishing fact from opinion
		Emergent reader skills:
		directionality, concept of "word,"
		sound/symbol relationships

groups for managing rotation through center-based activities. Although at some point, these same teachers may elect to encourage children to choose centers, this often leads to an overcrowding in one center and a dearth of participants in another. To help teachers manage the rotation of children through centers, a **flexible traveling group** can be formed. Flexible traveling groups are cohorts of children who are grouped together for the purpose of rotating or traveling through center activities in classrooms. These groups should include a mix of reading and writing ability levels to avoid the pitfalls associated with ability grouping. Flexible traveling groups should exist for no longer than a month at a time; then the children should be regrouped. A

When the classroom has multiple centers or stations, the teacher may place children into temporary groups for managing rotation through center activities.

group leader can be designated to oversee center cleanup, operation of cassette recorders, and other tasks. This grouping plan is flexible because it is regularly regrouped and is traveling because it forms a cohort group for traveling through station or center-based activities.

Adapting the Environment to Assist Children With Special Needs

Helping Students Develop a Sense of Ownership

Focus on two ways to structure the classroom literacy learning environment to help students with special needs.

For over two decades, teachers and schools have been under a legal mandate to provide the least restrictive learning environment possible for all children, especially those with handicapping conditions and other special needs. With the passage of Public Law 94-142, the Individuals with Disabilities Education Act, greater attention has been devoted to aspects of adapting typical classroom environments to accommodate the mainstreaming of children with special needs into the regular classroom. Teachers are searching for ways to be of greatest assistance all children in their classrooms.

Concerning the physical environment, classrooms should be broken into smaller, functional areas for specific activities. These should, according to Nordquist and Twardosz (1990) be bounded by low partitions or shelves. Literacy props selected for classroom activity areas should be selected based on "functionality" and "reactivity" to ensure maximal success. This means that props should be appropriate for the mental or chronological age of the individual child. Also, literacy props that temporarily sustain motion or produce sensory feedback such as read-along tapes, pop-up books and typewriters help to sustain appropriate classroom behaviors.

For children with attention deficit disorder, changing activity areas regularly, providing colorful props, inserting quiet, calming music, and furnishing activities that require engagement and an active response help these students maintain attention. In some cases, children may need to be given medical treatment to help them focus their attention on learning (Cooter, 1988; Zentall, 1993).

It is important that students with special needs feel fully accepted as part of the classroom community—a sense of ownership and belonging. Voltz and Damiano-Lantz (1993) have listed several strategies for helping children with special needs develop ownership for their classroom learning environment, which we have adapted as follows:

- Establish student-oriented bulletin boards where children create, use, and maintain these display areas.
- Solicit student input on how to organize the physical environment of the classroom.
- Provide a "suggestion box" where children can put their ideas on how to make the classroom a better place.
- Invite student input on classroom rules and policies.
- Link subject matter studies to real-world concerns outside the classroom and school.

- Use a thematic approach to learning that provides in-depth learning and helps children make connections across disciplines.
- Provide a variety of ways to engage and respond to learning activities that make use of different modalities such as touching, moving, seeing, hearing, and tasting.
- Invite children to set their own goals in relation to their learning.

Adapting the Environment to Assist Linguistically and Culturally Diverse Students

Garcia and Malkin (1993) suggest three major considerations in creating supportive learning environments for culturally and linguistically diverse students. First, teachers should carefully select and evaluate instructional materials. Figure 9.15 is a checklist offered by Garcia and Malkin (1993).

Also, teachers should be sure to incorporate children's language and culture into the ongoing activities of the classroom. Activities such as family histories can invite children to explore their own roots and come to appreciate the unique characteristics of their religious, geographical, gender, ethnic, and language background. Finally, teachers should encourage involvement and participation of the parents and the community. These individuals can add richness to the learning environment by sharing backgrounds, talents, knowledge, and cultural understandings. In some cases, parents and community members can help teachers by acting as translators for a period of time to facilitate communication for English as a second language students.

Focus on how parent involvement adds richness and variety to the classroom environment for all students and helps to validate each child's culture, language, etc.

Summary

Research has led to the development of clear guidelines or principles for creating supportive literacy learning environments. A four-part environmental model was presented and elaborated to help teachers understand these guiding principles. Next, the practical creation of learning spaces was discussed. Similar to homes, classroom space can be subdivided into functional areas to support specific instructional goals and activities. Whole-class learning, collaborative writing, silent reading, supported reading, conferences, and thematic studies areas may support reading, writing, and thematic studies in transitional and balanced literacy classrooms.

Basals, trade books, workbooks, volunteers, and computers are instructional resources available to the classroom teacher for supporting reading and writing instruction in the classroom. Examples of how computers can be used to support developing readers and writers include such recent developments as hypertext and hypermedia. Potential resources for implementing literacy volunteer programs include a volunteer sign-up form.

Evidence against continuing the practice of ability grouping students for reading instruction includes negative influences on teacher and student expectations, student self-concepts, and student friendship patterns. Literature-response groups, basal-

Figure 9.15

Checklist for selecting and evaluating materials for culturally and linguistically diverse learners

- Are the perspectives and contributions of people from diverse cultural and linguistic groups—both men and women, as well as people with disabilities—included in the curriculum?

- Are there curricula that will assist students in analyzing the various forms of the mass media for ethnocentrism, sexism, "handicapism," and stereotyping?

- Are men and women, diverse cultural/racial groups, and people with varying abilities shown in both active and passive roles?

- Are men and women, diverse cultural/racial groups, and people with disabilities shown in positions of power (i.e., the materials do not rely on the mainstream culture's character to achieve goals)?

- Do the materials identify strengths possessed by so-called "underachieving" diverse populations? Do they diminish the attention given to deficits, to reinforce positive behaviors that are desired and valued?

- Are members of diverse racial/cultural groups, men and women, and people with disabilities shown engaged in a broad range of social and professional activities?

- Are members of a particular culture or group depicted as having a range of physical features (e.g., hair color, hair texture, variations in facial characteristics and body build)?

- Do the materials represent historical events from the perspectives of the various groups involved or solely from the male, middle-class, and/or Western European perspective?

- Are the materials free from ethnocentric or sexist language patterns that may make implications about persons or groups based solely on their culture, race, gender, or disability?

- Will students from different ethnic and cultural backgrounds find the materials personally meaningful to their life experiences?

- Are a wide variety of culturally different examples, situations, scenarios, and anecdotes used throughout the curriculum design to illustrate major intellectual concepts and principles?

- Are culturally diverse content, examples, and experiences comparable in kind, significance, magnitude, and function to those selected from mainstream culture?

From "Toward Defining Programs and Services for Culturally and Linguistically Diverse Learners in Special Education" by S. B. Garcia and D. H. Malkin, 1993, *Teaching Exceptional Children, 26*(1), pp. 52–58. Copyright 1993 by the Council for Exceptional Children. Reprinted by permission.

reader visiting-response groups, whole-class, flexible traveling groups, and minilesson needs groups are alternatives to ability grouping students for reading instruction. Cooperative learning groups, such as jigsaw groups, buddy reading, focus trios, are additional alternatives to the practice of ability grouping. Finally, unique considerations for assisting children with special needs and those with cultural or linguistic differences were presented. (Figure 9.16 presents an overview of Chapter 9.)

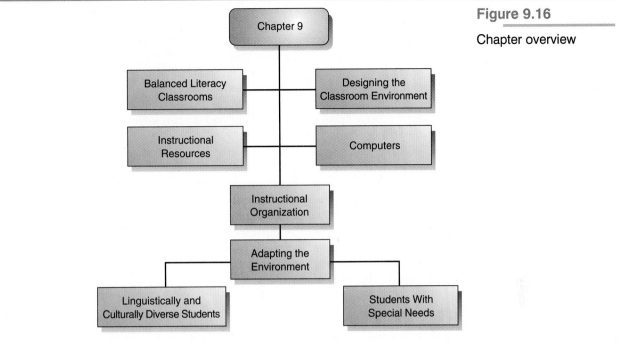

Figure 9.16

Chapter overview

CONCEPT APPLICATIONS

IN THE CLASSROOM

1. Make a layout map of how you intend to divide up your classroom space during your first year of teaching. Give a supporting rationale for the design you choose. (Keep in mind the idea of transitions—beginning simple and moving to more complex classroom arrangements!)

2. Create a 5-year plan for building a classroom library of trade books. Include in your plan a target total number of trade books and relevant target dates for accomplishment of your goals.

3. Choose a topic for conducting a minilesson in reading or writing. Defend the authenticity of your choice in terms of whether or not real readers or writers would ever need to use this skill or strategy outside the school setting.

4. Pick the grade level at which you hope to teach your first year. Devise a story like those found in the latter part of Chapter 5. In your story, detail your personal 5-year plan for making the transition in terms of your classroom design, curriculum, and lesson planning.

5. Analyze the cover of this text for qualities of design that are reflected in the research on creating literacy learning environments. What props are present? How are they arranged? Does this classroom provide for interaction and learning of literacy through demonstrations, engagement, and sensitivity? Is the classroom aesthetically pleasing; does it inform children; is it divided into functional areas; has the teacher used personal touches? You might make an analysis grid or evaluation instrument based on the principles presented in Chapter 9 to look at these questions for your own classroom.

IN THE FIELD

1. Visit at least two public or private school classrooms, and draw a layout map of the space in the classrooms and how it is used. Be sure to include bulletin boards and storage areas in your observations. Afterward, interview the teachers. Determine their reasons for the classroom arrangement and use.
2. Discuss with at least two parents the concept of volunteer work in schools. Determine whether or not parents would be willing to give their time to their local school. Invite them to fill out and discuss with you the volunteering for the school reading program form.
3. Visit two school classrooms, and note how teachers and children spend their time. On a separate paper, reflect in writing on your observations. Discuss relative advantages and disadvantages for your observations of teacher and student behaviors during reading instruction.
4. Interview at least two children in the above-average and below-average ability groups. Ask questions about how they like reading time, completing workbook and worksheet assignments, receiving books for presents, and reading aloud to their peers. Contrast your findings for the above-average and below-average readers.

RECOMMENDED READINGS

Au, K. (1991). Organizing for instruction [Special issue]. *The Reading Teacher, 44*(8).

Butler, A., & Turbill, J. (1984). *Towards a reading-writing classroom.* Portsmouth, NH: Heinemann.

Hagerty, P. (1992). *Reader's workshop: Real reading.* New York: Scholastic.

McVitty, W. (1986). *Getting it together: Organising the reading–writing classroom.* Portsmouth, NH: Heinemann.

Morrow, L. M., & Rand, M. K. (1991). Promoting literacy during play by designing early childhood classroom environments. *The Reading Teacher, 44(6),* 396–402.

Neuman, S. B., & Roskos, K. (1990). Play, print, and purpose: Enriching play environments for literacy development. *The Reading Teacher, 44(3),* 214–221.

Peterson, R., & Eeds, M. (1990). *Grand conversations: Literature groups in action.* New York: Scholastic.

Rasinski, T. (1989). Commentary: Reading the empowerment of parents. *The Reading Teacher, 43*(3), 226–231.

Reinking, D. (Ed.). (1987). *Computers and reading: Issues for theory and practice.* New York: Teachers College Press.

Slaughter, H. B. (1988). Indirect and direct teaching in a whole language program. *The Reading Teacher, 42*(1), 30–35.

Strickland, D. S., Feeley, J. T., & Wepner, S. B. (1987). *Using computers in the teaching of reading.* New York: Teachers College Press.

Van Manen, M. (1986). *The tone of teaching.* New York: Scholastic.

Whitaker, B. T., Schwartz, E., & Vockell, E. (1989). *The computer in the reading curriculum.* New York: McGraw-Hill.

COMPUTER SOFTWARE CITED

Bulletin board maker—Happy habitats: The pond. Fairfield, CT: Pelican, a division of Queue.

Choose your own adventure [series]. (1985). New York: Bantam Books.

Cosmic osmo. (1985). Menlo Park, CA: Activision.

MacWrite. (1984). Cupertino, CA: Apple Computer.

Playwriter. (1987). Old Bridge, NJ: Woodbury.

Science explorations: Nutrition. Jefferson City, MO: Scholastic.

Stories and more (1991). Atlanta, GA: International Business Machines.

Super story tree. (1989). Jefferson City, MO: Scholastic.

Talking text. (1986). Jefferson City, MO: Scholastic.

The Bank Street writer for the Macintosh (1991). Bank Street College of Education. Jefferson City, MO: Scholastic.

The puzzler. (1987). Pleasantville, NY: Sunburst Communications.

The semantic mapper. (1986). Gainesville, FL: Teacher Support Software.

The writing adventure. (1985). Allen, TX: Developmental Learning Materials (DLM).

WorldClassroom. (1988). Arlington, TX: Global Learning Corporation.

Chapter 10

Reading and Writing
in the Early Years

Focus Questions

When you are finished studying this chapter, you should be able to answer these questions:

1. What are the major elements of a balanced literacy program as outlined in this chapter?
2. What are six language routines that can be used to structure daily reading and writing experiences for young children?
3. How can young children be helped to make sense of printed language by learning the alphabetic principle?
4. How can young children be helped to develop an understanding of the function and structure of books and stories?
5. What are some strategies for helping young children respond to their reading through drawing and art?
6. How can young readers with special and multicultural/linguistic needs be helped?

Key Concepts

Balanced Literacy Program
Shared Book Experience
Predictable Book
Supported Reading
Guided Reading
Language Experience Approach
Big Books
Language Routines
Tune-in Routine
Old-Favorite Language Routine

Learning About Language
New-Story Routine
Independent Output Activities
Sharing Time
Print-Rich Environment
Directed Listening Thinking Activity (DLTA)
Story Retellings
Transmediation
Themed Studies

Teaching Reading and Writing to Young Children

Thirty-four bright-eyed and curious first-grade children gather around a kidney-bean-shaped table at the back of the room on the first day of school. The teacher places a soda bottle half-filled with white vinegar on the table. She says, "I am going to blow this balloon up with a soda bottle." The children giggle and watch intently as the teacher places a limp, red balloon over the lip of the bottle. She pulls the balloon tight over the lip and shakes the balloon back and forth a couple of times. A puff of white powder falls into the vinegar. The liquid inside the bottle begins to foam; at the same time, the balloon begins to fill with air. It grows bigger and bigger. The children move away from the bottle expecting the balloon to burst at any moment. Just as suddenly as it began, the liquid stops foaming and the balloon stops growing. "How did the bottle blow up the balloon?" asked the teacher. "Let's go over to the carpet for a minute, and I'll write down your ideas on this chart paper." For a few minutes, the teacher wrote down the children's ideas as they dictated them. Then, the teacher reread the ideas and asked the children to join in rereading the ideas with her. As this teacher recorded her students' ideas, she evidenced a concern and respect for children's thoughts and language.

Teachers play a critical role in creating the conditions that support the learning of young children.

Teachers play a critical role in creating the conditions that support the learning of young children. The way in which teachers interact with children every day is a living demonstration from which children may choose to learn. Albert Schweitzer once said, "Example isn't the best teacher, it is the only teacher!" When teachers listen carefully to children, they demonstrate sensitivity and value for children and their ideas. By surrounding children with books and other printed media and by encouraging them to engage in reading and writing collectively and individually, the teacher creates an environment in which children begin to view themselves as skilled readers and writers. Children learn to read and write by acting like skilled language users and doing the things that readers and writers do, namely, reading, writing, talking, playing, thinking, listening, and drawing. The information presented in this chapter is designed to assist teachers to make optimal use of trade books and process writing to help young children become joyful readers and writers.

Think of a time when you remember a child acting like a skilled language user. What was the child doing?

A Balanced Literacy Program: Reading TO, WITH, and BY Young Children

Deciding on the program elements necessary to provide children with successful and enriching literacy learning experiences is typically a teacher's first order of business. The elements of **balanced literacy programs** have been well defined for over two decades by literacy scholars and practitioners working in New Zealand and Australia (Holdaway, 1979; Mooney, 1990). These elements ensure that children will receive well-rounded and balanced experiences with reading and writing. School literacy programs typically focus heavily on developing reading and writing skills with students. Of course, speaking and listening are integrally related to and used as vehicles for teaching children to read and write.

The elements of balanced literacy programs have been well defined for over two decades by scholars and practitioners working in Australia and New Zealand.

In the next sections of this chapter, we describe the elements of balanced literacy programs. Even though literacy programs always integrate reading and writing (they are inseparable language processes), for purposes of clarity, we shall briefly focus on the elements of balanced reading and balanced writing programs separately. We begin by examining the major elements of balanced reading programs in Figure 10.1. Note that beneath each major element heading specific instructional practices are listed.

Balanced literacy programs, which include reading and writing, are easily defined with three important words: to, with, and by.

Reading TO Children

The question is sometimes raised why teachers spend valuable instructional time during a school day reading aloud to children. There are several good reasons to read aloud to children daily, if not more often! Trelease states,

> [The] reasons are the same reasons you talk to a child: to reassure, to entertain, to inform or explain, to arouse curiosity, and to inspire—and to do it all personally, not impersonally with a machine. All those experiences create or strengthen a positive attitude about reading (1989, p. 2)

Early research by Durkin (1966) revealed that children who read early often come from homes where parents read to them regularly. Further, it is through read-aloud activities that young children develop a sense of how stories are constructed (Morrow, 1993; Morrow & Roskos, 1993). An understanding of story structure among younger readers has been closely linked with effective reading comprehension (McGee, Ratliff, Sinex, Head, & LaCroix, 1984). During read alouds, children see teachers and others as models of the reading process and witness first-hand the enjoyment of reading (Mooney, 1990). Reading aloud provides children with an ever-expanding exposure to the world of printed language.

Read alouds expand children's understanding of the world around them. In short, through listening to texts read by teachers and parents, children can learn about ideas, concepts, and events that are within their ability to comprehend. Hence,

Name three do's and don'ts related to reading aloud to children.

Figure 10.1

Major elements of balanced reading programs

Reading TO Children
- Teacher Read Alouds
- Small-Group or One-to-One Reading

Reading WITH Children
- Shared Book Experience
- Shared Rhythm and Singing Experience
- Supported Reading
- Language Experience
- Guided Reading

Reading BY Children
- Readers' Theater
- Sustained Silent Reading (SSR) / Drop Everything and Read (DEAR)
- School and Class Libraries

teachers should read books to children that challenge their intellectual development but do not exceed their cognitive and emotional levels to comprehend. Consequently, books written at children's reading levels and that can be read on their own or with support should be reserved for reading with and by young children. Based on Trelease's (1989) *The New Read-Aloud Handbook,* several other "do's" and "don'ts" of read alouds for teachers are listed in Figure 10.2.

Figure 10.2

The do's and don'ts of read alouds

Do's

- Begin reading to children as soon as possible. The younger you start them, the better.
- Use Mother Goose rhymes and songs to stimulate children's language and listening.
- Read as often as you and the child (or class) have time for.
- Try to set aside at least one traditional time each day for a story.
- Picture books can be read easily to a family of children widely separated in age.
- Start with picture books, and build to storybooks and novels.
- Vary the length and subject matter of your readings.
- Follow through with your reading.
- Occasionally read above the children's intellectual level and challenge their minds.
- Remember that even sixth-grade students love a good picture book now and then.
- Allow time for class discussion after reading a story.
- Use plenty of expression when reading.
- The most common mistake in reading aloud is reading too fast. Read slowly enough for the child to build mental pictures.
- Bring the author to life, as well as her book.
- Add a third dimension to the book whenever possible.
- Reluctant readers or unusually active children frequently find it difficult to just sit and listen.
- Follow the suggestion of Dr. Caroline Bauer and post a reminder sign by your door: "Don't Forget Your *Flood* Book."
- Fathers should make an extra effort to read to their children.
- Lead by example.

Don'ts

- Don't read stories that you don't enjoy yourself.
- Don't continue reading a book once it is obvious that it was a poor choice. Admit the mistake and choose another.
- If you are a teacher, don't feel you have to tie every book to classwork.
- Don't read above a child's emotional level.
- Don't impose interpretations of a story on your audience.
- Don't confuse quantity with quality.
- Don't use the book as a threat, "If you don't pick up your room, no story tonight!"

Based on Trelease (1989).

Small-Group and One-to-One Reading

Although most read alouds take place with an entire group of children, Morrow (1988b) reminds teachers not to overlook the benefits and importance of reading aloud to smaller groups and individuals. One of the benefits associated with reading to children at home is the interaction between parent and child. This same benefit can be replicated in the school setting. Children whose reading development lags behind their peers can be helped a great deal by teachers who take time to read to them in small-group or individual settings. Children can stop the teacher to ask questions, make comments, or respond to the story. This seldom happens in whole groups. Morrow (1989) also suggests that individual readings be recorded and analyzed to provide diagnostic information to inform future instruction. The coding sheet in Figure 10.30 can be used to perform such analyses.

List two reasons why teachers should read aloud in small groups or one-to-one settings.

Reading WITH Children

Shared Book Experience

Many children have learned to read by having books read to them. These books were usually shared by parents or siblings during bedtime reading or lap reading. Although learning to read by being read to has been shown to be successful and meaningful, what was missing was a way to replicate in a classroom all of the important characteristics of the bedtime or lap-reading event. The **shared book experience** is the suggested solution to this problem (Holdaway, 1979, 1981).

A critical part of the shared book experience involves the selection of good, **predictable books** to be shared. Several criteria need to be observed. Books and stories chosen for sharing need to be those that have been proven to be loved by children. Any book or story (including those selections in basal readers) to be shared should have literary merit and engaging content. The pictures should match the text and tell or support the telling of the story in proper sequence. The text should be characterized by repetition, cumulative sequence, rhyme, and rhythm to entice the children and "hook" them on the language patterns. Books should be chosen that put reasonable demands on the reader. Put another way, the amount of print should not overburden the reader.

Predictable books *should have literary merit and engaging content, pictures that match the text, and the text should be characterized by repetition.*

For young children, shared reading is accomplished by reading big books.

Thus, in early books, the pictures should carry the story, with the print amounting to little more than a caption. Later, books in which the print and the picture carry nearly an equal share of the story can be selected. With practice and increased independence in reading, books can be selected in which the print carries the story and the illustrations simply augment the text. Finally, and perhaps most importantly, the books chosen for shared book experiences need to have a visual impact on 30 children similar to the impact that a standard-sized book would have on the knee of a child or in the lap of a parent. This requirement of the shared book experience led to the development, marketing, and use of big books for teaching young children to read (Figure 10.3). When all of these conditions are met, children and teachers truly share the reading experience. They share the discovery of good books, an awareness of how print works, and the power and humor of language. What is more, children gain a growing confidence in their ability to read (F. L. Barrett, 1982).

The shared book experience is begun by the teacher's introducing the book. If the book *The Gingerbread Man* (1985) is selected for sharing, the introduction may begin with children looking at the book cover and the teacher reading the title aloud. The teacher may talk about the front and back of the book and may demonstrate certain features of the book, such as author and illustrator names, publisher, copyright, and table of contents. Next, the teacher may ask, "What do you think this story may be about?" After looking at the cover and reading the title aloud, children may want to relate personal anecdotes or make predictions about the contents of the book. The sensitive teacher will not only tolerate these contributions to the discussion but will encourage and praise children. The intent of the introduction is to heighten

Figure 10.3

Big book and standard-sized version

Book cover from *Caps, Hats, Socks, and Mittens* by Louise Borden. Jacket illustration copyright © 1988 by Lillian Hoban. Reprinted by permission of Scholastic Inc.

children's desire to read the story and help them draw on their own experiences to enjoy and interpret the story.

Next, the teacher should read the story with "full dramatic punch, perhaps overdoing a little some of the best parts" (F. L. Barrett, 1982, p. 16). If the story possesses the characteristics outlined here that make the text predictable, soon after the teacher begins reading, the children will begin chiming in on the repetitive and predictable parts. In the story of *The Gingerbread Man* (1985), the children may join in on the phrase, "Run, run as fast as you can. You can't catch me; I'm the Gingerbread man!" At key points, the teacher may pause during reading to encourage children to predict what is coming next in the book.

After the first reading, a discussion usually ensues. Children often want to talk about their favorite parts, share their feelings and experiences, as well as discuss how well they were able to predict. The story can be reread on subsequent days and will eventually become a part of the stock of favorite stories to be requested for rereading. One means for increasing involvement on a second reading is to use hand movements or rhythm instruments (see the old-favorites routine described later). Research by Ribowsky (1985) compared the shared book experience approach to a phonics-emphasis approach, the J. B. Lippincott basal, and found that the shared book experience resulted in higher end-of-year achievement scores and phonic analysis subtest scores than did the direct-instruction phonics approach used in the Lippincott basal. In a recent study, Reutzel and others (1994) showed that the shared book experience resulted in substantial reading progress for second-grade children across measures of word recognition, vocabulary, comprehension, and fluency.

Shared Rhythm and Singing Experience

Music is a great motivator for reading! According to O'Bruba (1987), music broadens reading into a multisensory experience, heightens interest and involvement, brings variety and pleasure to reading, and reduces the tedium of repetition and drill. One variation of the shared book experience that involves music and rhythm is the shared rhythm and singing experience. Bill Harp (1988) suggests that teachers fill the classroom with inviting songs. In addition, we feel teachers should fill the classroom with exciting chants, poems, and raps. Whether song, poem, chant, or rap, each text selected for the shared rhythm and singing experience should have the potential to be loved by children. (Selected resources for songs, poems, chants, and raps to be used in the shared rhythm and singing experience are listed in the appendix.)

When songs, poems, chants, and raps are chosen for the shared rhythm and singing experience, those songs and texts selected should place reasonable demands on the reader. Any musical or rhythmic text selected should contain lyrics and text that emphasize repetition, cumulative sequence, rhyme, and rhythm. Next, the text of selected songs, poems, chants, and raps needs to be enlarged on charts or chalkboards, as in Figure 10.4.

The criteria for selecting songs, chants, poems, and raps are similar to those for choosing books to be shared in the shared book experience. Favorite songs such as "BINGO," "Oh My Aunt Came Back," and "On Top of Spaghetti" will be sung joyfully again and again by children. New words and lyrics can be substituted or invented by the children for the standard song lyrics and recorded on large charts or at the chalkboard. For example, the lyrics to the song "BINGO" can be replaced with new lyrics, such as "TEDDY," "MOMMY," or "DADDY." The lyrics to the song "Everybody Hates Me, Nobody Likes Me, Think I'll Go Eat Worms" can be changed

"After discussion, the teacher should read the story with full dramatic punch, perhaps overdoing a little some of the best parts" (F. L. Barrett, 1982, p. 16).

Increasing involvement on a second reading can be accomplished by adding hand movements or rhythm instruments.

Texts selected for the shared rhythm and singing experience should have the potential to be loved by children.

Favorite songs such as "BINGO," "Oh My Aunt Came Back," and "On Top of Spaghetti" will be sung joyfully again and again by children.

Figure 10.4

Song lyrics enlarged on
a chart

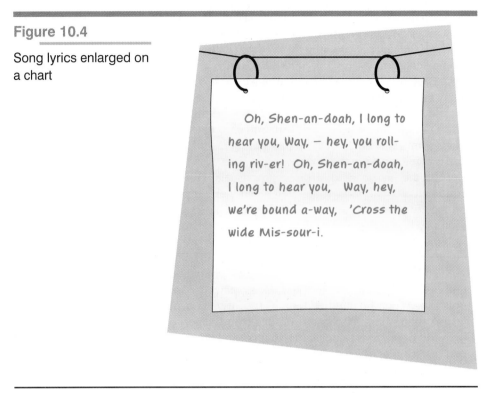

Oh, Shen-an-doah, I long to
hear you, Way, — hey, you roll-
ing riv-er! Oh, Shen-an-doah,
I long to hear you,   Way, hey,
we're bound a-way,   'Cross the
wide Mis-sour-i.

From *Heritage Songster* (p. 5) by L. Dallin and L. Dallin, 1980, Dubuque, IA: William C. Brown.

by substituting in other miserable things to eat, such as grasshoppers or flies. Beating out the rhythm of a favorite song, poem, rap, or chant by clapping or using rhythm instruments will make a joyful sound in every classroom. Poems such as "Warning" or "Sick" in Shel Silverstein's *Where the Sidewalk Ends* (1974) or *The New Kid on the Block* by Jack Prelutsky (1984) are just a few popular poems children may wish to put to rhythm. Chants such as "Squid Sauce" in Sonja Dunn's (1990) *Butterscotch Dreams* performed with actions and rhythm will elicit calls on a daily basis for more chants. Using dance, hand movements, and actions along with music and rhythm captures and sustains children's interest. Children delight in using rhythm instruments to accompany their singing and choral readings, although using these devices can be a very noisy enterprise!

Harp (1988) suggests that after several readings, children can be invited up to the chart to point out words pronounced by the teacher. Words could be copied on a word card the same size as the words on the chart. These word cards could be shuffled, and children could match the words on the cards back into the text of the song, poem, chant, or rap. The text of the songs, poems, raps, and chants on the charts could be copied on duplicating masters to produce small personal booklets of the text on the charts. These small individual booklets of songs, chants, poems, and raps then could be taken home to be read, shared, and sung with parents and siblings.

Children taught music on a daily basis had significantly higher reading growth scores than did children who were not taught music.

Research has demonstrated the positive effects of music on learning language, both oral and written. G. C. Taylor (1981) determined that music-centered language arts instruction resulted in enhanced listening, language awareness, and reading readiness skills. Eastlund (1980) found that music as a medium of language made learning and language acquisition easier for young children. McGuire (1984) reported that children taught music on a daily basis had significantly higher reading growth scores than did children who were not taught music. In short, the shared rhythm and singing experience is an entertaining and beneficial extension of the shared book experience, which enlivens and integrates learning to read with music and diverse genres of literature and texts.

Supported Reading: Read-Along Cassettes and Take-Home Books

Just as parents support their children with training wheels and holding onto the back of the seat when children learn to ride a bicycle, so teachers need to support the emergent reader through the process of learning to read. **Supported reading** strategies include the use of adult and child volunteers as well as mechanical support devices such as computers and read-along cassette tapes. Read-along cassettes can be used to effectively support readers through the reading of new or relatively unfamiliar books at all levels. This practice, however, seems to make best sense in the emergent or initial stages of learning to read. Read-along cassettes are now commercially available for a wide variety of predictable books. When tapes are not available, teachers may record their own read-along cassettes or involve parent volunteers in the production of read-along cassettes. These carefully paced, prerecorded readings support children through the reading of a book when the teacher is needed elsewhere in the classroom. Tapes can, for example, be color coded for varying text levels (e.g., green for emergent, yellow for easy reading, and blue for independent reading) and stored in specially designed cassette storage cases.

Supported reading strategies include the use of adult and child volunteers as well as mechanical support devices such as computers and read-along cassette tapes.

See Chapter 9 for ideas on recruiting volunteers.

Take-home books are a means for involving parents in supporting their children's reading. To construct take-home books for students, use published, predictable books as patterns. For example, the book *On Market Street* (Lobel, 1981) may have been selected. Next, rewrite the book with different words and illustrations for each alphabet letter (e.g., alligators, beds, etc.). The resulting version from patterning the take-home book after the original text is transcribed on a duplicating master and duplicated—enough for each child to have their own copy. Sometimes children can be asked to color the illustrations in these take-home books. To produce other take-home books, simply duplicate the text and encourage children to illustrate their own take-home books. When children finish illustrating or coloring their take-home books, they can be encouraged to take them home to share their emerging reading abilities with parents. Also, teachers can produce multiple copies of read-along cassette tapes to accompany these take-home books. Children can check out the read-along cassettes and take them home to practice their take-home books when parents are unable to assist.

Take-home books are a means for involving parents in supporting their children's reading.

Guided Reading

Guided reading is an important part of a balanced reading program. Unlike basal readers that claim to engage children and teachers in "guided reading" activities, the notion of guided reading in a balanced reading program focuses on reading books with children that would present too many challenges for them if they were to take full responsibility for the first reading. Thus, the purposes of guided reading are (a) to develop reading strategies and (b) to move children toward independent reading.

Children are sometimes grouped homogeneously by developmental levels that reflect a range of competencies, experiences, and interests (Mooney, 1990). The most

*During **guided reading**, children are grouped homogeneously by developmental levels and by the ability to handle specific reading materials.*

important consideration centers on the child's ability to successfully manipulate and process the text. Groups are typically thought to include the following four levels of children's reading development: (a) early emergent, (b) emergent, (c) early fluency, and (d) fluency. Developmental guided reading groups are composed of six to eight children who will work together for a period of time with the assistance of the teacher. *Groups change as children progress during the year.* This is a crucial point in using homogeneous groups, because failure to change groups can result in the "Eagles, Bluebirds, and Buzzards" form of ability grouping seen in previous decades: children in "lower" developmental groups can suffer self-esteem damage when their groups become fixed.

Before guided reading, great care is taken to match text and child to ensure that children can enjoy and control the story throughout the first reading. Texts chosen for each level should present children with a reasonable challenge but also with a high degree of potential success. Typically, children should be able to read 90% to 95% of the words correctly in a book for guided reading. Books used in early emergent guided reading should demonstrate a close match of text and pictures, gradual introduction of unfamiliar concepts and words, as well as sufficient repetition of predictable elements to provide support for novice readers. Peterson (1991, p. 135) has constructed a very helpful summary for selecting guided reading books, shown in Figure 10.5.

In Figure 10.5, levels 1 to 4 are linked to early emergent guided reading. Emergent reading is linked to levels 5 to 8. Levels 9 to 12 function as a bridge between the lower levels and upper levels, capturing elements of emergent and early fluent reading. For early fluent readers, levels 13 to 15 seem most appropriate, and levels 16 to 20 are aimed at fluent reader levels. During guided reading, teachers use questions and comments to help children access and use strategies and resources available within themselves and in the text.

Children should *not* be introduced to guided reading until they have had ample opportunities to listen to stories, poems, songs, and so on and to participate in shared reading experiences. The basic lesson pattern employed in guided reading lessons consists of *seven* phases. These phases are listed in Figure 10.6.

As teachers work with children in guided reading, they lead children to understand that there are three important cuing systems that good readers use to unlock text (Mooney, 1990). These are meaning, organization or order, and the letter–sound system, as shown in Figure 10.7.

To help young children access the cuing systems for fluent reading, teachers usually model these systems by asking questions and making comments that direct children to use one or more of the four major reading cuing strategies: predicting, sampling, confirming, and cross-checking to self-correct. Examples of questions and comments teachers use to direct or guide children to use the four reading cuing strategies are listed in Figure 10.8.

As children progress along the continuum of reading development in guided reading, teachers begin by taking responsibility for the first reading of the text with the children. Thus, early guided reading looks in practice much like the shared reading experience; the main difference is the size of the group. Over time and with development, children assume more of the responsibility for the first reading of the text with the teacher taking a supporting role through echoing, coaching, and helping where needed. The gradual release of responsibility for the first reading of a guided reading book generally occurs as teachers observe that children understand basic print concepts and have acquired a basic sight word vocabulary.

During these earliest stages and ages of reading development, children use their fingers to finger-point read (Ehri & Sweet, 1991). Finger-point reading involves children in voice pointing or indicating the one-to-one correspondence of spoken words

Books selected for guided reading should provide a reasonable challenge and potential for high success: 90% to 95% of the words should be easily read by students.

Guided reading should be introduced after children have enjoyed ample opportunities to participate in shared reading experiences.

Name four reading strategies to be developed during guided reading.

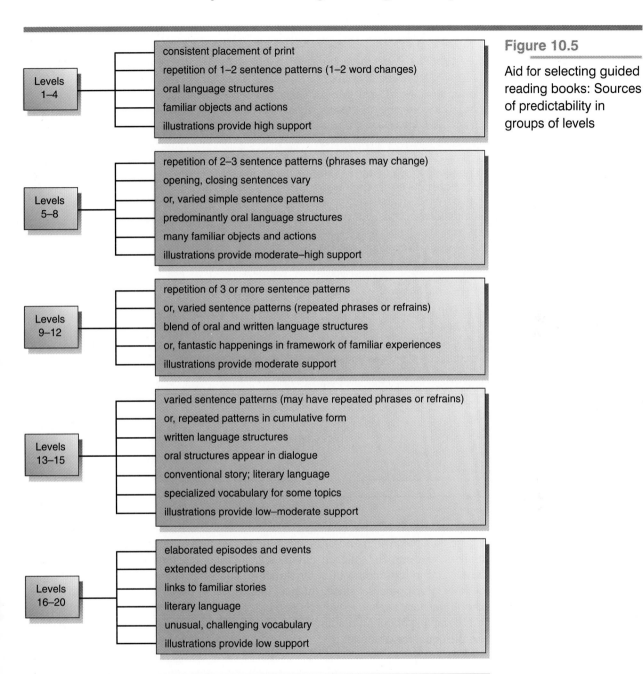

Figure 10.5

Aid for selecting guided reading books: Sources of predictability in groups of levels

Levels 1–4
- consistent placement of print
- repetition of 1–2 sentence patterns (1–2 word changes)
- oral language structures
- familiar objects and actions
- illustrations provide high support

Levels 5–8
- repetition of 2–3 sentence patterns (phrases may change)
- opening, closing sentences vary
- or, varied simple sentence patterns
- predominantly oral language structures
- many familiar objects and actions
- illustrations provide moderate–high support

Levels 9–12
- repetition of 3 or more sentence patterns
- or, varied sentence patterns (repeated phrases or refrains)
- blend of oral and written language structures
- or, fantastic happenings in framework of familiar experiences
- illustrations provide moderate support

Levels 13–15
- varied sentence patterns (may have repeated phrases or refrains)
- or, repeated patterns in cumulative form
- written language structures
- oral structures appear in dialogue
- conventional story; literary language
- specialized vocabulary for some topics
- illustrations provide low–moderate support

Levels 16–20
- elaborated episodes and events
- extended descriptions
- links to familiar stories
- literary language
- unusual, challenging vocabulary
- illustrations provide low support

with written words (Reutzel, 1995). Thus, during early emergent guided reading, teachers focus children's attention on *predictions* by *sampling* text features such as picture clues and known words. In addition, teachers focus early emergent readers' attention on print concepts such as directionality (left to right, top to bottom, etc.).

During emergent guided reading, teachers focus children's attention on processing text with the use of multiple strategies such as confirming, cross-checking, and

Figure 10.6

Picture Talk • Walk through a new book by looking at the pictures. Ask children, "What do you see?"

First Reading • Depending on the students' developmental levels, the first reading is initially done by the teacher with children following the lead. Later, the teacher gradually releases responsibility for the first reading to the children by sharing the reading role and then fading into one who encourages children to try it on their own.

Language Play • In this phase of the guided reading lesson, the teacher carefully analyzes the text to find specific elements associated with written language to teach children how language works. For early emergent readers, this may mean letter identification, punctuation, or directionality. In the fluency stage, children might identify text genre or compound words.

Rereading • Children read the text again with the assistance of the teacher, a peer, or a mechanical device such as a computer, tape, etc. Novice readers are encouraged to point to the text as they read, where fluent readers are encouraged to "read the text with your eyes" or silently.

Retelling • Children retell what they have read to their teacher or to their peers. Typically we say, "Can you tell me what you've read?" Sometimes we probe children's retellings with other questions to prompt recall.

Follow-up • The most effective follow-up activity to a guided reading lesson is to invite children to take guided reading books home for demonstrating their ability to parents and siblings. This provides needed practice time and promotes increased confidence and self-esteem among young readers.

Extensions • Extending books through performances, murals, artwork, and even music helps children deepen their understandings and increase their interpretations of text.

self-correcting. In addition, emergent guided reading groups are led by the teacher to engage in summarizing and/or retelling the text as well as engaging in the beginnings of silent reading. As children enter early fluency, teachers broaden guidance to include an understanding of story structure, characterization, and silent reading. In the final developmental stage, fluency, intermediate, upper elementary, and middle school teachers expand children's strategies and understandings of text to include considerations of genre, reading like a writer (stylistic examinations), literary devices, and dialogue, for example.

Reading with children in guided reading is an essential part of a balanced reading program—one that has been typically lacking in many early reading experiences asso-

Figure 10.7

Meaning: Semantics

Order and Organization: Syntax

Graphophonics: Letter Sounds

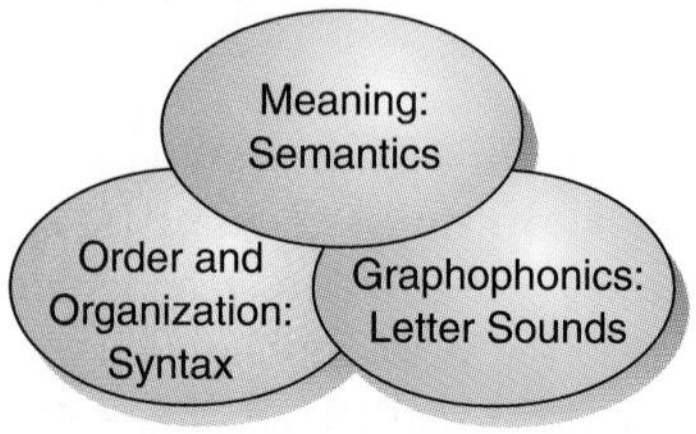

Predicting *Look at the pictures. What do you think the words will tell you?*
Sampling *Look at the print. What do you see? Read it with your (fingers) eyes.*
Confirming *How do you know? Can you show me by pointing and reading it to me?*
Cross Checking & Self Correcting *Does it make sense? Does it sound right? Does it look right?*

Figure 10.8

Teacher questions and comments to guide children to use the four reading cuing strategies

ciated with so-called whole language approaches. Teachers who understand the reading process also know that children learn to read from people, not from programs, materials, or even books, although each of these is important in their own place. Learning to read is a social process motivated primarily by a need to understand and be understood. In view of this, guided reading experiences, when coupled with individual reading conferences (described in Chapter 9) and assessed by the use of running records (described in Chapter 13), ensure that young children will receive the experiences and personal guidance necessary to develop into successful, fluent readers.

Language Experience

The **language experience approach** (LEA) is intended to develop and support children's reading and writing abilities. The essence of this approach is to use children's oral language and personal or vicarious experiences as the basis for creating personalized reading materials. These reading materials typically take the form of group experience charts, individually dictated books, or word banks for storing personal or group-selected high-interest, one-look, key vocabulary words (Ashton-Warner, 1963).

Lamoreaux and Lee (1943) trace the beginnings of the LEA approach to reading and writing instruction of the late 1930s and early 1940s. Another early contributor to the LEA approach was Ashton-Warner (1963), who worked with Maori children in New Zealand. Her approach to LEA, called organic reading, used children's personal words or key vocabulary to teach reading. Holdaway (1979) recommends LEA for early reading instruction because the most predictable text for a child to begin reading is a text transcribed from her oral dictation of a personally meaningful event or experience. Teachers who have used LEA have found that children's dictated stories about these personally important events can be recorded in at least three different ways:

The LEA uses children's oral language and personal experiences as the basis for creating personalized reading materials.

The most predictable text for a child to begin reading is a text transcribed from her oral dictation of a personally meaningful event or experience.

1. The group experience chart
2. The individual language experience story
3. The key vocabulary word bank

Creating the Group Experience Chart   The group experience chart is a means of recording the firsthand or vicarious experiences of an entire group of children. This means, of course, that the entire group of children would have shared an experience in common such as a field trip, a new book read aloud, or the visit of an outside expert on weaving. Although entire groups of children are often involved in the creation of group experience charts, it is also advisable to involve smaller groups of children periodically rather than the entire class to maximize the involvement of individual children. The typical course of events associated with the creation of a group experience chart follows:

1. The children participate in a shared experience.
2. Teachers and children discuss the shared experience.
3. Children dictate the chart, while the teacher transcribes the dictation.
4. Teachers and children share in reading the chart.
5. The chart is used to teach about words and learn other important language concepts.

Focus on why selecting an interesting and stimulating experience or topic for children can spell the success or failure of any LEA activity.

The selection of an interesting and stimulating experience or topic for children can spell the success or failure of any LEA activity. Topics and experiences simply must capture the interest of children to provide the motivation necessary for learning. The following activities, and the one that began this chapter (the science experiment using the balloon, bottle, soda, and vinegar), provide examples of activities for beginning a group experience chart:

• Our mother hamster had babies last night.
• Writing a new version of *The Napping House* (A. Wood, 1984).
• What mountain men did in the old days.
• What we want for Christmas.
• Planning our Valentine's Day party.
• What did Martin Luther King, Jr., do?
• Sometimes I have scary dreams. Once. . . .
• Once I got into trouble for. . . .
• A classmate is ill, make a get-well card from the class.

Discussing the experience or topic carefully can help children assess what they have learned about the topic, can help them make personal connections, and can motivate them to share with others their knowledge, experiences, and personal connections. The teacher should be careful not to dominate the discussion. Asking too many focused questions can turn what would otherwise be an open and exciting discussion into a dull exercise in knowledge interrogation. The teacher's questions should invite children to engage in dialogue rather than to give short, unelaborated responses. Many teachers make the mistake of beginning dictation too early in the discussion. If this is done, the results will reflect a dull, even robotic, recounting of the experience or topic.

Think of three questions that could be asked during a discussion of an LEA group chart that would invite children to engage in dialogue rather than to give short, unelaborated responses.

Imagine a teacher who has read aloud to her class the book *The Polar Express* by Chris Van Allsburg (1985). After inviting children to respond to the book, the teacher asks, "If you had been chosen by Santa to receive the first gift of Christmas, what would you have said?" The teacher calls on individual children to give their responses to the book. After plenty of discussion, she calls on children to respond to the book by dictating aloud their best ideas for responding to this question. The teacher records each child's dictation on the chart. With emergent readers, the teacher may record each child's dictation with different colored markers. The colors help children identify their own dictation more easily in the future. Later, the teacher may write the children's names by their dictation. When the chart is complete, the teacher typically reads the chart aloud to the children while pointing to each word as she reads. After the teacher has read the chart aloud, she invites the children to read along with her a second time. Next, she may ask individual children to read their own responses aloud or invite volunteers to read aloud the responses of other children.

The teacher may read aloud a certain line from the chart and ask for a child to come up to the chart and point to the line the teacher just read aloud. She may copy the lines of the chart on sentence strips and have children pick a sentence strip and match it to the line in the chart. Favorite words in the chart story can be copied onto word cards for matching activities as well. Thus, the text generated by the children for the chart story can be used in subsequent large- and small-group meetings to build the students' sight vocabulary of words in the chart, demonstrate word-recognition strategies, and even help children learn about letter sounds for decoding purposes. The chart also can be copied on a duplicating master and sent home with each child for individual practice.

Creating the Individual Language Experience Story   All children have a story to tell. While group experience charts serve a purpose for the entire group, each child in the classroom has her own set of experiences and as a result her own unique story to tell. The individual language experience story provides an opportunity for children to talk about their experiences and have these experiences recorded. Just as with writing, a steady diet of teacher-initiated topics and experiences used to produce group experience charts ignores the fact that children should be given opportunities to compose for their own purposes. Motivation for topic choices comes from many different sources in the child's life, both in and out of the classroom. Graves (1983) is adamant about the need for children to choose their own topics for writing. Perez (1983) describes composing as an inside-out process that adds justification for encouraging children to choose their own topic for the individual language experience story.

> *The individual experience story provides an opportunity for children to tell their own story and have these experiences recorded.*

We have found that it is helpful to have parent volunteers available when recording individual language experience stories. In our classrooms, we referred to this process as the make-a-book approach. An example appears in Figure 10.9.

We like to notarize individual language experience stories as we did all child-authored books, by placing a card pocket and library card in each child's book. These books can then be placed in the classroom library for other children to read. A story reader's chair or chairs can be designated for encouraging children to read their individual language experience stories aloud to peers in their own classroom and in other classrooms in the school.

A variation of individual language experience stories we particularly liked was shape stories (Figure 10.10). The cover and pages of the dictated individual language experience story is drawn and cut into the shape of the book topic. For example, if a child has just returned from Disneyland, the book might be cut into the shape of Mickey Mouse's head. A trip to Texas might be recorded in a book cut into the shape of the state of Texas. For most young children, no single individual is more important and exciting to talk or read about than themselves. This fact alone explains why individual language experience stories always provide meaningful, predictable stories for children to read: the stories are drawn from each child's own language and personal experiences.

Teaching Vocabulary and Word Recognition Using LEA: The Word Bank   Ashton-Warner (1963), in a book entitled *Teacher*, described how she taught young Maori children to read in New Zealand. With little more than a chalkboard, chalk, black crayons, and a few pieces of paper for word cards, this amazing teacher taught children to read. She believed that vocabulary building and learning to read were essentially very personal. Children needed to have a desire and reason to learn to read. Ashton-Warner also believed that learning to read should be a natural or organic process. Thus, when children had difficulty learning to read the high-frequency sight words typically found in primary basal readers, Ashton-Warner turned to

> *Key vocabulary words can be stored in a box called a word bank.*

Figure 10.9

An example of an individual language experience story: Make a book

asking children which words they wanted to learn to read instead! She found that while children had difficulty learning to recognize words like *come* and *look*, they had little difficulty recognizing their own words such as *knife* and *tigers*. Each day children were asked to come to school with a word they wanted to learn to read. Ashton-Warner listened to the word and wrote it on a card for each child. These key vocabulary words were stored in a box called a *word bank*. Children used these words to compose sentences and stories. They copied these words on the chalkboard, practiced them with peers, and played games with their cards from their word banks.

In our first-grade classrooms, we used two types of word banks with our students. First, we created a personalized word bank for each child. Similar to Ashton-Warner (1963), we asked children to tell us a word they wanted to have in their own word bank on a daily basis. These words were written on cards and stored in a small shoe, cigar, or index box in alphabetical order. Often, two or three children combined their word banks by dumping the word cards on the floor and mixing them together. The object of the game was to sort through the pile of words and find their own word cards again and place them back into their word banks. Children can combine the

Two types of word banks can be used with students: personalized or class word banks.

Figure 10.10

Examples of shape books

words from their own word banks with those of another child to write coauthored or collaborative sentences and stories. Thus, the use of personalized word banks serves several important functions for developing children's reading ability.

- Personalized word banks provide opportunity for children to integrate words from outside the classroom into their learning about reading and writing.
- These words provide repeated, meaningful exposures to a core of highly personal or one-look words.
- These words are used for word games, sentence-building activities, matching, and skill instruction.
- These words provide a reference for children to use during their own writing and spelling.

A second type of word bank we found useful is a class or group word bank. When group experience charts, big books, enlarged text of poems, songs, and the like were read by large or small groups of children, we asked our students to choose several favorite words taken from these sources to place into a group word bank. We took a piece of oak tag card stock and placed it beneath each word selected in the chart or book. While children watched, we copied the word on the word card and placed it into the group word bank. These cards were used later for matching and word-substitution activities, as well as for word-recognition and decoding instruction.

Activities using the group word bank are described in Chapter 7.

Research for many years now has substantiated the fact that the LEA is as effective as basal reader instruction (Bond & Dykstra, 1967; M. A. Hall, 1981). In fact, in a review of studies comparing basal reader instruction and LEA whole-language instruction, Stahl and Miller (1989) found a 0.6 standard deviation advantage for LEA whole-language approaches over basal reading instruction. A similar finding was reported by Reutzel and Cooter (1990) comparing whole-language to basal reader instruction on standardized reading achievement test performance.

Research has shown LEA to be as or more effective than basal reader instruction.

One criticism of LEA is that students will not gain as much vocabulary knowledge as using other approaches. M. A. Hall (1978) refutes this criticism in her review of the literature showing the LEA children acquire vocabulary as well as, if not better than, students taught with other methods. C. Chomsky (1971) also showed that LEA students usually became better spellers than students taught with basal readers. Although LEA is certainly not a panacea, it presents certain advantages that other approaches to reading instruction do not. Typical advantages and disadvantages of LEA are summarized in Figure 10.11.

Using LEA with basal reader instruction is discussed in Chapter 4.

LEA can be adapted and used successfully with basal reader stories. In fact, many current basal readers advocate supplementing the basal reader with language experience activities (Jones & Nessel, 1985; Reimer, 1983).

Reading BY Children

Sustained Silent Reading, or Drop Everything and Read

If children are going to improve as readers, they must have daily time to read as is provided in SSR or DEAR.

An important part of a balanced reading program is the inclusion of reading BY children. Children must be given opportunities to enjoy reading self-selected materials on a regular basis. Sustained silent reading (SSR), or drop everything and read (DEAR), is a structured approach that provides needed regular reading events for

Figure 10.11

Advantages and limitations of the language experience approach

Advantages

1. It enables children to conceptualize reading as "talk written down."
2. It ensures that children will have a background of experiences to bring to reading material.
3. It enables children to read their own language patterns.
4. It has a beneficial motivating effect when used with older disabled readers.
5. It stresses the interrelationships among the four language arts of listening, speaking, reading, and writing.
6. It stresses reading comprehension.
7. It enhances creativity of children.
8. It creates an interest in and love of reading.

Limitations

1. It lacks sequential skill development.
2. It offers little direct guidance for teachers.
3. It lacks vocabulary control.
4. It demands much teacher time (for transcribing stories and individual help).
5. It presupposes a well-equipped room and a rich and motivating classroom environment.
6. It cannot be used as a major method of teaching reading beyond the primary grades.

young children. Hunt (1970) explained that SSR is a structured activity in which children are given regular, fixed-time periods for silently reading self-selected materials. Put differently, SSR is an activity where everyone in the classroom—students, teachers, parents, volunteers—reads silently something they have personally selected for a designated period of time.

The purposes of SSR are grounded in the belief that anyone—children or adults—gets better at anything they practice regularly. We believe that the more children read, the more they will learn about the process of becoming a successful reader. R. Allington (1977) once raised the question, "If they don't read much, how they ever gonna get good?" Other purposes for engaging in SSR include encouraging children to read voluntarily material they have selected for enjoyment or information. To help children derive greater purpose and understanding from SSR, we display a chart much like the following (D. Spiegel, 1981).

> We will learn to enjoy reading more and try a variety of reading materials.
>
> We will learn about new places, new faces, and new ideas.
>
> We will get better at reading and learn to concentrate while reading.

McCracken and McCracken (1978) describe several positive reasons for implementing an SSR or DEAR classroom reading-by-children program:

- Reading books is important. Children come to understand what teachers value by taking note of what they are asked to do.
- Anyone can read a book. Readers with special needs do not feel singled out for attention when they engage in reading or looking at a book during SSR.
- Children learn that reading is interacting with an author through sustained engagement with a self-selected text.
- Children develop the ability to remain on task for an extended period of time during SSR.
- Books were meant to be read in large chunks for extended periods of time. Children may get the wrong idea that reading is done during small segments of time and focus on short texts such as those often found in basal readers.
- Comprehension is improved through SSR activities (Reutzel & Hollingsworth, 1991c).
- Finally, children learn to judge the appropriateness of the materials they select for reading during SSR. Timion commented that her first-grade students remarked, "choosing the books was the hardest part of learning to read" (1992, p. 204).

Notice at least four reasons for implementing a daily reading time.

Implementing an SSR program is a relatively straightforward process:

1. *Designate a specific daily time for reading.* Teachers have found that three time slots work well for SSR. The first is as children enter the classroom first thing in the morning. The second is following lunch or recess. And the third is right before children go home for the day. Typically, teachers allocate about 15 to 20 minutes per day for SSR. For younger children, teachers might begin with a 10-minute SSR time and lengthen this time throughout the year as children indicate a desire for more time. We have found that a cooking timer with a bell is a welcome addition for younger children so they do not become worried about watching the clock.

List the steps for implementing an effective SSR or DEAR classroom program.

2.   *Hold a procedural minilesson to describe the rules of SSR.* To set the stage for successful experiences with SSR, we suggest that teachers conduct a brief lesson on the rules and expectations associated with SSR time. Begin by stating the purposes of SSR shown previously. Second, review with children the rules for participation in SSR. We have found that enlarging these rules and placing them on a chart for the class helps students take responsibility for their own behavior. Finally, explain how students can ready themselves for this time each day. The rules for SSR are shown in Figure 10.12 in chart form.

3.   *Extend the experience through sharing.* Children can be asked to share their books with other students at the conclusion of SSR through a "say something" or "turn to your neighbor" activity. In addition to these informal share sessions, groups of children may organize a response to a book through art, drama, writing, or musical performances to be shared with others. In any case, beginning an SSR program with young children, even in kindergarten, convinces children of the value of reading and gives them important practice time. Clearly, SSR has the potential to help children develop life-long reading enjoyment and habits.

Reader's Theater and Dramatizations

In reader's theater, emphasis is placed on presenting an interpretation of literature read in dramatic style for an audience who imagines setting and actions.

Reader's theater is an effective and enjoyable strategy for developing oral reading fluency among young children. In reader's theater, children practice reading from a script and then share their oral interpretations with classmates and selected audiences (Hill, 1990b; Sloyer, 1982). Unlike for a play, students do not memorize lines, practice actions, or use elaborate stage sets to make their presentation. Instead, emphasis is placed on presenting an interpretation of literature read in a dramatic style for an audience who imagines setting and actions.

List three criteria for selecting texts to be read in reader's theater productions.

Easy texts are selected for reader's theater with young readers and should be drawn from tales originating from the oral tradition, poetry, or quality picture books designed to be read aloud. In some cases, information texts such as *The Popcorn Book* (dePaola, 1978) and *The Magic School Bus Lost in the Solar System* (Cole, 1990) may be used as reader's theater practice scripts (Young & Vardell, 1993). Selections should be packed with action, have an element of suspense, and comprise an entire meaningful story or episode. Also, texts selected for use in reader's theater should contain sufficient dialogue to make reading and preparing the text a challenge and involve several students as characters. A few examples of such texts include Mar-

Figure 10.12

The rules for sustained silent reading (SSR)

- Children must select their own books or reading materials.
- Changing books during sustained silent reading (SSR) is discouraged to avoid interruptions.
- Each individual in the classroom is expected to read silently without interruption during the fixed period of time for SSR.
- The teacher and other visitors in the classroom are expected to read silently materials of their own choosing as well.
- Children are not expected to make reports or answer teacher questions about the books they have been reading during SSR.

Drama helps deepen students' appreciation and enjoyment of their reading experiences.

tin and Archambault's *Knots on a Counting Rope* (1987), Viorst's *Alexander and the Terrible Horrible No Good Very Bad Day* (1972), and Barbara Robinson's *The Best Christmas Pageant Ever* (1972).

Minimal props are used in reader's theater. Masks, hats, or simple costumes can be used. If a story is selected for reading, students are assigned to read a character's part. If poems are selected for reader's theater, students may read alternating lines or groups of lines. *Reader's theater in-the-round*, where readers stand around the perimeter of the room and the audience is in the center surrounded by the readers, is a fun and interesting variation for both performers and audience.

Young or inexperienced readers will often benefit from a discussion before the first reading of a reader's theater script. This discussion is designed to help them make connections between their own background experiences and the text to be read. Also, young children benefit from listening to a previously recorded performance of the text as an oral language model before the initial reading of the script.

Hennings (1974) described a simplified procedure for preparing reader's theater scripts for classroom performance. First, the text to be performed is read silently by the individual students. Second, the text is read again orally, sometimes using choral reading in a group. After the second reading, children either choose their parts, or the teacher assigns parts to the children. We suggest that students be allowed to select their three most desired parts, write these choices on a slip of paper, and submit them to the teacher, and that teachers do everything possible to assign one of these three choices. The third reading is also an oral reading with students reading their parts with scripts in hand. Students may have several rehearsal readings as they prepare for the final reading or performance in front of the class or a selected audience.

The School Library

Our librarians always seemed to have a magical way with children. Their secret was their knowledge of books children loved! When it was announced that it was time to visit the library, our students snapped to attention. They were always anxious to hear the new story our librarian, Mrs. Harmer, would read. But better yet, they were anxious to spend uninterrupted time browsing through the shelves of books that captured their imagination and interest.

The school library and librarian should be a focal point for teachers, parents, and early readers.

The school library and librarian should be a focal point for teachers, parents, and early readers. In cooperation with the school librarian, a monthly newsletter could be sent home announcing new library acquisitions to parents and children while inviting both parents and children to make better use of the school library. In this newsletter, two or three of the new books could be highlighted for parents and children. For special occasions such as holidays, the newsletter may feature books about Halloween, Thanksgiving, Hanukkah, or Christmas.

Because teachers are often too busy to keep up on the newest myriad of children's books published, school librarians may be asked to present selected books at school faculty meetings. A children's choices book list from the school library could be published annually and made available to teachers and parents. By keeping teachers and parents better informed, librarians open the world of books to their patrons.

Parents and teachers should make sure each child uses the school library regularly. Beyond this, parents should be encouraged to take their children to the community library and acquire a library card for each of their children. A letter home from teachers and the school librarian to parents encouraging library visits as a family activity will contribute much to helping young children develop life-long library habits. Library visits also provide a setting for children to learn about book-selection strategies. Teachers, parents, and librarians can assist children in selecting books by brainstorming interests with them and by teaching children fundamental library skills such as using the card catalogue system. It is important to remember that children learn to use the library by using the library—frequently! In spite of busy school-day schedules, regular visits to the library should not be crowded out. Children should visit the school library at least twice weekly, and more often if possible. Libraries, if properly integrated into the school reading program, will become busy hubs of activity where children read for enjoyment and pleasure and a place where librarians, parents, and teachers share a love of books with their children and students.

Balanced Literacy Programs: Writing TO, WITH, and BY Young Children

The major elements of balanced writing programs include those listed in Figure 10.13. Beneath each major element heading, specific instructional practices are listed.

Figure 10.13

The major elements of balanced writing programs

Writing TO Children

- Dialogue Journals
- Message Boards

Writing WITH Children

- Shared Writing Experience
- Language Experience Approach
- Traveling Tales

Writing BY Children

- Journals
- Post Office Letter Writing
- Pocketbooks
- Reading Logs

Writing TO Children

Dialogue Journals

Writing TO children motivates both reading and writing development. Young children enjoy receiving written notes, letters, invitations, and so on from peers, but they particularly value receiving written communication from their teachers. In this spirit, we have found *dialogue journals* to be useful in sparking a written conversation between teachers and children in the early grades. Gambrell (1985) describes the use of dialogue journals as a number of steps, as outlined in Figure 10.14.

Dialogue journals form a perfect link between reading and writing while offering a direct and natural way for teachers to write TO their children. Teachers who have used dialogue journals have found them to be effective but also time-consuming. Gambrell (1985) suggests that teachers not try to write to the entire class but rather select a smaller group of children with whom they can communicate. In our experience, we have found that children are willing to write daily in their dialogue journals and also seem to be willing to accept an occasional but regular response from the teacher. For instance, we have responded to 20% to 25% of the children's daily journal entries each day to ameliorate the problem of having to respond to the entire class.

Dialogue journals form a perfect link between reading and writing while offering a direct and natural way for teachers to write TO their children.

Message Board

Children like to receive notes from their teachers. One means for communicating with a classroom of children is to display a message board that is set aside for writing notes to children. The notes left on the message center are compliments, comments, directions, and the like. These notes are often brief, and many children consult these notes at the beginning or throughout the school day. Our students enjoyed writing and reading responses to books posted in the book message center.

Figure 10.14

Steps in implementing dialogue journals with young children

1. Each day, children write something about an interest, concern, or experience.
2. Each day, the teacher responds to the child's journal entry by commenting, asking questions, and encouraging the children to continue their journal writing.
3. Use a bound composition book or other similarly bound writing book.
4. To start children writing, talk about how people write letters to one another. Describe how they write to you, and you write to them.
5. If children have a difficult time getting started, you may want to suggest some topics such as favorite foods, after-school activities, etc. You may also want want to provide stimulus sentence leads such as, "My favorite thing to do after school is. . . ."
6. Set aside about 10 to 15 minutes daily time for writing and reading in the dialogue journals.
7. Do not correct children's mechanical or grammatical errors, because dialogue journals are intended to encourage open communication. If children use incorrect mechanics or grammar, model the correct uses in your response.
8. Use comments in your responses that encourage children to write, e.g., "Tell me more about when . . ." or "you didn't answer my question last time about. . . ."
9. Children should be told that the information in the dialogue journal is private, just between the two of you.
10. If you or the children want to share information with others, each should ask the other for permission to share.

Adapted from "Dialogue Journals: Reading-Writing Instruction" by L. B. Gambrell, 1985, *The Reading Teacher, 38*(6), pp. 512–515. Copyright 1985 by the International Reading Association.

Writing WITH Children

Shared Writing Experience

Shared writing experiences develop writing strategies and expand options and modes of authorship.

Shared writing is an important part of a balanced writing program. The notion of shared writing in a balanced writing program focuses on exposing children to and writing WITH children a broad variety of potential writing genres to expand their horizons of authorship beyond that of stories, poems, and reports. Thus, the purposes of shared writing are

- To develop writing strategies
- To expand children's options and modes of authorship

In Figure 10.15 we list the various types of text that teachers and children may want to consider together during shared writing. These activities apply not just to early readers but to children across the grades.

Because children love big books,they want to write their own.

One example of shared writing in our classrooms focused on the production of big books. Because children love **big books**, it was not long before they wanted to write their own in our classrooms (Figure 10.16). We began responding to reading a big book by rewriting it as a whole group. During group discussions following the reading of a big book, we invited children to invent a different story line or problem based on the story in the big book. For example, after finishing reading the big book *Hubert Hunts His Hum* (Lock, 1980), we rewrote it as *Hubert Hunts His Hat.* Chil-

Figure 10.15

Writing activities across the grades

Personal		Public
1. Notes	34. Couplets	1. Maps
2. Friendly Letters	35. Triplets	2. Business Letters
3. Lists	36. Quatrain	3. Teachers to Administrators
4. Tasks	37. Cinquain	4. Notes from Teachers to Parents
5. Goals	38. Haiku	5. Resumes
6. Shopping Lists	39. Sonnets	6. Orders
7. Christmas	40. Limericks	7. Contracts
8. Wish Lists	41. Free Verse	8. Collection Notices
9. Labels	42. Tanka	9. Bills
10. Boxes	43. Septolet	10. Recommendations
11. Objects	44. Lantern	11. Promotional Letters
12. Clothing	45. Diamante	12. Instructional Letters
13. Treasure Hunt Clues	46. Messages	13. Birth Announcements
14. Assignments	47. Phone	14. Research Reports
15. Cards	48. Warning	15. Public Notices
16. Get Well	49. Information	16. Obituaries
17. Greeting	50. Family Management–Budgets	17. Newspapers
18. Holiday	51. Scrapbooks	18. Magazines
19. Sympathy	52. Baby Books	19. Books
20. Thank You	53. Travel Itineraries	20. Scripts
21. Romance	54. Applications	21. Musical Lyrics
22. Change of Address	55. Credit Cards	22. Critiques
23. Want Ads	56. Job	23. Evaluations
24. Interviews	57. Social Security	24. Tax Forms
25. Instructions	58. College Scholarships	25. Eulogies
26. Newsletters	59. Pagent	26. Court Orders
27. Postcards	60. Loan	27. Summons
28. Journals	61. Grants	28. Speeches
29. Dialogue Journal	62. Checks	29. Pamphlets
30. Graffiti		30. Wanted Posters
31. Diaries		31. Posters
32. Job Charts		32. Lesson Plans
33. Poems		33. Informational

dren contributed ideas for rewriting the big book as a group. We wrote these ideas on the blank pages of an empty big book. Later during the day, children illustrated a page for the book.

Later during the year, children, often in pairs, rewrote or condensed stories they had heard or read on their own into a big book to be shared with others. Older children (grades 2 and 3) were often invited to read their big books to younger children in the kindergarten and first grades. These coauthored big books were a popular way for our students to respond to their reading and to share their responses with others, and we were impressed with our student's interpretations and variations of the original stories they had read.

Figure 10.16

Child-authored big book

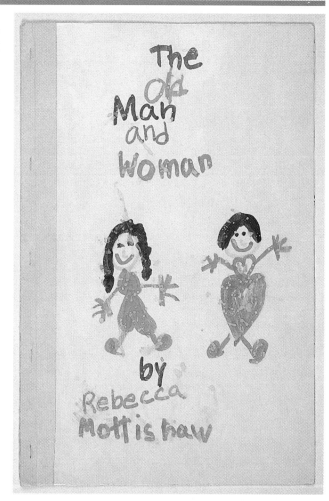

Language Experience Approach

For young writers, the process of composing is much less taxing than is the process of transcribing thoughts into the written code. Young children, by the time they enter school, are fairly adept at expressing thoughts through oral language. The LEA encourages teachers to capitalize on children's strengths by tapping into their ability to manipulate and compose using oral language. As described earlier, children use oral language and the assistance of others to orally collect interesting words in a word bank and to compose both group charts and individual stories. Using oral composition as a springboard, teachers can encourage children to write those very things they have seen written from their oral language. In other words, children can begin to watch for words they want to add to their word banks. Blank cards can be made available for children to copy these words from environmental displays and from books and other texts. Children can form authoring teams to work on producing a group experience chart to be shared with other children in the classroom. They can work together to make signs, captions, labels, or directions for objects and events that transpire in their classroom. Many children will choose to write for themselves when they see their dictation recorded and their art work come together in a book or story. In short, LEA exposes children to printed language in relevant, functional ways to promote curiosity about print that leads to selecting writing as an appealing, independent activity. Examples of LEA stories produced by first-graders are shown in Figure 10.17.

Traveling Tales

The traveling tales backpack (Figure 10.18) can be used to involve parents with their children in responding to books or stories through writing together (Reutzel & Fawson, 1990; Yellin & Blake, 1994). This traveling tales backpack is filled with writing media and guidelines for parents in working with their children at home to produce a written response to a favorite book. The contents of the backpack include:

A traveling tales backpack is used to involve parents with their children in writing together by including a short description of the writing process as well as a host of writing media.

Plain unlined paper	Scissors
Lined paper	Small stapler
Construction paper—multiple colors	Staples
Letter stencils	Brass fasteners
Drawing paper	Card stock
Poster paper	Hole punch
Crayons	Yarn
Watercolors	Wallpaper for book covers
Water-base markers	Glue stick
Colored pencils	Tape
Pencils	Paper clips
Felt-tip pens	Ruler
Felt-tip calligraphy pens	

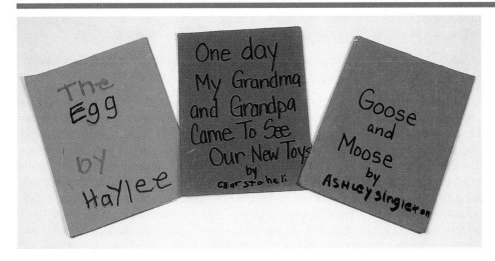

Figure 10.17

Examples of LEA stories produced by first-graders

Figure 10.18

Traveling tales backpack

The backpack is sent home with an individual child for two nights. Parents are contacted by phone or note before the backpack is sent home to maximize involvement and success. Parents and children can choose a variety of ways to respond to their favorite book: They can write shape stories, pocketbooks, accordion books, or cards. Included in the traveling tales backpack is a letter (Figure 10.19) to the parents with guidelines on how to engage their child in the writing process.

After completing the project, parent and child are invited to share their work with the entire group of children in the author's chair at school. After sharing, the written product is placed on display for the other children to read and enjoy.

Writing BY Children

One of the more effective applications of the writing process is through literature response activities. Readers deepen and extend their interpretation and understanding of stories when they respond in writing. Although writing should never be thought of as the only way to respond to a story, it certainly should be considered an effective and enjoyable alternative to discussion. In fact, discussions are often more productive when students have responded to their reading through writing. Writing encourages students to reflect on their insights and interpretations gained from reading as well as to reflect on the processes they used during reading to arrive at their interpretations. Also, writing about reading helps students become better readers. Calkins (1986) has said that writing helps children become insiders on the reading process. By constructing their own texts, children develop insights into how authors write. They begin to read other texts through the eyes of an author, noticing structure, sequence, and style. In this way, children become better readers because they are writers. Although the list of possible ways to respond to reading in writing is almost endless, we have selected several ways to respond to reading in writing that we have found to be successful when used with younger children.

Classroom Post Office for Letter Writing

A variation of the book message center is a classroom post office. Children like to write letters to each other, the teacher, and principal. We encouraged our students to write letters to their peers, the teacher, or a principal when they had read a particularly interesting book and wanted to share it with others. We set up a post office station with a slot for "in-class" and "out-of-class" mail. Children are invited to send letters about books they have read to students, faculty, and staff in the school. One student is selected to serve as post master and another as mail carrier. These responsibilities are rotated on a weekly basis to allow all children to participate in these roles. The post master sorts mail by classroom and fills the mail carrier's bag. The mail carriers take letters to the classrooms of other teachers and children as well as to the librarian and the principal. Teachers, staff members, students, and the principal enjoy reading the information about books, poems, and stories shared with them through the classroom post offices.

A classroom post office can be set up for students to write letters to their peers, the teacher, or a principal when they read a particularly interesting book and want to share it with others.

Wordless Picture Books

The wordless picture book is a relatively new arrival in the world of picture books (D. Norton, 1995). In these books, the illustrations tell the entire story. Wordless picture books offer teachers and children opportunities to compose their own print to accompany the pictures. Using wordless picture books in this fashion is much like using the LEA. Norton (1995, p. 220) offers several hints for selecting wordless picture books for sharing and instruction.

In wordless picture books, the illustrations tell the entire story.

- Do the pictures follow a sequentially organized plot?
- Is the depth of detail appropriate for the children's age levels?
- Do the children have enough experiential background to interpret the illustrations?
- Is the size of the book appropriate for group sharing?
- Is the subject one that will appeal to children?

Wordless picture books are ideal for involving children in oral composing and dictating stories. For example, the teacher may select the Caldecott Award-winning wordless picture book *Noah's Ark* (Spier, 1977) or *Just in Passing* (Bonners, 1989), physically cut it apart, and temporarily mount the pages on separate pieces of chart paper or place them inside an acetate story frame board. In addition to using wordless picture books for oral composing, books with illustrations on one page and words on the other may be used much like wordless picture books.

One disadvantage of the story frame board is the fact that two copies of the book are needed to display both sides of the pages. This disadvantage is offset, however, by the advantage of providing protection for the pictures in the book as well as the ease of clean up and use (Figure 10.20). A water-based pen can be used to record children's dictation on the acetate sheets of the story frame board and cleaned off with water and a dry rag. Chart paper is a little less easy to use and provides less protection for the original pages of the book.

Figure 10.19

Traveling tales parent
letter

From "Traveling Tales: Connecting Parents and Children
in Writing," by D. R. Reutzel
and P. C. Fawson, 1990, *The
Reading Teacher, 44,* pp.
222–227. Copyright 1990 by
the International Reading
Association. Reprinted by permission of D. Ray Reutzel and
the International Reading
Association.

Dear Parent(s):

Writing activities provided at home can have a great influence on your child's reading and writing development. Traveling Tales is a backpack that includes a variety of writing materials for use by you and your child. As per our conversation, we encourage you to work together cooperatively with your child to create a story that will be shared at school. *Please avoid competition or trying to outdo others.*

Your child has been given this backpack for two nights. If you need more time, please call us at XXX–XXXX. Otherwise, we will be looking forward to you and your child returning the Traveling Tales backpack in 2 days.

We would like to suggest some guidelines that may help you have a successful and enjoyable Traveling Tales experience with your child.

1.   Help your child brainstorm a list of ideas or topics by asking questions that will invite him or her to express ideas, interests, feelings, etc., about which he or she may wish to write. Stories about personal experiences (factual or fictional), information stories that tell of an area that your child finds interesting, biographies of family members or others, and stories of science or history are possible topics.

2.   After selecting a topic, help your child decide which of the writing materials included in the Traveling Tales backpack he or she will need to use to create his or her story. Suggest that the story may take several different forms. Some ideas include (1) poetry, (2) fold-out books, (3) puppet plays, (4) pocket books, (5) backward books, and (6) shape books.

3.   Help your child think through or rehearse the story before beginning writing. You may wish to write down some of the ideas your child expresses for him or her to use in writing the first draft.

4.   Remember, your child's first draft is a rough draft. It may contain misspellings, poor handwriting, and incomplete ideas. This should be expected. Be available to answer questions as your child works on the first draft. Be careful to encourage him or her to keep writing and not worry about spelling, punctuation, etc. Tell him or her to just do his or her best and both of you can work on correctness later. *This is the idea development stage of writing.*

5.   Once the first draft is completed, try to involve others in the household by asking them to listen to the first draft read aloud. Reading one's writing aloud helps

---

*Descriptions dictated by the
children can be written
beneath wordless picture
book pages on the chart or
on the story frame board.*

When the teacher introduces a wordless picture book like *Noah's Ark* (Spier, 1977), children and the teacher can begin by looking carefully at each picture in the book. They may discuss what they think is happening in each of the pictures. After this initial discussion, individual children may be called on to describe the events in a particular picture. The descriptions dictated by the children can be written beneath the wordless picture book pages on the chart or on the story frame board. The text of

writers determine the sensibility of the message. Be sure to tell those who are invited to listen to be encouraging rather than critical. Ask questions about ideas that were unclear or were poorly developed. Questions help a writer think about his or her writing without feeling defensive.

6.   Write down the questions and suggestions made by the home audience. Talk with your child about how a second draft could use these suggestions to make the story easier to understand or more exciting. Remember to be supportive and encouraging! Offer your help, but encourage your child to make his or her best efforts first.

7.   After the second draft is completed, your child may wish to read his or her writing to the family group again. If so, encourage it. If not, it is time to edit the writing. Now is the time to correct spellings, punctuation, etc. Praise your child for his or her attempts and tell him or her you want to help make his or her writing the best it can be. Show your child which words are misspelled and why. Do the same with punctuation and capitalization.

8.   With the editing complete, the writing is ready to be revised for the final time. When your child writes the final draft, encourage him or her to use neat handwriting as a courtesy to the reader. Feel free to help your child at any point as he or she makes final revisions.

9.   Once finished, encourage the members of your family or household to listen to the final story. This practice will instill confidence in your child as he or she shares his or her writing at school.

10. We cordially invite you to come to school with your child, if possible, to share the writing you have done together. Your child will appreciate the support, and we would like to talk with you.

Thank you for your help. We appreciate your involvement. If you have an interesting or special experience and are unable to come to school with your child, we would appreciate hearing about these. Please call us or send a note with your child. We will be glad to call back or visit with you. Thanks again for your support. We hope you enjoyed your experiences!

these dictated wordless picture book stories can be used for instruction in many of the same ways as the LEA group experience charts and big books.

Pocketbooks

For many years now, we have known that young children prefer small, soft-bound paperback books. Lowery and Grafft (1967) speculated that the improved attitudes

Figure 10.20

Artist's drawing of a story frame board

Pocketbooks are small books about 3½ inches wide by 4 inches long with condensed reproductions of a story or book.

of children who were given paperback books to read may be attributed to the size—thin books that could be read in a single sitting—and the coverings, which made books soft and easy to handle. Thus, we shared with our students another written response to books or stories they had read—the pocketbook. These books are 3½ inches wide and 4 inches long, with condensed reproductions of a story or book that has been read aloud as a whole group or in a small group. In spite of the small size, children enjoy making illustrations for these books. Pocketbooks are small enough to fit in students' and teachers' pockets. Children often swap their pocketbooks with other students. Through swapping pocketbooks, children become acquainted with a wide variety of books available for reading in the school and classroom libraries.

Teachers can use pocketbooks as rewards for outstanding individual achievements. Rather than giving out stickers or candy, teachers can reward children with a pocketbook from the teacher's pocket. Children enjoy pocketbooks as a means of responding in writing to their reading. An unexpected outcome of writing, sharing, and swapping pocketbooks among our students was an increased desire to read and write. Examples appear in Figure 10.21.

Reading Response Logs and Journals

One of many ways to invite children to respond to their reading of books is to use a reading log or journal. No particular format is required for these journals. For young children, we suggest that reading logs and journals be very open-ended by including unlined paper. In so doing, children can register their meanings for their reading through both drawing and writing. Reading logs and journals should be bound and the date for each entry should be registered. If each morning is begun by reviewing the calendar, day, and date, children can copy this information from a display in the classroom. As a counting activity, children can number the pages in their journals/logs from 1 to 10 and beyond. Early in the year, journal entries should be regular but not necessarily daily.

Reading response logs or journals are open-ended invitations to register one's feelings about a book in drawing, writing, or both.

Establishing Daily Reading and Writing Routines for Young Children

Children develop a sense of security when the school day revolves around an established daily routine. Many teachers rely heavily on basal readers for providing reading instruction. The reading lessons found in basal readers usually follow the format of the directed reading activity (DRA) authored by Betts (1946). The six-step format of the DRA offers an instructional scaffolding or structure for providing reading instruction. Although the DRA is one way of designing reading instruction, an alternative and effective scaffolding for structuring early reading instruction is called **language routines** (LRs). Language routines have been used extensively and successfully in New Zealand, Australia, and Canada.

Language routines provide an alternative organizational framework to the basal readers' directed reading activity.

Language routines are specific, short, teacher-organized language learning opportunities. In transitional and balanced literacy classrooms, teachers who use language routines establish a variety of subroutines for sharing language and literature with children. Although basal reader instruction often focuses on skill instruction, transitional and balanced literacy reading instruction focus on processing and responding to connected, meaningful language that naturally engages the interests of children.

Don Holdaway (1984) describes LRs for working with young children that have undergone years of extensive field testing by teachers in Australia, New Zealand, the United States, and Canada. An outline of adapted routines is found in Figure 10.22.

Figure 10.21

Children's pocketbooks

Figure 10.22

A whole-language lesson guide for reading instruction

Tune-In

(10% of allocated reading time or about 10 min.)

Enjoyment of favorite poems, songs, and jingles, displayed on enlarged text and chosen by request. There is likely to be a new piece for the day or a new activity, such as actions, for an old familiar piece.

Practices: Singing songs, poems, jingles, riddles, movement stories, puppetry, stories, chants, choral readings, naming, word rubber banding, playing with words and letters, dictations, etc.

Old Favorites

(10% of allocated reading time or about 10 min.)

The children choose an old favorite story, chart, poem, etc., which they have enjoyed in the enlarged format. Cloze and masking can be used to encourage predictions. Words and letters can also be discussed.

Practices: Shared book experience, group language experience approach (LEA) charts, overhead transparencies of poems or stories, and readers' theater scripts.

Learning About Language

(15% of allocated reading time or about 15 min.)

During this very brief period, something useful in decoding the new story today will be taught or something previously taught will be reviewed.

Practices: Minilessons on decoding, strategy instructions, drastic strategy, word rubber banding, predicting, brainstorming, mapping, webbing, organizing, zip cloze, etc.

Adapted from *Stability and Change in Literary Learning* (pp. 44–46) by D. Holdaway, 1984, Portsmouth, NH: Heinemann Educational Books. Copyright 1984 by Heinemann Educational Books.

Tune-In

Tune-in is a time for teachers to help children focus on language and acquaint them with the daily language learning opportunities.

Each school day is begun by warming children up or tuning them into language. The **tune-in routine** is a time for teachers to help children focus on language and acquaint them with the language learning opportunities for the day. Young children and teachers participate in reading poems, jingles, chants, word games, or singing songs for fun and instruction. Often, teachers select songs and chants to support specific reading instructional goals, such as learning the alphabet, recognizing words, and understanding letter–sound relationships. Gaming with language is also common during the tune-in routine. For example, using Sniglets (R. Hall, 1984) can be an intriguing way to help children to tune in to language. *Sniglets* are words that are not found in the dictionary but should be. For example, the Sniglet for the burnt, black rice krispy in the box of puffed rice cereal is a *rice roach.*

Pundles (Nash & Nash, 1980) can help children find enjoyment in exploring and playing with language. Can you tell what this Pundle means: iriigihiti? Look carefully. Can you see it represents the common phrase "right between the eyes"? Riddles and jokes are also very useful resources for sharing during the tune-in routine. (Many of these classroom-tested resources for tune-in are listed in the appendix, "Resources for Teachers.")

New Story

(10% to 15% of allocated reading time or about 10 to 15 min.)

Introducing a new story, generally in an enlarged format, or composing a new story from an old favorite.

Practices: Shared book experience, group LEA charts, and overheads of new books, poems, songs, etc.

Independent Reading and Writing

(50% of allocated reading and writing time, or about 50 min.)

This is the reason for all of the previous activity. Children and the environment are now ready for independent involvement and output activities. This period can be subdivided into two periods of reading and writing, for ease of administration.

Practices: Logo language, reading nook sustained silent reading (SSR), read-along tapes, older with younger, word banks (key vocabulary), paired reading, reading conferences, the writing workshop, drama center.

Reading Period: Logo language, reading nook, SSR, read-along tapes, older children reading with younger, word banks (key vocabulary), assisted reading, individual reading conferences, story corners, performances, and small-group strategy lessons.

Writing Period: Writing workshop, minilessons, peer conferences, editing, revising, publishing, authors' chairs, sustained silent writing (SSW) projects.

Closing Sharing Time

(5% of allocated reading time or about 5 min.)

Students share books they have read or writing projects published.

The teacher should enlarge any printed material selected for tune-in (poems, chants, songs, etc.) so that the entire group of children can read the print. Enlarging a text can be accomplished in any number of ways. If the text of a poem, song, or joke is to be used only a few times, the chalkboard may be used. If a text is to be used again and again, however, we suggest using a large chart or tablet displayed on an easel. With frequent use, these charts may become torn and frayed around the edges. To prevent this, 2-inch-wide library cellophane tape can be placed around the edges of each page on the tablet or charts. To provide easy access on later occasions, we also suggest that the first page or two of the chart or tablet be used as a table of contents. Tablets and charts may be read again and again by individuals or small groups of children during another LR called *independent output activities*.

Another means for enlarging the text of books, poems, or songs is to transcribe and place the text on overhead transparencies. Short books can be photocopied on overhead transparencies. From teacher experiences, children do not seem to enjoy the use of transparency texts and books as much as teacher-produced charts or big books.

When using the tune-in routine to introduce new songs, poems, or chants on a daily basis, teachers conscientiously provide time for expanding children's literary horizons while fanning the fires of language enjoyment. Because tune-in activities take place as a whole class, we have also found that the risks associated with learn-

Printed material selected for tune-in (poems, chants, songs, etc.) should be enlarged by the teacher so that the print can be read by the entire group of children.

ing to read become minimized while simultaneously children are rewarded with highly successful, motivating, and supportive language learning opportunities.

Old Favorites

The use of favorite books and "read it again" was one of the principles for creating effective language learning environments mentioned in Chapter 1.

The **old-favorite language routine** provides daily time to return to and reread favorite enlarged texts of songs, poems, chants, and books for enjoyment or to deepen understanding. In this way, the old-favorite routine provides children with massive and regular practice of familiar texts.

Because old-favorite books have been read for enjoyment on previous occasions, Holdaway (1981) suggests that this may be an appropriate time for deepening understanding of the reading process and for teaching the skills and strategies associated with reading in the context of a familiar book. When focusing on skills, caution should be exercised not to isolate skill instruction from a meaningful context if at all possible. In the Wellington, New Zealand, handbook for teachers entitled *Reading in Junior Classes* (Department of Education, 1985), teachers are told:

*The **old-favorite language routine** provides daily time to return to and reread favorite texts.*

> Children, learning to read, have to pay particular attention to print. It is sometimes necessary, then, to have them focus on detail. They may temporarily isolate, for example, a letter, and identify the sound usually associated with it. But any learning of separate items needs to be combined with other items of information, both in the text and in the reader, before its use is truly understood and applied. Separate items of learning need to be *taken back into reading,* i.e., teachers should ensure that any item which has been isolated for attention should be looked at again in its original context, and what has been learned applied later in other contexts. (Department of Education, 1985, p. 32)

A big book is an enlarged standard-sized trade book.

Helping children learn about the parts of a book and the way in which print functions can be explored within the pages of a big book. As mentioned, a big book is an enlargement of a standard-sized trade book. Teachers may begin book and print concept instruction by pointing out the front and back of a big book. Also, when the teacher points to the print during reading, children learn how the print moves in a linear direction from left to right and from top to bottom on a page. Recent research has shown that children learn as much about the concepts of printed language, such as directionality, or line movement, from this type of contextualized and natural demonstration in a big book as they do from isolated, direct instruction lessons on book parts and print directions (Reutzel, Oda, & Moore, 1989).

Using self-adhesive notes to cover up or mask selected words in a big book can encourage children to give careful attention to using context clues. Interesting words in big books can be copied from the book on cards and stored in a class word bank for later practice by children.

Techniques for helping children develop word-recognition and phonic skills are described in detail in Chapter 8.

Children's understanding of books can be deepened through dramatization. A favorite book may be dramatized as a play. Puppet plays are particularly exciting for young children. Children can role play parts of a story or certain characters. In the story "The Little Red Hen," a group of children might be given a stick puppet for each character—the dog, the cat, the goose, and the little red hen. When repetitive parts of a story are read, such as, " 'Not I,' said the . . . " the group of children given stick puppets for that character is prompted to hold them up and join in a unison or choral reading of that part of the book. Also, favorite stories can be turned into reader's theater scripts for dramatizing a story with minimum props. Rehearsing for a dramatization provides additional opportunities for reading practice. Thus, the old-favorites routine provides a time and a context for massive practice of favorite books and texts as well as time for teaching reading strategies and skills in the familiar context of a favorite book or text.

Learning About Language

Holdaway describes the **learning about language** routine as a time for teaching a "very brief skill lesson" (1984, p. 36). Such a skill lesson should not be an isolated skill and drill lesson; rather, it should be a short lesson provided in a meaningful situational and language context. Calkin's (1986) idea of a minilesson seems to have been created with a similar purpose in mind. For example, a teacher who wishes to teach her children about the alphabet may involve them in chants, games, rhymes, and songs emphasizing certain letter names. Children may be asked to bring environmental print to school, such as soda can logos, cereal box covers, and candy wrappers. These wrappers may be put into alphabet letter categories using beginning letter sounds. A group of *S* environmental print logos could be bound together on 5 by 7-inch index cards to help children learn about the *S* letter name and sound.

*The **learning about language** routine is a time for teaching a very brief skill lesson.*

Other learning about language lessons may center on pointing out and discussing the role of punctuation marks in enlarged print. Favorite words selected from familiar books can be placed on cards to be stored in a class word bank to teach word-recognition skills. The learning about language routine may also be an appropriate time to share and discuss various forms and genres of writing with children, such as notes, letters, books, cards, posters, fairy tales, and folktales, as well as to provide brief minilessons on handwriting, writing conventions and mechanics (i.e., punctuation, capitalization, spelling, etc.). The learning about language routine can be used to present and review the writing process approach to writing including drafting, conferencing, editing, and publishing. Most important, teachers should remember that when skill lessons for reading and writing are provided, four criteria should be considered and met if at all possible:

See Chapter 11 for a discussion of the writing process.

- The lesson should grow out of an observed need or desire to enrich children's literacy horizons and not just to teach the next skill on the basal or district skill list.
- A minilesson is not a maxilesson and as such should be brief—5 to 10 minutes maximum.
- The skill selected for instruction should be one that helps young children read better and with greater enjoyment. Lessons focusing on the syllabication, diacritical marks, the schwa, finding the accent, and so on do little to meet this criteria.
- Finally, any skill selected for instruction should be demonstrated with real texts and/or books the children have been reading or writing, thus providing a meaningful language context for instruction.

New Story

The **new-story routine** is often the highlight of the day and is a time for children to discover a brand-new story. Before introducing the new story, the teacher should select a book that contains interesting illustrations and language. Books such as *On Market Street* (Lobel, 1981), *The Carrot Seed* (Krauss, 1945), and *The Napping House* (A. Wood, 1984) are chosen because the illustrations match the text and the language is predictable, playful, and interesting. Because of increasing availability, many teachers are selecting information books more often, such as *Frogs* (Henwood,

*The **new-story** routine is a time for children to experience a brand-new story.*

1988), *A Checkup With the Doctor* (K. A. Smith, 1989), *Spiders* (N. S. Barrett, 1984), and *Trucks* (N. S. Barrett, 1989) for sharing during the new-story routine.

When introducing a new story, teachers may choose a big book and involve the entire group of children in a shared book experience, or they may chose to use several traditional-sized copies of a story in a basal with a small group of children. Teachers often begin the new story by talking about it. They may draw children's attention to the front and back covers of the book, the title page, the names of the author(s) and illustrator(s), the illustrations, and any interesting print displays. A question such as, "Have we read other books by this author or illustrator?" may be discussed. During the introduction of each new story, children may be asked to make predictions about the story by looking carefully at the book cover and illustrations. Prediction and other reading preparatory activities for younger readers are described in detail later in this chapter.

After introducing the new book or story, the teacher should read the story aloud straight through in a dramatic and enthusiastic fashion. After reading, children and teachers discuss the book, confirm or correct their predictions, elaborate on favorite parts, talk about any surprises, and relate the story to their own experiences. Following a discussion, time permitting, the book may be read a second time using hand actions or rhythm instruments to increase student involvement. Subsequent readings may be used to induce word-solving strategies in context and to focus on unfamiliar vocabulary words.

Independent Output Activities

*The **independent output activities** routine is aimed at involving individual children in reading, writing, and other language-output activities.*

The **independent output activities** routine is aimed at involving individual children in reading, writing, and other language-output activities. Providing independent reading and writing opportunities selected from a wide range of possibilities is the ideal. Teachers often create stations or centers around the room to involve children in a variety of reading and writing activities. During this time, the teacher may be occupied in a single center with a group of children conducting a minilesson or a reading response group. When not occupied with a single group of children, the teacher is free to move about the classroom during independent output activities time to engage in conferences with individual students, to offer help and suggestions, or to conduct informal evaluations of individual progress.

These stations are described in Chapter 9.

Several classroom centers may be arranged to require a minimum of teacher supervision. In fact, centers that require minimum teacher supervision are ideal and provide the teacher freedom and flexibility to meet individual student needs. A reading nook; a read-along table with cassette tapes of books, charts, and logo language collections; logo language walls; message boards; post offices; big books; a publishing area; and many other stations may be created to provide for children's varied output. Initially, some teachers may choose to place students in flexible traveling groups to rotate through certain stations on a time schedule. Rotation times may be determined by the school schedule or by a classroom-imposed time schedule. Rotations may be signaled by the ringing of a cooking timer bell, a school bell, or playing the first five notes of Beethoven's *Fifth Symphony* on a piano or electronic keyboard, as Ashton-Warner (1963) described in her book *Teacher.* The order of rotation through classroom stations can be prescribed by using a rotating wheel like the one shown in Figure 10.23.

Flexible traveling groups are described in detail in Chapter 9.

With time, experience, and effort, teachers and children may feel comfortable enough with each other to relax time and rotation schedules to encourage greater flexibility and spontaneity during the independent output activities routine.

Figure 10.23

Rotation wheel (SSR, sustained silent reading; SSW, sustained silent writing)

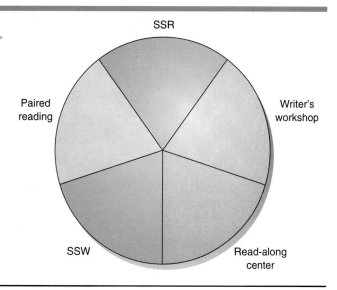

Sharing Time

As a concluding language routine, during **sharing time** children can be gathered together in a whole group or several smaller groups to share the things they have been reading or writing during the day. Several types of language sharing strategies have been developed and used successfully in elementary classrooms. First is the author's chair. A chair in the classroom can be designated, even decorated, as the author's chair. Children who have published their writing in one form or another can be given an opportunity to share their work with the class. Although a single author's chair is useful, we found that, as more and more children began writing and publishing in our own classrooms, a single author's chair was insufficient. Thus, our students proposed authors' corners.

Authors' corners provide more students with the opportunity to share their work with a smaller audience. Each author is invited by the teacher to stand in an assigned corner in the classroom. Authors are asked to share just a bit of their writing project with the group to capture the interest of their peers. Each student shares her project briefly. The remaining students in the classroom audience can select which of the authors' corners they want to attend that day.

A similar means of providing time for children to read their favorite book aloud to an audience is the reader's chair or readers' corners. These reading and sharing opportunities are important for those children who have read a particularly interesting book that day or who want to demonstrate to their peers their emerging ability to read.

A whole-group sharing approach, called the *sharing circle*, allows children time to share in abbreviated form how they have spent their time in the independent output activities time that day. Children briefly share the title of the book they have read or written, the play they have been working on, or even on occasion perform a play for the entire group when scheduled with the teacher. Typically, individual sharing progresses rapidly around the entire circle and class of participants. The only difficulty often experienced with sharing time is the children's apparent enjoyment. Stopping is always difficult!

Sharing time is a time when children gather together in a whole group or several smaller groups to share the things they have been reading or writing during the day.

Authors' chairs and corners provide children with multiple opportunities to share their written or published works.

Readers' chairs and corners provide younger students with opportunities to demonstrate their emerging abilities.

Children are actively engaged in reading and writing in a variety of independent activities at learning centers.

Strategies for Helping Young Children Make Sense of Print

For some time now, researchers have suggested that children can learn to read and write as naturally as they learned to speak if the right kind of conditions can be recreated in school classrooms (Clay, 1972; Hiebert, 1981). Perhaps Van Manen describes this belief best:

> As we walk into a classroom we like to feel that the atmosphere, even the sheer physical space, is sensitive to the need for intimacy, security, and shelter. . . . We soon have a sense of what pedagogy is practiced there. The atmosphere tells what vision the teacher has about what is a good space for children. The lived space of the classroom, its textural and spiritual qualities, first should remind us of what schools are for. School is a place where children explore aspects of the human world. An elementary classroom speaks of the ways children come to know their world: mathematically, socially, historically, musically, literally, aesthetically, and so forth. (1986, p. 34)

If the right conditions can be created in classrooms, children can learn to read and write as naturally as they learn to speak. No child should be led to believe that learning to read and write is something they cannot do.

Although teachers and instructional designers carefully plan instruction, procedures, and materials, the importance of carefully planning the classroom environment to support learning is often minimized. Failure to carefully consider how the classroom context or environment supports learning may lead to a problem described by Spivak (1973) called "setting deprivation." The classroom environment cannot be viewed by teachers as merely a backdrop or landscape for learning but must be viewed as comprising integral parts of the very contextual and social nature of the learning process.

Failure to carefully plan the classroom environment may result in a problem called setting deprivation.

N. E. Taylor, Blum, and Logsdon (1986) have identified and tested several critical variables associated with designing a print-rich classroom environment. The characteristics of a **print-rich environment** identified by Taylor et al. as well as other variables are presented in Figure 10.24. Teachers may wish to consult this listing as they plan their classroom environments and instructional activities.

Print-rich classrooms immerse children in an environment that serves as a ready reference for understanding written print. A good beginning point, Morrow (1989) suggests, is to label the classroom furniture, fixtures, and objects. We believe labeling objects or procedures in classrooms should be functional: for example, "Crayons in here," or "Open here," "Turn on here."

A message board can be placed in a prominent location in the classroom for teachers and children to write messages to one another. In a kindergarten, a message board can be placed by the telephone in the play kitchen area to take down messages, leave messages, or make lists for grocery shopping.

Classrooms should be rich in print and serve as a ready reference for understanding how to read and write.

On a daily basis, teachers often repeat the same phrases, requests, and directions. These common phrases and directions can be written on signs or direction cards. These cards should be large enough to hold up and to invite children to read. A hole can be cut into the card for a handle. See Figure 10.25 for examples. A method for signaling children's attention to the direction cards needs to be devised by the teacher. A hotel bell, whistle, or turning lights off and on can serve this purpose.

Songs, poems, jokes, riddles, dictation, and so on can be enlarged and placed on charts, as described in the tune-in language routine, to enrich the print environment. These charts can be placed around the room for children to read alone or together with peers. Displays should be designed that provide children pertinent information about directions for center activities, sign-up boards for conferences, classroom rules, lists for favorite TV programs, books, songs, and the like. Other dis-

Figure 10.24

Characteristics of a print-rich environment

Books and Stories

A. Commercially published trade books
B. Commercially published big books
C. Commercially published reference books
D. Commercially published informational trade books
E. Individually authored child stories, e.g., shape books, minibooks, big books, accordion books
F. Group-authored big books
G. Group-authored chart stories
H. Group-authored informational charts

Child-Authored Messages

A. Notes
B. Cards
C. Invitations
D. Letters
E. Announcements

Adult-Authored Messages

A. Notes
B. Cards
C. Invitations
D. Letters
E. Announcements

Reference, Informational, and Record-Keeping Lists

A. Sign-in board for attendance
B. Color chart
C. Numbers chart
D. Alphabet chart
E. Logo language wall
F. Words we know list
G. Songs we know list
H. Our favorite books
I. Lunch menu

Directions

A. Classroom rules
B. Use of centers
C. Activities directions
D. Recipes
E. Traffic, regulatory, and direction signs
F. Management schemes

Scheduling

A. Daily schedule
B. Calendar
C. Lunch time
D. Classroom helpers

Labeling

A. Location of centers
B. Objects in the classroom
C. Containers for children's personal belongings
D. Mailboxes
E. Coat racks
F. Objects from home
G. Captioned drawings
H. Contents of cupboards

Writing

A. Paper
B. Chalkboard
C. Blank chart paper
D. Blank big books
E. Pencils
F. Crayons
G. Markers
H. Three-hole punch
I. Binding materials
J. Stapler
K. Glue
L. Magnetic letters
M. Rubber letter stamps
N. Stencils, etc.

Supported or Self-Selected Reading

A. Shared reading experience
B. Group language experience
C. Read-along tapes and books
D. Older children reading with younger
E. Senior citizen volunteers
F. Parents
G. Library center, etc.

Adapted from "The Development of Written Language Awareness: Environmental Aspects and Program Characteristics," by N. E. Taylor, I. H. Blum, and D. M. Logsdon, 1986, *Reading Research Quarterly, 21*(2), pp. 132–149. Copyright 1986 by International Reading Association.

Figure 10.25

Direction card

plays can be placed about the room, providing information on color words and number words that children often need to consult during their writing.

Environmental Print

Old cereal boxes, signs, bumper stickers, and candy wrappers can be used in interesting ways to give children confidence in reading as well as to help them come to understand how print works. A display area, bulletin board, or wall can be designated as a logo language wall. Children can be asked to bring environmental print or product logos from home to put on the wall. Some teachers request that children bring environmental print that begins with a particular letter sound. Other teachers simply fill the wall with print children bring from home and can read.

Another way environmental print can be used is to make I-can-read books. Children select from a group of collected logos to make these books. I-can-read books are often dictated to the teacher or some other adult, and the product logos are used in place of specific dictated words. These books are easily read by every child and become a source of confidence building and enjoyment. Teachers can ask children to bring environmental print to school for a specific letter name and sound. These items can then be used for specific lessons on letter names and sounds while maintaining an authentic language context for learning the alphabetic principle. After discussing and displaying letter-specific environmental print, teachers and children can cut and paste environmental print items onto 5 by 7-inch plain index cards. These specific letter-name and -sound environmental print collections may be bound together with a clip or ring to be practiced in small groups or by individuals in center or station activities. Phonic generalizations can be taught from known environmental print such as the final, silent *e* generalization. Teachers can collect product logos and bind these items together, similar to the alphabet letter collections.

Children can use environmental print to produce classroom signs using logos to substitute for written word(s). Children can also cut up environmental print to send notes to each other or make word collages for an art activity.

Reading environmental print such as product labels, signs, or bumper stickers can give children an early sense of success in learning to read.

Children who were taught with environmental print learned significantly more letter names and sounds than did children who learned alphabet letters without using environmental print.

We have field tested these strategies with young children and have experienced exciting results. Hiebert and Ham (1981) documented that children who were taught with environmental print learned significantly more letter names and sounds than did children who learned alphabet letters without using environmental print. McGee, Lomax, and Head (1988) have also found that young children attend to print in environmental displays and are not just reading the entire context.

Learning the Alphabetic Principle

Children need to learn the alphabetic principle to become fluent and independent readers.

Past research has shown that children learn to read without being able to identify every letter of the alphabet (Teale, 1987). In fact, children are constantly learning how to read from birth. They pick up sight words off bathroom doors, cereal boxes, and billboards. Most children can write and recognize their own name without mastering the identification of every alphabet letter name and sound. Conversely, no sensible individual will argue against the fact that children need to learn the alphabetic principle to become fluent and independent readers. How does one learn the alphabetic principle, and what does this imply for teachers and parents? Learning letter names and sounds is most effectively done when it is enjoyable and meaningful for young children. Put another way, it must have a purpose and make sense to a 5-year-old!

The issues of how, when, how long, and how many phonics generalizations should be taught are discussed at length in Chapter 8.

In the reports *Becoming a Nation of Readers* (R. C. Anderson et al., 1985) and *Beginning to Read* (Adams, 1990b), disseminated by the Center for the Study of Reading in 1985 and 1990, the purpose of phonics instruction is to reveal the alphabetic principle, the concept that written letters roughly represent certain sounds used in spoken language. Phonics instruction should focus on only the most important letter–sound relationships. Learning the alphabetic principle does not necessarily imply that all letter–sound combinations, rules, and exceptions need to be explicitly taught one at a time for years on end. The fact is that young children do not need this amount of instructional overkill to induce the alphabetic principle.

There are many ways children can be made aware of letter names and sounds. One way to help children learn about the letters and sounds of the alphabet is to make use of environmental print. Labeling the classroom, using a child's name, and constructing personal word collections or word banks arranged in alphabetical order provide personally interesting and meaningful takeoff points for young children in learning the alphabet. A wall may be designated to display uppercase and lowercase alphabet letters. Children who bring environmental print items from home may place each logo underneath the appropriate alphabet letter display. This helps children become aware of the alphabet letters and alphabetical order in a natural way, one that extends beyond school boundaries. (Other suggestions for using environmental print were outlined in the previous section.)

An alphabet station or center that is stocked with alphabet puzzles, magnetic letters, sandpaper letters, alphabet games, stencils, flashcards, and alphabet charts should be part of every kindergarten or first-grade classroom.

An alphabet station or center stocked with alphabet puzzles, magnetic letters, sandpaper letters, alphabet games, stencils, flashcards, and alphabet charts should be a part of *every* kindergarten or first-grade classroom. In this station or center, children have an opportunity to explore the alphabet in a gaming and essentially risk-free setting. Inviting children to write, trace, or copy the alphabet letters in these centers can be accomplished without drill. This may be accomplished by furnishing the alphabet center with individual-sized chalkboards, dry-erase boards, clay trays, tracing paper, and painting easels, which naturally lead children toward copying, tracing, and experimenting with letters. More tasty approaches can be added to this rich alphabet menu. Periodic eating of alphabet soup, animal crackers, and cereal, and sorting the letters or animals into alphabet letter categories increases children's awareness of letters, sounds, and alphabetical order.

Teachers should acquire or have on hand in the school collections of quality alphabet trade books. Books like *On Market Street* (Lobel, 1981), *Animalia* (Base, 1986), and *The Z Was Zapped* (Van Allsburg, 1987) are just a few of the many delightful alphabet books that can be used to teach children the alphabet as a whole rather than a letter a week, or one at a time (Reutzel, 1992). Morrow specifically advises against the practice of teaching a letter a week: "Systematic teaching of the alphabet, one letter per week, is not as successful as teaching children letters that are meaningful to them" (1989, p. 131).

Morrow (1989) specifically advises against the practice of teaching a letter a week.

By reading and rereading a favorite alphabet book(s) over a period of weeks and months, children naturally learn the names of all the alphabet letters and begin to associate the letters with many of their related sounds.

Weaver (1988) says that many teachers who teach the alphabet select specific songs, poetry, raps, and chants to emphasize a selected letter of the alphabet. For example, if a teacher wanted to emphasize the letter *S* for a day or so, she might select and enlarge on a chart to be read by the group the text of "Sally Go Round the Sun" or "Squid Sauce" (S. Dunn, 1987), or "Miss Mary Mac, Mac, Mac" (Hill, 1990a). Songs such as "See Saw, Margery Daw" (Dallin & Dallin, 1980) or "Sandy Land" (Dallin & Dallin, 1980) could be selected and enlarged on charts for practice and group singing. Shel Silverstein's "Sister for Sale" (Silverstein, 1974) or Jack Prelutsky's (1984) "Sneaky Sue" poems could be likewise enlarged and used to emphasize the name and sound of the letter *S*. Sensory experiences can be integrated into this lesson as well. A sip of Sprite, a bite of a Snickers candy bar, a long spaghetti noodle to munch on, and a handful of Skittles to taste can successfully emphasize *S*. Art experiences, with children creating pictures using an *S*, can be used as the beginning point. Collages of things that begin with *S*, such as a sack, screw, safety pin, salt, silver, or sand, can be created and displayed. In this print-rich environment and through teacher-planned experiences with the alphabet, children learn the alphabet in natural, enjoyable, and meaningful ways. (See the appendix, "Resources for Teachers," for poetry, songs, chants, and other sources useful for conveying the alphabetic principle to emergent readers.)

A listing of poetry, song, and chant titles, and sources useful for conveying the alphabetic principle to emergent readers is found in the appendix.

Helping Young Children Develop a Sense of Story

Picture Schema Stories

Watson and Crowley (1988) describe schema stories as a reading strategy designed to require readers to "reconstruct the order of a text based on meaning and story grammar" (p. 263). A prelude to this strategy, appropriate for emergent readers, is a modification developed by Reutzel and Fawson (1987) known as *picture schema stories*. This approach uses wordless picture books or pictures copied from emergent-reader trade books. The pictures from the books are displayed in random order on a flannel board. Each picture is discussed. Questions about who is in the picture, what the character is doing, and so on may be asked. A picture from the display is handed to selected children. Who has the first picture in the story? The child who thinks she

Picture schema stories help students construct the order of a text based on meaning and comprehension of text.

has the first picture indicates this and explains why. The teacher places the pictures in linear order from top to bottom or left to right in the display. The teacher then reads the story aloud while the children watch their picture predictions at the board or on the chart. Much like the literature web, the picture schema story activity can be extended to include a dictation of responses to the story and possible language extensions. The picture schema story can be mounted on the top of chart paper for recording the children's responses (oral dictation) about the story. These responses can be read later.

Picture Story Frames

Fowler (1982) described a strategy for developing a sense of story called *story frames.* Reutzel and Fawson (1987) adapted this strategy to be used with emergent readers. Several paperback picture books and emergent-level trade books are purchased and physically cut apart. Old basal stories can also be used. If text accompanies the pictures, and it often does, the text is cut away. The pictures are placed in a story frame board covered with acetate sheets, as shown in Figure 10.20.

Pictures are selected (Reutzel & Fawson, 1987) to be used in the story frame board that portray the major story elements (i.e., setting, problems, attempts, etc.). These selected pictures are then placed in each frame of the story frame board in the proper story sequence. Each picture is placed near the top of the story frame, leaving room at the bottom of the frame to record children's descriptions of what the picture is about.

Picture story frame activities are ideally used with small groups for composing a story based on story structure knowledge.

The picture story frame activity is ideally used with smaller groups of children, ranging from five to eight. Before taking down any ideas on the acetate sheets of the story frame board, the teacher invites children to look at each picture of the story in order. She may direct the children to "Think about what the author may have written to tell this story as you look at the pictures." Next, the teacher invites one child to describe what she thought the author might have written about the first picture. This may be written with water-based felt-tipped markers, which can be cleaned off with a wet sponge. The teacher invites each child to build on the previous student's story line as well as to think about the author's point of view as shown in the picture. Once the children have composed the story from the pictures, the teacher reads the actual book aloud to the children. The two versions provide interesting discussions about point of view and other stylistic devices. Children seem to like reading their own version of the story as well as the author's!

Literature Webbing With Predictable Books

Literature webs can be used to help improve students' story structure knowledge and comprehension of text.

Reutzel and Fawson (1989) designed a successful strategy lesson to be used with predictable books for building children's understanding of story structure. A literature web is constructed from the major elements of a predictable book (Bromley, 1991). This is accomplished by selecting sentences from the book that tell about each major element of the story, that is, setting, characters, problems, attempts, and solution. These sentences are placed around the title of the book in random order on a chalkboard or a large bulletin board, as shown in Figure 10.26. Before reading the story, the children read the sentences aloud with the teacher. In the early part of the school year, the sentences selected for the web sentence strips are usually heavily augmented with hand-drawn or copied pictures from the book.

Figure 10.26

Artist's drawing of random order literature web

Children are divided into small groups, and each group is given the picture and sentence card from the board. The children are asked which group thinks they have the first part of the story. After discussion and group agreement is reached, the first sentence and picture card is placed at the one-o'clock position on the literature web. The remainder of the groups are asked which sentence and word card comes next, and the cards are placed around the literature web in clockwise order, as in Figure 10.27.

Next, the story is read from a traditional-sized trade book or big book. Children listen attentively to confirm or correct their literature web predictions. After the reading, corrections are made to the predictions in the literature web if necessary. Children respond to the story, and these responses are recorded near the end of the literature web. Other books similar to the one read may be discussed and recorded on the web. Finally, the children and teacher brainstorm together to produce some ideas about how to extend the reading of the book into the other language arts while recording these ideas on the web. A completed web appears in Figure 10.28.

Reutzel and Fawson (1989, 1991) and Reutzel and Hollingsworth (1991d) demonstrated that first-grade children, especially low-achieving first-grade children, who participate in the literature webbing of a predictable book learn to read these books with fewer reading miscues, fewer miscues that distort comprehension, and greater recall. They attribute this to the fact that children must impose an organization on their predictions when using literature webs, rather than simply making random predictions from story titles and pictures. Literature webs can also be designed to be linear rather than circular. Teachers should decide which way is best.

Figure 10.27

Artist's drawing of predicted literature web

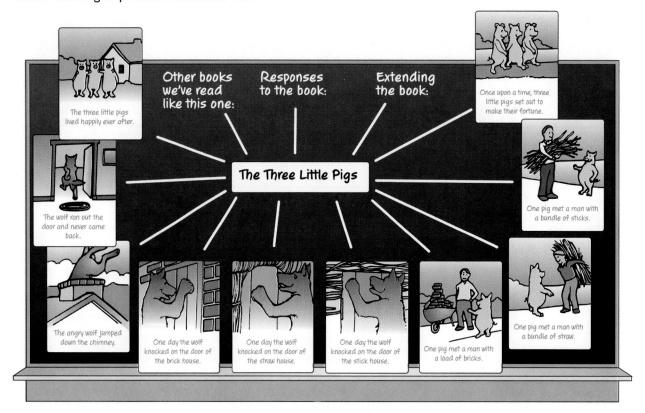

Directed Listening Thinking Activity

Directed reading thinking activity is presented in Chapter 4.

During DLTA, students listen, make predictions about a story, and listen again to confirm or correct their predictions.

The **directed listening thinking activity** (DLTA) is an adaptation of Russell Stauffer's (1975) directed reading thinking activity (DRTA). During DRTA, students read, made predictions about a story, and read on to confirm or correct their predictions. During DLTA, emergent readers listen to a story read aloud, predict, and continue to listen to confirm or correct their predictions. The DLTA has become a popular strategy to help emergent readers develop a sense of story (Morrow, 1984; Slaughter, 1988). The following steps illustrate the DLTA strategy:

Step 1: Introducing the Story and Predicting

Teachers can introduce a story like *The Three Billy Goats Gruff* by showing students the cover of the book and reading the title. After discussing the title, the cover, and some of the pictures, the teacher may ask students to make a prediction about the story. This is usually accomplished by asking a series of questions such as:

- What do you think this story may be about?
- What do you think might happen in this story?
- Do the pictures give you any clues about what might happen?

Sometimes the teacher may read the first few paragraphs of the story to provide students with enough information to make reasonable predictions. Following an initial discussion, students decide which of the predictions they wish to accept. This process can be also facilitated by asking questions such as:

- Which of the ideas about how the story will turn out do you think is most likely correct?
- Have you ever wished that you could live somewhere else?
- Have you ever thought some of your friends have a better life than you do?

Relating questions to the real-life experiences of the children helps them make vital connections with their background knowledge and experience to guide their predictions.

Step 2: Listening, Thinking, and Predicting

Once students commit to a prediction, they have in effect set their own purpose for listening as the teacher reads the story aloud. As the story unfolds during the reading, students begin to confirm, reject, or modify their predictions. The teacher usually stops at key points in the story and asks students more questions. These questions

Figure 10.28

Artist's drawing of completed literature web

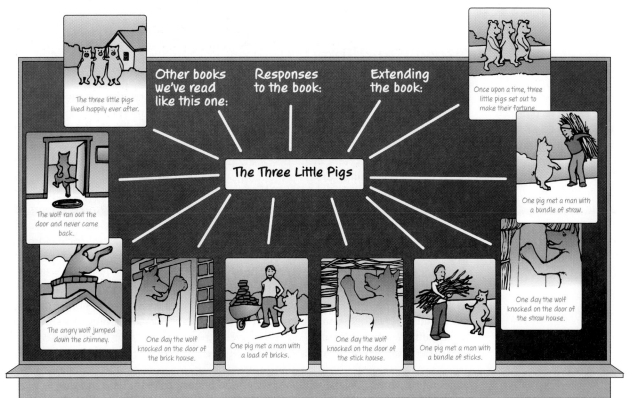

are meant to involve children in confirming, rejecting, or modifying their predictions using the new information they have heard. Teachers may ask questions such as:

- Have you changed your original predictions about how the story will turn out?
- What do you think will happen next?
- If . . . happens, how will that change your ideas?

The teacher continues to read the story aloud, stopping at key points in the story to repeat this procedure until the end of the story is reached.

Step 3: Supporting With Evidence

During the final part of the DLTA, the teacher asks students to remember information from the story to support their predictions. She may also ask students to recall which information in the story caused students to change their predictions. Again, the teacher uses questioning to invite students to respond to the story. Examples of such questions follow:

- Can you remember how many times your predictions changed?
- What happened in the story that caused you to change your predictions?

The DLTA provides teachers with a structure for introducing and discussing stories read aloud to children while supplying the children with a generalizable framework for listening to these stories.

The DLTA provides teachers with a structure for introducing and discussing stories read aloud to children while supplying the children with a generalizable framework for listening to these stories. Research has shown that using a DLTA significantly increases children's listening comprehension of a story (Morrow, 1984). With frequent use, young children can internalize the DLTA and transfer its use to new stories read aloud (R. C. Anderson, Mason, & Shirey, 1984).

Story Retellings

Story retellings ask children to retell a story orally. These can be recorded and examined for purposes of assessing comprehension.

In most elementary school classrooms, children are asked to answer a series of questions after completing the reading of a selection to assess reading comprehension. In many cases, these questions require students to recall bits and pieces of the story in a rather piecemeal or incoherent fashion. Asking children to retell a story involves them in reconstruction of the entire story. **Story retellings** require that students sequence the story, recall important elements of the plot, make inferences, and notice relevant details. Thus, retellings assess story comprehension in a holistic, sequenced, and organized manner when compared to typical questioning practices.

Children can quickly learn to retell stories with the help of demonstrations and practice, although retelling is not easy for young children (Morrow, 1985). The teacher may begin by demonstrating the retelling of a favorite story for children. A pre- and post-reading discussion of the story also can be helpful in preparing students for retelling. Morrow (1989) suggests that students be told before reading that they will be asked to retell a story. In addition, we suggest that individual children be given at least three reading rehearsals before they are to retell the story from their own reading. Teachers can ask children to pay attention to the sequence of the story or empathize with the main character(s) feelings to focus student attention on particular aspects of the story. In this way, retellings become much more than assessment.

Morrow suggests that teachers prompt children to begin story retellings with a statement such as, "A little while ago, we read a story called [*name the story*]. Would you retell the story as if you were telling it to a friend who has never heard it before?" (1985, p. 659). Other prompts during the recall may be framed as questions:

- How does the story begin? [or] Once upon a time. . . .
- What happens next?
- What happened to [the main character] when . . . ?
- Where did the story take place?
- When did the story take place?
- How did the main character solve the problem in the story?
- How did the story end?

Morrow (1989) is explicit in her advice that teachers offer only general prompts like those listed here rather than prompting specific details, ideas, or sequence of events in the story.

Assessment of children's story retellings can reveal much about their understanding of story structure, the order of story sequence, and the major elements of the story plot. Evaluating a story retelling is accomplished by first parsing a story into four categories: setting, theme, plot episodes, and resolution, as shown in Figure 10.29.

Second, a guide sheet for analyzing the story retellings can be constructed, much like the one illustrated in Figure 10.30, to accompany the parsed story outline. Children should be given credit for partial recall or recalling the gist of the story in the retelling. The guide sheet in Figure 10.31 also provides for analyzing a student's retelling for proper ordering of events. Thus, items included or omitted in recall as well as event order in the retelling are assessed. The information gleaned from the retelling may be used to help teachers focus their instruction in the future. The information may also indicate the nature of the information to be focused on in future retellings or the nature of the prompts to be given during retellings.

Evaluating a story retelling is accomplished by parsing a story into four categories: setting, theme, plot episodes, and resolution.

Drawing and Art: Young Children Responding

Teachers often invite children to respond to books and stories through discussion and other oral language activities, and increasing numbers of teachers of young children are beginning to appreciate the role of writing in responding to stories and books. When children are first given a pencil, pen, or crayon to write with, they seem to approach the paper with an intent to explore what will happen. These first encounters with writing generally result in what adults call *scribbling*. Scribble writing, however, usually gives way quickly to discovering lines, curves, circles, and other forms that may be used to represent objects and events in drawings. In the writing of very young children, drawing is typically used as one of the first symbol systems intended to carry a message (Clay, 1987; Ferreiro & Teberosky, 1982). Drawings represent the fact that children have come to understand the difference between the object or event itself and culturally recognized symbols that can be used to signify the object or event.

Drawing is typically used as one of the first symbol systems intended to carry a message.

During kindergarten and first grade, children use drawing a great deal. Research into the uses of drawing and its effect on writing development has shown that drawing seems to inform and enhance writing development initially but that writing also acts to embellish drawings later (Bissex, 1980; Calkins, 1986). Calkins (1986) relates an incident when she was visiting a first-grade classroom. She asked Chris, a first-grade boy, what he was going to write about. Chris looked at Calkins with astonishment and responded, "How should I know; I haven't drawed it yet!" (pp. 47, 50). Thus, drawing can help children rehearse for writing by providing a scaffolding from which a piece of writing can be constructed. Drawings can also be used to help children hold the world

Figure 10.29

Story grammar parsing of the story *The Little Red Hen*

The Setting

Once upon a time there was a little red hen who shared her cottage with a goose, a cat, and a dog.

The goose was a gossip. She chatted with the neighbors all day long.

The cat was very vain. She brushed her fur, straightened her whiskers, and polished her claws all day long.

The dog was always sleepy. He napped on the front porch swing all day long.

The Theme

The Little Red Hen ended up doing all the work around the house. She cooked. She cleaned. She washed the clothes and took out the trash. She mowed the lawn and raked the leaves. She even did all of the shopping.

The Events

One morning on her way to market, the Little Red Hen found a few grains of wheat. She put them in the pocket of her apron. When she got home she asked her friends, "Who will plant these grains of wheat?"

"Not I," said the goose.
"Not I," said the cat.
"Not I," said the dog.
"Then I will plant them myself," said the Little Red Hen.
And she did.

When the grains of wheat began to sprout, the Little Red Hen cried, "Look, the wheat I planted is coming up! Who will help me take care of it this summer?"

"Not I," said the goose.
"Not I," said the cat.
"Not I," said the dog.
"Then I will take care of it myself," said the Little Red Hen.
And she did.

All summer long she cared for the growing wheat. She made sure that it got enough water, and she hoed the weeds out carefully between each row. By the end of the summer the wheat had grown tall. And when it turned from green to gold, she asked her friends, "Who will help me cut and thresh this wheat?"

"Not I," said the goose.
"Not I," said the cat.
"Not I," said the dog.
"Then I will cut and thresh it myself," said the Little Red Hen.

And she did.

When all of the wheat had been cut and threshed the Little Red Hen scooped the wheat into a wheel barrow and said, "This wheat must be ground into flour. Who will help me take it to the mill?"

"Not I," said the goose.
"Not I," said the cat.
"Not I," said the dog.
"Then I will take it myself," said the Little Red Hen.
And she did.

The miller ground the wheat into flour and put it into a bag for the Little Red Hen. Then, all by herself, she pushed the bag home in the wheel barrow. One cool fall morning not many days later, the Little Red Hen got up early and said, "Today would be a perfect day to bake some bread. Who will help me bake a loaf of bread with the flour I brought home from the mill?"

"Not I," said the goose.
"Not I," said the cat.
"Not I," said the dog.
"Then I will bake the bread myself," said the Little Red Hen.
And she did.

She mixed the flour with milk and eggs and butter and salt. She kneaded the dough and shaped it into a nice plump loaf. Then she put the loaf in the oven and watched it as it baked.

The Resolution

The smell of baking bread soon filled the air. It smelled so delicious that the goose stopped chatting . . . The cat stopped brushing . . . The dog stopped napping. One by one they came into the kitchen. When the Little Red Hen took the freshly baked loaf of bread out of the oven, she said, "Who will help me eat this bread?"

"Oh, I will!" said the goose.
"And I will!" said the cat.
"And I will!" said the dog.
"You will?" said the Little Red Hen.

"Who planted the wheat and took care of it? I did. Who cut the wheat? Who threshed it and took it to the mill? I did. Who brought the flour home and baked this loaf of bread? I did. I did it all by myself. Now, I am going to eat it all by myself."

And that is exactly what she did.

Figure 10.30

Coding children's responses during story readings

Child's name _____ Date _____ Story _____

(Read one story to the child or a small group of children. Encourage the children to respond with questions and comments. Tape-record the session. Transcribe or listen to the tape, noting each child's responses by placing checks in the appropriate categories. A category may receive more than one check, and a single response may be credited to more than one category. Total the number of checks in each category.)

1. Focus on Story Structure
   a. Setting (time, place)   _____
   b. Characters   _____
   c. Theme (problem or goal)   _____
   d. Plot episodes (events leading toward problem solution   _____
      or goal attainment)
   e. Resolution   _____

2. Focus on Meaning
   a. Labeling   _____
   b. Detail   _____
   c. Interpreting (associations, elaborations)   _____
   d. Predicting   _____
   e. Drawing from one's experience   _____
   f. Seeking definitions of words   _____
   g. Using narrational behavior (reciting parts of the book   _____
      along with the teacher)

3. Focus on Print
   a. Questions or comments about letters   _____
   b. Questions or comments about sounds   _____
   c. Questions or comments about words   _____
   d. Reads words   _____
   e. Reads sentences   _____

4. Focus on Illustrations
   a. Responses and questions that are related to illustrations   _____

From *Literacy Development in the Early Years: Helping Children Read and Write* (p. 109) by L. M. Morrow, 1989, Boston: Allyn and Bacon. Copyright © by Allyn and Bacon. Reprinted by permission.

still for a moment—long enough to select a topic for writing. This may explain why drawing pictures often precedes the use of letters or words in children's writing. Drawings give children something to guide the selection of words for writing. In a sense, drawing appears to be a primordial form of representing the world to assist writing. Therefore, Calkins (1986) recommends particularly for kindergarten and first-grade children that drawing be used liberally to enhance children's development of writing.

Figure 10.31

Story retelling evalua-
tion guide sheet

Child's Name _____   Age _____

Title of Story _____   Date _____

General directions: Give 1 point for each element included as well as for "gist."
Give 1 point for each character named as well as for such words as *boy, girl,* or
dog. Credit plurals (friends, for instance) with 2 points under characters.

Sense of Story Structure

Setting
a. Begins story with an introduction   ____
b. Names main character   ____
c. Number of other characters named   ____
d. Actual number of other characters   ____
e. Score for "other characters" (c/d)   ____
f. Includes statement about time or place   ____

Theme
Refers to main character's primary goal or problem to be solved

Plot Episodes
a. Number of episodes recalled   ____
b. Number of episodes in story   ____
Score for "plot episodes" (a/b)   ____

Resolution
a. Names problem solution/goal attainment   ____
b. Ends story   ____

Sequence
Retells story in structural order: setting, theme, plot episodes,   ____
resolution. (Score 2 for proper, 1 for partial, 0 for no sequence
evident.)

Highest score possible: ____   Child's score   ____

Checks can be used instead of numbers to get a general sense of elements children include & progress over time. A quantitative analysis as shown above is
optional. Retellings can be evaluated for interpretive critical comments as well.

Excerpt from "Story Retelling Analysis" from "Retelling as a Diagnostic Tool," Lesley M. Morrow, *Re-examining Reading Diagnosis: New Trends and Procedures in Classrooms and Clinics,* Susan M. Glazer, Lynn W. Searfoss, and Lance M. Gentile (Eds.), 1988, Newark, DE: International Reading Association. Copyright 1988 by International Reading Association. Reprinted with permission of Lesley M. Morrow and the International Reading Association.

Most importantly, drawing helps children to understand that many symbol systems are available for communicating a message, that is, music, art, drama, writing, movement, and so on. Siegel (1983) claims that by taking what we have come to know from one communication or symbol system and recasting into another, new knowledge is generated. This process of recasting knowledge in alternative symbol systems is called **transmediation**. For example, inviting children to recast into draw-

*Taking what we have come
to know from one commu-
nication or symbol system
and recasting it into another
is called **transmediation**.*

Inviting children to draw about what they've read improves students' understanding and enjoyment of the story by allowing them many opportunities to plan and rehearse their writing ideas.

ings a story read aloud causes children to develop new insights for the story. Thus, drawing not only can help children become more proficient and expressive writers, it can help children respond to reading in a way that deepens their knowledge and leads to new insights and interpretations.

Sketch to Stretch

"Sketch to stretch" (Harste, Short, & Woodward, 1988; Siegel, 1983) offers a wonderful opportunity for students to draw pictures illustrating "what this story meant to me or my favorite part of the story." The procedure for using sketch to stretch follows:

1. Place children in groups of about four or five with multiple copies of the same story (either basal story or trade book).
2. After the children have read the story, each child independently reflects on the meaning of the story. Then, they draw their own interpretations of the story. Plenty of time should be given for students to complete their sketches. Remember that the emphasis is on meaning, not artistic ability.
3. Next, each student shares her sketch (without comment) and allows the other group members to speculate on its meaning as related to the book. Once the questions and comments of the other children are concluded, the artist has the final word.
4. After each child in the group has shared her sketch, the group may wish to pick one sketch to share with the class. The sketch chosen by the group usually offers a good synopsis of the book or story.

Sketch to stretch allows children the opportunity to represent the interpretation of a story in another symbolic system.

Sketch to stretch offers teachers an opportunity to discuss with students why each reader may have different interpretations of a story even though the gist is recognized by all. Sketch to stretch also helps encourage a spirit of risk taking among students as they see that there is no single "correct" response to stories and books but that interpretations depend on a reader's background knowledge and interests.

See Chapter 13 for a discussion of assessment portfolios.

Sketch to stretch has many follow-up possibilities. Sketches may be collected as part of the teacher's ongoing assessment portfolio, bound together into a group or class book, displayed on bulletin boards, or used as a metacognitive strategy to help students monitor their own comprehension of a story. Another possibility is that sketches may be collected and combined to create a kind of story map to depict major events in a story. Thus, sketch to stretch may:

- Aid students' story comprehension.
- Serve as an entree into the writing process.
- Provide documentation of students' reading comprehension and progress.

Murals

In Ms. Bonnell's kindergarten class, the children had just finished reading the story *Why Can't I Fly?* (Gelman, 1976). Ms. Bonnell wanted to extend the reading of the book into a class art project. Instinctively, she knew that inviting children to draw about what they had read would improve her students' understanding and enjoyment of the story. A mural was decided on as the class art project. Children busily worked in small groups and pairs, drawing and painting the characters from the story: a ladybug, a duck, and a monkey. A 30-foot-long light-blue roll of butcher paper was spread out in the hall of the school. The children and the teacher reviewed the sequence of the story before pasting the characters in sequence on the mural. Bubbles were added above the heads of the characters with the text copied from the story.

Ms. Bonnell noted that the children had internalized this story to the point of endearment and could read and write many of the words found in the story.

Murals provide a wonderful means for groups of children to register their response to literature.

As shown in Figure 10.32, murals can capture the sequence, the episodes, and the warmth of the original story. Moreover, murals display the added warmth of the children's hand-drawn characters or carefully selected excerpts of text copied from the original book.

Posters

Advertising a favorite book or character in the form of a poster is a simple yet popular idea for inviting children to respond to a book through drawing. Several varieties of posters can be suggested for children: "wanted" posters, missing person poster,

Figure 10.32

An example of a class-made mural, which can assist children's writing and reading development

This mural was based on *Appelemando's Dreams* by P. Polacco, 1991, New York: Philomel Books. Copyright 1991 by Patricia Polacco.

A poster is a simple yet popular idea for inviting children to respond to a book through drawing.

favorite character poster, and best book posters. At a local elementary school, the teachers and librarians invited children to make a poster about their favorite book. A display case in the library was used to display the posters during the year. Each time a book was checked out that was on display in the library display case that week, the librarian made note of it. At the end of the year, the authors of the five posters that had sparked the largest number of check outs from the library were each given a book certificate from a local bookstore.

"Wanted" or missing person posters (T. D. Johnson & Louis, 1987) are also a popular drawing or art-related response to a book or story. To begin, the teacher may display a poster of a book the children have already read in a prominent place in the classroom, one that will naturally foster curiosity and questions. A discussion may focus on the information contained in the poster, and a list could be made at the board. Before reading a story aloud, the teacher tells students to listen carefully for information that may be used in making a poster like the one displayed and discussed. After reading, a discussion about information for a "wanted" or missing person poster could be discussed and listed at the board. Children could then be sent to work in pairs or individually on their own poster for the book or story. Johnson and Louis point out that poster making involves the use of a number of important reading skills: "reading for a purpose as well as gathering, organizing, and synthesizing information and selecting main ideas and significant details" (1987, p. 84).

Character Mobiles

To make character mobiles, children illustrate the characters from the book or story and cut these drawings out and hang them on a piece of string.

A favorite among young children for using drawing and art to respond to books and stories is the creation of character mobiles. Children illustrate the characters from the book or story and cut these drawings out and hang them on a piece of string. The character strings can be hung on coat hangers or pipe cleaners, which are hung from the ceiling of the classroom. Usually, the title of the book or story is also written on the mobile. Each mobile represents a child's representation of the characters in the book or story. By drawing these characters, children review the story, deepen their understanding, and expand on interpretations.

The ideas described here for responding to books through art and drawing are just a few of many possibilities. Figure 10.33 lists several more suggestions for using drawing and art as a medium for responding to books and stories with young children.

Developing Fluency: Young Children Rereading

Radio Reading

Radio reading is a procedure for developing oral reading fluency in a group setting.

Radio reading (Searfoss, 1975) is a procedure for developing oral reading fluency in a group setting, a process that shields neophyte readers from the sometimes harsh emotional consequences from peers in response to their developing reading abilities. In radio reading, each student is given a "script" to read aloud. Selections can be drawn from any print media, such as newspapers, magazines, or any print source that can be converted into a news story. The student acts as a news broadcaster, and other students act as listeners. Only the reader and the teacher have copies of the scripts. Because other students have no script to follow, minor word recognition

Figure 10.33

Art and drawing litera-
ture response list

- Make character puppets.

- Draw an illustration of the setting of the story.

- Construct a shoe box diorama of the story setting.

- Prepare a comic strip version of the story events.

- Design a book jacket for a favorite book or chapter.

- Make a transparency story for use on the overhead.

- Trace a friend and illustrate her as a character from a book.

- Draw a picture from your favorite book or story. Cut it into a jigsaw puzzle for a friend to put together.

- Produce illustrated bookmarks.

- Model book's characters from soap, clay, or salt dough.

- Make place mats advertising your favorite book. Cover with clear contact paper and place in school cafeteria.

- Design character masks to be worn during a dramatization of a story or book.

errors will go unnoticed if the text is well presented. At-risk readers have enjoyed radio reading from *Know Your World*. This publication is well suited for use in radio reading activities because the content and level of difficulty make it possible for younger readers to read with ease and enjoyment.

Before reading aloud to the group, students should rehearse the story silently to themselves or aloud to the teacher until they have gained confidence. Emphasis is first placed on the meaning of the story so that the students can paraphrase any difficult portions of the text. Students are encouraged to keep the ideas flowing in the same way as a broadcaster would. In contrast to the typical "round-robin" reading method, in which all mistakes are apparent to anyone following along in the text, radio reading allows students to deviate from the text without embarrassment by stressing the idea that their reading should make sense.

Repeated Readings

Repeated readings simply engage students in reading interesting passages orally over and over again. The basic purpose is to enhance students' reading fluency (Dowhower, 1987; J. Samuels, 1979). Although it might seem that reading a text again and again may lead to boredom, it actually has just the opposite effect. Because in this exercise each reading is timed and then recorded on a chart or graph, students compete with themselves trying to better their reading rate and cut down on errors on each successive attempt. Also, with each attempt, students' comprehension and vocal inflections improve (Dowhower, 1987; Reutzel & Hollingsworth, 1993). Young readers find it reinforcing to see visible evidence of their improvement, such as a personal (and private) graph of their fluency progress in repeated readings.

The basic purpose of repeated readings is to enhance students' oral reading fluency.

Repeated readings help students by expanding the total number of words they can recognize instantaneously and, as previously mentioned, help improve students' comprehension and oral elocution with each succeeding attempt. This quickly leads students to improved confidence regarding reading aloud and positive attitudes toward the act of reading. Additionally, because high-frequency words (*the, and, but, was,* etc.) occur in literally all reading situations, the increase in automatic sight word knowledge developed through repeated readings transfers far beyond the practiced texts.

In the beginning, texts selected for repeated readings should be short, predictable, and easy. Examples of poetry we recommend for repeated readings with young readers include those authored by Shel Silverstein and Jack Prelutsky. Stories by Bill Martin such as *Brown Bear, Brown Bear, What Do You See?* or Eric Carle's *The Very Hungry Caterpillar* are also wonderful places to start this activity. When students attain adequate speed and accuracy with easy texts, the length and difficulty of the stories and poems can gradually be increased.

Students can tape-record their oral reading performances as a source of immediate feedback. If two cassette tape player/recorders are available, students can listen and read along with the taped version of the text using headphones, while at the same time, the second recorder is recording the student's oral reading. Another child can then either replay her version simultaneously with the teacher-recorded version to compare, or else simply listen to her own rendition alone. Either way, the feedback can be both instant and effective (Cooter, 1993).

Teachers can use the taped recording of repeated readings for further analysis of each young reader's improvement in fluency and comprehension. Using a tape recorder also frees the teacher to work with other students, thereby conserving precious instructional time and leaving behind an audit trail of student readings for later assessment and documentation. On occasion, teachers should listen to the tape with the reader present so that effective ways of reducing word-recognition errors and increasing reading rate can be modeled by the teacher.

Themed Studies With Young Children

Themed studies, also known as *topical studies,* are undertaken with young children for a purpose, a purpose that relates to the content to be studied and a personal or societal need to know (Weaver, Chaston, & Peterson, 1993). Children study about the development of *aviation* as a theme because it is important to know. Themed study is not just a thinly disguised excuse for learning to recognize certain words, to spell a list of 20 words, or to punctuate a sentence from a textbook. Because the processes for developing both literature-based and thematic studies units are described fully in Chapters 11 and 12, we will mention here only a few considerations crucial to the success of using themed studies with very young students.

Planning a themed studies unit begins with understanding what makes for a quality theme for study. Gamberg, Kwak, Hutchings, and Altheim (1988) describe 10 criteria that characterize a quality theme.

List 10 criteria that characterize the selection and development of a quality theme for thematic studies.

1. A theme is the focus of attention, not a curriculum goal or skill, such as reading and math.
2. A theme studies unit involves in-depth study.
3. A theme must be of interest to the children.

4. A theme must be broad enough to be subdivided into smaller subtopics also of interest to the children.
5. A theme and its relation to the subtopics must remain clear.
6. A theme must not be geographically or historically limiting.
7. A theme must lend itself to comparing and contrasting of ideas.
8. A theme must permit extensive investigation of concrete situations, materials, and resources.
9. A theme must be conducive to breaking down the wall of curriculum barriers in the school.
10. A theme must assist in breaking down the walls between the school and society.

To begin a themed studies unit, teachers select a theme from the universe of worthy and interesting themes such as oceanography, aviation, bones and bodies, transportation, weather, feelings, or magic. Teachers often initiate this process by brainstorming a number of theme ideas before making a selection. Once the theme is selected, teachers brainstorm resources such as print materials, hands-on materials, community resources, audiovisual resources, and human resources to support the theme.

Very often, teachers use an "I know" and "I wonder" webbing approach to invite children into the themed studies unit. Teachers ask children to brainstorm everything they know about the theme and record this on an "I know" web. Next, children are invited to brainstorm "I wonder" statements to be attached to the web to guide the exploration of the theme. For some teachers, a large "I wonder" wall chart organized into columns of "I wonder," "I found out," and "How I found out," works very well for children to organize and record information learned about the theme, as shown in Figure 10.34.

Teachers organize children into smaller groups to pursue specific subtopics of the theme or answer specific "I wonder" questions. The products of thematic study units

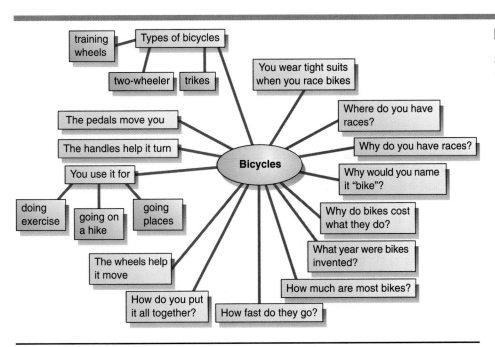

Figure 10.34

Second-grade students' "I know–I wonder" web

include, for example, written documents, murals, charts, graphs, as well as displays, fairs, speeches, demonstrations, plays, dioramas, and tours.

Two "Yes–But" issues loom large over teachers who question their own ability engage in thematic studies with young children. First, what about managing the classroom? And second, what about assessment? Organization, clear objectives, and flexibility are the keys to the first concern. Well-organized classroom centers with clear tasks and expectations make the classroom a much easier place to manage during themed studies. When problems occur, class meetings provide a democratic and useful forum for discussing and solving problems related to conduct and management in a classroom. The second concern, that of evaluating themed studies, is directly addressed by the use of authentic assessment. This approach to evaluation is fully described in Chapter 13.

Assisting Young Readers With Special Needs

When students in the early elementary grades have trouble with beginning literacy experiences, the effect can be far reaching. The child's self-esteem is usually damaged, life at home is affected, and a cycle of failure may develop. School systems spend many thousands of dollars trying to help at-risk students close the gap between them and their peers and get back on track with their education. Unfortunately, many students are never able to close the gap between their performance and potential. In this section, we summarize innovative practices relative to assisting early readers.

Reading Recovery

Reading recovery is one of the most successful early intervention reading programs.

In recent years, many reading researchers have called for direct and focused attention on beginning literacy problems in our schools. The idea is to "recover" early those children who are having problems in beginning reading. This can potentially spare children a lifetime of emotional and economic damage related to literacy problems, and schools can preserve valuable resources otherwise spent on remedial education.

One of the most successful early-intervention programs is Reading Recovery. Developed by Marie Clay (1985), an educator from New Zealand, Reading Recovery identifies at-risk children during their first year of reading instruction and provides them with individualized tutoring for 30 minutes each day. Reading Recovery has experienced success not only in New Zealand but in the United States as well (Pinnell, Fried, & Estice, 1990). In a recent study, Pinnell, Lyons, DeFord, Bryk, and Seltzer (1994) showed that Chapter 1 students assigned to Reading Recovery produced the only statistically significant gains on all reading measures used in the study as compared with three other treatment groups and a control group.

A typical tutoring session (Clay, 1985) includes each of the following activities:

See Chapter 13 for a complete description of running records.

- Rereading of two or more familiar books
- Rereading of yesterday's new book and taking a running record
- Letter identification (plastic letters on a magnetic board)
- Writing a story (including hearing sounds in words)
- Cut-up story to be rearranged
- New book introduced
- New book attempted

The Reading Recovery approach is effective with at-risk students for several reasons. First, Reading Recovery provides young children with a great deal of individual attention, which can be very beneficial for at-risk learners feeling insecure in a classroom setting. Also, Reading Recovery immerses children in pleasurable reading and writing opportunities. It promotes risk taking, attachment to favorite literature, self-selection of books, and creative writing production. Finally, teachers are better able to adjust the learning program and respond to student needs because of the one-on-one tutorial set-up.

In essence, Reading Recovery offers at-risk students a daily, individualized, balanced literacy teaching program with heavy emphasis on writing and reading in children's trade books. Teachers who enjoy adequate support from their school system should be able to achieve similar results as they construct transition programs of their own.

Helping Students With Special Cultural and Language Needs Succeed in the Early Years

Several researchers (Koskinen, Wilson, & Jensema, 1985; Neuman & Koskinen, 1992) have found that closed caption television is a particularly effective tool for motivating reluctant, language-minority students to learn to read and to improve fluency and comprehension. Closed caption television, which uses written subtitles, provides students with meaningful and motivating reading material set in the evolving context of a TV program. Materials necessary for using closed caption TV include (a) a video recorder/player, (b) a video monitor, (c) close captioning reader, and (d) videotapes.

The teacher begins by carefully selecting high-interest television programs, recording and previewing programs before making final selections, then introducing the program(s) to students with attention to vocabulary and prior knowledge factors (Koskinen, et al., 1985). Three elements should be considered in a successful closed caption lesson.

"The major advantage of captioned television is the multi-sensory stimulation of viewing the drama, hearing the sound, and seeing the captions." (Koskinen et al., 1985, p. 6)

1. The group watches a part of the captioned TV program together (5 to 10 minutes). The teachers stops the recorded tape and asks students to predict what will happen next in the program. Then the teacher continues showing the program so that students can check their predictions.
2. Students watch a segment of the program that has examples of certain kinds of phonic patterns, word uses, or punctuation. For example, students can be alerted to the use of quotation marks and the fact that these marks signal dialogue. Students can then watch the remainder of the tape to identify the dialogue using their knowledge of quotation marks.
3. After watching a closed caption TV program, students can practice reading aloud along with the captions. If necessary, both the auditory portion and the closed captioning can be played simultaneously to provide at-risk readers support through their initial attempts to read. At some later point, students can be allowed to practice reading the captioning without the auditory portion of the program.

Koskinen et al. add that they "do not recommend that the sound be turned off if this, in effect, turns off the children. The major advantage of captioned television is the multi-sensory stimulation of viewing the drama, hearing the sound, and seeing the captions" (1985, p. 6).

Summary

Language routines and strategies for structuring classroom reading and writing events involve children and teachers in, for example, sharing literacy, as during the tune-in routine. Repeated reading of favorite stories and text is provided during the old-favorites routine. The learning about language routine provides time for teachers to teach minilessons on strategies and skills that teachers have designated as useful for their students to learn to read. Predictable books and literature are shared daily during the new-story routine. And finally, children engage in a variety of independent reading and writing activities to deepen and extend their growing understanding and control of the reading and writing processes during the independent output activities routine.

Strategies for helping younger readers behave like skilled readers to the fullest extent possible from the very beginning of their experiences with reading and writing include using environmental print that children encounter daily in their lives. Teaching the alphabetic principle through regular encounters with whole books, poems, songs, and chants helps young children grasp the relationship between sounds, symbols, spoken words, and written words in a way that parallels their natural learning processes. A sense of story can be developed through using strategies that keep stories whole, connected, and meaningful for younger children. As young children encounter stories with the help of sensitive teachers, they internalize the structure of stories as well as the structures of various other literary genres. They can then use their understanding of story structure to make sense of unfamiliar stories and print.

Children need to respond to their reading to deepen and extend their understanding and interpretations. For emergent readers, response to a story can be elicited effectively and enjoyably by using drawing and art. Younger children are familiar with representing their meanings on paper through the symbol system of shapes and figures. With time and exposure to printed language, their drawing responses to reading gradually give way to using the symbol system of printed language. Ashton-Warner once said, "First words are different from first drawings only in medium" (1963, p. 28). Figure 10.35 provides an overview of the chapter.

CONCEPT APPLICATIONS

IN THE CLASSROOM

1. Start an alphabetized collection of environmental print. Arrange to meet with a child and make an I-can-read book.
2. Start a collection of favorite songs, poems, riddles, language games, and puzzles for use during the tune-in routine.

IN THE FIELD

1. Buy a wordless picture book. Make arrangements to meet with a small group of kindergarten children. Take down their dictation for the pictures. Help them to read their dictated story for the pictures.
2. Take a predictable book and make a literature web for this book. Arrange to meet with a group of first-grade children to use the literature web and read the predictable book.

Figure 10.35

Chapter overview

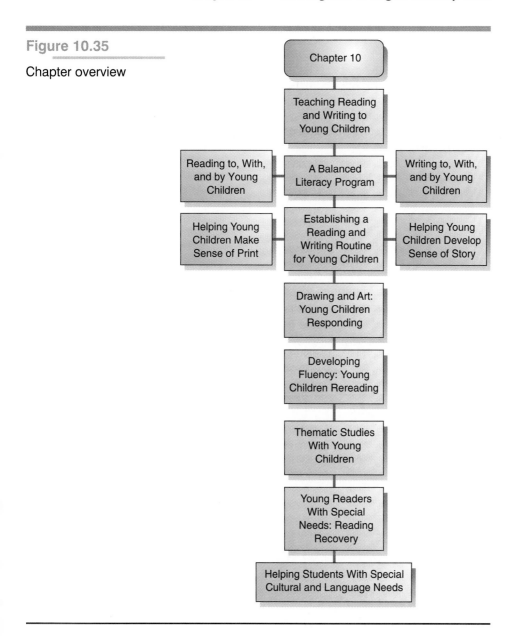

3. Arrange to meet with an individual child in first grade to read a book. Ask the child to retell the book, and record her retelling. Analyze the book and the retelling using Morrow's (1989) guides.

4. Read a predictable book to a group of kindergartners or first-grade children. Have them respond to the book by using the sketch-to-stretch activity. Write a brief summary of your observations from the experience.

5. Locate a teacher who uses Reading Recovery. Interview her. You may wish to ask how she became acquainted with Reading Recovery, where she received training, and if she is experiencing success.

RECOMMENDED READINGS

Barrett, F. L. (1982). *A teacher's guide to shared reading.* Ontario, Canada: Scholastic-TAB Publications.

Brown, H., & Cambourne, B. (1987). *Read and retell.* Portsmouth, NH: Heinemann.

Clay, M. (1985). *The early detection of reading difficulties* (3rd ed). Portsmouth, NH: Heinemann.

Gambrell, L. (1985). Dialogue journals: reading-writing interaction. *The Reading Teacher, 38(6),* 512–515.

Hill, S. (1989). *Books alive! Using literature in the classroom.* Portsmouth, NH: Heinemann.

Hill, S. (1990). *Raps and rhymes.* Portsmouth, NH: Heinemann.

Johnson, T. D., & Louis, D. R. (1990). *Bringing it all together: A program for literacy.* Portsmouth, NH: Heinemann.

Lynch, P. (1986). *Using big books and predictable books.* New York: Scholastic.

Nathan, R., Temple, F., Juntunen, K., & Temple, C. (1989). *Classroom strategies that work: An elementary teacher's guide to process writing.* Portsmouth, NH: Heinemann.

Parsons, L. (1990). *Response journals.* Portsmouth, NH: Heinemann.

Pinnell, G. S., Fried, M. D., & Estice, R. M. (1990). Reading recovery: Learning how to make a difference. *The Reading Teacher, 43(3),* 282–295.

Chapter **11**

Reading and Writing
in Grades 2 to 8

Focus Questions

When you are finished studying this chapter, you should be able to answer these questions:

1. What are the differences between core book units and themed literature units? In what ways are they similar?
2. What is the purpose of sharing time in the Reading Workshop?
3. During self-selected reading and response, teachers and students both have options. What are their choices?
4. What happens during individual reading conferences that helps teachers assess reading development and plan for instruction?
5. What is the purpose of a writing process approach to composition instruction?
6. In what ways are the Reading and Writing Workshops similar?
7. What is meant by "publishing"?
8. What are some of the benefits and liabilities of the *Writing to Read* computer program?
9. What is meant by "holistic integration of the curriculum"?
10. Are literature-based reading programs and writing workshops helpful with readers with learning problems? Is substantial modification necessary? If so, why?

Key Concepts

Core Books
Individualized Reading
Themed Literature Units
Reading Workshop
Fluency
Repeated Readings
Writing Process Approach

Prewriting
Drafting
Revising
Editing
Publishing
Writing Workshop
Themed Studies Approach

The Reading–Writing Connection: An Introduction

Reading and writing are reciprocal processes.

Reading and writing are basic reflections of the same language processes (Squire, 1983). For example, one aspect of the reading act is concerned with *decoding* graphic symbols into words, whereas writing is concerned, in part, with *encoding* meaning into graphic symbols. Similarly, writers create meaning in text, while readers interpret meaning from text.

From a language learning perspective, teachers understand that reading and writing are reciprocal processes (K. S. Goodman & Goodman, 1983; Shanahan, 1984). As children become authors, they also become better readers, because "writers must read and reread during writing" (K. S. Goodman & Goodman, 1983, p. 591). Indeed, it does not seem possible to positively affect one without improving the other. Reading quality text that is stimulating and writing for authentic purposes are crucial elements of a balanced reading program.

In Chapter 10 we saw how emerging reading and writing abilities are facilitated by literacy learning events in the classroom. As children move into intermediate and middle school years, their teachers seek ways of facilitating and advancing their literacy development to inspire life-long reading and writing abilities. Because of the complementary benefits of reading and writing instruction, teachers frequently seek ways of involving the two simultaneously. An integrated curriculum is a powerful vehicle for merging reading and writing instruction, problem-solving skills, cooperative learning, and other desirable curriculum elements in authentic learning situations.

Integrated curriculums are usually accomplished in two stages. At the first level of integration, the language arts curriculum (reading, writing, listening, speaking) makes the transition from a fragmented, segmented schedule to a more unified model. This is often accomplished through literature-based reading units. At the second level of curriculum integration, the language arts are integrated across the curriculum. This is often accomplished through interdisciplinary thematic units.

In this chapter we particularly concern ourselves with the first level of curriculum integration, specifically, how literature-based reading programs are constructed and how the writing process can be used effectively in upper elementary and middle school grades. Later in the chapter, we offer some fascinating ideas as to how integrated language arts programs can be used as a catalyst for substantive study of diverse cultures and to benefit readers with learning needs.

Literature-Based Reading Programs

It is possible for literature-based reading instruction to take several forms.

When we visited a publishers' exhibit at an annual conference of the International Reading Association, the "hot" topic that year seemed to be the rediscovery of children's books as a viable source for teaching reading. As this mammoth exhibit opened, thousands of teachers grabbed virtually every trade book in sight. They seemed motivated to update their classrooms with the latest materials and to feel a part of the literature-based movement. Teachers who want to use literature for reading instruction need to clearly understand how to use books in effective and coherent ways and how books can be used to foster children's love of literacy experiences.

The notion of literature-based reading units has matured into several viable instructional strategies. In reviewing studies of effective literature-based reading programs (Cox & Zarillo, 1993; Cooter & Griffith, 1989; Hiebert & Colt, 1989; Zarillo, 1989), three interpretations or program designs were found to be effective: (a) core books, (b) individualized or self-selected and self-pacing units, and (c) themed literature units. It is important for the reader to note that these options are organizational structures for the classroom having a common purpose: teaching reading using children's or adolescent literature. The components found in each are interchangeable.

In this section, we review the essential elements of core books and the individualized reading approach. In subsequent sections of this chapter, we present themed literature units and a fourth alternative, the Reading Workshop.

Core Books

Core books are defined as "those [literary] selections that are to be taught in the classroom, are given close reading and intensive consideration, and are likely to be an important stimulus for writing and discussion" (California State Department of Education, 1980, p. ix). With core book units, a single trade book title is selected and enough copies are acquired so each student has one to use. When used in conjunction with free reading and writing activities, core books offer teachers and students many enjoyable literacy experiences.

Core book units use multiple copies of a single book selection for an entire class.

Successful teachers of core book units have several things in common (Cox & Zarillo, 1993; Zarillo, 1989). First, they usually do not restrict students to a short list of "approved" books but allow them to select books of their own choosing or from an extensive list of popular literature. Teachers may find it helpful each year to consult such lists as the "Children's Choices" and "Teachers' Choices" for the best new books being released. These lists are published annually by the International Reading Association in its journal *The Reading Teacher.* Second, successful core book teachers present the selection to the class with enthusiasm and drama. Sometimes selected students are involved in introducing a book or book chapter through reader's theater. Teacher book talks and shared book experiences are also effective means of developing enthusiasm for the book. Most importantly, successful teachers use the core book as a springboard for independent reading and writing activities.

Perhaps the greatest concern related to using core books is the idea of requiring *all* children to read the same book. Although there are many books that educators hope children will not miss, there are probably none that should be required of *every* child (Huck, Helper, & Hickman, 1987; Zarillo, 1989). Whenever the element of choice is removed from students, teachers run the risk of alienating them from books. Further, the use of core books as the only method of instruction in a literature-based program ignores the importance of allowing children to match books to their individual interests.

Core books are used as a springboard for other reading and writing activities.

Another concern relates to allowing children to read the core book independently. Students should be allowed to read the book at their own pace. Sometimes children become so absorbed by a book that they want to read it quickly. Let them! There are plenty of other related books of high quality they can read while their classmates are still reading. On the other hand, some children may not get into the book without some direction. Many teachers assign goal pages each night to keep the class moving and to let readers know which part of the book will be discussed next in class.

Core book units usually have several constituent parts and tend to follow a common general sequence. Offered below is a kind of template we have used in constructing core book units. As with all teaching suggestions, these should be tried out in the classroom and adapted to suit the teacher's needs.

A Template for Planning Core Book Units

Background Preparations

- Confer with authoritative sources (other teachers, media specialists/librarians, lists of popular children's and adolescent books) concerning possible core books, then make your selection.
- Read the selected core book.
- Obtain background information about the book, author, and general theme of the book.
- Order multiple copies of the core book so that each student will have a copy. For bilingual classrooms and students early in their learning of English, obtain, if available, translated editions of the core book.
- Obtain a book jacket, pictures and other props to use in "selling" the book.
- Obtain extension materials related to the general theme of the book (these will be part of a temporary classroom library and/or reference center).
- Make a list of literature-reponse projects that may be suggested to students (numerous examples are suggested later in this chapter.

Part 1: Book and Author Introduction

The primary purpose is to introduce the core book and other books by the same author and/or suggest related books that might be enticing to students. Teachers should also describe in a general way choices that will be available to students pertaining to literature response, written reponses, and group collaborations. Following are typical activities that transpire in Phase 1:

- **Book introduction** using book jacket and other displays or props.
- **Sharing information** about the author and why he or she wrote the book (Note: for a great example, see Jerry Spinelli's 1991 article "Catching Maniac Magee" in which he explains his motives in writing this Newberry Award winning book.)
- **Book talk** — the teacher dramatically reads an interesting portion of the book leaing up to a thrilling point, then leaves the class hanging.
- **Distribution of the book**
- **Sustained Silent Reading (SSR)** to permit students to begin reading the core book and, hopefully, get hooked.
- **Description of initial choices for literature reponse,** which usually are of an individual nature (i.e., reading response journals, reading logs, story mapping, etc.).

Individualized Reading

Individualized reading units permit students to choose their own book from many choices.

Individualized reading (Veatch, 1978), also known as self-selected or self-paced reading, is virtually at the other end of the continuum of literature-based reading instruction from core books (Hiebert & Colt, 1989). Instead of reading a book chosen by the teacher, students are permitted to select for themselves from a library of trade books. Virtually all reading instruction springs from these books that students have self-selected.

Rule of thumb is an easy-to-use book selection strategy for children.

Individualized reading begins with students learning how to self-select books of interest. A procedure known as "rule of thumb" (also called the "sticky palm" and "greasy fingers" method) is taught to the class, enabling them to efficiently choose books that are "just right." First, the child finds a book that appeals to him. Second, he opens the book to any page with a lot of words and begins to read. Each time the child comes to a word he does not know, he puts a finger down. If, by the time he comes to the end of the page, all fingers on one hand have been used, then the book

- **Introduction of the library and resource centers,** which house additional free-reading materials for self-selected reading and research into related topics.
- **Assignment of goal pages** so that students are aware of minimal reading expect-tions for coming days.

Part 2: Reading and Reponse

In this phase, students read and discuss events in the book with the teacher and peers. Literature-reponse activities, including written reponse, commence. Phase 2 activities may include

- **Discussion of reponses** noted in reading journals pertaining to the goal pages.
- **Read alouds/choral rereadings** by the teacher or students who have rehearsed with a partner(s). Choral readings are intended to assist students in developing flu-ency.
- **Group response sessions** wherein students develop a project to demonstrate their comprehension of the book (e.g., discussion webs, "Novels in the News," dramatic portrayals).
- **Student-teacher conferences,** which permit one-on-one interaction for the purpose of ongoing assessment
- **SSR time** to allow students time to read portions of the core book during school hours and subtly remind students that "reading is a priority" in our education.
- **Literacy skill/strategy activities** in which teacher-led minilessons are presented to help students continue their development in such areas as vocabulary knowledge, comprehension strategies, study skills, decoding abilities, writing/composition, and fluency.

Part 3: Conclusion and Presentations

In the final phase, students complete the reading and analysis of the core book. Group and individual reponse projects are presented to the class. Phase 3 often involves

- **Class discussions** about the book and other related books read by class members.
- **Presentations of literature-response activities,** such as murals, posters, mobiles, dramatizations, or panel discussions, etc.
- **Closure activities** led by the teacher to help bring about a sense of completion and inspire a continuing desire to read other books by the same author or by other authors in the same genre.

is probably too hard, and he should put it back and find another he likes just as well. This procedure can be taught easily to students from primary grades on up.

Once a book has been selected, students engage in many activities, both independently and as a class. These include self-selected reading (SSR), whole-class language experience approach (LEA), writing workshop, and literature-response projects (skits, dioramas, writing new endings to stories). Teachers conduct conferences with each child to monitor and assess comprehension, to develop reading strategies, and to teach related literacy skills. Groups are formed on the basis of mutual need for learning specific reading skills or strategies. Individualized reading culminates with an opportunity for students to read aloud a favorite part of their book to the teacher or class.

Zarillo (1989) cites five common concerns educators often have related to individualized reading programs: (a) a lack of administrative support; (b) a shortage of books in classroom libraries; (c) fear among some teachers and administrators that individualized reading will lead to a chaotic environment; (d) concerns that students

Teachers meet with individuals or small groups of children in individualized reading to teach skills and strategies.

Students select books for themselves in the individualized reading approach.

will not fare as well on standardized reading tests; and (e) many teachers' feeling uninformed about how to implement individualized reading programs.

Themed literature units and the Reading Workshop are two additional organizational schemes that have been used with great success. As with core book and individualized reading units, themed literature units and the Reading Workshop have a common purpose: teaching reading using children's or adolescent literature. The components found in themed literature units and the Reading Workshop are quite interchangeable. Because of their comprehensive nature, they are presented in some detail in the following two sections.

Using a Themed Literature Units Approach

History of Common Elements of Themed Literature Units

Themed literature units
organize instruction around
a central theme or concept.

Themed literature units (Cooter & Griffith, 1989) organize reading and writing activities around a central concept or theme. They differ from a themed studies or thematic approach (discussed fully in Chapter 12) in the sense that themed studies integrate content areas (e.g., science, mathematics literature, social studies, etc.), whereas themed literature units pertain mainly to reading. In themed literature units, students are permitted to choose a book from a short list of book options. After reading the book, reader response groups (also called literature-response groups) are formed to develop a project that demonstrates their comprehension of the book.

As with many holistic approaches to reading instruction, the origin of themed literature units may be traced at least as far back as the Progressive Era in American education. However, this "new–old" way of thinking about reading instruction finds more recent support in the writings of Fish (1967) and Holland (1975). In essence, educators feel that the reader should be drawn into an emotional response with written language so as to create a bond between the book and student. Reader response is often seen as a very crucial element. According to Worby (1980), reader response supports the notion of literature being gathered into themes that mirror the conscious or unconscious desires and interests of the student.

Ways to extend thematic instruction across all curriculum areas are discussed in Chapter 12.

The professional literature concerning themed literature units suggests certain common elements. A brief description follows:

Themes are linked to quality literature or expository text. Themes help teachers select from the vast numbers of quality children's literature and nonfiction books available. A good theme is broad enough to allow for the selection of books that accommodate the wide range of reading interests and abilities in every classroom yet narrow enough to be manageable. Themes are not limited to fictional stories or narrative text but often involve content themes as well (e.g., in science, social studies, health, etc.). Several examples may help to clarify this point.

Journeys and courage are two popular themes selected by teachers.

One of the more successful themed literature units developed for upper elementary grades is called *journeys.* In planning a unit using the journeys theme, teachers first brainstorm as many different interpretations as possible for the theme and diagram them on paper in the form of a web (Figure 11.1). After subtopics have been identified, teachers search for popular children's books that might go along with each subtheme.

For instance, in children's literature, characters are often seen going on long journeys into "fantasy lands" full of mystery and danger. Such books as *The Lion, the Witch, and the Wardrobe* (Lewis, 1961), *The Phantom Tollbooth* (Juster, 1961), *Charlie and the Chocolate Factory* (Dahl, 1964), or the old favorite book by Frank Baum (1972) *The Wizard of Oz* all fit nicely into this interpretation of journeys. Figure 11.2 shows a fully completed web for the journeys theme with subtopics and possible book titles.

Figure 11.1

Journeys theme web

Figure 11.2

Completed journeys web

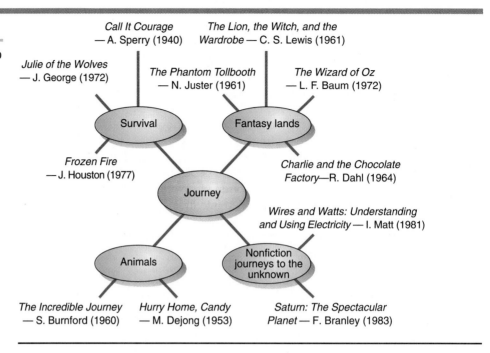

Think of some of the various forms of courage depicted in quality books.

Another popular theme is called *courage*. Courage is a superb theme because it may be interpreted in many ways yet allows teachers to choose books from a manageable body of literature. Again, teachers wishing to develop a themed literature unit using courage as the theme should begin by "webbing out" several interpretations or subtopics. For instance, there is the kind of courage demonstrated on a battlefield, which might be called "bravery in battle." Another interpretation might involve the kind of courage exhibited by persons having to cope with problems of the human condition. This subtopic might be called "overcoming adversity." Many times young people have to develop courage when dealing with "peer relationships." These are only a few interpretations that could be used in a themed literature unit titled "Courage." Figure 11.3 shows a fully developed web with book possibilities for a courage theme for upper elementary students.

A good theme is broadly interpretable and can be linked to quality books.

To review, a good theme is broadly interpretable and can be linked to quality children's books. When these criteria are met, planning a successful themed literature unit is possible. A number of viable themes have been collected from several school systems using themed literature units and are included in the following list. They have been classified into specific grade levels by in-service teachers (Table 11.1).

Student choice is a powerful motivator in themed literature units.

Students have the freedom to choose which books they wish to read. When possible, students should be permitted to select themes so as to enhance interest (Jacobs & Borland, 1986). Each theme should include a variety of choices that reflect the diversity of interests and ability levels in the classroom. This view of reading instruction is in sharp contrast to the overly structured "teacher as dictator" forms of teaching associated with the "mastery learning" movement. After previewing each of the book choices through teacher book talks, the student is then able to make his selection.

Literature response allows students to demonstrate what they have learned. In addition to answering teacher-generated comprehension questions, stu-

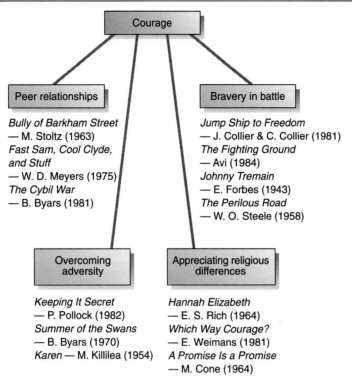

Figure 11.3

Completed courage theme web

dents complete special projects pertaining to the book's content. These projects may take the form of student dramas, creative writing projects, or other creative responses.

Team planning and collaboration help teachers efficiently develop themed literature units. In themed literature units, the teacher guides students toward new and exciting discoveries in a seemingly effortless fashion. The secret to a good themed literature unit, however, is adequate planning. Themed literature units are usually developed through team planning involving reading and language arts teachers at each grade level. Team planning allows teachers to develop units quicker and with greater depth. The old adage "two heads are better than one" definitely holds true here. Sometimes teachers from various academic disciplines join in to help plan interdisciplinary units. Some examples of interdisciplinary units are discussed later in the chapter and in Chapter 12.

An important consideration for the success of themed literature units is school system support. Developing effective themed literature units is a major undertaking requiring a great deal of teacher planning time, financial resources (primarily for the purchase of paperback books), and administrative approval. This means that school systems necessarily need to provide teachers with some form of compensated planning time after school hours or release time during the school day. It may be most desirable for school systems to address this need during the summer season when schools are usually not in session. Additionally, school systems should carefully select in-service leaders to assist teachers planning themed literature units for the first time. Leaders should be up to date on the professional literature concerning themed literature units and should have classroom experience using these procedures.

Students demonstrate their comprehension of text through literature response projects.

Notice that teachers building themed literature units prefer to do so collaboratively.

Administrative support is crucial in developing successful themed literature units.

Table 11.1

Selected themes by grade level: Prekindergarten through sixth grade

Selected Themes by Grade Level: Prekindergarten Through Sixth Grade		
Prekindergarten and Kindergarten ABC Color Community Helpers* Dinosaurs* Fairy tales Families* Friends Holidays* Monsters Pets* School* Seasons* **First Grade** Animals* Famous People* Feelings Food* Growing Up* Insects* Numbers Poems Travel* **Second Grade** Author (specific)* Birthdays Deserts* Fable Fairy Tales	Giants Grandparents* Native Americans* Sea* Space* Tall Tales Weather* **Third Grade** Adventure Beasts/Creatures Biographies* Culture* Folktales Legends Magic Mystery Pioneers* Sports* War* Western Stories Witches **Fourth Grade** Changes in Life* Explorers* Geographical Regions* Heroes* Mysteries Myths* Night Frights Space*	Tales–Tails Wheels* **Fifth Grade** Cultures* Fantasy–Fairy tales Friends Journeys Little People–Giants Monsters Occupations* Prejudices* Seasons of Life* Survival The Future* Transportation* **Sixth Grade** Adventure Animals* Cars and Motorcycles* Conflict* Family* Ghosts Heroes* Humor Music* Overcoming Adversity Seasonal Sports* Survival

Note: Many of the themes could be used at different grade levels
*Nonfiction and/or expository text.

Teaching Themed Literature Units: The Nuts and Bolts

Once themes have been chosen, teachers are ready to gather learning resources and plan for instruction. The next two sections describe which resources are needed for successful implementation of themed literature units and how required reading skills and strategies can be documented. In the last part of this section, a 5-week sample plan is presented.

Gathering Learning Resources

Once the teacher has selected a theme, resources must be assembled. Although large amounts of capital are not required, a substantial commitment of time and other assets is needed for full implementation. One school system using our approach began trials of themed literature units in a middle school consisting of several middle school classes with about $1,500, most of which was spent on multiple copies of paperback books. Following is a short "shopping list" of items needed for themed literature units:

- Multiple copies of books selected ("perma-bound" books are preferred)
- Classroom library related to theme (e.g., textbooks, trade books from the school library, filmstrips, recordings, etc.)
- Art supplies for literature-response projects (e.g., markers, scissors, tag board, rulers)
- Classroom computers
- Reference books (e.g., dictionaries, encyclopedia, thesaurus)

It is possible to begin themed literature units on a small budget, but quality programs require sufficient funding over time.

Documenting Progress in Required Reading and Study Skills

As mentioned in previous chapters, most school systems have mandated performance objectives for students that tend to be based on, or correlate highly with, basal reader scope and sequence charts and state curriculum requirements. A common concern among administrators when themed literature units or other holistic programs are being considered relates to documentation of these student performance objectives. This is one of the political realities to which teachers frequently must give some attention.

Nonnegotiable reading skills and strategies are figured into the earliest planning stages.

Teachers select books for their classroom library that are related to the theme.

Student performance objectives can easily be addressed in the early planning stages of a themed literature unit. Observing the following considerations will help teachers account for these performance objectives and avoid difficulties in justifying the themed literature program.

Ways of assessing reading are discussed in Chapter 13.

1. Secure a copy of the state and local curriculum guides and identify all required objectives for the grade level(s) involved.
2. Study the objectives thoroughly, and identify possible learning experiences that could satisfy the requirements. Be sure to consider alternative grouping patterns and materials for each learning experience.
3. As plans for the themed literature unit are drawn up, all objectives should be clearly stated and plans for assessing each objective described.

It is not unusual for teachers to discover that a few objectives cannot easily be satisfied in themed literature units. These objectives can be addressed through short-term, whole-group minilessons.

Themed Literature Unit Time Line: An Example

Themed literature units can be as short as 1 day or as long as 6 weeks. Factors such as grade or developmental level, the nature of the theme itself, and curriculum requirements usually help teachers decide what sort of time frame might be best. For illustrative purposes, a 5-week time line for upper elementary or middle school students has been selected. Figure 11.4 presents the time line and is followed by descriptions of each element.

Week 1: Introducing the Theme.   Many teachers like to begin themed literature units with introductory activities of some sort. The purposes are to activate students' prior knowledge and generate motivational feelings about the theme to be studied. Introductory activities might include a collage bulletin board depicting many interpretations of the new theme, role playing, a guest speaker, or group participation activities.

With a colleague, brainstorm ways students could be introduced to a theme.

One classroom about to begin work using the courage theme reviewed a teacher-made collage bulletin board. The teacher had clipped pictures from magazines depicting several interpretations of the word *courage*. These pictures included two police officers on patrol in their squad car, a young woman in a wheelchair, the

---

Figure 11.4

Themed literature unit time line for fifth- or sixth-grade students

WEEK 1:	Class introduction to the theme. Book talks and book selection. Self-selected reading (SSR).
WEEK 2:	Reading response groups are formed. Response projects approved by the teacher. Groups begin work on projects.
WEEKS 3 to 4:	Response project work continues. Teacher conducts minilessons (student performance objectives).
WEEK 5:	Students present response projects to class. Closure activities by the teacher and class.

President of the United States making a speech, and a soldier on a battlefield. The teacher and class had a most productive discussion about the theme, and the stage was set for the introduction of the books.

Another very similar kind of bulletin board could be constructed using jackets from the books to be introduced. For the courage theme, a teacher might simply display the word *courage* in bold letters at the center of the bulletin board. Lines could spiral out from the theme word in a web format and connect to each of the book jackets (similar to the designs of Figures 11.2 and 11.3). With this type of bulletin board, the teacher can introduce both the theme and book choices at once.

Many other theme introductions are possible. A guest speaker might come and talk to the class. For instance, before beginning a theme entitled "Animals," the teacher could invite a local veterinarian to visit the class and speak about specific animals portrayed in the selected books for the unit. In one instance we observed, the presenter brought along some of the instruments used for administering medicine to animals, talked about some of the myths and facts about the animals under study, and answered questions from the class. This experience produced a strong interest in the theme and resulted in a great deal of recreational reading in the library and student writing (in the form of language experience stories).

Other introductory activities may involve drama. Role playing, reader's theater, and even an occasional video production can be used for theme introduction. Once a mental mind set has been created for the theme, the teacher is ready to introduce the books.

Book Talks. One of the most enjoyable parts of a themed literature unit, for both teacher and students, is book talks (Fader, 1976). The object is to draw the children into the books and interest them deeply, so they will want to read. When the book talk is well executed, all children want to read several of the books mentioned. In fact, a little frustration may result as each student tries to choose the one book he most wants to read.

Book talks call on teachers to use their drama skills to draw children into choosing books.

The book talk activity is very easy to do. First, the teacher finds a most enticing section in each of the books to be used (about six titles for a class of 25, with five copies of each title available). We recommend that the section of the book to be emphasized take about 5 to 10 minutes to read and come from the first third of the book. Second, the teacher enthusiastically tells the class about each book, perhaps adding some background information about the author, then reads a juicy part of the book to the class. Naturally, the more drama and excitement a teacher puts into the book talk, the easier it will be to get the class hooked on each book. Third, the teacher should conclude the reading without giving away the plot. In other words, the book talk should be a cliffhanger. In fact, the suspense of not knowing what will happen to the characters in the story should create an almost overpowering urge to read the book. After each book has been introduced, the children are ready to make their selection.

Student Self-Selection. An important element for the success of any holistic reading program is for students to feel that they have choices. In themed literature units, students are allowed to choose which of the books they will read. As mentioned, about six titles (five copies of each title) usually are selected for a class of 25 children.

Students choose books on the basis of interest.

In helping children choose which book to read, a good way to avoid peer pressure among students is to have them select their books by secret ballot. Ask the children to write their names on a blank piece of paper, then list in order their first, second, and third choices. Inform them that they will be given one of their choices and, if at all possible, their first choice.

During the teacher's planning period, he simply lists on a sheet of paper the title for each book and writes the numbers from one to five under each title (this corresponds to the multiple copies acquired for each title). Next, the teacher opens the ballots and gives each child their first choice. Should the teacher run out of a given title, he simply gives the child their second choice. Even if the teacher has to give a child their second choice, the child still feels he was given a book of his own choosing instead of one chosen by the teacher. Figure 11.5 illustrates a typical class assignment chart. Sometimes only one child chooses a given title. In this event, the student simply works through the project alone. In fact, during the course of a school year, all children should have an opportunity to work alone at least once.

Self-Selected Reading. Once the book assignments have been announced, the children are ready to begin reading. It is recommended that the unit begin in earnest by allowing students time to read their books in an uninterrupted fashion. We call this reading period *self-selected reading (SSR),* rather than the usual label, *sustained silent reading,* simply because readers may want to share an exciting reading discovery with a friend during the period. These positive encounters with books should be encouraged as long as class disruption does not become a factor.

Children spend at least two class periods reading their new book selections.

The purpose of SSR in this situation is threefold. First, children are given time to read, an activity that improves reading ability over time. Second, the children are allowed to get involved with their books, which creates a strong motivation to continue reading. A third purpose is to allow children who may have selected a book that is too difficult time to change their minds and trade in their book for one of the remaining titles. Usually, a 24-hour grace period is allowed for exchanges. The equivalent of two reading class periods on consecutive days is a good start for SSR.

Time limits are usually set for students to finish reading their books.

A question teachers frequently ask relates to how long students should be expected to take to complete reading their books. Some teachers feel that when students are given a great deal of time to finish their books, say 3 to 4 weeks, students simply procrastinate finishing the book until 1 or 2 days before the deadline. This

Figure 11.5

Themed literature unit assignment chart example

Themed Unit Title: "Courage"	
Book: *Fast Sam, Cool Clyde and Stuff*	Book: *The Perilous Road*
1. Jason B.	1. Christen M.
2. Jina M.	2. Ramesh B.
3. Melanie C.	3. Michelle L.
4. Bill J.	4. Jason L.
5. Mark S.	5.
Book: *Summer of the Swans*	Book: *Which Way Courage?*
1. Austin K.	1. Skip C.
2. Sutton E.	2. Margarette S.
3. Jill E.	3. Julian G.
4. Emilio C.	4. Jason U.
5. Bruce W.	5.
Book: *Johnny Tremain*	Book: *The Cybil War*
1. Shelley P.	1. Toni G.
2. Jackson B.	2. Marion H.
3. Deb F.	3. Luis J.
4.	4. Jillian Y.
5.	5. Charesse D.

generally results in a not-so-pleasurable reading experience for the student, opposite of our intended purpose. To counteract this problem, some teachers prefer to use a shortened timetable for reading the book, say 5 to 7 days for books of about 120 pages. With this timetable comes a mild sense of urgency or feeling on the part of the student that "I better get busy reading or I won't be finished in time."

Some books naturally require more time than others for reading because of length or complexity. Usually, a formula can be worked out by the teacher to determine how many days should be allowed for the reading of each book. For instance, if the teacher feels that the average child could read 20 pages of a given book per night, then a 300-page book will require at least 15 days to read. Teachers should also consider such factors as print size, number of words per page, and the author's writing style when developing these formulas. Whatever the formula used, teachers should try to come up with reasonable limits that help students stay on task and enjoy the book.

Week 2: Beginning Literature-Response Projects.   As teachers well know, sometimes students can be very reluctant readers. Literature-response activities can be a wonderful vehicle for spurring interest in books and can create writing opportunities. During the second week, students begin work with their literature-response groups (LRGs). Children are grouped based on mutual interest, namely, which book they chose. For example, all students (up to four or five in number) who choose to read *Henry and Beezus* (Cleary, 1952) as part of a friendship theme become the Henry and Beezus Group. All children reading *The Lion, the Witch, and the Wardrobe* (Lewis, 1961) as part of the journeys theme become The Lion, the Witch, and the Wardrobe Group. This type of grouping capitalizes on students' intrinsic interests, needs, and motivations.

Students begin work in literature-response groups during the second week of the unit.

Students working in LRGs are required to conceive of a project that demonstrates their comprehension of their book. All project ideas are subject to approval by the teacher because refinement of some ideas will be required. We observed one group that read Lewis's *The Lion, the Witch, and the Wardrobe* and decided to create a "Narnia game." Constructed in the image of popular trivia games, contestants landing on certain spaces on the gameboard were required to answer questions related to the book. Because students in the LRG were required to write all questions and answers for the game (on a variety of cognitive levels), comprehension of the book seemed to be deeper than one might typically expect from, for example, workbook exercises.

Next, we discuss several popular LRG project ideas that have been successful with themed literature units. Some are rather extensive and take considerable preparation, while others may be accomplished in just one or two sessions.

Student Dramas.   Reenactment of major events in a book is a particularly popular LRG activity for students in elementary through middle school grades. These student dramas foster deeper understanding of story structures and narrative competence (Martinez, 1993), facilitate content mastery, and provide a marvelous forum in which to display oral fluency skills. Only minimal props and costumes are needed to help students participate.

Think about some of the advantages of LRG projects over traditional reading follow-up activities like completing worksheets.

Students begin by choosing a favorite part of the book to retell through drama. Next, they develop a script based on a combination of actual dialogue in the book and narration. Usually the narration is delivered by a reader or narrator, who explains such story elements as setting, problem, and other pertinent information. Typically, the drama is presented as a one-act play and concludes in the same way as a book talk—leave the audience in suspense. This often makes the audience (other students in the class) want to select the book themselves for recreational reading.

Martinez (1993) points out that modeling can be especially helpful in encouraging students to choose this option for literature response. Inviting a professional or amateur actor to explain to students some of the rudiments of performance is a good way to stimulate interest.

Students frequently choose to create dramas based on their selected books.

The accompanying box shows a script developed by students for the novel *Fast Sam, Cool Clyde, and Stuff* (Myers, 1975). This script includes dialogue excerpts from the book along with narration developed by the students.

Dialogue Retellings. Cudd and Roberts (1993) suggest another drama form using fables to help students better understand the importance of dialogue. First, the teacher selects a short fable having two characters and reads it to the class. Cudd and Roberts suggest Arnold Lobel's (1983) *Fables*. Second, the teacher chooses two students to orally retell the fable, each assuming the part of one character. The other students listen for story sequence and help supply any missing parts. The whole class has a discussion about how dialogue is important to story and character development. Third, the teacher provides each student with a copy of the fable for rereading and analysis of the dialogue mechanics in writing. Fourth, students working in pairs write a retelling of the

---

Script for *Fast Sam, Cool Clyde and Stuff*

Stuff: Sam and Clyde were going to enter the contest. Only, one of them was going to get decked out like a girl.

Sam: You can be the woman, and I'll be the man, and we can win this contest. Ain't nobody around going to beat us. And that's a f-a-c-t fact.

Clyde: How come I have to be the woman? You can be the woman, and I can be the guy.

Sam: I got to be the guy. Because I can't be no woman.

Clyde: Why not?

Sam: Because it messes with my image.

Clyde: And it messes with my image, too.

Sam: Anyway, I'm so manly that anybody looking at me could tell I was a man.

Stuff: We told Angel and Maria and it was decided that me, Angel, and Maria would decide who would be the girl and who would be the guy. Me and Angel figured the guy who was the more manly would be the guy and the other person would be the girl. Maria, Angel's sister, said the guy who was the most manly would be the girl "cause it wouldn't bother him as much being the girl." Which made sense in a funny kind of way. Anyway, we had a manly contest to see who was the most manly between Clyde and Sam.

The contest was simple. Whoever did the manliest thing was going to be the woman, and the other guy would be the man. We figured we had three votes, and it couldn't be a tie. But that was before we considered Maria.

Adapted from the text by R. Cooter, 1990.

fable from memory with each student assuming one of the character roles. As they write/retell the dialogue and their character speaks, the paper used to create the draft should be physically handed to the appropriate person so that they are constantly reminded to indent. In the final stages of this activity, students can share their dialogues with the class, then create their own original fables individually, in pairs, or groups.

Radio Play. Developing a radio play involves virtually the same process as any other student drama, except that it involves a purely oral–aural delivery. Students first write a one-act play based on their book as described in the preceding section. Next, materials are gathered for the purpose of creating needed sound effects (i.e., police whistles, recorded train sound effects, door opening/closing, etc.), and different human sounds are practiced (such as a girl's or boy's scream, tongue clicking noise, throat clearing, etc.). After thorough rehearsal of the script with sound effects, the radio play is taped on a cassette recorder and played over the school's public address system into the classroom.

Teachers may want to obtain recordings of old radio shows, such as "The Shadow," to help students better understand the concept. Another source is Garrison Keillor's radio program, "A Prairie Home Companion," which airs every Saturday night on American Public Radio stations and usually has several radio dramas each week.

Radio plays involve both reading and writing processes.

	Sam and Clyde, me, Angel, and Maria all met at Clyde's house. Sam was supposed to do his manly thing first.
Sam:	I am going to do 50 push-ups. Every time I go down I'll go all the way down until my *mustache* touches the floor.
Stuff:	When he said "mustache" he gave Clyde a look because Sam was the only one in the whole bunch who had even a little bit of a mustache.
Clyde:	He got his mustache by having a transplant from under his arms.
Sam:	Yeah, baby, but match these 50.
Stuff:	Sam then did 50 push-ups. I think he could have done more if he wanted to, too. Then it was Clyde's turn. Clyde announced that he was going to take any *torture* that Sam could dish out. Torture!!!
Angel:	You're going to let him torture you?
Clyde:	Right, and I'm going to take it without giving up.
Sam:	You got to be jiving, man. I'll put you through so many changes that you won't even remember your name. I'll put bamboo splinters under your eyelids and tap dance over your forehead. You might as well give it up, turkey, because you're going to be crying for mercy in the worse kind of way.
Stuff:	Clyde laid down on the floor and crossed his arms over his chest.
Clyde:	Sock it to me, and see what a real man can take.
Stuff:	Now, man. If you dudes want to know what came down next, you gotta read the book. You know man, if you wanna see the show you gotta pay the toll!

Think of ways parent volunteers could be included to help students develop their LRG projects.

Evening Newscast. Students enjoy acting out book summaries in the form of a nightly newscast, often titled something like the "10 O'clock Eyewitness Action News." Each student prepares a news story script (using the writing workshop method described later in this chapter) that retells an important event or piece of information in the book. After LRG members have helped each other refine their scripts, they dress up and rehearse as news reporters until the performance is ready for presentation to the class. The evening newscast can either be acted out before the class or recorded using a video camera, then replayed to the class on television.

Novels in the News. Rice (1991) describes an activity called *novels in the news,* which has students learn to combine the journalistic style found in newspaper headlines with the story structure of novels. The idea is to reduce major events in the novel or nonfiction book to simplest terms, then display these mock headlines on a bulletin board. Thus, one might see such headlines as LOCAL SCARECROW SEEKS BRAIN IMPLANT for *The Wizard of Oz* (Baum, 1972), COB STEALS TRUMPET FROM LOCAL MUSIC STORE for *The Trumpet of the Swan* (White, 1970), or LOCAL BOY BECOMES FOOTBALL HERO for *Forrest Gump* (Groom, 1986).

In a more advanced version of *novels in the news,* a mock newspaper front page is created. News stories are created with each LRG member acting as a writer/reporter in much the same way as explained in the evening newscast activity. Stories are typed at the computer, printed out, then pasted onto a large piece of poster board using a newspaper front-page style. The front page is then displayed in a prominent place and presented to the class. *Hint:* show the class a copy of the book *The True Story of the 3 Little Pigs, by A. Wolf* (Scieszka, 1989) which has an excellent example on the front cover.

Many popular authors are formula writers.

Formula Retelling. Many popular authors are *formula* writers; they have discovered a successful basic story line, which is altered in each book in terms of setting, characters, and problem. In *formula retelling* (Cooter, 1994), students in LRGs read two or three books by the same author, chart the basic story line, then respond through group writing to create their own short story using the author's formula.

For example, John Grisham, author of such popular books as *The Firm, The Pelican Brief,* and *The Client,* appears to have used a formula in creating these action/mystery stories (Brennan, 1994). These titles are also excellent choices for a themed literature unit with young adolescents because of their high-interest content, easy readability, and Grisham's relative avoidance of profanity and adult situations that might cause some parents to object. Group members (usually a group of five) begin by reading at least one of these titles, with all books being read by someone in the group. As the stories are read and the plots unfold, students begin a comparison grid detailing major points in the story. Eventually the books are completed, as is the comparison grid. After carefully examining the comparison grid and discussing similarities, the final step is for students to create their own short story using common elements from the author's formula.

Design your own comparison grid for three children's book authors who are formula writers.

In Figure 11.6, a completed formula retelling comparison grid is shown depicting Grisham's formula for the three novels mentioned, based on an analysis by Brennan (1994). The students' short story can be presented to the class using either a dramatic reading format, printed copies of the short story, radio play, or through drama.

Teachers in elementary grades may want to consider some of the works of such authors as E. B. White, C. S. Lewis, Beverly Cleary, and Betsy Byars for formula-retelling activities.

A Meeting of Minds. In the early days of television, Steve Allen hosted a program called "A Meeting of Minds." Famous people of the past were played by actors

Figure 11.6

Formula retelling comparison grid (plot similarities noted in italics)

	The Firm	*The Pelican Brief*	*The Client*	*Our Story*
The Hero	Mitch, *bright young guy, poor family,* beginning a *law* career	Darby, a *bright young* woman, *poor family, law* student	Mark, *bright young* man, *poor family,* hires a *lawyer*	
Hero's Problem	*Knows something he shouldn't* — firm run by gangsters — Mafia wants him dead	*Knows something she shouldn't* — oil billionaire paid to have two Supreme Court justices killed— oil billionaire wants her dead	*Knows something he shouldn't* — where a Mafia killer hid a murdered victim — Mafia wants him dead	
Villain(s)	*Corrupt lawyers and vicious hit men*	Oil billionaire, *corrupt lawyers and vicious hit men*	*Vicious hit men*	
The Government	FBI *wants Mitch to put himself at risk* by gathering evidence against the firm	FBI *wants Darby to put herself at risk* by turning herself in	U.S. attorney *wants Mark to put himself at risk* by testifying against the killer	
The hero doesn't because. . .	*He doesn't believe the FBI* will keep its word	*She doesn't believe the FBI* will keep its word because of corrupt advisers to the President	*He doesn't believe the FBI* can protect him	
In the end . . .	*The hero outsmarts everyone* (Mafia and the FBI)	*The hero outsmarts everyone* (billionaire and President's men)	*The hero outsmarts everyone* (Mafia and U.S. attorney	
But our hero. . .	*Is forced to give up* his job and start over	*Is forced to give up* her law studies and go into hiding	*Is forced to give up* his identity and enter the Witness Protection Program	

Based on an analysis by J. Brennan, 1994.

who held high-level discussions about issues of their time and problems they were trying to solve. Peggy Lathlaen (1993) has adapted "Meeting of Minds" in her classroom and found it especially useful with biographies.

List some popular TV shows of the past few years that could serve as a template for this kind of project.

Students begin by thoroughly researching their famous person from the past so that they can later "become" this person before the class. This involves careful reading of one or more books, construction of a time line for this person's life (which is then compared to a general time line recording significant inventions and world events at the time), research into costumes of the era, Venn diagrams comparing their person to others being researched in the LRGs, and searching Bartlett's *Familiar Quotations* for memorable quotes made by the individual. Reenactments of famous events and question–answer sessions are typical presentations made by students. Famous figures portrayed in Lathlaen's classroom include Thomas Jefferson, Queen Elizabeth I, Barbara Jordan, and George Bush.

Dioramas. A diorama is an important scene from the chosen book that is re-created for presentation. Students, usually working in pairs, often re-create the scene on a small scale using art materials. The diorama is presented to the class along with a prepared explanation as to why this scene was deemed important to the book. Multiple dioramas can be presented to portray a visual sequence retelling key scenes in the book.

Big Book or Predictable Book With Captions. A great response activity that can be constructed by either individuals or groups is a big book or predictable book version of the novel or nonfiction book. The idea is for students to create a simplified version of the book, which can be shared with kindergarten or first-grade audiences. One middle school student at a school adopting our themed literature units model decided to construct a multiple-page predictable book retelling the story line of *Huckleberry Finn* (Figure 11.7). After completion of his project, he shared his predictable book with first-grade classes at the neighboring elementary school—a treat for the young children and the author alike!

Rewriting chapters as books for first graders requires thorough comprehension and skillful writing.

Discussion Webs. Discussion webs are a kind of graphic aid for teaching students to look at both sides of an issue before making final judgments (Alvermann, 1991). They may be useful with novels and other narrative selections, but we feel they can be particularly useful with nonfiction materials. Adapted from the work of social studies teacher James Duthie (1986), there are basically five steps in using discussion webs. The first step is much like traditional reading activities in that a discussion is held to activate background knowledge, discuss new or challenging vocabulary and provide a purpose for reading. Students then read, or begin reading, the selection. The second step is to state the central question to be considered and introduce the discussion web. Students complete both the yes and no column individually, usually recording key thoughts, as opposed to complete sentences. The third step is for students to be paired for the purpose of comparing responses and begin working toward consensus. Later, the groups of two are paired to construct groups of four for the purpose of further consensus building. In the fourth step, a group spokesperson reports to the whole class which of the reasons best reflects the consensus of the group. Usually, a 3-minute period is allotted for reporting. The final step suggested is that students individually write a follow-up position paper about their judgment on the matter. In Figure 11.8, we present a discussion web completed by students researching whether television cameras should be permitted in courtrooms.

Home-Made Filmstrip. Home-made filmstrips are an interesting way for students to retell the sequence of a story. Pictures are made with captions that retell important parts of the book. The pictures are then taped together in sequence and

Figure 11.7

Student holding book
he made in class

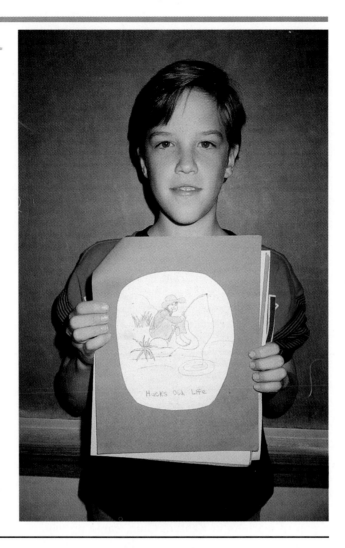

viewed with the aid of an opaque projector (if available). This activity is in some ways similar in purpose to the creation of big books or predictable books described earlier.

David Letterman or Oprah Talk Show. In a combination of drama, action news, and "A Meeting of Minds," students write a script for a TV talk show. One of the students is cast as a TV host or interviewer ("Dave" or "Oprah"), and the other team members represent characters from their chosen book being interviewed. The talk show can either be acted out in front of the class, followed by questions and answers, or videotaped and shown over television to the class using VCR/TV equipment. For schools not having video equipment, teachers can check with the high school football coach; coaches have such equipment and may be willing to make it available at convenient times.

Giant Comic Strips. Similar to a mural in size, giant comic strips are made by students to re-create and retell the main story line of a book they've read. First, the group sketches out a comic strip having, typically, six to eight panels, which retell an important part of a narrative story or facts explained in a nonfiction book. Next, the comic strip

Figure 11.8

Students' discussion web: TV cameras in courtrooms?

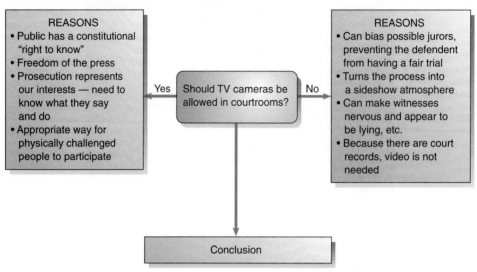

sketch is reviewed by the teacher for accuracy and approved for final stages. The group then reproduces the comic strip on a large sheet of butcher paper and displays it on a wall in the classroom. Giant comic strips are helpful in assessing understanding of sequence. Figure 11.9 shows a giant comic strip created by a middle school group.

Students must be shown appropriate group behavior; it doesn't occur naturally.

Group Etiquette for Successful Literature-Response Groups. Finally, note that students do not work in groups harmoniously by accident; some careful training must occur. Through role-playing experiences, children can be helped to understand appropriate kinds of behavior expected while working in LRGs. One group of teachers in Kenton, Ohio, came up with a wonderful idea for teaching "group etiquette." One day after school, teachers at each grade level met to dramatize both positive and negative group behavior. They dressed in the clothing styles of young adolescents and role played negative group behavior, then positive group behavior. These performances were recorded on videocassette tape and shown to their classes during the introduction to themed literature units. Students enjoyed the production and were able to identify "do's and don'ts" for their LRGs. Figure 11.10 shows some typical rules that might emerge from a discussion of group etiquette.

Minilessons are taught using examples drawn from the book selections, or other books consistent with the theme.

Weeks 3 and 4: LRG Projects and Minilessons.   Work continues on LRG projects in weeks 3 and 4, but the teacher claims part of the time for minilessons. Minilessons, as applied to themed literature units, allow teachers to (a) help students develop reading and study strategies within the context of the theme and (b) satisfy local or state mandates regarding student performance objectives. For example, if the class is reading books related to the theme "animal stories," then the teacher may prepare a related minilesson(s) about using the card catalog in the library to locate other books on animals.

In weeks 3 and 4 of the unit, students should be allowed approximately one half to two thirds of the time for working on LRG projects and SSR. Students who feel they require more time to work on their LRG projects should do so out of class as homework.

Figure 11.9

Student-made giant comic strip

Week 5: Project Presentations and Closure Activities.   The final week of themed literature units is set aside for students to present their projects to the class. These presentations serve two important functions. First, it is a kind of sharing time that provides LRGs with an opportunity to make public their efforts. Second, students in the class are reintroduced to the books they did not read, a process that often serves to stimulate further recreational reading.

Themes should be concluded with some sort of closure activity. Closure activities bring about a positive sense that the work is now complete and the class is ready to

Figure 11.10

Group etiquette rules (student generated)

Group Etiquette Rules

1. Remember that we are taking part in a discussion to learn and help others to learn.
2. We need to bring a paper and pencil to each meeting.
3. Listen to people without interrupting when they talk. Let everyone have their say.
4. Don't show off in a discussion.
5. Everyone has to take part in the discussion.
6. It's OK to change your mind when you have been proven wrong.
7. If someone is having trouble saying what they mean and you understand, help them say it in another way.
8. Always have one member of the group write down important ideas.

move on to something new. Closure activities might include a guest speaker, a field trip, or perhaps a film presentation related to the theme.

Evaluating Themed Literature Units

Themed literature units provide many assessment opportunities.

Teachers can accumulate evidence of student growth in themed literature units in many ways. Generally, a typical themed literature unit presents 5 to 10 assessment opportunities. The following list includes some of the potential sources for student assessments:

- *Book Tests:* Teachers often give a brief paper-and-pencil test for the middle and end of each book.
- *Literature-Response Projects:* Teachers quickly realize that a few students will sometimes attempt to let their fellow group members do all of the work, then claim their share of the credit. This attitude is rarely successful for very long, mainly as a result of peer pressure. Using the following evaluation scheme tends to produce fair and defensible grades:
  1. *Class Evaluations:* Each student in the class viewing the project presentations completes an evaluation form (teacher designed) for each group. Criteria for evaluating each group should be negotiated with the LRG at the beginning of week 2, then used by the class members as evaluation criteria during the class presentation.
  2. *Intragroup Evaluation:* Each member in the LRG should rate the productivity and contribution of each of the other group members.
  3. *Teacher's Evaluation:* Based on the above two criteria, the teacher awards each individual group member an LRG grade.
- *Minilesson Grades:* Summative grades and evaluations accumulated during minilessons become part of the overall assessment.
- *Student–Teacher Conferences:* These generally take the form described in the following section on the reading workshop.

Student–teacher conferences provide valuable teaching and assessment opportunities.

In Chapter 13, we discuss many other authentic assessment methods that apply to themed literature units.

The Reading Workshop: Organizing for Instruction

*The **reading workshop** is an alternative to themed literature units having many of the same elements along with some interesting twists.*

The **reading workshop** (Reutzel & Cooter, 1991) is an organizational scheme providing for the full integration of children's literature or basal stories into the classroom reading program. It is not intended to be prescriptive but rather to offer a functional and flexible instructional scaffolding for reading. The five main components are sharing time, minilesson, state of the class, reading workshop, and sharing time. Each of these components is explained in the following paragraphs and outlined in Figure 11.11.

Phase 1: Sharing Time (5 to 10 Minutes)

Sharing time is a teacher-conducted read-aloud period.

During sharing time, teachers share new discoveries they have made in children's literature (e.g., folktales, short stories, nonfiction, poetry). For example, the teacher may have been looking for spooky stories for the Halloween season and just discovered Jack Prelutsky's (1976) collection of poetry called *Nightmares: Poems to Trouble*

Figure 11.11

The reading workshop

Reading Workshop (70 min)		
Sharing Time (5–10 min) *Minilesson (5–10 min)* *State of the Class (5 min)*		
Self-Selected Reading and Response (SSR) (35–45 min)		

SSR
1. Self-selected book
2. Reading their goal pages for literature-response group
3. Responding to literature
4. Record keeping
  a. Book time and title logs
  b. Updating state of class
  c. Signing up for individual reading conference
 	
10 min
	Literature response
	1. Group meeting for response
	2. New meeting
	3. Determine new response mode
	
	15–20 min
		Individual reading conferences
		1. Two a day
		2. Running record
		  a. Taped
		  b. Retellings
		
		10–15 min

Sharing time (children) (5–10 min)		

From "Organizing for Effective Instruction: The Reading Workshop" by D. R. Reutzel and R. B. Cooter, Jr., 1991, *The Reading Teacher,* *44*(8), pp. 548–555. Copyright 1991 by International Reading Association. Reprinted by permission.

Your Sleep. With permission from the publisher, the teacher might make overhead transparencies of a few of the spooky pen and ink sketches from a few of the poems in the book and display them on the overhead screen while reading aloud the selections on vampires and ghouls! The idea is to spark interest in various literary genres for free reading. Good judgment on the teacher's part will dictate which selections should be used. Thus, the poems cited here may not be appropriate for some audiences (e.g., lower elementary children). Sometimes, the sharing time activity can serve as a catalyst for writing workshop projects (explained in the second half of this chapter) or as an introduction for the Reading Workshop minilesson.

Phase 2: Minilesson (5 to 10 Minutes)

Minilessons, as discussed in some detail in Chapters 8 and 9, are whole-group instructional sessions with the purpose of teaching reading strategies and preparing students for reading new books. Topics for discussion are usually drawn from the following:

- Demonstrated needs of students discovered during individual reading conferences (discussed more fully later in this section)
- Nonnegotiable skills list
- Literature preparation (prereading) activities to assist students with new books they are to begin reading

Think about the process one might go through in developing a nonnegotiable skills list.

The second source listed here, nonnegotiable skills list, requires further explanation as to how typical reading skills fit into the Reading Workshop minilesson. Reading teachers often feel "chained" to the skills. When examining why they feel this way, teachers often make an interesting discovery. School district-mandated competency tests in reading draw many of their test items from the skills lists found in adopted basal readers. Thus, many school districts require the use of basals so that students will be tested on material they have been taught, a factor in testing known as *content validity*. This policy, however, has at least two negative aspects. First, teachers feel obliged to use the reading series to make sure that their children know the skills. Second, mandating the basal program almost surely will result in children being placed in ability groups in reading, which can be very detrimental to their self-esteem and overall learning potential. The minilesson offers a wonderful way out of this dilemma.

Because a major reason for the use of basal readers is to maintain control over skill instruction, we suggest that required reading skills for all reading groups be taught in a whole-group format. This can easily be done during the minilesson period. Perhaps a brief story will help make the point.

Ms. Nelson Zings the Zinger!

Ms. Nelson teaches third grade in a large school district and wants to eliminate the three-ability-level group format for teaching reading in her class. For 2 years, she has been carefully putting together a literature-based reading program using the most up-to-date research-proven ideas she can find. Now she is ready to have a wonderful year with her class enjoying the reading process.

Unfortunately, the school system has just adopted a new basal reading system published by the Zinger Educational Reading Organization (ZERO) for all elementary schools, which is quite expensive. Needless to say, the administration is expecting teachers to use the new Zinger series. Part of their enthusiasm for buying the series in the first place is that it correlates so well with the Idaho Basic Skills Test (IBST), a standardized test used for determining educational growth in school districts.

Ms. Nelson has a real dilemma. Although her principal, Ms. Compton, is very supportive, she is not likely to go against her superiors in the central office. Ms. Nelson decides that she will be able to keep her new Reading Workshop plan by simply teaching the skills to be taught to her third graders in the Zinger series during the minilesson. Each week Ms. Nelson plans to teach a skill from the Zinger scope and sequence chart to the class following a whole-to-parts-to-whole format, followed by a test-wiseness lesson. Ms. Nelson will teach some 25 skills from the Zinger series during minilesson periods over the course of the school year.

What does Ms. Nelson gain using the minilesson in this way? Very simply, control over and independence from the basal reader. The skills are taught, her students will do well on the end-of-book tests required by the district, no reading groups based on "ability" are necessary, and Ms. Nelson can decide whether or not she wishes to use the basal reader. Thus, minilessons allow teachers to fulfill local mandates regarding student performance objectives and escape forced use of basal readers at the same time.

Another potential use of the minilesson is for literature preparation or prereading activities. The following activities are intended to assist students in drawing on past experiences or schemata before reading to enhance comprehension. Literature-preparation activities should also help create a stronger affective climate for students before reading (e.g., interest, positive attitude, motivation). These activities should be studied and earmarked for future classroom use.

Story Frames

Story frames (Fowler, 1982) are series of blanks hooked together by important "language elements" reflecting a specific line of thought. Examples of story frames are presented in Chapter 6.

Story Sequence Clothesline

Many teachers have found that having children predict what might happen in a story before reading boosts overall comprehension. Typically, the teacher has an introductory discussion to tap students' relevant prior experiences. Then predictions are made by students and recorded on the chalkboard. After reading, the story predictions are checked and revised for accuracy. A weakness of this procedure is that students generally attend to random story events without regard to sequence.

A story sequence clothesline is used to help students understand a sequence of events in texts.

One literature-preparation activity that helps students develop sequence comprehension strategies is the story sequence clothesline (Reutzel & Cooter, 1987). This activity requires a clothesline (strung across the front of the classroom), clothespins, tag board cut into large strips or rectangles, and a dark marker. The procedure follows:

1. The teacher conducts an activity intended to bring to the students' minds past experiences relevant to the story (e.g., discussion, role-playing activity, guest speaker, demonstration, etc.).
2. The teacher then introduces the selection, discusses troublesome new vocabulary with students, and asks students to predict what might happen in the story.
3. The teacher records predictions on the pieces of tag board and places them in front of the class, for example, on the chalkboard chalk tray, and asks students to predict the order in which events will occur.
4. As the class makes predictions as to what will happen first, second, and so on, the teacher pins the written predictions on tag board in order on the clothesline.
5. Students read the selection, revise and clarify predictions, and make corrections regarding the sequence of events as needed.

Figures 11.12 and 11.13 depict both a predicted sequence of events and the revised sequence for the wonderful Christmas book *The Polar Express* by Chris Van Allsburg (1985).

Books like The Polar Express (Van Allsburg, 1985) can be very useful in teaching sequence.

Schema Stories

Schema stories (Harste, Short, & Burke, 1988) challenge students to construct or reconstruct stories using meaning and story grammar. An explanation of schema stories is presented in Chapter 6.

Figure 11.12

Clothesline predictions for *The Polar Express* (Van Allsburg, 1985)

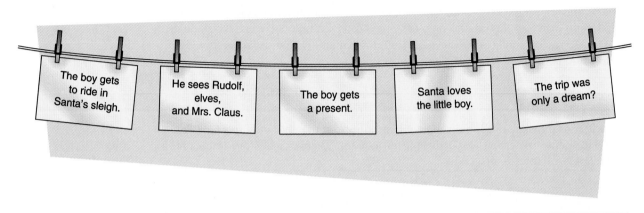

Phase 3: State of the Class (3 to 5 Minutes)

State of the class informs the teacher and reminds students what tasks they plan to do during the work-shop period.

One of the concerns for teachers trying out the Reading Workshop is monitoring what youngsters do during independent work periods. State of the class is a wonderful classroom management tool that informs teachers of student activities each day *and* reminds students of their responsibilities during the workshop period. Each day, students fill in a state of the class chart like the one shown in Figure 11.14, explaining their major activities for the next day. Just before the SSR and response period begins (see next section), the teacher reviews the chart with the students to help them remember what they are supposed to be doing and assign deadlines. Some teachers, like Nancy Atwell (1987), prefer to complete the chart themselves with the whole

Figure 11.13

Revised predictions for *The Polar Express* (Van Allsburg, 1985)

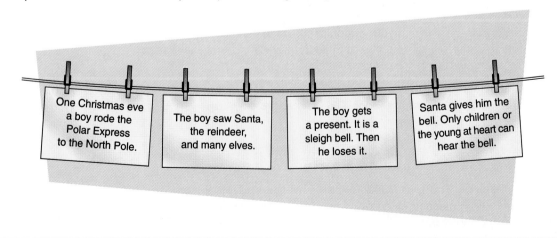

State of the Class Chart					
Student Name	M	T	W	TH	F
John	LR-GM	LR-GM			
Maria	LR-NM	IRC			
Jalissa	LR-NM	LR-GM			
Sue	IRC	LR-NM			
Miguel	SSR-LRG	SSR-LRG			
Yumiko	IRC	SSR-LRG			
Jamie Lee	LR-NM	LR-GM			
Seth	SSR-SSB	SSR-SSB			
Andrea	SSR-SSB	SSR-RL			
Martin	IRC	SSR-SSB			
Heather	SSR-SSB	SSR-SSB			
April	LR-NM	LR-GM			
Jason	ABSENT	SSR-SSB			
Malik	LR-GM	IRC			
Juanita	SSR-LRG	SSR-LRG			
J.T.	SSR-LRG	SSR-LRG			
Patrice	ABSENT	IRC			
Shelley	LR-NM	LR-GP			
Melanie	SSR-SSB	SSR-LRG			

Key
SSR: Self-selected reading
SSB: Self-selected book
LRG: Literature-response group goal pages
RL: Responding to literature
RK: Record keeping
LR: Literature-response group
GM: Group meeting for response
NM: New meeting
RM: Determining new response
IRC: Individual reading conference

From "Organizing for Effective Instruction: The Reading Workshop" by D. R. Reutzel and R. B. Cooter, Jr., 1991, *The Reading Teacher, 44*(8), pp. 548–555. Copyright 1991 by the International Reading Association. Reprinted by permission.

Figure 11.14

State of the class chart

class. Atwell describes state of the class as a brief (3 to 5 minutes) and effective way of "eavesdropping" on students' plans and activities during independent activity periods.

When problems are observed, such as a student's spending several days on one task with no apparent progress, then a "house call" or teacher–student conference is scheduled (see individual reading conferences in Figure 11.11). This simple process ensures that students having difficulty do not "fall through the cracks" and provides teachers with a daily audit trail of each student's work that can be referred to during conferences with parents and for planning minilessons.

Phase 4: Self-Selected Reading and Response (40 Minutes)

Note that a number of options are available for students during SSR&R.

The heart of the reading period is called *self-selected reading and response (SSR&R)*. It involves three student activities: SSR, literature response (LR), and individual reading conferences (IRC).

Self-Selected Reading

During SSR, students may become involved in one or more activities. To begin the workshop period, students and teachers engage in free reading of a book they have chosen for 10 minutes of SSR. Another option is for students to read goal pages established by their LRG. *Goal pages* are daily reading goals established by students themselves to accomplish the reading of a book within a given time frame.

Literature-response logs are ongoing records of students' reading activity.

Students who continue in SSR during the LRG meeting (discussed in the next section) may engage in four priority choices. First, they must complete their LRG goal pages. Next, they may complete LR projects. Literature-response logs are regular records, usually daily, that children keep as running diaries of their reading. Third, they may update their reading records. These include filling in book time and title logs, updating their activities on the state of the class chart, or signing up for an IRC with the teacher. When these three activities are completed, students may self-select a book of their own choice for recreational reading as a fourth choice.

Literature-Response Groups

Think about some of the reasons why adults choose to work together. How are those motivations like those of students in LRGs?

After the initial 10 minutes of SSR&R, one or more groups of children per day moves into an LRG by appointment while the remainder of the class continues working in SSR. As described earlier, literature-response groups are made up of students who come together by choice, not assignment, to read and respond to a chosen piece of literature and develop related projects. Teachers meet with one LRG each day to participate in and facilitate response activities. Some teachers like to act in the role of recorder for the group or wait in silence. This allows them to be quiet participants in the group's activities. Other LRGs may wish to meet at this same time without the teacher present to continue work on projects.

Harste and co-workers (1988) encourage using written conversations to talk about books of interest. This format provides for regular feedback to students and establishes an audit trail for student progress. Many authorities in the field recommend that children avoid simply summarizing their daily readings but rather react to what they have read (Parsons, 1990). At the conclusion of the LRG meeting, goals for continued reading in the book (goal pages) and the next group meeting date are arranged. Some examples of LR alternatives follow.

A Burgess summary is essentially a modified cloze activity.

Burgess Summary.   A kind of cloze passage, Burgess summaries (T. D. Johnson & Louis, 1987) are teacher constructed, using a summary of a selected story. Instead of blanks representing selected missing words from the story, nonsense words replace the missing words. The ratio suggested for replacement words to regular text is about 1:12. Burgess summaries may need to be simplified greatly when used with younger

> Lewis was a trumpeter swan born without a <u>blurber</u>. Lewis' father, the cob, decided that something must be done. If Lewis <u>ciz</u> ever to have a chance for a normal life he <u>wrost</u> need a trumpet, the kind humans play in a band. The cob flew into the nearest town, Billings, in <u>dweeb</u> of the needed trumpet. Then he saw it, a <u>renzee</u> store with a shiny, new trumpet with a dangling red cord hanging in <u>sas</u> window. Now was his chance to risk everything on one bold move.

Figure 11.15

Burgess summary for
The Trumpet of the Swan
(E. B. White, 1970)

children in the early stages of reading development. Figure 11.15 is a brief example of a passage developed from E. B. White's (1970) *The Trumpet of the Swan*.

Character and Author Report Cards.   Although children often have a great deal of anxiety concerning their own report cards, they enjoy giving grades to others. In this activity, students have the opportunity to grade the author or character(s) in the book they have been reading. Character and author report cards (T. D. Johnson & Louis, 1987) are developed by the teacher with appropriate categories for grading included. Students grade each aspect called for, then write a justification for the grade based on evidence from the book. Both explicit (factual) and implicit (inferred) justifications should be identified. Figure 11.16 offers a simple example of a character report card.

Clue Cards.   Clue cards (T. D. Johnson & Louis, 1987) are a relatively simple idea useful in developing vocabulary knowledge. The child draws cards from a deck specially prepared for that book. On the front of the card is a sentence summarizing

Clemmons School
Ms. Robert's Third Grade
Character Report Card

Figure 11.16

Character report card

Name: _____

Date: _____

Character: Lewis's Father

Book: *The Trumpet of the Swan*

Subject	Grade	Comments
Honesty		
Commitment		
Courage		
Love of family		

or defining the target word using context from the story. The word being emphasized is printed on the back so that children can self-monitor their prediction. Figure 11.17 offers several examples drawn from *The Red Pony* by John Steinbeck (1937).

The Unknown Character.   The Unknown Character is an activity patterned after the old familiar game of 20 Questions. The teacher assumes the role of one of the characters from a book or story. Students ask questions that can be answered with a simple "yes" or "no" response. Teachers find in this activity a natural vehicle for teaching children about characterization and inferential comprehension. (Teaching hint: A greater sense of drama can be created if the teacher puts on some sort of "Unknown Character" mask while in this role.)

Yakity-Yak involves both oral reading and retelling activities.

Yakity-Yak and ReQuest.   Yakity-Yak is a reciprocal retelling procedure involving groups of two students each. After the initial reading of the whole story, each pair of students sits together with copies of the same story. Students then take turns rereading sections, usually paragraphs, then stop to retell their partner what they have just read. Then the process is repeated by the other student using the next section of text. Yakity-Yak may be combined with Manzo's (1969) ReQuest procedure in upper elementary grades for comprehensive student analysis of the passage.

ReQuest.   ReQuest (Manzo, 1969) is very similar to Yakity-Yak in that it is also a reciprocal response procedure that follows an initial reading of the whole text. Typically, students working together in a one-to-one setting take turns rereading a portion of text silently. Next, one of the team members asks as many questions of his partner as possible about the portion of text just read. After the questioning is complete, the students continue reading the next unit of text and the second partner assumes the role of questioner. In Manzo's (1969) scheme, the story is reread sentence by sentence, but larger units of text are often preferred. Manzo also presents ReQuest as a procedure to be practiced between the teacher and one student, usually in a tutorial setting. However, questioning could easily be addressed in a whole-class minilesson, thus allowing students to work together.

Yakity-Yak and ReQuest could easily be combined in the following format:

1. Students read the entire selection or chapter independently.
2. Student groups of two each are created.
3. The children begin by rereading portions of the text. Then, one partner (called the "listener") says "Yakity-Yak!" indicating that the teller should retell the pas-

---

Figure 11.17

Clue cards for *The Red Pony* (Steinbeck, 1937)

Front of the card	*Back of the Card*
Sometimes I had to talk to Jody as though I was his father.	**Billy Buck**
Sounded the triangle in the morning and said irritably, "Don't you go out until you get a good breakfast in you."	**Jody's mother**

sage just read. After the retelling is complete, the "listener" asks his partner (the "teller") as many questions as possible related to story elements not mentioned.
4. The process is repeated over and over with the children switching roles each time.

Newspaper Reports.   Using various newspaper reporting styles offers motivating ways to help students develop many important comprehension abilities. Some of the forms that newspaper reports could take follow:

- Ads

WANTED—TIME TRAVELER!

Have mutant VCR capable of zapping people back in time. Need partner to help stop robbery and shooting of relative. No pay, just thrills. Phone Kelly at 293-4321. (Pfeffer, 1989)

- Headlines

  CHILDREN DISCOVER WORLD THROUGH OLD WARDROBE
  TRACK COACH RESNICK SAYS "TAKE A LONG JUMP"!
  JOHN HENRY BEATS STEAM HAMMER, WINS RACE!

- Crossword: Can be developed using *Henry and Beezus* (Cleary, 1952) using a Minnesota Educational Computing Consortium (MECC) computer program.

- Other stimulating literature-response projects using the newspaper motif include Letters to the Editor, Dear Gabby, editorials, sports, and cooking.

Newspaper reports have students summarize main ideas using brief and precise language.

Literature-Response Logs.   Literature-response logs are regular records, usually daily, that children keep as running diaries of their readings. As mentioned previously, many authorities in the field recommend that children avoid simply summarizing their daily readings but rather react to what they have read (Parsons, 1990).

Develop some literature-response log entries using popular children's books to use during introductory minilessons.

Individual Reading Conferences

During the last 10 to 15 minutes of each reading workshop, the teacher usually meets with two children for individual reading conferences (IRCs). Students make appointments on a sign-up board at least one day in advance, usually at the teacher's request during the state of the class period. The advance notice gives the teacher enough lead time to review the student's reading portfolio (see Chapter 13) and decide how to spend IRC time. We recommend (as a goal) that three individual conferences per quarter be conducted with each student. If students forget or avoid conferences, the teacher should inform them of their next appointment. During IRC time, students not involved return to the previously described activities to continue SSR&R. Assessment activities described earlier for themed literature units work just as well for IRC time in the Reading Workshop. In Chapter 13, we also discuss in great detail additional assessment activities that might be selected for IRC time.

Phase 5: Student Sharing Time (5 to 10 Minutes)

As a daily closing activity in the reading workshop, we recommend a sharing time for teachers and children to come together for a few minutes to share with the group activities, books, poetry, and projects with which they have been working. Student groups might share progress reports on their literature-response projects, such as play practices, murals, or reader's theater scripts. Some children may wish to share books they have been reading during SSR in the form of book talks. Others can share their responses to books discussed in their LRG. Teachers may comment in IRCs and celebrate the accomplishments of individual children or share a part of a book they themselves were reading during SSR. The only problem associated with this second block of sharing time is sticking to the 10-minute time limit because children sincerely enjoy this time for sharing their ideas, work, and discoveries.

Atwell (1987), in her book for middle school teachers, suggests that students write letters to the teacher about what they have read. Teachers write back to the students, sometimes asking questions or making clarifying remarks. This format provides for regular feedback to students and establishes an audit trail for student progress.

One of the 10 principles for encouraging literacy development discussed in Chapter 1 relates to the connection between reading and writing instruction. The writing process and ways of encouraging authorship are described in some detail in the second half of this chapter.

Fluent readers are better able to focus on passage meaning.

Developing Reading Fluency as Part of Literature-Based Reading Instruction

Fluency has to do with the ability to read accurately and at an appropriate rate. Research conducted in recent years indicates that students who can read fluently are better able to focus on the meaning of the passage (e.g., Homan, Klesius, & Hite, 1993; Walley, 1993). The opposite also seems to be true, which is to say that students having difficulty with reading often evidence slow, hesitant, and effortful reading (Mathes, Simmons, & Davis, 1992).

Several theories have been suggested as to the role fluency plays in reading success and the ability to comprehend the author's message. Perhaps most prominent is the "automaticity theory" described by LaBerge and Samuels (1974). This theory suggests that some readers have difficulty comprehending when reading because too much time and attention is consumed identifying words in print, whereas more fluent readers can identify words automatically without devoting conscious attention to the process. Fluent readers are therefore better able to process meaning at the same time words are being decoded. Said another way, word identification and comprehension cannot be performed simultaneously. For a reader to comprehend what is being read, word recognition must be automatic so that thinking resources can be devoted to comprehension (Homan et al., 1993). To the degree teachers help their students become fluent readers, they increase the likelihood of their students' success. In this section, we summarize ways of promoting reading fluency within the context of literature-based reading programs.

Repeated Readings and Other Fluency Strategies

Several strategies have been developed and tested through research that are intended to improve reading fluency. The strategy called **repeated readings** (S. J. Samuels, 1979) has received considerable attention and shown potential for improving not only fluency but also comprehension and motivation with students having reading problems. The repeated readings strategy usually involves the following steps:

List the steps for conducting ***repeated readings.***

Step 1:   The student reads a passage aloud while the teacher records any miscues (errors).

Step 2:   The student practices rereading the passage orally or silently several times.

Step 3:   The student rereads the passage for the teacher, who records time and any miscues.

Step 4:   The teacher and student prepare a graph showing the growth or improvement between the first and last reading.

A variation of repeated readings is oral previewing. Oral previewing begins by having the student preview the passage by listening to a fluent reader reading the passage first, such as a teacher, older student, parent volunteer, or instructional aide. After listening to the fluent reader model several times and after the student feels confident, he reads the passage independently. Rasinski (1990) has shown that oral previewing and repeated readings are equally effective in improving fluency.

Through recent research trials, a third class of strategies has emerged that seems to be effective in improving reading fluency and is known as *teacher-assisted nonrepetitive oral reading strategies*. They are considered nonrepetitive because students are not asked to repeat the text. Nonrepetitive oral reading strategies appear to be about as effective as repeated readings and offer several advantages over the latter (Homan et al., 1993):

The search for classroom methods that improve fluency has led to the discovery of effective nonrepetitive techniques.

- Because students read a passage only once, they are able to read a wider range of literature.
- Because students tend to acquire most new vocabulary through wide reading and this approach increases student encounters with books, greater vocabulary learning should result.
- Wide reading causes students to be exposed to wider range of topics and information.
- Exposure to a wider range of reading materials in this approach can improve such affective factors as interest, attitudes about reading, and motivation.

Echo reading and unison reading are two forms of nonrepetitive oral reading that have been thoroughly researched. In echo reading, the teacher or other fluent reader reads part of a passage, then the students read the same part back. In unison reading, the teacher and students read a passage together with the teacher assuming the lead role, that is, reading loud enough to be heard above the group. Both echo and unison reading are considered forms of choral reading, because students usually read together as a group rather than individually.

Echo and unison reading are two research-proven techniques for improving fluency.

Although repeated and nonrepetitive readings have proven to be effective in improving fluency in some readers and in carefully controlled settings, these methods (especially repeated readings) have some serious drawbacks, at least as recommended in the research literature. First, in most research into repeated and nonrepetitive readings, students have been given virtually no choice as to which passages will be read. Either a teacher-selected passage from a book or basal selections have been preselected without student input. Not only does this violate a fundamental principle for encouraging literacy development, choice (see Chapter 1), failing to let students self-select books tends to put a serious damper on interest and motivation. Thus, these methods might improve reading fluency but damage the student's basic interest in reading. Second, older students asked to engage in repeated readings sometimes view this activity as a punishment for not reading a selection well enough the first time (Homan et al., 1993). Homan and colleagues captured our sentiment in saying

Our overwhelming concern is that repeated readings will be overused as a means of remediating at-risk readers and will have a negative effect on their reading attitude. (1993, p. 98)

Maintaining interest and motivation while improving fluency is an important goal.

The fluency goal is clear: to gain the benefits of repeated and nonrepetitive readings in improving fluency while at the same time improving reading interest and motivation. Such literature-based reading strategies as core book units, themed literature units, and the Reading Workshop provide a wonderful backdrop for achieving this very goal.

Improving Fluency Through Literature-Based Reading Instruction

The primary context for improving fluency in literature-based reading units of instruction is through literature response. We have suggested in this chapter several literature-response activities that are easily adaptable to this purpose. In each instance, there are at least three main requirements to remember in selecting activities that will enhance fluency.

Think of a time when you read something repeatedly for a class assignment and felt motivated by the experience.

- The activity must provide a fluent model of reading. This may involve the teacher but could just as easily involve peer models, students from a higher grade classroom, adult volunteers, or instructional aids (e.g., tape recordings).
- The activity should involve repeated readings of text. This is often viewed as practice or rehearsal, as with radio plays and other student dramas.
- The element of choice should be involved. For example, students should have some say in the text or book to be used, as well as what portion of the chosen book will be practiced and read.

When adhered to, these three factors establish a fertile growth environment for improved fluency and promote positive attitudes about reading. Choral reading, a strategy previously described in earlier chapters, should be encouraged within LRGs as an ice breaker during the first session. For illustrative purposes, following are a few literature-response activities already named that meet these criteria.

Student Dramas

Stayter and Allington (1991) tell about a reader's theater activity for which a group of heterogeneously grouped seventh graders spent 5 days reading, rehearsing, and performing short dramas. After a first reading, students began to negotiate about which role they would read. More reticent students were permitted to opt for smaller parts, but everyone was required to participate. As time passed, the students critiqued each others' readings and made suggestions as to how they should sound (e.g., "You should sound like a snob"). The most common response in this experience related to how the repeated readings through drama helped them better understand the text. One student said,

> The first time I read to know what the words are. Then I read to know what the words say and later as I read I thought about how to say the words. . . . As I got to know the character better, I put more feeling in my voice. (Stayter & Allington, 1991, p. 145)

Dialogue Retellings

Fluency activities that involve both reading and writing are most effective.

We recommend that students adapt dialogue retellings, previously described, by first writing retellings of either fables or other narratives using as much actual dialogue as possible from the book, then prepare a puppet show for younger students. Participants should rehearse their parts until they are perfectly fluent and solicit suggestions from other LRGs before the day of performance. A book like *The Lion, the Witch, and the Wardrobe* by C. S. Lewis (1961) makes a great example for teachers to use in explaining this option. Walley (1993) recommends the use of cumulative stories, those having a minimum of plot and a maximum of rhythm and rhyme, in early elementary grades. Jane Yolen's (1976) *An Invitation to a Butterfly Ball* is one such example.

Evening Newscast

The evening newscast activity offers maximum opportunity for students to practice their roles using the kind of intonation characteristic of newscasters. Teachers may want to encourage students to adopt and adapt the particular style of a favorite personality, such as "Connie Chum" or "Peter Jokings."

The Unknown Character

In this adaptation of the Unknown Character activity, the student rehearses a number of key passages from the selected text. He reads them one by one until classmates guess the character or mystery book.

The Writing Process: Making Authors of Readers

Understanding the Writing Process

The **writing process approach** helps students learn to understand and use the phases and tools of authorship. Goals of writing process instruction include helping students understand the kinds of thinking processes skilled writers go through in producing different forms of text and helping students become authors themselves. Child-authors gain insights about words and language that cannot be gained through any other kind of experience. New perspectives are gained, because once a child has written a book, he becomes an "insider" with other authors (Calkins, 1986). As authors, children begin to read books in new ways: They notice how skillful writers paint pictures with words in the reader's mind, they discover words that convey just the right meaning for a given thought and phrases that capture the attention of readers. Through writing process instruction, children become wordsmiths and begin to enjoy the works of other authors on new and higher levels.

*The **writing process approach** helps children learn and use phases of authorship.*

Child-authors begin to feel like insiders in the world of books.

Writing instruction has changed significantly in recent years. Composition teachers of past decades typically assigned students the task of preparing a research paper or report as the primary mode of instruction. In this "one-draft mentality" (Calkins, 1986), students handed in their report, and the reports were graded by the teacher, returned, and most likely forgotten. In recent years, researcher-practitioners such as Donald Graves (1983) and Lucy Calkins (1994) have helped teachers (and students) understand that writing is a process instead of a one-time "quick and dirty" project. Children are taught to understand and use the phases of authorship.

Writers do not, strictly speaking, move rigidly from one stage to another. Rather, they sometimes move back and forth from one phase to another, or even quit in the middle of a writing project to start another. But for emergent writers in the elementary

In this approach to writing instruction, we seek to teach children to write in ways closely similar to those employed by professionals.

Prewriting *is the getting-ready stage.*

school, it is very instructive to examine the various modes or stages that writers go through in producing text: prewriting, drafting, revising and editing, and publishing.

The Prewriting Stage

Prewriting is the getting-ready-to-write stage (Tompkins, 1994). Writing begins with an idea or message. Many teachers help students begin the writing process by asking them to brainstorm a list of topics they might be interested in writing about at some point in the future. They should be topics that generate a certain amount of emotion for the student. Donald Graves, in his book *Writing: Teachers and Children at Work* (1983), suggests that teachers model each of the stages in the writing process to help children see adult examples. For this first step of brainstorming, the teacher might list at the overhead projector or chalkboard several topics that he is interested in writing about, possible topics such as sailing, collecting antiques, attending wrestling matches, traveling to South Pacific islands, or whatever else is stimulating to the teacher. It is important that teachers explain to the class why each topic is appealing. A brainstorming session sometimes helps children who are having difficulty to discover topics of interest. The key to success is helping students find topics that generate a certain amount of emotion so as to help "drive" the process until the composition is completed.

After students have selected a topic of interest, they should gather information or conduct their "research." Depending on the nature of the topic, students may need to make a trip to the library to gather background information, interview people in their family or community, or write to local, state, or federal agencies.

Opening sentences should grab and hold the reader.

Once the student-writer has settled on a topic and collected useful support information, he is ready to begin organizing ideas for presentation; in short, develop an outline of some kind. The outline's form is not really important; the writer simply should have some kind of organizational scheme for the composition. This step helps make the piece clear, concise, and thorough. Several outline formats depicting the story theme "Our Family's Trip to Universal Studios," written by a student named Jina, are presented as examples in Figures 11.18 through 11.20. Once the outline of

Gathering lists of correctly spelled words related to one's topic helps writers during the drafting stage.

Figure 11.18

Sample outline format

> ### My Birthday Trip to Universal Studios (by Jina)
>
> I. Arrival at Universal Studios
>   a. Came with Mom, Dad, Melanie, Michelle, and Rob, and Uncle Dan
>   b. Arrived in our new van
>   c. It was a hot day in August
>   d. We all rode the shuttle to the front gate
>   e. It was my birthday
> II. Sights of Special Interest
>   a. We saw the car from the movie *Back to the Future*
>   b. We saw the special effects studio for "Battlestar Galactica"
>   c. They have a special street on the back lot with houses from "Leave It to Beaver," "The Adams Family," and *Psycho*
>   d. King Kong jumps out at you at one point on the shuttle ride
>   e. We saw an action scene from "Miami Vice"
> III. Special Events That Happened on My Birthday Trip
>   a. I was chosen to ride on a bicycle on the set of *E.T.* The camera made it look like I was flying in mid-air.
>   b. Next, I was chosen to be in a film sequence in a boat. I got all wet!

ideas has been completed, it is often helpful for the writer to create several opening sentences for the story, or alternative leads. Having an interesting beginning, one that grabs the reader, helps create a successful composition. For example, in the story entitled "My Birthday Trip to Universal Studios," Jina may have begun her story thus . . .

> On my birthday my family and I went to Universal Studios. It was a very fun day that I will never forget.

On the other hand, if Jina wrote several alternative leads, then picked the most exciting one to begin her story, perhaps she would have come up with a beginning more like this . . .

> Imagine a birthday party with *King Kong, E.T.,* and the stars from *Miami Vice* as your guests! That's exactly what happened to me on my 13th birthday. If you think that's something, hold on to your seat while I tell you the rest of my story.

Sometimes children have a difficult time getting started with their composition, or even coming up with an idea compelling enough to commit to paper. In this situation, it is usually helpful to engage in free writing. *Free writing* simply means that students sit down for a sustained period of time and write down anything that comes to mind, anything at all. What often emerges is a rather rambling narrative with many idea fragments. Lucy Calkins (1986) has suggested that children might begin by simply listing things in their immediate environment until they come to an idea they wish to write about. After students have an organized set of ideas about which to write and have constructed alternative leads, they are ready for the drafting stage.

Free writing is a simple strategy for helping students come up with ideas for their compositions.

Figure 11.19

Semantic web

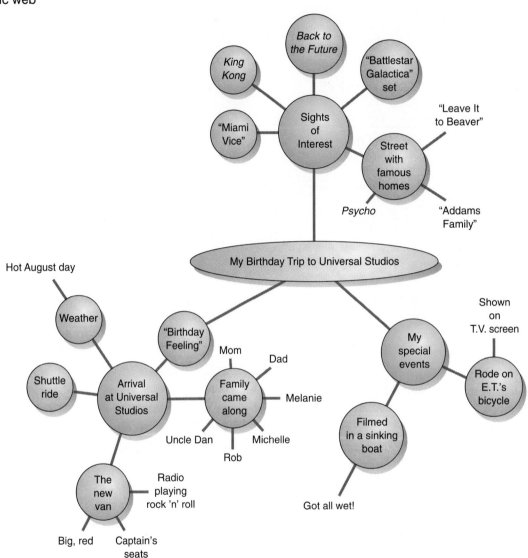

The Drafting Stage

The **drafting stage** represents a first attempt to get the ideas down on paper. Teachers should emphasize that the most important part of drafting is getting thoughts down, not mechanical correctness. Such fine points as verb–tense agreement or spelling correctness are not what is important at this stage; *ideas* are the most important consideration.

First drafts are often referred to as "sloppy copies."

It may be helpful for students to have a classroom bulletin board that lists many suggestions for each stage of the writing process. The following ideas may be useful

Figure 11.20

Structured overview

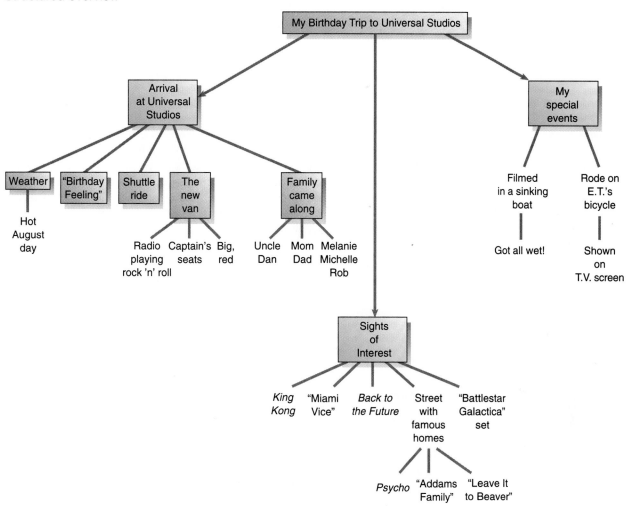

reminders for students as they are drafting. Some modification may be needed for clarity and to fit the maturity of the writer(s).

- Write as though you were telling a story to an interested friend.
- Use your own "voice" instead of trying to sound like your favorite author.
- Try to use words that create a picture in the reader's mind. Your words should be descriptive and clear.
- Be sure to describe sights, sounds, smells, and other sensory images that are important parts of the story you want to tell.
- Say what you want to say directly ("more" is not necessarily "better").

Some students may have difficulty getting ideas down on paper the first time or two they attempt drafting. Frequently, their handwriting ability is slower than the flow of ideas coming into their minds. There are at least two solutions to this kind of problem. One possibility is to have the student dictate his story into a tape recorder, then transcribe the story on paper later. This solution helps keep the student from becoming frustrated because of slow handwriting ability and also helps him improve those same skills as he transcribes the story on paper. A second possibility is to allow the student to dictate his story to an older student or peer tutor. The advantage here is that the storyteller can get valuable and immediate feedback from the peer tutor, aiding in the clarity of the composition.

Revising and Editing

Revising is a second look at one's composition and its message.

Once the draft has been completed, the author is ready to begin the final production stage of editing and revising. **Revising**, or "re-visioning," is the act of changing the manuscript to include any and all new ideas the author has discovered for improving the manuscript. **Editing** has to do with the process of reading and rereading the manuscript to find errors and omissions of one kind or another. Editing is usually a joint effort between the author and readers, who can offer constructive criticism.

The revision process can begin in many ways, each offering advantages for the student and teacher. Perhaps the most traditional method is the student–teacher writing conference. Students meet with the teacher after the teacher has read the composition. The teacher asks questions about the manuscript and offers suggestions for revising the manuscript. Some teachers like to use a form for recording their comments for the student as an aid in the revision process. Figure 11.21 offers one such form for this purpose.

Students work collaboratively in peer editing conferences.

Another option for helping students improve their compositions is peer editing. Many students prefer to get suggestions from their peers for improving their composi-

Figure 11.21

Writing evaluation form

Writing Evaluation Form

Student Name _____   Date _____
Title of Composition_____

Overall Evaluation of the Composition:

_____→

Underdeveloped   Partially Ready   Advanced   Excellent

Areas Needing Further Development

_____ Character development   _____ Spelling

_____ Setting   _____ Grammar

_____ Conflict description   _____ Punctuation

_____ Conflict resolution   _____ Capitalization

_____ Story closure

Text With Proofreader Markings	Explanation
injured Jamie carried the puppy home.	$\wedge$ is for inserting missing words
Let's go to Mark's house over.	$\cap$ for moving text
Let's go to Mark's house over.	ℓ for marking out text

Figure 11.22

Proofreaders' marks

tions before "publishing." Peer editing allows them to get suggestions in a collaborative and risk-free environment. Although some students may be able to work successfully one on one with their peers, peer editing is often more effective in small groups known as *teacherless writing teams* and/or *peer editing conferences*. These teams comprise three to four students who work together to develop the best compositions possible. At each stage of the writing process, students share their work with the team, then team members ask questions of the author and offer suggestions for improving the composition.

Editing involves careful review of the composition to check for such things as correct spellings, sentence constructions, topic sentences, awkward language, and whether the composition makes sense. Many teachers encourage children to use word banks or key word lists pertaining to the subject, a thesaurus, and dictionaries. Although some have advocated the use of reference tools during the drafting stage, Calkins (1986) recommends reserving them for the final stages of the writing process.

During the editing stage, it is often useful for writers to use proofreaders' marks. These are notations that an author marks on manuscripts to add, delete, or rearrange information. Figure 11.22 depicts a few examples teachers might consider demonstrating to young writers.

Finally, many schools provide students with word processing equipment for writing projects. Equipment such as the Apple Macintosh and IBM-PC makes the editing process both quick and relatively painless for young writers, although they must first learn keyboarding skills. Similarly, classroom computer word processing programs such as *Bank Street Writer* can convert existing computers into word processing-like systems. Computer applications for teaching writing are discussed in greater detail later in this chapter.

Showing students how to use proofreaders' marks will help make the process go more efficiently.

Publishing

The natural desire for most authors, young or old, is that their composition be shared with an audience. For children, **publishing** can take many exciting forms. One publishing experience common in elementary classrooms is called *author's chair*. Each day, at a designated time, young authors who have completed a composition and have been cleared by the teacher can sign up to share their most recent compositions in the author's chair. When the appointed time arrives, children take turns reading their creation to the class, answering questions about their story, and reaping generous applause. Other forms of publishing may include letter writing to pen pals, school officials, favorite authors, and media stars, or making stories into classroom books, news-

Publishing is a time for students to share their creations.

papers, and yearbooks. Information concerning publishing centers, which assist child-authors in preparing compositions for sharing, is presented in Chapter 9.

The key to success in publishing is that students feel their writing projects have a purpose and an audience beyond a teacher with a red grading pencil.

Using the Writing Workshop: Organizing for Instruction

*The **writing workshop** is a structure or scheme for implementing the writing process approach in classrooms.*

Once teachers understand the essential elements of the writing process, they are ready to begin planning for instruction. The **writing workshop** is an organizational structure for teaching–facilitating writing development. It is one model for instruction that can be modified as needed. Classroom periods could be organized to include five phases: teacher sharing time, minilesson, state of the class, workshop activities, and student sharing time. Figure 11.23 depicts the organizational scheme for the writing workshop. A description of each of the five phases follows.

Figure 11.23

The writing workshop

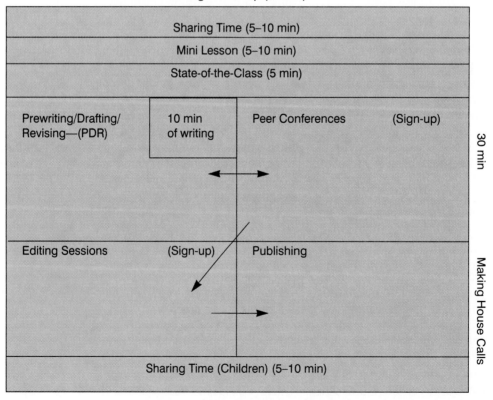

Writing Workshop (60 min)

| Sharing Time (5–10 min) |
| Mini Lesson (5–10 min) |
| State-of-the-Class (5 min) |

Prewriting/Drafting/Revising—(PDR) · 10 min of writing · Peer Conferences · (Sign-up) · 30 min

Editing Sessions · (Sign-up) · Publishing · Making House Calls

Sharing Time (Children) (5–10 min)

Phase 1: Teacher Sharing Time (5 to 10 Minutes)

The purpose of teacher sharing time is to present children with language and experiences through writing that stimulate the natural energies of thinking (Holdaway, 1984). The substance of these teacher-led presentations is usually an assortment of such writing products as brain-enticing poems, songs, stories, and exposition that have been written by the teacher. The goal is to inspire students to have an urge to strike out on new adventures in writing. This phase of instruction should be brief, perhaps 5 to 10 minutes, and serves as a stimulating introduction to the rest of the writing period.

Teachers show some of their own work during sharing time.

Phase 2: The Minilesson (5 to 10 Minutes)

The minilesson (Calkins, 1986) is a brief period of time set apart for offering student-writers tips from the teacher about good writing. Class discussions about topics such as selecting good ideas to write about, focusing topics, clustering information (webbing), gathering reference materials, conducting interviews, publishing, and many more writing-related ideas are all viable. A few examples of common minilesson topics suggested by Atwell (1987) follow:

Minilessons focus on all aspects of the writing process. For example, webbing, the use of proofreaders' marks, and invented spellings are common topics.

Illustrations	Narrative leads
Essay writing	Spelling
Form	Writing good fiction
Mythology	The dictionary
Resume writing	Genre
Writing conferences with yourself	Job applications
Correspondence	Punctuation
Focus	Style
Greek mythology	Writing short stories

Teachers usually use some of their own writing samples, and those volunteered by students, in teaching these brief minilessons. The main focus of the minilesson at all grade levels is helping students write with quality at their stage of development.

Phase 3: State of the Class (5 Minutes)

The state of the class phase for the Writing Workshop takes the same form as in the Reading Workshop (see Figure 11.14). The teacher simply lists each child's name on the left of the chart, and students fill in the blanks for each day, indicating what they will be doing (e.g., drafting, peer conferences, editing session, or publishing). Sometimes teachers, like Atwell (1987), prefer to complete the state of the class chart themselves in a whole-class setting and find the experience quite useful.

> I think the [state of the class] conference is worth three minutes of the whole class's time. I can't begin to know all the ways my students find ideas for writing, but I do know that eavesdropping is right up there. When they make their plans publicly, writers naturally teach each other about new options for topic and genre. (Atwell, 1987, p. 90)

By recording students' plans for writing and saving them over the weeks of the school year, teachers can see almost at a glance which students are failing to progress

(Atwell, 1987). State of the class helps teachers negotiate deadlines for key stages of the writing process with individual students, hold them accountable, and determine when house calls may be needed.

Phase 4: Workshop Activities (30 Minutes)

Four activities operate concurrently during the workshop activities phase: (a) prewriting, drafting, and revising; (b) peer editing conferences; (c) editing sessions (with the teacher); and (d) preparing for publishing. As mentioned in the previous section, students sign up for one of these activities each day and work accordingly during the workshop period. For descriptive purposes, it may be useful to distinguish between activities the teacher is engaged in versus those of the students.

Note that teachers have specific tasks to complete throughout the workshop activities period.

For the teacher, several activities take place during this time frame. The first 10 minutes or so of the writing workshop, teachers engage in sustained silent writing (SSW). While working on a written product of his choice, the teacher provides children with (a) a silent model of positive writing behavior and (b) needed examples for the teacher sharing time period previously described. After the teacher's SSW period, he is ready to move on to making individual house calls and working with students in private editing sessions.

Children are allowed to move at their own pace during the workshop activities and select from four alternatives. In the prewriting, drafting, and revising option, children choose topics for narratives, gather resources and references, conduct interviews, and/or make an outline or other scheme for organizing their stories, and eventually produce a draft.

Once children finish their first drafts, they are ready to sign up for a peer conference. Peer conferences are small groups of children, usually three or four, who sign up to read each others' first drafts and make recommendations to their peer authors for revisions. Peer conferences are sometimes known as "teacherless writing groups," because the teacher is not involved during this critique phase unless invited by the group for consulting purposes.

Teachers have told us that some students beginning to learn the writing workshop system seem to want to peer conference almost all the time. This can be problematic because a sincere goal of holistic teaching is to promote peer collaboration and cooperation. One solution to this dilemma might be to establish guidelines differentiating peer conferences from what might be termed "1-minute conferences." When children need a quick opinion on their composition, they can have a 1-minute conference with a peer. Students should not require more than three 1-minute conferences during a workshop activity period.

Group etiquette rules should be established early in the school year to ensure maximum productivity and to minimize conflicts. Role playing is one way to arrive at these rules. As mentioned previously, in one school, teachers made a videotape acting out positive and negative group behavior. Students had no problem coming up with a list of their own group etiquette rules, which functioned well in all group experiences. (Figure 11.10 shows some typical kinds of rules generated by students.)

Some teachers initially have difficulty accepting higher classroom noise levels. Think about what might be acceptable and why.

A word regarding classroom noise levels seems warranted as it relates to peer conferences and group work in general. Whenever teachers begin to experiment with modes of learning that allow children to work on their own or in small groups, the noise level invariably goes up. This may be a little distressing at first but should be carefully analyzed. If the class is unruly, then appropriate steps must be taken to maintain class control. But more often than not, the increase in classroom noise should be viewed as the sound of learning and creative interaction. Silvia Ashton-Warner (1963) refers to this kind of classroom hubbub as "peaceful noise."

Once the peer conference group meets and considers each child's manuscript, suggestions are made for improving the writing project. Of course, each child is free to accept or reject the suggestions according to the principle of choice and independence, as discussed in Chapter 1. Thus, manuscript revisions follow the peer conference in preparation for the editing session with the teacher.

Editing sessions are special times for students to meet with teachers to discuss their writing projects. To take part in the editing session, children should sign up the day before the conference and submit a copy of their writing project. This allows teachers time to read the project and make notes for the student. Teachers should avoid writing directly on the project. Instead, remarks should be made on a separate sheet of paper to prevent defacing the project. The teacher may wish to review a story grammar outline for narrative compositions to decide whether all important elements have been included. Semantic and syntactic considerations should also be discussed during this time.

Editing sessions are marvelous opportunities for teaching and extending.

After the editing session, students frequently need to edit or revise further before publishing. It may be desirable for the student and teacher to have an additional editing session before publishing to go over modifications.

A visit in the publishing center is the final option for the workshop activities period. The purpose is to prepare the writing project for publication.

One final point: Publishing does not necessarily happen with every writing project. Sometimes students will say to the teacher "I'm running out of interest for this story. May I work on another one?" Most writers occasionally run out of gas during a writing project and start a new one. Some may have several projects in process. It is not the number of publications a child produces during a given time period that is important, but the process itself. Although it is desirable for the child to reach closure on a regular basis with writing projects, it does not have to happen every time.

Sometimes young authors have more than one composition in process.

Phase 5: Sharing Time (5 to 10 Minutes)

The Writing Workshop concludes with student sharing time. This period is for sharing and publishing completed writing projects. Children proceed to sharing time only with the approval of the teacher during the editing session.

Even students who may be publishing their writing project outside of class (e.g., putting their book in the school library or submitting their story to a children's magazine) should take part in sharing time. This allows other children to see their finished product and enjoy the story. The most common format for sharing time for students is the author's chair experience, previously described in this chapter.

Student sharing time is an initial publishing experience before peers.

Using Computers to Teach Writing

When teachers think of computers, word processing often comes to mind. *Word processing* is the general term for software programs that permit someone to write, edit, store, and print text (Strickland, Feeley, & Wepner, 1987, p. 13). Word processing enables the computer to be used much like a typewriter but with all the added advantages a computer offers. In addition to standard word processing packages for elementary and middle school-age students, other related computer packages help students compose. In this section, we review several promising writing options that might be considered when developing balanced literacy programs. They are compatible with most IBM and Apple family computers commonly used in the classroom.

IBM's *Writing to Read* Program

Writing to Read is a popular computer-assisted program based on a modified alphabet system.

Writing to Read is a computerized beginning reading–writing program based on a modified alphabet idea (one symbol for each of 42 language sounds) for kindergarten and first-grade levels. Originally developed by John Henry Martin, a retired teacher and school administrator, *Writing to Read* was underwritten by IBM, which makes the computers and typewriters used in the program (Strickland et al., 1987). The typical routine, usually lasting 30 to 40 minutes per day, takes children through a five-station rotation in a special computer lab away from the regular classroom. Students begin with the computer station, where they are taught to type 42 phonemes (representing the English language sounds) using color images and synthesized speech. These lessons are repeated in a work journal, then students listen to a tape-recorded story while following along in a book in the listening library. These activities are followed by a typing–writing center, in which students can write compositions of their own choosing. The final center is called "make words," where other reinforcement activities are practiced.

Because of the nationwide publicity concerning *Writing to Read,* some teachers likely will be asked about its efficacy. Many advantages and disadvantages of *Writing to Read* have been described by researchers in this field. The major advantage seems to be improved interest and ability in writing (Collis, 1988; Ellison, 1989). Children involved in *Writing to Read* often spontaneously begin stories at home and bring them to school the next day to put on the computer. Because reading and writing are reciprocal processes, it is reasonable to assume that some benefit to students' reading development would also accrue, although research has thus far failed to prove this to be the case (Collis, 1988; Ellison, 1989).

Cost is often a barrier for schools wishing to add computer facilities.

The biggest drawback to *Writing to Read* relates to cost. This program requires the exclusive use of one brand of computer (IBM), which is sufficiently expensive to preclude the use of any other computers in most schools (Strickland et al., 1987; Whitaker et al., 1989). "Not many schools, for example, can install an IBM lab for reading, plus an Apple lab for mathematics literature. In addition, children must eventually 'unlearn' the modified alphabet and learn to use standard orthography" (Whitaker et al., 1989, p. 103).

Others criticize some of the *Writing to Read* activities as nothing more than electronic workbook activities (especially the work journal) and note that its writing instruction appears to be inconsistent with current research in the writing process (Ohanian, 1984; Strickland et al., 1987). Whatever the criticisms, *Writing to Read* appears to be a ground-breaking technology likely to be mimicked, and hopefully improved, in the future of writing education.

Word Processing Software

A number of interesting word processing software programs are now available for process writing.

Word processing software has been a major focal point for developers in recent years. These efforts have resulted in many affordable programs that help students develop and extend their authoring abilities. Listed here are a few programs that represent some of the technologies presently available.

Writing a Narrative (MECC, 1984): This is an easy-to-use program that helps students write about their own experiences. It contains two interactive tutorials having to do with brainstorming and drafting. *Writing a Narrative* is recommended for grades 9 through 12 but can be used successfully in many upper elementary classrooms. It is available for the Apple II family computers.

Author! Author!: A great way to merge reading and writing processes is to have students write their own plays, either individually or in groups. The *Author! Author!* (Mindplay, 1990) program, available for Apple and MS-DOS formats, is a playwriting package that helps students write scene-by-scene scripts and create accompanying stages complete with movable graphics of characters and props (Wepner, 1993).

Bank Street Writer (1990, Scholastic): One of the pioneering efforts in this field, *Bank Street Writer* is both easy to use and affordable. It is a menu-driven program that converts computers (Apple II family, Commodore 64, IBM, Atari) to word processors. It is suggested for grade 3 and up.

MacWrite (Apple, 1984): This program is designed to be used with Apple Macintosh computers and is well-known for its user-friendly capacity. It features word processing with a "mouse" pointer and pull-down help windows. The cost is free with the purchase of Macintosh computers, and it is recommended for all grade levels.

Quill (Heath): Another word processing program that has been on the education scene for several years, *Quill* features a prewriting section called "Planner," a message system called "Mailbag," and an editing feature known as "Writer's Assistant." Quill is available for Apple family computers and the TRS-80 Model III/IV.

The Language Arts and Themed Studies: Second-Level Integration Across the Curriculum

The teaching of reading and writing using holistic orientations has been the focus of this chapter. Although reading and writing have been presented as separate entities for the sake of clarity, holistic classrooms that have achieved advanced transitions development do not teach these literacy abilities as separate subjects. Rather, they are integrated across the curriculum such that these boundaries virtually cease to exist. In a fully holistic integration, reading and writing become integral parts of subject area investigations and vice versa. Frequently, classes move into expanded interdisciplinary themed studies, such as those mentioned earlier in this chapter. A theme such as journeys, for instance, can become an exciting classroom experience involving social studies, science, mathematics literature, art history, and other important areas of the curriculum. This **themed studies approach** is what balanced literacy teaching is all about in its purest form.

Integrating reading and writing across the curriculum is called second-level integration.

The advantages of curriculum integration are numerous. Reading and writing abilities are acquired and refined within a rich context of real world significance, which in turn inspires students to want to know more. Skills are no longer taught in isolation as rote drill but are learned as welcomed tools for communicating ideas. Holistic integration of the curriculum results in a blend of instruction in literacy communication skills and content as well as the planting of seeds for future searches for new knowledge.

In one description of successful themed studies in Canada, Gamberg and others (1988) identified a number of important characteristics. First, themed studies are in-

The themed studies approach has become the preferred mode of second-level integration.

depth investigations of a topic, concept, or theme—not reading, math, or science per se. They are high-interest topics that are broad enough to be divided into smaller subtopics. Themed studies are not geographically or historically limiting and help in breaking down the artificial curricular barriers. For elementary students, "The History of Buildings" and "Around the World in 60 Days" are two suggested themes that facilitate themed investigations.

Guidelines for Conducting Themed Studies

Themed studies are very similar to the themed literature units discussed earlier in this chapter, differing mainly at the level of curricular integration (language arts integration vs. total curriculum integration); thus, an exhaustive discussion of the key elements does not seem necessary. A brief summary of essential components of theme studies—as identified from the work of Paradis (1984) and Gamberg and co-workers (1988)—follows:

Think of some creative ways teachers could obtain needed resources for themed studies.

- *Theme Selection:* Themes should be chosen that meet the criteria previously described.
- *Identifying Resources:* Teaching and learning materials should be identified and collected by the teacher before beginning the unit. Examples include nonfiction books; other pertinent print media (e.g., documents, travel brochures, government publications, etc.); hands-on materials from the real world that pertain to the topic; community experts; nonprint media (videotapes, films, radio recordings); parent volunteers; relevant basal stories; and identification of possible field trips.
- *Brainstorming:* Themed studies involve brainstorming for both the teacher and students. Teachers brainstorm as part of the planning process to anticipate ways that curricula can be integrated into the unit and to assist in the selection of materials. Paradis (1984) offers a brainstorming web (Figure 11.24) to assist teachers in this process. Students are also encouraged to brainstorm as a way of becoming involved initially with the topic. Brainstorming helps students focus their thinking and value each of their peers' ideas, encourages collaboration, and reveals student interests and background knowledge.
- *Learning Demonstrations:* Students complete projects and tasks that demonstrate their newly acquired knowledge. Projects like those cited for themed literature units generally apply here. In addition, students may complete other products such as displays, speeches, demonstration fairs, and guided tours.

Figure 11.24

Teacher brainstorming web for theme studies

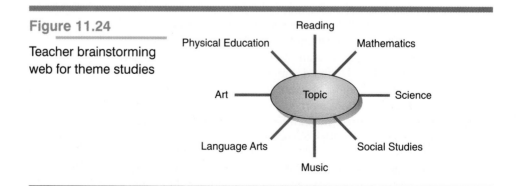

In Chapter 12, we describe more fully how language arts skills can be integrated across the expanse of the total curriculum. Of particular interest will be the application of reading and writing strategies in expository materials so that students have an opportunity to become literate in the fullest possible sense.

In Chapter 12, the construction of thematic units is discussed in detail.

Helping Readers With Learning Problems: Using Balanced Reading and Writing Strategies

Some teachers search for a "magic pill" in remedial teaching, some sort of previously unknown approach that they have somehow overlooked, which will lead to universal success in the classroom. Other teachers attempt to help children succeed by giving them more of what they have failed at before, only in larger doses. Yet the question remains, "Is there a better way to help children with reading problems, and if so, is holistic teaching really *it*?"

The answer to this question is an emphatic "maybe." We strongly feel that the methods outlined in this chapter represent examples of the very best forms of literacy education available for students having problems in literacy learning, as well as for those in the mainstream. The balanced literacy instruction alternative represents a serious challenge to more traditional modes of teaching. However, there are some important points to consider. Veatch and Cooter (1986), in a study of reading instruction in California, found that the most important factor in successful reading instruction is not so much the program, but the teacher. More specifically, when teachers have the freedom to choose their own program of instruction, one they believe to be the best, then their students tend to respond favorably. This is at the heart of what has been called "ownership of the curriculum." On the other hand, when teachers feel that the curriculum has been chosen or dictated by someone other than themselves, the feeling of ownership is missing, and their students tend to not perform as well. Therefore, even though balanced teaching practices may be superior to other forms of literacy education, they should not be forced on teachers who are not ready to accept them. This is why we have tried to make a case for *transitions,* or allowing teachers to move into balanced literacy instruction as far and as quickly as they see fit. If, however, one assumes that the teacher of children with reading problems makes curriculum decisions based on a balanced literacy perspective, then it is possible to make at least two concrete suggestions based on ideas presented in this chapter.

The search for the "best way" to teach reading has led to the realization that it is the teacher, not the program, that is most important.

First, all students, and especially children with reading problems, should spend quality time (20 to 30 minutes per day as a minimum) in the act of reading if they are to grow and progress. Children with reading problems often spend less time reading than do their "normally progressing" counterparts, which sometimes is due to a remedial reading curriculum using large numbers of skill-drill exercises. This chapter has presented many literature-based reading instruction alternatives that can foster increased reading by all students. We further recommend two procedures for readers with learning problems that may enhance their experiences with books: a group-assisted strategy and dyad reading groups.

To become better at reading, one must read often.

The term *group-assisted reading* (Eldredge, 1990) refers to teachers helping a group of students read text material in unison—emphasizing correct phrasing, intonation, and pitch. In group-assisted reading, teachers read each book many times with students until students can read it fluently with expression. In *dyad,* or buddy, reading groups, the teacher's role is filled with a peer "lead reader." Both group-assisted and dyad reading groups have been shown to be more effective in classroom settings with at-risk readers than more traditional methods (Eldredge, 1990; Eldredge & Quinn, 1988).

Daily writing is also crucial for improving literacy abilities.

It is also crucial that a writing workshop program be established as part of the balanced literacy program. Although not empirically tested, a writing-dyad system should be used with students having learning problems. Because of the reciprocal nature of reading and writing, the natural development of word-spelling knowledge and phonemic awareness fostered in students through the writing process and the concomitant interest in books and authors that springs from writing experiences make writing a mainstay in any literacy program for students having reading problems.

Helping Students With Special Language and Cultural Needs: Linking Bilingual Learners With Technology

In constructing balanced literacy programs like the ones described in this chapter, teachers often must consider the needs of culturally and linguistically different learners. We have discovered that emerging technologies available for classroom computers and computer labs offer some interesting alternatives. In this section, we highlight two possibilities as examples of what we mean: electronic dialoguing and an advanced program known as *The Bilingual Writing Center.*

Electronic Dialoguing: An Application of Interactive Telecommunications

Interactive telecommunications uses a computer network like a telephone exchange to transmit text messages. This technology links two computers at different locations with three essential components (M. Moore, 1991): (a) a modem, which allows one computer to communicate with a second computer via the telephone system; (b) a telecommunications software program, which allows the user to control the modem's transfer of information; and (c) a "host computer," which provides access to the network and stores, organizes, and displays information.

Electronic dialoguing facilitates long-distance written discussions using the computer.

Electronic dialoguing (M. Moore, 1991) uses interactive technology to link a student with another person to stimulate written communications. For bilingual learners, we see electronic dialoguing as a means of linking students with successful adults of their native culture in substantive conversations. M. Moore (1991) recommends the use of a poem as an ice breaker using the following basic format:

Grace

Daughter of Louis and Louise Rizzardi,
Lover of mom, dad, Casey (puppy), and SimAnt,
Who feels happy, athletic, anxious, and thrilled,
Who needs family, hiking, drawing, pizza, and boys,
Who fears drugs, scary movies, and being alone,
Who gives friendship, time to family, and time to artwork,
Who would like to see Italy, Hollywood, and a world with no homework!

Three major advantages result from electronic dialoguing. First, the student has an authentic reason to write and is motivated to do so because a real person is awaiting a communication. Second, electronic dialoguing permits the adult volunteer to communicate at his convenience and workplace. Finally, bilingual learners are offered a real-world opportunity to use their developing English skills with a sympathetic audience.

The Bilingual Writing Center

Some teachers become a little frustrated when, at last, they obtain computer equipment for the classroom and discover bilingual students are left out. That is, students having limited English proficiency can find the mysteries of computer technology coded in English terms (e.g., file, edit, format, tools, windows) insurmountable. With limited funds, purchasing word processing programs in two languages is usually not possible. One program for teachers working with students having Spanish as their native language is a program called *The Bilingual Writing Center.*

The Bilingual Writing Center (1992) is essentially a word processing program for speakers of English and Spanish. Two complete programs in one, a click on the menu bar changes all functions from one language to the other. This package features a spell checker (670,000 words in Spanish, 100,000 words in English), color graphics, bilingual documentation, activities for learners, blackline masters, and over 250 bicultural color graphics.

The Bilingual Writing Center is a wonderful option for teachers committed to inclusion of bilingual learning populations.

Summary

Reading and writing are closely related processes that have a reciprocal developmental influence. Balanced literacy programs depend heavily on these processes for overall language development. Four organizational schemes for literature-based reading instruction may be used: core books, individualized reading instruction, themed literature units, and the reading workshop. Core book units involve using a single book as the reading curriculum, and as a springboard for other reading and writing experiences. Individualized reading instruction allows each child to choose for himself the book he will read, then groups children based on need for reading skill instruction. Themed literature units combine the teaching convenience of core book units with the student self-selection of books from individualized reading units for an appealing third alternative. The reading workshop is a fourth alternative for teachers moving into advanced transitions and can be used with either basal readers or trade books.

The writing process approach helps students learn composition skills similar to those of professional writers. Children learn and progress through a series of writing process stages with each composition: prewriting, drafting, revising, editing, and publishing. The Writing Workshop is an organizational scheme offered to preservice and in-service teachers for implementing process writing in the elementary school.

As teachers become knowledgeable in reading and language arts integration and progress toward advanced transitions, they often adopt the themed studies approach. This organizational scheme leads to full curriculum integration, the ultimate goal of balanced literacy programs.

Readers with learning needs benefit from both literature-based reading programs and the writing process approach. Although many readers with learning needs respond well to these program models, as presented, some may require additional

Figure 11.25

Chapter overview

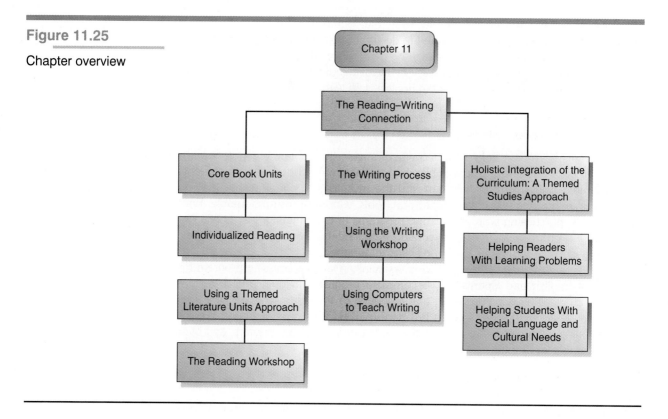

intervention strategies. One method particularly helpful in both reading and writing instruction is the use of dyads, or buddy systems: A peer example or leader becomes the model for children with reading problems, developing a true sense of collaboration and providing the at-risk student with an instructional safety net.

Finally, bilingual students and culturally different students can benefit from new technologies available to the classroom teacher. Electronic dialoguing is a motivational telecommunications technology that enables students to have running discussions over the computer with adult native language speakers. *The Bilingual Writing Center* is a word processing package that translates all functions from Spanish to English and vice versa.

Figure 11.25 provides an overview of the chapter.

CONCEPT APPLICATIONS

IN THE CLASSROOM

1. Identify an interested colleague and develop a themed literature unit using one of the following themes: courage, relationships, discovering new worlds, changes, or animals. Your plans should include a web of the unit, list of books chosen from popular children's literature, possible reading strategies to be taught in teacher-directed sessions, and suggested ideas for literature-response activities.

2. Develop plans for your own Writing Workshop. Sketch out how you will manage the program within the constraints of a typical classroom environment.

What physical facilities (furniture, space, etc.) will you need? Draw up a series of lessons plans for demonstrating or modeling to your class how the Writing Workshop will work.

3. Using the section in this chapter on Reading Workshops, map out plans and materials needed to get started. Identify children's literature to be used, sources of ideas for prereading activities and literature-response projects, and materials to be used in literature-response groups.

4. Prepare an annotated bibliography of computer software available for either the Apple II, Macintosh, IBM, or other computer of your choice that could be helpful in reading and writing instruction. You should develop a list of criteria by which each program may be judged, then evaluate the programs accordingly.

IN THE FIELD

1. Develop a writing and publishing center for your classroom. It should have a variety of writing instruments, different kinds of paper, an assortment of envelopes, and materials useful for binding stories into books. Solicit parent volunteers to help staff the station on selected days to assist students.

RECOMMENDED READINGS

Atwell, N. (1987). *In the middle: Writing, reading, and learning with adolescents.* Portsmouth, NH: Heinemann.

Calkins, L. M. (1994). *The art of teaching writing (new ed.).* Portsmouth, NH: Heinemann.

Calkins, L. M., & Harwayne, S. (1987). *The writing workshop: A world of difference.* Portsmouth, NH: Heinemann. (Note: An excellent videotape by the same name is available from the publisher for teacher education purposes.)

Cox, C., & Zarillo, J. (1993). *Teaching reading with children's literature.* Englewood Cliffs, NJ: Merrill/Prentice Hall.

Fader, D. N. (1976). *The new hooked on books.* New York: Berkley Publishing.

Lathlaen, P. (1993). A meeting of minds: Teaching using biographies. *The Reading Teacher, 46*(6), 529–531.

Martinez, M. (1993). Motivating dramatic story reenactments. *The Reading Teacher, 46*(8), 682–688.

Moore, M. A. (1991). Electronic dialoguing: An avenue to literacy. *The Reading Teacher, 45*(4), 280–286.

Tompkins, G. E. (1994). *Teaching writing: Balancing process and product* (2nd ed.). Englewood Cliffs, NJ: Merrill/Prentice Hall.

Veatch, J. (1978). *Reading in the elementary school* (2nd ed.). New York: Richard C. Owen.

COMPUTER SOFTWARE

The Bilingual Writing Center. (1992). Fremont, CA: The Learning Company. (Aidenwood Tech Park, 493 Kaiser Drive, Fremont, CA 94555, 1-800-852-2255)

Mindplay. (1990). *Author! Author!* Danvers, MA: Methods and Solutions.

Chapter 12

Content Area
Literacy Instruction

Focus Questions

When you are finished studying this chapter, you should be able to answer these questions:
1. How is the second level of curriculum integration achieved through thematic units?
2. Compare and contrast seamless integration and segmented integration.
3. How does concept load have an effect on the readability of content reading assignments?
4. What are the different expository text patterns used in textbook chapters or units of study?
5. How does one analyze a unit of study in terms of essential information to be conveyed to students?
6. What is the purpose of graphic organizers and study guides in content instruction?
7. What is the purpose of expository text response?
8. What are some specific efficient reading and study strategies that can be taught within the context of content instruction?
9. How can the writing process be used to facilitate the learning of new concepts and vocabulary related to a content unit?
10. How are readers with learning needs helped to succeed in content area classrooms?

Key Concepts

Narrative Text
Expository Text
Thematic Units
Seamless Integration
Segmented Integration
Global Coherence
Concept Load
Readability Formula
Content Analysis
Facts, Concepts, Generalizations
Graphic Organizers

Classroom Experience Pyramid
Study Guides
Three-Level Guides
Anticipation Guides
Expository Text Response
Efficient Reading Strategies
Cubes
Conceptual Word Knowledge
Concept Thinking Matrix
Content-Specific Vocabulary Cards

Helping students become independent learners is education's primary goal.

Building Comprehensive Literacy Programs Across the Curriculum

One of the major goals of education is to help people become knowledgeable and independent learners. This implies learning about who we are as human beings and how to keep educating ourselves throughout life. A high level of literacy is essential in maximizing life choices and assuming a valuable role in society.

In previous chapters, we have thoroughly reviewed ways students can be helped to become readers and writers. Teachers developing balanced literacy programs usually begin by integrating their language arts program first (listening, speaking, reading, and writing) and then progress toward the second level of integration: reading and writing across the curriculum. Reading and writing skills are applied in content area subjects, such as the sciences, social studies, and mathematics, so that literacy—in the broadest possible sense of that term—can be realized. This can be a formidable challenge for students because they must learn to master nonfiction forms of reading and writing while also learning new and unfamiliar concepts related to content fields.

An old adage in reading education states, "in the early elementary grades, students *learn to read,* and in the upper grades they *read to learn.*" The implication is that once youngsters master the rudimentary abilities associated with the reading act they are ready to apply these skills in materials that help them grow in their knowledge of the world around them. This reading to learn act, or in other words, the transmission of knowledge from one generation to the next, arguably is the end product and goal of reading/literacy education.

Narrative text tells a story.

Expository text is intended to explain.

As students begin to investigate the world of print, they discover that there are four different forms of composition: argumentation, description, exposition, and narration. In the elementary school, teachers are mostly concerned with helping students successfully read narrative and expository text. **Narrative text** is defined as a form of writing in which the author tells a story, either factual or fictional, in prose or verse (T. L. Harris & Hodges, 1981). **Expository text** is a writing form having the primary purpose of explaining. *A Dictionary of Reading and Related Terms* states that

> Good exposition in speech or writing is clear in conception, well-organized, and understandable. It may include limited amounts of argumentation, description, and narration to achieve this purpose. (Harris & Hodges, 1981, p. 111)

Reading in the content areas as a field is mainly concerned with helping students succeed with expository text. A prime role of teachers of content area subjects is to help students understand the unique characteristics and demands of expository text.

Our purpose in this chapter is twofold. First, we acquaint the reader with ways of achieving the second level or full curriculum integration using thematic units. We then describe some of the particular challenges teachers encounter with expository materials. Last, we describe study strategies students can use to effectively read and learn from exposition in the content areas.

Developing and Using Thematic Units

The goal of themed or **thematic units** is to integrate reading, writing, and other language skills across the curriculum (Savage, 1994). Teachers building thematic units search for ways to incorporate reading and other basic literacy skills into content subjects because they know that these processes help students deepen their knowledge of the real world. The synergism created in these cross-curricular units (Cox & Zarillo, 1993; Wepner & Feeley, 1993) is quite powerful and spawns many positive outcomes in the classroom including heightened interest in the subject matter and a sense of empowerment.

Thematic units integrate reading and writing across the curriculum.

After many years of helping school districts around the nation build thematic units, we have made a few important discoveries that tend to speed the process of curricular integration. The most efficient way to begin is by first constructing a themed literature unit using the process described in Chapter 11. This achieves full integration of the language arts within the context of great literature. Themed literature units also contain all essential elements for a balanced literacy program, such as daily reading and writing, the teaching of nonnegotiable skills, literature response, cooperative groups, opportunities to practice fluency, student self-evaluation, and so on. Once teachers build themed literature units as the curriculum core, it becomes a relatively simple matter to interlace the content areas. Finally, we have learned that once teachers go through the process we will describe in building thematic units, they better understand all the essential elements and can re-create the process in the future in their own way—keeping some elements, deleting others, to create a balanced learning system that meets the needs of their students.

Planning thematic units involves five major phases, which may be applied equally well in grades 3 through 8. These phases are theme selection, setting goals and objectives, webbing, choosing major activities and materials, and unit scaffolding.

Theme Selection

In many ways, the success of thematic units depends on the concept chosen to be the theme. It must be broad enough to accomplish linkage between the various content subjects, to address local and state requirements listed in curriculum guides (Pappas, Kiefer, & Levstik, 1990), include quality nonfiction and fictional literature, and still be interesting to youngsters. Topics like state history or nutrition can be far too confining for the kinds of engaging learning experiences we hope to craft. In Chapter 11, we suggested a large number of possible topics by grade level, which might give the reader a good starting point; these include legends, survival, heroes, changes, seasons, and journeys. If the theme selected is broad enough, teachers will discover creative and enticing ways to weave into the unit the various content subjects. To demonstrate more clearly ways thematic units can be constructed, in the remainder of this section, we build on the themed literature unit called *journeys*, introduced in Chapter 11.

The success of thematic units often begins with the selection of flexible and interesting themes.

Setting Goals and Objectives

Once the theme has been selected, teachers should consult the district curriculum guide and other available resources to determine possible goals and objectives. Some teachers prefer to do this first because themes occasionally grow logically out of the required curriculum. Whether done as a first or second step, establishing goals and objectives must come early so that appropriate learning activities and materials can be chosen.

Notice that selection of required skills and curricula to be included occurs after the theme is chosen.

Webbing

The next step in planning thematic units is webbing. *Webbing* is essentially the process of creating a schematic or schema map of the linkage between each aspect of the unit. By creating a web of the major aspects of the proposed unit, the teacher can gain a global view—the "big picture." Webs can also be revised and adapted later to use as an advance organizer for students at the beginning of the thematic unit. In Figure 12.1, we see an initial (not fully developed) thematic unit web for the journeys theme. Note that we have not "fleshed out" the language arts component, because it is fully described in Chapter 11 (see "Using a Themed Literature Units Approach"). The journeys theme now spans three additional content areas: social studies, science, and mathematics. Major activities have also been suggested, which is the next topic we explore.

Choosing Major Activities and Materials

The floodgates of creativity are opened when teachers introduce thematic units.

One of the joys of thematic units is that they infuse the curriculum with great ideas, activities, and materials that energize learners. What a great alternative this is for teachers ready for modest yet powerful change. In the following paragraphs, we describe just a few of the possibilities.

Figure 12.1

Initial thematic unit web: journeys

Thematic Unit Activities

Activities chosen for thematic units provide students with opportunities to apply literacy skills within a real-world context. Sometimes students complete these activities independently, other times as part of a problem-solving team. Occasions for personal exploration and reflection are also seen as valuable aspects of thematic unit activities.

In Figure 12.1, we include several interesting activities that fit the journeys theme nicely and allow the teacher great flexibility. Although it may not be obvious at first glance, various district curriculum requirements have been built into the journeys theme. These include studies of Greece, investigations into the solar system, and rudiments of geometry and algebra. A "problem/challenge" scheme has been selected as the means for discovering each curriculum objective within a real world context.

Social Studies   In the social studies component, the problem/challenge activity is for students working in groups of four to assume the role of travel agents charged with the responsibility of developing a "tour guide" for clients traveling to Greece. Required parts of the tour guide involve information about ancient Greece, Greek cuisine, and information about the original founding of the Olympics in ancient Greece. Students in each group present what they have learned to the class, or other classes, in the form of an enlarged travel brochure.

Brainstorm a list of possible problems/challenges for social studies.

Science   The problem/challenge activity for science has student groups assume the role of astronauts aboard a space shuttle. Their mission is to travel to a planet of their choosing in the solar system and establish a colony. This involves scientific research into such things as what humans need to sustain life, surface conditions on the selected planet, as well as any useful natural resources (if any), and information about the building of life-supporting human environments (biospheres). To present their findings, students in each group will draft a report in the form of a book using the writing process, and construct a model of the biosphere they propose to build on the planet surface.

Mathematics   The problem/challenge activity for mathematics is for students to assume the role of sea voyagers who must navigate their ship to Greece from the United States. This is an individual project or may be conducted in pairs. Skills involved include basics in map reading, geometry as related to navigation, translation of miles per hour to knots, and journal writing. The product is a ship's log, which details daily destinations, map coordinates, travel times, and (if desired) some brief information about what they see at each port.

Thematic Unit Materials

The preceding examples clearly alert us to the fact that many and diverse materials are needed. Both fiction and nonfiction materials are needed to plan rich and interesting activities. The core materials are books, lots of books of every kind. Pappas et al. (1990) got it just right when they said, "as with chocolate, you never have enough books!" Essential are reference materials, fictional books to read aloud and awaken imaginations, and books to read aloud. Teachers will also need to locate what are known by historians as "primary source materials"—factual, original sources of information. Later in this chapter, we mention a number of time-saving resources for locating specialty books and other media.

" . . . as with chocolate, you never have enough books" (Pappas et al., 1990)

Unit Scaffolding

Assembling the basic daily plans of thematic units is the process known as unit scaffolding.

The final stage of planning is what we term *unit scaffolding.* At this point, the teacher determines just how long the unit should run and makes final decisions about which activities to include. Typically, thematic units last 1 to 2 weeks in the lower grades (Wiseman, 1992) and up to 4 or 5 weeks in the upper grades. The teacher should resist the temptation to run units for months at a time, because this usually becomes too much of a good thing and turns high student interest into boredom.

***Seamless integration** depends heavily on schedule flexibility.*

One of the decisions to be made is whether the unit is to be fully integrated and presented as a seamless curriculum. Some teachers choose to operate in a nondepartmentalized fashion. In this case, our journeys unit may operate for a few days or a week strictly focusing on the social studies problem/challenge. When the social studies portion is concluded, the class may move on to the science problem/challenge, focusing on that aspect for whole days at a time. The mathematics problem/challenge may come next. The value of **seamless integration** is that students pursue problems in much the same way as adults in the professional world, incorporating literacy skills throughout the day. Another benefit is that students can move from one problem/challenge to another every few days, thus maintaining a higher level of interest. Unfortunately, seamless integration cannot be achieved very easily in departmentalized schools—self-contained classrooms are generally necessary.

***Segmented integration** of the curriculum works best in departmentalized schools.*

Another option for organizing thematic units that may be used either in self-contained or departmentalized situations is called **segmented integration**. In segmented integration, each content area portion is developed concurrently by either the self-contained teacher or content specialists. A sample daily schedule depicting how this might occur in a departmentalized middle school setting is shown in Figure 12.2. Segmented integration permits teachers in fully departmentalized schools to develop thematic units collaboratively as faculty teams. Sometimes all teachers in a departmentalized team will choose to take part in the thematic unit. On other occasions, one or two teachers may feel a need to do something different to satisfy district or state mandates. Participation should be a matter of choice. Further, one teacher may decide to run a thematic unit in her classroom for 3 weeks, while other teachers may have the unit run for 4 or 5 weeks. Whenever possible, however, it is usually a good thing to begin and end the unit at the same time to achieve proper closure.

Figure 12.2

Segmented integration for journeys theme

8:30–9:30	**Language Arts:** Themed Literature Unit on Journeys
9:30–10:45	**Social Studies:** Greece/Tour Guide
10:55–11:30	Computer Lab
11:30–12:30	**Science:** Solar System/Biosphere Model
12:30–1:00	Lunch
1:00–2:15	Specials: Library, P.E.
2:30–3:25	**Mathematics:** Sea Navigation

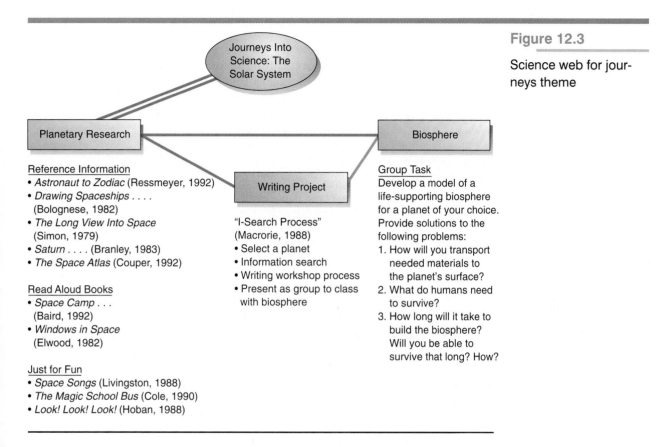

Figure 12.3

Science web for journeys theme

We have found that planning daily activities is greatly facilitated by webbing each content component separately. Teachers should include in the web such information as key reference books, computer software, important questions to be answered, special activities, and demonstrations that teachers may wish to perform. In Figure 12.3, we share a web used in the science portion of the journeys theme.

A key to the success of any learning adventure in the content areas is helping students develop strategies for coping with the demands of expository text. These strategies are applied within the context of thematic units, not to mention the necessity in traditional content classrooms. In the next section, we explore this important topic in some detail.

Understanding the Differing Text Demands of Content Area Reading

The successful teaching of expository text requires extensive preparation and planning on the part of the teacher. Three major concerns that should be addressed when planning for instruction are the organizational structure of the text, concept load, and readability considerations. In this section, each of these concerns is discussed from the point of view of what teachers must do to prepare for instruction.

Analyzing Text Structures

Global coherence per-tains to the overall organiza-tion of texts.

A great deal of research has been conducted in recent years related to **global coher-ence** (Armbruster, 1984), or the overall structure or organization of different forms of text. Narrative text has been described using a story grammar scheme, which includes such common elements as setting, theme, characterization, plot, and resolu-tion. Expository text, however, is quite different. The structure of expository text tends to be much more compact, detailed, and explanatory (Heilman, Blair, & Rup-ley, 1990). Similar to the story grammar research for narrative text, five common expository text structures have been described by Meyer and Freedle (1984): descrip-tion, collection, causation, problem/solution, and comparison.

Teachers, in preparing to teach units in the content areas, need to establish which expository text structures are used and organize for instruction accordingly. Next, Meyer and Freedle's (1984) five expository text patterns are described along with examples taken from content textbooks:

Examine an elementary sci-ence book. How many expository text patterns can you find?

Description: Explains something about a topic or presents a characteristic or setting for a topic.

Decimals are another way to write fractions when the denominators are 10, 100, and so on. (From *Merrill Mathematics* [Grade 5], 1985, p. 247.)

Collection: A number of descriptions (specifics, characteristics, or settings) pre-sented together.

WATER HABITATS

Freshwater habitats are found in ponds, bogs, swamps, lakes, and rivers. Each fresh-water habitat has special kinds of plants and animals that live there. Some plants and animals live in waters that are very cold. Others live in waters that are warm. Some plants and animals adapt to waters that flow fast. Others adapt to still water. (From *Merrill Science* [Grade 3], 1989, p. 226)

Causation includes a time element.

Causation: Elements grouped according to time sequence with a cause–effect relationship specified.

AMERICA ENTERS THE WAR

On Sunday, December 7, 1941, World War II came to the United States. At 7:55 A.M. Japanese warplanes swooped through the clouds above Pearl Harbor. Pearl Harbor was the American naval base in the Hawaiian Islands. A deadly load of bombs was dropped on the American ships and airfield. It was a day, Roosevelt said, that would "live in infamy." *Infamy* (IN·fuh·mee) means remembered for being evil.

The United States had been attacked. That meant war. (From The *United States: Its History and Neighbors* [Grade 5], Harcourt Brace Jovanovich, 1985, p. 493)

Problem/Solution: Includes a relationship (between a problem and its possible causes[s]) and a set of solution possibilities, one of which can break the link between the problem and its cause.

AGREEMENT BY COMPROMISE
(EVENTS THAT LED TO THE CIVIL WAR)

For a while there was an equal number of Southern and Northern states. That meant that there were just as many Senators in Congress from slave states as from free states. Neither had more votes in the Senate, so they usually reached agreement on new laws by compromise. (From *The United States and the Other Americas* [Grade 5], Macmillan, 1980, p. 190)

Comparison: Organizes factors on the basis of differences and similarities. Comparison does not contain elements of sequence or causality.

Students often have difficulty making comparisons. Why do you think this is so?

Segregation

Segregation laws said that blacks had to live separate, or apart, from whites. Like whites, during segregation blacks had their own parks, hospitals, and swimming pools. Theaters, buses, and trains were segregated.

Many people said that the segregation laws were unfair. But in 1896, the Supreme Court ruled segregation legal if the separate facilities for blacks were equal to those for whites. "Separate but equal" became the law in many parts of the country.

But separate was not equal. . . . One of the most serious problems was education. Black parents felt that their children were not receiving an equal education in segregated schools. Sometimes the segregated schools had teachers who were not as well educated as teachers in the white schools. Textbooks were often very old and out-of-date, if they had any books at all. But in many of the white schools the books were the newest ones. Without a good education, the blacks argued, their children would not be able to get good jobs as adults.

Finally in 1954, the Supreme Court changed the law. (Adapted from *The American People* [Grade 6], American Book Company, 1982, p. 364)

Concept Load

Concept load (also called *concept density*) has to do with the number of new ideas and technical vocabulary introduced by an author (Singer & Donlan, 1989). This means that sentences of equal length may, in fact, require very different comprehension skills from a reader. Expository reading materials found in content classrooms are often much more difficult to understand than narrative/story readings because of greater concept load (Harris & Sipay, 1990). The reason this is usually true is that story writers usually present information gradually and build to a conclusion or climax. Elements such as setting, plot, and characterization are laced with information quite familiar to most readers. Expository writers, however, usually present new and abstract information unfamiliar to the reader, which requires the building of new schemata or memory structures in the brain. Authors who introduce several new concepts in a single sentence (high concept load) create a situation that is extremely difficult for all but the best readers.

Concept load is the number of new ideas introduced by an author.

Teachers should obviously consider concept load when they think about ordering or adopting new learning materials. High concept load reading materials will create a major obstacle for readers lacking in fluency. One alternative to selecting conceptually dense textbooks is to select several smaller books that specialize on just a few topics and cover them in some depth. If this is not possible, the teacher can have students read through materials in dyads (groups of two) and write summaries of key points using good paragraph structure to flesh things out: a topic sentence, which tells the key idea; supportive sentences, which explain the key idea in greater detail; several examples; and a closing summative sentence.

Think of strategies you use to cope with high concept load texts.

Readability Considerations

Another concern of teachers preparing content material for instruction is text difficulty. Text difficulty is most often measured using a **readability formula**. The purpose of a readability formula is to assign a grade-level equivalent, or approximate

Readability formulas help teachers determine the relative difficulty of books.

difficulty level, for narrative or expository reading material used to teach children. Sentence length and complexity of vocabulary used are two elements often measured in readability formulas.

A number of readability formulas are available for classroom use. The Fry (1977) readability formula (Figure 12.4) is one of the more popular formulas available and bases its estimates on sentence and word length. Another formula that is significantly quicker and easier to use (Baldwin & Kaufman, 1979) is the Raygor (1977) readability graph (Figure 12.5). Instead of having to count the number of syllables contained in a 100-word passage, teachers merely count the number of words having six or more letters.

One problem with readability formulas is that they fail to account for student interest.

The problem with readability formulas in general is that they are too narrow in scope and simplistic. Many factors determine whether or not students can read a given passage effectively. Klare (1963) concluded that some 289 factors influence readability, 20 of which were found to be significant. Typical readability formulas, such as the Fry (1977) and Raygor (1977), account for only two factors. An important factor affecting both readability and comprehension is interest (Cooter, 1994). If a student is highly interested in a subject, say *cooking,* then such words as *cuisine, parfait, pastry, pasta,* and *guacamole* likely will be immediately recognizable, even if the text is found to be several years above the student's so-called reading level. Another student at the same point of reading development who is disinterested in cooking may find the same words incomprehensible. This is so because interest in a subject usually corresponds directly to a student's background and vocabulary knowledge in that subject area. In summary, readability formulas may be helpful in determining a very general difficulty level, but they should not be considered anything more than a gross estimate.

Teaching Successful Content Units: A Process Approach

Interesting, informative, and compelling content area units do not come together by accident; they require deliberate planning and certain key elements. These key elements are developed naturally from something called a *content analysis* and help students build lasting memories of the content material. They include graphic organizers, vocabulary and concepts, study guides, and expository text response activities.

Performing a Content Analysis

*A **content analysis** helps teachers determine important facts, concepts, and generalizations.*

Perhaps the best way to begin planning for instruction in any of the content areas is to perform a **content analysis**. The purpose of a content analysis is to help teachers identify the important facts, concepts, and generalizations presented in a given unit of study. This is an essential process for establishing curriculum objectives and learning activities for children (Martorella, 1985). By carefully analyzing new information to be presented, the teacher is better able to locate important information, disregard useless trivia, and determine which areas of the unit require deeper development for students. The end result of this process is a cohesive unit of study that builds new schemata or memory structures for students. In explaining the significance of analyzing units for these mental building blocks, Martorella stated the following:

> What we regard as an individual's knowledge consists of a complex network of the elements of reflection. The fact of our date of birth, for example, is linked in some

Figure 12.4

The Fry readability for-mula

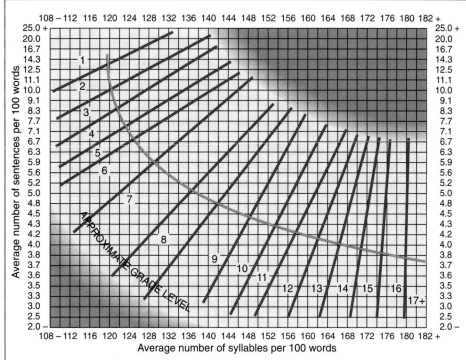

Average number of sentences per 100 words

Average number of syllables per 100 words

APPROXIMATE GRADE LEVEL

Expanded Directions for Working Readability Graph

1. Randomly select (3) three sample passages and count out exactly 100 words each, beginning with the beginning of a sentence. Do count proper nouns, initializations, and numerals.

2. Count the number of sentences in the 100 words, estimating length of the fraction of the last sentence to the nearest one-tenth.

3. Count the total number of syllables in the 100 word passage. If you don't have a hand counter available, an easy way is to simply put a mark above every syllable over one in each word: then when you get to the end of the passage, count the number of marks and add 100. Small calculators can also be used as counters by pushing numeral 1, then push the + sign for each word or syllable when counting.

4. Enter graph with *average* sentence length and *average* number of syllables: plot dot where the two lines intersect. Area where dot is plotted will give you the approximate grade level.

5. If a great deal of variability is found in syllable count or sentence count, putting more samples into the average is desirable.

6. A word is defined as a group of symbols with a space on either side: thus, *Joe, IRA, 1945*, and *&* are each one word.

7. A syllable is defined as a phonic syllable. Generally, there are as many syllables as vowel sounds. For example, *stopped* is one syllable and *wanted* is two syllables. When counting syllables for numerals and initualizations, count one syllable for each symbol. For example, *1945* is four syllables, *IRA* is three syllables, and *&* is one syllable.

From "Fry's Readability Graph: Clarifications, Validity, and Extension to Level 17" by Edward Fry, 1977, *Journal of Reading, 21,* pp. 242–252.

Figure 12.5

The Raygor readability formula

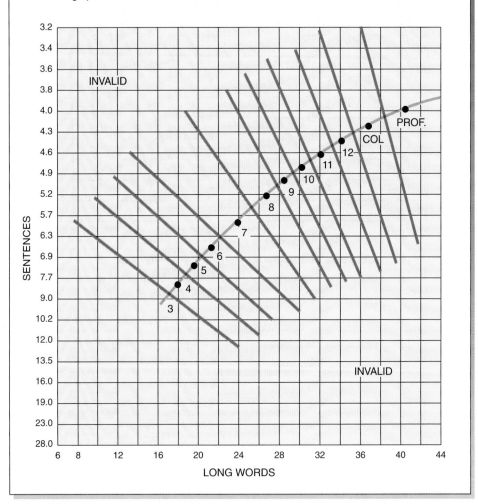

1. Count out three 100-word passages at the beginning, middle, and end of a selection or book. Count proper nouns but not numerals.
2. Count sentences in each passage, estimating to the nearest tenth.
3. Count words with six or more letters.
4. Average the sentence length and word length over three samples, and plot the average on the graph.

From "The Raygor Readability Estimate: A Quick and Easy Way to Determine Difficulty" by A. L. Raygor, in *Reading: Theory, Research and Practice, Twenty-Sixth Yearbook of the National Reading Conference* (pp. 259–263) edited by P. D. Pearson, 1977, Clemson, SC: National Reading Conference.

way to our concept of *birthday*. As further reflection occurs, we incorporate the new information into our network and it becomes related with the old knowledge. (1985, pp. 69–70) [*Authors' note:* This is the stage at which a new generalization is created.]

Facts are details presented in a unit of study.

Facts are individual bits of information, or details, presented in a unit under study. In a science unit dealing with our solar system, some of the facts to be learned might include atmosphere, satellite, and planet. For a history unit pertaining to events surrounding the American Civil War, possible important facts might include General Robert E. Lee, Second Manassas, and states' rights.

Concepts are categories into which we group all facts or phenomena known through our experiences (Martorella, 1985). In the previous example of a unit about the solar system, satellite and planet could be grouped into a single concept called "objects orbiting around the sun." Concepts are usually stated in a simple phrase, word, or sentence that captures the main idea.

Concepts are clusters of related facts.

A **generalization** is a principle or conclusion that applies to the entire class or sample being examined (T. L. Harris & Hodges, 1981). In this instance, a generalization is teacher generated, is written in the language of the students, and is expressed in a complete sentence(s). Generalizations organize and summarize a large amount of information, often an entire unit. Two examples of generalizations follow:

Generalizations are principles or conclusions that relate to an entire unit of study.

There are many different reasons why the American Civil War happened.

Our solar system is made up of many different things.

Once facts, concepts, and generalizations have been identified, the teacher should organize them into some sort of graphic representation. This could take the form of a traditional outline, semantic web, structured overview, or some other preferred form. Arranging information in this way allows the teacher to size up the unit and begin making decisions related to organizing for instruction. A typical question related to instructional decision making follows:

Question: What should a teacher do if the adopted textbook contains information that is not relevant to any of the major concepts?

Answer: If the information helps build background understandings for the students that are important to the facts, concepts, and generalizations taught, then teachers should keep and use that information. If the information serves no real purpose, however, it should not be included in unit activities or discussion.

Figures 12.6 and 12.7 are examples of partially finished content analysis graphic representations by two teachers. Notice that they are essentially schema maps.

Graphic Organizers

A **graphic organizer** is essentially a map or graph that summarizes information to be learned and the relationship between ideas (Alvermann & Phelps, 1994; Barron, 1969). It provides a means for presenting new technical vocabulary and their relationship to larger concepts and generalizations, and it helps content teachers clarify teaching goals (Tierney, Readence, & Dishner, 1990). Graphic organizers are generally used as an introductory instrument to begin a unit of study, are referred to regularly during the course of the unit, and are used as a review instrument near the end of a unit of study. Although very instructive, graphic organizers should not be viewed as the mainstay of a content area program (Earle & Barron, 1973; Tierney, et al., 1990).

*How are **graphic organizers** and schema maps alike?*

Graphic organizers are especially useful at the beginning and end of units of study.

Constructing a Graphic Organizer

Constructing a graphic organizer is a simple matter once a content analysis has been completed. Basically, all that need be done is to simplify or condense the facts, concepts, and generalizations in the unit by reducing each to a single word or phrase, then arrange them graphically in the same hierarchical pattern as the content analy-

Figure 12.6

Partial content analysis of matter

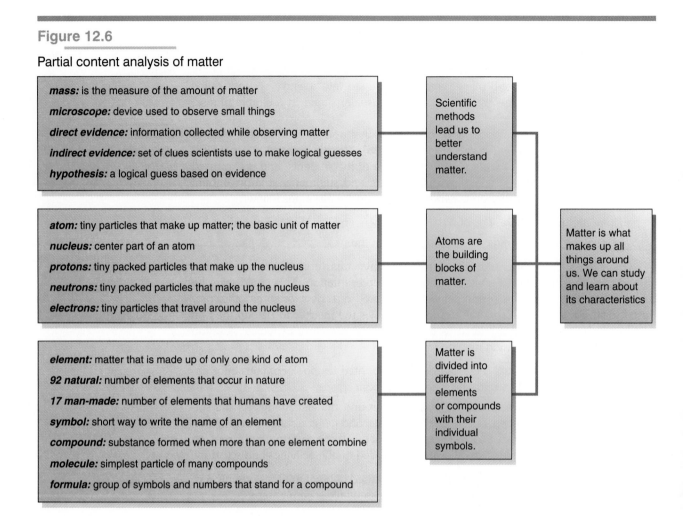

Courtesy of David Harlan, Fifth-Grade Teacher, Sage Creek Elementary School, Springville, UT.

sis. If a thorough content analysis is not possible, however, the following steps may be used to develop a graphic organizer (adapted from Barron, 1969):

1. The teacher should identify all facts and vocabulary she feels are essential to understanding the unit under study. This forms the bottom layer of information, or subordinate concepts (Thelen, 1984). For the sake of consistency with the content analysis idea discussed earlier in the chapter, we refer to these subordinate concepts as *facts*.
2. After listing the preceding information, the teacher groups related facts into clusters. These clusters form a second layer of understanding in the unit we refer to as *concepts*.
3. Finally, concepts that relate to each other should be grouped under the major heading for the unit we refer to as a *generalization*. Most often, the unit will have only a single generalization, but occasionally, two or more generalizations may be needed especially for large or complex units.

Figure 12.7

Partial content analysis of events leading to the Civil War

Generalization

Differences between states in the North and South led to the Civil War.

Concept

The northern economy was based on industry; the southern economy was based on agriculture.

Facts

Samuel Slater built many factories in the North.

In these factories, Slater discovered that machines could be used instead of people to make things more quickly and cheaply.

Soon, things made in northern factories were being sold to people living in southern states.

Farmers discovered that cotton could be processed more quickly and easily with the cotton gin than by hand.

Many southern farmers grew cotton and sold it to people living in northern states.

Many immigrants became factory workers; many slaves were forced to work in cotton fields.

Concept

Both the North and the South fought for control of the government.

Facts

The North wanted laws favoring business and industry; the South wanted laws favoring farming and slavery.

Northerners wanted any new states entering the Union to be free states.

Southerners wanted any new states entering the Union to be slave states.

In 1820, when Missouri asked to become a state, there were 11 free and 11 slave states in the Union.

Northerners wanted Missouri to be a free state; Southerners wanted Missouri to be a slave state.

Courtesy of Laurie McNeal, Fifth-Grade Unit, Brigham Young University.

Teachers may wish to use a variety of graphic formats to depict the different units covered each year. One style is not particularly better than another, but using a different style for each unit may help hold students' attention. Several popular formats for graphic organizers are shown in Figures 12.8 through 12.11 for an elementary unit pertaining to the structure of American government.

Graphic organizers can take many forms.

Teaching Vocabulary and Concepts

A fundamental challenge for *every* elementary teacher is helping students learn previously unknown concepts and vocabulary. New vocabulary consists simply of words or "labels" that represent concepts (R. T. Vacca & Vacca, 1989). For a detailed discussion of vocabulary instruction, see Chapter 7.

New vocabulary consists of "labels" or captions for new content learning.

Figure 12.8

Traditional outline

> ***Structure of American Government***
> 1. Constitution provides for three branches
>   A. Executive Branch
>   1. President
>   B. Legislative Branch
>   1. House of Representatives
>   2. Senate
>   C. Judicial Branch
>   1. Supreme Court

There are four acquired vocabularies. List some examples of each.

Vocabulary knowledge is developmental and is based on background experiences (Heilman et al., 1990). Teachers need to lead their students through four levels of vocabulary knowledge if new content or specialized vocabulary words are to become part of their permanent memory: listening, speaking, reading, and writing. *Listening vocabulary,* the largest of the four vocabularies, is made up of all words people can hear and understand. This includes not only the words we use in our everyday speech but also those words we can understand only when used in context. For instance, while listening to an evening news report, a child in sixth grade may hear about the latest breakthrough in cancer research. Although the youngster may be able to hear and understand the news report, she probably would not be able to reproduce the specialized medical terms used (e.g., carcinomas, metastasis, chemotherapy). Some have speculated that entering first-grade students may have a listening vocabulary of around 20 thousand words! The sec-

Figure 12.9

Structured overview

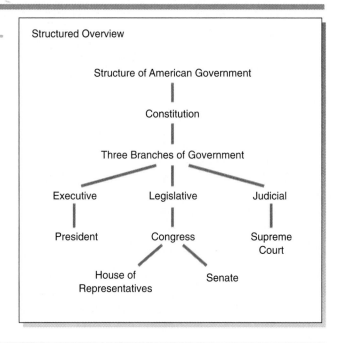

Figure 12.10

Pyramid outline

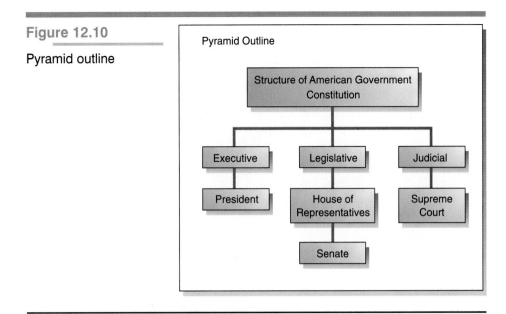

ond level of vocabulary knowledge is called the *speaking vocabulary.* This consists of words we not only can hear and understand but also can use in our everyday speech. A third level of vocabulary knowledge is called *reading vocabulary.* These are words we can hear and understand, use as part of our speech communications, and recognize in print. The final level, *writing vocabulary,* is made up of words we can understand on all these levels, listening, speaking, and reading, and likewise use in our written communications. In teaching new technical vocabulary like that found in typical content readings, a primary goal is to bring students through each of these levels of vocabulary knowledge.

The best way to teach children about new ideas is through concrete, or "hands-on," experience. For example, if one wanted to teach students from rural Wyoming

Figure 12.11

Semantic web

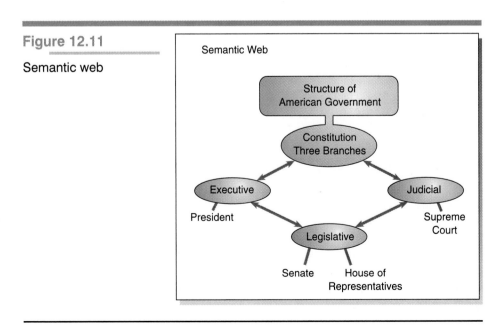

Read alouds are an effective means for helping students develop a listening vocabulary.

One goal of instruction is to bring students through each level of vocabulary knowledge.

*The **pyramid of classroom experiences** reveals the range and hierarchy of learning activities.*

about life in New York City, then the most effective way to do so would be to take them there for a visit. Similarly, the very best way one could teach children about the space shuttle would be to put them through astronaut training and then send them into space on a future mission! Obviously, neither of these experiences is feasible in today's schools, so we must seek the best concrete experiences within our reach as teachers.

Some educators (Dale, 1969; Estes & Vaughan, 1978) have suggested hierarchies for typical classroom activities, ranging from concrete to abstract experiences. Such hierarchies help prospective teachers select concept and vocabulary development activities of a more concrete nature, and help practicing teachers review their past practices for evaluative and curriculum redesign purposes. We have developed a composite version of these hierarchies, which is presented in Figure 12.12. Notice that, as one ascends toward the top of the **classroom experiences pyramid**, activities become more concrete and thus easier for children to assimilate.

According to recent studies of vocabulary development (Nagy, 1988), effective vocabulary development in content classes seems to include three important properties: (a) integration of new words with known experiences and concepts, (b) sufficient repetition so that students will recognize words as they read, and (c) meaningful use of new words brought about through stimulating practice experiences. In light of these requirements, we offer several examples of vocabulary development activities for whole-group and individual teaching situations.

Whole Group

When teaching in large- or small-group situations, the teacher's primary vehicle for integrating new vocabulary with known experiences, which was discussed earlier in this chapter, is the graphic organizer. Graphic organizers (e.g., semantic web, pyramid, etc.) can be used to introduce and review new words throughout the unit. Because of their schema-like nature, they are ideal for this type of learning situation.

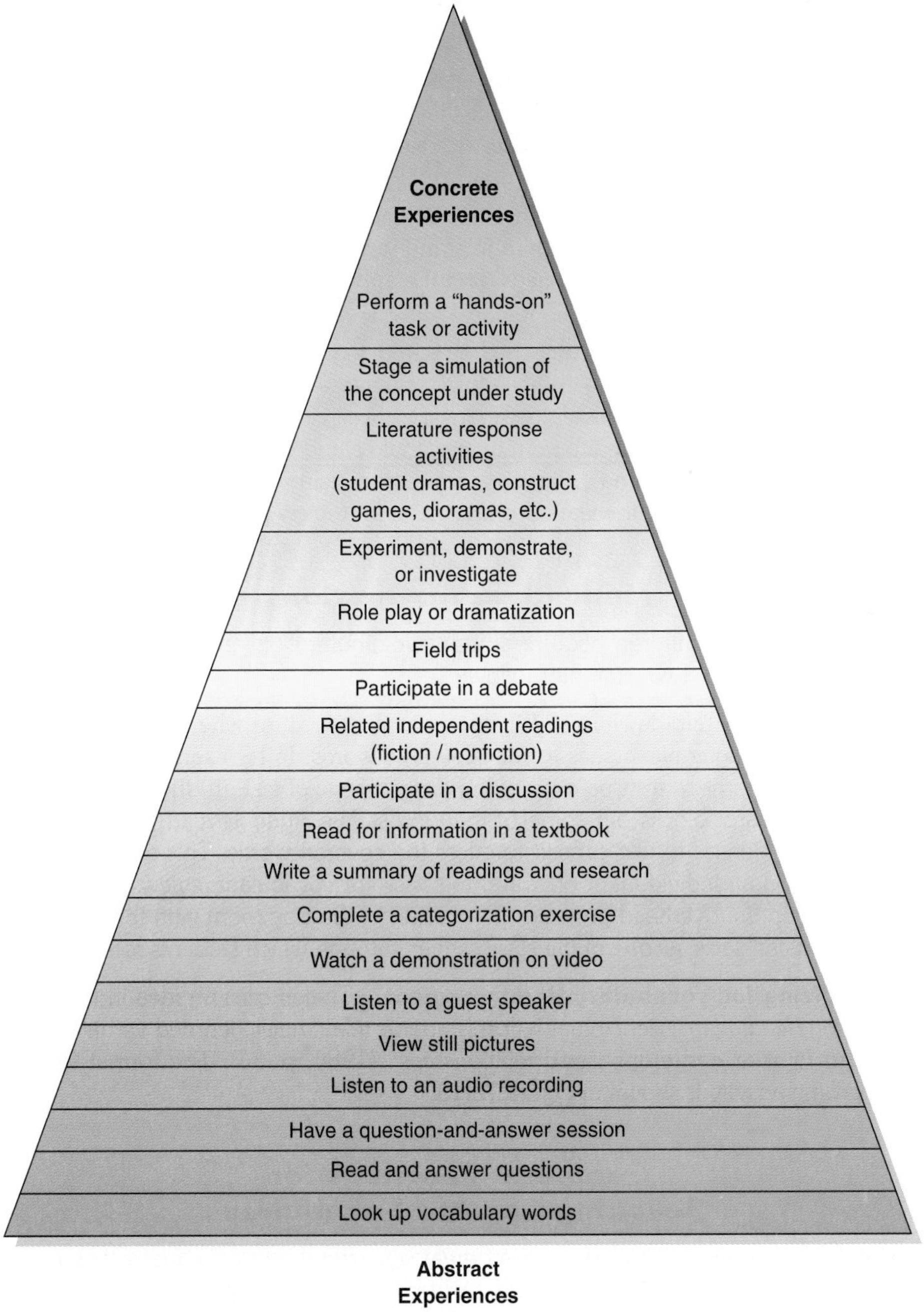
Concrete Experiences
Perform a "hands-on" task or activity
Stage a simulation of the concept under study
Literature response activities (student dramas, construct games, dioramas, etc.)
Experiment, demonstrate, or investigate
Role play or dramatization
Field trips
Participate in a debate
Related independent readings (fiction / nonfiction)
Participate in a discussion
Read for information in a textbook
Write a summary of readings and research
Complete a categorization exercise
Watch a demonstration on video
Listen to a guest speaker
View still pictures
Listen to an audio recording
Have a question-and-answer session
Read and answer questions
Look up vocabulary words
Abstract Experiences

Figure 12.12
Pyramid of classroom experiences

Another way to approach vocabulary instruction is through whole-group vocabulary minilessons. The idea is to involve the entire class in an activity that demonstrates the meaning of new vocabulary. Whole-group vocabulary minilessons will not work with all new vocabulary but may be helpful on an occasional basis. The idea is to provide concrete understanding for abstract ideas. Following is an example for fifth graders learning about the basic components of an atom.

Atomic Kid Power!

Step 1:   The teacher introduces key information about atomic structure (e.g., nucleus made up of protons and neutrons, electrons orbiting the nucleus, etc.).

Step 2:   The teacher takes the class out to the play area and assigns children to a role-playing situation wherein they take turns being subatomic particles (e.g., protons, neutrons, electrons). Protons could wear a special hat, colored purple, neutrons wear a white hat, and electrons wear a bright orange hat.

Step 3:   A circle is drawn with chalk on the playground surface large enough for approximately six children to stand within. Several children are assigned to play the part of the nucleus, and the appropriate number of child(ren) will be the electron(s).

Step 4:   Finally, the nucleus children stand together in the circle, hopping up and down simulating a live atomic nucleus. The electron child(ren) run around the nucleus, keeping about a 20-foot distance at all times. For extra instructional benefit, a parent helper could stand on a ladder (or perhaps the roof of the building), film the simulation using a video camcorder, and replay the film to the class at a later time for review purposes.

Individual Instruction

Teachers can help children acquire content vocabulary on an individual basis in many creative ways. Two examples follow:

Word Masking   Holdaway (1979) discusses a procedure whereby students can gain practice using context clues to rehearse new words. In his example, the teacher (a) makes an overhead transparency of the desired page of text, (b) then, using a long strip of cardboard, blocks out some of the words. The students read the uncovered words and sentences to use context to guess the covered words. This activity can be done easily on an individual or peer tutoring basis for vocabulary review. The teacher simply sets up the overhead projector in a corner of the classroom with the necessary materials. It can serve as one of the class centers through which students rotate.

Categorizing for Vocabulary Reinforcement   Thelen cites an idea in her book *Improving Reading in Science* that helps "students relate newly learned verbal associations to familiar and emphasized relationships" (1984, p. 36). The format for this categorizing activity is shown in Figure 12.13.

Computer Programs for Teaching Content Vocabulary

The microcomputer, or PC, offers many great opportunities for the future of content area instruction. Although there is great potential for classroom use, truly creative and beneficial software programs for teaching content vocabulary are few and far

Functions of Cells: Vocabulary Review*

Name _____

1. _____   3. _____

    neutrons   diffusion osmosis

    protons   active transport

    electrons   pinocytosis

2. _____   4. _____

    light reaction   metabolism

    chlorophyll   respiration

    nutrients from soil   homeostasis

*Answers: 1. atoms, 2. photosynthesis, 3. transport, 4. cell functions

Figure 12.13

Vocabulary reinforcement: Functions of cells

between. Most programs available tend to be computerized workbook exercises. Indeed, it is quite possible to decrease efficiency in the classroom through the use of computers (Wessells, 1990).

A review of vocabulary software offerings indicates that the present possibilities are very limited. Most are of a drill and practice nature, such as Hangman, "Scrabble," and crossword puzzles. One of the best options for educators at this time is to seek computer software through the Minnesota Educational Computing Consortium (MECC). See Chapter 9 for the address for MECC and additional information on computers in the classroom.

Making and Using Study Guides

Study guides, also known as reading guides (A. Manzo & Manzo, 1990; R.T. Vacca & Vacca, 1989), are teacher-made activities intended to help students move successfully through a unit of study. They somewhat resemble workbook activities but may be used before, during, and/or after reading the unit materials (Manzo & Manzo, 1990). Frequently, they consist of a series of key questions or problems for students to work through, followed by page references to text materials used in the unit. Students use the references to seek out answers and become familiar with the content. Tutolo (1977) describes two types of study guides: interlocking and noninterlocking. An *interlocking* study guide groups questions according to three comprehension levels: literal, interpretative, and applied. A *noninterlocking* study guide does not use a hierarchical relationship for questions. Tutolo (1977) feels that with some text selections the reader may need to move from the literal level to the application level and back to the literal level. Thus, grouping of study questions in this situation might be inappropriate.

Many useful study guide formats are appropriate for elementary classrooms. We recommend that teachers use a combination of (a) interlocking or noninterlocking guides for students to use independently, along with (b) whole-group activities such as the anticipation guide or prereading plan (PReP). Descriptions of a few examples follow.

Study guides are teacher-made activities intended to help students chart a successful course through units of study.

Three-Level Guide

A **three-level guide** (Herber, 1978) is a classic interlocking guide in that it leads students from basic levels of comprehension to more advanced levels (Manzo & Manzo,

*A **three-level guide** is an interlocking guide that moves students from basic to advanced comprehension levels.*

1990). The first level (literal) of the guide helps students understand what the author said, the second level (interpretative) helps students understand what the author means, and the third level (applied) helps students understand how this information can be applied (Manzo & Manzo, 1990). Although three-level guides have traditionally been constructed using declarative statements, we feel that it may be just as appropriate to use a question or problem-solving format.

In constructing a three-level guide, we suggest the following guidelines, which have been adapted from R. T. Vacca and Vacca (1989):

1. The teacher should begin constructing the study guide at the second, or interpretative, level by determining what the author means. The teacher should write inferences that make sense and fit the content objectives. Then the teacher should revise her statements so that they are simple and clear. Part 2 of the guide is now completed.

2. Next, the teacher searches the text for explicit pieces of information (details, facts, and propositions) that support inferences she has chosen for the second part of the guide. Put these into statement, question, or problem form. Part 1 of the guide is now completed.

3. Next the teacher develops statements, questions, or problems for the applied level of the guide, part 3. They should represent additional insights or principles that may be drawn when analyzing parts 1 and 2 of the guide. Part 3 should help students connect what they already know with what they have learned from the study of the unit.

The format for three-level guides should be varied to hold students' attention.

When using a three-level guide, teachers should try to be flexible. The format should be varied from unit to unit to help hold students' attention. It may also be a good idea to occasionally put in distracter or "foil" items (those not directly pertinent to the subject). Distracters sometimes prevent students from indiscriminately focusing on every item and cause them to focus on the information search more carefully (R. T. Vacca & Vacca, 1989).

Finally, we recommend that teachers include page numbers in parentheses following each question, problem, or statement where answers may be found. This alerts students to key ideas found on each page and enables them to screen out irrelevant information.

Anticipation Guides

__Anticipation guides__ survey students' prior knowledge of a given topic.

Anticipation guides are prereading activities used to survey students' prior knowledge and attitudes about a given subject or topic. They usually consist of three to five teacher-prepared declarative statements that students read and react to before reading. The statements may be either true or false. The important factor is for students to respond to the statements based on their own experiences (Wiesendanger, 1986). Figure 12.14 shows a sample anticipation guide for "Our Picture of the Universe" (Hawking, 1988).

Prereading Plan

PReP has both instructional and assessment benefits.

The prereading plan (PReP) was developed by Judith Langer (1981) and provides both instructional and assessment benefits. In this three-step process, the teacher first identifies key concepts in the reading selection for the students. Next, the teacher asks students to discuss their associations with each of these terms or concepts. Their

> **Our Picture of the Universe**
>
> **Directions:** Read each statement below and decide whether you agree or disagree with the statement. If you agree with a statement, put an "X" in the **Before I Read** blank before that statement. If you disagree, put an "O" in the blank. After you have finished reading "Our Picture of the Universe," complete the blanks labeled **Hawking's Views,** indicating how you think the author would answer those same questions.
>
> **Before I Read**   **Hawking's Views**
>
> _____   Many of the early scientists, like Aristotle (340 B.C.),   _____
>   believed the Earth was round instead of flat.
>
> _____   The universe was created at some point in time in   _____
>   the past more or less as we observe it today.
>
> _____   An expanding universe theory (big bang) does not   _____
>   preclude a creator.
>
> _____   Knowing how the universe came about millions of   _____
>   years ago can help mankind to survive in the future.

Figure 12.14

Anticipation guide based on "Our Picture of the Universe" from Stephen W. Hawking's *A Brief History of Time* (1988)

associations might be displayed on the chalkboard using a web or structured overview format. Once the group has discussed the different student associations, the teacher "reforms" the associations by asking students if they have any new interpretations to suggest about the major concepts and terms before reading the selection.

PReP helps teachers assess what students already know about the topic before reading and helps students who may have inadequate knowledge about the topic under study to acquire more background knowledge from their peers and teacher before reading.

Trade Books as Bridges to Textbooks

Sparking an abiding interest in a subject is perhaps the greatest challenge for teachers as they help students gain content expertise. This is no small feat when dealing with a curriculum that is typically fragmented, fact laden, and broken into boring microbits to be memorized (Brozo & Simpson, 1995). Small wonder that students do not think of science, mathematics, or social studies as interesting reading. Let's face it— the tradition of lecture–test teaching is about as effective in content instruction as leeches are in the medical profession. The result of lecture–test teaching is that students are turned off to advanced content studies, and much of what is presented is forgotten. There is no better place to begin forging new and exciting models of teaching exposition than with the addition of quality literature to content classes using trade books. As Pappas et al. summarize,

The addition of quality literature to content classes can breathe life into a sometimes boring curriculum.

> Research has shown that . . . today's textbooks are often dry, uninteresting, and even poorly written. Thematic units assist teachers in including many of the excellent works of fiction, information books, and periodicals published for children. . . . In addition, these well-written works provide children with excellent models for their own writing. (1990, p. 53)

Trade books can breathe life into content investigations while also providing needed background information for best comprehension and schema building (Wepner & Feeley, 1993).

The key to success in weaving good literature into the content curriculum is remembering that books can be read aesthetically for enjoyment or afferently to learn new information (Cox & Zarillo, 1993). Both purposes are important to encourage the symbiosis that is possible between good books and content learning. Cox and Zarillo (1993) recommend a second-sweep approach whenever using trade books as part of content instruction. The first reading, or sweep, should be strictly for enjoyment or aesthetic purposes. The purpose of a second sweep is to identify important concepts, facts, or vocabulary the author has embedded in the book that relate to the unit under investigation in the content class.

Reading daily to students from relevant trade books is a highly recommended practice.

A good beginning is for the teacher to read a relevant trade book daily to students for about 15 to 20 minutes (Brozo & Simpson, 1995). For example, if a unit on Japan is underway and the teacher decides that some knowledge of feudal times is important, she may choose to read aloud *The Coming of the Bear* by Lensey Namioka (1992). In a science class focusing on robotics and mechanization, the teacher could select *Jed's Junior Space Patrol* (Marzollo & Marzollo, 1982), *The White Mountain* (Christopher, 1967), or Simon Watson's (1976) *No Man's Land*. Reading aloud great books such as these sparks interest in the subject matter and makes complex ideas more accessible to students.

It is equally important that students be encouraged to read trade books pertaining to the subject under study themselves. Three literature-based reading methods described in Chapter 11—core books, themed literature units, and individualized reading instruction—have been recommended for adaptation in content classes (Brozo & Simpson, 1995; Cox & Zarillo, 1993). In core book designs, the entire class reads the same trade book selection, whereas in themed literature formats, students are given a choice between several preselected titles. Individualized reading permits students to make their own book selections from a school or classroom library. Regardless of the format used to incorporate trade books in content classes, we favor the second-sweep method so that students can enjoy books as literature before seeking needed information.

A number of important resources exist for teachers of content.

Teachers can use several resources to locate appropriate trade books for content classes. Here are just a few that we have found helpful.

- *Journal of Reading.* International Reading Association. A periodical for middle school and secondary teachers that features a "Books for Adolescents" column each year. Substantial summaries presented in these issues are most helpful in planning units.
- Lima, C., & Lima, J. (1993). *A to Zoo: Subject Access to Children's Picture Books.* New York: Bowker. A reference tool useful in locating books for specific topics and themes.
- Norton, D. E. (1995). *Through the Eyes of a Child: An Introduction to Children's Literature* (4th ed.). Englewood Cliffs, NJ: Merrill/Prentice Hall. An up-to-date textbook that offers brief descriptions of trade books and their uses for read alouds, themed studies, and other possible uses.
- *The Newberry and Caldecott Awards: A Guide to Medal and Honor Books.* American Library Association. Provides helpful information regarding some of the most celebrated trade books available.
- *The Reading Teacher.* International Reading Association. A periodical for elementary teachers that publishes a list of popular books each year called "Children's

Choices" (October issue) and "Teachers' Choices" (November issue). Substantial summaries presented in these issues are most helpful in planning units.

Expository Text-Response Activities

Content area teachers in the 1990s are attempting to create classrooms similar to those described throughout this book. That is, they are moving away from the typical lecture–test modes of teaching of the past and blending elements of balanced literacy programs into their content classrooms. An important part of this transformation process is the inclusion of response activities.

Expository text-response activities are those exercises that cause students to reflect on new knowledge and apply this information in novel ways. They are problem-solving experiences that integrate and apply what has been discovered in the classroom. Summarized in this section are a few examples of expository text-response activities.

Expository text-response activities cause students to reflect on and apply new knowledge.

Real-World Application Projects

Real-world application projects cause students to apply new knowledge in unique ways. Borrowed from the Progressive Era of American education of the early 20th century, real-world projects require students in groups of three to five to take and apply new knowledge within the context of their environment. As with most teaching, these project ideas are limited only by the imaginations and resources of the classroom teacher and her students. Figure 12.15 illustrates the spirit of real-world application projects. This project is intended for sixth-grade students who have been learning about bacteria and how they cause disease. The students' project is to solve a health problem for a rural and very depressed community known as "Eagleville."

Real-world projects are an idea borrowed from the Progressive Ear discovery projects of the early 20th century.

A wonderful benefit of real-world projects is that they require students to read and learn beyond material covered in class. These projects involve students with

---

Outhouses Are OUT!

Problem: Eagleville relies on well water for most of its drinking and cooking needs. Because of the large number of outhouses in Eagleville, the underground water supply is rapidly becoming contaminated, resulting in epidemics. Students in this group are to find answers to the following:

1. What bacteria and diseases are likely to emerge as the ground water is conta minated by the outhouses? Name at least three bacteria and three diseases. Explain or justify your responses.

2. What can the community do for the immediate future (1 to 2 years) to solve this problem? Develop a plan that could be presented to the city council for action.

3. Design a long-term plan for doing away with outhouses that includes a new state-of-the-art sewage system. Note: Use the map of Eagleville provided to draw in your new sewage system.

Figure 12.15

Sample application project: Outhouses are OUT!

library research skills, foster supplemental reading, encourage learner responsibility and collaboration, and result in creative applications of new learning.

Writing Projects

One of the fundamental elements of balanced literacy programs is the writing process. We know that reading and writing are reciprocal processes; as we help students to become better writers, they likewise improve as readers. Additionally, writing projects in the content areas help students internalize new knowledge about the content area. Because much of what is learned in the content areas is rather abstract and difficult to learn, writing can be an important addition to the curriculum. Following are several writing projects that may be helpful in content classrooms.

Content-Focused Melodrama   One procedure (Cooter & Chilcoat, 1990–1991) has students in history classes write and perform their own melodramas as text response. The procedure follows.[*]

(1) Implementation of content-focused melodramas in history classes begins with the teacher identifying important issues found in the unit. For example, in a unit dealing with events leading up to the American Civil War some relevant issues for discussion might include slavery, issues pertaining to states' rights, economic differences between Northern and Southern states, and political figures of the period.

(2) During the first day or two of the unit the teacher should introduce each potential topic to the class. Topic introduction can be accomplished through the use of video productions, guest speakers dressed in clothing of the period, or reader's theatre productions. One stimulating way used to introduce topics is through book talks (Donelson & Nilsen, 1985; Fader, 1976). This involves dramatic readings from either fiction or nonfiction books that help create a better understanding of important historical events. For example, with the above pre-Civil War theme the teacher might use such books as *The Drinking Gourd* (Monjo, 1970) or *The Slave Dancer* (Fox, 1973) to introduce the slavery issue.

(3) Once the topics have been introduced students should be allowed to select for themselves a topic of interest. Allowing students the opportunity for self-selection helps create a sense of ownership in the process, improves learner attention, increases motivation and tends to reduce classroom management problems. In order to avoid conflict, some teachers have students write their first and second choices of topics on a slip of paper and turn it in anonymously.

(4) Once the teacher has had an opportunity to collect and collate the student topic requests s/he is ready to form groups based on their choices. In the unit suggested above there would likely be several groups of students interested in the slavery issue, some interested in politicians of the era, and so on. We recommend that size of the groups not exceed six in number so as to keep group discussions productive and manageable.

Groups will need some training and direction when first implementing melodramas. There should be an elected group leader and a recorder. Ground rules for group behavior and expectations should likewise be discussed. We find that role playing positive and negative group behaviors is desirable leading to the development of their own group etiquette rules. Collaboration and cooperation within the group is the ultimate goal.

---

[*]From "Content-Focused Melodrama: Dramatic Renderings of Historical Text" by R. B. Cooter and G. Chilcoat, 1990–1991, *Journal of Reading, 34*(4), pp. 275-276. Copyright 1990 International Reading Association. Used by permission of authors and International Reading Association.

(5) Production of the melodrama is the chief task of the group. The first time the teacher introduces melodrama in the classroom it is often desirable to offer some very specific examples which illustrate the elements of melodrama. One entertaining and informative way is to show the class an old movie where features of melodrama are easy to identify. Some possible examples from this genre include *It's a Wonderful Life* starring Jimmy Stewart and Donna Reed, or *African Queen* with Humphrey Bogart and Katharine Hepburn. One of the great silent film classics, *Wings* for example, may also be a good choice.

The production of the melodrama involves writing the plot, developing characterization, and the making of scenery. We recommend that in developing the script students follow the writing process format (Atwell, 1987; Graves, 1983). This essentially means that students will go through 1.) a *prewriting* stage where they research the topic thoroughly, organize facts, and develop the characters; 2.) produce an initial *draft* of the script; and 3.) go through a revising and editing stage where the students, sometimes with the aid of the teacher, polish and perfect the script.

Once students have created their melodrama scripts and had a chance to rehearse, the play is performed for the class. Following the performance, the teacher should lead a class discussion to compare and contrast the melodramatized version of the facts with history as we know it. This will reduce the possibility of learning erroneous information.

The Eyewitness Action Nightly News   Another stimulating activity is for students to take information learned in the unit and write a news program based on that information. As with the melodrama, a script must be written that presents the information in a clever and interesting way. The student playing the news anchor is taped using a video camera for replay to the class. Other group members can act out on the scene accounts of relevant news related to the newscast.

Nightly news activities involve reading and writing processes as well as creative expression.

This activity need not involve large outlays of money for equipment or materials. Costumes should be designed by the children involved, using their own wardrobes or borrowed items. If the school does not own a video camera, then one can usually be borrowed from the high school athletic director (who uses them to film football

How do expository text response activities allow more student interaction between literacy and content materials?

games and other sporting events). We have had local video stores donate blank or used videotapes and other equipment for occasional school use.

Big book projects involve use of summarization and retelling skills.

Making Big Books   Many elementary students enjoy creating their own big books based on newly learned expository information. Lower elementary students create books on such topics as how cows make milk or how plants grow. Older students develop big books about such things as the differences between stars and planets or wetlands of the world. Whatever the topic, students are required to study and process new information, mentally manipulate the language of the new concepts, and represent their understandings in written language form.

Reading and Study Skill Instruction: Helping Students Succeed With Expository Materials

During the 1960s and 1970s, many educators became interested in finding ways to help students succeed with content area materials. Speed reading, note taking, and other reading and study strategies became permanent additions to the education agenda. Through research, the field of education has been able to deduce which strategies are most effective and worthy of classroom instructional time. This section briefly discusses some of the more prominent and useful strategies for elementary settings.

Efficient (Speed) Reading Strategies

One of the characteristics of successful mature readers is that they read selectively instead of word by word. In fact, mature reading has been characterized as a "psycholinguistic guessing game" (K. S. Goodman, 1967). This means that **efficient reading strategies** are a conscious or unconscious search for meaning in the text, not a word-by-word laborious process.

Efficient reading strategies save time and generally improve self-esteem and comprehension.

Even though much of efficient reading is an unconscious process carried out automatically by the brain (LaBerge & Samuels, 1974), it is desirable for teachers to show students several efficient reading strategies that, when practiced, become internalized in the student over time, resulting in improved reading fluency and comprehension. A discussion of several of these strategies follows.

Skimming and Scanning

Think of times when you find yourself skimming materials.

Skimming is an easy strategy to learn and can be useful with a variety of reading materials. It is very helpful with periodicals, popular press materials, and with most science and social studies textbooks. Skimming can be used to preview materials or for review purposes. The object of skimming is quite simple. Students practice forcing their eyes to move quickly across each line of print. As they do so, they try to attend to a few key words from each line. Sometimes it is helpful for students to move their finger rapidly under each line of text following the text with their eyes (this is called *pacing*). At first, comprehension will drop off dramatically, because students are concentrating more on the physical movement of their eyes than on the meaning of the text. But over time and with practice, students are able to perform the skimming operation with as much or more comprehension than usual.

The teacher should lead students through some practice exercises with the class. Emphasis should be on the fact that the key words on each line will tend to be nouns, verbs, and adjectives—in other words, the meaning-carrying words. Articles, conjunctions, and other function words in the sentence add little to the comprehension process and can essentially be ignored.

Scanning, on the other hand, is a much simpler strategy to teach and learn. The idea is to have students visually sweep or scan a page of text to locate information, such as an important date, key words, or answers to a specific question. Instead of attempting to comprehend all information on the page, the reader is simply trying to locate an information bit. Teachers should be able to demonstrate this strategy through simple modeling.

Scanning is a speedy search for a known type of information, for example, dates and keywords.

Previewing

Previewing is especially useful for getting a general idea of heavy reading, such as nonfiction books (Cosby, 1987). One of the true speed-reading strategies, previewing allows readers to cover nonfiction material in a fraction of the usual time with up to 50% comprehension. For example, a student proficient in previewing should be able to cover a typical chapter in social studies, say 25 pages, in about 15 minutes or less. The procedure is simple to teach and learn but may take quite a bit of practice to achieve useful and practical comprehension levels.

The first step of previewing is to read the entire first two paragraphs of the chapter or selection. Most professional writers provide the reader with an overview of the chapter in the first couple of paragraphs, so reading every word of the first two paragraphs is essential. The second step is for students to read only the first sentence of each paragraph thereafter. Again, most professional writers of textbooks and nonfiction texts begin paragraphs with a topic sentence, which summarizes the main idea of each paragraph. Thus, reading the first sentence in each paragraph will provide crucial information to the reader, but remember that some of the important details that follow will be missed. Finally, the student reads the final two paragraphs of the chapter or selection. This provides the reader with a summary of major points covered. If the final section is labeled "Summary," "Conclusions," or something similar, then the student should read the entire section.

Previewing is useful with heavy reading assignments and yields general comprehension.

Varying Reading Rate

Another important efficient reading lesson is varying reading rate. Reading rate is the speed at which readers attempt to process text. Different types of content (e.g., mathematics, geography, American literature, earth science) usually require a different reading speed for best comprehension to occur. For example, some students may be able to read a *Hardy Boys* mystery at a very fast reading rate. After all, not every word is crucial to understanding the author's message in a book of this kind, and a previewing or skimming strategy may be sufficient for good comprehension. On the other hand, when students read a story problem in mathematics, it is important to read each word carefully at a reading rate much slower than with a mystery story. Therefore, students need to be made aware of the need to consciously vary their reading rate to match the style and purpose of the text they are reading. Minilessons should be prepared in each of the content fields wherein the teacher and students practice and discuss reading rate strategies that can be used to achieve the best comprehension.

Children must learn to vary their reading rate according to purpose and type of text.

A Recommended Efficient Reading Strategy

After working with many students in elementary and secondary grades, we have arrived at an efficient reading strategy that appears to be comprehensive and helpful with most expository and narrative materials. The one exception is mathematics, which requires more specialized strategies. The procedure is a combination of previewing and skimming, as previously described. Here are the steps to follow:

1. Read the first two paragraphs of the selection to get an overview of the piece.
2. Next, read the first sentence of each successive paragraph. Then, after reading the first sentence of each paragraph, skim the remainder of the paragraph to get important supporting details for each topic sentence.
3. Read the final two paragraphs of the selection to review main ideas.

This procedure has yielded comprehension rates of up to 80% with mature readers but requires only about one third the time of normal reading.

This efficient reading strategy combines previewing and skimming strategies.

Proven Study Strategies

In addition to the efficient reading strategies just introduced in this chapter, educational research has supported the use of many other tactics helpful to students in their content area pursuits. It seems that when students understand *what* to study, *how* to study quickly and efficiently, and *why* the information is pertinent to their world, classroom performance is improved. We have chosen some of the more popular study strategies for brief discussion in this section.

SQ3R

SQ3R is a widely taught study strategy that has met with some success.

Perhaps the most widely used study system is SQ3R (Robinson, 1946), which is an acronym for survey, question, read, recite, review. Especially effective with expository text, SQ3R provides students with a step by step study method that ensures multiple exposures to the new material to be learned. Many students also find that they can trim their study time using SQ3R and still earn better grades.

SQ3R is best taught through teacher modeling followed by a whole-class walkthrough. Each step of SQ3R is explained in the following list:

- *Survey:*   To survey a chapter in a textbook, students read and think about the title, headings and subheadings, captions under any pictures, vocabulary in bold print, side entries on each page (if there are any), and the summary.
- *Question:*   Next, students use the survey information, particularly headings and subheadings, to write prediction questions about what they are about to read. Students frequently need teacher assistance the first few times they use SQ3R in developing questions that will alert them to important concepts in the unit.
- *Read:*   The third step is for students to read actively (Manzo & Manzo, 1990), looking for answers to their questions. They should also attend to boldface type, graphs, charts, and any other comprehension aid provided.
- *Recite:*   Once the material has been read and the questions answered fully, the student should test herself on the material. Anything difficult to remember should be rehearsed aloud or recited. This multisensory experience helps the difficult material to move into short-term, and with practice, long-term, memory.
- *Review:*   The final step is to periodically review the information learned. This can be done orally with a peer, through rewriting notes from memory and

comparing to the students' master set of notes, or with mock quizzes developed by a peer or the teacher.

SQRQCQ

Although the SQ3R method can be very effective with most expository texts, it is difficult to apply to mathematics. A similar plan developed especially for mathematics story problems (Fay, 1965) is known as SQRQCQ: survey, question, read, question, compute, question. As with SQ3R, the teacher should model SQRQCQ with the class and conduct whole-class practice before expecting students to attempt the procedure on their own (P. C. Burns, Roe, & Ross, 1988). The steps of this procedure follow:

SQRQCQ is designed for use with mathematics texts.

- *Survey:*   Read through the story problem quickly to get a general feel for what the problem is about.
- *Question:*   Next, the student should ask herself general questions related to problem solving such as, "What is the problem to be solved?" "What do I need to find out?" and "What important information is provided in the story problem?"
- *Read:*   Read the problem again carefully, giving close attention to details and relationships that will assist in the problem-solving process.
- *Question:*   Answer the question, "What mathematical operation is needed to solve this problem?"
- *Compute:*   Do the computation associated with the operation decided on in the previous step.
- *Question:*   Answer the question, "Does this answer make sense?" If not, then the student may need to repeat some or all of the process.

Metacognition

Metacognition, or comprehension monitoring, has to do with helping students recognize what they know or need to know about what they are learning. Research suggests that good readers can describe their methods for reading and getting meaning, but poor readers seem virtually unaware of strategies that can be employed (A. Brown, 1982). F. Smith (1967) found that poor readers fail to adjust their reading behavior when reading for different purposes, such as reading for specific details or general impressions. A crucial role for the content area reading teacher is to help students (a) become aware of their own reading comprehension abilities and needs (called *metacognitive awareness*), and (b) learn specific strategies that can be used to fit their own comprehension needs at any given time.

Metacognition has to do with self-monitoring of thinking and learning processes.

A. Brown makes an eloquent case as to why we need to include metacognitive instruction as a fundamental part of study skill instruction:

> I emphasize the need for "cognitive training with awareness" because the whole history of attempts to instill study strategies in ineffectual learners attests to the futility of having students execute some strategy in the absence of a concomitant understanding of why or how that activity works. [For example] . . . we see that outlining itself is not a desired end product, and merely telling students it would be a good idea to outline, underline, or take notes is not going to help them become more effective studiers (A. Brown & Smiley, 1978). Detailed, *informed* instruction of the purposes of outlining and methods of using the strategy intelligently are needed before sizable benefits accrue. (1982, pp. 46–47)

A. Brown (1982) has developed a tetrahedral model for teaching students metacognitive processes that includes the following four steps:

1. *Nature of the material to be learned:*   Students should review the text—for example, using the previewing method described earlier in this chapter (*see* SQ3R)—to learn what kind of material it is (narrative, expository, etc.). Most content area texts and materials in each of the subject areas follow a fairly well-defined pattern. Understanding the pattern involved at the outset helps the reader to anticipate reading demands and expectations.

2. *Consider the essential task involved:*   Students need to understand what they are looking for in the text. What is the critical information that will likely appear on tests and other assessment activities? T. H. Anderson and Armbruster (1980) indicate that when students modify their study plans accordingly they tend to learn more than if the criterion task remains vague.

3. *Consider your own strengths and weaknesses:*   As A. Brown (1982) points out, some students are good at numbers or have a good rote memory, while others may have trouble remembering details or learning new languages (foreign, computer, scientific, etc.). In general, the task is to make new, abstract ideas familiar and memorable. Learners need to assess their own strengths and weaknesses in each of the content fields they study in preparation for the final phase of the four-step sequence.

4. *Employ appropriate strategies to overcome learning weaknesses:*   Once students understand where they have specific learning difficulties, remedial action to overcome these weaknesses is essential. Such strategies as look-backs, rereading, reading ahead, highlighting, note taking, summary writing, webbing, and outlining suddenly become of great interest to students when taught in connection with their new metacognitive self-awareness.

Students should keep in mind what they need to know from texts.

Consciously employing appropriate strategies to overcome learning problems, such as rereading parts not understood, dramatically affects learning.

Writing Expository Texts to Deepen Content Knowledge

Of the many ways to help readers succeed with content materials, teaching them to become authors of expository texts may be the most powerful. There is something about creating our own texts that clarifies and embeds permanently the new concepts, facts, and vocabulary in our minds. It also appears that our interest frequently increases in content information as we gain mastery over it in writing. In this section, we suggest a few ways students create expository texts and, by doing so, become more competent and fluent readers.

Paraphrase Writing

Writing clarifies our learning.

Shelley M. Gahn (1989), an eighth-grade language arts teacher in Ohio, recommends paraphrase writing as one way students can re-create content information found in textbooks. The basic idea is that information is restated in their own words, which tends to keep the vocabulary simple and the resulting material brief. This helps students to clarify their personal understanding of what has been studied. Gahn suggests three types of paraphrase writing: rephrasing, summarizing, and elaborating. Rephrasing involves rewording relatively short paragraphs from content textbook chapters. Summarizing calls on students to identify the text's major points. Elaborating requires students to compare information in the new text to previous knowledge, sometimes using graphs, charts, or comparison grids. Paraphrase writing is often most effective when students write in small groups or pairs. It is also crucial that teachers model each type of writing for students, showing examples of acceptable paraphrases and those that are flawed.

Using Text Structures

Earlier in this chapter, we discussed expository text patterns (Meyer & Freedle, 1984) frequently found in textbooks. Because these patterns can be difficult for many readers to comprehend, teaching students to write using expository text patterns can often lead to wonderful breakthroughs in understanding. We advocate a four-step process for teaching students how to become authors of these forms of expository writing.

This strategy puts theory by Meyer and Freedle (1984) into practice.

Step 1: The teacher describes the five expository text patterns. The teacher explains the differences between description, collection, causation, problem/solution, and comparison. The teacher presents examples of each using the overhead projector or chalkboard.

Step 2: The teacher identifies these patterns in content textbooks. Using previously researched materials, the teacher asks students to help her locate examples of each expository text pattern on photocopies supplied to them for this purpose.

Step 3: The teacher models the writing of one of the expository text patterns. Beginning with description, the teacher creates an example of a description passage at the overhead projector or chalkboard based on text materials that the class has been reading. The teacher encourages students to coach her through premeditated mistakes in her example. The teacher should be sure to think aloud as she creates the example, because this is the key element of modeling.

Step 4: The teacher asks students to now create their own example. Step 3 is repeated, but this time, the teacher asks students to do the work. As with many writing and reading tasks, it may be profitable for students to work in pairs. Volunteers should be asked to share their examples with the class.

As students become comfortable creating simple expository text structures, they should be encouraged to combine structures in creating more lengthy compositions and projects. Using multiple structures in lengthy pieces is an essential tool for writers. This fact can easily be examined in the adopted textbook.

Student-authors of expository texts gain much deeper understandings of the content.

Cubes

G. Tompkins (1994) recommends **cubes** as an expository writing activity. She explains that a cube has six sides, and in this activity, students review what they are learning about a topic from six sides, or perspectives, using the following tasks:

Cubes is an activity that helps students review ideas from six perspectives.

- Describe it.
- Compare it to other things you know about.
- Associate it to things it makes you think of.
- Analyze it as to what it is composed of.
- Apply it by explaining what you can do with it.
- Argue for or against it using reasons you have discovered through your investigation.

We offer an example from a fifth-grade class investigating the concept *democracy:*

> **Democracy**
>
> 1. *Describe it.*
>
> A democracy is a government that is run by the people in that country. They make up all the laws and decide how things are going to be.
>
> 2. *Compare it.*
>
> Countries like Canada, the United States, and Great Britain have democracy because their leaders are elected by the people and are supposed to do what the people say.
>
> 3. *Associate it.*
>
> Democracy reminds me of what we do in scouts when we elect a patrol leader and stuff like that. We pick someone who thinks like we do and wants the same things. It's better that way.
>
> 4. *Analyze it.*
>
> Most democracies have something like our Constitution that sets up an organization like our Congress. Congress has representatives elected by the people who write the laws and make sure things like the Army and Navy are organized. They also act as a watchdog over other branches of government, like the president and the Supreme Court. In England, their congress is called a Parliament, and they do the same kinds of things.
>
> 5. *Apply it.*
>
> Probably the most important thing about a democracy is for people to vote. In the United States people can vote when they become 18 years old. It is important for people to vote for a democracy to work.
>
> 6. *Argue for or against it.*
>
> I think living in a democratic country is best. If we didn't have a democracy, then we might end up having a king or dictator like they have had in countries like Haiti, Cuba, Russia, and Nazi Germany. I like being able to vote for the people who will make our laws, and vote for someone else if they don't do a good job. It might not be a perfect system, but I haven't heard of a better one.

Readers with learning problems often have trouble in content materials because of low self-esteem, poor organization, and general reading difficulty.

Helping Readers With Learning Problems: Content Area Reading Assistance

Readers with learning problems often face feelings of discouragement and bewilderment in content area classes. Reflecting on our own past experiences as classroom and remedial teachers, we have observed many similarities with readers having learning problems that sometimes compound their learning difficulties. First, and probably most troubling, is an attitude that says "I'm dumb and can't do the work!" This feeling has usually developed over a period of months or years and is due to unsuccessful experiences in the classroom. For these children, the safety net (mentioned in Chapter 1) has not been established or maintained, and risk taking is not as likely to occur. Second, elementary students who struggle with content area subjects are usually poorly organized. When children are helped to become systematic in their reading and thinking strategies, positive results follow. Third, readers with learning problems tend to have weak overall reading ability, especially as demonstrated by a very slow reading rate. Fortunately, problems of attitude, organization, and reading rate can be remedied within the regular elementary classroom.

Resolving Problems of Attitude, Organization, and Reading Rate

To show how problems in attitude, organization, and reading rate can be remedied by classroom teachers, we offer the following case history:

Jason Masters the "Slam Dunk" in Science

Several years ago, a middle school-aged boy came to the Maryville College Learning Center (Tennessee) for help with his studies in science. Jason was bright and articulate, but had not enjoyed much success in his schooling. Generally, his grades were C's and D's, and this concerned and frustrated his parents greatly. Jason's mother wanted him tested to determine whether he had a learning disability and to have an appropriate tutorial program developed.

The assessment battery test results indicated that this eighth grader was, according to standardized tests, performing on about a fourth-grade level in reading (about 4 years behind most of his peers). Perhaps more importantly, however, we learned quite a bit about his interests and knowledge of the world in which he lived. Above all, Jason had quite an interest in basketball. He carried around a basketball almost everywhere he went. His idols were celebrities like Michael "Air" Jordan, Larry Bird, and "Magic" Johnson. This seemed to be a great piece of information for the teacher.

During the first tutorial session, which was really an organizational period, Jason and his teacher discussed Jason's school record and results on the assessment battery. It was pointed out that Jason did not, in fact, have any permanent learning problems and that the problems he experienced could be corrected fairly easily. The essence of the program was (a) to improve his reading rate and interest through a daily recreational reading program involving basketball magazines and related sports material and (b) to improve his organizational and study patterns by teaching him to use the SQ3R procedure. Jason readily embraced the program. After all, he was being allowed to read material for pleasure he already knew a lot about, and SQ3R would allow him to spend less time studying and make better grades in the process.

What made this program work was individual one-on-one intervention and follow-up. These sessions did not require a great deal of time, once the ground rules were laid, and resulted in feelings of achievement and success in science. After 6 weeks of using this program, Jason's reading proficiency (according to standardized measures) jumped almost 2 years. In science, Jason went from a "D" grade to a "B." More importantly, Jason began to enjoy reading, to complete books he was reading for pleasure, and to feel that he was in control of his science class.

All students need to read at least 20 to 30 minutes per day to realize substantial reading ability growth.

Some teachers reading this case history have asked how long Jason read each day. Jason was asked to read at least 20 minutes per day, reading whatever he was interested in knowing more about. We pointed out that even Michael "Air" Jordan did not become great in basketball overnight, that it took regular practice almost every day of his teenage life. Reading is the same—we get better at the skill of reading only when we practice. Time-on-task pays off in reading.

Jason's program used popular adolescent reading material especially keyed to his interests to stimulate an interest in reading. His consistent efforts resulted in improved reading rate and attitude. SQ3R helped this poorly organized student to understand what was required to be successful in science. And the whole process was relatively painless for both teacher and student. In the remainder of this chapter, we offer a few other ideas that may be helpful in working with readers with learning problems. Two of the suggestions relate to direct instruction offered by the teacher; one concerns student initiatives.

Selected Strategies for Readers Having Learning Problems With Content Materials

Inference Awareness

Inference awareness helps students understand implicit, or "reading between the lines," types of information.

The inference-awareness procedure, described by C. J. Gordon (1985), can be most helpful in showing students how to locate information found only implicitly (Pearson & Johnson, 1978) in content selections. We recommend that inference awareness be used during reading to answer teacher-posed questions and to complete independent assignments. The steps to teaching inference awareness follow:

1. The teacher defines for the class the skill of inference making as using clues from a paragraph or selection along with background knowledge that is stored in memory to reasonably guess what the author has meant but has not directly stated.
2. Next, the teacher models inference making by reading a selection from the content materials, poses an inference question, then provides the answer and the reasoning involved.
3. In the next phase of instruction, called *providing the evidence,* students join in the modeling process. The teacher poses a new inference question and gives the answer. Students are asked to find in the text supporting evidence that supports (or refutes) the teacher-provided answers. Students are encouraged to engage in discussion to explain the thinking processes used to find their responses. This form of teacher- and peer-supported guided practice can be a very beneficial intermediate step for readers with learning problems.
4. The fourth step, called *reversing the process,* has students write answers to inference questions with the teacher providing the evidence. A teacher–student discussion follows to justify responses and supporting evidence.
5. Total student responsibility is the final step in inference awareness. Now that students are thoroughly familiar with the steps of this strategy, the teacher only

asks inference questions and the students do the rest. They answer the question, find supporting evidence (clues), and explain the reasoning involved.

Listen–Read–Discuss

Manzo and Casale (1985) propose the teaching model heuristic listen–read–discuss (L-R-D), which can provide the kind of varied repetition readers with learning problems need for classroom success. The process follows:

Notice the modalities used by students in L-R-D.

- Listen: The teacher begins by selecting a portion of text to be emphasized. This section is presented in a favored format, often a lecture format, for about half the class period.
- Read: Next, students read the section just covered by the teacher in class.
- Discuss: The teacher conducts a classroom discussion about the material the students have just read. The purpose of the discussion should be, first, to answer questions about what was read and, second, to raise new questions of an application nature. The questions might look something like these:
  What did you understand from what you read and heard?
  Which parts did you have difficulty understanding?
  What new questions did this lesson raise in your mind?

Paper Chase Groups

Readers with learning problems, and other students as well, can find a great deal of academic support by forming paper chase groups. Essentially, they are groups of students who meet together on a regular basis to work on assignments and share the work load. Paper chase groups typically range in size from two to five members. Membership in these groups is generally determined by the students themselves but could be arranged by the teacher to achieve a balance of abilities and personalities.

Paper chase group members come together to review key information presented or researched in content classes. Sometimes members develop questions on a certain area for the purpose of quizzing each other. Similarly, students may take an assigned number of study questions provided by other group members or the teacher and research them thoroughly, making clear and legible notes. At the next meeting, photocopies of research information gained by each group member are distributed and discussed with other group members. In this way, everyone in the group gets a full set of notes from which to study and has an opportunity to have misunderstandings about information cleared up. The paper chase group is a most effective peer tutoring strategy.

Paper chase groups are a kind of academic support group.

Strategy Families

Dana (1989) has grouped several effective reading comprehension strategies for readers with learning problems into what she refers to as *strategy families*. They can be used with relative ease, in minimal time, and have similar or complementary functions in aiding comprehension. The first strategy family mentioned here, *SIP* (summarize, imaging, predict) helps students focus on content, and the second strategy, called *EEEZ* (take it easy, explain, explore, expand), is a set of elaborative strategies that can be used as a postreading experience to "help anchor the content in memory" (Dana, 1989, p. 32). In each of these strategy families, the acronym reminds students of important steps they are to follow.

Note the similarities and differences in these comprehension strategies.

SIP: The SIP set of strategies is reportedly consistent with R. C. Anderson's (1970) findings indicating that students benefit from learning task activities that require attention to content and active engagement in processing. The steps for SIP follow:

S reminds students to summarize the content of each page or naturally divided section of the text. This summarization of text invites students to reflect on and interact with the content in producing a summarized version.

I represents the notion of *imaging.* This is a reminder that students should form an internal visual display of the content while reading, which provides a second imprint of the text's content.

P reminds students to *predict* while reading. As each page or naturally divided section is read, students should pause to predict what they may learn next. While reading the section predicted, students verify, revise, or modify predictions according to what they learned. This process of predicting and verifying can carry students through entire selections and help hold their interest.

EEEZ: The second strategy gets students to elaborate mentally on new content information to facilitate long-term retention. In her introduction to this strategy, Dana explains

> After reading, it is recommended that students review what they have read in light of the purpose that was set for the reading assignment. Students are told that after reading they should "take it easy" (EEEZ) and make an attempt to *explain* (E) the content in a manner commensurate with the purpose set for reading. They might have to answer questions, generate questions, define a concept, or provide a summary. (1989, p. 33)

The other ideas represented by the EEEZ acronym are

E: Explore the same content material as it has been described by other authors of different texts. These comparisons often help students to clarify important ideas.

E: Expand the subject matter by reading other texts that go beyond the content covered by the original text.

After expanding, students should respond to the original purpose for reading the assignment given by the teacher and should embellish their responses with additional content discovered during the EEEZ process.

Helping Students With Special Language and Cultural Needs: Learning New Content Concepts and Vocabulary

A major challenge for students reading content materials is comprehending new concepts and vocabulary related to the subject being studied. This can be all the more troublesome for culturally and linguistically different students who may still be learning to cope with relatively basic language demands in the classroom. Content teachers know that all students must be helped to learn new vocabulary beyond rote memorization of definitions.

Conceptual word knowledge involves four levels of understanding.

Nist and Simpson (1993) explain that we must help students get to know words and concepts on four distinct levels; what they term **conceptual word knowledge**. The first level is usually the word's basic definition. Level two includes understanding of synonyms, antonyms, examples, and nonexamples. Level three involves an understanding of connotations and characteristics of the word. The fourth level of understanding involves applying the word to personal and new situations apart from the original encounter in the content area classroom. Nist and Simpson liken these levels of understanding to an iceberg; the top level that we see first is the dictionary definition, but the bigger picture by far is composed of the three other levels of conceptual word knowledge lying beneath the surface.

Helping culturally and linguistically different students attain deeper knowledge of new concepts in the content classroom is our primary task. This level of understanding opens the door to academic success and enhanced life opportunities for all learners. In this section, we offer two teacher-tested ideas that help achieve this goal.

Thinking Matrix

Originally suggested by McTighe and Lyman (1988), the thinking matrix can be used to help students generate their own questions, as an end-of-unit review, or in helping student groups lead class discussions (Alvermann & Phelps, 1994). A **concept thinking matrix** can be easily adapted to vocabulary learning using the Nist and Simpson (1993) scheme for conceptual word knowledge by simply listing key concepts and words to be learned down one axis and the four levels of understanding across the top columns. In Figure 12.16, we illustrate a concept thinking matrix using terms from a lesson on African-American art. Completion of the matrix necessitates higher order analysis of each concept or term and is a perfect opportunity for student collaboration.

Content-Specific Vocabulary Cards

Another idea suggested by Nist and Simpson (1993) is the **content-specific vocabulary card**. Vocabulary cards are personal dictionaries developed by students and kept on 3 x 5 index cards in plastic recipe boxes or bound together using steel rings. Nist and Simpson tell us that students typically keep two types of vocabulary cards: general and content-specific. General vocabulary cards are for more common everyday language, whereas content-specific vocabulary cards, as the name implies, are to assist with learning specialized content terms.

*Students create their own dictionaries with **content-specific vocabulary cards**.*

The procedure is simple. On one side, the student writes the term or concept to be learned. On the backside, students write pertinent information about its meaning, such as a definition, synonyms, antonyms, examples, and so forth. Figure 12.17 presents an example of a content-specific vocabulary card for the word *contaminant* from a unit on air pollution.

Summary

Full curriculum integration is the ultimate goal for many teachers interested in building balanced literacy programs. This means, in part, weaving advanced literacy instruction into content area presentations so that instead of simply *learning to read* students *read to learn*. One way full curriculum integration is accomplished is through thematic units. In this chapter, we learned how thematic units are constructed. They begin with the construction of themed literature units as the curricular core, then encompass appropriate content areas. Thematic units may be delivered using ongoing uninterrupted sessions that mirror real-world problem-solving strate-

Figure 12.16

Concept thinking matrix: Lesson on African-American art

Concepts/ Vocabulary	Dictionary Definition	Synonyms, Antonyms, Examples, Nonexamples	Connotations, Characteristics	Other Uses of the Word(s)
race consciousness		Syn.: Ant.: Ex./nonex.:	Connot.: Char.:	
African-American "art idiom"		Syn.: Ant.: Ex./nonex.:	Connot.: Char.:	
images		Syn.: Ant.: Ex./nonex.:	Connot.: Char.:	
flattened space		Syn.: Ant.: Ex./nonex.:	Connot.: Char.:	
compressed gestures		Syn.: Ant.: Ex./nonex.:	Connot.: Char.:	
controlled palette		Syn.: Ant.: Ex./nonex.:	Connot.: Char.:	

gies in the workplace, or seamless integration, or as more traditional departmentalized content area sessions called *segmented integration.*

Expository texts, the staple of content instruction, present students with new challenges. Unlike narrative texts, expository materials use less familiar vocabulary and concepts, may be written using different composition patterns, and have greater concept load per sentence. For these reasons, students must be taught coping strategies to assist in comprehension. A number of such strategies that may be used by students have been presented, as well as tools for teachers in preparing lessons. Graphic organizers, study guides, and anticipation guides are but a few of the suggestions offered.

One of the things teachers can do to help students acquire and retain content knowledge is through proper organization of units. Developing a thorough content analysis helps teachers to identify important facts, concepts, and generalizations to be delivered. The content analysis helps teachers organize schematically so that it may be presented in the most logical and comprehensible way possible.

Another important area discussed pertained to the teaching of reading and study strategies. Students conducting content-related research must often pore over great

Figure 12.17

Content-specific vocabulary card

contaminant

def. something that soils or corrupts by contact.

syn.– taint, pollute, defile

ex. – acid rain, industrial chemicals dumped into a river, an open cesspool.

volumes of print material ranging from textbooks to periodicals. Efficient reading strategies, such as skimming, scanning, and previewing, can be most helpful in this pursuit and done so without significant loss of comprehension, if done correctly. Other proven study strategies were presented, including SQ3R, SQRQCQ, and metacognition. Additionally, inclusion of the writing process is seen as an important asset by teachers who feel that as students become authors of expository texts they automatically become more insightful readers of that genre as well. Cubes was one of the expository text writing activities recommended.

Finally, the academic concerns of students with learning needs can be compounded in content materials because of concept load and readability problems. We offered several teaching and learning strategies that benefit learning needs students, including inference awareness, L-R-D, SIP, and paper chase groups.

Figure 12.18 provides an overview of the chapter.

CONCEPT APPLICATIONS

IN THE CLASSROOM

1. Select a chapter from an elementary social studies book on the level of your choice. Using the descriptors for expository text patterns discussed in this chapter, identify as many patterns (e.g., description, comparison, etc.) as possible in the unit and answer the following questions: Which patterns do you find? How often do they occur in the unit? Are any patterns missing? If so, what could you do as the classroom teacher to compensate for these omissions? Is it possible that omission of some patterns could lead to learning difficulties for some children? If so, why?

2. Developing a thorough content analysis is the foundation for successful teaching in content area subjects. To practice and refine this ability, try the following: Form an adult paper chase group with several of your colleagues. Select several lengthy magazine articles having to do with various topics relevant to elementary content subjects. You may want to consider such magazines as *Air & Space*

Figure 12.18

Chapter overview

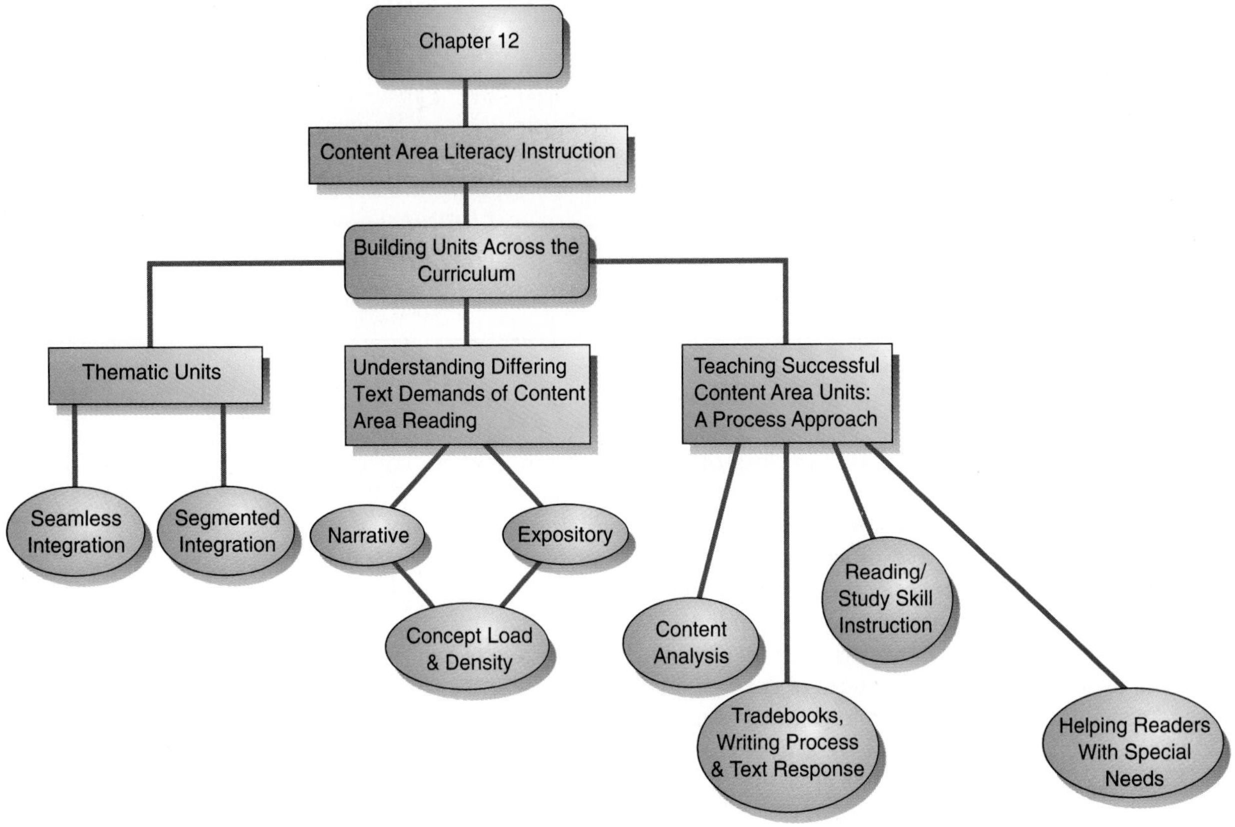

or *National Geographic* for these articles. After reading these articles, each person should develop a content analysis to present to the rest of the group. By comparing analyses, it will be possible to detect whether important bits of information (or for that matter, superfluous information) have been included.

IN THE FIELD

1. Computer science applications in education account for one of the fastest growing industries in the world. Perform a library search, and compile a list of the latest software available for the teaching of content area vocabulary and concepts. Perhaps a computer specialist at your school can assist you in this effort. After your list has been compiled, write to the various companies, requesting detailed information about their programs and, if possible, a sample disk for review. This process will help you to determine which programs are most beneficial, and it may be possible to order new software for your school library in the future.

RECOMMENDED READINGS

Alvermann, D. E., & Phelps, S. F. (1994). *Content reading and literacy.* Boston: Allyn & Bacon.

Brozo, W. G., & Simpson, M. L. (1995). *Readers, teachers, learners: Expanding literacy in secondary schools* (2nd ed.). Englewood Cliffs, NJ: Merrill/Prentice Hall.

Gahn, S. M. (1989). A practical guide for teaching writing in the content areas. *Journal of Reading, 33,* 525–531.

Martorella, P. H. (1985). *Elementary social studies: Developing reflective, competent, and concerned citizens.* Boston: Little, Brown.

Pappas, C. C., Kiefer, B. Z., & Levstik, L. S. (1990). *An integrated language perspective in the elementary school.* New York: Longman.

Reinking, D. (Ed.). (1987). *Reading and computers: Issues for theory and practice.* New York: Teachers College Press.

Thelen, J. N. (1984). *Improving reading in science.* Newark, DE: International Reading Association.

Wepner, S. B., & Feeley, J. T. (1993). *Moving forward with literature: Basals, books, and beyond.* Englewood Cliffs, NJ: Merrill/Prentice Hall.

Chapter 13

Assessing Progress
in Literacy

Focus Questions

When you are finished studying this chapter, you should be able to answer these questions:
1. What are the basic principles of effective classroom literacy assessment?
2. How do traditional assessment procedures differ from authentic assessment procedures?
3. What commercial reading tests are available for classroom use?
4. How can authentic assessment strategies be used in the reading classroom to inform instruction?
5. How can teachers derive grades from authentic assessment strategies?
6. Describe some of the present and future trends in reading assessment.

Key Concepts

Authentic Reading Assessment
Principles of Classroom Assessment
Traditional Reading Assessment
Reliability
Norm-Referenced Tests
Criterion-Referenced Tests
Portfolio Assessment
Kid Watching
Reading Development Milestones

Running Records
Rubrics
Anchor Papers
Reporting Progress to Families
Ungraded Background Profiles
Graded Background Profiles
Authentic Grading
Affective Factors
Conative Factors

Assessments are frequently conducted to satisfy political realities.

Authentic reading assessments *inform instruction.*

Reading assessment conducted by the classroom teacher generally serves one of two purposes. One rationale for reading assessment is to satisfy what are sometimes referred to as *political realities.* That is, teachers are frequently required by district, state, and federal officials to document student growth and achievement in their classrooms in some sort of formal way (usually with standardized achievement tests). A second, and perhaps more constructive, purpose is to *inform teaching.* Assessment practices fitted to this purpose are usually informal, analyze reading using real books, provide natural experiences with text, and are more concerned with carefully analyzing overall student growth in the reading process. **Authentic reading assessments**, as they are known, provide teachers with invaluable information for making instructional decisions in balanced literacy programs. Differences between traditional and authentic assessment perspectives in reading may be likened to the differences between a black-and-white photograph and a color movie. Traditional assessment at best provides teachers and administrators with a very quick and limited view of readers (like a "snapshot" of the child), whereas authentic assessment provides teachers with a much clearer and more comprehensive view of the learner (like a movie with Dolby® sound).

In this chapter, we describe forms of traditional and authentic reading measures and examples of each and we discuss some future trends in reading assessment. First, however, we explore some basic principles of classroom reading assessment that should apply to any form of reading assessment.

*The **principles of classroom assessment** help teachers select valid and useful strategies.*

Principles of Classroom Assessment

The following **principles of classroom assessment** are intended to help elementary teachers decide which assessment strategies should be adopted to improve classroom instruction. They are based on classroom experience, research in the field, and opinions expressed to us by teachers in the field.

Principle 1: Assessment Procedures Should Help Teachers Discover What Children Can Do, Not What They Cannot Do

Reading assessment in recent decades followed what has been called a *medical* or *clinical model.* The clinical model was used to cloak reading assessment in the robes of science and precision. An implied assumption was that children getting off to a rough beginning must have something organically wrong preventing their literacy development in reading. The idea was that whenever a teacher discovered a student having difficulty with reading, a "diagnosis" of the child's problem areas should be developed using reading tests. From this assessment of strengths and, more importantly, weaknesses, a "prescription," or remediation program was developed. After several decades of following this medical model and the establishment of federally sponsored remedial programs (Chapter 1 and Special Education resource rooms), very little impact has been registered on at-risk students (Mullis, Campbell, & Farstrup, 1993). A new perspective in assessment seems warranted.

Rather than spending precious classroom time trying to identify what students *cannot* do, many educators are finding that time is better spent finding out what students *can* do. When teachers understand student abilities, it becomes much easier to decide which new learning experiences should be offered to help them develop further. Not only is this a more constructive point of view, but students benefit in other important ways. As Cousin, Weekly, and Gerard (1993, p. 555) summarize, "positive atmospheres are created in classrooms where mistakes are viewed as ways to learn rather than opportunities to ridicule."

Principle 2: Assessment Procedures Should Help Identify Zones of Proximal Development

In the real world of elementary teaching, most assessments conducted are very informal. From the first day of school in late summer, teachers begin to form judgments about the children in their class—some correct, some erroneous. On balance, however, experienced teacher judgment has been regarded as reasonably reliable and accurate. Families and students tend to put a great deal of credence into what a competent teacher has to say. Therefore, when teacher pronouncements are made about a student's growth and ability in reading, they should be based on consistent patterns of behavior.

Assessments should help teachers learn students' stage of development to aid in planning appropriate instructions.

In Chapter 2, we discussed Vygotsky's (1962, 1978) notion of a *zone of proximal development,* or the area of potential growth in reading that can occur with appropriate teacher and peer intervention. To identify students' zone of proximal development, teachers need to look for relatively consistent behaviors to determine accurately what children can do and which new experiences they are ready to try. For example, in a kindergarten or first-grade classroom, children who can create story lines for wordless picture books, and have been doing so for some time, should be ready for predictable books containing simple and predictable text.

Teachers also need to watch for any problem areas a student may be having. Whether only one student or many students seem to have the same reading problem, the teacher should offer a minilesson to help them over the hurdle. In other words, the reading curriculum should be responsive and flexible according to students' demonstrated needs and patterns of ability.

Principle 3: Every Assessment Procedure Should Have a Specific Purpose

It is easy for teachers to fall into the habit of giving tests simply because of tradition within a school or school system. This is especially so with standardized tests, which tend to offer little, if any, classroom utility. This could also be true, however, with the assessment of children who seem to be having significant reading problems. For example, at a school where one of the authors taught, it was common practice to give all children who had reading difficulties the following battery, or cluster of tests:

Think of times when you performed tasks needlessly simply because of past practices.

- *Woodcock Reading Mastery Tests—Revised* (Woodcock, Mather, & Barnes, 1987)
- *Brigance® Diagnostic Inventories* (Brigance, 1983)
- *Peabody Individual Achievement Test* (L. M. Dunn & Markwardt, 1970)
- *Slosson Intelligence Test* (Slosson, 1971)
- *Auditory Discrimination Test* (Wepman, 1973)

The problem with this sort of "shotgun" approach is that all children receive the same battery of tests without regard to known student abilities or anticipated needs. In addition, these tests provided very little information that would be helpful to the classroom teacher and once again reflected the assumption that all reading problems are to be

"Shotgun" approaches to assessment waste time, resources, and are stressful to children.

found in the reader. If the locus of the reading problem resides in the curriculum or classroom environment, then a standardized reading test will be of little or no value. This brings us to our next principle pertaining to reading process versus products.

Principle 4: Classroom Assessment Should Provide Insights Into the Process of Reading, Not Only the Product

Traditional tests tend to view reading from a skills perspective (see Chapter 2 for a review of the various instructional models). This is clearly reflected in the kinds of information provided by the tests themselves. For example, the *Woodcock Reading Mastery Tests—Revised* (Woodcock et al., 1987) has many subtests that measure such elements as word identification, word attack (applied phonics knowledge), and letter identification. Any conclusions that may be reached using this type of test will dictate the kind of remedial teaching strategies to be used, namely skills-oriented intervention.

Fortunately, some promising assessment instruments now seem to view reading from a more authentic perspective. Clay (1985), for instance, has developed an assessment procedure for primary level children known as the Concepts About Print Test. This instrument assesses the print awareness of emerging readers and can be used to assess what they know about fundamental print concepts (Heathington, 1990). Clay has also suggested the use of running records for assessing reading ability more authentically. Other authentic assessment procedures are discussed later in this chapter.

Principle 5: Assessment Should Inform Teaching

Assessment should help teachers plan future instructional directions.

When considering whether or not to perform any sort of reading assessment, the teacher should ask himself, "Will this procedure help me make educational decisions regarding this student's reading needs?" The procedure should yield rich insights as to approaches, materials, and environmental concerns that can positively affect literacy growth. To achieve this end, assessments begin with a careful survey of what is known about the student using information available (i.e., home surveys, cumulative records, informal assessments, student self-assessments, etc.). Next, the teacher begins to form hypotheses (Bintz, 1991) about where the student is in her reading development. The next task is to select assessment procedures that will help the teacher better understand the student's abilities and confirm or reject earlier hypotheses. Armed with the information obtained from the above processes, the teacher teaches lessons aimed at helping the student develop further. Figure 13.1 depicts this assessment-teaching process.

Principle 6: Assessment Strategies Should Not Supplant Instruction

Assessment should not take the place of quality instruction.

New trends in reading assessment often seem to overpower the teacher and take over the classroom. One case in point is the idea of portfolio assessment discussed later in this chapter. If the teacher loses sight of the purpose of classroom assessment, namely, to inform and influence instruction, then he may well move into the role of *teacher as*

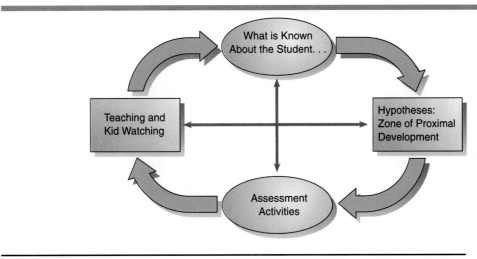

Figure 13.1

Assessment–teaching process

manager rather than *teacher as teacher* (Pearson, 1985). Thus, the assessment program should complement the instructional program and grow naturally from it.

Principle 7: The Holistic Context of Instruction Should Be Considered and Assessed

As previously mentioned, much of traditional assessment in reading has operated under the assumption that the sole, or at least principal, locus of reading progress or failure is the child. But in truth, many other factors may have a direct impact on how well children acquire reading abilities. These factors include the home environment (e.g., availability of books, family attitudes toward reading and schooling in general, siblings who model positive reading behavior), and the classroom environment (e.g., noise level, teacher attitude and perceptions regarding the child, organizational and/or philosophical perspective of the teacher, peer collaboration opportunities). Especially of concern in the classroom environment are the programs and approaches to reading. These, too, should be assessed. To omit home and classroom factors from consideration is to see only half the picture and risk an inaccurate assessment of the teaching–learning context.

List some of the factors that might influence a child's reading performance.

Principle 8: The Only Truly Valid and Competent Assessment Is Individual Assessment

Whole-group assessment tends to provide gross estimations of reading program effectiveness. Neither individual student needs nor valid conclusions regarding the reading program can be determined using such procedures. Teachers need to be able to watch, listen, and interact with individual students, one at a time, to develop clear understandings of their abilities.

Individual assessment is the best assessment.

In the remainder of this chapter, we survey assessment practices as they pertain to reading instruction. We begin with an analysis of traditional reading assessment practices because they remain prevalent and, in some cases, useful. Later, we take a more in-depth look at authentic reading assessment options and related issues.

Teachers learn most about student development in one-on-one encounters.

Traditional Reading Assessment

Traditional reading assessment in the United States has served the primary purpose of satisfying the political reality of providing district-wide or national comparisons of children using commercial reading tests. Although this information may prove helpful in measuring gross aspects of program efficiency, traditional reading tests offer teachers little insight into meaningful program change. Nevertheless, these tests are still widely used and should be understood by teachers.

In this section, several questions regarding traditional reading assessment are addressed. First, what is the typical scheme for classifying students who appear to be having difficulty in reading? Second, what kinds of commercial reading tests are commonly available to teachers and what are some examples of each? Finally, what are some of the major problems encountered by teachers who rely exclusively on these kinds of reading tests?

Traditional Classifications of Reading Ability: Developmental, Corrective, and Remedial Readers

In traditional and some transitional reading programs, differences in reading ability often become so great as to require some curricular adjustments. Most of the time, these adjustments can and should be made within the regular classroom. On some occasions, however, reading problems may become so pronounced as to require some additional intervention. The question that emerges for teachers is, When have problems become so severe as to warrant referral to a remedial reading program?

We subscribe to the position that children experiencing reading problems should be helped in the regular classroom by the teacher they are most familiar with—the classroom teacher. Referral to remedial reading programs should be viewed as a last resort for several reasons, discussed next.

Most adjustments for students with learning needs should occur in the regular classroom.

Classroom Teachers Are in the Best Position to Help

Although there are many competent remedial teachers, classroom teachers usually know their children better than anyone else educationally. They have the opportunity to assess their students' development every day and fine tune the curriculum for the benefit of individual students. Because students know their teacher well, and are usually comfortable with him, there is little or no emotional disruption associated with classroom intervention. For teachers with large class sizes that do not permit as much one-on-one work with students, classroom intervention strategies often can be delegated to parent volunteers or others such as "adopted grandparents" from the community who like to help out (e.g., listening to children retell a story just read, working with word banks, helping with word recognition or phonics strategies).

Teachers know students best and are in a better position to deliver intervention strategies.

Additionally, classroom teachers are better able to coordinate what is going on in the daily reading groups or whole-class minilessons in reading with in-class remedial efforts. For instance, if in a whole class minilesson, the teacher has been developing the use of context clues as part of a word-recognition strategy, he can develop additional experiences for children needing more practice. In classroom intervention programs, this is relatively easy for the teacher to plan into the daily routine.

The Stigma of Labeling Is Damaging to Children

Unfortunately, to have children admitted to special remedial programs, most notably special education classes that are federally funded, students must endure the humiliation of labeling. No matter how hard school systems try to shield children from the adverse effects of labeling, these efforts never seem to be enough. A child's self-esteem is badly damaged when educators associate children with such labels as learning disabled (LD), developmentally handicapped (DH), attention deficit disordered (ADD), behaviorally handicapped, dyslexic, or emotionally disabled. Thus, these children must not only attempt to survive in a classroom environment in which they already feel inadequate, but they have to face the additional barrier of the label itself. This is a most discouraging situation for anyone to have to face, let alone a young child. One must carefully weigh the costs of labeling against potential benefits of remedial programs.

Labeling is damaging to children's self-esteem.

Family Discouragement Often Results

Adult family members of children in remedial pull-out classes often seem to give up on their own children. That is, once a child is placed in a classroom that is perceived as highly specialized and that caters to children with disabilities, adult family members tend to retreat. They may feel inadequate at that point to provide even basic educational support in the home. Even worse, they may begin to treat and speak openly about the child in ways that say "you are disabled, and we cannot expect as much from you as other children." Again, the child is further handicapped by the stigma of labeling and placement in a program intended to help.

Although there are many reasons for caution, sometimes it does become necessary to refer children for special remedial reading services. Classroom teachers, however, should be sure that they have done all in their power to help the child within the regular classroom before making the referral. Similarly, special help teachers should not accept referrals unless an appropriate program of classroom assessment and intervention has been carefully carried out and documented by the classroom teacher.

Teachers need to help parents remain optimistic about their children, especially when they are having difficulty.

Fortunately, the trend in helping students with learning needs has moved away from so-called pull-out programs (remedial programs in which the child must leave the classroom to receive help in a special education or Chapter 1 program) to more classroom-based *inclusion* programs. This is good news for most classroom teachers and students because pull-out programs are a much less efficient or effective way to deliver needed instruction than classroom-based interventions. Now classroom teachers can have special education and Chapter 1 teachers assist them with special needs learners directly in their own classrooms. This assistance may take the form of helpful suggestions from these specially trained teachers to actual team teaching situations in which the student(s) with learning needs receives small group or one-on-one assistance within the regular classroom environment.

Remediating Unsuccessful Readers

Remediating unsuccessful readers in a traditional program has usually implied highly individualized instruction that takes place outside the regular classroom in a special class (T. L. Harris & Hodges, 1981). The special help teacher has usually completed some graduate education in either reading or special education. Qualification for remedial services is typically determined after extensive assessment and review of classroom performance.

Some remedial programs, like resource programs, take the place of regular classroom instruction.

Remedial instruction is intended to either supplement or supplant the regular classroom reading program. For example, Chapter 1 reading programs are federally funded in the United States and, by definition, are intended to supplement the regular classroom reading program. That is, students still participate in the daily classroom reading program and receive Chapter 1 instruction as an extra support system. Special education programs, also known as *Resource,* are intended to supplant or replace the regular classroom program in reading (and possibly other subject areas such as mathematics). Usually, the degree of difficulty the child is experiencing dictates which program will be used, Chapter 1 being the lesser intervention. In most states, the child must be performing significantly below his reading expectancy level according to some designated standardized measures. Just how far below expectancy is considered "significant" varies from district to district.

Many girls need extra help in reading but are never identified. Why do you think that is?

How many students can be expected to need remedial services? Some feel that in the United States the overall percentage of schoolchildren requiring some form of remedial services ranges from 5% to 12%. The percentage in disadvantaged areas may even reach 50% or higher (Alexander & Heathington, 1988). Remember, however, that most of these reading problems can and should be handled within the regular classroom. Asher's (1977) research indicates that in the United States 70% to

75% of the students referred to remedial programs are boys. One reason may be social and behavioral, in that when some young boys have difficulty in school, they tend to misbehave, whereas many low-achieving girls tend to become more reclusive. The actual ratio of boys to girls having reading problems is believed to be nearly even—about 3:2 (Naiden, 1976). Thus, it may well be that many young girls having reading problems may go unnoticed.

Ultimately, the goal of all remedial programs is to help children cope with and enjoy reading, whether in the classroom or for pleasure and self-learning.

Commercial Reading Tests and Their Uses in Traditional Assessment

Although many educators feel that reading assessment should be performed using only informal teacher-devised procedures, most assessments in traditional public and private school settings rely extensively on commercial reading tests (Cooter, 1990). In this section, we describe several types of commercial reading tests, their specific uses, and a few examples of each.

Informal Reading Inventories

An informal reading inventory (IRI) is typically an individually administered (though a few may be given to groups of children) reading test, usually composed of graded word lists and story passages. Emmett A. Betts (Johns & Lunn, 1983) is generally considered to be the original developer of the IRI; however, several other individuals contributed to its development as far back as the early 1900s.

IRIs tend to be more like reading in real books than most other commercial reading tests.

The Teacher's Guide to Reading Tests (Cooter, 1990) cites several advantages and unique features of IRIs that help to explain, in part, why teachers continue to find them useful. One advantage is that IRIs provide for more holistic assessments of the reading act, at least when compared to many of the other reading tests that splinter reading into various component skills (e.g., phonics knowledge, context clues, structural analysis, etc.). Students are better able to "put it all together" by reading whole stories or passages. Another advantage of IRIs is that they usually provide a systematic procedure for studying student miscues or errors (see the discussion of running records later in this chapter for examples of miscues).

IRIs are rather unusual when compared to other forms of reading assessment. First, because they are informal, no norms, reliability data, or validity information is usually available. This is often seen as a disadvantage by some public school educators, especially those in special education who need reliable figures for accountability purposes. **Reliability** has to do with how consistently a test measures what it is designed to measure. In fact, IRIs are notorious for being rather unreliable. That is, two teachers testing the same child with the same IRI may well get very different assessment results. Second, IRIs offer information that is often quite helpful to teachers in making curricular decisions, especially those who place students into ability groups (a practice we oppose). IRIs provide an approximation of each child's ability in graded reading materials, such as basal readers. These approximations, or reading levels, are interpreted as independent level (easy or recreational), instructional level, or frustration level (failure or difficult). It is important to note that even though these reading level distinctions are widely used in American schools, a research base supporting the use of such levels does not presently exist. A third characteristic is that the

__Reliability__ is a measure of the consistency of tests.

Teacher-constructed IRIs have the greatest degree of curricular validity.

various IRIs available tend to be quite different from each other. Beyond the usual graded word lists and passages, IRIs vary a great deal in additional subtests offered (e.g., silent reading passages, phonics, interest inventories, auditory discrimination) and in the scoring criteria used to assess miscues. Finally, some argue that the best IRIs are those constructed by classroom teachers themselves using reading materials from their own classrooms (a form of content or curricular validity). Several examples of IRIs now used in many school systems follow:

- *Classroom Reading Inventory (CRI)* (Silvaroli, 1986). One of the oldest and most commonly used commercial IRIs, the "Silvaroli" (as it is commonly called) uses the classic graded word lists and passages combination. Unlike most of its competitors, the CRI also features illustrations that go along with each passage at the elementary levels. The test includes four forms (A, B, C, D), which cover elementary grades (1 to 6, on forms A and B), middle or junior high (form C), and high school students or adults (form D).

The Flynt/Cooter Reading Inventory for the Classroom incorporates recent research on assessment with high-interest passages.

- *The Flynt/Cooter Reading Inventory for the Classroom, Second Edition* (Flynt & Cooter, 1995). The Flynt-Cooter Reading Inventory for the Classroom (RIC) is an updated version of traditional IRIs. The authors incorporate recent research on comprehension processes and miscue analysis into a more effective authentic assessment. They include prompted recall and story grammar comprehension evaluation, high-interest selections, authentic length passages, both expository and narrative passages, and a time-efficient miscue grid system for quick analyses of running records.

Group Reading Tests

Norm-referenced tests compare students to other children who have taken the same test.

Sometimes it is desirable to assess the reading abilities of children in group situations and attain norm-referenced information. **Norm-referenced tests** compare student performance to a cross section of students in other areas of the country who were administered the same test. Group reading tests in this section feature norm-referenced data and offer a few other advantages. For example, these tests are available in different forms, thus allowing school systems and researchers to assess children at the beginning of the school year or program and then assess again at the conclusion to determine growth. Group reading tests usually have several levels available, allowing learners at different grade and ability levels to be matched with a test of appropriate difficulty.

The major disadvantage of norm-referenced group reading tests is that they provide little or no usable information for modifying the classroom teacher's curriculum (i.e., informing instruction). Most information yielded by these tests tends to come in the form of stanines, percentile rankings, and grade equivalents. In more recent years, educators have begun to turn away from such statistics as grade equivalents in favor of the more meaningful normal curve equivalents. These data inform the school system in a very general way as to how their students compare to other students nationally who have taken the same test, but that is about all. One example of a typical group test follows.

- *Gates-MacGinitie Reading Tests, Third Edition* (MacGinitie & MacGinitie, 1989). A most popular instrument with school systems and reading researchers, the Gates-MacGinitie assesses children ranging from prereading levels through grade 12. The prereading, readiness, and level one (kindergarten to 1.9 grade levels) have only one form available, but levels two through 10/12 (grades 1.5 to

12.9) have two forms each (Aaron & Gillespie, 1990). Levels two through 10/12 have essentially two measures of reading: vocabulary and comprehension.

Individual Diagnostic Reading Tests

School districts sometimes feel it is necessary to assess an individual student's reading ability using norm-referenced measures. This often happens when new students move into a school district without their permanent records file or when students are being considered for special help programs such as Chapter 1 reading or special education options.

Individual diagnostic reading tests, for the most part, remain rooted in bottom-up forms of assessment and break the reading act into components or subskills. This results in suggestions for intervention that use a parts-to-whole teaching perspective and an emphasis on what the child cannot do rather than what he can do.

Individual diagnostic readings are sometimes used when children with suspected learning problems move into a school district and their permanent records are not yet available.

Many of these tests have attempted to establish norms to support claims of validity and reliability. Some have done so in a more rigorous way, like the Woodcock Reading Mastery Tests—Revised (Woodcock et al., 1987), but others have not gone to such impressive lengths (Cooter, 1990).

• *Woodcock Reading Mastery Tests—Revised* (Woodcock et al., 1987). The Woodcock Reading Mastery Tests—Revised (WRMT-R) is a battery of six individually administered subtests intended to measure reading abilities from kindergarten through adult levels. Its design reveals a skills perspective of reading, dividing the assessment into three "clusters" appropriate to age and ability levels: readiness, basic skills, and reading comprehension. The WRMT-R reports norm-referenced data for each of its two forms, as well as insights into remediation oriented toward a skills perspective. Results may be calculated either manually or using the convenient scoring program developed for microcomputers. This test is frequently used by teachers in special education, Chapter 1 reading, and sometimes teachers assigned to regular classrooms.

Other Reading-Related Tests

Finally, many tests, although they may not all be reading tests per se, provide classroom teachers with some insights into children's reading behavior. An example of one follows:

• *Kaufman Test of Educational Achievement* (Kaufman & Kaufman, 1985). Sometimes teachers require norm-referenced data to determine how a child is progressing compared to other children nationally. This is sometimes the case when a teacher is working with a population of students who are performing at atypically high or low levels. That is, working with these students over a long period of time may tend to give teachers a distorted view of what "normal" achievement looks like. The Kaufman Test of Educational Achievement (K-TEA) can provide useful insights in these situations. The K-TEA is a norm-referenced test yielding information in the areas of reading, mathematics, and spelling. Intended for students in grades 1 to 12, the K-TEA is available in both a brief form for quick assessments (when only standardized data are needed) and a comprehensive form (provides both standardized data and insights into classroom remediation). Strictly speaking, alternate forms are not available, but the authors suggest that the two versions may be used as such for pretest–post-test measures.

The K-TEA is an individually administered achievement test.

Use of Skill Sheets and Ditto Masters: Avoiding the "Purple Plague"

CRTs measure whether a child can perform a task at a prescribed performance level.

The most traditional and frequently used reading assessment devices are skill sheets and ditto masters. Many teachers have been led to believe by basal publishers that skill sheets and ditto masters are useful for *teaching* various reading skills. In reality, they do not teach, they are simply a form of **criterion-referenced tests (CRTs)**. A CRT is designed to measure whether a student can perform a given task at some predetermined proficiency level, or "criterion." Thus, it is easy to see that skill sheets and workbook pages may most accurately be described as CRTs rather than as instructional activities.

There is some debate as to whether "test-wiseness" should be part of the curriculum.

Skill sheets and ditto masters do have at least one legitimate instructional use in the classroom, however. Teachers should use these instruments as a vehicle for teaching the format of district- or state-required tests of reading skills knowledge. This is what is called teaching *test-wiseness*. For example, let's say that a second-grade teacher, Ms. Guenther, has decided to teach a minilesson having to do with using context clues. Her motivation for teaching the lesson is twofold: (a) Context is a valuable tool for helping beginning readers develop fluency and identify new words in print, and (b) using context clues is listed as one of the required reading strategies to be taught in second grade according to the school system's curriculum guide (political realities). Guenther will first teach context clues as a whole-class minilesson using holistic principles (whole to parts to whole), then offer a whole-group test-wiseness lesson. Notice how and when she will use workbook pages in the following teaching summary:

Modeling is essentially an activity during which the teacher thinks aloud.

Step 1:   Demonstration Reading and Modeling. First, the minilesson begins as Guenther shares a new book entitled *The True Story of the 3 Little Pigs! by A. Wolf* (Scieszka, 1989).

Step 2:   Statement of the Problem. Guenther explains that good readers sometimes come to words they do not recognize. One strategy is to use the other words in the story, and especially in the same sentence, to help figure out what the unknown word might be (context clues).

Step 3:   Modeling and Guided Group Application. Next, Guenther places a transparency on the overhead projector that has been adapted from *The True Story of the 3 Little Pigs!* Several of the words in the story have been covered using self-stick memo notes. Guenther reads aloud the passage saying "blank" when she comes to one of the covered words. The text might go as follows:

> Way back in Once Upon a [blank] time,
> I was making a [blank] cake
> for my dear old [blank].
> I had a terrible sneezing [blank].
> I ran out of sugar. (Scieszka, 1989, p. 6)

As Guenther rereads the passage, she "thinks aloud" (modeling) as she completes the first two blanks for the class. Class members are then invited to assist the teacher as she attempts to complete the remaining two blanks. Remember that the essence of reading is meaning. Therefore, synonyms suggested by students, as well as naming the exact words used by the author, are to be encouraged and praised.

Worksheets are sometimes useful in test-wiseness lessons.

As a final step in guided practice, Guenther asks students to complete another similar page from the book that is shown on the overhead projector or given to students as a duplicated worksheet. Guenther can score the latter option to identify students needing further help.

Step 4:   Test-Wiseness Lesson. The last activity is to show students how context clues are represented on basal mastery tests required by the school system. Once again, Guenther may want to demonstrate an example or two at the overhead projector, then ask students to complete a workbook page or worksheet at their desks. She then collects these papers and scores them to determine which children require extra assistance.

In this example, Guenther used two worksheets to help students understand how the strategy (context clues) they had just learned appears on required tests. Notice that the test-wiseness lesson came after students had already acquired the new strategy. Thus, worksheets were not used to teach the strategy or to "teach to the test," but simply to help the children apply what they already knew in the required test format.

Problems With Traditional Reading Assessment

In this section, we have examined some of the traditional forms of reading assessment prevalent in many American schools. As previously mentioned, the primary strength of these instruments and procedures is their usefulness for documenting general reading performance for the sake of satisfying political realities. It has also been stated that compared to authentic assessment, which is discussed in the next section, traditional assessment seems woefully inadequate. Following is a discussion of a few of the specific problems or shortcomings of traditional assessment:

1. *Traditional assessment mirrors outdated views of the reading process.* Although much of reading research of the recent decade has confirmed the holistic and transactional nature of the reading act, traditional reading assessment has remained in the relative dark ages of skills-based teaching. Traditional reading assessment stubbornly clings to the notion that reading can be conveniently divided into constituent pieces and that reading is only concerned with discrete elements such as phonics knowledge, hierarchical comprehension elements such as literal and inferential thinking, and some reading and study skills. What has been ignored is situational contexts of reading such as background knowledge, motivation to read, the classroom environment, and reading program elements. In short, traditional reading assessment is fragmented, limited, and simplistic in nature, and yields data of questionable utility.

Traditional assessment tends to be based on outdated views of reading processes.

2. *Much of traditional reading assessment fails to assist teachers in helping children succeed.* As shown in this section, much of traditional assessment yields information of little help from a classroom teaching point of view. Norm-referenced data (e.g., stanines, grade equivalents, percentiles) tell the teacher nothing about which strategies a child is or is not using during reading. Many tests, such as group tests and skill sheets, do not allow the teacher to interact with children as they read. Many of the so-called reading passages on IRIs are too short and uninteresting for children to yield useful information regarding authentic reading tasks.

3. *Traditional reading assessment fails to use authentic reading tasks.* Frequently, children are assessed in reading using only snippets of real reading passages, words and sounds in isolation, or objective question formats. Reading assessment, if it is good assessment (Valencia, 1990), will look like real reading. It should use different forms of text including narrative, informational text, and environmental print. It should have students reading for different purposes.

4. *Traditional reading assessments are actually another name for testing—incomplete assessments of reading ability.* Most traditional assessments are, in fact, paper-and-pencil tests that focus on only a few aspects of the reading act. Important parts of reading—such as interest, motivation, and ability to decode when reading self-selected books—are not usually investigated. Developing informed teaching opportunities for students is difficult with such limited information.

5. *Traditional assessments, especially standardized tests, are frequently viewed negatively by classroom teachers for a number of important reasons.* Many teachers have found that standardized tests create a negative affect in their classrooms and often hinder learning. Two classroom teachers (Nolan & Berry) spoke out on this point in a recent article:

> [We] resented how the district's standardized tests intruded on class time, created an atmosphere of anxiety, and failed to reflect the complexity of the literate learning, the quality and presentation of the text, or the conditions of collaboration and discussion that are valued in [a teacher's] classroom. (1993, p. 606)

These are just some of the needed features of reading assessment that are generally ignored, in part or whole, in traditional reading assessment. These concerns and others are more effectively addressed in authentic assessment, the subject of the next section.

Many teachers feel that traditional assessment creates a negative affect in their classrooms and yields an incomplete picture of a child's ability.

Authentic Reading Assessment

Traditional reading assessment, as described earlier in this chapter, is often termed *formal* or *product assessment.* That is, most of the information yielded from these assessments is oriented toward bottom-line comparisons of children and offers the classroom teacher little that informs instruction (Cambourne & Turbill, 1990; Clay, 1990). Authentic reading assessment is much more *informal* or *process-oriented,* describing clearly what students do as they read. These procedures survey student development in reading and writing-based developmental theory and research and are typically teacher initiated, and teacher developed.

Authentic reading assessment paints a clearer picture of what students do while reading.

Werner (1991) has described four purposes of process-oriented assessment as applied to writing, which seem to have general applicability to authentic reading assessment.

Authentic reading assessment shows where students are in terms of their development.

1. A process view of assessment shows where students are in terms of development and creates a record of progress.
2. Process assessment helps teachers determine areas of strength and need for planning instruction.
3. Process assessment can be used to assist teachers in giving grades. Although the notion of grading is not usually considered consistent with a holistic philosophical view, grades can be derived from some forms of process assessment to satisfy political realities.
4. Process-oriented assessment helps teachers in their own classroom-based research. Specifically, process assessment helps teachers learn more about the reading process and how children can be assisted to become successful readers.

A portfolio is a place for gathering learning artifacts.

Portfolio assessment programs are a popular and extremely effective vehicle for authentically assessing reading development (Farr, 1991; Glazer & Brown, 1993; Tierney, Carter, & Desai, 1991; Valencia, McGinley, & Pearson, 1990). A portfolio is simply a folder or other storage place for gathering student products, reflecting the whole picture of their reading development (Jongsma, 1989). It is both a *philosophy,* or way of viewing assessment, and a *place* for gathering pieces of evidence indicating student growth and development in reading (Valencia, 1990). Cooter and Flynt (in press) explain that

> the *philosophy* of portfolios suggests that we should consider all factors related to reading when assessing students. Portfolios are consistent with newer curriculum designs (Farr, 1991, p. 2) that emphasize the integration of the language arts (listening, speaking, reading and writing). They focus on the processes of constructing meaning, use of quality literature and other information aids, problem solving and application skills, and student collaborations. Therefore, portfolios are a means for dynamic and ongoing assessment (Tierney, 1992).
>
> Portfolios also represent a *place* for collecting student work samples that provide "windows" on the strategies used by students when reading and writing (Farr, 1991; Farr & Tone, 1994; Tierney, 1992). File folders, storage boxes, hanging files, and notebooks are a few of the common portfolio containers used to hold daily samples or "evidence" of student learning. This puts the responsibility and control for [reading] assessment back into the hands of those most affected by it—teachers and students (Valencia, 1990, p. 5), and provides the foundation for teacher/student conferences (Farr, 1991).

List some of the learning artifacts produced by students.

Two sets of portfolios are often maintained in the classroom (Cooter & Flynt, in press), student portfolios and file portfolios. *Student portfolios* are kept in the possession of students and may be added to by either the student or teacher. *File portfolios* are year-long files kept by the teacher on each student, which include representative samples of student development over time.

Portfolio assessment methods create a vivid picture of how students are progressing from one reading milestone to the next. Portfolios are not necessarily the *only* way to conduct authentic reading assessments, but they do represent a convenient and popular mode for many teachers. Numerous informal reading assessment options may be included in reading portfolios, some of which are described in the next section. The following is not intended to be an exhaustive listing but to serve as a starting point.

Portfolios help teachers and parents see the growth of a child from one reading milestone to another.

Kid Watching: Classroom Observations of Children and Reading

For many teachers, the first authentic assessment strategy is systematic and careful observations of children engaged in the reading act, or **kid watching** (K. S. Goodman, 1986). Clay, in her book *The Early Detection of Reading Difficulties,* explains her philosophy concerning observations:

Kid watching involves careful and systematic observations of children's reading behaviors.

> I am looking for movement in appropriate directions. . . . For if I do not watch what [the student] is doing, and if I do not capture what is happening in records of some kind, Johnny, who never gets under my feet and who never comes really into a situation where I can truly see what he is doing, may, in fact, for six months or even a year, practice behaviours that will handicap him in reading. (1985, p. 49)

Thus, observation is a critical tool at the teacher's disposal for early assessment of students and their abilities.

There appears to be a certain degree of consensus among balanced literacy program experts (Clay, 1985; Holdaway, 1979; Rhodes & Dudley-Marling, 1988) concerning critical features of observation. A summary of these important points follows:

What are some of the reading milestones to look for in kid watching?

Kid watchers are child researchers.

• *Adopt an attitude of researcher rather than teacher.* It is important when making observations to step out of the normal directive role of teacher and into a more participant–observer role. As teachers, we tend to interact and react. But to be an effective observer, we must resist the natural impulse to make midcourse corrections in the child's educational program. In other words, we need to "let it happen" and take notes accordingly. In many ways, we adopt the posture of a scientist in the laboratory.

• *Know which strategies are appropriate for the child to use.* To make effective observations, teachers must be aware of developmental trends in reading—which reading strategies are appropriate for the child's age and environment. For example, the following strategies might be considered appropriate for early readers (Clay, 1985): exhibits left-to-right progression across a page of text, knows the meaning of a period, knows concept of first and last part of a story, and knows where to start reading a book or story. Unless the teacher understands what to look for, observations will probably not be very insightful.

Numerous observations are necessary before valid conclusions can be drawn.

• *Make multiple observations over time (longitudinal).* Observations cannot be what is sometimes referred to as "quick and dirty." Teachers should look at reading behaviors over time to detect patterns of ability, or problems. One-shot observations tend to be unreliable indicators of student ability or growth. By making many observations over time, the teacher will be able to document growth and identify areas needing further development during group or individual minilessons. As a rule of thumb, the younger the child and the poorer the reader, the more time teachers will need to spend both observing and pondering observations (Clay, 1985, p. 50).

• *Observe real reading in varied situations.* Many commercial reading tests require students to read in very artificial situations. The text may be boring, use stilted language, and may be limited to the reading of narrative (story) compositions. If teachers are to make instructional decisions that carry some force of validity, then children should be observed with self-selected reading materials as well as district-required reading materials. In addition, varied settings (whole-class readings, teacher–student conferences, small reading group) for sampling reading behavior are desirable.

• *Document observations with regularity and clarity.* To satisfy accountability requirements, not to mention teaching efficiency, observations should be recorded promptly and regularly. If written recording–response methods are used, all entries should be easy to read. In fact, another teacher should be able to read and interpret comments without difficulty. In most situations, it is not necessary for others to be able to read these records; however, clear, concise records will aid the teacher who took them months later to recall the observation and piece together a record of student achievement. In addition to written recording–response records, many teachers now include observation guides and videotape or audiotape recordings of student observations in their assessment portfolio. Figure 13.2 is an example of one observation guide that might be used to document a kid-watching experience.

Observations should be documented clearly and often.

Although kid watching is usually considered to be an informal assessment activity, more formal options do exist. One example is *The Burke Reading Interview* (Burke, 1987), which provides insights into how students perceive themselves as readers and the reading task in general. The following questions have been adapted from the Burke instrument for more formal kid-watching observations.

Think of ways that kid watching could become part of one's assessment program.

- When you are reading and come to a word or something else you don't know, what do you do? What else can you do?
- Which of your friends is a good reader? What makes him or her a good reader?
- Do you think your teacher ever comes to a word or something else he or she doesn't know when reading? What do you think he or she does when that happens?
- If you knew that one of your friends was having problems with their reading, what could you tell your friend that would help?
- How would a teacher help your friend with reading problems?
- How do you think you learned to read?
- Are you a good reader?
- What would you like to be able to do better as a reader?

Diffily (1994) has recommended a number of other methods that may be used to document observations. These include checklists of reading behaviors that are observable, rating scales that make use of Likert scales (1 to 5), daily work samples, photographs that document reading development, audiotapes that record oral reading and retellings, as well as videotapes of children performing a variety of reading activities. In the next section, we present several observation checklists and scales that may be useful as a starting point for kid-watching activities.

Observation Checklists and Scales: Noting Reading Development Milestones

Authentic assessment in many ways begins with an understanding of **reading development milestones** (Cooter, Diffily, Gist-Evans, & Sacken, 1994). These are stages of reading development through which most students progress as they move toward independent reading. It is essential that teachers come to know well these observable

*Authentic assessment is grounded in an understanding of **reading development milestones**.*

Kid-Watching Guide
Ms. Conger's Sixth Grade

Student name _____

Date _____

I.   Nature of Reading Task Observed

Self-selected reading _____

Literature response (class activity) _____

Literature response (individual) _____

Literature response (group) _____

Content area reading _____ Which subject? _____

Oral reading _____

Other _____

II.   Description/Evidence of Reading Fluency Abilities Demonstrated

Self-monitoring of comprehension

Identification of new or difficult words

Rate and fluency of oral reading

Adjusting rate to different text demands

Retellings

Miscues corrected

III.   Other relevant observations

---

behaviors and abilities because this enables teachers to (a) describe where students are in their development, and (b) plan future instruction fitted to the students' respective zones of proximal development. For example, Linda Lamme and Cecilia Hysmith (1991, p. 632) recommend a kind of scale that can be used to identify developmental milestones in emergent readers. It describes 11 levels often seen in the elementary school. Following is a slight adaptation of that scale:

Level 11:   The student can read fluently from books and other reading materials.

Level 10:   The student seeks out new sources of information. He volunteers to share information from books with other children.

Level 9:   The student has developed the ability to independently use context clues, sentence structure, structural analysis, and phonic analysis to read new passages.

Level 8:   The student reads unfamiliar stories haltingly (not fluently), but requires little adult assistance.

Level 7:   The student reads familiar stories fluently.

Level 6:   The student reads word-by-word. He recognizes words in a new context.

Level 5:   The student memorizes text and can pretend to "read" a story.

Level 4:   The student participates in reading by doing such things as supplying words that rhyme and predictable text.

Level 3:   The student talks about or describes pictures. He pretends to read (storytelling). He makes up words that go along with pictures.

Level 2:   The student watches pictures as an adult reads a story.

Level 1:   The student listens to a story but does not look at the pictures.

Some teachers find it helpful to use checklists as a quick reference tool that incorporates what we know about reading development. We have experimented with one such checklist, which is based on the research of Cochrane et al. (1984) and Sulzby (1985), discussed in Chapter 3 (Figure 13.3). Bear in mind that checklists are only intended as a beginning point in a comprehensive assessment program.

Checklists are efficient tools that help us incorporate valuable research into classroom assessment programs.

Some teachers find that checklists that include a kind of Likert scale can be useful in student portfolios, because many reading behaviors become more fluent over time. Deborah Diffily (1994) developed one such scale for use with her elementary students, which is shown in Figure 13.4.

Although the reading behaviors listed in any scale or checklist naturally vary according to the grade level, these formats have been quite helpful. Armed with a knowledge of reading developmental milestones, teachers are ready to begin making careful and constructive kid-watching observations.

Reading Logs

Reading logs are daily records of student reading habits and interests, usually during self-selected reading (SSR) periods (Cambourne & Turbill, 1990). Students keep these records for the teacher by completing simple forms kept in a reading log folder at students' desks or other appropriate locations.

Running Records

Clay (1985) describes the **running record** as an informal assessment procedure with high reliability (.90 on error reliabilities) that can inform teachers as to where students are in their reading development. The procedure is not difficult but requires practice. Clay (1985) estimates that it takes about 2 hours of practice for teachers to become relatively proficient at running records.

*Assessment of oral reading is often accomplished through the use of **running records**.*

For critical curriculum decisions, Clay (1985) recommends that three running records be obtained for each child on various levels of difficulty. Clay's criteria for oral reading evaluation are based on words correctly read aloud:

Figure 13.3

Reading milestones checklist

Reading Milestones Checklist for Emergent Reading (Abbreviated Version)

Student: _____   Year: _____

Teacher: _____   School: _____

Directions: *Write in the date(s) as child exhibits the behaviors listed below.*

A.   PRE-INDEPENDENT READING STAGES

Date Observed:

    1.   *Magical Stage (Sulzby's "Story Not Formed" occurs here and before)*

____ Displays an interest in handling books.

____ Listens to print read to him for extended periods of time.

____ Begins to notice print in environmental context (signs, labels).

____ Letters may appear in his drawings.

____ Likes to "name" the pictures in a book, e.g., "lion," "rabbit."

    2.   *Self Concepting Stage (Sulzby's "Story Formed" level begins here)*

____ "Reads" or reconstructs content of familiar storybooks.

____ Recognizes his name and some other words in high environmental contexts (signs, labels).

____ His writing may display phonetic influence, i.e., wtbo = Wally, hr = her.

____ Can construct story meaning from pictorial clues.

____ Cannot pick words out of print consistently.

____ Rhymes words.

    3.   *Bridging Stage (Sulzby's "Story Formed" to "Written Language-Like")*

____ Can write and read back his own writing.

____ Can pick out individual words and letters.

____ Can read familiar books or poems which could not be totally repeated without the print.

____ Words read in one context may not be read in another.

____ Increasing control over visual cuing system.

Adapted from *Reading, Writing, and Caring* by Cochrane, O., Cochrane, D., Scalena, D., and Buchanan, E., 1988, New York: Richard C. Owen and from "Assessment of Emergent Literacy: Storybook Reading" by E. Sulzby, 1991, *The Reading Teacher, 44*(7), pp. 498–500.

An easy (independent) text	95% to 100% correct
An instructional text	90% to 94% correct
A hard (frustration) text	80% to 89% correct

Usually, books children are presently reading tend to fall at the instructional level. Running records are taken without having to mark a prepared script and may be recorded on a sheet of paper and require about 10 minutes to transcribe. Guidelines for administration follow:

Oral reading errors are called miscues.

1. A sample from the book(s) used is needed that is 100 to 200 words in length. For early readers, the text may fall below 100 words.
2. The teacher completes a record for each page of the three books, making "tick" marks on a sheet of blank paper for each word said correctly. Errors should be described fully. Figure 13.5 shows an example of one running

_____ Can match or pick out words of poems or chants that have been internalized.

B. INDEPENDENT READING STAGES

　　1.　*Take-Off Stage (Sulzby's "Print Watched" to "Holistic")*

_____ Wants to read to you often.

_____ Realizes that print is the base for constructing meaning.

_____ Aware of and reads aloud much environmental print (signs, labels, etc.).

_____ May exhibit temporary tunnel vision (concentrates on words and letters).

_____ Oral reading may be word-centered rather than meaning-centered.

　　2.　*Independent Reading (Sulzby's "Holistic" level)*

_____ Characterized by comprehension of the author's message by reader.

_____ Desire to read books to himself for pleasure.

_____ Reads orally with meaning and expression.

_____ May see print as literal truth. What the print says is right (legalized).

_____ Has internalized several different print grammars, i.e., fairy tales, general problem-centered stories, simple exposition.

　　3.　*Skilled Reader*

_____ Processes material further and further removed from his own experience.

_____ Reading content and vocabulary become a part of his experience.

_____ Can use a variety of print forms for pleasure.

_____ Can discuss several aspects of a story.

_____ Can read at varying and appropriate rates.

_____ Can make inferences from print.

_____ Challenges the validity of print content.

_____ Can focus on or use the appropriate grammar or structuring of varying forms of print, e.g., stories, science experiments, menus, diagrams, histories.

record taken from the early reading book *If You Give a Mouse a Cookie* (Numeroff, 1985, pp. 1–6).

Examples of errors in oral reading, or miscues, and how to code them follow (based on Clay, 1985):

1. Word-call errors: The student says a word that is different from the text in the book. The teacher writes the incorrect response(s) with the correct text under it.

    Student: *happen*
    Text: *house*

2. Attempted decoding: The student tries several times to say a word. The teacher records each attempt with the correct text under the trials.

    Student: *cake . . . c— . . . cook*
    Text: *cookie*

3. Self-correction: The student corrects an error himself. Self-corrections are noted by writing "SC."

    Student: *mike money* SC
    Text: *monkey*

Figure 13.4

Diffily's literacy development checklist

Student's Name _____ Date

Literacy Development Checklist

	Seldom				Often
Chooses books for personal enjoyment	1	2	3	4	5
Knows print/picture difference	1	2	3	4	5
Knows print is read from left to right	1	2	3	4	5
Asks to be read to	1	2	3	4	5
Asks that story be read again	1	2	3	4	5
Listens attentively during story time	1	2	3	4	5
Knows what a title is	1	2	3	4	5
Knows what an author is	1	2	3	4	5
Knows what an illustrator is	1	2	3	4	5
In retellings, repeats 2+ details	1	2	3	4	5
Tells beginning, middle, end	1	2	3	4	5
Can read logos	1	2	3	4	5
Uses text in functional ways	1	2	3	4	5
"Reads" familiar books to self/others	1	2	3	4	5
Can read personal words	1	2	3	4	5
Can read sight words from books	1	2	3	4	5
Willing to "write"	1	2	3	4	5
Willing to "read" personal story	1	2	3	4	5
Willing to dictate story to adult	1	2	3	4	5

Gratefully used by the authors with the permission of Deborah Diffily, Ph.D., Alice Carlson Applied Learning Center, Ft. Worth, TX.

4. If no word is given, then the error is noted with a dash.
5. Insertions: A word is added that is not in the text. An insertion symbol (a caret) is recorded between the two appropriate words, and the inserted word is placed above the insertion symbol.
    Student: *have a*
    Text: *He'll want to ˄look in the mirror.*
6. Teacher assistance: The student is "stuck" on a word he cannot call, and the teacher pronounces the word for him. The teacher records the incident as "TA" (teacher-assisted).
    Student: TA
    Text: *automobile*
7. Repetition: Sometimes children repeat words or phrases. These repetitions are not scored as an error but may be noted by drawing a line under the word that was repeated.

Running records provide teachers with numerous insights about reading development.

> Student: *He's going to* ask you for a glass of milk.
> Text: *He's going to ask you for a glass of milk.*

By noting the percentage of miscues or oral reading errors and by studying the errors for repeating patterns, the teacher can deduce how reading development is progressing for each child and which minilesson should be offered. In the next section, we show how running records can be used to inform teaching using a streamlined process.

Interpreting Running Records Using the Flynt/Cooter Scoring System.   Flynt and Cooter (1993, 1995) have developed a method of scoring running records that makes the process both time efficient and useful to classroom teachers. Employed in their informal reading inventory, The Flynt/Cooter Reading Inventory for the Classroom, this system involves the use of what they call a "miscue grid." They state that this system can be extremely effective when used with authentic text selections matched to student interests.

The miscue grid by Flynt and Cooter (1995) makes interpreting miscues much more efficient.

In the following excerpt from the Flynt/Cooter Reading Inventory (Figure 13.6), you will notice how miscues can be noted on the left side of the grid, then later tallied in appropriate columns to the right according to miscue type. This process not only makes the administration quicker but also enables teachers to quickly identify error patterns for each oral reading. We find that the "grid" idea can easily be adapted by teachers for use with excerpts from authentic literature samples.

Figure 13.5

Running record

Text	Record
If you give a mouse a cookie,	✓ ✓ ✓ ✓ ✓ ✓ ✓
he's going to ask for a glass of milk.	✓ ✓ ✓ ✓ ✓ ✓ *cup* ✓ ✓
When you give him the milk,	✓ ✓ ✓ ✓ ✓ ✓
he'll probably ask you for a straw.	✓ (SC) *premly* ✓ ✓ ✓ ✓ ✓
When he's finished, he'll ask for a napkin.	✓ ✓ *through* ✓ ✓ ✓ ✓ ✓
Then he'll want to look in a mirror	✓ ✓ ✓ ✓ ✓ ✓ ✓
to make sure he doesn't	✓ ✓ ✓ ✓ ✓
have a milk mustache.	✓ ✓ ✓ ✓

From *If You Give a Mouse a Cookie* (pp. 1–6) by L. J. Numeroff, 1985, New York: Scholastic. Copyright 1985 by Scholastic. Reprinted by permission.

For best assessments, students should be able to choose the book to be read themselves.

The process for administering running records using the Flynt/Cooter system begins, as usual, by having students select and read a passage from a book of interest. Flynt and Cooter recommend that teachers have students select the passage a day ahead of the actual reading so that the first 100 words may be transcribed onto the left-hand side of a blank grid patterned after the one shown in Figure 13.6. During the oral reading, the teacher tape-records the session for convenience and accuracy of transcription. Miscues are noted in the right-hand column. After all miscues are noted, the teacher examines each miscue and determines its type (e.g., mispronunciation, substitution, insertion, etc.), then puts a mark in the appropriate grid. Once this is done, each column is tallied. In Figure 13.6, note that the reader had two mispronunciations, two insertions, and so on. When the student has read several passages for the teacher over time, it is not difficult to identify error patterns—types of miscues that happen regularly—and to plan appropriate minilessons for classroom-based intervention.

Retellings

Unaided recall is a form of retelling.

One of the best ways to find out if a child understands a story he has read is through retellings (Gambrell, Pfeiffer, & Wilson, 1985; Morrow, 1985). The teacher elicits a retelling not by simply asking, "Do you understand the story?" but by asking him to retell the story in his own words. This may be accomplished in many ways. First, the teacher may wish to use pictures from the story as memory prompts. As the teacher flashes pictures sequentially from the book or story, the child retells the story as remembered. This is a form of aided recall and may be especially useful with beginning readers or students with reading problems who are just beginning to learn the retelling format. A second option is unaided recall, or retelling without pictures. We recommend a two-step process. The teacher begins by having the student retell everything he can remember about the passage. If it is a narrative passage, the teacher can use a record sheet like the one shown in Figure 13.7 to record critical elements of the story grammar the student has recalled. After the student stops retelling the first time, the teacher asks, "What else can you remember?" Usually, the

Figure 13.6

Flynt/Cooter running record scoring system

	Mispronounce	Substitute	Self-correct	Insertions	Teacher assist	Omissions	Other
Hot Shoes							
The guys at (the) I.B. Belcher						1	
lived (SC) Elementary School ~~loved~~ all the			1				
wib new sport shoes. Some ~~wore~~ the	1						
" Sky High" model by Nicky.							
really *buy* Others who‸couldn't afford Sky		1		1			
another Highs would settle for ~~a lesser~~		1					
shoe. Some liked the "Street							
Smarts" by Concave, or (the)						1	
s "Uptown-Downtown" by Beebop.				1			
go The Belcher boys ~~got~~ to the point		1					
with their shoes that they could							
impea ~~identify~~ their friends just by	1						
shoes (SC) looking at their ~~feet~~. But the boy			1				
every who was the ~~envy~~ of all the fifth		1					
grade was Jamie Lee. He had a							
pair of "High Five Pump'em Ups"							
by Adeedee. The only thing Belcher							
boys loved as *ll much as their*							
shoes was basketball.							
TOTALS	2	4	2	2	0	2	0

student will remember one or two other bits of information. The teacher continues to ask the child, "What else do you remember?" until he cannot remember anything else. Then, the teacher refers to the story grammar record sheet for any categories (e.g., setting, characters) not addressed by the student and asks him direct questions about the unaddressed areas. This is another form of aided recall.

Story Maps

Story maps (Beck & McKeown, 1981; Routman, 1988) may be used to determine whether a child understands the basic key elements of a narrative text or passage. Like the story grammar retelling record sheet discussed previously, the same story

A story grammar retelling record sheet is useful during unaided recall assessments.

Figure 13.7

Story grammar retelling record sheet

Student's Name _____	Date _____

Story _____

Source/Book _____

Category	Prompt Questions (After Retelling)	Student's Retelling
Setting	Where did this story take place?	
	When did this story happen?	
Characters	Who were the characters in this story?	
	Who was the main character(s) in the story?	
	Describe _____ in the story.	
Challenge	What is the main challenge or problem in the story?	
	What were the characters trying to do?	
Events	What were the most important things that happened in the story?	
	What did _____ do in the story?	
Solution	How was the challenge/problem solved?	
	What did _____ do to solve the problem?	
	How did the other characters solve their problems?	
Theme	What was this author trying to tell us?	
	What did _____ learn at the end of the story?	

grammar elements may be used. The task is for students to complete a story map (Figure 13.8) after the completion of a story. A generic format, like the one shown, may be used and applied to almost any narrative text.

Teacher-Made Cloze Tests

Cloze passages may be used for either instructional or assessment purposes.

A most common and effective authentic assessment strategy is the use of teacher-made cloze tests. Cloze tests (derived from the word *closure*) cause students to use their knowledge of word order (syntax) and sentence meaning (semantics) to successfully guess a missing or familiar word in print. A cloze passage is constructed as follows:

1. The teacher selects a passage from either narrative or expository text.
2. The teacher types the passage, either on a typewriter or computer. The first sentence should be typed exactly as it appears in the original text. Beginning with the second sentence, one of the first five words is deleted and replaced with a blank. Then, *every* fifth word is deleted and replaced with a blank.

3. Students read the passage all the way through once silently before attempting to fill in the blanks.
4. The teacher scores the cloze passage using a one-third to one-half formula. If students correctly guess more than one-half of the deleted words, then the passage is easy reading. If a student correctly guesses less than one-third of the missing words, then the passage is too difficult for classroom instruction at this time. Scores falling between the one-third to one-half criteria are within the students' zone of proximal development, or the instructional range. With help from the teacher or peers, the student can succeed in that level passage.

Another form of the cloze test, called "Burgess summary," is discussed in Chapter 11.

Another form of the cloze test, called "Burgess summary," is discussed in Chapter 11.

Figure 13.8

Story map form

Story Map

Name _____   Date _____

Title _____   Author _____

Setting (Where and when did this story take place?)

Characters (Who were the main characters in this story?)

Challenge (What is the main challenge or problem in the story?)

Events (What were the events that happened in the story to solve the problem/challenge?)

    Event 1.

    Event 2.

    Event 3.

(List all the important events that happened.)

Solution (How was the challenge/problem solved or not solved?)

Theme (What was this author trying to tell us?)

Adapted from *Transitions: From Literature to Literacy* by R. Routman, 1988, Portsmouth, NH: Heinemann.

Print-Awareness Tests

When working with emergent readers, it is necessary to find out how much they know and understand about the world of print. Although some might say that this can be determined through casual observation, this practice is not very reliable, comprehensive, or efficient. Print-awareness tests, such as Clay's (1985) Concepts About Print Test, provide a viable solution to this assessment need. Clay's test assesses some 24 fundamental print awareness elements, which include the following: front of a book, print versus pictures, left-to-right progression, changes in word order, changes in letter order in words, meaning of a period, and location of a capital letter. The assessment is carried out using one of two available books called *Sand* and *Stones,* thus providing an authentic reading setting. Once teachers have reviewed this procedure, they should be able to construct their own print-awareness tests using real books from the classroom library, if desired.

Alphabet Knowledge (Early Readers)

Knowledge of the alphabet is essential in early reading instruction. It provides teachers and students with common language for discussing graphophonic relationships. Assessment of alphabet knowledge should occur in two contexts: letter recognition within words and sentences, and letters in isolation. We recommend that alphabet knowledge be assessed as part of the print awareness test discussed previously.

Questioning

Questioning is a most basic and effective means of assessing reading comprehension and is dealt with at some length in Chapter 6.

Family Surveys of Reading Habits

We recently observed a friend of ours who has a heart condition going through his normal daily activities with a small radio-like device attached to his belt. When asked what this gadget was, he indicated that it was a heart monitor. He went on to say that the device constantly measured his heart rate for an entire day to provide the doctor with a reliable account of his normal heart rhythms in the real-world of daily activity. Traditional reading assessment has often failed to give teachers a real-world look at students' reading ability by restricting the assessment to school settings. So the question posed here is, "How do we acquire information about a student's reading habits and abilities away from the somewhat artificial environment of the school?" One way is to assess what is happening in the home, using family surveys.

Family surveys are *brief* (too long and they'll never be answered!) questionnaires sent to adult family members periodically to provide teachers insights into reading behavior at home. Taken into consideration with other assessment evidence from the classroom, family surveys enable teachers to develop a reliable profile of the child's reading ability. One example of a family survey is provided in Figure 13.9.

Evaluating Program

Authentic assessment implies that teachers look not only at the child but also at all other relevant factors in the teaching–learning process. Teachers should logically develop a careful analysis of the classroom reading program to determine whether or

Figure 13.9

Family survey

September 6, 199__

Dear Adult Family Member:

   As we begin the new school year, I would like to know a little more about your child's reading habits at home. This information will help me provide the best possible learning plan for your child this year. Please take a few minutes to answer the questions below and return in the self-addressed stamped envelope provided. Should you have any questions, feel free to phone me at XXX–XXXX.

Cordially,

Mrs. Shelley

---

1. My child like to read the following at least once a week (check all that apply):

   Comic books _____   Sports page _____

   Magazines (example: *Highlights*) _____   Library books _____

   Cereal boxes _____   Cooking recipes _____

   T.V. Guide _____   Funny papers _____

   Others (please name):

2. Have you noticed your child having any reading problems? If so, please explain briefly.

3. What are some of your child's favorite books?

4. If you would like a conference to discuss your child's reading ability, please indicate which days and times (after school) would be most convenient.

---

not it meets the needs of all children. We suggest an analysis that at least begins by looking at the following:

- *Theoretical orientation:* What do you believe about how children learn to read? To which theoretical view of the reading process do you subscribe? (See Chapter 2). To which instructional model do you subscribe (subskills, skills, whole language, transitional)?

Sometimes children having problems learning are fully capable but are disabled by the curriculum.

- *Alignment of theory and practice:* After examining each major element of the reading program (for all students), how well does your program align with your theoretical beliefs? Are there any elements that do not seem to fit? If so, can they be justified using any of the 10 principles? (See Chapter 1.)
- *Resources:* What resources are available for your program that have not already been tapped (e.g., family volunteers, Reading Is Fundamental [R.I.F.] books, funds for purchasing books from the PTA, etc.)?
- *Readers with special needs:* What is your procedure for readers with special needs? Do you have a "revaluing" (intervention) program established in your classroom for recovering at-risk readers? If so, how well does it align with your stated philosophy, theory, and practice for other readers?

Evaluating Classroom Environments

In Chapter 9, we discussed how a teacher in various stages of the transition may wish to arrange the classroom environment. This is an important concern because the classroom environment affects student comfort while reading and, hence, reading performance. Ideally, the classroom environment should approach the comfort level of a home environment if one is to maximize learning potential. A careful description and mapping of the present classroom environment contrasted to those descriptions presented in Chapter 9 will help the teacher determine whether classroom modifications are needed.

Self-Rating Scales

Don't forget the obvious. Ask children what they feel their special needs are.

No one knows better how he is doing in reading than the reader himself. A teacher carrying out an assessment agenda should never overlook the obvious: Ask the kid how he's doing! Although this may be best achieved in a one-on-one discussion setting, large class sizes frequently make this a prohibitive practice. A good alternative to one-on-one interviews for older elementary children is a student self-rating scale. Students complete a questionnaire custom-tailored to obtain specific information about the reader from the reader's point of view. One example is illustrated in Figure 13.10 for a teacher interested in reading and study strategies used with social studies readings. The teacher should remember to keep self-rating scales focused and brief.

Additional Suggestions for Developing Reading Portfolios

The implementation of authentic assessment programs using portfolios can be challenging to new teachers as well as for seasoned veterans accustomed to more traditional schemes. In our experience, attention to several details not previously mentioned can lead to an efficient and successful experience. These include developing a plan for implementation, record-keeping systems, and use of time management strategies. There are also a few pitfalls to avoid when constructing authentic assessment programs. In this section, we discuss what we have learned in our teaching about constructing reading portfolios, as well as helpful ideas written about portfolios in the professional literature.

Reading Social Studies

Name _____ Date _____

1. The first three things I usually do when I begin reading a chapter in social studies are (number 1, 2, 3):

____ Look at the pictures.

____ Read the chapter through one time silently.

____ Look at the new terms and definitions.

____ Read the questions at the end of the chapter.

____ Read the first paragraph or introduction.

____ Skip around and read the most interesting parts.

____ Skim the chapter.

____ Preview the chapter.

2. What is hardest for me about social studies is . . .

3. The easiest thing about social studies is . . .

4. The thing(s) I like best about reading social studies is (are) . . .

Figure 13.10

Self-rating scale: Reading social studies

Develop a Plan for Constructing Reading Portfolios

Implementation of a reading portfolios assessment system can often seem overwhelming to many teachers just getting started. Success usually depends on having a simple logic to guide one's choices in this otherwise complex process. Margaret Puckett and Janet Black (1994) have described some key considerations for teachers as they begin to construct a portfolio system of assessment. They suggest that teachers decide which basic components or framework will be used, scrutinize information already at hand to decide what additional information may be needed to implement the authentic assessment plan, and outline the management process (how portfolios are used to inform teaching and to report progress to families).

Developing a deliberate plan for implementation of authentic assessment strategies is important.

Rubrics

Rubrics are scoring guides or rating systems used in performance-based assessment (Farr & Tone, 1994; Webb & Willoughby, 1993). The intent of rubrics is to assist teachers in two ways: (a) Make the analysis of literacy learning artifacts (i.e., reading

Rubrics are scoring guides.

and writing) simpler, and (b) make the rating process more reliable and objective (i.e., consistent). This is a tall order, indeed, because any assessment process is rarely objective, value free, or theoretically neutral (Bintz, 1991). Webb and Willoughby (1993, p. 14) explain that "the same rubric may be used for many tasks [once established] as long as the tasks require the same skills."

Although a rubric may be established in any number of ways, Farr and Tone (1994) have suggested a seven-step method that may be adapted to reading assessment. We have modified the process slightly to conform to reading assessment needs and shortened it to five relatively easy steps.

Anchor papers help teachers understand the range of performance across a group of students.

Step 1: Identify Anchor Papers.   The teacher begins by collecting and sorting into several stacks literacy learning artifacts (e.g., reading response activities, student self-analysis papers, content reading responses, etc.) according to quality. These are known as **anchor papers**. The teacher analyzes why he feels that certain artifacts represent more advanced development in reading than others and also why some artifacts cannot be characterized as belonging in the more advanced categories.

Step 2: Choose a Scoring Scale for the Rubric.   Usually a three-, four-, or five-point scoring system is used. A three-point scale may be more reliable, meaning that if more than one teacher were to examine the same reading artifacts they would be likely to arrive at the same rubric score (1, 2, or 3). However, when multiple criteria are being considered, a five-point scale or greater may be easier to apply. A major problem with reading rubrics is that they imply a hierarchy of skills that does not really seem to exist in many cases. (For example, in the upper grades, is the ability to skim text for information a higher or lower level skill than scanning text for information? Probably neither.) This brings us to Farr and Tone's (1994) next suggestion.

Scoring criteria should reflect your beliefs about reading development.

Step 3: Choose Scoring Criteria That Reflect What You Believe About Reading Development.   Two points relative to reading rubrics need to be considered in Step 3: scoring and learning milestones. First, a rubric is usually scored in a hierarchical fashion. That is, if on a five-point scale, a student fulfills requirements for a 1, 2, and 3 score, but not the criteria for a 4, then even if he may fulfill the criteria for a 5, he would still be ranked as a 3. That may work fairly well in areas such as mathematics where certain skills can be ranked hierarchically in a developmental sense. For example, for a student to progress to the point of performing long division, he will need to be able to do the more basic skills of multiplying, carrying numbers, and subtraction. Because, however, many reading skills cannot be ranked that clearly, we recommend that a procedure slightly different than typically recommended in reading. If a five-point rubric is being used, the teacher should survey all five reading skills or strategies identified in the rubric when reviewing artifacts found in the portfolio. If the student has the ability to do four of them, the teacher ranks the student as a 4, regardless of where those skills are situated in the rubric. We hasten to add that this modification may not always be appropriate, especially with emergent readers, among whom clearer developmental milestones are evident. This brings us to the second point.

As already mentioned, teachers need to know well the major literacy learning milestones identified through classroom-based research. This knowledge can be applied as one constructs rubrics in collaboration with other teachers. Keeping literacy learning milestones in mind as one constructs is the only way of ensuring validity in the process.

Step 4: Select Sample Reading Development Artifacts for Each Level of the Rubric and Write Descriptive Annotations.   It is important for teachers to have samples of each performance criterion in mind when attempting to use a rubric. From the Stage 1 process where range papers or other kinds of artifacts (e.g., running records, literature-response activities, story grammar maps, etc.) were identified, the teacher will have good examples of each reading skill or strategy being surveyed. As mentioned, these are what Farr and Tone (1994) call "anchor papers." After a careful review of these papers, it is possible to write short descriptive statements for each level in the rubric that summarize what the teacher is searching for in the assessment.

Exemplars help teachers better understand what is possible for a group of students.

Figure 13.11 shows a sample rubric developed for a fifth-grade class wherein students are to describe (orally and through written response) cause–effect relationships based on in-class readings about water pollution.

Step 5: Modify the Rubric Criteria as Necessary.   In any assessment, the teacher should feel free to modify a rubric's criteria as new information emerges. This is another way of maintaining validity in the process.

Rubrics can be modified as new information becomes available.

Reporting Progress to Families: What About Grades?

In this section on authentic assessment, we have listed several ways that children's growth in reading can be measured. Frequently, however, teachers become a little per-

---

Cause-Effect Relationships: Scale for Oral and Written Response

Level 4:   Student clearly describes a cause and effect of water pollution, and provides concrete examples of each.

S/he can provide an example not found in the readings.

"We read about how sometimes toxic wastes are dumped into rivers by factories and most of the fish die. I remember hearing about how there was an oil spill in Alaska that did the same thing to fish and birds living in the area."

Level 3:   Student describes a cause and effect of water pollution found in the readings.

Student can define "pollution."

"I remember reading about how factories sometimes dump poisonous chemicals into rivers and all the fish die. Pollution means that someone makes a place so dirty that animals can't live there anymore."

Level 2:   Student can provide examples of water pollution or effects pollution had on the environment found in the readings.

"I remember reading that having enough clean water to drink is a problem in some places because of garbage being dumped into the rivers."

Level 1:   Student is not able to offer voluntarily information about the cause and effects of pollution found in the readings.

Figure 13.11

Sample rubric for a fifth-grade reading class

plexed about how to report progress to families and convert these assessment data into grades. Some say that although authentic measures are more valid than traditional procedures, they are also more difficult to quantify or translate into grades required by many school districts. Teachers sometimes complain that authentic assessment, when it comes to grading, is too "touchy-feely." We believe the solution to this problem is to develop a new perspective for reporting and grading, and to learn how, when necessary, to derive traditional grades from these nontraditional assessment schemes.

Some elements of the reading portfolio are never graded—for example, alphabet knowledge and family surveys.

First, it may be helpful to distinguish between **graded performance profiles,** which relate to gradable tasks that demonstrate students' knowledge of reading strategies, and **ungraded background profiles,** which provide information about the student that would be utterly inappropriate to grade. Both ungraded and graded assessment options are included in the umbrella term *portfolio assessment* because the teacher uses all of this information to inform instruction. Each of the authentic reading assessment procedures discussed in this chapter are categorized in the following lists:

Authentic/Portfolio Assessment

Graded Performance Profiles	**Ungraded Background Profiles**
Reading logs	Print-awareness tests
Running records	Alphabet knowledge tests
Retellings (unaided and aided recall)	Family surveys
Literature-response projects	Self-rating scales
Cloze passages	Story maps
Questioning	
Evaluation forms	

Ungraded background profiles provide teachers with background information to help inform instruction, especially during the first few weeks of school. Ungraded background profiles cannot, and should not, be viewed as a source for grades. For instance, it would be absurd to "grade" a family survey form and use such information to score a child's performance at school! Teachers therefore use ungraded background profile information to inform instruction and provide insights into what students already know or have been exposed to in the past.

Graded performance profiles provide valid measures of student growth to satisfy accountability requirements.

Grades can be derived from graded performance profiles, as listed. In the remainder of this section, we discuss ways each of these assessment procedures can yield quantitative scores or grades. As with other examples throughout this book, we offer this information as merely one way of getting the job done, not the only way or the best way. (An alternate system for reporting called *authentic grading* is discussed later in the chapter.)

Reading Logs

Although some would say that reading logs should be ungraded, it is possible to add to this reading diary the element of retelling in a reading conference setting and derive grades. Following is an example that could be used with a third-grade classroom.

A = 4 or more books read along with a reading conference with the teacher

B = 3 books read along with a reading conference with the teacher

C = 2 books read along with a reading conference with the teacher

D = 1 book read along with a reading conference with the teacher

Running Records

As with reading logs, some teachers wonder whether running records should be used for grading. Our position is that this is one of many professional judgment calls for teachers to make. Running records should be done with each student about three times per quarter, or once about every 3 weeks. If running records are to be used as a grading source, grades may be derived from (a) the number of oral reading miscues and (b) combining the running record information with retellings (discussed next).

To use the running record for grading purposes, it is usually necessary to do an initial ungraded reading that is used as a baseline. After several rereadings of the text (e.g., 3 weeks apart), the student's performance can be compared to the baseline performance, then contrasted to a predetermined criterion to establish a grade. For example, earlier in the chapter, we provided a sample passage and analysis taken from *If You Give a Mouse a Cookie* (Numeroff, 1985). Let us assume that, after an initial baseline reading and several subsequent individual reading conferences in a first-grade classroom, the student Annie had the results shown in Table 13.1 as she read this popular children's book.

Running records can be used for grading some aspects of reading growth.

One Criterion for Running Records

If You Give a Mouse a Cookie, approximately 289 words

A = (98% correct oral reading) 6 miscues or less

B = (95% to 97%) 9 to 13 miscues

C = (90% to 94%) 17 to 29 miscues

Annie's grade could be computed easily at each of the rereading intervals using the preceding criteria. The criteria in this example are arbitrary and should be adjusted to suit the teacher's belief system. Annie's first reading would place her at the top of the "C" range, her second rereading at the top of the "B" range, and the third rereading is at the "A" level. After two or three rereadings for grading purposes, a new book thought to be more challenging would be selected for a new baseline measurement. To assess comprehension, retellings would be used.

Table 13.1

Annie's running record summary

Miscue Category Student: Annie	Baseline (9/12/95)	1st Rereading (10/3/95)	2nd Rereading (10/25/95)	3rd Rereading (11/10/95)
Book: *If You Give a Mouse . . .*				
1. Word call errors	3	1	0	0
2. Attempted decoding	6	4	3	1
3. Self-correction	2	1	1	1
4. Insertions	4	2	1	1
5. Teacher assistance	6	4	2	2
6. Repetition	4	5	2	1
Totals	**25**	**17**	**9**	**6**

Retellings

A retelling record sheet can be constructed in such a way as to be useful for grading.

Retellings, as mentioned earlier, are a two-step proposition involving both unaided and aided recall. For grading purposes, we recommend that teachers construct a checklist of important elements from the selection. For narrative selections, the checklist can be generic, like the one previously shown in Figure 13.7. As the student retells (unaided recall) the story, the teacher records elements remembered relating to setting, characters, challenge, and so on. After the retelling is complete, the teacher then asks questions from those story grammar categories not addressed in the retelling by the student (aided recall). At the conclusion of the retelling process, criteria such as the following (or others established by the teacher) could be used to convert the comprehension performance (combined unaided and aided recall) into a letter grade:

A = 95% recall or better
B = 88% recall
C = 80% recall
D = 75% recall

If students in, for example, upper elementary grades are reading long passages or books, we recommend that only a portion of the text be selected for the retelling exercise.

Literature-Response Projects

The literature-response category is perhaps the most subjective to grade. Also, just how much weight literature-response project grades should carry in the overall portfolio will vary according to how much effort was involved. Two very different projects are presented here that carry different values in the overall portfolio because of levels of difficulty: a literary poster (T. D. Johnson & Louis, 1987) and a group-developed radio play.

Literary posters are literature response activities created around some aspect of a story.

A literary poster has students create a poster around some aspect of a story. Some of the poster types suggested by T. D. Johnson and Louis (1987) are "missing persons," "greatest hero," and "wall of fame." This literature-response activity is done by students as seat work and does not require collaboration with peers. Typically, literary posters require about 20 minutes to complete. The essence of the poster is recalling several important bits of information from the text. To grade such a project, or any other literature-response project for that matter, the teacher must once again decide what is to be measured by naming the criteria. Figure 13.12 shows one possible set of criteria for the upper elementary level book *Fast Sam, Cool Clyde, and Stuff* (Myers, 1975).

Radio plays can involve three-way grading.

A radio play is a drama written by a small group of students (three to five) drawn from a key incident in a book they have all read. The drama, once written, is then read aloud into a tape recorder by the student-actors, complete with sound effects. Radio plays in finished form are usually played for the entire class over the public address system in the school, giving the impression of an actual radio production. Grading for this kind of literature-response activity is often triangulated, or three-way. A description of the three grade sources follows:

- *Within-group grade:* Students in the radio play group grade each other. This tends to prevent one or more students from "goofing off" and still getting full credit for the project.
- *Class evaluation:* All members of the class not associated with the project grade the radio play according to criteria outlined by the teacher. Each of the

Figure 13.12

Criteria for "wall of fame" poster

Criteria for *Fast Sam, Cool Clyde, and Stuff* (Myers, 1975)

"Wall of Fame Poster"

Ms. Holden's Sixth Grade

Directions: To qualify for the grade you want, you must not only have the total number of ideas required but also *have at least one idea from each of the story grammar categories* (setting, characters, challenge, events, solution, theme).

Grade Desired	Requirement
A	12 or more ideas recalled
B	9–11 ideas recalled
C	7–8 ideas recalled
D	6 ideas recalled (one idea from each of the story grammar categories)

criteria grades is tabulated by the teacher, and an average or mean grade is calculated based on the overall class evaluation.

- *Teacher grade:* Naturally, the teacher has veto power over any portion of the process if he feels the children were not just in their assessment. Additionally, the teacher grades the performance and factors in his grade as one third of the overall group grade. Based on the within-group grade, the teacher then decides if all students in the group get the same grade, or not, based on their contribution.

Cloze Tests

Cloze tests can serve a dual function: as a teaching activity for such reading strategies as context clues or inferential forms of comprehension or as an assessment procedure. Typically, most teachers using cloze modify the passage so that specific elements are deleted, such as character names, facts related to setting, key events in the story, and so on. Grading is simply a matter of applying the classroom criteria to the percentage of correct responses (e.g., 94% to 100% = A, 85% to 93% = B, etc.).

Cloze tests are easily graded using standard classroom-based criteria.

Questioning

Questioning is explained in some depth in Chapter 6. For grading purposes, we suggest (a) establishing basic minimum criteria, such as, the child must correctly identify at least one element from each of the story grammar criteria during questioning, and (b) applying the overall percentage correct to the classroom grading criteria, just as was explained for cloze texts.

Evaluation Forms

Valencia (1990) suggests that good evaluation begins with a knowledge of what is to be assessed and how to interpret the performance. Evaluation forms may take many forms, reflecting the diversity of teachers in various stages of the transition. For exam-

Evaluation forms can be useful in observation-oriented grading.

ple, some teachers in early-to-intermediate transitions may elect to use some of the skill sheets supplied by the basal reader as evaluation forms for grading. Why? Because skill sheets tend to focus on discrete, definable reading strategies and easily lend themselves to grading (e.g., 5 of 5 correct = A, 4 of 5 correct = B, etc.). For advanced transition teachers, skill sheets may not be an acceptable alternative, because they divorce the reader from more authentic reading activities. These teachers may prefer an evaluation form that is based on teacher observations while the child is reading whole text. Figure 13.13 is one example of an evaluation form that might be used to grade content reading strategies (based in part on Kemp, 1987).

Potential Pitfalls in Using Portfolios

In working with teachers experimenting with literacy portfolios in their classrooms, we have been struck by certain commonalties when they encounter problems. They are the same problems we have encountered ourselves as teachers when returning to work with children to try out new ideas. In this section, we alert readers to some of these rather predictable difficulties.

Overcommitment to Daily Entries

For example, weekly running records for all children is usually an unrealistic goal.

When teachers discover just how informative reading conferences with students can be, it becomes a natural impulse to want to conduct these conferences more and more often! We frequently encounter teachers who want to have daily reading con-

Figure 13.13

Content reading evaluation form

Name _____   Date _____

Text _____   Pages _____

Content Reading Strategies Practiced After Whole Group Minilessons

1. Follows class instructions given orally
2. Follows written instructions
3. Uses previewing strategy
4. Scans for important information on request
5. Surveys text before reading
6. Completes task on time
7. Can justify inferences drawn from text
8. Distinguishes between relevant and irrelevant facts
9. Other observations

Criteria:

A = Observed competence in this area and was used at appropriate times

B = Observed ability, but missed an opportunity to correctly apply the strategy

C = Used the strategy only once and/or missed obvious opportunities to apply

D = Appears to not fully understand the strategy or when to apply it

Based in part on Kemp, 1987.

ferences with every child. Even though assessment strategies like running records, story retellings, and discussions about different strategies that may be used are indeed powerful, attempting such regular conferences is not a very reasonable expectation to set for oneself. Most teachers find that weekly or bi-weekly reading conferences are sufficient.

Spending Too Much Time Managing Portfolios

Trying to manage portfolio assessment systems can become an almost crushing burden when added to the myriad other responsibilities of classroom teachers. Frankly, there is no easy solution to this problem, but a couple of strategies do seem to help. Many teachers find that using some of the various checklists available by publishers can help organize kid-watching observations.

Too Many Contributions by Students

Although we want students to make contributions to their reading and writing portfolios, sometimes students have trouble knowing "how much is too much!?" When this happens, teachers will notice students putting nearly everything they can think of into their portfolios, making it difficult for teachers to manage. Whole-group instruction sessions where the teacher shares the contents of an exemplary portfolio from a previous year or from a student volunteer can usually help students develop perspective.

Think of some ways students could be taught to select only the most useful learning artifacts.

Use of Portfolios as Traditional Assessment

A key advantage of portfolios is that one can use them to observe the growth of language processes. They permit us to get away from the mentality of grading everything a student does in school. Because reading and writing are developmental by nature—you get better at them over time and with practice—process assessment strategies such as portfolios are by nature preferred. This viewpoint puts us somewhat at odds with those expounding on the advantages of portfolios. For example, in a recent essay, Elbow states

Portfolio assessment programs are inherently developmental in philosophy. Grading work samples and making "good work–bad work" judgments run counter to that view.

> Portfolio assessment that occurs at the end of the semester helps us be ally to students for virtually all of the semester: students don't need to fight us as the enemy, because the more help they get from us, the better their portfolios will be and the higher their grades. (1994, p. 41)

This would seem to indicate that the purpose of the portfolio (in this instance, a writing portfolio) is to prove how "good" one is rather than to document growth in reading or writing ability over time. Elbow's statement in the same essay, "I'm suggesting, then, that portfolios might justify giving two holistic scores: EXCELLENT and POOR/UNSATISFACTORY" (p. 49), seems to confirm this good–poor mentality, although Elbow states it is quite the contrary. Reading and writing milestone behaviors are not inherently good or poor but rather are points on a developmental continuum.

Perhaps there is an underlying question concerning portfolios and grades: How should teachers respond to the often political reality of grading? Can portfolios be used for more valid and reliable grading or reporting systems, as Elbow (1994) alludes in his essay? In the next section, we suggest some ways that teachers can report progress in reading using some of the artifacts collected in the portfolio.

Current Trends in Reading Assessment

Reading assessment in American education has essentially followed a skills-based medical model since the 1930s. Reading assessment has been viewed as the act of diagnosing strengths and weaknesses and defining which skills are known, to be learned, or remediated. After decades following this model, many educators, public officials, and adult family members feel that little significant gains in literacy have resulted. Results of the National Assessment of Educational Progress report (Mullis et al., 1993) verify that only modest gains have been registered in overall reading development in recent years. Many people concerned with literacy development are calling for new approaches to both reading assessment and instruction. The authentic assessment movement alone has spawned numerous books and articles over the past few years. In this section, we briefly discuss a few ideas that are presently being explored in reading assessment. Note that some of the topics discussed remain at the idea stage and have not been fully developed.

Authentic Grading

Teachers and researchers advocating the use of portfolio assessment in process-reading classrooms are frequently opposed to any form of grading. They feel it is inappropriate to grade an area of language development because its very nature is student specific. Nevertheless, many if not most school districts still require grades for elementary school reading instruction.

Authentic grading offers the informative benefits of authentic assessment while satisfying political realities.

Cooter and Flynt (in press) have proposed a compromise system for reporting grades to families called **authentic grading**. This procedure (many will no doubt say that "authentic grading" is an oxymoron) has the potential dual benefit of satisfying the political reality of grading expected in many school districts and helping teachers who believe reading is a developmental process feel their reporting to families is more valid. Cooter and Flynt suggest a new type of reporting system that would contain the following information:

- A letter grade that reflects how well the student has progressed during the grading period (comparing the student to himself).
- A summary explaining in some detail what the student has achieved during this grading period and what he might accomplish next (zone of proximal development).
- A rating and explanation that reflect how the student compares to others at this level.

These three components would constitute full reporting of student progress and would likely satisfy the requirement to inform adult family members, students, and school administrators. In Figure 13.14, we suggest our conceptualization of an authentic grading report form.

Some whole language educators may object to a system like the one proposed, but the issue of reporting to families in a way that makes use of portfolio learning artifacts is certainly needed. We encourage the reader to continue pondering this dilemma and searching for acceptable solutions.

Standardized Tests of Reading

Valencia and Pearson (1987) note that standardized, norm-referenced tests are the most commonly used measures in U.S. schools. They indicate that a top priority in

Figure 13.14

Authentic grading
report form

Reading Report Form
Oxford Elementary School

Student's Name _____ Grade _____

Teacher _____ School _____

Grading Period _____

Part I: How your child has progressed in reading this grading period.

a.   Grade _____

b.   What your child has learned about reading this grading period . . .

c.   What we hope your child will be able to do next in reading . . .

d.   Things you can do at home to help his/her growth in reading . . .

Part II: How your child compares to other children his/her age or grade level in reading.

a.   How your child compares to other students at this grade level:

_____

Early in   Usual   Advanced
Development   Development   Development

b.   Comments:

Figure 13.14

Authentic grading report form

reading assessment research should be to develop and evaluate new assessment techniques that are consistent with our present understanding of the reading process and amenable to large-scale testing (p. 730). These researchers have been experimenting with several novel assessment formats that include summary writing, metacognitive tasks, question selection (choosing questions that best represent important ideas in a selection), multiple acceptable responses, and prior knowledge assessment (measuring ideas and vocabulary relatedness to central concepts).

In a related area, several statewide initiatives have begun that seek to develop reading tests that are more consistent with current theory (Winograd, Paris, & Bridge, 1991; Wixson, Peters, Weber, & Roeber, 1987). In Michigan, for example, policymakers, curriculum specialists, researchers, the state reading association, and teachers have been

Some states are experimenting with new, more authentic forms of standardized tests.

working together to redefine reading objectives and develop more authentic measures. The Michigan Department of Education scheduled full statewide implementation of their new reading tests in the fall of 1989. The new test objectives had three major categories: constructing meaning, knowledge about reading, and attitudes and self-perceptions.

Assessing Affective and Conative Factors in Reading

Interest, attitude, and motivation all have profound effects on reading success.

One of the most important (and elusive) aspects of reading assessment is **affect**, which deals with feelings about the reading act (Mathewson, 1985). Attitude, motivation, interest, beliefs, and values are all aspects of affect that have profound effects on reading development. In the past, affect has been discussed very little in reading assessment and usually has been limited to the administration of interest inventories (Figure 13.15 shows one example of a reading interest inventory), observation checklists, and attitude surveys (Walker, 1991). Teachers building balanced literacy programs require information in student portfolios that provides insights not only into reading materials and teaching strategies that may be employed but also into positive affective aspects that drive the reading process (Werner & Cooter, 1991). Ultimately, selection of materials and strategies should be based, at least in part, on affective considerations.

Authentic assessment can provide teachers with affective insights into reading, but skills and procedures for gaining this information require some investment of time and study on the part of the teacher. Two steps are generally required for teachers to effect this process. First, teachers must become knowledgeable as to affective aspects of reading. Second, teachers need to carefully review each naturalistic assessment strategy used for evidence of these affective aspects of reading in students. Further discussion and examples of these two points may help teachers begin to discover new ways of focusing on affective dimensions.

Mathewson (1985) identified four affective variables that drive the reading process: attitude, motives, feelings, and physical sensation. These variables may affect one's reading by influencing the decision to read, attention, comprehension, recall, and other factors. In addition, Mathewson identified eight motives that also appear to affect students' decision to read and reading behavior. Because Mathewson delineated these affective variables, scant attention has been paid to affect in literacy research in general, and assessment research in particular. With basic knowledge of some of these relevant affective reading variables, one may subjectively analyze selected portfolio assessment strategies for their potential to yield insights into students' motivations to read. Werner and Cooter (1991) attempted this process by subjectively comparing Mathewson's eight motives affecting decision to read with nine reading activities frequently used as authentic assessment strategies. Although their specific conclusions (represented in Table 13.2) may be debatable to some, they demonstrate that it may be possible to learn valuable affective reading behavior information through procedures already known and practiced. Future research by classroom teachers and others into affective connections in reading assessment and instruction seems warranted.

Persistence and determination are called **conative factors**.

A related area of research pertains to **conative factors** (Berlak, 1992; Raven, 1992). Conative factors include such aspects of human behavior as determination, persistence, and will. As Berlak (1992) stated in summarizing Raven's work in this area:

> [Students] can enjoy doing something without being determined to see it through, and he or she can hate doing something, but still be determined to do it . . . taking initiative (which would be categorized as an "affective" outcome in Bloom's Taxonomy) is inseparable from intellectual or cognitive functioning, and from action. (p. 17)

Figure 13.15

Interest inventory

Interest Inventory

Student's Name _____

Date _____

Instructions: Please answer the following questions on a separate sheet of paper.

1. If you could have three wishes, what would they be?
2. What would you do with $50,000?
3. What things in life bother you most?
4. What kind of person would you like to be when you are older?
5. What are your favorite classes at school, and why?
6. Who do you think is the greatest person? Why do you think so?
7. Who is your favorite person? Why?
8. What do you like to do with your free time?
9. Do you read any parts of the newspaper? Which parts?
10. How much TV do you watch each day? What are your favorite shows, and why?
11. What magazines do you like to read?
12. Name three of your favorite movies.
13. What do you like best about your home?
14. What books have you enjoyed reading?
15. What kind of books would you like to read in the future?

These researchers believe that conative factors have been falsely subsumed under the affective label and actually constitute a separate domain of human behavior.

Cooter (1994) attempted to translate Raven's (1992) conative research into authentic assessment applications in reading. He raises a few questions for further classroom-based research when he asks:

> If it is true that teachers and students moving in positive affective/conative directions can result in learning success, what happens when the teacher and student(s) are moving in opposite directions? For example, will a highly motivated student who is determined to learn to read mathematics materials more effectively but who encounters a teacher disinterested in her students still be able to learn? What about the reverse—where a student is disinterested in an academic task, but who encounters a highly motivated and inspiring teacher? It is difficult to predict in either case whether students will learn. It may be that the answer lies with how strong the affective and conative drives are for students and teachers alike.
>
> Another assessment question combines the role of affective and conative factors when students read expository versus narrative texts. Classroom experience suggests that interest, motivation, determination, and persistence tend to diminish when students read many expository materials, especially textbooks. Is this less true when using expository trade books? Can these feelings can be reversed if enticing text response activities are used? (Cooter, 1994, p. 89)

Some researchers wonder whether interest declines when students read expository materials. If so, what could be done to improve student affect?

Table 13.2

Motives affecting decision to read that may be discernible through authentic assessment measures

	Belong/ Love	Curiosity	Compe- tence	Achieve- ment	Esteem	Self-actu- alization	Desire to know	Aesthetic
Reading Logs	X	X	O	X	X	X	X	X
Running Records	O	O	X	X	O	O	O	O
Retellings	X	X	X	O	X	X	X	X
Radio Play	X	X	X	O	O	X	X	X
Wanted Poster	O	X	X	X	O	O	X	X
Burgess Summary	O	O	X	X	O	O	X	O
Diorama	X	X	X	X	O	X	X	X
Schema Map	X	X	X	X	O	O	X	X
Comic Strip	X	X	X	X	X	X	X	X

From "Affective Connections of Selected Naturalistic Assessment Strategies in Reading," by P .H. Werner and R. B. Cooter, May 1991, presented at the 36th Annual Conference of the International Reading Association, Las Vegas, NV. Copyright 1991 by P. H. Werner and R. B. Cooter. Reprinted by permission.

Although answers to these and other questions concerning affective and conative factors are yet to be resolved, they are essential to the effectiveness of any authentic assessment program. To ignore such factors as interest, motivation, and determination is to have an incomplete assessment. As Cooter summarizes, it would be "somewhat akin to a mechanic claiming to have done a complete assessment of an automobile after only checking tire pressures!" (1994, p. 86).

Measuring Prior Knowledge

Prior knowledge is one of the more difficult aspects to assess.

Prior knowledge is closely associated with reading comprehension. One dilemma to be resolved is deciding whether to assess a child's overall or gross prior knowledge or to measure specific prior knowledge related to each reading selection used in a testing situation. Another larger problem in both instances is how to assess prior knowledge comprehensively.

Measuring Reading Comprehension

Cognitive researchers have a great deal of difficulty agreeing on the nature of reading comprehension. Some feel that comprehension is hierarchical and can be represented adequately in terms of literal, inferential, and evaluative thinking, or some comparable system. Others feel that reading comprehension is not hierarchical but is holistic and might be described in terms of story grammars for narrative passages or similar patterns for expository text. Until reading comprehension processes are better understood, reading comprehension will be difficult to measure.

Metacognitive Strategies

Metacognition concerns students understanding their own reading abilities, demands of different texts, and matching reading abilities to text demands for effective comprehension. Future reading assessment needs to find better ways to assess a student's ability to vary reading strategies to fit the text.

Summary

Although traditional assessment modes may help satisfy political realities, they offer little information to teachers that informs classroom instruction. That is, they do not assess what people value as real reading (Valencia, 1990). Authentic reading assessment, on the other hand, generally does a better job of measuring real-world reading tasks but may not be viewed by some as a reliable or consistent indicator of individual student abilities. Establishment of clearly defined rubrics can help authentic assessment be more trustworthy to adult family members and administrators.

Current trends in reading assessment focus on process-oriented views of reading, as well as cognitive and affective aspects. Of particular interest to researchers at present is the measurement of students' prior knowledge and comprehension. Teachers who can accurately assess the depth and scope of students' knowledge about a topic can develop instructional lessons that address student needs more effectively. However obvious this conclusion may seem, the troubling question remaining is how to assess such knowledge. Other equally perplexing problems in reading assessment for future study relate to metacognition, the affective domain, and conative factors. As with the study of prior knowledge, the benefits of assessing such information seem obvious.

Figure 13.16 shows an overview of the chapter.

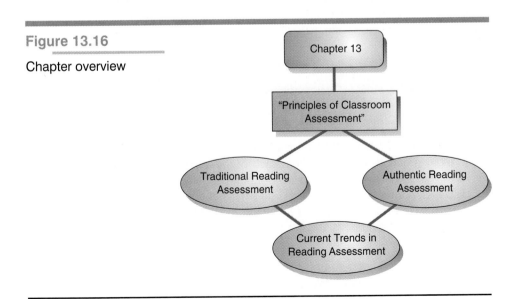

Figure 13.16

Chapter overview

CONCEPT APPLICATIONS

IN THE CLASSROOM

1. As a review, complete the following comparison grid analyzing the differences and similarities between traditional and authentic assessment perspectives:

Factors/Comparison	Traditional Assessment	Authentic Assessment
View(s) of the student		
Sources or types of reading diffculty (for students)		
Teacher's role		
Methods of assessment		

2. Develop a schedule for your classroom that includes time for corrective reading instruction. Remember that each of the corrective students has individual needs as well as some needs in common with all of the other students.
3. Develop three evaluation checklist forms that could be used in your classroom or a grade level you specify for reading comprehension, word identification, and content reading strategies. Include a possible rubric.

IN THE FIELD

1. Arrange through your college instructor, or through a neighborhood school, to work with an elementary-age student who is reportedly having difficulty in

reading. The following two major assignments can be completed with your assigned student.

Part 1: Complete the following informal assessment procedures

- A running record and miscue analysis using the Flynt/Cooter scoring system and text from a book chosen by the student
- A commercial informal reading inventory of your choice
- An oral retelling of a book read by the student
- Three classroom observations of the student in various classroom settings, such as reading group, content area materials, and free reading
- An interest inventory, which you have constructed or adapted from the one in this chapter

Part 2: After compiling and summarizing the preceding information, construct a reading profile of the student that includes the following:

- Approximate reading level (instructional)
- Reading strategies that appear to be strengths for the child
- Reading strategies that need development
- A list of trade books correlated to the interests of the child
- A list of possible literature-response activities the child might consider in connection with the trade books

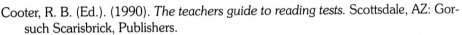

RECOMMENDED READINGS

Cooter, R. B. (Ed.). (1990). *The teachers guide to reading tests.* Scottsdale, AZ: Gorsuch Scarisbrick, Publishers.

Flynt, E. S., & Cooter, R. B., Jr. (1995). *The Flynt/Cooter reading inventory for the classroom* (2nd ed.). Scottsdale, AZ: Gorsuch Scarisbrick Publishers.

Lamme, L. L., & Hysmith, C. (1991). One school's adventure into portfolio assessment. *Language Arts, 68,* 629–640.

Puckett, M. B., & Black, J. K. (1994). *Authentic assessment of the young child: Celebrating development and learning.* Englewood Cliffs, NJ: Merrill/Prentice Hall.

Rhodes, L. K. (Ed.) (1993). *Literacy assessment: A handbook of instruments.* Portsmouth, NH: Heinemann.

APPENDIX

Selected Resources for Teachers

Long-Lasting Literature

Aardema, V. (1975). *Why mosquitoes buzz in people's ears.* New York: Scholastic.

Ahlberg, J., & Ahlberg, A. (1986). *The jolly postman or other people's letters.* Boston: Little, Brown.

Andersen, H. C. (1965). *The ugly duckling* (R. P. Keigwin, Translator, & A. Adams, Illustrator). New York: Scribner.

Asbjornsen, P. C. (1973). *The three billy goats gruff* (P. Galdone, Illustrator). New York: Seaburry Press.

Avi, W. (1984). *The fighting ground.* Philadelphia: J. B. Lippincott.

Aylesworth, J. (1992). *Old black fly* (S. Gammell, Illustrator). New York: Holt.

Barrett, J. (1978). *Cloudy with a chance of meatballs* (R. Barrett, Illustrator). Hartford, CT: Atheneum.

Barrett, N. S. (1984). *Trucks* (T. Bryan, Illustrator). London, NY: F. Watts.

Barrett, N. S. (1989). *Spiders.* London, NY: F. Watts.

Base, G. (1986). *Animalia.* New York: Harry Abrams.

Baum, L. F. (1972). *The Wizard of Oz.* Chicago: World.

Bonne, R. (1985). *I know an old lady.* New York: Scholastic.

Bourgeois, P., & Clark, B. (1986). *Franklin in the dark.* New York: Scholastic.

Branley, F. (1983). *Saturn: The spectacular planet.* New York: HarperCollins.

Brown, M. (1947). *Stone soup.* New York: Scribner.

Bunting, E. (1990). *The wall.* New York: Clarion.

Burnford, S. (1960). *The incredible journey.* Boston: Little, Brown.

Byars, B. (1970). *The summer of the swans.* New York: Viking.

Byars, B. (1981). *The Cybil war.* New York: Viking.

Carle, E. (1986). *The grouchy ladybug.* New York: Harper-Collins.

Carle, E. (1993). *Today is Monday.* New York: Philomel.

Chase, R. (1948). *Grandfather tales.* Boston: Houghton Mifflin.

Cherry, L. (1992). *A river ran wild: An environmental history.* San Diego: Gulliver/Harcourt Brace.

Christelow, E. (1992). *Don't wake up Mama! Another five little monkeys story.* New York: Clarion.

Cleary, B. (1952). *Henry and Beezus.* New York: William Morrow.

Cohn, A. L. (1994). *From sea to shining sea: A treasury of American folklore and folk songs.* New York: Scholastic.

Cole, J. (1992). *The magic school bus on the ocean floor* (B. Degen, Illustrator). New York: Scholastic.

Collier, J., & Collier, C. (1981). *Jump ship to freedom.* New York: Delacorte.

Collins, D. (1992). *Malcolm X: Black rage.* Minneapolis, MN: Dillon Press.

Cone, M. (1964). *A promise is a promise.* Boston: Houghton Mifflin.

Conroy, P. (1990). *The water is wide.* Atlanta, GA: Old New York Book Shop Press.

Cowley, J. (1980). *Hairy bear.* San Diego, CA: The Wright Group.

Cowley, J. (1982). *What a mess!* San Diego, CA: The Wright Group.

Dahl, R. (1961). *James and the giant peach: A children's story* (N. E. Burkert, Illustrator). New York: Alfred A. Knopf.

Dahl, R. (1964). *Charlie and the chocolate factory.* New York: Alfred A. Knopf.

Dakos, K. (1992). *Don't read this book, whatever you do! More poems about school* (G. B. Karas, Illustrator). New York: Four Winds.

Davis, D. (1990). *Listening for the crack of dawn.* Little Rock, AR: August House.

DeJong, M. (1953). *Hurry home, Candy.* New York: Harper.

Drew, D. (1989). *The life of the butterfly.* Crystal Lake, IL: Rigby.

Duke, K. (1992). *Aunt Isabel tells a good one.* New York: Dutton.

Fisher-Nagel, H. (1987). *The life of a butterfly.* Minneapolis, MN: Carolrhoda Books.

Fleischman, S. (1986). *The whipping boy.* Mahwah, NJ: Troll Associates.

Forbes, E. (1943). *Johnny Tremain.* Boston: Houghton Mifflin.

Fox, P. (1973). *The slave dancer.* New York: Bradbury.

Fox, P. (1986). *The moonlight man.* New York: Bradbury.

Garner, J. F. (1994). *Politically correct bedtime stories.* New York: Macmillan.

Gelman, R. G. (1976). *Why can't I fly?* (J. Kent, Illustrator). New York: Scholastic.

Gelman, R. G. (1977). *More spaghetti, I say!* New York: Scholastic.

Gelman, R. G. (1985). *Cats and mice.* New York: Scholastic.

George, J. (1972). *Julie of the wolves.* New York: Harper-Collins.

The Gingerbread Man. (1985). K. Schmidt, Illustrator. New York: Scholastic.

Goble, P. (1993). *The lost children.* New York: Bradbury.

Gwynne, F. (1970). *A chocolate moose for dinner.* New York: Windmill Books.

Gwynne, F. (1976). *The king who rained.* New York: Windmill Books.

Harlow, R., & Morgan, G. (1992). *Amazing nature experiments* (Kuo Kan Chen, Illustrator). New York: Random House.

Haskins, J. (1992). *I have a dream: The life and words of Martin Luther King, Jr.* Brookfield, CT: Millbrook.

Henwood, C. (1988). *Frogs* (B. Watts, Photographer). London, NY: Franklin Watts.

Houston, J. (1977). *Frozen fire.* New York: Atheneum.

Hurwitz, J. (1985). *The adventures of Ali Babba Bernstein.* New York: Scholastic.

Johnson, D. W. (1976). *Jack and the beanstalk* (D. W. Johnson, Illustrator). Boston: Little, Brown.

Juster, N. (1961). *The phantom tollbooth.* New York: Random House.

Killilea, M. (1954). *Karen.* New York: Dodd, Mead.

Kinsey-Warnock, N., & Kinsey, H. (1993). *The bear that heard crying.* New York: Cobblehill.

Krauss, R. (1945). *The carrot seed* (C. Johnson, Illustrator). New York: Scholastic.

Krumgold, J. (1953). *. . . and now Miguel.* New York: Harper Trophy.

L'Engle, M. (1962). *A wrinkle in time.* New York: Dell.

Lewis, C. S. (1961). *The lion, the witch, and the wardrobe.* New York: Macmillan.

Lisle, J. T. (1989). *Afternoon of the elves.* New York: Franklin Watts.

The Little Red Hen. (1985). L. McQueen, Illustrator. New York: Scholastic.

Littlejohn, C. (1988). *The lion and the mouse.* New York: Dial Books for Young Readers.

Lobel, A. (1981). *On Market Street* (Anita Lobel, Illustrator). New York: Scholastic.

Lock, S. (1980). *Hubert hunts his hum* (J. Newnham, Illustrator). Sydney, Australia: Ashton Scholastic.

Lowry, L. (1993). *The giver.* Boston: Houghton Mifflin.

Martin, B. (1983). *Brown Bear, Brown Bear, what do you see?* (E. Carle, Illustrator). New York: Henry Holt.

Martin, J. R., & Marx, P. (1993). *Now everybody really hates me* (R. Chast, Illustrator). New York: HarperCollins.

Math, I. (1981). *Wires and watts: Understanding and using electricity.* New York: Charles Scribner's Sons.

Mayer, M. (1976). *Ah-Choo.* New York: Dial Books for Young Readers.

Mayer, M. (1976). *Hiccup.* New York: Dial Books for Young Readers.

McKissack, P. C. (1986). *Flossie & the fox.* New York: Dial Books for Young Readers.

Monjo, F. N. (1970). *The drinking gourd.* New York: Harper & Row.

Myers, W. D. (1975). *Fast Sam, Cool Clyde, and Stuff.* New York: Puffin Books.

Numeroff, L. J. (1985). *If you give a mouse a cookie.* New York: Scholastic.

Parish, P. (1980). *Good work, Amelia Bedelia* (L. Sweat, Illustrator). New York: Avon Books.

Paulsen, G. (1991). *The river.* New York: Delacourt.

Perlman, J. (1993). *Cinderella Penguin* (J. Perlman, Illustrator). New York: Viking.

Pfeffer, S. B. (1989). *Claire at sixteen.* New York: Bantam Books.

Pollack, P. (1982). *Keeping it secret.* New York: Putnam.

Porter, B. J. (1990). *Grandpa and me and the wishing star.* Salt Lake, UT: Deseret Book.

Potter, B. (1953). *The tale of Peter Rabbit* (R. Ruth, Illustrator). Racine, WI: Golden Press.

Provensen, A., & Provensen, M. (1983). *The glorious flight: Across the channel with Louis Bleriot.* New York: Viking Penguin.

Reuter, E. (1993). *Best friends* (A. Becker, Illustrator). Pitspopany Press.

Rice, J. (1992). *Texas night before Christmas.* Gretna, LA: Pelican.

Rich, E. S. (1964). *Hannah Elizabeth.* New York: Harper-Collins.

Ross, T. (1986). *I want my potty.* Brooklyn, NY: Kane/Miller.

Schwartz, D. M. (1985). *How much is a million?* Richard Hill, Ontario: Scholastic-TAB.

Scieszka, J. (1989). *The true story of the 3 little pigs! By A. Wolf.* New York: Viking Kestrel.

Scieszka, J. (1992). *The stinky cheese man and other fairly stupid tales* (L. Smith, Illustrator). New York: Viking.

Sendak, M. (1962). *Chicken soup with rice.* New York: Scholastic.

Sendak, M. (1963). *Where the wild things are.* New York: HarperCollins.

Seuss, D. (1954). *Horton hears a Who!* New York: Random House.

Sharmat, M. W. (1980). *Gila monsters meet you at the airport.* New York: Aladdin.

Skaar, G. (1972). *What do the animals say?* New York: Scholastic.

Smith, K. A. (1989). *A checkup with the doctor.* New York: McDougal, Littell.

Smith, R. K. (1981). *Jelly belly.* New York: Dell.

Speare, E. G. (1958). *The witch of Blackbird Pond.* New York: Dell.

Sperry, A. (1940). *Call it courage.* New York: Macmillan.

Spier, P. (1977). *Noah's ark.* Garden City, NY: Doubleday.

Steele, W. O. (1958). *The perilous road.* Orlando, FL: Harcourt, Brace.

Steinbeck, J. (1937). *The red pony.* New York: Bantam Books.

Stolz, M. (1963). *Bully on Barkham Street.* New York: Harper.

Thaler, M. (1989). *The teacher from the black lagoon.* New York: Scholastic.

Thompson, C. (1992). *The paper bag prince.* New York: Knopf.

Van Allsburg, C. (1985). *The polar express.* Boston: Houghton Mifflin.

Van Allsburg, C. (1987). *The Z was zapped.* Boston: Houghton Mifflin.

Viorst, J. (1972). *Alexander and the terrible horrible no good very bad day* (R. Cruz, Illustrator). New York: Atheneum.

Vozar, D. (1993). *Yo, hungry wolf!* (B. Lewin, Illustrator). Garden City, NY: Doubleday/Bantam Doubleday Dell.

Weimans, E. (1981). *Which way courage?* New York: Atheneum.

Wells, R. (1973). *Noisy Nora.* New York: Scholastic.

White, E. B. (1952). *Charlotte's web.* New York: HarperCollins.

White, E. B. (1970). *The trumpet of the swan.* New York: HarperCollins.

Wood, A. (1984). *The napping house.* (D. Wood, Illustrator). San Diego: Harcourt Brace.

Wood, A. (1990). *Weird parents.* New York: Dial Books for Young Readers.

Young, E. (1992). *Seven blind mice.* New York: Philomel.

Alphabet Books

Anno, M. (1975). *Anno's alphabet: An adventure in imagination.* New York: Crowell.

Baldwin, R. M. (1972). *One hundred nineteenth-century rhyming alphabets in English.* Carbondale, IL: Southern Illinois University.

Brent, I. (1993). *An alphabet of animals.* Boston: Little, Brown.

Chwast, S. (1991). *Alphabet parade.* Fort Worth, TX: Harcourt Brace.

Crowther, R. (1978). *The most amazing hide-and-seek alphabet book.* New York: Viking.

Ehlert, L. (1989). *Eating the alphabet: Fruits and vegetables from A to Z.* Fort Worth, TX: Harcourt Brace.

Emberley, E. (1978). *Ed Emberley's ABC.* Boston: Little, Brown.

Feelings, M. (1974). *Jambo meets Hello: Swahili alphabet book.* New York: Dial.

Hoban, T. (1987). *26 letters and 99 cents.* New York: Greenwillow.

Hunt, J. (1989). *Illuminations.* New York: Bradbury.

Jonas, A. (1990). *Disembark.* New York: Greenwillow.

Kitchen, B. (1984). *Animal alphabet.* New York: Dial.

Lobel, A. (1990). *Alison's zinnia.* New York: Greenwillow.

Merriam, E. (1987). *Halloween ABC.* New York: Macmillan.

Musgrove, M. (1976). *Ashanti to Zulu: African traditions.* New York: Dial.

Provensen, A., & Provensen, M. (1978). *A peaceable kingdom: The Shaker abecedarius.* New York: Viking.

Ressmeyer, R. (1992). *Astronaut to zodiac.* New York: Crown.

Thornhill, J. (1990). *The wildlife ABC: A nature alphabet book.* New York: Simon & Schuster.

Fantastic Fun and Facts

Burns, M. (1987). *The I hate mathematics book* (M. Hairston, Illustrator). Cambridge, MA: Cambridge University Press.

Cullinan, B. E. (1987). *Children's literature in the reading program.* Newark, DE: International Reading Association.

Gallant, M. G. (1986). *More fun with Dick and Jane.* New York, NY: Penguin Books.

Kobrin, B. (1988). *Eyeopeners!* New York: Penguin Books.

Lipson, E. R. (1988). *Parent's guide to the best books for children.* New York: Times Books.

Norton, D. (1995). *Through the eyes of a child: An introduction to children's literature* (4th ed.). Englewood Cliffs, NJ: Merrill/Prentice Hall.

Ohanian, S. (1984). Hot new item or same old stew? *Classroom Computer Learning, 5,* 30–31.

Reed, A. (1988). *Comics to classics.* Newark, DE: International Reading Association.

Trelease, J. (1989). *The new read-aloud handbook.* New York: Penguin Books.

Wankelman, W., Wigg, P., & Wigg, M. (1968). *A handbook of arts and crafts.* Dubuque, IA: W. C. Brown.

Wacky and Weighty Words

Hall, R. (1984). *Sniglets.* New York: Macmillan.

Levitt, P. M., Burger, D. A., & Guralnick, E. S. (1985). *The weighty word book.* Longmont, CO: Bookmakers Guild.

Nash, B., & Nash, G. (1980). *Pundles.* New York: Stone Song Press.

Poetry, Rhythm, and Rhyme

Adoff, A. (1991). *In for winter, out for spring.* Fort Worth, TX: Harcourt Brace.

Baracca, D., & Baracca, S. (1990). *Taxi dog.* New York: Dial.

Carle, E. (1989). *Eric Carle's animals, animals.* New York: Philomel.

Cassidy, S. (1987). *Roomrimes.* New York: Crowell.

Coe, W. (1979). *Dinosaurs and beasts of yore.* New York: Philomel Books.

Demi. (Ed.). (1992). *In the eyes of the cat. Japanese poetry for all seasons.* New York: Holt.

Fleishman, P. (1988). *Joyful noise: Poems for two voices.* New York: HarperCollins.

Hudson, W. (1993). *Pass it on: African-American poetry for children.* New York: Scholastic.

Kennedy, X. J., & Kennedy, D. (Eds.). (1982). *Knock at a star: A child's introduction to poetry.* Boston: Little, Brown.

Lear, E. (1982). *A book of bosh.* New York: Penguin.

Loveday, J. (Ed.). (1981). *Over the bridge: An anthology of new poems.* New York: Kestrel, Penguin.

Mahy, M. (1989). *Nonstop nonsense.* New York: Macmillan.

Morton, M. (Ed.). (1972). *The moon is like a silver sickle: A celebration of poetry by Russian children.* New York: Simon & Schuster.

O'Neill, M. (1961). *Hailstones and halibut bones.* Garden City, NY: Doubleday.

Poems teachers ask for. (1979). New York: Granger Book.

Prelutsky, J. (1984). *The new kid on the block.* New York: Greenwillow Books.

Prelutsky, J. (1976). *Nightmares: Poems to trouble your sleep.* New York: Greenwillow Books.

Prelutsky, J. (Ed.). (1983). *The Random House book of poetry for children.* New York: Random House.

Prelutsky, J. (1986). *Ride a purple pelican.* New York: Greenwillow Books.

Prelutsky, J. (1988). *Tyrannosaurus was a beast: Dinosaur poems.* New York: Greenwillow Books.

Prelutsky, J. (1990). *Something big has been here.* New York: Greenwillow Books.

Prelutsky, J. (1991). *For laughing out loud: Poems to tickle your funnybone.* New York: Alfred A. Knopf.

Schwartz, A. (1992). *And the green grass grew all around: Folk poetry from everyone.* New York: HarperCollins.

Silverstein, S. (1974). *Where the sidewalk ends.* New York: HarperCollins.

Silverstein, S. (1981). *A light in the attic.* New York: Harper-Collins.

Sky-Peck, K. (Ed.). (1991). *Who has seen the wind? An illustrated collection of poetry for young people.* Boston: Museum of Fine Arts, Boston, & Rizzoli.

Wilner, I. (Ed.). (1977). *The poetry troupe: An anthology to read aloud.* New York: Charles Scribner's Sons.

Wordless Books

Anno, M. (1982). *Anno's Britain.* New York: Philomel.

Anno, M. (1980). *Anno's Italy.* New York: Collins.

Collington, P. (1987). *The angel and the soldier boy.* New York: Alfred A. Knopf.

dePaola, T. (1978). *Pancakes for breakfast.* Fort Worth, TX: Harcourt Brace.

Drescher, H. (1987). *The yellow umbrella.* New York: Bradbury.

Goodall, J. (1987). *The story of a main street.* New York: Macmillan.

McCully, E. A. (1987). *School.* New York: HarperCollins.

McCully, E. A. (1988). *New baby.* New York: HarperCollins.

Spier, P. (1977). *Noah's ark.* Garden City, NY: Doubleday.

Wiesner, D. (1988). *Free fall.* New York: Lothrop, Lee & Shepard.

Wiesner, D. (1991). *Tuesday.* New York: Clarion.

Almost Wordless Books

Dubanevich, A. (1983). *Pigs in hiding.* New York: Four Winds.

Martin, R. (1989). *Will's mammoth.* New York: Putnam.

Munro, R. (1987). *The inside-out book of Washington, D.C.* New York: E. P. Dutton.

Tafuri, N. (1983). *Early morning in the barn.* New York: Greenwillow.

Sing and Read Books

Bierhorst, J. (1979). *A cry from the earth: Music of the North American Indians.* New York: Four Winds.

Carroll, L. (1979). *Songs from Alice.* New York: Holiday House.

Cohn, A. L. (Ed.). (1993). *From sea to shining sea: A treasury of American folklore and folk songs.* New York: Scholastic.

Dallin, L., & Dallin, L. (1980). *Heritage songster.* Dubuque, IA: Wm. C. Brown.

Delacre, L. (1989). *Arroz con leche: Popular songs and rhymes from Latin America.* New York: Scholastic.

Fox, D. (Ed.). (1987). *Go in and out the window: An illustrated songbook for young people.* New York: Metropolitan Museum of Art & Holt, Rinehart & Winston.

Glazer, T. (1988). *Treasury of songs for children.* Garden City, NY: Doubleday.

Johnson, J. W. (1993). *Lift every voice and sing.* New York: Walker.

Keller, C. (1976). *The silly song book.* Englewood Cliffs, NJ: Prentice Hall.

Knight, H. (1981). *Hillary Knight's the twelve days of Christmas.* New York: Macmillan.

Nye, V. (1983). *Music for young children.* Dubuque, IA: Wm. C. Brown.

Pankake, M., & Pankake, J. (1988). *A Prairie Home Companion folk song book.* New York: Viking.

Peek, M. (1987). *The balancing act: A counting song.* New York: Clarion.

Rubin, R. (1980). *The all-year-long song book.* New York: Scholastic.

Seeger, R. C. (1948). *American folksongs for children—In home, school, and nursery school.* New York: Doubleday.

Spier, P. (1970). *The Erie canal.* New York: Doubleday.

Spier, P. (1970). *The fox went out on a chilly night.* New York: Doubleday.

Surplus, R. W. (1963). *The alphabet of music.* Minneapolis: Lerner.

Yolen, J. (Ed.). (1986). *The lullaby songbook.* Fort Worth, TX: Harcourt Brace.

Yolen, J. (1991). *Hark! A Christmas sampler.* New York: Putnam.

Zinar, R. (1983). *Music in your classroom.* New York: Parker.

Chanting With Children

Cole, J., & Calmenson, S. (1990). *Mary Mack and other children's street rhymes.* New York: Morrow Junior Books.

Colgin, M. L. (Compiler). (1982). *Chants for children.* Manlius, NY: Colgin.

Dunn, S. (1987). *Butterscotch dreams.* Markham, Ontario: Pembroke.

Dunn, S. (1990). *Crackers and crumbs: Chants for whole language.* Portsmouth, NH: Heinemann.

REFERENCES

Aardema, V. (1975). *Why mosquitoes buzz in people's ears.* New York: Scholastic.

Aaron, R. L., & Gillespie, C. (1990). Gates-MacGinitie Reading Tests, third edition [Test review]. In R. B. Cooter, Jr. (Ed.), *The teacher's guide to reading tests.* Scottsdale, AZ: Gorsuch Scarisbrick.

Adams, M. J. (1990a). *Beginning to read: Thinking and learning about print.* Cambridge, MA: MIT Press.

Adams, M. J. (1990b). *Beginning to read: Thinking and learning about print (Summary).* Urbana-Champaign, IL: Center for the Study of Reading.

Adams, M. J. (1994). *Beginning to read: Thinking and learning about print.* Cambridge, MA: MIT Press.

Adams, M. J., Allington, R. L., Chaney, J. H., Goodman, Y. M., Kapinus, B. A., McGee, L. M., Richgels, D. J., Schwartz, S. J., Shannon, P., Smitten, B., & Williams, J. P. (1991). Beginning to read: A critique by literacy professionals and a response by Marilyn Jager Adams. *The Reading Teacher, 44*(6), 370–395.

Ahlberg, J., & Ahlberg, A. (1986). *The jolly postman or other people's letters.* Boston: Little, Brown.

Alexander, J. E. (Ed.). (1983). *Teaching reading* (2nd ed.). Boston: Little, Brown.

Alexander, J. E., & Heathington, B. S. (1988). *Assessing and correcting classroom reading problems.* Glenview, IL: Scott, Foresman.

Allan, K. K. (1982). The development of young children's metalinguistic understanding of the word. *Journal of Educational Research, 76,* 89–93.

Allington, R. L. (1977). If they don't read much, how they ever gonna get good? *Journal of Reading, 21,* 57–61.

Allington, R. L. (1980). Teacher interruption behaviors during primary grade oral reading. *Journal of Educational Psychology, 72,* 371–372.

Allington, R. L. (1983). The reading instruction provided readers of differing reading ability. *Elementary School Journal, 83,* 255–265.

Altwerger, B., Edelsky, C., & Flores, B. M. (1987). Whole language: What's new? *The Reading Teacher, 41*(2), 144–154.

Altwerger, B., & Flores, B. (1989). Abandoning the basal: some aspects of the change process. *Theory Into Practice, 28*(4), 288–294.

Alvermann, D. E. (1991). The discussion web: A graphic aid for learning across the curriculum. *The Reading Teacher, 45*(2), 92–99.

Alvermann, D. E., & Boothby, P. R. (1982). Text differences: Children's perceptions at the transition stage in reading. *The Reading Teacher, 36*(3), 298–302.

Alvermann, D. E., Dillon, D. R., & O'Brien, D. G. (1987). *Using discussion to promote reading comprehension.* Newark, DE: International Reading Association.

Alvermann, D. E., & Phelps, S. F. (1994). *Content reading and literacy.* Boston: Allyn & Bacon.

Alvermann, D. E., Smith, L. C., & Readence, J. E. (1985). Prior knowledge activation and the comprehension of compatible and incompatible text. *Reading Research Quarterly, 20*(4), 420–436.

Ancona, G. (1994). *The piñata maker: Piñatero.* San Diego, CA: Harcourt Brace.

The American people (Grade 6). (1982). New York: American.

Andersen, H. C. (1965). *The ugly duckling* (R. P. Keigwin, Trans., & A. Adams, Illustrator). New York: Scribner.

Anderson, L., Evertson, C., & Brophy, J. (1979). An experimental study of effective teaching in first-grade reading groups. *The Elementary School Journal, 79,* 193–222.

Anderson, R. C. (1970). Control of student mediating processes during verbal learning and instruction. *Review of Educational Research, 40,* 349–369.

Anderson, R. C., & Freebody, P. (1981). Vocabulary knowledge. In J.T. Guthrie (Ed.), *Comprehension and teaching: Research reviews* (pp. 80–82). Newark, DE: International Reading Association.

Anderson, R. C., Hiebert, E. F., Scott, J. A., & Wilkinson, I. A. G. (1985). *Becoming a nation of readers: The report of the commission on reading.* Washington, D. C.: The National Institute of Education.

Anderson, R. C., Mason, J., & Shirey, L. (1984). The reading group: An experimental investigation of a labyrinth. *Reading Research Quarterly, 20*(1), 6–38.

Anderson, R. C., Osborn, J., & Tierney, R. J. (1984). *Learning to read in American schools.* Hillsdale, NJ: Erlbaum.

Anderson, R. C., & Pearson, P. D. (1984). A schema-theoretic view of basic processes in reading. In D. P. Pearson (Ed.), *Handbook of reading research* (pp. 255–291). New York: Longman.

Anderson, R. C., Reynolds, R. E., Schallert, D. L., & Goetz, E. T. (1977). Frameworks for comprehending discourse. *American Educational Research Journal, 14,* 367–382.

Anderson, R. C., Wilson, P. T., & Fielding, L. G. (1988). Growth in reading and how children spend their time outside of school. *Reading Research Quarterly, 23*(3), 285–303.

Anderson, T. H., & Armbruster, B. B. (1980). Studying. In P. D. Pearson (Ed.), *Handbook of reading research* (pp. 657–680). New York: Longman.

Apple Computer. (1984). *Macwrite* [Computer program]. Cupertino, CA: Author.

Applebee, A. N. (1979). *The child's concept of story: Ages two to seventeen.* Chicago, IL: The University of Chicago Press.

Applebee, A. N., Langer, J. A., & Mullis, I. V. S. (1988). *Who reads best.* Princeton, NJ: Educational Testing Service.

Armbruster, B. B. (1984). The problem of "inconsiderate text." In G. G. Duffy, L. R. Roehler, & J. Mason (Eds.), *Comprehension instruction: Perspective and suggestions.* New York: Longman.

Armbruster, B., & Anderson, T. (1981). *Content area textbooks* (Reading Education Report No. 23). Urbana-Champaign: University of Illinois at Urbana-Champaign, Center for the Study of Reading.

Asbjornsen, P. C. (1973). *The three billy goats gruff* (Paul Galdone, Illustrator). New York: Seaburry Press.

Asheim, L., Baker, D. P., & Mathews, V. H. (1983). *Reading and successful living: The family school partnership.* Hamden, CT: Library Professional.

Asher, S. R. (1977). *Sex differences in reading achievement.* Reading Education Report number 2. Champaign, IL: Center for the Study of Reading, University of Illinois.

Asher, S. R. (1980). Topic interest and children's reading comprehension. In Spiro, R. J., Bruce, B. C., & Brewer, W. F. (Eds.), *Theoretical issues in reading comprehension* (pp. 525–534). Hillsdale, NJ: Erlbaum.

Ashton-Warner, S. (1963). *Teacher.* New York: Simon & Schuster.

Atwell, N. (1987). *In the middle: Writing, reading, and learning with adolescents.* Portsmouth, NH: Heinemann.

Au, K. H. (1993). *Literacy instruction in multicultural settings.* Fort Worth, TX: Harcourt Brace College.

Aukerman, R. (1981). *The basal reader approach to reading.* New York: John Wiley & Sons.

Ausubel, D. P. (1959). Viewpoints from related disciplines: Human growth and development. *Teachers College Record, 60,* 245–254.

Avi, W. (1984). *The fighting ground.* Philadelphia: J. B. Lippincott.

Bacharach, N., & Alexander, P. (1986). Basal reader manuals: What do teachers think of them? *Reading Psychology, 3,* 163–172.

Bader, L. A. (1984). Instructional adjustments to vision problems. *The Reading Teacher, 37*(7), 566–569.

Baker, L., & Brown, A. L. (1984). Cognitive monitoring in reading. In J. Flood (Ed.), *Understanding reading comprehension* (pp. 21–44). Newark, DE: International Reading Association.

Baldwin, R. S., & Kaufman, R. K. (1979). A concurrent validity study of the Raygor readability estimate. *Journal of Reading, 23,* 148–153.

Bank Street writer [Computer program]. (1990). Jefferson City, MO: Scholastic Software.

Bantam. (1985). *Choose your own adventure.* New York: Bantam.

Barker, R. (1978). Stream of individual behavior. In R. Barker & Associates (Eds.), *Habitats, environments, and human behavior* (pp. 3–16). San Francisco: Jossey-Bass.

Barracca, D., & Barracca, S. (1990). *Taxi dog.* New York: Dial Books.

Barrett, F. L. (1982). *A teacher's guide to shared reading.* Richmond Hill, Ontario, Canada: Scholastic-TAB Publications.

Barrett, J. (1978). *Cloudy with a chance of meatballs* (R. Barrett, Illustrator). Hartford, CT: Atheneum.

Barrett, N. S. (1984). *Trucks* (Tony Bryan, Illustrator). London, NY: F. Watts.

Barrett, N. S. (1989). *Spiders.* London, NY: F. Watts.

Barrett, T. (1972). Taxonomy of reading comprehension. *Reading 360 Monograph.* Boston: Ginn.

Barron, R. F. (1969). The use of vocabulary as an advance organizer. In H. L. Herber & P. L. Sanders (Eds.), *Research in reading in the content areas: First year report.* Syracuse, NY: Reading and Language Arts Center, Syracuse University.

Bartlett, B. J. (1978). *Top-level structure as an organizational strategy for recall of classroom text.* Unpublished doctoral dissertation, Arizona State University.

Barton, D., Miller, R., & Macken, M. A. (1980). Do children treat clusters as one unit or two? *Papers and Reports on Child Language Development, 18,* 137.

Basal reading texts. What's in them to comprehend? (1984, November). *The Reading Teacher,* pp. 194–195.

Base, G. (1986). *Animalia.* New York: Harry N. Abrams.

Baum, L. F. (1972). *The Wizard of Oz.* World.

Baumann, J. F. (1993). Letters to the editor: Is it "You just don't understand," or am I simply confused? A response to Shannon. *Reading Research Quarterly, 28*(2), 86–87.

Baumann, J. F. (1992). Basal reading programs and the deskilling of teachers: A critical examination of the argument. *Reading Research Quarterly, 27*(4), 390–398.

Baumann, J. F., Jones, L. A., & Siefert-Kessell, N. (1993). Using think alouds to enhance children's comprehension monitoring abilities. *The Reading Teacher, 47*(3), 184–193.

Baumann, J. F., & Stevenson, J. A. (1986). Teaching students to comprehend anaphoric relations. In J. W. Irwin (Ed.), *Understanding and teaching cohesion comprehension* (pp. 3–8). Newark, DE: International Reading Association.

Baylor, B. (1976). *Hawk, I'm your brother.* New York: Macmillan.

Beck, I. L. (1986). Using research on reading. *Educational Leadership, 43*(7), 13–15.

Beck, I. L., Armbruster, B., Raphael, T., McKeown, M. G., Ringler, L., & Ogle, D. (1989). *Reading today and tomorrow: Treasures. Level 3.* New York: Holt, Rinehart & Winston.

Beck, I. L., & McKeown, M. G. (1981). Developing questions that promote comprehension: The story map. *Language Arts, 58,* 913–918.

Beck, I. L., McKeown, M. G., Omanson, R. C., & Pople, M. T. (1984). Improving the comprehensibility of stories: The effects of revisions that improve coherence. *Reading Research Quarterly, 19,* 263–277.

Beck, I. L., Omanson, R. C., & McKeown, M. G. (1982). An instructional redesign of reading lessons: Effects on comprehension. *Reading Research Quarterly, 17,* 462–481.

Berlak, H. (1992). The need for a new science of assessment. In H. Berlak et al., *Toward a new science of educational testing and assessment.* New York: State University of New York Press.

Betts, E. A. (1946). *Foundation of reading instruction.* New York: American Book.

The bilingual writing center. (1992). Fremont, CA: The Learning Company (Aidenwood Tech Park, 493 Kaiser Drive, Fremont, CA 94555, (800) 852-2255).

Bintz, W. P. (1991). Staying connected—Exploring new functions for assessment. *Contemporary Education, 62*(4), 307–312.

Bissex, G. L. (1980). *Gnys at wrk: A child learns to write and read.* Cambridge, MA: Harvard University Press.

Blachman, B. A. (1984). Relationship of rapid naming ability and language analysis skills to kindergarten and first-grade reading achievement. *Journal of Educational Psychology, 76,* 610–622.

Blachowicz, C. L. Z. (1977). Cloze activities for primary readers. *The Reading Teacher, 31*(3), 300–302.

Blachowicz, C. L. Z. (1986). Making connections: Alternatives to the vocabulary notebook. *Journal of Reading, 29*(7), 643–649.

Blanchard, J. S., Mason, G. E., & Daniel, D. (1987). *Computer applications in reading.* Newark, DE: International Reading Association.

Blanchard, J., & Rottenberg, C. J. (1990). Hypertext and hypermedia: Discovering and creating meaningful learning environments. *The Reading Teacher, 43*(9), 656–661.

Blanton, W. E., & Moorman, G. B. (1985). *Presentation of reading lessons. Technical Report No. 1.* Boone, NC: Center for Excellence on Teacher Education, Appalachian State University.

Blanton, W. E., Moorman, G. B., & Wood, K. D. (1986). A model of direct instruction applied to the basal skills lesson. *The Reading Teacher, 40,* 299–305.

Bleich, D. (1978). *Subjective criticism.* Baltimore, MD: Johns Hopkins University Press.

Block, J. H. (1989). *Building effective mastery learning schools.* New York: Longman.

Bloom, A. (1987). *The closing of the American mind: How higher education has failed democracy and impoverished the souls of today's students.* New York: Simon & Schuster.

Bloom, B. (1956). *Taxonomy of educational objectives.* New York: David McKay.

Blume, J. (1972). *Tales of a fourth grade nothing.* New York: Dell.

Bohning, G. (1986). The McGuffey eclectic readers: 1836–1986. *The Reading Teacher, 40,* 263–269.

Bond, G. L., & Dykstra, R. (1967). The cooperative research program in first-grade reading instruction. *Reading Research Quarterly, 2,* 5–142.

Bonne, R. (1985). *I know an old lady.* New York: Scholastic.

Bonners, S. (1989). *Just in passing.* New York: Lothrop, Lee & Shepard.

Booth, J., et al. (1985). *Impressions.* Toronto, CA: Holt, Rinehart & Winston.

Bourgeois, P., & Clark, B. (1986). *Franklin in the dark.* New York: Scholastic.

Brackett, G. (1989). *Super story tree.* Jefferson City, MO: Scholastic.

Branley, F. (1983). *Saturn: The spectacular planet.* New York: HarperCollins.

Bransford, J. C., & Johnson, M. K. (1972). Contextual prerequisites for understanding: Some investigations of comprehension and recall. *Journal of Verbal Learning and Verbal Behavior, 11,* 717–726.

Bransford, J. D., & Franks, J. J. (1971). The abstraction of linguistic ideas. *Cognitive Psychology, 2,* 331–350.

Braun, C. (1969). Interest-loading and modality effects on textual response acquisition. *Reading Research Quarterly, 4,* 428–444.

Brennan, J. (1994, September 3). Been there done that: Three John Grisham stories, one John Grisham plot. *Fort Worth Star Telegram,* p. 1E.

Bridge, C. (1978). Predictable materials for beginning readers. *Language Arts, 55,* 593–597.

Brigance, A. H. (1983). *Brigance® diagnostic comprehensive inventory of basic skills.* North Billerica, MA: Curriculum Associates.

Brimner, L. D. (1992). *A migrant family.* Minneapolis, NM: Lerner Publications.

Brofenbrenner, U. (1977). Toward an experimental ecology of human development. *American Psychologist, 32,* 513–531.

Bromley, K. D. (1991). *Webbing with literature: Creating story maps with children's books.* Boston: Allyn & Bacon.

Brown, A. (1982). Learning how to learn from reading. In J. A. Langer & M.T. Smith-Burke (Eds.), *Reader meets author: Bridging the gap* (pp. 26–54). Newark, DE: International Reading Association.

Brown, A., & Smiley, S. S. (1978). The development of strategies for studying texts. *Child Development, 49,* 1076–1088.

Brown, D. J., Engin, A. W., & Wallbrown, F. J. (1979). Developmental changes in reading attitudes during the intermediate grades. *Journal of Experimental Education, 47,* 262–279.

Brown, M. (1947). *Stone soup.* New York: Scribner.

Brown, T. (1986). *Hello, amigos.* New York: Holt, Rinehart & Winston.

Brozo, W. G, & Simpson, M. L. (1995). *Readers, teachers, learners: Expanding literacy in secondary schools.* Englewood Cliffs, NJ: Merrill/Prentice Hall.

Burke, C. (1987). Burke reading interview. In Goodman, Y., Watson, D., & Burke, C. (Eds.), *Reading miscue inventory: Alternative procedures.* New York: Richard C. Owens.

Burnford, S. (1960). *The incredible journey.* Boston: Little, Brown.

Burns, M. (1987). *The I hate mathematics book* (Martha Hairston, Illustrator). Cambridge, MA: Cambridge University Press.

Burns, P. C., Roe, B. D., & Ross, E. P. (1988). *Teaching reading in today's elementary schools* (4th ed.). Dallas: Houghton Mifflin.

Burns, P. C., Roe, B. D., & Ross, E. P. (1992). *Teaching reading in today's elementary schools* (5th ed.). Dallas: Houghton Mifflin.

Byars, B. (1970). *The summer of the swans.* New York: Viking.

Byars, B. (1981). *The Cybil war.* New York: Viking.

Byrne, B., & Fielding-Barnsley, R. (1989). Phonemic awareness and letter knowledge in the child's acquisition of the alphabetic principle. *Journal of Educational Psychology, 81,* 313–321.

Byrne, B., & Fielding-Barnsley, R. (1990). Acquiring the alphabetic principle: A case for teaching recognition of phoneme identity. *Journal of Educational Psychology, 82*(4), 805–812.

Byrne, B., Freebody, P., & Gates, A. (1992). Longitudianl data on the relations of word-reading strategies to comprehension, reading time, and phonemic awareness. *Reading Research Quarterly, 27*(2), 140–151.

California State Department of Education. (1980). *Report on the special studies of selected ECE schools with increasing and decreasing reading scores.* (Available from Publication Sales, California State Department of Education, P.O. Box 271, Sacramento, CA 95802.)

Calkins, L. (1986). *The art of teaching writing.* Portsmouth, NH: Heinemann Educational Books.

Calkins, L. (1994). *The art of teaching writing* (new ed.). Portsmouth, NH: Heinemann Educational Books.

Calkins, L. M. (1980). When children want to punctuate: Basic skills belong in context. *Language Arts, 57,* 567–573.

Calkins, L. M., & Harwayne, S. (1987). *The writing workshop: a world of difference* [Video]. Portsmouth, NH: Heinemann Educational Books.

Cambourne, B. (1988). *The whole story: Natural learning and the acquisition of literacy in the classroom.* New York: Ashton-Scholastic.

Cambourne, B., & Turbill, J. (1990). Assessment in whole-language classrooms: Theory into practice. *Elementary School Journal, 90*(3), 337–349.

Canney, G., & Winograd, P. (1979). *Schemata for reading and reading comprehension performance* (Technical Report No. 120). Urbana, IL: University of Illinois Center for the Study of Reading. (ERIC Document Reproduction Service No. ED 109 520)

Carbo, M. (1988). The evidence supporting reading styles: A response to Stahl. *Phi Delta Kappan, 70,* 323–327.

Carle, E. (1986). *The grouchy ladybug.* New York: Harper-Collins.

Carr, E. (1985). The vocabulary overview guide: A metacognitive strategy to improve vocabulary comprehension and retention. *Journal of Reading, 28*(8), 684–689.

Carr, E., Dewitz, P., & Patberg, J. (1989). Using cloze for inference training with expository text. *The Reading Teacher, 43*(6), 380–385.

Carr, E., & Wixson, K. K. (1986). Guidelines for evaluating vocabulary instruction. *Journal of Reading, 29*(7), 588–589.

Carr, H. K. (1986). *Developing metacognitive skills: The key to success in reading and learning.* For the MERIT, Chapter 2 project, The School District of Philadelphia, H. K. Carr, MERIT supervisor. Philadelphia: School Distric of Philadelphia.

Carroll, J. B., Davies, P., & Richman, B. (1971). *Word frequency book.* Boston: Houghton Mifflin.

Carroll, L. (1872) *Through the looking glass.* New York: Macmillan.

Cassidy, J. (1981). Grey power in the reading program—a direction for the eighties. *The Reading Teacher, 35,* 287–291.

Cattell, J. M. (1885). Ueber die Zeit der Erkennung und Bennenung von Schriftzeichen, Bildern und Farben. *Philosophische Studien, 2,* 635–650.

Caverly, D. C., & Buswell, J. (1988). Computer assisted instruction that supports whole language instruction. *Colorado Communicator, 11*(3), 6–7.

Chall, J. S. (1967). *Learning to read: The great debate.* New York: McGraw-Hill.

Chall, J. S. (1979). The great debate: Ten years later, with a modest proposal for reading stages. In Resnick, L. B., & Weaver, P. A. (Eds.), *Theory and practice of early reading* (pp. 29–55). Hillsdale, NJ: Erlbaum.

Chall, J. S. (1983). *Stages of reading development.* New York: McGraw-Hill.

Chapman, L. J., & Hoffman, M. (1977). *Developing fluent reading.* Milton Keynes, England: Open University Press.

Chase, R. (1948). *Grandfather tales.* Boston: Houghton Mifflin.

Chisom, F. P. (1989). *Jump start: The federal role in adult literacy.* Southport, CT: Southport Institute for Policy Analysis.

Choi, S. N. (1991). *Year of impossible goodbyes.* Boston: Houghton Mifflin.

Chomsky, C. (1971). Write first, read later. *Childhood Education, 47,* 230–237.

Chomsky, N. (1974). *Aspects of the theory of syntax.* Cambridge, MA: MIT Press.

Chomsky, N. (1975). *The logical structure of linguistic theory.* Chicago: The University of Chicago Press.

Chomsky, N. (1979). Human language and other semiotic systems. *Semiotica, 25,* 31–44.

Christopher, J. (1967). *The white mountains.* New York: Macmillan.

Clarke, M. A. (1989). Negotiating agendas: Preliminary considerations. *Language Arts, 66*(4), 370–380.

Clay, M. M. (1967). The reading behaviour of five year old children: A research report. *New Zealand Journal of Educational Studies, 2*(1), 11–31.

Clay, M. M. (1972). *Reading: The patterning of complex behaviour.* Exeter, NH: Heinemann Educational Books.

Clay, M. M. (1975). *What did I write? Beginning writing behaviour.* Portsmouth, NH: Heinemann Educational Books.

Clay, M. M. (1985). *The early detection of reading difficulties* (3rd ed.). Portsmouth, NH: Heinemann.

Clay, M. M. (1987). *Writing begins at home: Preparing children for writing before they go to school.* Portsmouth, NH: Heinemann Publishers.

Clay, M. M. (1990). What is and what might be in evaluation (Research currents). *Language Arts, 67*(3), 288–298.

Cleary, B. (1952). *Henry and Beezus.* New York: William Morrow.

Cochrane, O., Cochrane, D., Scalena, D., & Buchanan, E. (1984). *Reading, writing and caring.* New York: Richard C. Owen.

Cole, B. (1983). *The trouble with mom.* New York: Coward-McCann.

Cole, J. (1986). *This is the place for me.* New York: Scholastic.

Cole J. (1990). *The magic school bus lost in the solar system.* New York: Scholastic.

Cole, J., & Calmenson, S. (1990). *Miss Mary Mack.* New York: Morrow Junior Books.

Collier, J., & Collier, C. (1981). *Jump ship to freedom.* New York: Delacorte.

Collins, A., & Smith, E. (1980). *Teaching the process of reading comprehension* (Tech. Rep. No. 182). Urbana, IL: University of Illinois, Center for the Study of Reading.

Collins, A. M., & Quillian, M. R. (1969). Retrieval time from semantic memory. *Journal of Verbal Learning and Verbal Behavior, 8,* 240–247.

Collis, B. (1988). Research windows. *The Computing Teacher, 15,* 15–16, 61.

Cone, M. (1964). *A promise is a promise.* Boston: Houghton Mifflin.

Cooter, R. B., Jr. (1988). Effects of Ritalin on reading. *Academic Therapy, 23,* 461–468.

Cooter, R. B., Jr. (Ed.). (1990). *The teacher's guide to reading tests.* Scottsdale, AZ: Gorsuch Scarisbrick, Publishers.

Cooter, R. B., Jr. (1993). *Improving oral reading fluency through repeated readings using simultaneous recordings.* Unpublished manuscript, PDS Urban Schools Project, Texas Christian University.

Cooter, R. B., Jr. (1994). Assessing affective and conative factors in reading. *Reading Psychology, 15*(2), 77–90.

Cooter, R. B., Jr., & Chilcoat, G. W. (1990–1991). Content-focused melodrama: Dramatic renderings of historical text. *Journal of Reading, 34*(4), 274–277.

Cooter, R. B., Jr., Diffily, D., Gist-Evans, D., & Sacken, M. A. (1994). *Literacy development milestones research project* (Report No. 94-100). Unpublished manuscript, Texas Christian University, Fort Worth, TX.

Cooter, R. B., & Flynt, E. S. (1989). Blending basal reader and whole language instruction. *Reading Horizons, 29*(4), 275–282.

Cooter, R. B., Jr., & Flynt, E. S. (in press). *Teaching reading in the content areas: Developing content literacy for all students.* Englewood Cliffs, NJ: Merrill/Prentice Hall.

Cooter, R. B., & Griffith, R. (1989). Thematic units for middle school: An honorable seduction. *Journal of Reading, 32*(8), 676–681.

Cooter, R. B., Jr., Joseph, D. G., & Flynt, E. S. (1987). Eliminating the literal pursuit in reading comprehension. *Journal of Clinical Reading, 2*(1), 9–11.

Cooter, R. B., Jr., & Reutzel, D. R. (1987). Teaching reading skills for mastery. *Academic Therapy, 23*(2), 127–134.

Cooter, R. B., Jr., & Reutzel, D. R. (1990). *Yakity-yak: A reciprocal response procedure for improving reading comprehension.* Unpublished manuscript, Brigham Young University, Department of Elementary Education, Provo, UT.

Cosby, B. (1987). *How to read faster.* (Available from "Power of the Printed Word," International Paper Company, Dept. 3, Box 954, Madison Square Station, New York, NY 10010.)

Cousin, P. T., Weekly, T., & Gerard, J. (1993). The functional uses of language and literacy by students with severe language and learning problems. *Language Arts, 70*(7), 548–556.

Cowley, J. (1980). *Hairy bear.* San Diego, CA: The Wright Group.

Cowley, J. (1982). *What a mess!* San Diego, CA: The Wright Group.

Cox, C., & Zarillo, J. (1993). *Teaching reading with children's literature.* Englewood Cliffs, NJ: Merrill/Prentice Hall.

Craft, H., & Krout, J. (1970). *The adventure of the American people.* Chicago, IL: Rand McNally.

Crist, B. I. (1975). One capsule a week—A painless remedy for vocabulary ills. *Journal of Reading, 19*(2), 147–149.

Cudd, E. T., & Roberts, L. L. (1987). Using story frames to develop reading comprehension in a 1st grade classroom. *The Reading Teacher, 41*(1), 74–81.

Cudd, E. T., & Roberts., L. L. (1993). A scaffolding technique to develop sentence sense and vocabulary. *Reading Teacher, 47*(4), 346–349.

Cunningham, P. (1980). Teaching were, with, what, and other "four-letter" words. *The Reading Teaching, 34,* 160–163.

Dahl, R. (1961). *James and the giant peach: A children's story* (Nancy Ekholm Burkert, Illustrator). New York: Alfred A. Knopf.

Dahl, R. (1964). *Charlie and the chocolate factory.* New York: Alfred A. Knopf.

Dale, E. (1969). *Audiovisual methods in teaching* (3rd ed.). New York: Holt, Rinehart & Winston.

Dallin, L., & Dallin, L. (1980). *Heritage songster.* Dubuque, IA: William C. Brown.

Dana, C. (1989). Strategy families for disabled readers. *Journal of Reading, 33*(1), 30–35.

Davis, D. (1990). *Listening for the crack of dawn.* Little Rock, AR: August House.

Day, K. C., & Day, H. D. (1979). Development of kindergarten children's understanding of concepts about print and oral language. In M. L. Damil & A. H. Moe (Eds.), *Twenty-eighth yearbook of the National Reading Conference* (pp. 19–22). Clemson, SC: National Reading Conference.

Dechant, E. V. (1970). *Improving the teaching of reading* (2nd ed.). Englewood Cliffs, NJ: Prentice Hall.

DeFord, D., & Harste, J. C. (1982). Child language research and curriculum. *Language Arts, 59*(6), 590–601.

DeFord, D. E. (1985). Validating the construct of theoretical orientation in reading instruction. *Reading Research Quarterly, 20*(3), 351–367.

DeGroff, L. (1990). Is there a place for computers in whole language classrooms? *The Reading Teacher, 43*(8), 568–572.

DeJong, M. (1953). *Hurry home, Candy.* New York: Harper.

Delpit, L. D. (1988). The silenced dialogue: Power and pedagogy in educating other people's children. *Harvard Educational Review, 58*(3), 280–298.

dePaola, T. (1978). *The popcorn book.* New York: Holiday House.

Department of Education. (1985). *Reading in junior classes. Wellington, New Zealand.* New York: Richard C. Owens.

D.E.S. (1975). *A language for life (The Bullock Report),* H.M.S.O.

Developmental Learning Materials. (1985). *The writing adventure.* Allen, TX: Developmental Learning Materials.

Dewey, J., & Bentley, A. F. (1949). *Knowing and the known.* Boston: Beacon Press.

Dewitz, P., & Carr, E. M. (1987, December). Teaching comprehension as a student directed process. In P. Dewitz (Chair), *Teaching reading comprehension, summarizing and writing in content area.* Symposium conducted at the National Reading Conference, Florida.

DeWitz, P., Stammer, J., & Jensen, J. (1980). *The development of linguistic awareness in young children from label reading to word recognition.* Paper presented at the annual meeting of the National Reading Conference, San Diego, CA.

Diffily, D. (1994, April). *Portfolio assessment in early literacy settings.* Paper presented at a professional development schools workshop at Texas Christian University, Fort Worth, TX.

Dillner, M. (1993–1994). Using hypermedia to enhance content area instruction. *Journal of Reading, 37(4),* 260–270.

Doctorow, M., Wittrock, M. C., & Marks, C. (1978). Generative processes in reading comprehension. *Journal of Educational Psychology, 70*(2), 109–118.

D'Odorico, L. (1984). Nonsegmental features in prelinguistic communications: An analysis of some types of infant cry and noncry vocalizations. *Journal of Child Language, 11,* 17–27.

Dole, J. A., Rogers, T., & Osborn, J. (1987). Improving the selection of basal reading programs: A report of the textbook adoption guidelines project. *Elementary School Journal, 87,* 282–298.

Donelson, K. L., & Nilsen, A. P. (1985). *Literature for today's young adults.* Boston: Scott, Foresman.

Dowd, C. A., & Sinatra, R. (1990). Computer programs and the learning of text structure. *Journal of Reading, 34*(2), 104–112.

Dowhower, S. (1987). Effects of repeated readings on second-grade transitional readers' fluency and comprehension. *Reading Research Quarterly, 22,* 389–406.

Downing, J. (1977). How society creates reading disability. *The Elementary School Journal, 77,* 274–279.

Downing, J., & Oliver, P. (1973). The child's concept of a word. *Reading Research Quarterly, 9,* 568–582.

Downing, J., & Thomson, D. (1977). Sex role stereotypes in learning to read. *Research in the Teaching of English, 11*, 149–155.

Doyle, C. (1988). Creative applications of computer assisted reading and writing instruction. *Journal of Reading, 32*(3), 236–239.

Dreher, M. J., & Gambrell, L. B. (1985). Teaching children to use a self-questioning strategy for studying expository prose. *Reading Improvement, 22*, 2–7.

Drew, D. (1989). *The life of the butterfly.* Crystal Lake, IL: Rigby.

Duffy, G. G., Roehler, L. R., & Putnam, J. (1987). Putting the teacher in control: Basal reading textbooks and instructional decision making. *The Elementary School Journal, 87*(3), 357–366.

Dunn, L. M., & Markwardt, F. C. (1970). *Peabody individual achievement test.* Circle Pines, MN: American Guidance Service.

Dunn, R. (1988). Teaching students through their perceptual strengths or preferences. *Journal of Reading, 31,* 304–309.

Dunn, S. (1987). *Butterscotch dreams.* Markham, Ontario: Pembroke.

Durkin, D. (1966). *Children who read early: Two longitudinal studies.* New York: Teachers College Press.

Durkin, D. (1978). What classroom observations reveal about reading comprehension instruction. *Reading Research Quarterly, 14*(4), 482–533.

Durkin, D. (1981a). Reading comprehension in five basal reader series. *Reading Research Quarterly, 16*(4), 515–543.

Durkin, D. (1981b). What is the value of the new interest in reading comprehension? *Language Arts, 58,* 23–43.

Durkin, D. (1983). *Reading comprehension instruction: What the research says.* Presentation at the first annual Tarleton State University Reading Conference, Stephenville, TX.

Durkin, D. (1984). Is there a match between what elementary teachers do and what basal reader manuals recommend? *The Reading Teacher, 37,* 734–745.

Durkin, D. (1987). *Teaching young children to read* (4th ed.). New York: Allyn & Bacon.

Durkin, D. (1989). *Teaching them to read* (5th ed.). New York: Allyn & Bacon.

Durrell, D. D. (1940). *Improvement of basic reading abilities.* New York: World Book.

Duthie, J. (1986). The web: A powerful tool for the teaching and evaluation of the expository essay. *The History and Social Science Teacher, 21,* 232–236.

Earle, R. A., & Barron, R. F. (1973). An approach for testing vocabulary in content subjects. In H.L. Herber & R. F. Barron (Eds.), *Research in reading in the content areas: Second year report.* Syracuse, NY: Reading and Language Arts Center, Syracuse University.

Eastlund, J. (1980). Working with the language deficient child. *Music Educators Journal, 67*(3), 60–65.

Eckhoff, B. (1983). How reading affects children's writing. *Language Arts, 60*(5), 607–616.

Edelsky, C. (1988). Living in the author's world: Analyzing the author's craft. *The California Reader, 21,* 14–17.

Edelsky, C., Altwerger, B., & Flores, B. (1991). *Whole language: What's the difference?* Portsmouth, NH: Heinemann Educational Publishing.

Eder, D. (1983). Ability grouping and student's academic self-concepts: A case study. *The Elementary School Journal, 84,* 149–161.

Educational Testing Service. (1988). *Who reads best?* Princeton, NJ: Educational Testing Service.

Ehri, L. C. (1984). How orthography alters spoken language competencies in children. In J. Downing & R. Valtin (Eds.), *Language awareness and learning to read* (pp. 118–147). New York: Springer-Verlag.

Ehri, L. C., & Sweet, J. (1991). Fingerpoint-reading of memorized text: What enables beginners to process the print? *Reading Research Quarterly, 26,* 442–462.

Ehri, L. C., & Wilce, L. C. (1980). The influence of orthography on readers' conceptualization of the phonemic structure of words. *Applied Psycholinguistics, 1,* 371–385.

Ehri, L. C., & Wilce, L. C. (1985). Movement into reading: Is the first stage of printed word learning visual or phonetic? *Reading Research Quarterly, 20,* 163–179.

Ekwall, E. E., & Shanker, J. L. (1989). *Teaching reading in the elementary school* (2nd ed.). Englewood Cliffs, NJ: Merrill/Prentice Hall.

Elbow, P. (1994). Will the virtues of portfolios blind us to their potential dangers? In L. Black, D. Daiker, J. Sommers, & G. Stygall (Eds.), *New directions in portfolio assessment* (pp. 40–55). Portsmouth, NH: Boynton/Cook Publishers.

Eldredge, J. L. (1990). Increasing the performance of poor readers in the third grade with a group assisted strategy. *Journal of Educational Research, 84*(2), 69–77.

Eldredge, J. L., & Quinn, D. W. (1988). Increasing reading performance of low-achieving second graders with dyad reading groups. *Journal of Educational Research, 82,* 40–46.

Eldredge, J. L., Reutzel, D. R., & Hollingsworth, P. M. (in press). Round room reading versus the shared book experience: Examining changes in oral reading practice. *Journal of Literacy Research.*

Ellis, A. K., & Fouts, J. T. (1993). *Research on educational innovations.* Princeton Junction, NJ: Eye on Education.

Ellison, C. (1989, January). PCs in the schools: An American tragedy. *PC/Computing,* 96–104.

Engelmann, S., & Bruner, E. C. (1995). *Reading mastery I, presentation book A* (rainbow edition). Columbus, OH: McGraw-Hill/SRA.

Engelmann, S., & Hanner, S. (1983). *Reading mastery.* Chicago: Science Research Associates.

Ervin, J. (1982). *How to have a successful parents and reading program: A practical guide.* New York: Allyn & Bacon.

Esch, M. (1991, February 17). Whole language teaches reading. *The Daily Herald* (Provo, UT), p. D1.

Estes, T. H., & Vaughn, J. L. (1978). *Reading and learning in the content classroom*. Boston: Allyn & Bacon.

Fader, D. N. (1976). *The new hooked on books*. New York: Berkley Publishing.

Farr, R. (1991). *Portfolios: Assessment in the language arts*. ED334603.

Farr, R., & Tone, B. (1994). *Portfolio and performance assessment*. Fort Worth, TX: Harcourt Brace College Publishers.

Farr, R., & Tulley, M. (1989). State level adoption of basal readers: Goals, processes, and recommendations. *Theory Into Practice, 28*(4), 248–253.

Farr, R., Tulley, M. A., & Powell, D. (1987). The evaluation and selection of basal readers. *The Elementary School Journal, 87,* 267–281.

Farrar, M. T. (1984). Asking better questions. *The Reading Teacher, 38,* 10–17.

Fay, L. (1965). Reading study skills: Math and science. In J. A. Figurel (Ed.), *Reading and inquiry*. Newark, DE: International Reading Association.

Felmlee, D., & Eder, D. (1983). Contextual effects in the classroom: The impact of ability groups on student attention. *Sociology of Education, 56,* 77–87.

Ferreiro, E., & Teberosky, A. (1982). *Literacy before schooling*. Portsmouth, NH: Heinemann.

Fish, S. E. (1967). *Surprised by sin: The reader in Paradise Lost*. Englewood Cliffs, NJ: Merrill/Prentice Hall.

Fisher-Nagel, H. (1987). *The life of a butterfly*. Minneapolis: Carolrhoda Books.

Fleischman, S. (1986). *The whipping boy*. Mahwah, NJ: Troll Associates.

Flesch, R. (1955). *Why Johnny can't read*. New York: HarperCollins.

Flesch, R. (1979, November 1). Why Johhny still can't read. *Family Circle, 26,* 43–46.

Flesch, R. (1981). *Why Johnny still can't read*. New York: HarperCollins.

Flood, J., & Lapp, D. (1986). Types of texts: The match between what students read in basals and what they encounter in tests. *Reading Research Quarterly, 21,* 284–297.

Flynt, E. S., & Cooter, R. B., Jr. (1993). *The Flynt/Cooter reading inventory for the classroom*. Scottsdale, AZ: Gorsuch Scarisbrick.

Flynt, E. S., & Cooter, R. B., Jr. (1995). *The Flynt/Cooter reading inventory for the classroom* (2nd ed.). Scottsdale, AZ: Gorsuch Scarisbrick.

Follett, R. (1985). The school textbook adoption process. *Book Research Quarterly, 1,* 19–23.

Forbes, E. (1943). *Johnny Tremain*. Boston: Houghton Mifflin.

Fowler, G. L. (1982). Developing comprehension skills in primary students through the use of story frames. *The Reading Teacher, 36*(2), 176–179.

Fox, P. (1973). *The slave dancer*. New York: Bradbury.

Fox, P. (1986). *The moonlight man*. New York: Bradbury.

Fredericks, A. D., & Rasinski, T. V. (1990). Working with parents: Involving the uninvolved: How to. *The Reading Teacher, 43*(6), 424–425.

Freeman, Y. S., & Freeman, D. E. (1992). *Whole language for second language learners*. Portsmouth, NH: Heinemann Educational Books.

Fry, E. (1977). Fry's readability graph: Clarifications, validity, and extension to level 17. *Journal of Reading, 21,* 242–252.

Fry, E. (1980). The new instant word list. *The Reading Teacher, 34,* 284–289.

Fry, E. B., Polk, J. K., & Fountoukidis, D. (1984). *The reading teacher's book of lists*. Englewood Cliffs, NJ: Prentice-Hall.

Gahn, S. M. (1989). A practical guide for teaching writing in the content areas. *Journal of Reading, 33,* 525-531.

Gall, M. D., Ward, B. A., Berliner, D. C., Cahen, L. S., Crown, K. A., Elashoff, J. D., Stanton, G. C., & Winne, P. H. (1975). *The effects of teacher use of questioning techniques on student achievement and attitude*. San Francisco: Far West Laboratory for Educational Research and Development.

Gallant, M. G. (1986). *More fun with Dick and Jane*. New York: Penguin Books.

Gallup, G. (1969). *The Gallup poll*. New York: American Institute of Public Opinion.

Gamberg, R., Kwak, W., Hutchings, M., & Altheim, J. (1988). *Learning and loving it: Theme studies in the classroom*. Portsmouth, NH: Heinemann Educational Publishers.

Gambrell, L. B. (1985). Dialogue journals: Reading-writing instruction. *The Reading Teacher, 38*(6), 512–515.

Gambrell, L. B., Pfeiffer, W., & Wilson, R. (1985). The effects of retelling upon reading comprehension and recall of text information. *Journal of Educational Research, 78,* 216–220.

Gambrell, L. B., Wilson, R. M., & Gnatt, W. N. (1981). Classroom observations of task-attending behaviors of good and poor readers. *Journal of Educational Research, 74,* 400–404.

Garcia, S. B., & Malkin, D. H. (1993). Toward defining programs and services for culturally and linguistically diverse learners in special education. *Teaching Exceptional Children, (Fall),* 52–58.

Garza, C. L. (1990). *Cuadros de familia: Family pictures*. San Francisco: Children's Book Press.

Gates, A. I. (1921). An experimental and statistical study of reading and reading tests (in three parts). *Journal of Educational Psychology, 12,* 303–314, 378–391, 445–465.

Gates, A. I. (1937). The necessary mental age for beginning reading. *Elementary School Journal, 37,* 497–508.

Gates, A. I. (1961). Sex differences in reading ability. *Elementary School Journal, 61,* 431–434.

Gelman, R. G. (1976). *Why can't I fly?* New York: Scholastic, Inc.

Gelman, R. G. (1977). *More spaghetti, I say!* New York: Scholastic.

Gelman, R. G. (1985). *Cats and mice.* New York: Scholastic.

Gentry, R. (1987). *Spel . . . is a four-letter word.* Portsmouth, NH: Heinemann.

George, J. (1972). *Julie of the wolves.* New York: HarperCollins.

Gibson, E. J., & Levin, H. (1975). *The psychology of reading.* Cambridge, MA: MIT Press.

Gillet, J. W., & Temple, C. (1986). *Understanding reading problems: Assessment and instruction.* Boston: Little, Brown.

The gingerbread man. (1985). Karen Schmidt, Illustrator. New York: Scholastic.

Gipe, J. P. (1980). Use of a relevant context helps kids learn new word meanings. *The Reading Teacher, 33,* 398–402.

Gipe, J. P. (1987). *Corrective reading techniques for the classroom teacher.* Scottsdale, AZ: Gorsuch Scarisbrick.

Glatthorn, A. A. (1993). Outcome-based education: Reform and the curriculum process. *Journal of Curriculum and Supervision, 8*(4), 354–363.

Glazer, S. M. (1989). Oral language and literacy development. In D. S. Strickland & L. M. Morrow (Eds.), *Emerging literacy: Young children learn to read and write* (pp. 16–26). Newark, DE: International Reading Association.

Glazer, S. M., & Brown, C. S. (1993). *Portfolios and beyond: Collaborative assessment in reading and writing.* Norwood, MA: Christopher-Gordon.

Gleason, J. B. (1989). *The development of language* (2nd ed.) Englewood Cliffs, NJ: Merrill/Prentice Hall.

Goetz, E. T., Reynolds, R. E., Schallert, D. L., & Radin, D. I. (1983). Reading in perspective: What real cops and pretend burglars look for in a story. *Journal of Educational Psychology, 75*(4), 500–510.

Golden, J. M. (1992). The growth of story meaning. *Language Arts, 69*(1), 22–27.

Good, T. (1979). Teacher effectiveness in the elementary school. *The Journal of Teacher Education, 30,* 52–64.

Goodman, K., Shannon, P., Freeman, Y., & Murphy, S. (1988). *Report card on basal readers.* Katona, NY: Richard C. Owen.

Goodman, K., Smith, E. B., Meredith, R., & Goodman, Y. M. (1987). *Language and thinking in school: A whole-language curriculum.* Katona, NY: Richard C. Owen.

Goodman, K. S. (1967). Reading: A psycholinguistic guessing game. *Journal of the Reading Specialist, 6,* 126–135.

Goodman, K. S. (1968). *Study of children's behavior while reading orally* (Final Report, Project No. S 425). Washington, DC: U.S. Department of Health, Education, and Welfare.

Goodman, K. S. (1976). Behind the eye: What happens in reading. In H. Singer & R. B. Ruddell (Eds), *Theoretical models and processes of reading* (2nd ed., pp. 470–496). Newark, DE: International Reading Association.

Goodman, K. S. (1985). Unity in reading. In H. Singer & R. B. Ruddell (Eds.), *Theoretical models and processes of reading* (3rd. ed.). Newark, DE: International Reading Association.

Goodman, K. S. (1986). *What's whole in whole language?* Ontario, Canada: Scholastic.

Goodman, K. S. (1987). Look what they've done to Judy Blume!: The "basalization" of children's literature. *The New Advocate, 1*(1), 29–41.

Goodman, K. S., & Goodman, Y. M. (1983). Reading and writing relationships: Pragmatic functions. *Language Arts, 60*(5), 590-599.

Goodman, Y. M. (1986). Children coming to know literacy. In W. H. Teale & E. Sulzby (Eds.), *Emergent literacy: Writing and reading* (pp. 1–14). Norwood, NJ: Ablex Publishing.

Goodman, Y. M., & Altwerger, B. (1981). *Print awareness in preschool children: A study of the development of literacy in preschool children.* Occasional paper, Program in Language and Literacy. Tucson, AZ: University of Arizona.

Gordon, C. J. (1985). Modeling inference awareness across the curriculum. *Journal of Reading, 28*(5), 444–447.

Gordon, C. J., & Braun, C. (1983). Using story schema as an aid to reading and writing. *The Reading Teacher, 37*(2), 116–121.

Gordon, N. (Ed.). (1984). *Classroom experiences: The writing process in action.* Exeter, NH: Heinemann Educational Books.

Goswami, U., & Mead, F. (1992). Onset and rime awareness and analogies in reading. *Reading Research Quarterly, 27*(2), 152–163.

Gough, P. B. (1972). One second of reading. In J. F. Kavanagh & I. G. Mattingly (Eds.), *Language by ear and by eye.* Cambridge, MA: MIT Press.

Gove, M. K. (1983). Clarifying teacher's beliefs about reading. *The Reading Teacher, 37*(3), 261–268.

Graves, D. H. (1983). *Writing: Teachers and children at work.* Portsmouth, NH: Heinemann Educational Books.

Greaney, V. (1994). World illiteracy. In F. Lehr & J. Osborn (Eds.), *Reading, language, and literacy: Instruction for the twenty-first century.* Hillsdale, NJ: Erlbaum.

Greene, F. P. (1973). *OPIN.* Unpublished paper, McGill University, Montreal, Quebec, Canada.

Griffith, P. L., & Olson, M. W. (1992). Phonemic awareness helps beginning readers break the code. *The Reading Teacher, 45,* 516–523.

Groff, P. J. (1984). Resolving the letter name controversy. *The Reading Teacher, 37*(4), 384–389.

Groom (1986). *Forrest Gump.* New York: Pocket Books.

Gross, A. D. (1978). The relationship between sex differences and reading ability in an Israeli kibbutz system. In D. Feitelson (Ed.), *Cross-cultural perspectives on reading and reading research* (pp. 72–88). Newark, DE: International Reading Association.

Guilfoile, E. (1957). *Nobody listens to Andrew*. Cleveland, OH: Modern Curriculum Press.

Gunderson, L. (1991). *ESL literacy instruction: A guidebook to theory and practice*. Englewood Cliffs, NJ: Prentice Hall.

Guszak, F. J. (1967). Teacher questioning and reading. *The Reading Teacher, 21,* 227–234.

Guthrie, J. T. (1982). Effective teching practices. *The Reading Teacher, 35*(7), 766–768.

Guthrie, J. T., Seifert, M., Burnham, N. A., & Caplan, R. J. (1974). The maze technique to assess and monitor reading comprehension. *The Reading Teacher, 28*(2), 161–168.

Gwynne, F. (1970). *A chocolate moose for dinner*. New York: Windmill Books.

Gwynne, F. (1976). *The king who rained*. New York: Windmill Books.

Hagerty, P. (1992). *Reader's workshop: Real reading*. New York: Scholastic.

Haggard, M. R. (1986). The vocabulary self-collection strategy: Using student interest and world knowledge to enhance vocabulary growth. *Journal of Reading, 29*(7), 634–642.

Hall, M. A. (1978). *The language experience approach for teaching reading: A research perspective*. Newark, DE: International Reading Association.

Hall, M. A. (1981). *Teaching reading as a language experience* (3rd ed.). Englewood Cliffs, NJ: Merrill/Prentice Hall.

Hall, N. (1987). *The emergence of literacy*. Portsmouth, NH: Heinemann.

Hall, R. (1984). *Sniglets*. Englewood Cliffs, NJ: Merrill/Prentice Hall.

Haller, E. J., & Waterman, M. (1985). The criteria of reading group assignments. *The Reading Teacher, 38,* 772–781.

Halliday, M. A. K. (1975). *Learning how to mean: Explorations in the development of language*. London: Edward Arnold.

Hallinan, M. T., & Sorensen, A. B. (1985). Ability grouping and student friendships. *American Educational Research Journal, 22,* 485–499.

Hammill, D., & Larsen, S. C. (1974). The relationship of selected auditory perceptual skills and reading ability. *Journal of Learning Disabilities, 7,* 429–435.

Hansen, J. (1987). *When writers read*. Portsmouth, NH: Heinemann.

Harp, B. (1988). When the principal asks: "Why are your kids singing during reading time?" *The Reading Teacher, 41*(4), 454–457.

Harp, B. (1989a). What do we do in the place of ability grouping? *The Reading Teacher, 42,* 534–535.

Harp, B. (1989b). When the principal asks: "Why don't you ask comprehension questions?" *The Reading Teacher, 42*(8), 638–639.

Harris, A. J., & Sipay, E. R. (1990). *How to increase reading ability* (9th ed.). New York: Longman.

Harris, T., et al. (1975). *Keys to reading*. Oklahoma City: Economy Co.

Harris, T. L., & Hodges, R. E. (Eds.). (1981). *A dictionary of reading and related terms*. Newark, DE: International Reading Association.

Harste, J. C., & Burke, C. L. (1977). A new hypothesis for reading teacher research: Both the teaching and learning of reading are theoretically based. In Pearson, D. P. (Ed.). *Reading: Theory, research, and practice* (pp. 32–40). Clemson, SC: National Reading Conference.

Harste, J. C., Short, K. G., & Burke, C. (1988). *Creating classrooms for authors: The reading writing connection*. Portsmouth, NH: Heinemann.

Harste, J. C., Woodward, V. A., & Burke, C. L. (1984). *Language stories and literacy lessons*. Portsmouth, NH: Heinemann.

Hasbrouck, J. E., & Tindal, G. (1992). Curriculum-based oral reading fluency for students in grades 2 through 5. *Teaching Exceptional Children, 24*(3), 41–44.

Hawking, S. W. (1988). *A brief history of time: From the big bang to black holes*. Toronto: Bantam.

Heald-Taylor, G. (1989). *The administrator's guide to whole language*. Katona, NY: Richard C. Owen.

Heald-Taylor, G. (1991). *Whole language strategies for ESL students*. San Diego, CA: Dominie Press.

Heath. (no date). *Quill* [computer program]. Lexington, MA: D. C. Heath.

Heathington, B. S. (1990). Test review: Concepts about print test. In R. B. Cooter (Ed.), *The teacher's guide to reading tests* (pp. 110–114). Scottsdale, AZ: Gorsuch Scarisbrick.

Heide, F. P., & Gilliland, J. H. (1990). *Day of Ahmed's secret*. New York: Lothrop, Lee & Shepard Books.

Heilman, A. W., Blair, T. R., & Rupley, W. H. (1990). *Principles and practices of teaching reading*. Englewood Cliffs, NJ: Merrill/Prentice Hall.

Henk, W. A., & Holmes, B. C. (1988). Effects of content-related attitude on the comprehension and retention of expository text. *Reading Psychology, 9*(3), 203–225.

Hennings, K. (1974). Drama reading, an on-going classroom activity at the elementary school level. *Elementary English, 51,* 48–51.

Henwood, C. (1988). *Frogs* (Barrie Watts, Photographer). London, NY: Franklin Watts.

Herber, H. L. (1978). *Teaching reading in the content areas* (2nd ed.). Englewood Cliffs, NJ: Prentice Hall.

Heymsfeld, C. R. (1989, March). Filling the hole in whole language. *Educational Leadership,* pp. 65–68.

Hiebert, E. (1978). Preschool children's understanding of written language. *Child Development, 49,* 1231–1241.

Hiebert, E. (1981). Developmental patterns and interrelationships of preschool children's print awareness. *Reading Research Quarterly, 16,* 236–260.

Hiebert, E. H. (1983). An examination of ability grouping for reading instruction. *Reading Research Quarterly, 18,* 231–255.

Hiebert, E. H., & Colt, J. (1989). Patterns of literature-based reading. *The Reading Teacher, 43*(1), 14–20.

Hiebert, E., & Ham, D. (1981). *Young children and environmental print.* Paper presented at the annual meeting of the National Reading Conference, Dallas, TX.

Hill, B., & Ruptic, C. (1994). *Practical aspects of authentic assessment: Putting the pieces together.* Norwood, MA: Christopher-Gordon.

Hill, S. (1990a). *Raps and rhymes.* Armadale, Victoria, Australia: Eleanor Curtain.

Hill, S. (1990b). *Readers theatre: Performing the text.* Armadale, Victoria, Australia: Eleanor Curtain.

Hirsch, E. D. (1987). *Cultural literacy: What every American needs to know.* Boston: Houghton Mifflin.

Hirschfelder, A. B., & Singer, B. R. (1992). *Rising voices: Writing of young Native Americans.* New York: Scribner's.

Hoffman, J. V. (1987). Rethinking the role of oral reading in basal instruction. *The Elementary School Journal, 87*(3), 367–374.

Hoffman, J. V., & Segel, K. W. (1982). *Oral reading instruction: A century of controversy.* (ERIC Document Reproduction Service No. ED 239 277)

Hoffman, M. (1991). *Amazing grace.* New York: Dial Books for Young Readers.

Holdaway, D. (1979). *The foundations of literacy.* New York: Ashton Scholastic.

Holdaway, D. (1981). Shared book experience: Teaching reading using favorite books. *Theory Into Practice, 21,* 293–300.

Holdaway, D. (1984). *Stability and change in literacy learning.* Portsmouth, NH: Heinemann.

Holland, N. (1975). *Five readers reading.* New Haven, CT: Yale University Press.

Hollingsworth, P. H. (1978). An experimental approach to the impress method of teaching reading. *The Reading Teacher, 31,* 624–626.

Hollingsworth, P. M., & Reutzel, D. R. (1988). Get a grip on comprehension. *Reading Horizons, 29*(1), 71–78.

Holmes, J. A. (1953). *The substrata-factor theory of reading.* Berkeley, CA: California Book.

Homan, S. P., Klesius, J. P., & Hite, C. (1993). Effects of repeated readings and nonrepetetive strategies on students' fluency and comprehension. *Journal of Educational Research, 87*(2), 94–99.

Hopkins, C. (1979). Using every-pupil response techniques in reading instruction. *The Reading Teacher, 33,* 173–175.

Hoskisson, K., & Tompkins, G. E. (1987). *Language arts: Content and teaching strategies.* Englewood Cliffs, NJ: Merrill/Prentice Hall.

Houston, J. (1977). *Frozen fire.* New York: Atheneum.

Huck, C. S., Helper, S., & Hickman, J. (1987). *Children's literature in the elementary school.* New York: Holt, Rinehart & Winston.

Hughes, T. O. (1975). *Sentence-combining: A means of increasing reading comprehension.* Kalamazoo: Western Michigan University, Department of English.

Hull, M. A. (1989). *Phonics for the teacher of reading.* Englewood Cliffs, NJ: Merrill/Prentice Hall.

Hunt, L. C. (1970). Effect of self-selection, interest, and motivation upon independent, instructional, and frustrational levels. *Reading Teacher, 24,* 146–151.

Hunter, M. (1984). Knowing, teaching and supervising. In P. L. Hosford (Ed.), *Using what we know about teaching.* Alexandria, VA: Association for Supervision and Curriculum Development.

Hymes, D. (Ed.). (1964). *Language in culture and society.* New York: HarperCollins.

Jachym, N. K., Allington, R. L., & Broikou, K. A. (1989). Estimating the cost of seatwork. *The Reading Teacher, 43,* 30–37.

Jacobs, H. H., & Borland, J. H. (1986). The interdisciplinary concept model: Theory and practice. *Gifted Child Quarterly, 30*(4), 159–163.

Jaffe, N. (1993). *The uninvited guest and other Jewish holiday tales.* New York: Scholastic.

Jenkins, R. (1990). *Whole language in Australia.* Scholastic Co. workshop at Brigham Young University, Provo, UT.

Jobe, F. W. (1976). *Screening vision in schools.* Newark, DE: International Reading Association.

Johns, J. L. (1980). First graders' concepts about print. *Reading Research Quarterly, 15,* 529–549.

Johns, J. L. (1986). Students: Perceptions of reading: Thirty years of inquiry. In D. B. Yaden, Jr. & S. Templeton (Eds.), *Awareness and beginning literacy: Conceptualizing what it means to read and write* (pp. 31–40). Portsmouth, NH: Heinemann Educational Books.

Johns, J. L., & Ellis, D. W. (1976). Reading: Children tell it like it is. *Reading World, 16,* 115–128.

Johns, J. L., & Johns, A. L. (1971). How do children in the elementary school view the reading process? *The Michigan Reading Journal, 5,* 44–53.

Johns, J. L., & Lunn, M. K. (1983). The informal reading inventory: 1910–1980. *Reading World, 23*(1), 8–18.

Johnson, D. (1989). *Pressing problems in world literacy: The plight of the homeless.* Paper presented at the 23rd annual meeting of the Utah Council of the International Reading Association, Salt Lake City, UT.

Johnson, D. D. (1973). Sex differences in reading across cultures. *Reading Research Quarterly, 9*(1), 67–86.

Johnson, D. D., & Baumann, J. F. (1984). Word identification. In P.D. Pearson (Ed.), *Handbook of reading research* (pp. 583–608). New York: Longman.

Johnson, D. D., & Pearson, P. D. (1975). Skills management systems: A critique. *The Reading Teacher, 28,* 757–764.

Johnson, D. D., & Pearson, P. D. (1984). *Teaching reading vocabulary.* New York: Holt, Rinehart & Winston.

Johnson, D. W. (1976). *Jack and the beanstalk* (D. William Johnson, Illustrator). Boston: Little, Brown.

Johnson, D. W., Maruyama, G., Johnson, R. T., Nelson, D., & Skon, L. (1981). Effects of cooperative, competitive and individualistic goal structures on achievement: A meta-analysis. *Psychological Bulletin, 89,* 47–62.

Johnson, T. D., & Louis, D. R. (1987). *Literacy through literature.* Portsmouth, NH: Heinemann Educational Books.

Jones, M. B., & Nessel, D. D. (1985). Enhancing the curriculum with experience stories. *The Reading Teacher, 39,* 18423.

Jongsma, K. S. (1989). Questions & answers: Portfolio assessment. *The Reading Teacher, 43*(3), 264–265.

Jongsma, K. S. (1990). Collaborative Learning (Questions and Answers). *The Reading Teacher, 43*(4), 346–347.

Joseph, D. G., Flynt, E. S., & Cooter, R. B. (1987, March). *Diagnosis and correction of reading difficulties: A new model.* Paper presented at the National Association of School Psychologists annual convention, New Orleans, LA.

Juster, N. (1961). *The phantom tollbooth.* Random House.

Kagan, J. (1966). Reflection-impulsivity: The generality and dynamics of conceptual tempo. *Journal of Abnormal Psychology, 71,* 17–24.

Karlsen, B., & Gardner, E. F. (1984). *Stanford diagnostic reading test* (3rd ed.). New York: Harcourt Brace.

Kaufman, A., & Kaufman, N. (1985). *Kaufman test of educational achievement.* Circle Pines, MN: American Guidance Service.

Kearsley, R. (1973). The newborn's response to auditory stimulation: A demonstration of orienting and defensive behavior. *Child Development, 44,* 582–590.

Keegan, M. (1991). *Pueblo boy: Growing up in two worlds.* New York: Cobblehill Books.

Keith, S. (1981). *Politics of textbook selection* (Research report No. 81-AT). Stanford, CA: Stanford University School of Education, Institute for Research on School Finance and Governance.

Kemp, M. (1987). *Watching children read and write.* Portsmouth, NH: Heinemann.

Kessen, W., Levine, J., & Wendrich, K. (1979). The imitation of pitch in infants. *Infant Behavior and Development, 2,* 93–100.

Killilea, M. (1954). *Karen.* New York: Dodd, Mead.

Kirsch, I. S., Jungeblut, A, Jenkins, L., & Kolstad, A. (1993). *Adult literacy in America: A first look at the results of the national adult literacy survey.* Washington, DC: National Center for Educational Statistics.

Klare, G. R. (1963). Assessing readability. *Reading Research Quarterly, 10,* 62–102.

Koskinen, P., Wilson, R., & Jensema, C. (1985). Closed-captioned television: A new tool for reading instruction. *Reading World, 24,* 1–7.

Kownslar, A. O. (1977). *People and our world: A study of world history.* New York: Holt, Rinehart & Winston.

Kozol, J. (1985). *Illiterate America.* New York: New American Library.

Krashen, S., & Biber, D. (1988). *On course.* Sacramento, CA: CABE.

Krauss, R. (1945). *The carrot seed* (Crockett Johnson, Illustrator). New York: Scholastic.

Kuchinskas, G., & Radencich, M. C. (1986). *The semantic mapper.* Gainesville, FL: Teacher Support Software.

Kulik, C. C., & Kulik, J. A. (1982). Effects of ability grouping on secondary students: A meta-analysis of evaluation findings. *American Educational Research Journal, 19,* 415–428.

LaBerge, D., & Samuels, S. J. (1974). Toward a theory of automatic information processing in reading. *Cognitive Psychology, 6,* 293–323.

LaBerge, D., & Samuels, S. J. (1985). Toward a theory of automatic information processing in reading. In H. Singer & R. B. Ruddell (Eds.), *Theoretical models and processes of reading* (pp. 689–718). Newark, DE: International Reading Association.

Lamme, L. L., & Hysmith (1991). One school's adventure into portfolio assessment. *Language Arts, 68,* 629–640.

Lamoreaux, L., & Lee, D. M. (1943). *Learning to read through experience.* New York: Appleton-Century-Crofts.

Langer, J. (1981). From theory to practice: A prereading plan. *Journal of Reading, 25,* 152–156.

Langer, J. A. (1984). Examining background knowledge and text comprehension. *Reading Research Quarterly, 19,* 468–481.

Langer, P., Kalk, J. M., & Searls, D. T. (1984). Age of admission and trends in achievement: A comparison of blacks and Caucasians. *American Educational Research Journal, 21,* 61–78.

Larsen, N. (1994). *The publisher's chopping block: What happens to children's trade books when they are published in a basal reading series?* Unpublished master's project, Brigham Young University.

Lass, B., & Davis, B. (1985). *The remedial reading handbook.* Englewood Cliffs, NJ: Prentice-Hall.

Lathlaen, P. (1993). A meeting of minds: Teaching using biographies. *The Reading Teacher, 46*(6), 529–531.

Law, B., & Eckes, M. (1990). *The more than just surviving handbook: ESL for every classroom teacher.* Winnipeg, Canada: Peguis.

Leinhardt, G., Zigmond, N., & Cooley, W. (1981). Reading instruction and its effects. *American Educational Research Journal, 18,* 343–361.

L'Engle, M. (1962). *A wrinkle in time.* New York: Dell.

Lenneberg, E. H. (1964). *New directions in the study of language.* Cambridge, MA: MIT Press.

Levin, J. R., Johnson, D. D., Pittelman, S. D., Levin, K., Shriberg, L. K., Toms-Bronowski, S., & Hayes, B. (1984).

A comparison of semantic- and mnemonic-based vocabulary-learning strategies. *Reading Psychology, 5,* 1–15.

Levin, J. R., Levin, M. E., Glasman, L. D., & Nordwall, M. B. (1992). Mnemonic vocabulary instruction: Additional effectiveness evidence. *Contemporary Educational Psychology, 17,* 156–174.

Levine, S. S. (1976). *The effect of transformational sentence-combining exercises on the reading comprehension and written composition of third-grade children.* Unpublished doctoral dissertation, Hofstra University.

Lewis, C. S. (1961). *The lion, the witch, and the wardrobe.* New York: Macmillan.

Liberman, I. Y., Shankweiler, D., Liberman, A., Fowler, C., & Fischer, F. (1977). Phonetic segmentation and decoding in the beginning reader. In A. S. Reber & D. L. Scarborough (Eds.), *Toward a psychology of reading* (pp. 207–225). Hillsdale, NJ: Erlbaum.

Lima, C., & Lima, J. (1993). *A to zoo: A subject access to children's picture books.* New York: Bowker.

Lindsay, P. H., & Norman, D. A. (1977). *Human information processing: An introduction to psychology.* New York: Academic Press.

Lipson, M. Y. (1983). The influence of religious affiliation on children's memory for text information. *Reading Research Quarterly, 18*(4), 448–457.

Lipson, M. Y. (1984). Some unexpected issues in prior knowledge and comprehension. *The Reading Teacher, 37*(8), 760–764.

Lisle, J. T. (1989). *Afternoon of the elves.* New York: Franklin Watts.

The little red hen. (1985). L. McQueen, Illustrator. New York: Scholastic.

Littlejohn, C. (1988). *The lion and the mouse.* New York: Dial Books for Young Readers.

Livingston, N., & Birrell, J. R. (1994). Learning about cultural diversity through literature. *BYU Children's Book Review, 54*(5), 1–6.

Lobel, A. (1981). *On Market Street* (Pictures by Anita Lobel). New York: Scholastic.

Lobel, A. (1983). *Fables.* New York: Harper & Row.

Lock, S. (1980). *Hubert hunts his hum* (J. Newnham, Illustrator). Sydney, Australia: Ashton Scholastic.

Lomax, R. G., & McGee, L. M. (1987). Young children's concepts about print and reading: Toward a model of word reading acquisition. *Reading Research Quarterly, 22*(2), 237–256.

Loughlin, C. E., & Martin, M. D. (1987). *Supporting literacy: Developing effective learning environments.* New York: Teachers College Columbia Press.

Lowery, L. F., & Grafft, W. (1967). Paperback books and reading attitudes. *The Reading Teacher, 21*(7), 618–623.

Lyman, F. (1988). Think-Pair-Share, Wait time two, and on. . . . *Mid-Atlantic Association for Cooperation in Education Cooperative News, 2,* 1.

Lyon, R. (1977). Auditory-perceptual training: The state of the art. *Journal of Learning Disabilities, 10,* 564–572.

MacGinitie, W. H. (1969). Evaluating readiness for learning to read: A critical review and evaluation of research. *Reading Research Quarterly, 4,* 396–410.

MacGinitie, W. H., & MacGinitie, R. K. (1989). *Gates-MacGinitie reading tests, third edition.* Chicago: Riverside.

Macmillan/McGraw-Hill. (1993). *Macmillan/McGraw-Hill reading/language: A new view.* New York: Author.

Manarino-Leggett, P., & Salomon, P. A. (1989, April–May). *Cooperation vs. competition: Techniques for keeping your classroom alive but not endangered.* Paper presented at the thirty-fourth annual convention of the International Reading Association, New Orleans, LA.

Mandler, J. M., & Johnson, N. S. (1977). Remembrance of things parsed: Story structure and recall. *Cognitive Psychology, 9,* 111–151.

Manzo, A. V. (1969). The request procedure. *The Journal of Reading, 13,* 123–126.

Manzo, A. V., & Casale, U. P. (1985). Listen-read-discuss: A content reading heuristic. *Journal of Reading, 28,* 732–734.

Manzo, A. V., & Manzo, U. C. (1990). *Content area reading: A heuristic approach.* Englewood Cliffs, NJ: Merrill/Prentice Hall.

Marchionini, G. (1988). Hypermedia and learning: Freedom and chaos. *Educational Technology, 28,* 8–12.

Martin, B. (1983). *Brown Bear, Brown Bear, What do you see?* New York: Henry Holt.

Martin, B., & Archaumbalt, J. (1987). *Knots on a counting rope.* New York: Holt, Rinehart & Winston.

Martin, J. H. (1987). *Writing to read* [Computer program]. Boca Raton, FL: IBM.

Martinez, M. (1993). Motivating dramatic story reenactments. *The Reading Teacher, 46*(8), 682–688.

Martinez, M., & Nash, M. F. (1990). Bookalogues: Talking about children's literature. *Language Arts, 67,* 576–580.

Martorella, P. H. (1985). *Elementary social studies.* Boston: Little, Brown.

Marzano, R. J. (1993–1994). When two world views collide. *Educational Leadership, 51*(4), 6–11.

Marzollo, J., & Marzollo, C. (1982). *Jed's junior space patrol: A science fiction easy to read.* New York: Dial.

Mason, J. (1983). An examination of reading instruction in third and fourth grades. *The Reading Teacher, 36*(9), 906–913.

Mason, J. M. (1980). When do children begin to read: An exploration of four-year-old children's letter and word reading competencies. *Reading Research Quarterly, 15,* 203–227.

Masonheimer, P. E., Drum, P. A., & Ehri, L. C. (1984). Does environmental print identification lead children into word reading? *Journal of Reading Behavior, 16,* 257–271.

Math, I. (1981). *Wires and watts: Understanding and using electricity.* New York: Charles Scribner's Sons.

Mathes, P. G., Simmons, D. C., & Davis, B. I. (1992). Assisted reading techniques for developing reading fluency. *Reading Research and Instruction, 31*(4), 70–77.

Mathewson, G. C. (1985). Toward a comprehensive model of affect in the reading process. In H. Singer & R. B. Ruddell (Eds.), *Theoretical models and processes of reading* (3rd ed., pp. 841–856). Newark, DE: International Reading Association.

Mathewson, G. C. (1994). Model of attitude influence upon reading and learning to read. In H. Singer & R. B. Ruddell (Eds.), *Theoretical models and processes of reading* (4th ed., pp. 1131–1161). Newark, DE: International Reading Association.

Maxim, G. (1989). *The very young: Guiding children from infancy through the early years* (3rd ed.). Englewood Cliffs, NJ: Merrill/Prentice Hall.

May, F. B., & Elliot, S. B. (1978). *To help children read: Mastery performance modules for teachers in training* (2nd ed.). Englewood Cliffs, NJ: Merrill/Prentice Hall.

Mayer, M. (1976). *Ah-choo.* New York: Dial Books.

Mayer, M. (1976). *Hiccup.* New York: Dial Books.

McCallum, R. D. (1988). Don't throw the basals out with the bath water. *The Reading Teacher, 42,* 204–209.

McCormick, C. E., & Mason, J. (1986). Intervention procedures for increasing preschool children's interest in and knowledge about reading. In W. H. Teale & E. Sulzby (Eds.), *Emergent literacy: Writing and reading* (pp. 90–115). Norwood, NJ: Ablex Publishing.

McCormick, S. (1995). *Instructing students who have literacy problems.* Englewood Cliffs, NJ: Merrill/Prentice Hall.

McCracken, R. A., & McCracken, M. J. (1978). Modeling is the key to sustained reading. *Reading Teacher, 31,* 406–408.

McDermott, G. (1993). *Raven: Trickster tale from the Pacific Northwest.* San Diego, CA: Harcourt Brace.

McGee, L. M., Lomax, R. G., & Head, M. H. (1988). Young children's written language knowledge: What environmental and functional print reading reveals. *Journal of Reading Behavior, 20*(2), 99–118.

McGee, L. M., Ratliff, J. L., Sinex, A., Head, M., & LaCroix, K. (1984). Influence of story schema and concept of story on children's story compositions. In J. A. Niles & L. A. Harris (Eds.), *Thirty-third yearbook of the National Reading Conference* (pp. 270–277). Rochester, NY: National Reading Conference.

McGee, L. M., & Richgels, D. J. (1990). *Literacy's beginnings: Supporting young readers and writers.* Boston: Allyn & Bacon.

McGuire, F. N. (1984). How arts instruction affects reading and language: Theory and research. *The Reading Teacher, 37*(9), 835–839.

McInnes, J. (1983). *Networks.* Toronto, Canada: Nelson of Canada.

McKee, D. (1990). *Elmer.* London: Red Fox.

McKeown, M. G., & Beck, I. L. (1988). Learning vocabulary: Different ways for different goals. *Remedial and Special Education, 9*(1), 42–52.

McKissack, P. C. (1986). *Flossie & the fox.* New York: Dial Books for Young Readers.

McKuen, R. (1990). Ten books on CD ROM. *MacWorld, 7*(12), 217–218.

McNeil, J. D. (1987). *Reading comprehension* (2nd ed.). Glenview, IL: Scott, Foresman.

McTighe, J., & Lyman, F. T. (1988). Cueing thinking the classroom: The promise of theory-embedded tools. *Educational Leadership, 45*(7), 18–24.

Meade, E. L. (1973). The first R—A point of view. *Reading World, 12,* 169–180.

MECC. (1984). *Writing a narrative* [computer program]. St. Paul, MN: Minnesota Educational Computing Consortium (MECC).

Menyuk, P. (1988). *Language development knowledge and use.* Glenview, IL: Scott, Foresman/Little, Brown College Division.

Merrill Mathematics (Grade 5). (1985). Englewood Cliffs, NJ: Merrill/Prentice Hall.

Merrill Science (Grade 3). (1989). Englewood Cliffs, NJ: Merrill/Prentice Hall.

Meyer, B., Brandt, D., & Bluth, G. (1980). Use of top-level structure in text for reading comprehension of ninth-grade students. *Reading Research Quarterly, 16,* 72–103.

Meyer, B. J. (1979). Organizational patterns in prose and their use in reading. In M. L. Kamil & A. J. Moe (Eds.), *Reading research: Studies and applications* (pp. 109–117). Twenty-eighth Yearbook of the National Reading Conference.

Meyer, B. J. F., & Freedle, R. O. (1984). Effects of discourse type on recall. *American Educational Research Journal, 21*(1), 121–143.

Mezynski, K. (1983). Issues concerning the acquisition of knowledge: Effects of vocabulary training on reading comprehension. *Review of Educational Research, 53*(2), 253–279.

Miller, B. F., Rosenberg, E. B., & Stackowski, B. L. (1971). *Investigating your health.* Boston: Houghton Mifflin.

Mindplay. (1990). *Author! Author!* Danvers, MA: Methods and Solutions.

Moe, A. J., & Irwin, J. W. (1986). Cohesion, coherence, and comprehension. In J. W. Irwin (Ed.), *Understanding and teaching cohesion comprehension* (pp. 3–8). Newark, DE: International Reading Association.

Moffett, J. (1983). *Teaching the universe of discourse.* Boston: Houghton Mifflin.

Moffett, J., & Wagner, B. J. (1976). *Student-centered language arts and reading K–13. A handbook for teachers* (2nd ed.). Boston: Houghton Mifflin.

Monjo, F. N. (1970). *The drinking gourd.* New York: HarperCollins.

Mooney, M. E. (1990). *Reading to, with, and by children.* Katonah, NY: Richard C. Owens.

Moore, M. A. (1991). Electronic dialoguing: An avenue to literacy. *The Reading Teacher, 45*(4), 280–286.

Morphett, M. V., & Washburne, C. (1931). When should children begin to read? *Elementary School Journal, 31,* 496–503.

Morrow, L. M. (1984). Reading stories to young children: Effects of story structure and traditional questioning strategies on comprehension. *Journal of Reading Behavior, 16,* 273–288.

Morrow, L. M. (1985). Retelling stories: A strategy for improving children's comprehension, concept of story structure and oral language complexity. *Elementary School Journal, 85,* 647–661.

Morrow, L. M. (1988a). Retelling as a diagnostic tool. In S. M. Glazer, L. W. Searfoss, & L. Gentile (Eds.), *Re-examining reading diagnosis: New trends and procedures in classrooms and clinics* (pp. 128–149). Newark, DE: International Reading Association.

Morrow, L. M. (1988b). Young children's responses to one-to-one story reading in school settings. *The Reading Teacher, 23*(1), 89–107.

Morrow, L. M. (1989). *Literacy development in the early years: Helping children read and write.* Englewood Cliffs, NJ: Prentice Hall.

Morrow, L. M. (1993). *Literacy development in the early years: Helping children read and write* (2nd ed). Needham Heights, MA: Allyn & Bacon.

Morrow, L. M., & Rand, M. K. (1991). Promoting literacy during play by designing early childhood classroom environments. *The Reading Teacher, 44*(6), 396–402.

Mosenthal, P. B. (1989a). From random events to predictive reading models. *The Reading Teacher, 42*(7), 524–525.

Mosenthal, P. B. (1989b). The whole language approach: Teachers between a rock and a hard place. *The Reading Teacher, 42*(8), 628–629.

Mullis, I. V. S., Campbell, J. R., & Farstrup, A. E. (Eds.). (1993). *NAEP 1992 reading report card for the nation and the states* (Report No. 23-ST06). Washington, DC: National Center for Education Statistics, USDOE.

Munsch, R. (1980). *The paper bag princess.* Toronto, Canada: Annick Press.

Muth, K. D. (1989). *Children's comprehension of text: Research into practice.* Newark, DE: International Reading Association.

Myers, W. D. (1975). *Fast Sam, Cool Clyde, and Stuff.* New York: Puffin Books.

Nagy, W. (1988). *Teaching vocabulary to improve reading comprehension.* Unpublished manuscript, Champaign, IL: Center for the Study of Reading.

Nagy, W. E., & Anderson, R. C. (1984). How many words are there in printed school English? *Reading Research Quarterly, 19*(3), 304–330.

Naiden, N. (1976). Ratio of boys to girls among disabled readers. *The Reading Teacher, 29*(6), 439–442.

Namioka, L. (1992). *Yang the youngest and his terrible ear.* Boston: Little, Brown.

Nash, B., & Nash, G. (1980). *Pundles.* New York: Stone Song Press.

Naslund, J. C., & Samuel, J. S. (1992). Automatic access to word sounds and meaning in decoding written text. *Reading and Writing Quarterly, 8*(2), 135–156.

National Assessment of Educational Progress. (1990). *Learning to read in our nation's schools: Instruction and achievement in 1988 at grades 4, 8, and 12.* Princeton, NJ: Author.

National Association for the Education of Young Children. (1986). Position statement on developmentally appropriate practice in programs for 4- and 5-year-olds. *Young Children, 41*(6), 20–29.

Nelson, T. (1988, January). Managing immense storage. *Byte,* 225–238.

Neuman, S., & Koskinen, P. (1992). Captioned television as comprehensible input: Effects of incidental word learning from context for language minority students. *Reading Research Quarterly, 27*(3), 94–106.

Neuman, S., & Roskos, K. (1992). Literacy objects as cultural tools: Effects on children's literacy behaviors in play. *Reading Research Quarterly, 27*(3), 203–225.

Neuman, S. B. (1981). Effect of teaching auditory perceptual skill on reading achievement in first grade. *The Reading Teacher, 34,* 422–426.

Neuman, S. B., & Roskos, K. (1990). Play, print, and purpose: Enriching play environments for literacy development. *The Reading Teacher, 44*(3), 214–221.

Neuman, S. B., & Roskos, K. (1993). *Language and literacy learning in the early years: An integrated approach.* New York: Harcourt, Brace.

Newman, J. M. (1985a). Yes, that's an interesting idea, but. . . . In J. M. Newman (Ed.), *Whole language theory in use* (pp. 181–186). Portsmouth, NH: Heinemann.

Newman, J. M. (Ed.). (1985b). *Whole language: Theory in use.* Portsmouth, NH: Heinemann.

Newman, J. M., & Church, S. M. (1990). Commentary: Myths of whole language. *The Reading Teacher, 44*(1), 20–26.

Nichols, J. (1980). Using paragraph frames to help remedial high school students with written assignments. *Journal of Reading, 24,* 228–231.

Nist, S. L., & Simpson, M. L. (1993). *Developing vocabulary concepts for college thinking.* Lexington, MA: Heath.

Nolan, E. A., & Berry, M. (1993). Learning to listen. *The Reading Teacher, 46*(7), 606–608.

Nordquist, V. M., & Twardosz, S. (1990). Preventing behavior problems in early childhood special education classrooms through environmental organization. *Education and Treatment of Children, 13(4),* 274–287.

Norton, D. E. (1993). *The effective teaching of language arts* (4th ed.). Englewood Cliffs, NJ: Merrill/Prentice Hall.

Norton, D. E. (1995). *Through the eyes of a child: An introduction to children's literature* (4th ed.). Englewood Cliffs, NJ: Merrill/Prentice Hall.

Numeroff, L. J. (1985). *If you give a mouse a cookie.* New York: Scholastic.

Nurss, J. R., Hough, R. A., & Goodson, M. S. (1981). Pre-reading/language development in two day care centers. *Journal of Reading Behavior, 13,* 23–31.

Oakes, J. (1992). Can tracking research inform practice? *Educational Researcher, 21*(4), 12–21.

O'Bruba, W. S. (1987). Reading through the creative arts. *Reading Horizons, 27*(3), 170–177.

Ogle, D. M. (1986). K-W-L: A teaching model that develops active reading of expository text. *The Reading Teacher, 39*(6), 564–570.

Ohanian, S. (1984). Hot new item or same old stew? *Classroom Computer Learning, 5,* 30–31.

O'Huigin, S. (1988). *Scary poems for rotten kids.* New York: Firefly Books.

Olson, M. W., & Gee, T. C. (1988). Understanding narratives: A review of story grammar research. *Childhood Education, 64*(4), 302–306.

Olson, M. W., & Longnion, B. (1982). Pattern guides: A workable alternative for content teachers. *Journal of Reading, 25,* 736–741.

Osborn, J. (1984). The purposes, uses, and contents of workbooks and some guidelines for publishers. In R. C. Anderson, J. Osborn, & R. J. Tierney (Eds.), *Learning to read in American schools* (pp. 45–112). Hillsdale, NJ: Erlbaum.

Osborn, J. (1985). Workbooks: Counting, matching, and judging. In J. Osborn, P. T. Wilson, & R. C. Anderson (Eds.), *Reading education: Foundations for a literate America* (pp. 11–28). Lexington, MA: Lexington Books.

Otto, J. (1982). The new debate in reading. *The Reading Teacher, 36*(1), 14–18.

Palincsar, A., & Brown, A. (1985). Reciprocal teaching: A means to a meaningful end. In Osborn, J., Wilson, P. T., & Anderson, R. C. (Eds.), *Reading education: Foundations for a Literate America* (pp. 299–310). Lexington, MA: D. C. Heath.

Pankake, M., & Pankake, J. (1988). *A Prairie Home Companion folk song book.* New York: Viking.

Pappas, C. C., Kiefer, B. Z., & Levstik, L. S. (1990). *An integrated language perspective in the elementary school.* New York: Longman.

Paradis, E., & Peterson, J. (1975). Readiness training implications from research. *The Reading Teacher, 28*(5), 445–448.

Paradis, E. E. (1974). The appropriateness of visual discrimination exercises in reading readiness materials. *Journal of Educational Research, 67,* 276–278.

Paradis, E. E. (1984). *Comprehension: thematic units* [videotape]. University of Wyoming, Laramie.

Paris, S. G., Lipson, M. Y., & Wixson, K. K. (1983). Issues concerning the acquisition of knowledge: Effects of vocabulary training on reading comprehension. *Review of Educational Research, 53,* 293–316.

Parish, P. (1963). *Amelia Bedelia.* New York: HarperCollins.

Parker, A., & Paradis, E. (1986). Attitude development toward reading in grades one through six. *Journal of Educational Research, 79*(5), 313–315.

Parsons, L. (1990). *Response journals.* Portsmouth, NH: Heinemann.

Paterson, K. (1977). *Bridge to Terabithia.* New York: Thomas Y. Crowell.

Pearson, P. D. (1974). The effects of grammatical complexity on children's comprehension, recall, and conception of certain semantic relations. *Reading Research Quarterly, 10*(2), 155–192.

Pearson, P. D. (1985). Changing the face of reading comprehension instruction. *The Reading Teacher, 38*(8), 724–738.

Pearson, P. D. (1989a). *Improving national reading assessment: The key to improved reading instruction.* Paper presented at the 1989 annual reading conference of the Utah Council of the International Reading Association, Salt Lake City, UT.

Pearson, P. D. (1989b). Reading the whole language movement. *Elementary School Journal, 90*(2), 231–242.

Pearson, P. D. (1989c). Whole language. *The Elementary School Journal, 90*(2), 231–242.

Pearson, P. D., & Fielding, L. (1982). Listening comprehension. *Language Arts, 59*(6), 617–629.

Pearson, P. D., & Gallagher, M. C. (1983). The instruction of reading comprehension. *Contemporary Educational Psychology, 8*(3), 317–344.

Pearson, P. D., Hansen, J., & Gordon, C. (1979). The effect of background knowledge on children's comprehension of implicit and explicit information. *Journal of Reading Behavior, 11*(3), 201–209.

Pearson, P. D., & Johnson, D. D. (1978). *Teaching reading comprehension.* New York: Holt, Rinehart & Winston.

Peregoy, S. F., & Boyle, O. F. (1993). *Reading, writing, and learning in ESL.* New York: Longman.

Perez, S. A. (1983). Teaching writing from the inside: Teachers as writers. *Language Arts, 60*(7), 847–850.

Perfetti, C. A., & Lesgold, A. M. (1977). Discourse comprehension and sources of individual differences. In M. A. Just & P. A. Carpenter (Eds.), *Cognitive processes in comprehension* (pp. 141–184). Hillsdale, NJ: Erlbaum.

Peterson, B. (1991). Selecting books for beginning readers. In D. E. DeFord, C. A. Lyons, & G. S. Pinnell (Eds.), *Bridges to literacy: Learning from reading recovery* (pp. 119–147). Portsmouth, NH: Heinemann.

Peterson, R., & Eeds, M. (1990). *Grand conversations: Literature groups in action.* New York: Scholastic.

Pfeffer, S. B. (1989). *Future forward.* New York: Holt.

Piaget, J. (1955). *The language and thought of the child.* New York: World.

Pikulski, J. J. (1985). Questions and answers. *The Reading Teacher, 39*(1), 127–128.

Pinkney, A. D. (1993). *Alvin Ailey.* New York: Hyperion Books for Children.

Pinnell, G. S., Fried, M. D., & Estice, R. M. (1990). Reading recovery: Learning how to make a difference. *The Reading Teacher, 43,* 282–295.

Pinnell, G. S., Lyons, C. A., DeFord, D. E., Bryk, A. S., & Seltzer, M. (1994). Comparing instructional models for the literacy education of high-risk first graders. *Reading Research Quarterly, 29*(1), 8–39.

Pino, E. (1978). *Schools are out of proportion to man.* Seminar on discipline, Utah State University, Logan, UT.

Point/counterpoint. The value of basal readers. (1989, August–September). *Reading Today, 7,* 18.

Pollack, P. (1982). *Keeping it secret.* New York: Putnam.

Potter, B. (1903). *The tale of Peter Rabbit.* New York: F. Warne.

Powell, D. A. (1986). *Retrospective case studies of individual and group decision making in district-level elementary reading textbook selection.* Unpublished doctoral dissertation, Indiana University, Bloomington, IN.

Prelutsky, J. (1976). *Nightmares: Poems to trouble your sleep.* New York: Greenwillow Books.

Prelutsky, J. (1984). *The new kid on the block.* New York: Greenwillow Books.

Prelutsky, J. (1990). *Something big has been here.* New York: Greenwillow Books.

Prelutsky, J. (1991). *Poems for laughing out loud.* New York: Alfred A. Knopf.

Prince, A. T., & Mancus, D. S. (1987). Enriching comprehension: A schema altered basal reading lesson. *Reading Research and Instruction, 27,* 45–53.

Provensen, A., & Provensen, M. (1983). *The glorious flight: Across the channel with Louis Bleriot.* New York: Viking Penguin.

Puckett, M. B., & Black, J. K. (1994). *Authentic assessment of the young child.* Englewood Cliffs, NJ: Merrill/Prentice Hall.

Pulver, C. J. (1986). Teaching students to understand explicit and implicit connectives. In J. W. Irwin (Ed.), *Understanding and teaching cohesion comprehension* (pp. 3–8). Newark, DE: International Reading Association.

Ramirez, G., & Ramirez, J. L. (1994). *Multiethnic literature.* Albany, NY: Delmar.

Raphael, T. E. (1982). Question-answering strategies for children. *The Reading Teacher, 36,* 186–191.

Raphael, T. E. (1986). Teaching question answer relationships, revisited. *The Reading Teacher, 39*(6), 516–523.

Raphael, T. E., & Pearson, P. D. (1982). *The effect of metacognitive awareness training on children's question answering behavior* (Tech. Rep. No. 238). Urbana, IL: University of Illinois, Center for the Study of Reading.

Rasinski, T. V. (1990). Effects of repeated reading and listening-while-reading on reading fluency. *Journal of Educational Research, 83,* 147–150.

Rasinski, T. V., & Fredericks, A. D. (1988). Sharing literacy: Guiding principles and practices for parent involvement. *The Reading Teacher, 41,* 508–512.

Rasinski, T. V., & Fredericks, A. D. (1989). Working with parents: What do parents think about reading in the schools. *The Reading Teacher, 43*(3), 262–263.

Rasinski, T., & Padak, N. D. (1990). Multicultural learning through children's literature. *Language Arts, 69,* 14–20.

Raven, J. (1992). A model of competence, motivation, and behavior, and a paradigm for assessment. In H. Berlak, et al., *Toward a new science of educational testing and assessment.* New York: State University of New York Press.

Ravitch, D., & Finn, C. E., Jr. (1987). *What do our 17-year-olds know?* New York: HarperCollins.

Rawls, W. (1961). *Where the red fern grows.* New York: Doubleday.

Raygor, A. L. (1977). The Raygor readability estimate: A quick and easy way to determine difficulty. In P. D. Pearson (Ed.), *Reading: Theory, research and practice* (pp. 259–263). Clemson, SC: National Reading Conference.

Read, C. (1971). Preschool children's knowledge of English phonology. *Harvard Educational Review, 41,* 1–34.

Read, S. J., & Rosson, M. B. (1982). Rewriting history: The biasing effects of attitudes on memory. *Social Cognition, 1,* 240–255.

Reid, J. F. (1966). Learning to think about reading. *Educational Research, 9,* 56–62.

Reimer, B. L. (1983). Recipes for language experience stories. *The Reading Teacher, 36*(4), 396–401.

Reinking, D. (Ed.). (1987). *Computers and reading: Issues for theory and practice.* New York: Teachers College Press.

Reinking, D., & Rickman, S. S. (1990). The effects of computer-mediated texts on the vocabulary learning and comprehension of intermediate-grade readers. *Journal of Reading Behavior, 22*(4), 395–409.

Reutzel, D. R. (1985a). Reconciling schema theory and the basal reading lesson. *The Reading Teacher, 39,* 194–197.

Reutzel, D. R. (1985b). Story maps improve comprehension. *The Reading Teacher, 38*(4), 400–405.

Reutzel, D. R. (1986a). Clozing in on comprehension: The cloze story map. *The Reading Teacher, 39*(6), 524–529.

Reutzel, D. R. (1986b). Investigating a synthesized comprehension instructional strategy: The cloze story map. *The Journal of Educational Research, 79*(6), 343–349.

Reutzel, D. R. (1986c). The reading basal: A sentence combining composing book. *The Reading Teacher, 40*(2), 194–199.

Reutzel, D. R. (1991). Understanding and using basal readers effectively. In Bernard L. Hayes (Ed.), *Reading instruction and the effective teacher* (pp. 254–280). New York: Allyn & Bacon.

Reutzel, D. R. (1992). Breaking the letter a week tradition: Conveying the alphabetic principle to young children. *Childhood Education, 69*(1), 20–23.

Reutzel, D. R. (1995). Fingerpoint-reading and beyond: Learning about print strategies (LAPS). *Reading Horizons,* in press.

Reutzel, D. R., & Cooter, R. B., Jr. (1987). Teaching reading skills for mastery. *Academic Therapy, 23*(2), 127–134.

Reutzel, D. R., & Cooter, R. B., Jr. (1988). Research implications for improving basal skill insturction. *Reading Horizons, 28,* 208–216.

Reutzel, D. R., & Cooter, R. B., Jr. (1990). Whole language: Comparative effects on first-grade reading achievement. *Journal of Educational Research, 83,* 252–257.

Reutzel, D. R., & Cooter, R. B., Jr. (1991). Organizing for effective instruction: The reading workshop. *The Reading Teacher, 44*(8), 548–555.

Reutzel, D. R., & Daines, D. (1987a). The instructional cohesion of reading lessons in seven basal reading series. *Reading Psychology, 8,* 33–44.

Reutzel, D. R., & Daines, D. (1987b). The text-relatedness of seven basal reading series. *Reading Research and Instruction, 27,* 26–35.

Reutzel, D. R., & Fawson, P. C. (1987). *A professor returns to the classroom: Implementing whole language.* Unpublished research update, Brigham Young University, Provo, UT.

Reutzel, D. R., & Fawson, P. C. (1989). Using a literature webbing strategy lesson with predictable books. *The Reading Teacher, 43*(3), 208–215.

Reutzel, D. R., & Fawson, P. C. (1990). Traveling tales: Connecting parents and children in writing. *The Reading Teacher, 44,* 222–227.

Reutzel, D. R., & Fawson, P. C. (1991). Literature webbing predictable books: A prediction strategy that helps below-average, first-grade readers. *Reading Research and Instruction, 30*(4), 20–30.

Reutzel, D. R., & Hollingsworth, P. M. (1988a). Highlighting key vocabulary: A generative-reciprocal procedure for teaching selected inference types. *Reading Research Quarterly, 23*(3), 358–378.

Reutzel, D. R., & Hollingsworth, P. M. (1988b). Whole language and the practitioner. *Academic Therapy, 23*(4), 405–416.

Reutzel, D. R., & Hollingsworth, P. M. (1991a). Investigating the development of topic-related attitude: Effect on children's reading and remembering text. *Journal of Educational Research, 84*(5), 334–344.

Reutzel, D. R., & Hollingsworth, P. M. (1991b). Reading comprehension skills: Testing the skills distinctiveness hypothesis. *Reading Research and Instruction, 30*(2), 32–46.

Reutzel, D. R., & Hollingsworth, P. (1991c). Reading time in school: Effect on fourth graders' performance on a criterion-referenced comprehension test. *Journal of Educational Research, 84*(3), 170–176.

Reutzel, D. R., & Hollingsworth, P. M. (1991d). Using literature webbing for books with predictable narrative: Improving young readers' predictions, comprehension, & story structure knowledge. *Reading Psychology, 12*(4), 319–333.

Reutzel, D. R., & Hollingsworth, P. M. (1993). Effects of fluency training on second grader's reading comprehension. *Journal of Educational Research, 86*(6), 325–331.

Reutzel, D. R., Hollingsworth, P. M., & Eldredge, J. L. (1994). Oral reading instruction: The impact on student reading development. *Reading Research Quarterly, 23*(1), 40–62.

Reutzel, D. R., & Morgan, B. C. (1990). Effects of prior knowledge, explicitness, and clause order on children's comprehension of causal relationships. *Reading Psychology: An International Quarterly, 11,* 93–114.

Reutzel, D. R., Oda, L. K., & Moore, B. H. (1989). Developing print awareness: The effect of three instructional approaches on kindergartners; print awareness, reading readiness, and word reading. *Journal of Reading Behavior, 21*(3), 197–217.

Reutzel, D. R., & Sabey, B. (in press). Teacher beliefs about reading and children's conceptions: Are there connections? *Reading Research and Instruction.*

Rhodes, L. K., & Dudley-Marling, C. (1988). *Readers and writers with a difference.* Portsmouth, NH: Heinemann.

Rhodes, L. K., & Shanklin, N. (1993). *Windows into literacy: Assessing learners K–8.* Portsmouth, NH: Heinemann.

Ribowsky, H. (1985). *The effects of a code emphasis approach and a whole language approach upon emergent literacy of kindergarten children* (Report No. CS-008-397). (ERIC Document Reproduction Service No. ED 269 720)

Rice, P. E. (1991). Novels in the news. *The Reading Teacher, 45*(2), 159–160.

Rich, E. S. (1964). *Hannah Elizabeth.* New York: HarperCollins.

Richek, M. A. (1978). Readiness skills that predict initial word learning using 2 different methods of instruction. *Reading Research Quarterly, 13,* 200–222.

Riley, R. E. (1993). *Adult literacy in America.* Washington, DC: United States Department of of Education.

Roberts, B. (1992). The evolution of the young child's concept of word as a unit of spoken and written language. *Reading Research Quarterly, 27*(2), 124–139.

Roberts, T. (1975). Skills of analysis and synthesis in the early stages of reading. *British Journal of Educational Psychology, 45,* 3–9.

Robinson, B. (1972). *The best Christmas pagent ever.* New York: HarperCollins.

Robinson, F. (1946). *Effective study.* New York: Harper Brothers.

Robinson, H. M. (1972). Perceptual training—does it result in reading improvement? In R. C. Aukerman (Ed.), *Some persistent questions on beginning reading* (pp. 135–150). Newark, DE: International Reading Association.

Romero, G. G. (1983). *Print awareness of the preschool bilingual Spanish English speaking child.* Unpublished doctoral dissertation, University of Arizona Tucson.

Rosenbaum, J. (1980). *Making inequality: The hidden curriculum of high school tracking.* New York: Wiley.

Rosenblatt, L. M. (1978). *The reader, the text, and the poem.* Carbondale, IL: Southern Illinois University Press.

Rosenshine, B. V. (1980). Skill hierarchies in reading comprehension. In Spiro, R. J., Bruce, B. C., & Brewer, W. F. (Eds.), *Theoretical issues in reading comprehension* (pp. 535–554). Hillsdale, NJ: Erlbaum.

Roser, N. L., Hoffman, J. V., & Farest, C. (1990). Language, literature, and at-risk children. *The Reading Teacher, 43*(8), 554–561.

Routman, R. (1988). *Transitions: From literature to literacy.* Portsmouth, NH: Heinemann.

Rowe, M. B. (1974). Wait-time and rewards as instructional variables, their influence of language, logic, and fate control: Part one—wait time. *Journal of Research in Science Teaching, 11,* 81–94.

Ruddell, R. (1974). *Reading-language instruction: Innovative practices.* Englewood Cliffs, NJ: Prentice-Hall.

Rumelhart, D. E. (1975). Notes on a schema for stories. In D. G. Bobrow & A. Collins (Eds.), *Representation and understanding: Studies in cognitive science* (pp. 211–236). New York: Academic Press.

Rumelhart, D. E. (1980). Schemata: The building blocks of cognition. In R. J. Spiro, *Theoretical issues in reading comprehension* (pp. 33–58). Hillsdale, NJ: Erlbaum.

Rumelhart, D. E. (1981). Schemata: The building blocks of cognition. In Guthrie, J. T. (Ed.), *Comprehension and teaching: Research reviews* (pp. 3–26). Newark, DE: International Reading Association.

Rumelhart, D. E. (1984). Understanding understanding. In J. Flood (Ed.), *Understanding reading comprehension* (pp. 1–20). Newark, DE: International Reading Association.

Rupley, W. H., & Blair, T. R. (1978). Teacher effectiveness in reading instruction. *The Reading Teacher, 31,* 970–973.

Rupley, W., & Blair, T. (1987). Assignment and supervison of reading seatwork: Looking in on 12 primary teachers. *The Reading Teacher, 40*(4), 391–393.

Rye, J. (1982). *Cloze procedure and the teaching of reading.* Portsmouth, NH: Heinemann.

Sadow, M. W. (1982). The use of story grammar in the design of questions. *The Reading Teacher, 35,* 518–523.

Samuels, S. J. (1970). Effects of pictures on learning to read, comprehension, and attitudes. *Review of Educational Research, 40,* 397–408.

Samuels, S. J. (1967). Attentional process in reading: The effect of pictures on the acquisition of reading responses. *Journal of Educational Psychology, 58,* 337–342.

Samuels, S. J. (1979). The method of repeated readings. *The Reading Teacher, 32*(4), 403–408.

Sanford, A. J., & Garrod, S. C. (1981). *Understanding written language.* New York: John Wiley & Sons.

Santa, C. (1990). *Reporting on the Montana Teacher Change Project: Kallispell reading/language initiative.* Utah Council of the International Reading Association, Salt Lake City, UT.

Savage, J. F. (1994). *Teaching reading using literature.* Madison, WS: Brown & Benchmark.

Scholastic. (1986). *Talking text* [computer program]. Jefferson City, MO: Scholastic.

Scholastic. (1990). *Bank Street writer III* [computer program]. Jefferson City, MO: Scholastic Software.

Scholastic. (1995). *Literary place program.* New York: Author.

Schwartz, D. M. (1985). *How much is a million?* Richard Hill, Ontario: Scholastic-TAB.

Schwartz, R. M., & Raphael, T. E. (1985). Concept of definition: A key to improving students' vocabulary. *The Reading Teacher, 39*(2), 198–205.

Scieszka, J. (1989). *The true story of the 3 little pigs: By A. Wolf.* New York: Viking Kestrel.

Searfoss, L. W. (1975). Radio reading. *Reading Teacher, 29,* 295–296.

Searfoss, L. W., & Readence, J. E. (1989). *Helping children learn to read* (2nd ed.). Englewood Cliffs, NJ: Prentice Hall.

Seefeldt, C., & Barbour, N. (1986). *Early childhood education: An introduction.* Englewood Cliffs, NJ: Merrill/Prentice Hall.

Sendak, M. (1962). *Chicken soup with rice.* New York: Scholastic.

Sendak, M. (1963). *Where the wild things are.* New York: HarperCollins.

Senechal, M., & Cornell, E. H. (1993). Vocabulary acquisition through shared reading experiences. *Reading Research Quarterly, 28*(4), 361–373.

Seuss, D. (1954). *Horton hears a Who!* New York: Random House.

Shake, M. C., & Allington, R. L. (1985). Where do teacher's questions come from. *The Reading Teacher, 38,* 432–439.

Shanahan, T. (1984). Nature of the reading–writing relation: An exploratory multivariate analysis. *Journal of Educational Psychology, 76,* 466–477.

Shanahan, T., & Lomax, R. G. (1986). An analysis and comparison of theoretical models of the reading–writing relationship. *Journal of Educational Psychology, 78,* 116–123.

Shanklin, N. L., & Rhodes, L. K. (1989). Comprehension instruction as sharing and extending. *The Reading Teacher, 43*(7), 496–500.

Shannon, P. (1983). The use of commercial reading materials in American elementary schools. *Reading Research Quarterly, 19,* 68–85.

Shannon, P. (1989). Basal readers: Three perspectives. *Theory Into Practice, 28*(4), 235–239.

Shannon, P. (1989). *Broken promises.* Granby, MA: Bergin & Garvey.

Shannon, P. (1992). *Becoming political: Readings and writings in the politics of literacy education.* Portsmouth, NH: Heinemann.

Shannon, P. (1993). Letters to the editor: Comments on Baumann. *Reading Research Quarterly, 28*(2), 86.

Sharmat, M. W. (1980). *Gila monsters meet you at the airport.* New York: Aladdin.

Siegel, M. (1983). *Reading as signification.* Unpublished doctoral dissertation, Indiana University.

Silvaroli, N. J. (1986). *Classroom reading inventory* (5th ed.). Dubuque, IA: William C. Brown.

Silverstein, S. (1974). *Where the sidewalk ends.* New York: HarperCollins.

Singer, H. (1960). *Conceptual ability in the substrata-factor theory of reading.* Unpublished doctoral dissertation, University of California at Berkeley.

Singer, H. (1978a). Active comprehension: From answering to asking questions. *The Reading Teacher, 31,* 901–908.

Singer, H. (1978b). Research in reading that should make a difference in classroom instruction. In *What research has to say about reading instruction* (pp. 57–71). Newark, DE: International Reading Association.

Singer, H., & Donlan, D. (1989). *Reading and learning from text* (2nd ed.). Hillsdale, NJ: Erlbaum.

Skaar, G. (1972). *What do the animals say?* New York: Scholastic.

Slaughter, H. B. (1988). Indirect and direct teaching in a whole language program. *The Reading Teacher, 42,* 30–35.

Slavin, R. E. (1991). Are cooperative learning and "untracking" harmful to the gifted? *Education Leadership, 48*(6), 68–71.

Slavin, R. E. (1988). Cooperative learning and student achievement. *Educational Leadership, 45,* 31–33.

Slosson, R. L. (1971). *Slosson intelligence test.* East Aurora, NY: Slosson Educational Publications.

Sloyer, S. (1982). *Reader's theater: Story dramatization in the classroom.* Urbana, IL: National Council of Teachers of English.

Smith, D. E. P. (1967). *Learning to learn.* New York: Harcourt Brace.

Smith, E. B., Goodman, K. S., & Meredith, R. (1976). *Language and thinking in school* (2nd ed.). New York: Holt, Rinehart & Winston.

Smith, F. (1977). The uses of language. *Language Arts, 54*(6), 638–644.

Smith, F. (1983). *Essays into literacy.* Exeter, NH: Heinemann.

Smith, F. (1985). *Reading without nonsense* (2nd ed.). New York: Teachers College Press.

Smith, F. (1987). *Insult to intelligence.* New York: Arbor House.

Smith, F. (1988). *Understanding reading* (4th ed.). Hillsdale, NJ: Erlbaum.

Smith, K. A. (1989). *A checkup with the doctor.* New York: McDougal, Littell.

Smith, N. B. (1965). *American reading instruction.* Newark, DE: International Reading Association.

Smith, N. B. (1986). *American Reading Instruction.* Newark, DE: International Reading Association.

Smith, R. K. (1981). *Jelly belly.* New York: Dell.

Smoot, R. C., & Price, J. (1975). *Chemistry, a modern course.* Englewood Cliffs, NJ: Merrill/Prentice Hall.

Soto, G. (1993). *Local news.* San Diego, CA: Harcourt Brace.

Spache, G., & Spache, E. (1977). *Reading in the elementary school* (4th ed.). Boston: Allyn & Bacon.

Spady, W., & Marshall, K. J. (1991). Beyond traditional outcome-based education. *Educational Leadership, 48,* 67–72.

Spangler, K. L. (1983). Reading interests vs. reading preferences: Using the research. *The Reading Teacher, 36*(9), 876–878.

Speare, E. G. (1958). *The witch of Blackbird Pond.* New York: Dell.

Sperry, A. (1940). *Call it courage.* New York: Macmillan.

Spiegel, D. L. (1981). Six alternatives to the directed reading activity. *Reading Teacher, 34,* 914–922.

Spier, P. (1977). *Noah's ark.* Garden City, NY: Doubleday.

Spinelli, J. (1991). Catching Maniac Magee. *The Reading Teacher, 45*(3), 174–176.

Spivak, M. (1973). Archetypal place. *Architectural Forum, 140,* 44–49.

Squire, J. R. (1983). Composing and comprehending: Two sides of the same basic process. *Language Arts, 60*(5), 581–589.

Squire, J. R. (1989). A reading program for all seasons. *Theory Into Practice, 28*(4), 254–257.

Stahl, S. A. (1986). Three principles of effective vocabulary instruction. *Journal of Reading, 29*(7), 662–668.

Stahl, S. A., Hare, V. C., Sinatra, R., & Gregory, J. F. (1991). Defining the role of prior knowledge and vocabulary in reading comprehension: The retiring of number 41. *Journal of Reading Behavior, 23*(4), 487–507.

Stahl, S. A., & Jacobson, M. G. (1986). Vocabulary difficulty, prior knowledge, and text comprehension. *Journal of Reading Behavior, 18*(4), 309–319.

Stahl, S. A., & Miller, P. D. (1989). Whole language and language experience approaches for beginning reading: A quantitative research synthesis. *Review of Educational Research, 59,* 87–116.

Stanovich, K. (1980). Toward an interactive-compensatory model of individual differences in the development of reading fluency. *Reading Research Quarterly, 16*(1), 37–71.

Stauffer, R. G. (1969). *Directing reading maturity as a cognitive process.* New York: HarperCollins.

Stauffer, R. G. (1975). *Directing the reading-thinking process.* New York: HarperCollins.

Stayter, F. Z., & Allington, R. L. (1991). Fluency and the understanding of texts. *Theory Into Practice, 30*(3), 143–148.

Steele, W. O. (1958). *The perilous road.* Orlando, FL: Harcourt, Brace.

Stein, N. L., & Glenn, C. G. (1979). An analysis of story comprehension in elementary school children. In R. O. Freedle (Ed.), *New directions in discourse processing* (pp. 53–120). Hillsdale, NJ: Erlbaum.

Steinbeck, J. (1937). *The red pony.* New York: Bantam Books.

Steptoe, J. (1987). *Mufaro's beautiful daughters: An African tale.* New York: Lothrop, Lee, & Shepard Books.

Stern, D. N., & Wasserman, G. A. (1979). *Maternal language to infants.* Paper presented at a meeting of the Society for Research in Child Development.

Stevens, R. J., Madden, N. A., Slavin, R. E., & Farnish, A. (1987a). *Cooperative Integrated Reading and Composition: A brief overview of the CIRC program.* Johns Hopkins University, Center for Research on Elementary and Middle Schools.

Stevens, R. J., Madden, N. A., Slavin, R. E., & Farnish, A. M. (1987b). Cooperative integrated reading and composition: Two field experiments. *Reading Research Quarterly, 22*(4), 433–454.

Stevens, R., & Rosenshine, B. (1981). Advances in research on teaching. *Exceptional Education Quarterly, 2,* 1–9.

Stolz, M. (1963). *Bully on Barkham Street.* New York: HarperCollins.

Stoodt, B. D. (1989). *Reading instruction.* New York: HarperCollins.

Strickland, D. S., Feeley, J. T., & Wepner, S. B. (1987). *Using computers in the teaching of reading.* New York: Teachers College Press.

Sucher, F., & Allred, R. A. (1986). *Sucher-Allred group reading placement test.* Oklahoma City: Economy.

Sukhomlinsky, V. (1981). *To children I give my heart* (pp. 125–126). Moscow, USSR: Progress Publishers.

Sulzby, E. (1985). Children's emergent reading of favorite storybooks: A developmental study. *Reading Research Quarterly, 20*(4), 458–481.

Sulzby, E. (1991). Assessment of emergent literacy: Storybook reading. *The Reading Teacher, 44*(7), 498–500.

Sulzby, E., Hoffman, J., Niles, J., Shanahan, T., & Teale, W. (1989). *McGraw-Hill reading.* New York: McGraw-Hill.

Sunburst. (1987). *The puzzler.* Pleasantville, NY: Sunburst Communications.

Taba, H. (1975). *Teacher's handbook for elementary social studies.* Reading, MA: Addison-Wesley.

Tarver, S. G., & Dawson, M. M. (1978). Modality preference and the teaching of reading: A review. *Journal of Learning Disabilities, 11*(1), 5–17.

Taxel, J. (1993). The politics of children's literature: Reflections on multiculturalism and Christopher Columbus. In V. J. Harris (Ed.), *Teaching multicultural literature in grades K–8* (pp. 1–36). Norwood, MA: Christopher Gordon Publishers.

Taylor, B., Harris, L. A., & Pearson, P. D. (1988). *Reading difficulties: Instruction and assessment.* New York: Random House.

Taylor, B. M., Frye, B. J., & Gaetz, T. M. (1990). Reducing the number of reading skill activities in the elementary classroom. *Journal of Reading Behavior, 22*(2), 167–180.

Taylor, D. (1983). *Family literacy: Young children learning to read and write.* Portsmouth, NH: Heinemann.

Taylor, D., & Strickland, D. S. (1986). *Family storybook reading.* Porstmouth, NH: Heinemann.

Taylor, G. C. (1981). ERIC/RCS report: Music in language arts instruction. *Language Arts, 58,* 363–368.

Taylor, M. D. (1990). *Road to Memphis.* New York: Dial Books.

Taylor, N. E. (1986). Developing beginning literacy concepts: Content and context. In D. B. Yaden, Jr., & S. Templeton (Eds.), *Metalinguistic awareness and beginning literacy* (pp. 173–184). Portsmouth, NH: Heinemann.

Taylor, N. E., Blum, I. H., & Logsdon, M. (1986). The development of written language awareness: Environmental aspects and program characteristics. *Reading Research Quarterly, 21*(2), 132–149.

Taylor, W. L. (1953). Cloze procedure: A new tool for measuring readability. *Journalism Quarterly, 30,* 415–433.

Teale, W. H. (1987). Emergent literacy: Reading and writing development in early childhood. In Readence, J. E., Baldwin, R. S., Konopak, J. P., & Newton, H. (Eds.), *Research in literacy: Merging perspectives* (pp. 45–74). Rochester, NY: National Reading Conference.

Teale, W. H., & Sulzby, E. (1986). *Emergent literacy: Writing and reading.* Norwood, NJ: Ablex.

Temple, C., Nathan, R., Burris, N., & Temple, F. (1988). *The beginnings of writing* (2nd ed.). Newton, MA: Allyn & Bacon.

Thaler, M. (1989). *The teacher from the Black Lagoon.* New York: Scholastic.

Thelen, J. N. (1984). *Improving reading in science.* Newark, DE: International Reading Association.

Thomas, D. G., & Readence, J. E. (1988). Effects of differential vocabulary instruction and lesson frameworks on the reading comprehension of primary children. *Reading Research and Instruction, 28,* 1–13.

Thorndike, R. L. (1973). *Reading comprehension education in fifteen countries: An empirical study.* New York: John Wiley & Sons.

Thorndyke, P. N. (1977). Cognitive structure in comprehension and memory of narrative discourse. *Cognitive Psychology, 9*(1), 77–110.

Tierney, R. J. (1992). Setting a new agenda for assessment. *Learning, 21*(2), 61–64.

Tierney, R. J., Carter, M. A., & Desai, L. E. (1991). *Portfolio assessment in the reading–writing classroom.* Norwood, MA: Christopher-Gordon.

Tierney, R. J., & Cunningham, J. W. (1984). Research on teaching reading comprehension. In P. D. Pearson (Ed.), *Reading research handbook* (pp. 609–656). New York: Longman.

Tierney, R. J., & Pearson, P. D. (1983). Toward a composing model of reading. *Language Arts, 60*(5), 568–580.

Tierney, R. J., Readence, J. E., & Dishner, E. K. (1985). *Reading strategies and practices: A compendium* (2nd ed.). Boston: Allyn & Bacon.

Tierney, R. J., Readence, J. E., & Dishner, E. K. (1990). *Reading strategies and practices: A compendium* (3rd ed.). Boston: Allyn & Bacon.

Timion, C. S. (1992). Children's book selection strategies. In J. W. Irwin & M. A. Doyle (Eds.), *Reading/writing connections: Learning from research* (pp. 204–222). Newark, DE: International Reading Association.

Tompkins, G. E. (1990). *Teaching writing: Balancing process and product.* Englewood Cliffs, NJ: Merrill/Prentice Hall.

Tompkins, G. E. (1994). *Teaching writing: Balancing process and product* (2nd ed.). Englewood Cliffs, NJ: Merrill/Prentice Hall.

Tompkins, G. E., & Hoskisson, K. (1991). *Language arts: Content and teaching strategies.* Englewood Cliffs, NJ: Merrill/Prentice Hall.

Tompkins, G. E., & Hoskisson, K. (1995). *Language arts: Content and teaching strategies* (3rd ed.). Englewood Cliffs, NJ: Merrill/Prentice Hall.

Topping, K. (1989). Peer tutoring and paired reading: Combining two powerful techniques. *The Reading Teacher, 42,* 488–494.

Torrey, J. W. (1979). Reading that comes naturally. In G. Waller & G. E. MacKinnon (Eds.), *Reading research: Advance in theory and practice* (Vol. 1, pp. 115–144). New York: Academic Press.

Tovey, D. R., & Kerber, J. E. (Eds.). (1986). *Roles in literacy learning.* Newark, DE: International Reading Association.

Towers, J. M. (1992). Outcome-based education: Another educational bandwagon. *Educational Forum, 56*(3), 291–305.

Towle, (1993). *The real McCoy: The life of an African American inventor.* New York: Scholastic.

Treiman, R. (1985). Onsets and rimes as units of spoken syllables: Evidence from children. *Journal of Experimental Child Psychology, 39,* 161–181.

Trelease, J. (1989). *The new read-aloud handbook.* New York: Penguin.

Tunnell, M. O., & Jacobs, J. S. (1989). Using "real" books: Research findings on literature based reading instruction. *The Reading Teacher, 42,* 470–477.

Tutolo, D. (1977). The study guide: Types, purpose and value. *Journal of Reading, 20,* 503–507.

The United States and the other Americas (Grade 5). (1980). Englewood Cliffs, NJ: Merrill/Prentice Hall.

The United States: Its history and neighbors (Grade 5). (1985). San Diego, CA: Harcourt Brace.

Vacca, J. L., Vacca, R. T., & Gove, M. K. (1987). *Reading and learning to read.* Boston: Little, Brown.

Vacca, J. L., Vacca, R. T., & Gove, M. K. (1991). *Reading and learning to read* (2nd ed.). Boston: Little, Brown.

Vacca, R. T., & Vacca, J. L. (1989). *Content area reading* (3rd ed.). Glenview, IL: Scott, Foresman.

Valencia, S. (1990). A portfolio approach to classroom reading assessment: The whys, whats, and hows. *The Reading Teacher, 43*(4), 338–340.

Valencia, S., McGinley, W., & Pearson, P. D. (1990). *Assessing reading and writing: Building a more complete picture for middle school assessment* (Tech. Rep. No. 500). Urbana, IL: Center for the Study of Reading. (ERIC Document Reproduction Service No. ED 320 121)

Valencia, S., & Pearson, P. D. (1987). Reading assessment: Time for a change. *The Reading Teacher, 40*(8), 726–733.

Van Allsburg, C. (1985). *The polar express.* Boston: Houghton Mifflin.

Van Allsburg, C. (1987). *The Z was zapped.* Boston: Houghton Mifflin.

Van Manen, M. (1986). *The tone of teaching.* Ontario, Canada: Scholastic.

Varble, M. E. (1990). Analysis of writing samples of students taught by teachers using whole language and traditional approaches. *The Journal of Educational Research, 83*(5), 245–251.

Veatch, J. (1968). *How to teach reading with children's books.* New York: Richard C. Owen.

Veatch, J. (1978). *Reading in the elementary school* (2nd ed.). New York: Richard C. Owen.

Veatch, J., & Cooter, R. B. (1986). The effect of teacher selection on reading achievement. *Language Arts, 63*(4), 364–368.

Viorst, J. (1972). *Alexander and the terrible horrible no good very bad day* (Ray Cruz, Illustrator). New York: Atheneum.

Viorst, J. (1990). *Earrings!* (Nola Langer Malone, Illustrator). New York: Atheneum/Macmillan.

Voltz, D. L., & Demiano-Lantz, M. (1993, Summer). Developing ownership in learning. *Teaching Exceptional Children,* pp. 18–22.

Vygotsky, L. S. (1962). *Thought and language.* Cambridge, MA: MIT Press.

Vygotsky, L. S. (1978). *Mind in society.* Cambridge, MA: Harvard University Press.

Walker, J. E. (1991, May). *Affect in naturalistic assessment: Implementation and implications.* Paper presented at the 36th annual convention of the International Reading Association, Las Vegas, NV.

Wallach, L., Wallach, M. A., Dozier, M. G., & Kaplan, N. E. (1977). Poor children learning to read do not have trouble with auditory discrimination but do have trouble with phoneme recognition. *Journal of Educational Psychology, 69,* 36–39.

Walley, C. (1993). An invitation to reading fluency. *The Reading Teacher, 46*(6), 526–527.

Walters, K., & Gunderson, L. (1985). Effects of parent volunteers reading first language (L1) books to ESL students. *The Reading Teacher, 20,* 313–318.

Watson, D., & Crowley, P. (1988). How can we implement a whole-language approach. In C. Weaver (Ed.), *Reading process and practice* (pp. 232–279). Portsmouth, NH: Heinemann.

Watson, S. (1976). *No man's land.* New York: Greenwillow.

Weaver, C. (1988). *Reading process and practice: From socio-psycholinguistics to whole language.* Portsmouth, NH: Heinemann.

Weaver, C., Chaston, J., & Peterson, S. (1993). *Theme exploration: A voyage of discovery.* Portsmouth, NH: Heinemann.

Webb, K., & Willoughby, N. (1993). An analytic rubric for scoring graphs. *The Texas School Teacher, 22*(3), 14–15.

Webb, M., & Schwartz, W. (1988, October). Children teaching children: A good way to learn. *PTA Today,* pp. 16–17.

Weimans, E. (1981). *Which way courage?* New York: Atheneum.

Weinstein, R. S. (1976). Reading group membership in first grade: Teacher behaviors and pupil experience over time. *Journal of Educational Psychology, 68,* 103–116.

Weintraub, S., & Denny, T. P. (1965). What do beginning first graders say about reading? *Childhood Education, 41,* 326–327.

Wells, R. (1973). *Noisy Nora.* New York: Scholastic.

Wepman, J. M. (1973). *Auditory discrimination test* (rev. ed.). Chicago: Language Research Associates.

Wepner, S. B. (1990). Holistic computer applications in literature-based classrooms. *The Reading Teacher, 44*(1), 12–19.

Wepner, S. B. (1992). Technology and text sets. *The Reading Teacher, 46*(1), 68–71.

Wepner, S. B. (1993). Technology and thematic units: An elementary example on Japan. *The Reading Teacher, 46*(5), 442–445.

Wepner, S. B., & Feeley, J. T. (1993). *Moving forward with literature: Basals, books, and beyond.* Englewood Cliffs, NJ: Merrill/Prentice Hall.

Werner, P. H. (1990). Computers in a university reading clinic motivate reluctant readers and writers. *The Tech Edge, 10*(1), 14–15.

Werner, P. H. (1991). *Purposes of writing assessment: A process view.* Unpublished manuscript, Southwest Texas State University, San Marcos, TX.

Werner, P. H., & Cooter, R. B. (1991, May). *Affective connections of selected nauralistic assessment strategies in reading.* Paper presented at the 36th annual conference of the International Reading Association, Las Vegas, NV.

Wessells, M. G. (1990). *Computer, self, and society.* Englewood Cliffs, NJ: Prentice Hall.

Whaley, J. F. (1981). Readers' expectations for story structures. *Reading Research Quarterly, 17,* 90–114.

Wheatley, E. A., Muller, D. H., & Miller, R. B. (1993). Computer-assisted vocabulary instruction. *Journal of Reading, 37*(2), 92–102.

Whitaker, B. T., Schwartz, E., & Vockell, E. (1989). *The computer in the reading curriculum.* New York: McGraw-Hill.

White, C. S. (1983). Learning style and reading instruction. *The Reading Teacher, 36,* 842–845.

White, E. B. (1952). *Charlotte's web.* New York: HarperCollins.

White, E. B. (1970). *The trumpet of the swan.* New York: HarperCollins.

Wiesendanger, W. D. (1986). Durkin revisited. *Reading Horizons, 26,* 89–97.

Wilson, R. M., & Gambrell, L. B. (1988). *Reading comprehension in the elementary school.* Boston: Allyn & Bacon.

Winograd, P. (1989a). Improving basal reading instruction: Beyond the carrot and the stick. *Theory Into Practice, 28*(4), 240–247.

Winograd, P. N. (1989b). Introduction: Understanding reading instruction. In Winograd, P. N., Wixson, K. K., & Lipson, M. Y. (Eds.). *Improving basal reader instruction* (pp. 1–20). New York: Teachers College Press.

Winograd, P. N., Paris, S., & Bridge, C. (1991). Improving the assessment of literacy. *The Reading Teacher, 45*(2), 108–116.

Winograd, P. N., Wixson, K. K., & Lipson, M. Y. (Eds.). (1989). *Improving basal reader instruction.* New York: Teachers College Press.

Wiseman, D. L. (1992). *Learning to read with literature.* Boston: Allyn & Bacon.

Wittrock, M. C. (1974). Learning as a generative process. *Educational Psychologist, 11,* 87–95.

Wixson, K. K., Peters, C. W., Weber, E. M., & Roeber, E. D. (1987). New directions in statewide reading assessment. *The Reading Teacher, 40*(8), 749–755.

Wong, J. W., & Au, K. H. (1985). The concept-text-application approach: Helping elementary students comprehend expository text. *The Reading Teacher, 38*(7), 612–618.

Wood, A. (1984). *The napping house* (Don Wood, Illustrator). San Diego, CA: Harcourt Brace.

Wood, A. (1990). *Weird parents.* New York: Dial Books for Young Readers.

Wood, K. D. (1983). A variation on an old theme: 4-way oral reading. *The Reading Teacher, 37*(1), 38–41.

Wood, K. D. (1987). Fostering cooperative learning in middle and secondary level classrooms. *Journal of Reading, 31,* 10–18.

Woodcock, R., Mather, N., & Barnes, E. K. (1987). *Woodcock reading mastery tests—revised.* Circle Pines, MN: American Guidance Service.

Worby, D. Z. (1980). *An honorable seduction: Thematic studies in literature.* Arlington, VA: ERIC Document Reproduction Service. (ERIC Document Reproduction Service No. ED 100 723)

Yaden, D. B., Jr. (1982). A multivariate analysis of first graders' print awareness as related to reading achievement, intelligence, and gender. *Dissertation Abstracts International, 43,* 1912A. (University Microfilms No. 82-25, 520)

Yashima, T. (1983). *Crow boy.* New York: Viking.

Yellin, D., & Blake, M. E. (1994). *Integrating language arts: A holistic approach.* New York: HarperCollins.

Yep, L. (1989). *The rainbow people.* New York: HarperCollins.

Ylisto, I. P. (1967). An empirical investigation of early reading responses of young children (doctoral dissertation, The University of Michigan, 1967). *Dissertation Abstracts International, 28,* 2153A. (University Microfilms No. 67-15, 728)

Yolen, J. (1976) *An invitation to a butterfly ball: A counting rhyme.* New York: Philomel.

Yolen, J. (1988). *The devil's arithmetic.* New York: Viking Kestrel.

Yopp, H. K. (1988). The validity and reliability of phonemic awareness tests. *Reading Research Quarterly, 23,* 159–177.

Yopp, H. K. (1992). Developing phonemic awareness in young children. *The Reading Teacher, 45*(9), 696–703.

Yopp, H. K., & Troyer, S. (1992). *Training phonemic awareness in young children.* Unpublished manuscript.

Young, E. (1989). *Lon Po Po.* New York: Philomel Books.

Young, T. A., & Vardell, S. (1993). Weaving readers theatre and nonfiction into the curriculum. *Reading Teacher, 46,* 396–406.

Zarillo, J. (1989). Teachers' interpretations of literature-based reading. *The Reading Teacher, 43*(1), 22–29.

Zentall, S. S. (1993). Research on the educational implications of attention deficit hyperactivity disorder. *Exceptional Children, 60*(2), 143–153.

Zintz, M. V., & Maggart, Z. R. (1989). *The reading process: The teacher and the learner.* Dubuque, IA: William C. Brown.

Zlatos, B. (1993). Outcomes-based outrage. *Executive Educator, 15*(9), 12–16.

NAME INDEX

SUBJECT INDEX